Cadwallader Colden, 1688–1776

Cadwallader Colden with a coat of arms and his signature.

Cadwallader Colden, 1688–1776

A Life between Revolutions

by
Philip Ranlet

Hamilton Books
Lanham • Boulder • New York • Toronto • London

Frontispiece: Cadwallader Colden with a coat of arms and his signature. This portrait was a frequent illustration during the nineteenth century. Engraved. Portrait File PR 052. ID77063d.*Collection of the New-York Historical Society.*

Copyright © 2020 by The Rowman & Littlefield Publishing Group, Inc.
An imprint of The Rowman & Littlefield Publishing Group, Inc.
4501 Forbes Boulevard, Suite 200, Lanham, Maryland 20706
Hamilton Books Acquisitions Department (301) 459-3366

6 Tinworth Street, London SE11 5AL, United Kingdom

All rights reserved
Printed in the United States of America
British Library Cataloguing in Publication Information Available

Library of Congress Control Number: 2019913698

ISBN: 978-0-7618-7141-5 (pbk. : alk. paper)
ISBN: 978-0-7618-7142-2 (electronic)

This book is dedicated to the memory of
a great historian of New York, Milton M. Klein,
who was very happy that I planned to write it.

Contents

List of Illustrations	ix
Acknowledgments	xi
Abbreviations for Notes	xiii
Introduction	1
1 The Drummer	7
2 New York	25
3 Sylvan Retreat	45
4 Tyrant	71
5 Enlightenment	97
6 Revolts	121
7 Jennie and Davie	143
8 The Empire Calls	161
9 The Ottoman Family	187
10 Coldengham Under Siege	213
11 The Intelligent Being	241
12 Phoenix	265
13 Lawyers	297
14 Civil War	319
15 Out, In, and Out Again	343
16 Drunkard	377
17 Finis	405

Afterword	435
Bibliography	445
Index	477
About the Author	487

List of Illustrations

Fig. 1.1 *Mrs. Cadwallader Colden*, c. 1749-52 by John Wollaston.

Fig. 2.1 James Alexander. Colden's greatest friend.

Fig. 5.1 *Cadwallader Colden*, by an unknown artist based on an original by Matthew Pratt.

Fig. 8.1 *Cadwallader Colden*, c. 1749-52 by John Wollaston.

Fig. 12.1 Spring Hill. Photo by A. J. Wall.

Fig. 16.1 *Cadwallader Colden*, by Matthew Pratt.

Acknowledgments

This is not your grandfather's Colden. In the writing of this book, I have had the help of the late James Baughman, who read the entire text. Alden Vaughan read some of the material as did Florene Memegalos, my authority on all things British. I was the beneficiary of grants from the City University of New York Professional Staff Congress Adjunct Professional Development Fund, which primarily paid for my research trip to Ann Arbor. I thank the Newberry Library, Chicago, for permission to quote from the Ayer Collection. And special thanks go to my brother David.

Milton Klein was the first reader when I sought to publish my dissertation. Although I never met him, we corresponded and became friends. He was truly happy when I told him of my plan to write a biography of Colden, and was downright enthused when I mentioned I would write a biography of Klein's mentor, Richard B. Morris. Milton died shortly before my Morris book was published. As for the present book, I, once again, must hope that he would have liked it.

Abbreviations for Notes

AC	Alexander Colden (son)
ANB	*American National Biography*, 24 vols. (New York: Oxford University Press, 1999).
BF	Benjamin Franklin
Cad	Cadwallader Colden Jr.
CC	Cadwallader Colden
CC, *History*	Cadwallader Colden, *The History of the Five Indian Nations Depending on the Province of New-York in America* (1727, Part 1; 1747, Part 2) (New York: T. H. Morrell, 1866; repr. Ithaca, NY: Great Seal Books, 1958).
CL	Clements Library, Ann Arbor, Michigan
CLB	Cadwallader Colden, *The Colden Letter Books, 1760–1775*, New York Historical Society, *Collections*, 9–10 (1876–1877).
CO	Colonial Office (transcripts and microfilm of Great Britain)
Coll./Coll.	*Collections* (non-italics indicates not published).
CP	Cadwallader Colden, *The Letters and Papers of Cadwallader Colden*, 9 vols. (New York: New York Historical Society, 1918–1937); within *Collections of the New-York Historical Society*, vols. 50–56, 67–68 (New York: New York Historical Society, 1917–1923, 1934–1935).
CPU	Colden Papers (unpublished), New York Historical Society (microfilm).

Abbreviations for Notes

DH	Edmund B. O'Callaghan, ed. *The Documentary History of the State of New-York; Arranged Under Direction of the Hon. Christopher Morgan, Secretary of State* 4 vols. (Albany, NY: Weed, Parsons, 1849–1851), short page.
FP	Leonard W. Labaree and others, eds., *The Papers of Benjamin Franklin*, 43 vols. to date (New Haven, CT: Yale University Press, 1959–2019).
GC	Admiral George Clinton
HSP	Historical Society of Pennsylvania, Philadelphia
JA	James Alexander
JP	James Sullivan and others, eds., *The Papers of Sir William Johnson*, 14 vols. (Albany: University of the State of New York, 1921–1965).
LC	Library of Congress, Washington, DC.
NYCD	John Romeyn Brodhead, *Documents Relative to the Colonial History of the State of New-York*, ed. Edmund B. O'Callaghan and Berthold Fernow, 15 vols. (Albany, NY: Weed, Parsons, 1853–1887).
NYHS	New York Historical Society, New York City
NYPL	New York Public Library, New York City
Oxford DNB	*Oxford Dictionary of National Biography*, 61 vols. (New York: Oxford University Press, 2004).
PRO *Cal.*	Public Record Office, *Calendar*, Great Britain National Archives
RP	Rutherfurd Papers, New York Historical Society
SM	William Smith, Jr., *Historical Memoirs ... of William Smith, 1763–1783*, ed. William H. W. Sabine. 3 vols. (New York: New York Times, Arno Press, 1956–1971).

Introduction

In the 1870s genealogist Edwin R. Purple looked "in vain" for a sign of the reported grave site of his subject, Cadwallader Colden. "In turning away from the spot," "sadness" overwhelmed Purple "that one of New York's most gifted sons . . . was sleeping without monument or memorial, in a neglected and almost forgotten grave." The site looked no better in 1899. Years earlier, in the 1860s, John Gilmary Shea had lambasted New Yorkers: "It reflects little credit on New York that none of her sons have endeavored to present . . . the life of Cadwallader Colden . . . except to antiquaries and collectors, his very existence almost a myth."[1]

In 1879, Moses Coit Tyler insisted that Colden did have a memorial, if not one of marble. His monument consisted of "the vast mass of his writings, published and unpublished, which deal, acutely and philosophically, with almost every great topic of human interest—divinity, ethics, metaphysics, politics, mathematics, history, geology, botany, optics, zoology, medicine, agriculture, and even . . . the mechanic arts."[2]

While impressive in quantity, Colden's many writings could not alleviate the major reason for his obscurity among the general public. As Milton M. Klein commented, Colden constituted the very "archetype of the loyal servant of the Crown and the staunch defender of royal prerogative." Despite the fact that his two major fields of endeavor in New York—the colony's curious land system and his involvement in relations with the powerful Iroquois Indians—logically made him a royalist, nothing seemed enough to excuse his backing of the losing side in the American Revolution. His opposition to the supposed friends of liberty, New York's lawyers, saw him called "psychotic," "a belligerent clod," and a man possessed of a "classic paranoid style" as noted in a 2008 article, rather harsh terms even for a description of Cadwallader Colden.[3]

Colden's reputation had little chance to survive the War of Independence, the opening of which he lived to see, and had no chance at all to withstand the writings of the early nationalist historians. These patriotic Americans saw the Revolution as a struggle for liberty that emanated from the colonial assemblies, all the way back to the founding of the very first, Virginia's House of Burgesses. New York's General Assembly, therefore, formed an important cog in the development and nurturing of the spirit of liberty. No matter that, as the American republic grew older, its various legislatures often seemed corrupt and power-mad, the colonial assemblies had to be different. A royal official such as Colden, a supporter of the king's authority, had to be a foe of freedom itself and a dreaded role model for admirers of the American republic.

In reality, though, was New York's Assembly a bastion of liberty or something else entirely? In 1729, New York's Attorney-General Richard Bradley, not part of Colden's social circle, felt compelled to compile a report for his British superiors titled "Relating to Assemblys in the Plantations aiming at an Independency of the Crown." He related how the members of New York's Council, the other branch of the colonial legislature, two years before, had been threatened with "being Mobbed and pulled to pieces, and even privately murdered, and their estates ruined by actions at law" if they tried to thwart "the measures of the Assembly." The Assembly was so powerful, Bradley warned, that Britain had to change its system of colonial administration and appoint a special royal commissioner, as in Scotland, to examine all the Assembly's acts and to void any that went too far.[4]

If this advice was not followed, Bradley described what seemed to be inevitable. Reminding his readers of how hard it had been to suppress Virginia's Bacon's Rebellion in 1676, Bradley explained what would happen "if several" of the American colonies "should even at this time join in such a conspiracy (and could these Assemblys openly do more tho' they had actually so engaged)," the British would find it "extremely difficult and expensive if not impractical at this distance and in such a thicket of wood and Trees . . . to reduce them to their duty and obedience." America, a place "where people multiply so fast," was "of so vast extent" that British victory could not "be sure."[5]

During Colden's more than half-century long political career, he formed very clear opinions about colonial assemblies. Commiserating with a fellow sufferer from Massachusetts, Colden remarked: "You know Sir What kind of Creature an American assembly is." Colden understood, as he explained to his eldest son, that "The assemblies are at all times fond of power and to have their Governor dependent on them tho' they cover this view with different pretences." A cry for liberty, for example, would confuse their constituents into believing their assemblymen acted for the interests of the people. Generally, Colden believed, assemblymen "as a body they think themselves not accountable to any other authority and for that reason often act very unaccountably" and "spread alander and calumny with impunity." There Colden truly spoke from sad experience. These slanderers really had less "credit" than "private persons."[6]

Cadwallader Colden thought a great deal about the structure of government and can be considered a political scientist, one term that Tyler forgot. Writing a few years after Bradley, Colden, not as pessimistic as Bradley (then at least), did warn that the "Democratical or Popular part" of New York's government, the Assembly, "is too strong for the other parts"—the governor and Council—"and that in time it may swallow them both up." It took "no deep Skill in Politics" to realize that this imbalance would "in time like to endanger the Dependence" of the American colonies upon the mother country. Still, only "Very great Provocations and Hardships" would bring about such a separation.[7]

In the 1740s, Colden reiterated his belief in the importance of "a proper Ballance" found in the English Constitution as created by the "wise men and lovers of their Country" who were victorious over the Stuart James II in the Glorious Revolution of 1688, the year of Colden's birth. The Glorious Revolution ended any chance that England would dissolve into "an absolute Monarchy" like that of the powerful Tudor king Henry VIII. The monarch no longer presented a threat to balance. Instead, the "Democratical" branch, which the people were so "fond" of, created "more danger" to the essential balance. Colden's devotion to an earlier revolution did not endear him to supporters of a second.[8]

Despite Colden's backing of George III, after some time passed, interest in his life began to blossom. In 1805, Benjamin S. Barton, a Pennsylvania doctor with similar interests to Colden, declared his intention to write about him, but, alone among potential Colden biographers, Barton could not find enough material. In fairness to Barton, only four years later did Colden's grandson, Cadwallader D. Colden, announce that he had his illustrious forebear's papers—no one had known their whereabouts—and in 1811 came the report that he would write the great man's biography. It never appeared.[9]

In that year, another essay on Colden, often-cited, graced a journal devoted to medicine. A few other lesser publications had also appeared. William Allen's *Dictionary* of 1809, which had several editions in the nineteenth century, included a positive biography of the "respectable" Colden. Then in 1813, Gulian C. Verplanck penned what would be the most quoted essay on Colden—sometimes acknowledged, sometimes not—through the century. Calling the piece "hastily drawn up," Verplanck praised his subject as being far more influential than had been realized. "A mind thus powerful and active," he explained, "could not have failed to produce great effect on the character of that society in which he moved; and we doubtless now enjoy many beneficial, although remote effects of his labours, without being always able to trace them to their true source." The following year, a biography of Colden surfaced in an antiquarian collection with the help of one of his descendants, presumably Cadwallader D. Colden. And in 1850, the renowned documentary editor of New York, Edmund B. O'Callaghan, added his own (and influential) sketch of Colden.[10]

After the New York Historical Society obtained Colden's manuscripts in 1852—donated by a great-grandson—it started publishing them, finishing in the twentieth century with a total of eleven volumes plus some separate letters.[11]

Finally, some 130 years after Cadwallader Colden's death, an academic biography appeared, originating as a dissertation at Columbia University by Alice M. Keys under the sponsorship of Herbert L. Osgood, a prominent colonial historian of the day. The year 1906 was in the midst of the Progressive Era, and Keys treated Colden as if he had been a tool of the robber barons. Branding Colden "a faithful, if bigoted, servant" of the Crown, Keys went on insulting her subject. He was "a martinet, an intolerant theorist, an implacable stickler for the letter of the law, while tact and common sense became qualities to him unknown." Colden even lost "his humanity" by serving the British kings and government. Progressives had no liking for supporters of the royal prerogative.[12]

A biographer who detests her subject is truly a rarity. The tome today seems very quaint. Written in a superficial, nineteenth-century style, Keys's book printed large extracts of Colden's letters giving scholars a potential excuse not to read the originals. If anything, the book aged very fast and in 1956 Lawrence H. Leder savaged it. "Alice M. Keys' work may be taken by future biographers as the classic example of how not to write a biography." Adding to that stunning dismissal, Leder commented: "hardly one iota of his personality comes through after Miss Keys finished with him." Ten years later, Milton M. Klein complained about the lack of another biography of Cadwallader Colden, "a giant by reason of his virtuosity," who was "memorialized only by a [then] half-century old life which has been aptly characterized as a classic example of how not to write a biography."[13]

Despite this agreement by two leading scholars of early New York, no rush developed to write a new biography of Colden. The last decades of the twentieth century saw a decline in scholarly interest in biographies. Historians were drawn instead to increasingly-narrow aspects of social history. Alfred R. Hoermann did write an interesting account of Colden's scientific accomplishments but found something to praise in Keys's book. He also made some use of Keys's biography for Colden's political career, including her comment on his lack of humanity. Reviewing Hoermann's book, a scholar wrote that "a full-bodied and broad minded life of Cadwallader Colden, linking his interests with his intellect, is still very much needed."[14]

More than changing interests is responsible, however. Colden can be referred to as a polymath, a genius who divides his attention over many fields instead of only one. Andrew Robinson, who wrote a biography of a somewhat later polymath, Dr. Thomas Young, shrewdly remarked that "There can be little doubt that polymathy is exhausting, both for polymaths and for those who study them." Young passed away at 55 years old—Cadwallader Colden a few months short of 89 years of age. And his career was about as varied as it could be. Tyler's long list did not include Colden's over fifty-year political career that involved everyone from James Alexander to John Peter Zenger. No one could accuse Colden of being one of those colonial "governors who came and went."[15] Colden's voluminous manuscripts make writing a full biography of him very complex, to say the least.

Nonetheless, after a century a thorough and complete biography is long overdue. This book will look at the life of Cadwallader Colden, Scottish Whig and American Tory. It was possible for one man to be both.

NOTES

1. Edwin R. Purple, "Notes, Biographical and Genealogical, of the Colden Family, and of Some of Its Collateral Branches in America," *New York Genealogical and Biographical Record* 4 (1873): 167–68; John Gilmary Shea, introduction to Cadwallader Colden, *The History of the Five Indian Nations Depending on the Province of New-York* (New York: Bradford, 1727; rept. New York: T. H. Morrell, 1866), iii-iv; Henry D. Waller, *History of the Town of Flushing, Long Island, New York* (Flushing, NY: J. H. Ridenour, 1899), 115. Cadwallader Colden will be hereafter cited as CC in the notes. Some quotations have been slightly mondernized.

2. Moses Coit Tyler, *A History of American Literature: 1676–1765* (New York: G. P. Putnam, 1879), vol. 2, 213.

3. Milton M. Klein, "Prelude to Revolution in New York: Jury Trials and Judicial Tenure," *William and Mary Quarterly* 3rd ser., 17, no. 4 (1960): 443–44; Evarts B. Greene, "New York and the Old Empire," *Quarterly Journal of the New York State Historical Association* 8, no. 2 (1927): 125–26; Gregory Afinogenov, "Lawyers and Politics in Eighteenth-Century New York," *New York History* 89, no. 2 (2008): 143, 159, 162.

4. Richard Bradley, "Relating to Assemblys in the Plantations aiming at an Independency of the Crown," November 22, 1729, in John Romeyn Brodhead, *Documents Relative to the Colonial History of the State of New-York*, ed. Edmund B. O'Callaghan and Berthold Fernow (Albany, NY: Weed, Parsons, 1853–1887), vol. 5, 902–3 (hereafter cited *NYCD*).

5. Bradley, "Relating to Assemblys," in *NYCD*, vol. 5, 902–3.

6. CC to William Shirley, July 25, 1749, in Cadwallader Colden, *The Letters and Papers of Cadwallader Colden*, 9 vols. (New York: New York Historical Society, 1918–1937) (hereafter cited *CP*), vol. 4, 120 21; CC to Alexander Colden (son, hereafter cited AC), n.d., *CP*, vol. 5, 316–17; CC, "The Colden Letters on Smith's History," New York Historical Society (hereafter ctied NYHS), *Collections* (hereafter cited *Coll*/Coll., non-italics indicates not published)., vol. 1, (1868), 201.

7. CC, "Comments on government in general," n.d., Colden Papers (unpublished), New York Historical Society (microfilm) (hereafter cited CPU), reel 2; Paul M. Hamlin, ed., "'He Is Gone and Peace to His Shade': William Smith, Historian, Posthumously Boils Lieutenant Governor Cadwallader Colden in Oil," *New York Historical Society Quarterly* 36, no. 2 (1952): 162. For an excellent account of CC's political ideas, see Carole Shammas, "Cadwallader

Colden and the Role of the King's Prerogative," *New York Historical Society Quarterly* 53, no. 2 (1969): 110–15.

8. CC, "Publick affairs 1744–45," *CP*, vol. 9, 251–53; CC, "A Letter about Governors," August 1, 1737, *CP*, vol. 9, 243.

9. Benjamin S. Barton to Mrs. [Heart?], January 28, 1805, Benjamin S. Barton Papers, Historical Society of Pennsylvania, Philadelphia (hereafter cited HSP); *American National Biography* (New York: Oxford University Press, 1999), in 24 vols. (hereafter cited *ANB*), s.v. Barton, Benjamin Smith; Cadwallader D. Colden to Dr. Mitchell, September 25, 1809 (New York: Oxford University Press, 1999); Cadwallader D. Colden, "For the Port Folio," *Port Folio*, n.s., 3rd ser., 3 (January 1810): 33–34; "Biographical Sketch of the late Honourable Cadwallader Colden, formerly Lieutenant-Governor of New-York, with an Account of His Writings," *American Medical and Philosophical Register* 1 (January 1811): 301–3.

10. "Biographical Sketch," 297–303; William Allen, *An American Biographical and Historical Dictionary* (Cambridge, MA: William Hillard, 1809), 198; V [Gulian C. Verplanck], "Biographical Memoir of Cadwallader Colden, M.D. F.R.S. Lieutenant-Governor of the Colony of New York," *Monthly Recorder* (June 1813): 150, 153; Robert W. July, *The Essential New Yorker: Gulian Crommelin Verplanck* (Durham, NC: Duke University Press, 1951), 100; Timothy Alden, *A Collection of American Epitaphs and Inscriptions with Occasional Notes* (New York: [S. Marks, Printer], 1814), vol. 5, 268–75; *The Documentary History of the State of New-York; Arranged Under Direction of the Hon. Christopher Morgan, Secretary of State*, ed. Edmund B. O'Callaghan (Albany, NY: Weed, Parsons, 1849–1851), vol. 4, 829n-834n (hereafter cited *DH*).

11. *CP*, vol. 8, vii.

12. Alice Mapelsden Keys, *Cadwallader Colden: A Representative Eighteenth-Century Official* (New York: Columbia University Press, 1906; repr. New York: AMS Press, 1967), viii, 365, 368–69. For a similar Progressive attack see Everett Kimball, *The Public Life of Joseph Dudley: A Study of Colonial Policy of the Stuarts in New England, 1660–1715* (New York: Longmans, Green, 1911).

13. Lawrence H. Leder, "A Neglected Aspect of New York's Forgotten Century," *New York History* 37, no. 3 (1956): 262; Milton M. Klein, "Politics and Personalities in Colonial New York," *New York History* 47, no. 1 (1966): 12–13. See also Charles W. Akers, review of *The Reinterpretation of Early American History: Essays in Honor of John Edwin Pomfret*, by Ray Allen Billington, *Journal of American History* 54, no. 1 (1967): 89; and *The Empire State: A History of New York*, ed. Milton M. Klein (Ithaca, NY: Cornell University Press, 2001), 746.

14. Alfred R. Hoermann, *Cadwallader Colden: A Figure of the American Enlightenment* (Westport, CT: Greenwood Press, 2002), xii, 177, 181, 184, 187, 188n9–10, 189n21, 189n35, 190n46–47; Wayne Bodle, review of *Cadwallader Colden: A Figure of the American Enlightenment*, by Alfred R. Hoermann, *William and Mary Quarterly*, 3rd ser., 60, no. 2 (2003): 446–48. Two recent books on Colden, first by Seymour I. Schwartz, then by John M. Dixon, have not been consulted for the present study. In this I have followed the example of Forrest McDonald, who did not examine Robert E. Brown's book with a similar topic until his own work was published.

15. "Biographical Sketch," 299; Andrew Robinson, *The Last Man Who Knew Everything: Thomas Young, the Anonymous Genius Who Proved Newton Wrong and Deciphered the Rosetta Stone, Among Other Surprising Feats* (New York: Plume, 2006), 10; Alexander C. Flick, *History of the State of New York* (New York: Columbia University Press, 1933–1937), vol. 3, 135–36.

Chapter One

The Drummer

Reportedly, the Scottish name Colden derived from a place called Cowden in the shire of Midlothian and, in Scotland, Colden seems "to have been pronounced Couden or Cowdon." Perhaps, though, Cadwallader Colden gave a real clue to his family's origins when he named his country home in New York Coldingham (as it was first spelled).[1]

The original Coldingham, a famed monastery in Scotland, had been established in the middle of the seventh century. Its great age led to great wealth for the priory, creating numerous disputes over who controlled its revenue. Popes, kings, and nobles seemed preoccupied with Coldingham. One Scottish king, James III—who had meddled with its wealth—was murdered. Another, James V, deposited one of his illegitimate children there. Adding to Coldingham's importance, by the thirteenth century it stood about one day's march for an English army that had crossed the Scottish border.[2]

Cadwallader Colden had no love for the Catholic monastic tradition so, logically, there may have been an ancestral link. Some Scottish nobles had added "of Coldingham" to their names. Perhaps the Coldens originated as a cadet branch of a noble family or had branched off as an illegitimate line. Many churchmen had been at the monastery too. Given the sad state of Scottish Catholicism, one of them may have fathered a child, a common enough event, whose last name was shortened to Colden. In any case, the truth is unlikely to be discovered.[3]

What is known is that Coldens were drawn to the ministry of the Presbyterian Church and were opposed to the Stuart kings' attempts to make it compatible to the Church of England. A Rev. John Colden of Borthwick would so infuriate James VI of Scotland (James I of England), who had tried to restore bishops to Scotland, that in 1607 Colden was warded, that is jailed.[4]

However, the connection of Rev. John Colden to Cadwallader Colden (along with that of a Thomas Colden, a minister in 1669) is unknown. With the Rev. Robert Colden, the ancestral link is certain. A graduate of St. Andrews in 1626, Robert Colden had ministered to a Presbyterian flock in Ireland. In 1641 some of the hated Protestants suffered "brutal attack" along with "pillage" at the hands of the Catholic Irish, making Colden and his family flee. By 1643 they were refugees in Dunfermline. In 1650 Colden became the minister at Bunkle in Scotland. Four years later, his child, Alexander Colden, was born. Alexander Colden, in turn, became the father of Cadwallader Colden.[5]

Following an apparent family tradition, Alexander Colden, after graduating from the University of Edinburgh in 1675, sought to become a minister. Yet he would not be ordained until 1683 and that would be in Ireland. Jobs were scarce in Scotland, a country marked by dire poverty and plagued by gangs of violent beggars. This economic distress persisted long after Cadwallader Colden emigrated to America. When Alexander Colden was a new college graduate, Scots tended to seek their fortune in Ireland—from which his own father had fled. Exactly where the young man journeyed is uncertain; all his son said later was that his father was "in Ireland" during 1681. Presumably, the locale was Enniscorthy, the site of his future ordination. Most likely, he served as a school teacher, common work for an unemployed college man inclined to the ministry. Being in Enniscorthy, County Wexford, in southeastern Ireland, involved Alexander Colden in dramatic events important both to the future of the British Isles and his yet unborn son. Alexander Colden would forge a strong link between his family and powerful nobles, the Campbells, who held the earldom (and later dukedom) of Argyle.[6]

In 1681, the Scottish Parliament passed a *Test Act* that put the king in charge of the Presbyterian Church. As a further complication, next in line to the Stuart Charles II stood his Catholic brother James, the Duke of York. Meanwhile, some Scottish ministers switched to the Anglican Church, including Gilbert Burnet who became a bishop.[7]

A prominent Scottish nobleman, Archibald Campbell, the ninth earl of Argyle, refused to obey the *Test Act*. Convicted of treason and confined to Edinburgh Castle, he awaited his execution. "No sentence in our age was more universally cried out on than this," insisted Bishop Burnet. On December 20, 1681, Argyle's stepdaughter visited him and he changed into the "livery cloaths" of her page. Carrying "up her train behind her" as she left, Argyle coolly started to walk out of the castle but dropped the train in mud. His calm daughter yelled at her father, a "careless loon," and threw the mud-covered cloth at his face, obscuring it. Befitting the lowly status of a page, the mud-splattered earl stood on the rear of her coach and rode away. Once beyond the castle grounds, the earl slipped away and disappeared. Proclaimed a fugitive the next day, anyone who aided Argyle would suffer the "highest pains." If any accomplices resisted arrest and were killed, the law officers could not be touched by the law. What happened to Argyle from that point on was a mystery to those who knew nothing about Alexander Colden.[8]

According to some historians, William Veitch, an "outed" minister, a true sufferer at the hands of the Stuarts, saved the fugitive earl. Veitch, who wildly exaggerated his role, claimed that he led the earl on a dangerous trip through England and had many adventures, getting the nobleman safely to London. There, Argyle talked with supporters and wrote much bad poetry before finally going into exile in Holland.[9]

By 1718, though, the unhappy Veitch complained that he had gotten little to show for his dangerous undercover work. The ninth earl of Argyle, for whom he had risked so much, had promised "him a suitable reward in money" and "a free farm." In July 1718 Veitch wrote to the ninth earl's grandson, John Campbell, the second duke of Argyle, who made "many repeated promises to reimburse him . . . yet never was there anything done."[10]

The earliest writers about Veitch, often ministers themselves, fell for his story. As Robert Wodrow declared, Veitch penned dramatic accounts of his services "interspersed with several very remarkable appearances of providence in his behalf." Who could suspect a minister deposed by the Stuarts whose life showed the intervention of the hand of God? Writing in 1718, after the death of both the ninth earl and his son with the same name, the first duke of Argyle, Veitch must have been surprised by the stalling of the second duke who had been reluctant to be honest with Veitch. Although Veitch probably aided the earl in London, Duke John knew Cadwallader Colden—this duke had "all the fine Spirit and good Sense natural to the family" he thought—and, more important, knew that Alexander Colden—not William Veitch—had gotten his grandfather to safety in 1681.[11]

Years later, Cadwallader Colden explained to a friend, Dr. John Mitchell, then staying at the Argyle estates, about "the great regard my father always had to that noble family." The ninth earl had escaped to Ireland and "discovered himself to my father" who "was of some use to him in assisting him to go from Ireland to Holland." Colden, here relating events before his birth, got a detail wrong. The earl of Argyle stayed in London for a time; everyone knew it too, even Charles II, who refused to permit a search for the earl in the city. Surely there were more ships leaving Enniscorthy (or some other place in Ireland) headed to London than to Holland.[12]

Alexander Colden's role in rescuing the earl helps explain the course of future events. In 1683 Colden, at last, became a minister at Enniscorthy, a probable reward for services rendered. And his "considerable interest with many of the Nobility" seems to be another result of the assistance. His son recalled that the first duke of Argyle made several visits to Rev. Colden in Scotland while Cadwallader was young. Why would a Highland noble show such "esteem" to a borderer in Scotland—someone who lived far away near the English border? There is only one explanation: Alexander Colden had endeared himself to the Campbells by helping the earl.[13]

Alexander Colden's bravery in opposing the Stuarts explains some events in his son's life as well. Colden's long-lasting friendship with Lord Jedburgh, the third marquess of Lothian, no longer seems surprising; Jedburgh's father had married into the Argyle family after the Stuarts outlawed it. When Colden was in political trouble, Archibald Campbell, the third duke of Argyle, was expected to drop everything and rush to his assistance. That one of the most influential men in Great Britain would willingly help a colonial official in distant New York—who had been away for decades—no longer appears so remarkable. Colden's success in holding on to his offices for so long, even during the administration of New York's tyrannical governor William Cosby, partly happened because of his father's bravery in helping a fugitive earl.[14]

Contrast such facts with the unproven assertions of William Veitch. Along with the story's unbelievable nature, his wife's diary does not confirm that he guided the earl, despite the assertion of her editor. The family's credibility is further strained by the escapades of Samuel Vetch, their son, who emigrated to America. Caught trading with the French enemy during wartime, Vetch sparked a political crisis in Massachusetts.[15]

Now that Alexander Colden had secure employment as a minister, he married Jane Hughes in 1687. A year later, on February 7, 1688, Cadwallader Colden was born in Enniscorthy, Ireland.[16] The family grew quickly and the eldest child gained three brothers, Ebenezer, William, and James, and a sister, Elizabeth. William reportedly immigrated to America and died there. Nothing is known about Cadwallader's other siblings except for James, who followed in their father's footsteps and entered the ministry in 1722.[17]

Much had changed politically after Alexander Colden's ordination in 1683. The earl of Argyle, to thwart the "popish design" of the Catholic James VII (James II of England) in Scotland, launched an inept invasion of the Highlands in 1685. Captured, this time he was executed.[18]

Yet James II had not ended all opposition to his reign. His enemies invited William of Orange, the husband of James's daughter, Mary, to take power. Late in 1688 Prince William invaded Britain, King James fled, and William and Mary ruled jointly. Because of this Glorious Revolution, the English Constitution now became a shining, Whiggish example of liberty. Parliament gained power while the king's was weakened.[19]

In 1690 Alexander Colden moved his family to Bunkle in Scotland, his father's old post, and became its minister. Three years later, Rev. Colden shifted to Duns. Finally, in 1700 he settled in Oxnam, outside of Kelso, where he preached until his death.[20]

Cadwallader Colden's parents handled his early education. As the eldest son, his father, whose own ministerial reputation kept growing, expected him to enter the traditional occupation of the Colden family, the Presbyterian ministry. Young Colden entered his father's alma mater, the University of Edinburgh, a school not polluted by a papist foundation, in 1703.[21]

Despite Scotland's poverty, the universities were very different from England's class conscious ones, Oxford and Cambridge. In Scotland, even students such as Colden from a poor background could attend. The great esteem his father had gained did not change the low salary he earned. "The clergy were allowed almost to starve," a minister moaned. Luckily, Colden's father had been able to meet all of his son's expenses at Edinburgh.[22]

By all appearances, Colden received a superb education at Edinburgh. William Law taught the latest scientific theories of Sir Isaac Newton contained in his *Principia Mathematica* and another new book, his *Opticks*. And at Edinburgh, "Natural History" went hand-in-hand with medicine, which Colden was drawn to.[23]

Colden always remained vague as to why he had abandoned the goal of becoming a minister. After some time at college, "my inclinations were averse to entering into orders in the church." Although his mother appears to have known the truth, he would never tell his father. Rev. Colden, as late as 1717, still hoped that his eldest would change his mind about the ministry as a career. Cadwallader Colden had come to doubt the truth of the Trinity, a basic concept of Christianity. That heresy made a ministerial career impossible for him—even though, because of his father's reputation, his success in the Presbyterian Church had been assured. Having become a deist, something Cadwallader Colden shared with Newton, he rejected the other-worldly aspects of Christianity although not the existence of God.[24]

Finishing all the requirements for a M.A. degree in April 1705, Colden now had to obtain the necessary expertise to practice medicine. Although the University of Edinburgh did not then have a medical school, it granted its first M.D. degree barely a month after Colden graduated. Therefore, Colden could have stayed at Edinburgh and undertaken his medical training there. But he had had enough of a university setting. As he observed years later, "The Professors generally are sollicitous to establish an opinion of their great knowledge, but are not sufficiently careful to shew to their Pupils how far their knowledge is deficient." Instead, Colden moved to London and attended anatomy and chemistry courses with doctors, a system still in place at the end of the eighteenth century.[25]

Sometime before Colden finished his medical training— probably long before—he met Alice Chrystie, his future wife. Alfred R. Hoermann's suggestion that he met her in 1715 is wrong. She was the sister of his best friend from college, James Chrystie, who also graduated in 1705. It is inconceivable that Colden would not have discovered that his best friend, whose family lived in nearby Kelso, had a marriageable sister two years younger than him. In fact, Colden's son, Cadwallader Colden Jr. wrote that his parents had been "pre-engaged" long before their marriage. This love between Alice and her future husband, and his ardent desire to marry her, explain upcoming events. Cadwallader Colden is frozen into history as an old man, yet he was once a young man and deeply in love with his intended.[26]

In 1710 Colden wanted to marry Alice and raise a family, but he needed money to do so. His father's resources had been all but wiped out by his medical training. Could Colden quickly raise the necessary cash by practicing medicine? The answer was no. To start a practice in London, a doctor needed sufficient money "to make that figure which it is necessary for a young Physician to do in Great Britain." Thomas Young, also from a poor family, had a wealthy great-uncle who provided the funds needed to start Young's London practice. Colden had no such uncle. Nor was Scotland a viable alternative. A doctor there was usually so poor he had to be a trader too. That would not do.[27]

Scotland remained as poor a place as when Alexander Colden had emigrated to Ireland. Some Scots journeyed to Scandinavia—Cadwallader Colden had two brothers-in-law who settled in Norway. However, by 1710, when Colden had to make a decision, North America seemed a good alternative. The *Act of Union* (1707) had united the two kingdoms of England and Scotland, thus opening the English colonies to Scottish immigrants. (Some decades later, Scots would be drawn to India.) Colden picked the colony of Pennsylvania. Although he did not have a rich uncle, he did have a well-off aunt, Elizabeth Hill, a Quaker merchant, in Philadelphia. Now a widow and childless, she had invited him to join her. As a further inducement, a merchant could set up a business in Philadelphia for about £400; a trader in Britain needed thousands more.[28]

Arriving in Philadelphia in 1710, Colden left behind no account of his reactions to America. He might have agreed with a Swedish immigrant who sailed to Philadelphia a few years afterward. Although the city was sickly—ague was common—still "this city is very beautiful and lovely and abundant with God's blessings on both land and sea." Peaches were one of those blessings as were the trees. "The forest is very lovely and beautiful, there is no garden in Sweden so wonderful to walk in, as the forest here in America and smells so good."[29]

Colden lost no time in jumping into the business world. He sold everything, dry goods, flour, herring, currants—whatever was available. He does not seem to have had any time for medicine. The year after his arrival he undertook a trading voyage to Jamaica, sailed all around the Gulf of Mexico, then showed up in Charleston, South Carolina, where he made contacts and learned what items were in demand there. Philadelphia's trade was poor, as the merchants had imported too much from Britain, causing an oversupply, leaving all the traders with inventory they could not dispose of at any price. Nor did enemy privateers hovering off the coast—Queen Anne's War

(1702–1713) was underway—help. To make business even worse, some English merchants had sent shiploads of goods to Philadelphia, then dumped them into the market by selling them at cost. Colden was reduced to sending goods into the countryside to try to sell something. In 1713 he tried another Caribbean voyage, this time to Antigua.[30]

Despite Colden's determined interest in earning the money he needed, his restless mind remained intrigued by science. On one of his Caribbean cruises, he witnessed numerous waterspouts; one came within 120 feet of his ship. Far in the future, he used these observations to theorize how they were created.[31]

Science, however, remained a secondary concern. Already, in 1712, Colden wondered about the shaky finances of many Philadelphia merchants. By May 1714 things had improved somewhat; Philadelphia now had "an Indifferent good Market." But in November 1714, everything went bust. The spectacular bankruptcy of a female merchant—she owed more than £3000—cascaded through Philadelphia, hurting other traders. Colden lost something less than £200. Little could be regained as the bankrupt had transferred her property to a relative, and Pennsylvania had no law that could void the transfer.[32]

Despite that disaster, Colden's finances had not been damaged too much. As he later wrote, by 1714 he "had sufficient for" his goal and on December 2, 1714, he was set for a trip back to London and Scotland (with a stopover in Lisbon). He planned to be away for a year. Colden, as he left Philadelphia around April 1715, knew that the next twelve months would be memorable for him. Yet he could not have guessed that year would be just as memorable for Great Britain.[33]

After Colden's arrival in London, he traveled to Kelso with William Kerr, Lord Jedburgh, the heir to the earldom of Lothian. In the future, Kerr was known to be "much addicted to debauchery," a proclivity he shared with his father, "a Thorough Libertine." Although the two young men had known each other as children, their traveling together was not only due to friendship but safety as well. In September 1715 an uprising by Jacobites, supporters of the Catholic Stuart heirs of deposed monarch James VII, had caused "confusion" in Scotland as Rev. Colden revealed to his son. Because of the weakness of the new Hanoverian dynasty and government, which had only 6,000 soldiers in Britain itself, Jedburgh, a Whiggish military man and a colonel of the Scots Foot Guards, had been ordered "to raise volunteers for the King's service against the Rebels" in Scotland. Jedburgh's soldiers, who stayed in England to protect its southern coast from possible French attack, would have been handy to have in Scotland.[34]

When back with the Coldens in Oxnam, Cadwallader attended his father's church as usual on Sunday, October 20, 1715, when he was handed a letter from Jedburgh alerting him that a large force of Jacobites had landed. Asking him to gather as many supporters of the Hanoverians as he could, Jedburgh told him to rejoin him in Kelso. Colden "beat a drum . . . by his Father's order in the Church Gard." Someone who beat a drum in such a fashion was recruiting men for military service in both Britain and her American colonies. Gathering about seventy volunteers—the largest single group Jedburgh received—they joined the colonel in Kelso, whose citizens opposed the "Popish Pretender, and all his abettors." Colden became an officer of the assembled force, probably numbering about 300.[35]

What the eager loyalists did not realize (and Jedburgh soon discovered) was that Jacobite forces in Scotland planned to rendezvous at Kelso. Some 1,500 Jacobites vastly outnumbered the Kelso loyalists. As an experienced soldier, Jedburgh knew the hopelessness of a five to one disadvantage and ordered Colden and the others to go home. A few supposed Kelso Jacobites—probably really men who wanted to save their town from destruction—told the approaching rebels that no fighting was needed to take it. During the English wars, as a border town, Kelso had been burned every time the enemy seized it, leading a local historian to write that "No town in Scotland has been more frequently visited by fire . . . than the town of Kelso." The residents, not "congenial" to the Stuart pretender to the throne, knew that Jedburgh had been right—resistance was futile. When the Jacobites occupied the town with no bloodshed, they proclaimed the pretender to be king and yelled "No union! No malt! No salt-tax!" On October 27, 1715, the Jacobites abandoned still-intact Kelso, ending a very dangerous week for the Coldens, and marched off to total defeat elsewhere.[36]

Throughout Scotland, areas where the Presbyterian Church was strong saw the greatest support for the Protestant Hanoverians. Not surprisingly, the Rev. Alexander Colden, a vigorous foe of the Stuarts, had backed the German rulers of Hanover. Rev. Colden saw the Hanoverian dynasty as the surest way to preserve Protestantism in Britain forever. Although the son had drifted away from his father's religious faith, Cadwallader Colden remained true to his father's political beliefs and Hanoverian leaning. In the 1760s, Cadwallader commented that "tho' old," he was "able still to beat the Drum" for the king—the Hanoverian George III.[37]

With the Jacobites gone from Kelso, Colden now could accomplish what he had returned to Scotland for. On November 11, 1715 he married Alice; their "Honey Month" followed. Colden's mother, seeing "the good hand of God" in the marriage, believed that Alice was "the most fit wife" for her son. A descendent agreed, writing that Alice "performed the duties of a Wife, Mother, and Mistress with peculiar propriety." Alice's father, David Chrystie, is always referred to as a minister usually of Kelso. But, in 1715, Chrystie was not Kelso's minister; a "Mr. Ramsey" was. Nor is Chrystie listed in the compendious *Fasti Ecclesiae Scoticanae*. As Kelso lacked a settled minister from 1699 to 1707, he could have filled the pulpit occasionally. Perhaps he taught at the Kelso grammar school, part of the religious establishment. After his daughter's marriage, he was appointed the governor of Edinburgh's Heriot's Hospital which, despite its name, was a school. Whatever his occupation, Chrystie's letters show him to be deeply religious.[38]

Now a married man, Colden journeyed to London. There he met Dr. Edmund Halley (of comet fame) and other authorities in mathematics, then Colden's chief interest. Impressed by the young man, Halley, on January 12, 1716, read a paper by Colden on the "Animal Oeconomy"—which theorized how bodies worked—and tried to explain fevers and their cure to the Royal Society. The excited Colden kept hoping to hear if Halley had "taken any further notice" of his work. That never happened.[39]

Colden had another exploit planned while in London. By early February 1716 he sought to become a licentiate of the Royal College of Physicians of London. Getting a license from the College would allow him to practice medicine in the capital. Of course, he could not afford to stay there, but being a licentiate, a honor marking the elite of the profession, would set him above most doctors—especially in the colonies. No doubt to his surprise, Colden failed the examination. Considering that he had been preoccupied for years selling things instead of studying medicine, the result seems predictable. However, Scots traditionally had difficulties with the Royal College of Physicians; some were so disturbed by their experience that they became midwives. Naturally, being from Oxford or Cambridge or an Anglican helped a prospective licentiate. This setback may explain why Colden complained about the "assurance"—over-confidence—college students obtain from their education.[40]

Disappointing as such a failure had to have been, Colden had received other, more exciting news. Alice was pregnant. By early January, her being with child was certain; the ladies decided among themselves that it was a boy. A female friend urged Alice to remember them after her departure and, because they could then no longer gossip over tea, she had to bring her son back to Scotland soon for a visit.[41]

The prospect of a grandchild stirred the feelings of her parents and in-laws. Her mother, who "cannot digest the loss of her daughter," took parental concern to an extreme. She insisted on knowing exactly when the child was due, intending to sail to Philadelphia in time to help in the birth.[42]

Meanwhile, Alexander Colden, disturbed by the lessening in the volume of letters from his son, feared that the marriage had lessened his son's love for his parents. Rev. Colden soon made a "sincere" proposal to his son, one that must have startled him. Only the general outline is known. If the son did not go back to America, his father would give him such a substantial financial settlement that it would all but impoverish his parents. "I would rather Straiten myself than that you should be straitened," the minister wrote. His son could not accept prospering by plunging his parents into poverty. Sad-

Figure 1.1. *Mrs. Cadwallader Colden*, c. 1749-52 by John Wollaston (c. 1710-c. 1767). Alice about 1750, long after her marriage to Cadwallader Colden. Oil on canvas, 30 x 25 in. Bequest of Grace Wilkes, 1922 (22.45.7) ART463381. *The Metropolitan Museum of Art. Image copyright © The Metropolitan Museum of Art. Image source: Art Resource, New York.*

dened by the failure of the scheme to keep the young couple in Scotland, Rev. Colden asked that his son let them know when they arrived safely in far-off America.[43]

The Chrysties, acting in collusion with the Coldens, tried to convince the young couple to return to Scotland soon. Targeting Alice, her mother, Alison Hamilton, tried to overwhelm her with guilt. A letter from her daughter had brought joy mixed with disappointment because God had "thought fit to remove you at so great a distance from me." Experiencing "great grief," she regretted "parting with such a dutiful daughter," whom she had hoped would be "the light of my old age." At least her daughter had promised to return, and Hamilton brought up her mother-in-law's wish that Elizabeth Hill come back to Scotland too. That reunion would eliminate any "fear" of the couple staying in America. (Deprived of Hill's financial support, they probably would have had little choice but to return, delighting both the Colden and Chrystie families.) Finally, Alice's mother let loose her anger at Cadwallader Colden: "I had almost forgot to call him my son or rather he would not allow me to do so for he gives his respects to Mistress Chrystie instead of mother," she screamed in writing. "I think I deserve that title seeing I have not kept back my only daughter from being his wife."[44]

The Chrysties kept pelting Alice with guilt in the future. On September 9, 1717, well after her departure, her father mentioned that her brother James had become a minister in a poor place, but her parents were happy he was nearby unlike Alice and her other brothers. And her mother's health had gotten worse. The same day James Chrystie urged his sister that, once she had some more children, bring "your whole cargo" on a trip to Scotland.[45]

Despite the familial pressures, neither Cadwallader nor Alice were deterred from leaving Scotland. On March 3, 1716 they took passage on the *Gloucester*, which sailed from Land's End, the westernmost part of England, to the American colony of Maryland. The trip across the Atlantic saw a commonplace event during a long sea voyage—a mysterious "stubborn" fever broke out infecting nineteen of the twenty-six people on board. Apparently, neither Colden nor the pregnant Alice were among the sufferers. All of those ill eventually asked Colden for his aid, but some who had trusted to their own remedies almost waited too long. Dr. Colden's treatment was based on his paper read at the Royal Society. Few drugs were prescribed; the essential thing was "Catching the Critical Moment and knowing . . . what Secretion" had to be employed. His patients willingly allowed their doctor to experiment—"purging or sweating" used when urine was still clear failed. He performed bloodletting "freely" when necessary. Keeping the ill "cool" was essential. All of his patients survived and disembarked in Maryland on April 10. As Dr. Colden would write a year later: "I have been very lucky in my practice."[46]

Arriving in Philadelphia on May 7, 1716, Colden immediately rushed back into trade. By September 1716 he had managed to pay off his London landlady and a considerable personal loan. He did discover that the Philadelphia market was "more over-glutted with goods than ever."[47]

The erratic market in Philadelphia did not surprise Colden. Before he had set out for Britain, he had decided to change his focus. He had sold wheat at his stop in Portugal to help pay some expenses. While in London he arranged to sell medicines in Portugal. When back in Philadelphia he began to practice medicine seriously and, at the same time, continued to trade various articles. But now, in response to the market, he would specialize in selling medications—a line of goods unlikely to be dumped in Philadelphia by British merchants. In America, the price of imported drugs might be jacked up by as much as 300 percent. Insisting on a wholesale price, he ordered larger quantities than he could use quickly in his own practice. Among the medical supplies ordered were three dozen spectacles, "white sugar Candy" and "choice" rhubarb, used as a laxative.[48]

Although Colden's imported elixir did not sell well in Philadelphia, his combination of medicine and trade did lead to more purchases. His personal imports from Britain demonstrate in what directions his mind would be heading: a barometer, a thermometer, various books including one on astronomy, and the very latest version of Newton's *Opticks*. And Colden could now afford to become a slaveholder. He sold a sassy kitchen slave to Barbados, away from her children, so that she would not ruin them for work. The West Indies was a good place for her, her former master believed, because "the Custom of the country . . . will not allow us to use our Negroes as you do in Barbados."[49]

The success of Colden's dual careers came at the right time as his first son was born on August 13, 1716. Because of all the help Aunt Elizabeth had provided, the parents had given her the opportunity of naming the boy. The Coldens, both in Philadelphia and Scotland, expected her to christen him John, her late spouse's name. To the surprise of everyone, Elizabeth Hill called him Alexander, after Cadwallader's father, following the Scottish tradition that an eldest son gave his first son the name of the child's paternal grandfather. Her decision went over very well in Oxnam. Rev. Colden sent his thanks to his sister-in-law and praised his son too but also reminded him of his responsibility for the souls of not only his family but those of his slaves. Cadwallader's eldest would be called Sandie, a common nickname for a Scottish boy with red hair.[50]

Elizabeth Hill's stock in Oxnam rose even higher with another generous act. She promised that, if Rev. Colden died before her, she would help the Scottish Coldens. As James Colden was then studying at the University of Edinburgh, this promise of financial assistance meant a great deal to the family. Nonetheless, the Coldens still hoped to have their family united again. In 1718 his mother, distressed to hear that her sister had been very ill, reminded her son of the possible consequences of his aunt's death: "what a grief would it have been to us if God had taken her from you when you and your poor young babs are so far from us."[51]

That distressing prospect had not happened, however, and Colden's business successes had given him some leisure time. He filled it with intellectual pursuits, often in league with Alice's cousin, James Logan, a Quaker and one of the founders of Pennsylvania. His family had fled from persecution in Europe. Another polymath, Logan studied everything including mathematics. Corresponding with other like-minded individuals, Logan had a special affinity with Brigadier Robert Hunter, governor of New York and New Jersey since 1710, also the year of Colden's arrival. Hunter shared Logan's interest in Latin, the classics, and science. In 1717 Logan informed the governor that Colden was then busily revising his Royal Society paper and "is certainly very happy in his Speculations." Colden gave his comrade an account of some of his ideas about secretions to pass on to the intellectual soldier in New York.[52]

Meanwhile, Colden had already sought Logan's aid in improving both his financial situation and the dismal cultural atmosphere in Philadelphia. As Logan related, Colden had sought the passage of a law giving him a salary "as physician for the poor of this place," an idea that Logan really liked. But Colden wanted the prospective bill to do more. Included on his agenda was the establishment of "a public physical lecture" in the city, somewhat like what was done in London, and payment for a doctor to examine all corpses. The colonial assembly refused to approve Colden's suggested innovations.[53]

Just as unsuccessful was a joint Logan-Colden project—an investigation of "our great American eclipse" of the sun in 1717. The two would-be astronomers wished to get readings about a principle called "parallax"—how the apparent location of stars is affected by this planet's movement. They set a telescope the proper way but, because of "an unlucky accident," the device was knocked akilter when it was needed. Unable to correct the problem quickly, the experiment was ruined. The pair could watch the end of the solar event using "a smoked Glass"—to protect their eyes—and a telescope.[54]

Colden, in 1717, had no idea that his stay in Pennsylvania would soon be eclipsed. A visit to New York City would change both his destiny and that of the colony of New York.

NOTES

1. George F. Black, *The Surnames of Scotland: Their Origin, Meaning, and History* (New York: New York Public Library, 1946), 161; Timothy Alden, *A Collection of American Epitaphs and Inscriptions with Occasional Notes* (New York: [S. Marks, Printer], 1814), vol. 5, 268–75.

2. William Croft Dickinson, *Scotland from the Earliest Times to 1603* (New York: Th. Nelson, 1961), 47, 228–29, 270, 270n3; Michael Brown, *The Wars of Scotland, 1214–1371* (Edinburgh: Edinburgh University Press, 2004), 122; Norman Macdougall, *James III: A Political Study* (Edinburgh: John Donald, Humanities Press, 1982), 236–37; R. L. Mackie, *King James IV of Scotland: A Brief Survey of His Life and Times* (Edinburgh: Oliver and Boyd, 1958), 33, 35, 39; "Journal of the Movements of King Edward in Scotland," in *Documents*

Illustrative of the History of Scotland, ed. Joseph Stevenson (Edinburgh: H. M. General Register House, 1870), vol. 2, 26. For CC's name spelled as "Colding" in 1718 before his home was named, see New York State, *Calendar of N.Y. Colonial Manuscripts Indorsed Land Papers in the Office of the Secretary of State of New York, 1643–1803*, comp. E. B. O'Callaghan (Albany, NY: Weed, Parsons, 1864; repr. Harrison, NY: Harbor-Hill Books, 1987), 126.

3. "Diary of John Knox," in *Scottish Diaries and Memoirs, 1550–1746*, ed. J. G. Fyfe (Stirling, Scotland: E. Mackay, 1928), 19; Peter Fry and Fiona Somerset, *The History of Scotland* (London: Routledge, 1982; repr. New York: Routledge, 1995), 130.

4. *Fasti Ecclesiae Scoticanae: The Succession of Ministers in the Church of Scotland From the Reformation*, 2nd ed., ed. Hew Scott (Edinburgh: Oliver & Boyd, 1915–1950), vol. 5, 65; Alan R. MacDonald, *The Jacobean Kirk, 1567–1625: Sovereignty, Polity, and Liturgy* (Brookfield, VT: Ashgate, 1998), 119, 124, 131, 131n28; *A Glossary of Tudor and Stuart Words Especially from the Dramatists*, ed. Walter W. Skeat and A. L. Mayhew (Oxford: Clarendon Press, 1914; repr. New York: Burt Franklin, 1968), 441; *Oxford English Dictionary* (Oxford: Clarendon Press, 1961), s. v. "ward."

5. *Fasti*, ed. Scott, vol. 2, 4, 136; vol. 7, 526, vol. 8, 203; Patrick J. Corish, "The Rising of 1641 and the Catholic Confederacy 1641–5," in *A New History of Ireland, Volume III: Early Modern Ireland, 1534–1691*, ed. T. W. Moody et al. (repr. with corrections; Oxford: Clarendon Press, 1978), 291–92; David Finnegan, "What Do the Depositions Say About the Outbreak of the 1641 Rising?" in *The 1641 Depositions and the Irish Rebellion*, ed. Eamon Darcy et al. (London: Brookfield, 2012), 24; Inga Jones, "'Holy War'? Religion, Ethnicity and Massacre During the Irish Rebellion, 1641–2," in *1641 Depositions*, ed. Darcy, 141; John Gibney, *The Shadow of a Year: The 1641 Rebellion in Irish History and Memory* (Madison: University of Wisconsin Press, 2013), 26.

6. *Fasti*, ed. Scott, vol. 3, 136; CC to John Mitchell, July 6, 1749, *CP*, vol. 9, 19; Saul Jarcho, "Biographical and Bibliographical Notes on Cadwallader Colden," *Bulletin of the History of Medicine* 32, no. 4 (1958): 324; Elaine G. Breslaw, *Dr. Alexander Hamilton and Provincial America: Expanding the Orbit of Scottish Culture* (Baton Rouge: Louisiana State University Press, 2008), 10; Ned C. Landsman, *Scotland and Its First American Colony, 1683–1765* (Princeton, NJ: Princeton University Press, 1985), 18; John Clive and Bernard Bailyn, "England's Cultural Provinces: Scotland and America," *William and Mary Quarterly*, 3rd ser., 11 (1954): 201; Alexander Gray, "The Old Schools and Universities in Scotland," *Scottish Historical Review* 9, no. 34 (1912): 114.

7. Ian B. Cowan, *The Scottish Covenanters, 1660–1688* (London: V. Gollancz, 1976), 108–10.

8. Robert Law, *Memorialls; Or, The Memorable Things that Fell Out Within This Island of Brittain from 1638 to 1684*, ed. Charles Kirkpatrick Sharpe (Edinburgh: Archibald Constable, 1818), 210–13; Gilbert Burnet, *Bishop Burnet's History of His Own Time*, 2nd ed. enlarged (Oxford: Oxford University Press, 1833), vol. 2, 320; Robert Wodrow, *The History of the Sufferings of the Church of Scotland from the Restoration to the Revolution*, ed. Robert Burns (Glasgow: Blackie, Fullarton, 1828–1830), vol. 3, 339n-340n; John Willcock, *A Scots Earl in Covenanting Times: Being Life and Times of Archibald 9th Earl of Argyll (1629–1685)* (Edinburgh: A Ellot, 1907), 274, 278–81; Clare Jackson, *Restoration Scotland, 1660–1690: Royalist Politics, Religion and Ideas* (Rochester, NY: Boydell Press, 2003), 150, 154. For the lives of the various Archibald Campbells, see the sketches in *Oxford Dictionary of National Biography* (New York: Oxford University Press, 2004), in 61 vols. (hereafter cited *Oxford DNB*).

9. Wodrow, *History of Sufferings*, vol. 3, 6–7; vol. 4, 224; Willcock, *Scots Earl*, 283, 286–93; G. M. Waller, *Samuel Vetch: Colonial Enterpriser* (Chapel Hill: University of North Carolina Press, 1960), 4, 9.

10. *Memoirs of Mr. William Veitch and George Brysson, Written by Themselves*, ed. Thomas M'Crie (Edinburgh: W. Blackwood, 1825), 152–55.

11. Wodrow, *History of Sufferings*, vol. 3, 6–7; "Biographical Notes of 198 English Peers," c. 1703, 51, CPU, reel 2.

12. CC to Mitchell, July 6, 1749, *CP*, vol. 9, 19; Burnet, *History*, vol. 2, 321–22; Ronald Hutton, *Charles the Second: King of England, Scotland, and Ireland* (New York: Clarendon Press, 1989), 412–13.

13. CC to Peter Kalm, February 1751, *CP*, vol. 4, 258; CC to Mitchell, July 6, 1749, *CP*, vol. 9, 19; Jarcho, "Biographical," 324; D. Hay, "England, Scotland and Europe: The Problem of the Frontier," Royal Historical Society, *Transactions*, 5th ser., 25 (1975): 79, 84–85, 87.

14. "Biographical Notes of Peers," c. 1703, 53, CPU, reel 2; John Rutherfurd to CC, August 16, 1751, *CP*, vol. 4, 287; Richard B. Sher, "Scotland Transformed: The Eighteenth Century," in *Scotland: A History*, ed. Jenny Wormald (New York: Oxford University Press, 2005), 186, 192; *Debrett's Peerage and Baronetage*, ed. Charles Kidd and David Williamson (London: MacMillan, 2003), 1003, 1005.

15. *Memoirs of Mrs. William Veitch, Mr. Thomas Hog of Kiltearn, Mr. Henry Erskine and Mr. John Carstairs* (Edinburgh: [Free Church of Scotland], 1846), i–iii, 8, 8n; *Memoirs*, ed. M'Crie, 251–52; Philip Ranlet, *Enemies of the Bay Colony: Puritan Massachusetts and Its Foes*, 2nd ed. (Lanham, MD: University Press of America, 2006), 199–201.

16. T. Alden, *Collection*, vol. 5, 268–75. Under the Julian calendar then used in England, Colden was born in the Julian year 1687; this corresponds with the Gregorian calendar year 1688 (or as it is sometimes written 1687/8). Confusion arose when the *ANB* put his birth year as 1689, which was accepted by *Oxford DNB* and was followed by John Dixon, "Cadwallader Colden and the Scottish Enlightenment in Transatlantic Context," *Eighteenth-Century Scotland: The Newsletter of the Eighteenth-Century Scottish Studies Society* 23 (Spring 2009): 7; and Paul Tonks, "Empire and Authority in Colonial New York: The Political Thought of Archibald Kennedy and Cadwallader Colden," *New York History* 91, no. 1 (2010): 25. There is no doubt that Colden was born in the Gregorian year 1688. See Jarcho, "Biographical," 323. Although reference sources list CC's mother's name as Janet, she signed her letters Jane Colden. See, for example, Jane Colden to CC, February 5, 1717; and Jane Colden to Mrs. CC, February 5, 1717, *CP*, vol. 8, 17–20.

17. Jane Colden gave birth to twelve children of whom only CC and James still lived in 1724. Mrs. A. Colden to Mrs. CC, [1724], *CP*, vol. 8, 96; *Fasti*, ed. Scott, vol. 2, 64, 136. The Coldens in Scotland would be a rich topic for a genealogist.

18. Argyle to Laird of Lusse, May 22, 1685, in *The Argyle Papers*, [ed. J. Maidment] (Edinburgh: T. G. Stevenson, 1834), 31–32; Jackson, *Restoration*, 156–57; Jenny Wormald, "Confidence and Perplexity: The Seventeenth Century," in *Scotland*, ed. Wormald, 163, 165.

19. Norman Davies, *The Isles: A History* (New York: Oxford University Press, 1999), 613–14; Goldwin Smith, *England: A Short History* (New York: Scribner, 1971), 193–97.

20. *Fasti*, ed. Scott, vol. 2, 5, 9.

21. CC to Peter Collinson, May 1742, *CP*, vol. 2, 261–63; Gray, "Old Schools," 115–17; Alfred R. Hoermann, *Cadwallader Colden: A Figure of the American Enlightenment* (Westport, CT: Greenwood Press, 2002), 76.

22. CC to Kalm, February 1751, *CP*, vol. 4, 259; Alexander Carlyle, *The Autobiography of Dr. Alexander Carlyle of Inveresk, 1722–1805*, ed. John Hill Burton (London: T. N. Foulis, 1910; repr. Bristol, UK: Thoemmes, 1990), 527; Gray, "Old Schools," 114–15, 126–28; William C. Lehmann, *John Millar of Glasgow, 1735–1801: His Life and Thought and His Contributions to Sociological Analysis* (Cambridge: Cambridge University Press, 1960), 14.

23. Hoermann, *Colden*, 76–77; Roy N. Lokken, "Cadwallader Colden's Attempt to Advance Natural Philosophy Beyond the Eighteenth-Century Mechanistic Paradigm," American Philosophical Society, *Proceedings* 122, no. 6 (December 1978): 365; Alexander Grant, *The Story of the University of Edinburgh During Its First Three Hundred Years* (London: Longmans, Green, 1884), vol. 1, 226–29.

24. CC to Collinson, May 1742, *CP*, vol. 2, 261–63; CC to Kalm, February 1751, *CP*, vol. 4, 258–59; Rev. A. Colden to CC and wife, February 14, 1717, *CP*, vol. 8, 20–21; Mrs. Jane Colden to CC and Mrs. CC, February 5, 1717, *CP*, vol. 8, 19; CC, "The Reading of an Elaborate Treatise on the Eye, by the Learned and Ingenious Dr. Porterfield Is the Occasion of the Following Reflections," in *The Philosophical Writings of Cadwallader Colden*, ed. Scott L. Pratt and John Ryder (Amherst, NY: Humanity Books, 2002), 144; Robert H. Hurlbutt III, *Hume, Newton, and The Design Argument*, rev. ed., 2nd Landmark ed. (Lincoln: University of Nebraska Press, 1965), 65–66, 83.

25. CC to Dr. Bard, July 5, 1758, *CP*, vol. 5, 240; CC to Kalm, February 1751, *CP*, vol. 4, 258–59; John D. Comrie, *History of Scottish Medicine*, 2nd ed. (London: Baillière, Tindall &

Cox, Wellcome Historical Medical Museum, 1932), vol. 1, 300; Jarcho, "Biographical," 324, 334n86; William R. Brock and C. Helen Brock, *Scotus Americanus: A Survey of the Sources for Links between Scotland and America in the Eighteenth Century* (Edinburgh: Edinburgh University Press, 1982), 114; Andrew Robinson, *The Last Man Who Knew Everything: Thomas Young, the Anonymous Genius Who Proved Newton Wrong and Deciphered the Rosetta Stone, Among Other Surprising Feats* (New York: Plume, 2006), 22. CC's Edinburgh diploma is in Colden Family Papers, Library of Congress, Washington, DC (hereafter cited as LC).

26. James Chrystie to CC, April 22, 1715, *CP*, vol. 1, 81–82; Edwin R. Purple, "Notes, Biographical and Genealogical, of the Colden Family, and of Some of Its Collateral Branches in America," *New York Genealogical and Biographical Record* 4 (1873): 165; Hoermann, *Colden*, 5–6; "A Copy of a Letter Written by Cadwallader Colden of Coldenham, to a cousin in Scotland," April 27, 1796, in Samuel W. Eager, *An Outline History of Orange County* (Newburgh, NY: S. T. Callahan, 1846–1847), 245; *Fasti*, ed. Scott, vol. 2, 81. CC's son was never called Cadwallader Colden II. His name was always given as Cadwallader Colden, Jr. After his father's death, he dropped the junior as is customary. He will always be referred to here by his nickname, Cad, to avoid confusing him with his father. See Abbreviations for Notes.

27. CC to Kalm, February 1751, *CP*, vol. 4, 259; CC to Collinson, May 1742, *CP*, vol. 2, 261–63; Robinson, *Last Man*, 31; Helen Brock, "North America, a Western Outpost of European Medicine," in *The Medical Enlightenment of the Eighteenth Century*, ed. Andrew Cunningham and Roger French (Cambridge and New York: Cambridge University Press, 1990), 198–99.

28. Another brother-in-law, burdened by debts and attracted by the substantial money earned in the slave trade (including "head money," a bonus given for every living slave delivered across the ocean), became ill on a voyage from Africa. He died in 1718, along with much of the crew, when the ship docked in Virginia. David Chrystie to CC, January 15, 1718, *CP*, vol. 8, 42–43; D. Chrystie to Mrs. CC, March 9, 1719, *CP*, vol. 8, 48; CC to Kalm, February 1751, *CP*, vol. 4, 259; T. M. Devine, *The Scottish Nation, 1700–2000* (New York: Penguin Books, 1999), 52; H. Brock, "North American," 197–98; John M. MacKenzie, "Empire and National Identities: The Case of Scotland," Royal Historical Society, *Transactions*, 6th ser., 8 (1998): 221; Gordon S. Wood, *The Radicalism of The American Revolution* (New York: A. A. Knopf, 1992), 120.

29. Gustavus Hesselius to his mother, June 26, 1714, "'With God's Blessings on Both Land and Sea': Gustavus Hesselius Describes the New World to the Old in a Letter from Philadelphia in 1714," trans. Carin K. Arnborg, *American Art Journal* 21, no. 3 (1989): 5, 7; CC to his son, July 5, 1759, CC, "Letter on Smith's History," NYHS, *Coll.* 2 (1869): 206.

30. CC to Benjamin LeBerquier, December 24, 1711, *CP*, vol. 1, 5–6; various letters of CC to Philadelphia merchants, *CP*, vol. 1, 3–5; letters of CC to William Dry, 1712–1713, *CP*, vol. 1, 10–13; CC to Thomas Bruce, May 25, June 25, 1712, April 1, 1713, *CP*, vol. 1, 10–12; CC to John Tounsend, May 29, 1714, *CP*, vol. 1, 13–14.

31. "Water," enclosure in CC to Benjamin Franklin (hereafter cited BF), November 29, 1753, in *The Papers of Benjamin Franklin*, ed. Leonard W. Labaree et al. (New Haven, CT: Yale University Press, 1959–2019), vol. 5, 125 (hereafter cited *FP*).

32. CC to Dry, n.d., *CP*, vol. 1, 11–12; CC to Jacob Valverde, n.d., November 26, 1714, *CP*, vol. 1, 14, 24–25; CC to Jacob Franco, November 30, 1714, *CP*, vol. 1, 26.

33. CC to Amos Garrett, December 2, 1714, *CP*, vol. 1, 27; CC to Valverde, April 19, 1715, *CP*, vol. 1, 28–29; CC to Tounsend, April 28, 1715, *CP*, vol. 1, 28; CC to Collinson, May 1742, *CP*, vol. 2, 261–63.

34. "Biographical Notes of Peers," c. 1703, 53, CPU, reel 2; CC to Duke of Newcastle, March 21, 1747/8, *CP*, vol. 4, 21–25; "A Narrative of some facts relative to Mr. Colden," c. Dec. 1765, in CC, *The Colden Letter Books, 1760–1775*, New York Historical Society, *Collections*, 9–10 (1876–1877). vol. 2, 63–64 (hereafter cited *CLB*); Rev. A. Colden to CC, September [?], 1715, *CP*, vol. 8, 1–2; George E. Cokayne, *The Complete Peerage Or a History of the House of Lords and All Its Members from the Earliest Times*, rev. ed., ed. Vicary Gibbs et al. (London: St. Catherine Press, 1932), vol. 8,152; Alexander Carlyle, *Anecdotes and Characters of the Times*, ed. James Kinsley (London: Oxford University Press, 1973), 9; Archibald K. Murray, *History of the Scottish Regiments in the British Army* (Glasgow: Thomas Murray,

1862), 50, 60; G. Smith, *England*, 212; J. H. Plumb and others, *The English Heritage* (St. Louis, MO: Forum Press, 1978), 193; Charles Messenger, *History of the British Army* (Greenwich, CT: Brompton Books, 1986), 34–35.

35. "A Narrative of some facts," c. December 1765, *CLB*, vol. 2, 63–64; CC to Newcastle, March 21, 1747/8, *CP*, vol. 4, 21–25; William Smith, Jr., *Historical Memoirs . . . of William Smith, 1763–1783*, ed. William H. W. Sabine (New York: New York Times, Arno Press, 1956–1971), vol. 2, 31 (hereafter cited *SM*); James Haig, *Topographical and Historical Account of the Town of Kelso, and of the Town and Castle of Roxburgh* (Edinburgh: Fairbairn, 1825), 85n-86n. For American examples of beating the drum, see John Rutherfurd to CC, June 26, 1746, *CP*, vol. 3, 218–19; and Kyle F. Zelner, *A Rabble in Arms: Massachusetts Towns and Militiamen during King Philip's War* (New York: New York University Press, 2009), 50–51.

36. "A Narrative of some facts," c. December 1765, *CLB*, vol. 2, 63–64; Haig, *Town of Kelso*, 81–87, 84n-85n; Robert Patten, *The History of the Rebellion in the Year 1715*, 4th ed. (London: James Roberts, 1745), 30, 37–39; Daniel Szechi, *1715: The Great Jacobite Rebellion* (New Haven, CT: Yale University Press, 2006), 171.

37. *SM*, vol. 2, 31; Rev. A. Colden to CC and wife, February 14, 1717, *CP*, vol. 8, 25; Sher, "Scotland Transformed," 186.

38. James Colden to CC, December 31, 1715, *CP*, vol. 8, 4–5; Rev. A. Colden to CC, January 24, 1716, *CP*, vol. 8, 10; Purple, "Notes," 161; Alden, *Collection*, vol. 5, 268–75; Alice Colden Wadsworth, "A Sketch of my father's and mother's family," 4–5, in Gordon Lester Ford Collection, New York Public Library, New York City (archive hereafter cited NYPL); Haig, *Town of Kelso*, 85n–86n, 124. For Rev. James Ramsay, see *Fasti*, ed. Scott, vol. 2, 72. David Chrystie witnessed a baptism and did not perform it. At the hospital, he may have filled in for an absent teacher. See James Chrystie to CC, September 9, 1720, *CP*, vol. 8, 54; David Chrystie to CC, August 17, 1720, July 24, 1722, *CP*, vol. 8, 51, 70; *The Encyclopedia Britannica: A Dictionary of Arts, Sciences, and General Literature*, 9th ed. (Edinburgh: Adam and Charles Black, 1880), vol. 11, 738.

39. CC to Kalm, February 1751, *CP*, vol. 4, 259; CC to Hugh Graham, May 25, 1716, in "The Correspondence of Cadwallader Colden and Hugh Graham on Infectious Fevers (1716–1719)," ed. Saul Jarcho. *Bulletin of the History of Medicine* 30, no. 3 (1956): 202; Raymond Phineas Stearns, *Science in the British Colonies of America* (Urbana: University of Illinois Press, 1970), 496; Jarcho, "Biographical," 325.

40. Rev. A. Colden to CC, February 9, 1716, *CP*, vol. 1, 90–91; CC to Dr. Bard, July 5, 1758, *CP*, vol. 5, 240; Roy Porter, *Disease, Medicine and Society in England, 1550–1860*, 2nd ed. (Cambridge: Cambridge University Press, 1993), 28, 38, 40; Roy Porter, *Health for Sale: Quackery in England, 1660–1850* (Manchester, UK: Manchester University Press, 1989), 5, 26–27, 28–29; Sir George Clark, *A History of the Royal College of Physicians of London* (Oxford: Clarendon Press for the Royal College of Physicians, 1964–1972), vol. 2, 509; H. Brock, "North American," 196. CC is not listed in *The Roll of the Royal College of Physicians of London*, 2nd ed., ed. William Munk (London, 1878), vol. 2: *1701–1800*.

41. Ann Goudie to Mrs. CC, January 7, 1716, *CP*, vol. 8, 6.

42. James Chrystie to CC, January 7, 1716, *CP*, vol. 8, 7.

43. James Colden to CC, December 31, 1715, *CP*, vol. 8, 4–5; Rev. A. Colden to CC, February 9, 1716, *CP*, vol. 1, 90–91.

44. Alison Hamilton to [Mrs. CC], February 2, 1716, *CP*, vol. 1, 87–89. Scottish wives sometimes kept their maiden names. See Landsman, *Scotland*, 46.

45. David Chrystie to Alice Colden, September 9, 1717, Gratz Collection, HSP; James Chrystie to Alice Colden and CC, September 9, 1717, Gratz Collection, HSP.

46. CC, "An Account of the fever . . . on board the *Gloucester* . . . ," c. April 1716, in "Correspondence," ed. Jarcho, 203–4; CC to Graham, June 1717, in "Correspondence," ed. Jarcho, 208.

47. CC to Valverde, May 17, 1716, *CP*, vol. 1, 30; CC to Richard Hill, September 13, November 22, 1716, *CP*, vol. 1, 31,33.

48. CC to Kalm, February 1751, *CP*, vol. 4, 259; James Chrystie to CC, October 4, 1715, *CP*, vol. 8, 3–4; CC to R. Hill, November 22, 1716, *CP*, vol. 1, 33; CC to John Fair, January 22, 1716/7, *CP*, vol. 1, 36–39; CC to Mr. Innys, December 3, 1716, *CP*, vol. 1, 34; "Copy of

Invoice of Drugs sent . . . to Lisbon," *CP*, vol. 1, 35; CC to Capt. John Waldron, July 13, 1721, CC, "Dr. Colden's Cure," ed. Jacob Judd, *New York Historical Society Quarterly* 45, no. 3 (1961): 253; J. Worth Estes, "Therapeutic Practice in Colonial New England," in *Medicine in Colonial Massachusetts, 1620–1820*, Colonial Society of Massachusetts, *Publications* 57 (1980): 383.

49. CC to R. Hill, November 22, 1716, *CP*, vol. 1, 33; CC to Mr. Jordan, March 26, 1717, *CP*, vol. 1, 39; CC to Fair, August 6, 1718, *CP*, vol. 1, 40–41.

50. Rev. A. Colden to CC and Mrs. CC, February 14, 1717, *CP*, vol. 8, 20–27; Mrs. Jane Colden to CC and Mrs. CC, February 5, 1717, *CP*, vol. 8, 18; Purple, "Notes," 170; Landsman, *Scotland*, 46; Breslaw, *Dr. Alexander Hamilton*, 9. Young Alexander Colden will be called Sandie, long after his childish name was abandoned, to avoid confusion with his grandfather and his father's friend, James Alexander.

51. Rev. A. Colden to Madam Hill, February 15, 1717, *CP*, vol. 8, 28; Mrs. J. Colden to CC, November 17, 1718, *CP*, vol. 8, 46. Another son had been born but died very young.

52. James Logan to CC, March 17, 1719/20, James Logan Papers, Logan Letter Books, vol., 2, 220–21, HSP; Logan to Robert Hunter, October 24, 31, 1717, James Logan Papers, Logan Letter Books, vol. 2, 167, 168, HSP; Brooke Hindle, "The Quaker Background and Science in Colonial Philadelphia," *Isis* 46, no. 3 (1955): 249; Hindle, *The Pursuit of Science in Revolutionary America, 1735–1789* (Chapel Hill: University of North Carolina Press, 1956), 39; Louis Leonard Gitin, "Cadwallader Colden As Scientist and Philosopher," *New York History* 16, no. 2 (1935): 171; Frederick B. Tolles, *James Logan and the Culture of Provincial America* (Boston: Little, Brown, 1957), 97–98; Tolles, *Meeting House and Counting House: The Quaker Merchants of Colonial Philadelphia, 1682–1763* (Chapel Hill: University of North Carolina Press, 1948), 194, 194n84; Tolles, "Philadelphia's First Scientist: James Logan," *Isis* 47, no. 1 (1956): 24; Martha J. Lamb, *History of the City of New York: Its Origin, Rise, and Progress* (New York: A. S. Barnes, 1877; repr. New York: Valentine's Manual, 1921), vol. 1, 481; Mary Lou Lustig, *Robert Hunter, 1666–1734: New York's Augustan Statesman* (Syracuse, NY: Syracuse University Press, 1983), 146.

53. Logan to _____, May 1, 1717, in Francis R. Packard, *History of Medicine in the United States* (New York, 1931), vol. 1, 286, 297; Porter, *Disease*, 38.

54. CC to William Jones, September 25, 1717, CPU, reel 2; Tolles, "Philadelphia's First Scientist," 25.

Chapter Two

New York

In October 1717 the notorious pirate Edward Teach blockaded Philadelphia. Seizing, plundering, or destroying ship after ship, Teach—better known as Blackbeard—had appeared a second time to harvest the easy pickings off the shore of the Quaker city. With such a distraction, most Philadelphians would not notice an upcoming change in the life of a young Scottish doctor that soon saw him become a vital part of another colony's government and society.[1]

Shortly before Blackbeard's return to Philadelphia, Dr. Cadwallader Colden had journeyed to New York City. "Curiosity" prompted the trip he recalled but, as a new father, Colden felt increased pressure to provide for his family. Seeing New York would lead to more trade connections and so bring in more income.[2]

Gentlemanly visitors to New York were expected to make a courtesy call on the governor, Robert Hunter, even for the short span of three days Colden planned to stay. Already known to Governor Hunter through James Logan, Colden would never have avoided this obligation. Although no specifics exist about Colden's initial encounter with the brigadier, it should have been similar to that of the soldier John Fontaine, who met Hunter about a year earlier. Calling on the governor, Fontaine "was received very kindly" and invited to dinner. After the meal Hunter gave his fellow officer a tour of the inadequate fort the governor lived in. "It is but a weak place and badly contrived," Fontaine thought. During his somewhat longish stay in New York, Fontaine met with Hunter three more times.[3]

By any standard, Governor Hunter was scintillating company. A prominent member of the British literary scene, Hunter was a close friend of Jonathan Swift and Joseph Addison among others. Hunter's own well done literary efforts won him renown within his circle but, as was usually the case, were anonymous. And, as Colden wrote, the personable Robert Hunter, whom he talked with twice on this trip, "had an . . . entertaining manner of telling a Tale and was a most agreeable companion."[4]

Colden was taken with both Hunter and New York, a colony that seemed more intellectually and financially interesting than Pennsylvania. Public office and the wealth that went with it seemed open to Colden in New York City, unlike in Philadelphia where his ideas had already been rejected. Governor Hunter could be a superb mentor to a budding philosopher. As historian Brooke Hindle commented, Colden "never neglected his own best interests."[5]

After Colden's return to Philadelphia, he yearned for some sort of sinecure which would give him the time to pursue his "Studies." He hoped for someone who could be "a Lesser prophet"—a powerful mentor—and Robert Hunter would be perfect. Logan wished that Colden could better his prospects in Philadelphia and "that he would think less of N. York than he Seems to do Since his Return." Logan noted that "His preferring Brigadier Hunter to all persons whatever into whose Company he has fallen" demonstrated "his good Sense." When Logan showed Colden what Hunter had written about him in a letter, the young Scotsman begged his friend to recommend him to New York's governor. Logan turned him down explaining he could not bear to lose one of the few intellectuals in mercenary Philadelphia.[6]

What Colden never learned was that Logan changed his mind and did write Hunter as his friend had asked. As far as Colden knew, a letter to him from the governor just suddenly appeared, two weeks after his departure from New York, inviting him to return with promises, not only of "friendship," but an "offer to an office of Profit." Hunter's letter has not been found but it was probably similar to one that he wrote Swift urging him to come to America as the first colonial bishop: "Here is the finest air to live upon in the universe, and if our trees and birds could speak, and our assemblymen be silent, the finest conversation too." Unlike Swift, Colden jumped at the invitation and, in 1718, took his little family to Hunter's domain.[7]

Colden soon discovered that he was greatly missed in Philadelphia, and not just by Logan. The city had a great shortage of doctors, a problem aggravated by Colden's departure. Five years later, he still was receiving letters from former patients—including Logan—begging him for his help. "Eat bread and butter with a Little sage for breakfast," he advised an old friend, "but drink no more Tea than what is necessary to make your bread and butter go downe." To another, he pointed out the difficulty of diagnosing and treating a more serious condition from far away.[8]

Whatever qualms Colden felt at leaving his friends and Aunt Elizabeth behind, Colden knew that Governor Hunter had kept his promises. On May 15, 1718 he appointed Colden the "director of the Weigh House," that is, the customs house of New York harbor, a job (which could be done by a deputy) involving the weighing of trade goods to determine the duty on them. At first Colden did the work of the weighmaster himself and in November demanded the payment of unpaid accounts. The commission for that office, though written with standard wording, proved to be prophetic about Colden. The governor had "special trust and Confidence in your integrity, ability and firm intentions to do his Majesty's Good and faithfull Service." Hunter also made him a "master" of New York's chancery court, whose responsibility was to determine factual information that the court needed to know.[9]

The friendship of the governor and the cash these two offices brought in helped compensate Colden for the hostility he faced from some of New York's doctors, who resented the presence of the Scot with his young ideas. And the birth of his first daughter, Elizabeth, on February 5, 1720, reminded her father of the benefit of additional income. Because Aunt Elizabeth was nicknamed Ely, the little girl became Bettie.[10]

Colden was but one of several people Hunter either brought into New York or raised to high office who dominated political life in the colony for decades. The first, Lewis Morris, ("a very sensible and good man" Fontaine related) would be made chief justice by the governor. Morris, a very wealthy pillar among the colony's landed proprietors, had helped the governor obtain, from the Assembly, a salary grant for five years. Morris even assisted Hunter in the writing of a play based on his political problems in New York. Called *Androborus* (translated as "man eater" by Colden), it mocked the governor's enemies in and out of the Assembly. The first play written in America to be published there, this farce made the anti-Hunter faction seem laughable, gaining much popular support for the governor in the process.[11]

Another, more shadowy, Hunter ally, the Scot Archibald Kennedy, may have arrived with the governor, a Scot himself. Originally an army officer, Kennedy abandoned the military to hold various royal offices in New York, the most important and lucrative being the collectorship of the port of New York. So lucrative it made him wealthy, Kennedy would do nothing to rile any faction enough to endanger the collectorship. In the future, he would be described as "a timorous Gentleman and apt to be frightened." Although usually an ally of Colden and other supporters of the royal governor, Kennedy preferred to keep his assistance out of sight.[12]

In sharp contrast to Kennedy, another Scot, James Alexander, would take on anybody in either a court of law or politics. He came to America in 1715 and settled in New Jersey as a lawyer serving the interests of the old proprietors of the colony who, despite surrendering its government, retained their land. Hunter, a family friend, brought Alexander into his other government, New York. Unlike Colden, Alexander remained a significant force in both colonies.[13]

A great lawyer who lacked spoken eloquence, Alexander's intelligence and great knowledge of the law—aided by his huge law library—made him a dominating figure in the bars of New York and New Jersey. His legal skills brought him great wealth, but his broad intellect extended beyond law. He engaged in the same sort of scientific and philosophical pursuits that intrigued Cadwallader Colden. To Colden, Alexander was "the most intimate friend I have."[14]

Alexander was so dangerous an opponent that his enemies had to resort to anonymous smears. The only governor who detested him, William Cosby,

Figure 2.1. James Alexander. Colden's greatest friend. Portrait File PR 052. ID3181. *Collection of the New-York Historical Society.*

insisted that, according to his sources in the province, Alexander had been a Jacobite in the revolt of 1715, a common slur against eighteenth-century Scots. Even Governor Hunter employed the tactic at times. There can be no truth in the report as the noble backers he shared with Colden, the dukes of Argyle, would never have aided a Jacobite. Besides, Alexander was already in America when the revolt took place. And even Cosby admitted he did not know if his sources were accurate.[15]

Governor Hunter had great need for able allies such as Colden and his colleagues. There is substantial agreement with Colden's declaration that Hunter was a superb governor, but his administration of New York was beset with troubles from the very start.[16]

When Hunter left Britain for New York, he brought with him Protestants from a German state, the Palatines, whom the government had decided to resettle in Hunter's territory. In order to help "these distressed Protestant Brethren," Hunter spent much money obtained with his personal credit. Then the governor discovered that his Whiggish allies had been tossed out of office and that the British government, controlled by his foes, refused to compensate him for the huge expenses incurred, destroying the whole project. No wonder Hunter suspected, as he confided in Colden, "that he expected to die in a Jail." What to do with the Palatines continued to perplex the colony well into the 1720s.[17]

After Colden's move to New York, Hunter turned to him as a confidante to whom he could unburden himself. In still another revelation to Colden, Hunter admitted that at his arrival he had naively believed "that an American Assembly might be governed by reason, but experience taught him that it was a vain imagination." New York's Assembly battled him endlessly over financial matters, finally giving Hunter a multi-year grant, which, more or less, solved the dispute for twenty years. Still, in 1714 Hunter complained to Addison, then in the government, that "I have suffered beyond the force of human Nature."[18]

By the time Colden settled in New York, Hunter's friends had regained power in London so the political problems he faced lessened a bit. Then his health collapsed. Colden diagnosed the governor's crippling ailment as "a violent Rheumatism . . . which ended in an obstinate sciatica." Hunter had had enough and decided to depart in 1719, supposedly on a leave of absence. On June 24, 1719 Hunter graciously told the Assembly of his leaving "But with a firm Resolution to Return to you again" if the king agreed.[19]

Colden knew more about Hunter's feelings. Hunter had earlier complained to Swift: "The truth of the matter is this: I am used like a dog after having done all that is in the power of man to deserve a better treatment." But right before the governor's final Assembly speech, he was inspired to be far more graphic to Colden: "People think it is a fine thing to be a governor. A governor by _____ a Tom Turdman's is a better office than to rake in the dunghill of these peoples vile affections." The New York Assembly stirred up interesting emotions in the colony's governors; Hunter's health kept improving the farther away he got from New York.[20]

With the great man gone, Colden reconnected with his old friends in Philadelphia, partly to find out if anything had been learned about Hunter's safe arrival. Logan and Colden had fallen out, but the Quaker had written to Alice to try to reconcile with her husband. Taking advantage of the opportunity, Colden engaged Logan in scientific discussion and begged for any news of Hunter; he had landed in London, New Yorkers knew, but that was all they knew. Logan had no news of the brigadier, but their correspondence did revive as did that with Pennsylvania's lieutenant governor, Sir William Keith, who related events in Philadelphia. There infuriated German immigrants, angry that one of them, a counterfeiter, had been hanged, gave him a "most extraordinary pompous Funeral" that did not go over well. Nor could Colden have been pleased either. In New York he was annoyed that the New York Assembly included several "dutch boors grossly ignorant and rude who could neither write or read nor speak English."[21]

Logan had hoped that Colden was now "easie" in his "circumstances." His offices had helped his finances, but the doctor was still trading for part of his income and had to deal with bad markets. In contrast to Quaker Philadelphia, he latched on to more expensive items, gold buttons, silk laces, "the best Dundee snuff," and the like, which appealed to the more fashionable New Yorkers, who also had more of a taste for his imported elixir. New Yorkers, however, had no interest in strangely colored stockings, which had to be dyed black. Alice, for the first time, pushed such unpopular items with her female friends, but New York men would not touch such "odd" goods.[22]

Colden's medical practice kept him busy too and he stayed well stocked with rhubarb. Offered the position of doctor for the naval ships in New York harbor, he declined because the funds offered in payment simply did not cover the expenses involved. Whether Colden received the money he wanted is not known; perhaps somebody else took the job. Dr. Colden did have some success in treating the ill children of Hunter's replacement, William Burnet, but none with the governor's sickly wife some years later. And the doctor must have been exasperated when Kennedy informed him that Mrs. Kennedy had decided to ignore all his medical advice, despite her improvement, and rely instead on "old womens Recipes."[23]

When Colden could start a correspondence with Hunter at last, the doctor chose to expound upon how medicine could be improved, as astronomy could be. Astronomers, generally, Colden believed, were gentlemen who possessed "the Soul of Discovery" as well as "Leisure and money enough to make the necessary experiments." Along with such gentlemen-scholars were "Skillful and Laborious men maintained and rewarded at the Public charge." On the other hand, in medicine the "Hopes of sordid Gain" drew too many

"Ignorant of all the Sciences, of Obscure . . . or no Education." These pretenders write "the greatest number of . . . bulky Volumes" making practitioners seem "Contemptible" and giving medicine the reputation of being "a Jungle of Hard Words without any certain Foundation." Furthermore, "God suffers Quacks like Plague and Pestilence to Destroy his People," and Colden referred to the ancient writer Galen who insisted that too often "the cleverer flatterer" gained the most renown among doctors. Colden also revealed that he had been contemplating heat, inspired by the work of Sir Isaac Newton.[24]

Finally, Colden informed his mentor that he thought this letter to be "the most effectual Method in my power of showing my gratitude to you for your Extraordinary Favours whose obligations shall [last] as long as I live." Hunter wrote back assuring Colden that he would continue to enjoy reading his philosophical musings on any subject.[25]

Although Hunter had departed from New York so soon after Colden settled there, he was pleased to say in 1751 that "I had the good fortune to be in favour with all his Successors one only excepted." And the exception would not be William Burnet.[26] Pushed by Hunter as his successor, Burnet was already well known because of his late father, Bishop Gilbert Burnet, a major supporter of the Glorious Revolution; his son was an early friend of the Hanoverians. Keith knew and admired him. Governor Burnet, whose personal wealth had been devastated by a great economic disaster in British history, the South Sea Bubble (generated by "Mysterious Credit"), needed to come to New York to make some money. Burnet may have planned to settle down in America as he wed a New Yorker and started a family.[27]

A friend of Colden congratulated him: "You have the good fortune to have Successively Gentlemen of Genius and Learning for Governours." By all appearances, William Burnet possessed innumerable good qualities. Sociable with good taste in wine (he delegated Colden to obtain fine wine from Philadelphia), he also loved books and learning. Nor did he neglect the ladies, who were delighted by his conversations. The new governor had good morals and was very religious, too religious Colden thought. Burnet's devotion to divine prophecy, which he insisted had been instilled in him by Newton himself, made him try to convince Colden that "Prophecies are perpetual miracles." Colden and his friends, including Chief Justice Morris, were put off by the governor's mystical views, but the doctor did his best to explain them away as a typical failing of "Studious men." Why, even the "great Sir Isaac Newton in some instances is thought to have fallen into this misfortune."[28]

Brigadier Hunter did his best to create practically a seamless transition to the new administration. Not only did Hunter recommend prominent men such as the chief justice and James Logan, he urged Burnet, "in the strongest manner," to align himself with his younger allies, Kennedy, Alexander, and his newest friend Cadwallader Colden, who was quickly "so much in favour" with Burnet. All three gained important posts under the new governor.[29]

Burnet, just like Hunter, had to take great interest in relations with New York's Indians (primarily the Iroquois), the French in Canada, and the merchants of Albany who controlled the profitable fur trade because of their nearness to the Iroquois. Only New York, due to its geography, could contest with the French for dominance over the vast wealth generated by beaver pelts.[30]

Colden, who became the first British chronicler of Indian affairs in New York, related the sad tale of the sheer greed of Albany's fur merchants. Before he came to New York, Colden had been intrigued by the original inhabitants of America. While still in Philadelphia, he journeyed to a tribe only two miles away to investigate their religious beliefs. In due course he would learn much more about the culture and witness the history of the Indians in New York.[31]

Indians in Colden's new colonial base had made no secret of resenting their treatment in Albany. Their reports of force used to get their pelts there did not move the local authorities to seek justice. And Albany's complaints about drunken Indians brought an angry retort from native leaders, who had pleaded that liquor not be used to trade for furs: "the Beavers you have got from us for Rum if they were to be laid on one heap would reach the Clouds."[32]

Governor Hunter, interested in the Indians along with hosts of other subjects, also had his duty to perform. For many years, even during war between the French and English, substantial smuggling had been going on between the French in Canada who bought Indian trade goods from Albany dealers, and then swapped the items for furs from Indians. Neutrality, it seems, was very profitable to Albany; making money on trade goods was easier than getting furs themselves. To protect this illegal profiteering, interpreters hired by Albany officials deliberately misrepresented Hunter to the Indians to give them "a harsh opinion" of the governor. Learning what was happening, Hunter realized "the Secret spring that moves all that Engine." From that time on, he made sure to have a Frenchwoman married to an Indian at his side at all conferences to keep the Albany interpreters honest. In 1717 Hunter promised the natives that he would stop the smuggling, but this task would be left to his successor.[33]

Before acting, Governor Burnet made a point of reading New York's official records. When meeting with the Iroquois, he praised them for their "notions of Liberty" and for being "a free people" like the British. He warned the natives that a tyrannical king controlled the French, making them slaves. The French traders, themselves enslaved, would try to enslave their customers too. As for the Albany smugglers, what Colden called "a severe Law" of 1720 banned the sale of trade goods to the French to direct most of the pelts to British traders, not the French. What injured the French aided the imperial interests of Great Britain and so delighted Colden.[34]

The Albany smugglers had mercantile allies in New York City, who sold them the trade goods in the first place. The greatest of them all, Stephen DeLancey, was also one of the richest. DeLancey and his accomplices used their connections in London to try to overturn Burnet's policy. Colden, Alexander, and the governor's other friends defended the hard-pressed governor, pointing out that the smugglers would stoop to anything to save their questionable profits which gained them "Estates by trading many Years to Canada." By outlawing such trade, Burnet had managed to calm and extend the colony's frontier and the French had lost their easy supply of "strouds"—blankets—that had gained them so many pelts. It had become essential to demonstrate "the good Effects" of Burnet's policy.[35]

Governor Burnet asked Colden, now New York's surveyor-general, to answer the merchants. Colden then produced one of his most important writings, his report on New York's fur trade, as well as a version of his famous map of the colony. Sent to London in November 1724, the report was quickly published.[36]

Colden lamented that the French had seized almost total control of the fur trade, which not only diverted great wealth away from Britain, but endangered her colonies too. French possession of both the St. Lawrence and Mississippi rivers encircled the British mainland colonies and aided French acquisition of furs as Indians mostly depended on rivers to transport pelts. A French map even claimed much English territory as part of the French empire. Colden had studied how New Yorkers could seize the fur trade away from their enemies. Without that lucrative source of wealth, the frozen Canadian lands had little else.[37]

But this French trading empire was vulnerable, Colden believed. The St. Lawrence River was too far north to be a good conduit of trade. Terrible weather, fog, difficult currents, and rocks hidden below its surface made the river all but impassable except in summer unlike the benevolent geography of New York. Its waterways provided a far easier path to the Atlantic for beaver furs. Besides, the blankets, woolens, and trinkets that Indians coveted for their furs cost twice as much in Canada than in New York, so New Yorkers should be able to "reap twice the Profit they do." Therefore, the smuggling based in Albany was foolish. With no war raging, nothing should stop New Yorkers gaining not only pelts gathered by the Iroquois but also those possessed by Indians far to the west. Pushing New York's borders to the Great Lakes would not only bring in furs, but lead to new settlements. Those western lands seemed perfect for growing hemp and were filled with trees perfect for masts needed by the British navy.[38]

Colden had demonstrated how Burnet, unlike his trader foes, had only acted to better the imperial interests of Great Britain. By 1727 Burnet also managed to establish a post, Oswego, on Lake Ontario. The governor did so "at first chiefly with his Money, Credit and Risk." Years later, Colden justly claimed "a considerable share" in Oswego's creation. The post, possessed of enormous strategic value, controlled access to the mysterious western parts of North America.[39]

The Iroquois had long declared "that the French built their Forts with English Strouds." Because of Burnet's dedication—and Colden's astute defense of his policy—that would change. Oswego boomed and Indian tribes New Yorkers had never heard of before found their way there with their furs. Instead of getting English products "second hand" in Canada, the natives could find them far cheaper at Oswego than at Montreal. Colden's report became so influential that Parliament insisted on reviewing his description of the St. Lawrence in the 1730s when discussing colonial trade.[40]

As Colden had done so well with his report, and the fight at London had not yet been won, Burnet decided that a history of the Iroquois would help too. Therefore, the governor opened up official records to Colden, which proved to be a revelation to him. With nothing done by English authors, Colden discovered the inaccuracy of the only available books—written by the French. It was essential to reveal, Colden thought, what bad neighbors the French in Canada were, and "how dreadful the Consequences may be" if they succeeded in alienating the Five Nations—the Iroquois—from Great Britain. "We ought to be on our Guard," he warned. Reminding his readers that this was a pioneering effort, he vowed to correct any mistakes and also explained why such small skirmishes and ambushes were detailed. The book "would be very lame" without such "Private Adventures" because that was the style of warfare—"The whole Country being one continued Forest."[41]

In the eighteenth century, Colden's history was a sensation, nothing at all like any other book of the day. It especially attracted Scottish writers such as Tobias Smollett and others who knew American Indian society and culture from it alone. Even the American rebels during the War of Independence cited it with respect.[42]

Yet the nineteenth century came to different conclusions. In 1865 New England antiquarian Samuel G. Drake revealed he did "not value it much as a history." Some time later, in 1879, Moses Coit Tyler, three years after the death of George Custer at the Little Big Horn, dismissed Colden's "not in the least interesting" history "of sundry parcels of savages." It was "impossible," Tyler insisted, for Colden "to redeem his book from the curse of being a history of what deserves no history." Compared to that, Alice M. Keys's description of it as "both dull and confused" seems mild. As the twentieth century wore on, *The History of the Five Indian Nations* regained its reputation as a work valuable for its anthropological and historical insights.[43]

Nonetheless, Colden's report and his book failed in their ultimate purpose—convincing the British government to support Burnet's suppression of the smuggling. Despite Hunter seconding everything Burnet and Colden wrote about the fur trade and the Albany smugglers, the Lords of Trade, responsible for advising the government about the colonies, rejected the law in question. Although the Lords also rejected the smugglers' argument that their illegal activities actually helped the British Empire, the law was too draconian because the smugglers had to take an oath and so "are obliged to accuse themselves" or commit perjury; failure to take the oath resulted in jail and a heavy fine. And the oath could be administered by a "Common Soldier." Therefore, the Lords recommended that the law be voided by the king. In 1729, when Burnet no longer governed New York, the king overturned all New York laws related to Burnet's anti-smuggling campaign.[44]

William Smith Jr. had to comment in his history years after that startling result: "To whose intrigues this event is to be ascribed cannot be certainly determined." No logic seemed to justify this apparent helping of the hated French rival and obvious illegality committed by those who profited from smuggling.[45]

Colden agreed. As he wrote in 1760, "it was surprising to me how easily the Board of Trade . . . were induced to recommend . . . the repealing of the laws . . . after all that had been laid before them by Mr. Burnet on that head" such as Colden's report. But this comment, in a series of historical letters meant for his descendants, seems to reflect Colden's habit in such writings of cleaning up the past somewhat. In the same letter Colden also mentioned that "Mr. DeLancey had the advantage of his own private trade in view which was very considerable." Putting the two remarks together, Colden seems to have thought that the Lords of Trade were "induced" because DeLancey spread a good chunk of his ill-gotten smuggling gains to various Board of Trade members as bribes, not unusual for the time, thus explaining the mysterious outcome.[46]

Despite the importance of the fur trade, it was not the only imperial issue Colden delved into. In his "Report on Trade" of 1723, he had suggested ways to make New York "more useful" to the mother country. The colony, already a leader in the production of grain, would be more valuable if New Yorkers also pushed the development of naval stores such as the white pine for masts as well as tar and hemp. Colden urged New Yorkers not to listen to complainers who feared they would lose "the fundamental English Privilege of being tried by their country." After all, Britain, "the nursery of Liberty," would never "loose the surest tie she has upon the affections of the people in the Plantations." He continued: "free subjects are more useful to their Prince than Slaves."[47]

The glories of Britain, however, could not wipe out political disputes in the colony. Governor Burnet had three major critics within his own Council. The most senior of them, Peter Schuyler, the president of the Council, had become acting governor with the departure of Hunter. Although known to be brave, he was totally under the influence of a crafty politician, Adolph Philipse, also on the Council. In violation of all procedure, Schuyler allowed Philipse to keep the official seal and violated his instructions in other ways. Burnet asked that the home government remove both men from the Council and replace them with Colden and Alexander; less trouble would ensue if the order came from London rather than the governor, who could fire Council members. The death of another councilor moved the governor to recommend the appointment of the son of the chief justice, Lewis Morris Jr.[48]

Burnet did not even try to tangle with his third critic on the Council, George Clarke. Also the secretary of the province, Clarke had powerful connections in Britain making his position practically invulnerable. A great landholder in a colony filled with them, Clarke bitterly opposed any suggestion of land reform, something dear to the heart of Cadwallader Colden. As compensation for having to deal with Clarke, in 1721 the governor welcomed Colden and Alexander to the Council along with young Morris. Both Lord Jedburgh and the Duke of Argyle had been pushing for Colden's advancement.[49]

The governor's political difficulties became more intense in 1725. That year, in August, Philipse entered the Assembly. Only a month later DeLancey succeeded a deceased assemblyman. Burnet then made a colossal political mistake. Concerned by the sudden rise in the power of his enemies, Burnet demanded of DeLancey, an immigrant Huguenot, "How he became a Subject of the Crown?," thus doubting the British citizenship of DeLancey, a native of France, and thus his right to sit in the Assembly. A French Protestant, he had fled to England where he received denization, which gave him the right to live and work in British territory. Political rights, however, only came with naturalization, which he had not obtained when he immigrated to New York. The Assembly, by law, had naturalized him and others during Hunter's administration. And, DeLancey had already served in the Assembly.[50]

Unfortunately for Burnet's peace of mind, Colden had been away or he would have warned the governor about what seems to have been a reckless act. By doubting DeLancey's right to serve, Burnet had worried the many New Yorkers who were either foreign-born or children of immigrants. Could other rights be threatened, they feared. Every assemblyman, even the governor's friends, were "in a ferment." Burnet had threatened the Assembly's privilege of being sole judge of "the qualifications of its own members." DeLancey would be seated. Colden, who would have advised the governor not to contest the issue, only returned a day after Burnet's blunder and could not repair the damage, which Philipse took advantage of. Not surprisingly, the next year the Assembly, with Philipse as speaker, took aim at the governor's right, as established by the royal prerogative, to dispense money by a warrant and appoint and pay various government officials. Colden and the rest of the Council opposed this power play of the Assembly.[51]

In another dispute of the day Colden played an important, if anonymous, role. How should the expenses of the government be paid—through assorted taxes on trade or a land tax? Burnet's forces favored taxing trade, while merchants—such as DeLancey—wanted the great landowners, many of whom were in Burnet's corner, to bear the brunt of taxation.[52]

Colden's pamphlet, *The Interest of the Country in Laying Duties*, laid out the argument behind duties on trade. To Colden, the question was how could the necessary expenses of a government be met "with the least Prejudice to Trade and Industry." Obviously, "the less Charge upon Trade, the greater the Profit to the Province." It came down to two words—tax "Vice." That was far superior to taxing "Labour and Manufactures . . . the Foundation of all Trade without which it cannot be carried on."[53]

What a contrast between the country folk and city dwellers, Colden observed. In the countryside, no luxuries existed and the inhabitants worked very hard to make their living by selling choice meats and "Dainties" to "the rich Townsmen." In contrast, gaze at the cities, he urged. "If we look along the Streets, in what rich Silks, Head-dresses and unnecessary Cloaths shall we see the Women" and in the taverns you would spot "People Gameing or Drinking to Excess." All of this behavior was "highly prejudicial" to "the Good of the Country." A countryman would tell the city dwellers, "You [merchants] can much better afford to pay the Duties than we can." They want to make us their "Drudges," the country folk would argue, adding that the merchants also wanted "to get all our Lands Mortgaged." Nor was a land tax a good idea, Colden declared. In Britain, such taxes targeted "the Gentleman," but in America land taxes "fall upon the Farmers, the Labourers and the Manufacturers."[54]

Of course not everyone agreed. One author insisted that trade duties would be passed on to Colden's virtuous countrymen, who in the end actually would pay them. "Free Trade" would be more beneficial. "A general Tax on Men's Estates, in both City and Country" would solve the problem and not hurt the colony's trade. In an unpublished manuscript, Colden responded that the French king levied such a tax which produced "Vexations." Why imitate an absolute monarch? Why experiment when New Yorkers already knew a great deal about trade duties? Colden and his friends won the argument, but the merchants continued to argue their case.[55]

Another issue turned out to be even more divisive. A valuable weapon included in the royal prerogative, the chancery court, operated outside the courts of the English common law. Without juries, a chancery court sought to bring about justice when the niceties of the common law got in the way; chancery courts targeted the rich and powerful who could manipulate the legal system for their own advantage. However, chancery proceedings tended to be time-consuming and expensive.[56]

In New York, the governor served as the chancellor and presided over the chancery court. Hunter acted as chancellor, but Burnet, who knew law well, made much greater use of the chancery court and also tried to limit what the lawyers charged for service in that court.[57]

As events played out, one of the biggest abusers of the legal system was Philipse, the man of the people. At one point he signed a bond with a man called Coddrington, a business partner, for some £1,500. After his death, Philipse refused to pay anything at all, even interest, to the widowed lady "who had few or no Friends to stand between her and the powerful Influence of so popular a Man." Mrs. Coddrington then sued him in a common law court for the money owed. Philipse's defense was strange, to say the least: "the bond was paid [back] before it was given." Nonsensical, it became the leading piece of gossip in the city, including a coffeehouse Colden entered. There, Colden related, "I asked Mr. Philipse's attorney who happened to be present, what he meant by such a plea?" The lawyer, not surprisingly, assured him that "it was none of his, he knew better, that he was obliged to put it in by his client." The court rejected that absurdity, ordering Philipse to pay £2,000, which included interest.[58]

Rather than pay "a poor Widow," Philipse then hatched another scheme. He thought he could win in the chancery court. Suddenly, Philipse began visiting Governor Burnet, acting as if they had always been the best of friends; Burnet reciprocated. When sitting as chancellor, however, Burnet dismissed Philipse's still absurd defense and refused to interfere with the common law court. Philipse would have his revenge; he was "A Patriot" after all.[59]

On November 25, 1727, the last scheduled meeting of the Assembly for that session, few members attended as their work had been concluded—or so they thought. But Philipse had tipped off his supporters about his plan. The Assembly's Committee of Grievances then gave a report—written by Philipse—which was voted on and approved without any debate. The governor's party, totally surprised, had no idea what to do. The resolves of the committee branded New York's chancery court as a violation of English law, "a manifest Oppression," and dangerous to the "Liberties and Properties" of the people. Furthermore, the Assembly resolved that all acts of that court were "illegal, null and void." Upon learning what had been done, the governor dissolved the house, thus ending its existence.[60]

Disgusted, Burnet complained to the Duke of Newcastle about the resolves, insisting that "His Majesties Prerogative" had been "highly insulted" by the Assembly. The Council, with Colden present, defended the chancery court and complained "how much Differences and Jealousies industriously fomented" disturbed the "Harmony and Impartiality" needed to serve the public.[61]

Colden, however, also would employ his pen against the malicious Philipse in a "free manner," urging him to defend himself "for throwing of Dirt from a hidden Corner." Writing anonymously, Colden predicted "that when this Mighty dust shall be Blown away, people will be Surprised to find all the dirt sticking to your Self."[62]

James Alexander, who thought Colden's tone and language of the first letter to Ape—the moniker inspired by Adolph Philipse Esq.'s initials by which the two friends mocked him—to be too extreme, passed on to Colden interesting gossip about Ape. Asked about his silence regarding the broadside, Philipse boasted that "he will Answer by the voice of the people." Hopefully, Alexander believed, when New Yorkers learned the truth, Philipse would be exposed for what he was (although hostile rumors about Burnet seemed "more vile and base than any before").[63]

Colden intended to expose Philipse in a second anonymous letter to him, "a Selfish-man setting up for a Patriot," who only wanted "to serve himself." Why did no one raise an "Out-cry" when Philipse brought Mrs. Coddrington into the supposedly unconstitutional court? There had been an outcry

> When some Jews (Men that some suppose to have very little honour) prayed Relief against a Bond, which was fraudulently obtained from them by a Man of Wealth; and at the same Time every one is easy when Mr. Philipse prays Relief, not only against a Bond, but likewise against a Judgment at Common Law.[64]

Philipse, though, had still another defeat in the chancery court. Some of his neighbors in Westchester had brought him before Chancellor Burnet to settle the boundaries of their property. Philipse lost, this time "Lands of great Value," and raised "Clamours."[65]

Not surprisingly, the new Assembly added more fuel to the fire. After Burnet's departure from the governorship, the representatives of the people insisted that its predecessor's members had been "very ruffly used." Complaining that an investigation (launched to determine what Philipse and his allies had done before the dissolution) displayed Burnet's "high Hand," the present Assembly authorized its Committee of Grievances to investigate Burnet's investigation. Colden and other councilors expressed their astonishment at the scene of an Assembly "Blindly giving up their Judgments to the Will of one man without the Least regard to Justice or to the truth."[66]

The continued actions of the assemblymen, constantly chipping away at the prerogative, disturbed Colden. In 1727 he predicted:

> In short if they shall be allowed to go on without some speedy remedy to put a stop to them, it is to be feared that a resolve of the House of Representatives

will in time be lookt on as of more force than his Majesty's most positive command, or even perhaps than an act of Parliament if it be not accompanied with sufficient force to put it in execution.[67]

Colden would live to see his prediction come true.

NOTES

1. Logan to Hunter, October 24, 1717, James Logan Papers, Logan Letter Books, vol. 2, 167, HSP.
2. CC to Kalm, February 1751, *CP*, vol. 4, 259; CC to Collinson, May 1742, *CP*, vol. 2, 261–63.
3. CC to Kalm, February 1751, *CP*, vol. 4, 259; John Fontaine, *The Journal of John Fontaine: An Irish Huguenot Son in Spain and Virginia, 1710–1719*, ed. Edward Porter Alexander (Williamsburg: Colonial Williamsburg Foundation, University Press of Virginia, 1972), 114–17.
4. CC to his son, September 25, 1759, CC, "The Colden Letters on Smith's History," New York Historical Society, *Collections* 1 (1868): 192; Anthony Henley to Swift, September 16, 1708, Jonathan Swift, *The Correspondence of Jonathan Swift, D.D.*, ed. Francis Elrington Ball (London: G. Bell and Sons, 1910–1914), vol. 1, 113; Swift to Hunter, January 12, 1708/9, Swift, *Correspondence*, vol. 1, 135; CC to Kalm, February 1751, *CP*, vol. 4, 259; James Edward Scanlon, "British Intrigue and the Governorship of Robert Hunter," *New York Historical Society Quarterly* 57, no. 3 (1973): 204, 211.
5. CC to his son, September 25, 1759, CC, "Letters on Smith," 192; Brooke Hindle, "A Colonial Governor's Family: The Coldens of Coldengham," *New York Historical Society Quarterly* 45, no. 3 (1961): 236.
6. Logan to Hunter, November 7, 1717, James Logan Papers, Logan Letter Books, vol. 2, 169, HSP.
7. Logan to Hunter, November 7, 1717, James Logan Papers, Logan Letter Books, vol. 2, 169, HSP; CC to Collinson, May 1742, *CP*, vol. 2, 261–63; CC to Kalm, February 1751, *CP*, vol. 4, 259; Hunter to Swift, March 14, 1712/3, Swift, *Correspondence*, vol. 2, 42–43; Jordan D. Fiore, "Jonathan Swift and the American Episcopate," *William and Mary Quarterly*, 3rd ser., 11 (1954): 428, 430. CC wrote that he first met Hunter in New York during 1718 but his memory failed him.
8. Sir William Keith to CC, August 13, 1719, *CP*, vol. 1, 100; CC to John Kearsley, c. July-August 1723, *CP*, vol. 1, 149; Thomas Hooton to CC, n.d., CPU, reel 2; CC to Mr. Arbuthnotte, November 23, 1719, CPU, reel 2; Logan to CC, February 7, 1720/1, James Logan Papers, Logan Letter Books, vol. 3, 5–6, HSP.
9. "Robert Hunter Esqr. . . . To Cadwallader Colden Esqr.," May 15, 1718, Colden Family Papers, LC; CC, Account of Col. Robert Livingston, April 10, 1719, GLC03107.01234, Gilder Lehrman Coll., Gilder Lehrman Institute of American History, New York City; New York Colony, *Calendar of New York Colonial Commissions, 1680–1770*, comp. E. B. O'Callaghan (New York: New York Historical Society, 1929), 16; New York Colony, Council, *Calendar of Council Minutes, 1668–1783*, comp. Berthold Fernow (Albany: University of the State of New York, 1902; repr. Harrison, NY: Harbor Hill Books, 1987), 269; Alfred R. Hoermann, *Cadwallader Colden: A Figure of the American Enlightenment* (Westport, CT: Greenwood Press, 2002), 10; Arthur Everett Peterson, *New York As An Eighteenth Century Municipality Prior to 1731* (New York: Longmans, Green, 1917; rept. New York: AMS Press, 1968), 108. In 1724, for example, CC determined for the court the value of various currencies used in New York more than twenty years before. See CC, "Money Circulating in New York Prior to 1704," ed. Paul M. Hamlin, *New York Historical Society Quarterly* 40, no. 4 (1956): 361–67.
10. CC to Dr. Moncktone, August 11, 1718, *CP*, vol. 1, 42; CC to R. Hill, July 1720, *CP*, vol. 1, 47; Mrs. Jane Colden to CC, November 17, 1718, *CP*, vol. 8, 46; Edwin R. Purple, "Notes, Biographical and Genealogical, of the Colden Family, and of Some of Its Collateral

Branches in America," *New York Genealogical and Biographical Record* 4 (1873): 170; William R. Brock and C. Helen Brock, *Scotus Americanus: A Survey of the Sources for Links between Scotland and America in the Eighteenth Century* (Edinburgh: Edinburgh University Press, 1982), 116.

11. Fontaine, *Journal*, 114–15; CC to his son, October 15, 1759, CC, "Letters on Smith," 202; James A. Henretta, *"Salutary Neglect": Colonial Administration Under the Duke of Newcastle* (Princeton NJ: Princeton University Press, 1972), 29; Gregory Afinogenov, "Lawyers and Politics in Eighteenth-Century New York," *New York History* 89, no. 2 (2008): 150; Frederick B. Tolles, *James Logan and the Culture of Provincial America* (Boston: Little, Brown, 1957), 97–98; Lawrence H. Leder, ed., "Robert Hunter's *Androboros*," *Bulletin of the New York Public Library* 68 (1964): 153–90.

12. AC to George Harison, October 14, 1756, Richard Harison Papers, box 2, NYHS; Milton M. Klein, "Archibald Kennedy: Imperial Pamphleteer," in *The Colonial Legacy, Some Eighteenth-Century Commentators*, ed. Lawrence H. Leder (New York, 1971), vol. 2, 77, 81–82, 86–87.

13. Milton M. Klein, *The American Whig: William Livingston of New York* (New York: Garland, 1990), 61; Martha J. Lamb, *History of the City of New York: Its Origin, Rise, and Progress.* (New York: A. S. Barnes, 1877–1896; repr. New York: Valentine's Manual, 1921), vol. 1, 503; Mary Lou Lustig, *Robert Hunter, 1666–1734: New York's Augustan Statesman* (Syracuse, NY: Syracuse University Press, 1983), 145; Ned C. Landsman, *Scotland and Its First American Colony, 1683–1765* (Princeton, NJ: Princeton University Press, 1985), 210.

14. Klein, *American Whig*, 61; CC to Mitchell, November 7, [1745], *CP*, vol. 8, 335–36.

15. Alan Valentine, *Lord Stirling* (New York: Oxford University Press, 1969), 6–7; William Cosby to Lords of Trade, December 6, 1734, New Jersey Colony, *Documents Relating to the Colonial History of the State of New Jersey*, ed. William A. Whitehead (Newark, NJ: Daily Advertiser Printing House, 1880–1928), vol. 5, 395–99; Alison Gilbert Olson, "Governor Robert Hunter and the Anglican Church in New York," in *Statesmen, Scholars and Merchants: Essays in Eighteenth-Century History presented to Dame Lucy Sutherland*, ed. Anne Whiteman et al. (Oxford: Clarendon Press, 1973), 59–60.

16. CC to his son, September 25, 1759, CC, "Letters on Smith," 196–97; Anne Grant, *Memoirs of an American Lady with Sketches of Manners and Scenery in America as They Existed Previous to the Revolution* (London: Longman, Hurst, Rees, and Orme, 1808; repr. New York: Research Reprints, 1970), vol. 1, 161; William A. Whitehead, *Contributions to the Early History of Perth Amboy and Adjoining Country* (New York: D. Appleton, 1856), 149.

17. Daniel Defoe, *A Brief History of the Poor Palatine Refugees* (London: J. Baker, 1709); repr. Los Angeles: William Andrews Clark Memorial Library, University of California, 1964), 2; CC to his son, October 15, 1759, CC, "Letters on Smith," 201–2; CC to William Burnet, August 26, 1724, *DH*, vol. 3, 723–24; Olson, "Governor Robert Hunter," 51; H. T. Dickinson, "The Poor Palatines and the Parties," *English Historical Review* 82,no. 324 (1967): 481–83; Philip Otterness, *Becoming German: The 1709 Palatine Migration to New York* (Ithaca, NY: Cornell University Press, 2004), 111; Walter Allen Knittle, *Early Eighteenth Century Palatine Emigration: A British Government Redemptioner Project to Manufacture Naval Stores* (Philadelphia: Dorrance, 1937), 183–85; Beverly McAnear, *The Income of the Colonial Governors of British North America* (New York: Pageant Press, 1967), 27–28.

18. CC to his son, October 15, 1759, CC, "Letters on Smith," 205–6; Hunter to Joseph Addison, November 8, 1714, in Joseph Addison, *The Letters of Joseph Addison*, ed. Walter Graham (Oxford: Oxford University Press, 1941), 493–94; McAnear, *Income*, 12; Knittle, *Palatine Emigration*, 185–86.

19. Olson, "Governor Robert Hunter," 62; Scanlon, "British Intrigue," 210; CC to his son, October 15, 1759, CC, "Letters on Smith," 204–5; Hunter speech to Council and Assembly, June 24, 1719, in New York Colony, *Journal of the Legislative Council of the Colony of New York, Began the 9th day of April, 1691; and ended the [3d of April, 1775]*, ed. E. B. O'Callaghan (Albany, NY: Weed, Parsons, 1861), vol. 1, 447.

20. Hunter to Charles De La Fay, Esq., October 19, 1719, Colonial Office (transcripts and microfilm of Great Britain), 5/1085/no. 26 (hereafter cited CO), LC transcript; Hunter to Swift,

c. Jan 1712/3, Swift, *Correspondence*, vol. 2, 11; CC to his son, October 15, 1759, CC, "Letters on Smith," 205.

21. CC to Logan, March 13, 1719/20, CPU, reel 2; Logan to CC, March 17, 1719/20, James Logan Papers, Logan Letter Books, vol. 2, 220–21, HSP; Logan to CC, April 11, 1720, Gratz Collection, HSP; Keith to CC, November 24, 1720, Gratz Collection, HSP; Keith to CC, March 8, 1719/20, *CP*, vol. 1, 101; Logan to CC, July 14, 1720, *CP*, vol. 1, 102–3; CC to his son, October 15, 1759, CC, "Letters on Smith," 205. During the administration of Lord Bellomont (1698–1701), the Dutch came close to eliminating the use of English in official business. See Philip Ranlet, "A Safe Haven for Witches? Colonial New York's Politics and Relations with New England in the 1690s," *New York History* 90, no. 1 (2009), 53–54.

22. Logan to CC, July 14, 1720, *CP*, vol. 1, 102–3; CC to Fair, October 16, 1719, *CP*, vol. 1, 43–44; CC to R. Hill, July, December 10, 1720, *CP*, vol. 1, 47–50, 54; CC to John Falconer, November 14, 1724, *CP*, vol. 1, 57–59.

23. CC to Fair, October 16, 1719, *CP*, vol. 1, 43–44; CC to Waldron, July 13, 1721, in CC, "Dr. Colden's Cure," ed. Jacob Judd, *New York Historical Society Quarterly* 45, no. 3 (1961): 251–53; William Burnet to CC, October 4, 25, 1723, *CP*, vol. 1, 155–56; John Johnston to CC, February 9, 1726/7, *CP*, vol. 1, 194; Archibald Kennedy to CC, January 17, 1735/6, *CP*, vol. 2, 146.

24. CC to Hunter, January 26, 1720, CPU, reel 2; Galen, *Galen on the Therapeutic Method, Books I and II*, trans. R. J. Hankinson (Oxford: Clarendon Press, 1991), 3–5, 81–82.

25. CC to Hunter, January 26, 1720, CPU, reel 2; Hunter to CC, July 11, 1720, *CP*, vol. 8, 157.

26. CC to Kalm, February 1751, *CP*, vol. 4, 259.

27. Keith to CC, July 14, September 22, December 13, 1720, *CP*, vol. 1, 103–4, 106–7; William Smith, Jr., *The History of the Province of New York*, ed. Michael Kammen (Cambridge, MA: Belknap Press of Harvard University Press, 1972), vol. 2, 294; Esther Singleton, *Social New York under the Georges, 1714–1776* (New York: D. Appleton, 1902), 55; William Nelson, *William Burnet, Governor of New York and New Jersey, 1720–1728: A Sketch of his Administration in New York* (New York: N.p., 1892), 151–52; Henretta, *Salutary Neglect*, 108; *Oxford DNB*, s.v. Burnet, William (1688–1729).

28. W. Smith, *History*, vol. 1, 165; William Douglass to CC, February 20, 1720/1, *CP*, vol. 1, 114–16; Logan to Burnet, January 23, 1720/1, James Logan Papers, Logan Letter Books, vol. 3, 1, HSP; Logan to CC, January 24, 1720/1, James Logan Papers, Logan Letter Books, vol. 3, 2, HSP; CC to his son, December 31, 1759, CC, "Letters on Smith," 214–15; Lewis Morris, *The Papers of Lewis Morris*, ed. Eugene R. Sheridan (Newark, NJ: New Jersey Historical Society, 1991–1993), vol. 1, 312, 325n56.

29. Logan to [Hunter], October 1, 1720, James Logan Papers, Logan Letter Books, vol. 2, 226–28, HSP; Alexander and James Colden to CC, October 3, 1721, *CP*, vol. 8, 57; W. Smith, *History*, vol. 1, 166; James Alexander (hereafter cited JA) to Collinson, June 4, 1739, in New Jersey Colony, *Documents Relating to Colonial History*, vol. 6, 71–77.

30. CC, "Cadwallader Colden on the Trade of New York; 1723," *DH*, vol. 1, 716; James Birket, *Some Cursory Remarks Made by James Birket in his Voyage to North America, 1750–1751* (New Haven, CT: Yale University Press, 1916; repr. Freeport, NY: Books for Libraries Press, 1971), 46–47.

31. CC to Graham, December 7, 1718, CPU, reel 2.

32. CC, "Continuation of Colden's History of the Five Indian Nations, for the years 1707 through 1720," *CP*, vol. 9, 371–72, 383–84.

33. Hunter to Kilian van Rensslaer, May 15, 1712, Robert Hunter Papers, box 1, f. 2, NYHS; CC, "Continuation," *CP*, vol. 9, 425, 430; CC to his son, October 15, 1759, CC, "Letters on Smith," 200; Arthur H. Buffington, "The Policy of Albany and English Westward Expansion," *Mississippi Valley Historical Review* 8, no. 4 (1922): 334, 362–63.

34. CC, *The History of the Five Indian Nations Depending on the Province of New-York in America* (1727, Part 1; 1747, Part 2) (New York: T. H. Morrell, 1866; repr. Ithaca, NY: Great Seal Books, 1958), 77 (hereafter cited CC, *History*); CC, "Colden's account of the Conference between Gov. Burnet and the Five Nations, 1721," *CP*, vol. 1, 128–34; CC, "Cadwallader Colden on the Trade of New York; 1723," in *The Documentary History of the State of New-*

York; Arranged Under Direction of the Hon. Christopher Morgan, Secretary of State, ed. Edmund B. O'Callaghan (Albany, NY: Weed, Parsons, 1849), vol. 1, 716–17; Thomas Elliot Norton, *The Fur Trade in Colonial New York, 1686–1776* (Madison: University of Wisconsin Press, 1974), 64; Patricia U. Bonomi, *A Factious People: Politics and Society in Colonial New York* (New York: Columbia University Press, 1971), 90–91.

35. CC, JA and others to Burnet, n.d., W. Smith, *History*, vol. 1, 174–76, 178–79; Buffington, "Policy of Albany," 361; David L. Preston, *The Texture of Contact: European and Indian Settler Communities on the Frontiers of Iroquoia, 1667–1783* (Lincoln: University of Nebraska Press, 2009), 54.

36. Burnet to Lords of Trade, November 11, 1724, *NYCD*, vol. 4, 725; Burnet to Council of Trade, November 11, 1724, Public Record Office, *Calendar*, Great Britain National Archives (hereafter cited PRO *Cal.*), vol. 34, 251; Burnet to Duke of Newcastle, November 21, 1724, PRO *Cal.*, vol. 34, 271; Buffington, "Policy of Albany," 360; Lawrence H. Leder, *Robert Livingston, 1654–1728, and the Politics of Colonial New York* (Chapel Hill: University of North Carolina Press, 1961), 281; T. E. Norton, *Fur Trade*, 143.

37. CC, *A Memorial concerning the Furr-Trade of the Province of New York Presented to his Excellency William Burnet, Esq; . . . by Cadwallader Colden, Surveyor General of the said Province, the 10th of November, 1724*, in Papers relating to an act of the Assembly of the Province of New York (New York: William Bradford, 1724), 15–17.

38. CC, *Memorial concerning the Furr-Trade*, 17–24.

39. John Mitchell, *The Contest in America between Great Britain and France with Its Consequences and Importance* (London: A. Millar, 1757; repr. New York: Johnson, 1965), 165; J. A. Esq. to Mr. P. C. of London, 1740, CC, *The History of the Five Indian Nations of Canada*, 3rd ed. (London: Lockyer Davis, 1755), vol. 1, 256; CC to Collinson, May 1742, *CP*, vol. 2, 261–63; Buffington, "Policy of Albany," 360, 363; Klein, "Kennedy," 81; Preston, *Texture*, 68.

40. Mitchell, *Contest in America*, 30; CC, *History*, 78; CC, *History*, 3rd ed., vol. 1, 256–57; Alexander C. Flick, *History of the State of New York* (New York: Columbia University Press, 1933–1937), vol. 2, 224–25; PRO *Cal.*, vol. 38, 52, 84, vol. 39, 90; "List of papers directed to be laid before . . . the House of Lords by the Commissioners for Trade and Plantations," April 15, 1731, House of Lords Papers, The Tower, 2i, 2i.1, reel 7, microfilm at Columbia University, New York City.

41. CC, *History*, v, ix–x, xii, 78.

42. Samuel Wharton to Simon Kollock, June 10, 1782, in *Letters of Delegates to Congress, 1774–1789*, ed. Paul H. Smith et al. (Washington, DC: GPO, 1976–2000), vol. 18, 571; *Oxford DNB*, s.v. Colden, Cadwallader; Louis B. Wright, *The Cultural Life of the American Colonies, 1607–1763* (New York: Harper & Row, 1962), 164–65; Wilbur R. Jacobs, "Cadwallader Colden's Noble Iroquois Savages," in *The Colonial Legacy: Historians of Nature*, ed. Lawrence H. Leder (New York: Harper & Row, 1973), vol. 3, 35, 57–58; Lawrence C. Wroth, *An American Bookshelf, 1755* (London: Oxford University Press, 1934; rept. New York: Arno Press, New York Times, 1969), 92, 94, 178–83.

43. Samuel G. Drake to Thomas H. Morrell, July 13, 1865, Ms. 2187, Manuscript Collection, Boston Public Library, Boston, MA; Moses Coit Tyler, *A History of American Literature, 1676–1765* (New York: G. P. Putnam, 1879), vol. 2, 213–15; *Dictionary of American Biography* (New York: Charles Scribner, 1928–1958), s.v. Colden, Cadwallader; James M. Morse, "Colonial Historians of New York," *New York History* 23, no. 4 (1942): 403–4; Michael Kraus and Davis D. Joyce, *The Writing of American History*, 2nd rev. ed. (Norman: University of Oklahoma Press, 1985), 38.

44. Representation of the Lords of Trade on the New-York Indian Trade Acts, June 16, 1725, *NYCD*, vol. 5, 760–63; W. Smith, *History*, vol. 1, 189.

45. W. Smith, *History*, vol. 1, 189.

46. CC to his son, January 31, 1760, CC, "Letters on Smith," 220–21; John M. Beattie, *The English Court in the Reign of George I* (Cambridge: Cambridge University Press, 1967), 164.

47. CC, "Colden on Trade," 1723, *DH*, vol. 1, 717–20.

48. CC to his son, October 15, 1759, CC, "Letters on Smith," 199–200; CC to AC, n.d., *CP*, vol. 5, 310–12; Burnet to Council of Trade, November 26, 1720, PRO *Cal.*, vol. 32, 202–5; and *NYCD*, vol. 5, 579; Burnet to Lords of Trade, March 9, 1720/1, *NYCD*, vol. 5, 584.

49. CC, "Vindication of Governour Burnet," n. d., Rutherfurd Papers, reel 1, NYHS; Lords of Trade to Burnet, June 6, 1722, *NYCD*, vol. 5, 647; Rev. A. Colden to CC, January 27, 1720/1, *CP*, vol. 1, 109–14; New York Colony, *Calendar of Council Minutes*, comp. Fernow, 281. The various comings and goings in both the Council and Assembly can all be determined in the useful appendixes in Bonomi, *Factious People*, 295–316.

50. New York Colony, *Journal of the Votes and Proceedings of the General Assembly of the Colony of New York, 1691–1765* (New York: Hugh Gaine, 1764–1766), vol. 1, 514; W. Smith, *History*, vol. 1, 181–82; Bonomi, *Factious People*, 93; Leder, *Robert Livingston*, 284–86; Philip Ranlet, ed., "Richard B. Morris's James DeLancey: Portrait in Loyalism," *New York History* 80, no. 2 (1999): 193, 193n17.

51. CC to AC, n. d., *CP*, vol. 5, 315–16; Draft of a Report of a Committee of Council, October 13, 1726, *CP*, vol. 1, 191–93; Assembly to Gov. Burnet, October 13, 1726, in New York Colony, *Journal of the Votes and Proceedings of the General Assembly*, vol. 1, 549–50; Bonomi, *Factious People*, 93.

52. Bonomi, *Factious People*, 94–95.

53. CC, *The Interest of the Country in Laying Duties: Or A Discourse, showing how Duties on some Sorts of Merchandize may make the Province of New-York richer than it would be without them* (New York: J. Peter Zenger, 1726), 4–8.

54. CC, *Interest of the Country in Laying Duties*, 10–11, 13–16.

55. *The Interest of City and Country To Lay No Duties* (New York: John Peter Zenger, 1726), 6, 15, 18; CC, "The Second Part of The Interest of the Country in Laying Dutys Addressed more particularly to the City," in *The Letters and Papers of Cadwallader Colden* (New York: New York Historical Society, 1937) vol. 9, 269–70, 273; Bonomi, *Factious People*, 94–95.

56. Stanley N. Katz, "The Politics of Law in Colonial America: Controversies over Chancery Courts and Equity Law in the Eighteenth Century," *Perspectives in American History* 5 (1971): 258–61.

57. Katz, "Politics of Law," 274–75; Joseph H. Smith and Leo Hershkowitz, "Courts of Equity in the Province of New York: The Cosby Controversy, 1732–1736," *American Journal of Legal History* 16, no. 1 (1972), 12.

58. CC to AC, n.d., *CP*, vol. 5, 317–18; CC, *Sir, In my Former I frankly informed you . . .* ([New York: John Peter Zenger], 1728).

59. CC to AC, n.d., *CP*, vol. 5, 317–18; CC, *Sir, In my Former*.

60. CC to AC, n.d., *CP*, vol. 5, 317–18; New York Colony, *Journal of the Votes and Proceedings of the General Assembly*, vol. 1, 571–72; CC, *To the Honourable Adolph Philipse, Esq.* ([New York, John Peters Zenger], 1728).

61. Burnet to Newcastle, December 21, 1727, CO 5/ 1092 / 219, LC transcript; Council minutes, December 5, 1727, CO 5/ 1092 / 225–27, reel 28, NYHS.

62. CC, *To the Honourable*.

63. JA to CC, May 5, 1728, *CP*, vol. 1, 259–61; Mary Lou Lustig, *Privilege and Prerogative: New York's Provincial Elite, 1710–1776* (Madison, NJ: Fairleigh Dickinson University Press, 1995), 38.

64. CC, *Sir, In my Former*.

65. Obadiah Palmer and others, *Obadiah Palmer, Nehemiah Palmer, Sylvanus Palmer . . . and Henry Cock, Complainants Against Jacobus van Cortland and Adolph Philipse, Defendants, In Cancellarie Novae Eborac* (New York: William Bradford, 1728), 55; R. Walter, CC, and others to Gov. John Montgomerie, August 27, 1728, in New York Colony, *Journal of the Legislative Council*, vol. 1, 568–71.

66. New York Colony, *Journal of the Votes and Proceedings of the General Assembly*, vol. 1, 576–77; Walter, CC, and others to Montgomerie, August 27, 1728, in New York Colony, *Journal of the Legislative Council*, vol. 1, 568–71.

67. CC to Mr. Popple, December 15, 1727, PRO *Cal.*, vol. 35, 418.

Chapter Three

Sylvan Retreat

Trying to lure Scots-Irish immigrants away from Ireland and to New York in the 1770s, William Smith Jr. dismissed the southern colonies as "hot and sickly." New York's "too crowded" northern competitors paled before his province, which, he claimed, had "Millions of acres that remain to be cultivated."[1]

A typical lawyer, Smith chose his words carefully and downplayed the truth. New York did have millions of uncultivated acres, but only distant lands on its frontier could be easily purchased by immigrants seeking family farms. Close to New York City and along much of the Hudson River, what James Logan called "old Exorbitant Grants" had enabled a few privileged families to engross much land, making those areas "very Thinly Inhabited." Even the *Independent Reflector* (which Smith had a hand in writing) admitted that these grants to "a few Gentlemen" had discouraged "the Improvement of the Lands within those Grants." Such lands could only be leased from their owners.[2]

Smith, therefore, fooled only the most uninformed immigrants. Astute newcomers settled in Long Island towns such as Newtown and Flushing, communities free from those great landlords. Tourists noticed the aristocratic pretentions of New York's manor lords: "They were like German princes, who after furnishing their contingent to the Emperor, might make war on him when they chose." Immigrants often sought to escape from such a setting.[3]

Nor did some of New York's leaders fail to see what effect the monopolizing of lands had on the colony. Before Cadwallader Colden's move to New York, Governor Robert Hunter explained that young people had to flee the colony if they wanted land, made into a scarce commodity by the huge amounts controlled by the privileged. Colden would not be the first critic of the manor lords, but he proved to be the most determined and long lasting.[4]

In 1732 Colden prepared a report on New York's land system—detailing the abuses committed by the great landlords—for Governor William Cosby, himself no stranger to abuses. New York land grants issued before 1708 did not include a quitrent, a fee that went to the king. But at least the earliest governors such as Sir Edmund Andros and Thomas Dongan, most of the time, made sure surveys were conducted to create definite boundaries. Nonetheless, when reading a grant of 1686, made under Dongan to a small landholder, Colden moaned: "There is no making sense of his Patent according to his Description of his Boundaries." And a tree with initials carved on it, an easy thing to dispose of and replace, could still be an important part of a boundary. The pattern of confusion lasted through the years, even involving Colden. The much later Governor John Montgomerie gave him a bizarre grant, every inch of which was "claimed by some one or other"; some sections had two other supposed owners.[5]

Everything worsened during the administration of Benjamin Fletcher (1692–1698). Colden realized governors employed land grants, one of their important tools, to win allies, but Fletcher abused his power. Colden related that Fletcher "was a generous man, and gave the King's Lands by parcels of upwards of One hundred thousand Acres to a man, and to some particular favourites four or five times that quantity." Fletcher's successor, Lord Bellomont, ordered to undo Fletcher's giveaway, acted very politically, vacating some grants but leaving other huge ones untouched. Lord Cornbury (1702–1708), Bellomont's successor, went back to Fletcher's extravagant grants. During Cornbury's administration, George Clarke began building his empire of landholdings. Only in 1708 did London, in writing, insist that land grants could be at most 2,000 acres (in 1753 the maximum was lowered to 1,000 acres).[6]

The great landlords knew how to milk their grants for everything they could get. Colden explained their technique. If a number of acres was listed, the words "Be it more or less" enabled the owner to take whatever he wanted. In other cases, boundaries were given with "Indian names of Brooks, Rivulets, Hills, Ponds, Falls of water etc. which were and still are known to very few Christians." Sometimes these names were generic, say "Large Brook or broad Brook, or small Brook" which were often changed by the natives and so impossible to fix on a map. An Indian could always be found to swear to the truth of whatever name the landlord wanted "for the small reward of a Blanket or Bottle of rum." These frauds proved difficult to contradict and so the size of the grants wildly expanded. In one case a grant of 300 acres managed to create an estate of 60,000. And the owners had to pay the king minimal quitrents as, for example, "five beaver skins, one other skin one fat Buck and twenty shillings."[7]

Such abuses were not limited to New York and had occurred in all the English colonies soon after their establishment. Both Virginia and Pennsylvania, for example, at one time had bizarre and erratic systems. However, reform had taken place—all lands were re-surveyed restoring rationality. But in New York the manor lords employed their political influence to keep the status quo in place because they benefited from it. Colden raised the possibility that these "great Lordships with large dependencies and revenues" could "endanger the Dependency of the Colonies on their Mother Country." He believed that "great changes" usually were brought about "by Rich and powerful men; any other commotions generally produced only some short lived disorders and Confusions."[8]

Governor Hunter thrust Colden directly into the maelstrom of New York's land system. After Hunter's departure, New York's surveyor-general, Augustine Graham, died. President of the Council Schuyler appointed an ineffective replacement, Captain Allane Jarratt, to that important post. Supposedly "the best and Ablest Mathematician," Jarratt had been picked by Hunter to survey the New York-New Jersey border, a task that had been shut down after complaints. Reportedly, Jarratt had tried surveying during such "Foggy Cloudy and Rainy Weather"—unknown "in the Memory of Man"—when essential sightings of the sun could not be done. Instead, he got his "Information" from nearby residents. Topping everything, Jarratt discovered that his small quadrant was wildly inaccurate and had no idea how to correct it. When Hunter, still New York's governor, learned about Graham's demise, he had someone else in mind for the job—Colden. Hunter procured a royal warrant dated February 2, 1720 for Colden which nullified Schuyler's pick. On April 21, 1720 Colden received his commission for the office. In December of that year the Council ordered him to check Jarratt's faulty quadrant.[9]

Colden saw his position of surveyor-general as a "Trust" from the king. As Colden had "higher standards of honesty than many of his fellow officials," the laxity and "imperfect Drafts" that had been tolerated in that office for so long at last came to an end. In 1720 he sought the strongest surveyor chain available and, eventually, tried to create an improved quadrant. Although his inventing skills did not pass muster, his land surveys did. He had two Latin textbooks from 1706 on geometry and trigonometry for guidance and kept accurate field notes from 1721 on—the apparent start of his extensive trekking in the wilderness where he was "often obliged to sleep in the woods far from any house without any covering."[10]

Colden was not always working in a deserted forest because not all his surveying was far afield. In 1722 he did a survey on Staten Island. He also did work for New York City. During 1724 when city lots were subdivided before their renting, Colden's expertise was called upon. When in 1727 a street was extended because of the further development of a dock, his surveying was needed, and during 1730 the city government employed him again.[11]

Of course Colden did not do all the surveying in the colony himself. One of his most trusted deputy surveyors beginning in the 1730s, Charles Clinton, became a very close associate (his son became the first rebel governor of the state). Historian Thomas Jones called Clinton "a surveyor of note." And when a survey was conducted by someone Colden trusted, he did not check it over and rushed the paperwork for the land grant through.[12]

Surveying could also be dangerous, especially when it involved Indians. During William Burnet's administration in 1721, as Catharyna Brett of Poughkeepsie wrote in 1762, some colonists stirred up the Wappinger Indians against her and she was "in Danger of my Life." Governor William Burnet summoned all parties together, and the Indians accepted that the natives who had signed her deed were "the First Proprietors." So "the Governor Reproved them and made them" cease. Then he issued a "Special Warrant" and sent Colden himself to do the survey, but he

> was Soon Repulsed by a Company of Drunken Indians . . . who threatened to Break his Compass and was Stopped. He Sent for me and I went to him and fould Old Nimham [,the sachem of the Wappingers,] and his two Sons with Mr. Colden, persuading of them to Lett it be Surveyed, but in Vain, and then I Agreed with them to pay them if they Would See it Done and with much Difficulty Mr. Colden proceeded.[13]

As that case demonstrates, Colden did have to travel because of being on the Council along with his surveying trips, which put a crimp in his doctoring. The sometimes long separations caused a mixture of loneliness and fear. In 1722 Colden, anxious that Alice had not responded to his last three letters from Albany, reminded his wife that her last letter had mentioned that the children were ill and she had cut her hand. "I for my share cannot help fearing the worst from your not writing and no account (except that of Death) could make me more uneasy." He added: "I know your Love to me makes you fond of giving me all the agreeable news of your self and the Children you can." So why this "Neglect?"[14] The separations and the fears would continue.

Yet a major survey would, eventually, lessen the separations somewhat. One of Fletcher's most notorious land grants, the Evans Patent, had given some 150,000 acres to Captain John Evans and stretched over both Ulster and Orange counties. The huge grant, however, was revoked in 1699 because of "its magnitude, uncertainty and want of consideration" and so became "the King's land." Governor Hunter had ordered the then surveyor-general launch a survey of the borders of the patent but "his Indisposition and death at last kept that matter from being so much as begun" Colden would explain.[15]

Reports spread that the Evans Patent had been encroached upon by other landholders—to the sum of 50,000 acres. When Governor Burnet arrived, he and the new surveyor-general Colden wanted to investigate but Clarke bitterly resisted in the Council. Clarke had been among those "concerned in the land" next to the old grant. He admitted it. Then the governor, "justly offended," rebuked him for abusing his offices in such a manner "without any manner of threatening or opprobrious language." Clarke did not take it well. Colden revealed that Burnet soon experienced the "Displeasure and the resentments" of Clarke and the other "rich men that are concerned with him in the Large Grants." Colden even came to suspect that James Alexander, whom Burnet had made attorney-general, had been replaced by a British appointee due to the influence of those same rich men. Alexander, Colden believed, had been targeted for "appearing Vigorous in discovering the abuses in the large grants of Land." Despite the opposition, the governor directed the surveyor-general to determine the true boundaries of the Evans Patent.[16]

Surveyor-General Colden generated still more ire from the great landholders in 1721. By law the great family estates were "joint partnerships," making passing them on to the next generation somewhat difficult although the collection of quitrents by the king's government was also difficult. In 1721 the landlords pushed for the passage of a special bill, "an Act for facilitating the Partition of Lands in joint Tenancy." Landholders, without having to go to court or pay heavy fees, could split the grant among themselves as a private matter between partners or, as was often the case, other family members. Winning the approval of the Assembly, it breezed through the Council.[17]

At this point, Colden intervened. In July 1721 Colden presented a "Representation" to the governor, giving his objections to the proposed act. The surveyor-general asked that his office conduct surveys of such joint partnerships, and that the surveys not be done by the partners themselves. Although the Council had no interest in Colden's complaints, he expanded them with another representation in November which declared that the bill might "enable" the landholders "to hide their Deceits." Governor Burnet thought that "these two representations contain so fully the prejudice that may accrue" to the New York quitrents "from this act that I have nothing to add."[18]

Colden had come up with an argument that would end any doubt about the bill's fate. He pointed out to the governor that, in 1719, the king had repudiated a similar bill. Burnet checked the published record of New York's laws and discovered that the king had indeed done so in July 1719. Then Burnet asked if he could sign a bill so close to one the king had already rejected. The Lords of Trade told Burnet what he already knew, that his written instructions prohibited his approving such a bill. Having now obtained some political protection, Burnet rejected the bill. Colden had won.[19]

When the political climate changed, so did Burnet. In 1726 the great landholders tried again to secure a law to aid in the partition of joint partnerships. At a Council meeting Colden complained that the uncertain borders of the old grants bred confusion causing legal problems. He stated to the Council: "the neighbours adjoined to these great Tracts almost every where complain of the Encroachments of the Grantees of these great Tracts and severall are now at Law in those Disputes." The king's interest was sure to suffer too. Lands held by the royal government, which had no owner watching over them, were certain to suffer "greater encroachments." He requested that the Council committee handling the bill amend it to include a proper survey before any partition—just as he had called for in 1721. But Clarke led the fight against Colden's amendment, stirring up opposition to it in the Council. Also heading the relevant committee, Clarke produced a revised bill that ignored Colden's opinion completely. The Assembly soon approved Clarke's version.[20]

Once again, on December 4, 1726, Colden created another report attacking a partition law. That law, Colden complained, created a "new Method" which "may in my Opinion, introduce so many Inconveniencies and give room to so much Fraud, that it ought not to be Enacted into a Law."[21]

This time Governor Burnet abandoned Colden. Admitting that the large estates drove people away from New York and the 1718 law had been revoked by the king, Burnet insisted that this act of 1726 was different. It "is conceived in terms less liable to objections than any of the former." When a clause had been inserted in the bill delaying its operation until the king could rule on it, Burnet signed it on November 11, 1726 and sent it off to London the next month.[22]

Colden seems to have had no idea why Burnet acted as he did. From what Colden stated in 1728, he apparently believed that forces in London, where Clarke remained influential, were responsible for the turnabout. It did not change the surveyor-general's opinion of the governor or damage their friendship. If Colden had known that Burnet's successor as governor, Montgomerie, lobbied the Council of Trade in London, pushing for the approval of the partition bill, it would have strengthened his suspicion.[23]

If Colden was anything, he was a determined man. Despite the setback, he had no intention of letting the great landholders win this contest. He immediately sent his report of December 4 off to the Council of Trade, blaming the governor's surrender on his dependence on the New York Assembly for his salary. The necessary "Balance" needed "to keep that House within Bounds" had been "very much weakened" he insisted. This distressing situation threatened the British Empire. "How far this may in time affect the Dependency of this Province on Great Britain their Lordships are more proper Judges than I am."[24]

The impact of Colden's latest report is unclear; the Lords of Trade already had his earlier reports regarding the old law of 1721. And in 1727, a year later, Colden was filled with impatience to find out where the Lords of Trade stood. On February 15, 1728, the king disallowed the partition law of 1726. This time, even Colden had to write: "The Disallowance of the Partition act surprises." Still, it was a pleasant surprise for him, if not for Clarke and the Assembly.[25]

Nor were the great manor lords thrilled with Colden. Before this defeat, in 1724 Robert Livingston, the proprietor of one of the great estates in the province, Livingston Manor, the great bedrock of that family's power, complained to Governor Burnet about being badly treated. Why, back in his youth, landholders had to be persuaded "to take up Land in So wild a wilderness and Settle it." Back then it did not make sense to spend decades clearing land. "If Mr. Colden had been here then," both he and the governor—or anybody for that matter—would have been able to obtain as much as he had. His neighbors had far more and they were not even British; Livingston claimed he would have done better as a merchant. In the 1750s Livingston's son, Judge Robert R. Livingston, insisted that "the Proprietors of large Tracts are not such mischievous Animals as their Enemies represent."[26]

Despite the Livingstons' attempts to vindicate themselves and their fellow manor lords, New York's bizarre land system seemed humorous to outsiders. In a fictitious 1741 letter to "C.C."—obviously meant to be Colden—both sides were heaped with ridicule. A tenant explained that his rent consisted of "a Rose every Year" for a decade, then a tooth off and on. Things became dicey when he ran out of teeth. As for quitrent collectors, one was described as looking suitable for "his invidious Imployment": "He has a prodigious Stomach"— "whatever he gets, it all goes into his unrighteous Maw."[27]

While the great landlords profited from this system, was Colden just as mischievous and unrighteous? Did he profit as well? There is no denying that Colden profited from being surveyor-general. If the great estates were all resurveyed, Colden's fees would have been considerable. Yet, even more substantial would have been the tremendous increase in quitrents that the royal government could have collected. Such a windfall in quitrents likely would have changed the political balance in New York. With a large, independent source of revenue, the governors' strength as compared to the Assembly's would have increased substantially. As it was, Colden's dogged investigation into New York's confused land system increased the collection of quitrents. And Colden's suggestion that all lands pay a standard quitrent would have not only brought in more income, but would have destroyed the "truly extravagant" grants. Colden believed "that the most honest and surest way to establish my Credit with my Masters was to promote their Interest in a diligent prosecution of my Duty."[28]

Nor should it be forgotten why Colden depended on fees from land surveys. Except for a short period, his office had no salary. When there were many hardy pioneers who wanted to settle on New York's frontiers, the fees going to Colden and other officials were substantial. However, when war loomed on the frontier or Indian trouble appeared likely, that income quickly disappeared, which explains Colden's long and unsuccessful campaign to affix a salary to the office of surveyor-general. Colden saw no conflict with his public stands which might benefit himself. As one scholar has commented, "Colden believed himself to be a man of incorruptible virtue."[29]

Furthermore, Colden did not hesitate to jump into what was a common way to seek wealth in the American colonies, land speculation. These so-called "landjobbers" included many New York royal officials, such as Colden, who willingly took their fees in land from a grant in lieu of cash. If any of New York's governors did not indulge in this, it would be remarkable. But no one exceeded George Clarke's land acquisition. When he became lieutenant governor he sometimes took as much as half of a land grant. Clarke's holdings in the New York countryside totaled almost 118,000 acres. Political rivals such as Clarke, Colden, and James DeLancey all were willing to become partners in land grants of their own as well. Addressing Clarke in 1731, Colden assured him that "It will double my pleasure in advancing my own Interest if I can at the same time promote yours."[30]

Exactly how much speculative land Colden held is not certain. The number 40,000 has been given although that amount comes from the confiscated estate of his son David, which did not all come from his father. Determining Colden's landholdings is difficult because when he needed money, fairly often before he became lieutenant governor, he sold land. If a potential buyer had ready cash, Colden signed the land over to him. But, as was usually the case on the frontier, a man wanting a farm in his own name had to be patient. Colden explained the practice in New York: "The common method of selling lands in this Province is either in small farms to poor people who make several payments at distant times." In effect, the buyer got what amounted to a mortgage, but "the sale and payments are both slow and precarious." Otherwise, land would be sold to another speculator who planned "to sell it out afterwards to such poor people with profit." If no buyer expressed interest, a farmer might be given "a Verbal lease" for a short period.[31]

Precarious does describe land speculation in New York. Once New York's governors got land, they often were stuck with it after their administrations were over. Locals such as Clarke and Colden looked for what one scholar has called "long-term values rather than quick profits." One keen observer explained that Colden "enriched his family in a manner on the whole not objectionable" by showing patience. "He allowed this mine of future wealth to lie quietly ripening to its value, till the lands near it were, in process of time, settled, and it became a desirable object to purchase or hold on lease."[32]

When land available for speculation near New York City grew small, the landjobbers turned their attention to very rich land closer to Iroquois territory along the Mohawk River. This frontier land varied in price depending on geography. Even uncleared land could fetch a good price if located near a river that could be navigated by boats. Because that fortunate placement allowed for water transport of agricultural goods, prospective farmers expected quick profits from their hard work. On the other hand, land without good transport prospects had little chance of sale. But even good land might seem too dangerous. In 1732, for example, Colden told Alexander how "pleased" he was with Alexander's efforts to sell some land they had bought "in the Mohawk's Country for I am desirous to sell. If a War should happen with France it may not sell for many Years."[33]

Overall, "absurdly optimistic" estimates of speculative profits—such as those given by William Smith Jr.—should not be taken seriously. Land speculators often did well but few of them depended on it for most of their income; Colden certainly did not. He knew it was a risky occupation. "I find offers for land precarious," he observed in 1743, "so that when an offer is slipt it may take a long time before the same or a like offer be made." A good speculator could not miss an opportunity. Colden knew "how in affairs of land Humour prevails and how convenient it is to take people in the Humour." Although he was not as wealthy as his landholdings might suggest, in 1742 he was pleased to write: "I have been enabled to live above want to keep free of Debt so as never to suffer a labouring man to go from my house without his wages." For someone who had lived in the midst of dire poverty in Scotland, that was no mean achievement.[34]

In spite of Colden not having anywhere near the resources of a manor lord or a great merchant or lawyer in the city, he did have his own country estate, Coldingham (or, as it later came to be spelled, Coldengham), some sixty miles from New York City. Despite the grand name, Coldingham was really a large farm house. It would be a working farm, but "the grounds are rough and of no superior quality" according to a nineteenth-century source. In fact, farming was not all that successful in Ulster County, far from the Hudson as Coldingham was. Yet Coldingham was not intended to be a great source of wealth. Government, not farming, was the family business; the crops from Colden's sylvan retreat supplemented the proceeds from his offices.[35]

The move to Ulster was prompted by the great expenses incurred in living in New York City, a problem worsened by having to maintain a standard compatible with the leaders of the province. Being farther north made sense because most of his surveying took place on the frontier.

On April 9, 1719 Colden applied for a grant of 2,000 acres of the old Evans Patent in Ulster, which he received the same day. Both Alexander and Archibald Kennedy sought land there too, but Colden picked a site near the homestead of Jacobus Bruyn whom he knew well. In the years ahead, Bruyn would be "a very kind Neighbour" to the Coldens.[36]

Colden sought still more land for Coldingham. Although the Crown had specified that land grants could be for no more than 2,000 acres per person, the directive was completely ignored, even by the governors. Everyone who could afford the costs of additional land used the names of friends or associates willing to either sign over or sell to them. Official records, therefore, can not be used to determine who exactly was buying what. In Colden's case, on August 6, 1719, another neighbor, John Johnson, and others sought another grant of 6,000 acres in the Evans Patent. Some 1,000 acres of that grant went to Colden, making Coldingham a unified tract of 3,000 acres.[37]

The mere act of obtaining a country estate did not make it into a farm. Years of work had to be done before the land had real value. A nineteenth-century scholar described Coldingham in 1719: "it was solitary, uncultivated, and the country around it absolutely a wilderness, without roads, or with such only, as were almost impassable." Coldingham was a frontier.[38]

By all appearances, Colden tackled the task quickly. On July 7, 1719 he was named a "Ranger of the County of Ulster," suggesting that he was already spending much time there, probably in a makeshift shelter. Nonetheless, his official duties kept him busy. In 1721 Colden ordered the purchase of two young male slaves. "I design them for Labour and would have them strong and well made." Being thrifty, he suggested a simple paperwork trick to have "Less trouble" with the import tax on slaves. Everyone in New York tried to avoid paying these tariffs; smuggling of slaves imported into New York was common.[39]

As of 1724 the work at Coldingham had progressed. Colden was constructing what he called a "small house" with a cool cellar for storing and protecting butter and other dairy products during the summer heat. At this point he wanted to stay there several times a year for a few weeks to keep an eye on the wasteful builders he had hired. Luckily, he at least had a very able slave. Disturbed by the money they had squandered, Colden believed that, ultimately, the money he had plowed into his farm would be a good investment which would be passed on to his now young children. Colden envisioned it as a "retreat" if things went bad financially. Colden's inept manager, meanwhile, had "lost" a batch of horses and many pigs. Thankfully, Coldingham still had a herd of excellent horses. Things had not improved by 1726, when the available carpenters refused to expand the house.[40]

Exactly when the Coldens moved to Coldingham is unclear because Colden contradicted himself. In 1751 he said it was in 1729, which is improbable, while in 1742 he commented that they moved when Governor Burnet was "removed." But what did he mean by removed? Burnet's successor replaced him in New York during 1728; a gubernatorial commission for New York replacing Burnet was drawn up in 1727. Colden's farm journal starts in August 1727 but is silent about his family's whereabouts. The spring of 1728 seems like a reasonable guess.[41]

Farming, though, started at Coldingham at least by the summer of 1727. What is clear is that Colden had no idea what he was doing. Sometimes a plant was placed too deeply in the soil; other times it was not deep enough. Some fruit trees had their roots so exposed that cold weather killed them.

Some apple trees were placed too close together. Imported grass got choked by native types. Sometimes the plowing was poor or a crop was sowed out of season. There is no evidence that Colden had ever farmed on a large scale. He might have helped his father grow plants on a glebe—church land given to a minister to grow crops—but that would have been the extent of it.[42]

What is more remarkable is that his employees knew even less than he did. One man ruined a wheat crop by sowing it improperly. Colden believed his excuse about not knowing American conditions—one doubts he had ever done it in Europe either. And Colden's overseer displayed incompetence. After returning to Coldingham, Colden discovered that he had "thrown all my work strangely behind hand."[43]

Despite such inexperience, Colden gradually learned the finer points of agriculture. Coldingham brought forth a host of crops, from the basics such as wheat, corn, onions, peas, carrots, lettuce, apples, plums, pumpkins, kale, and turnips but also two plants most likely grown because of medicinal properties—poppies and tobacco. The farm had numerous pigs as well. He also learned to let wild weasels deal with troublesome rats.[44]

Colden figured out the solution to a problem that plagued all the nearby farmers. In rural areas with few people, farmers let their cattle graze among trees until the winter months. The animals fed on the plentiful acorns on the ground. Pregnant cows, however, often died upon eating acorns. Colden decided to keep his cows away from acorns. "By this," he wrote, "I have always avoided this dangerous disease, to which my neighbours cows were yearly incident, when they did not take the same precaution." In addition, Colden's ministrations with pig lard cured sheep that had been poisoned by another deadly plant, and a steer suffering from a snakebite.[45]

Farmer Colden still could not escape the perils of weather—in 1735 excessive rain endangered his entire wheat crop. Still, he found consolation in the benefits that "A Country Life" offered. A man such as himself, battered by politics, could escape and enjoy "the quiet and innocent pleasures that Nature freely offers in every step that he treds in the woods and fields." A sylvan retreat, however, also held perils. In 1749 Coldingham, several times, stood in danger from forest fires that encouraged Colden to consider buying his own fire engine, which, in safer times, could also water the garden.[46]

For Alice, not as interested in nature as her husband, Coldingham could be a bit too isolated especially when he was away for a long period. She had to take charge of the farm in his absence —Colden had total confidence in her judgment— and he knew she faced "a tedious Solitaryness in the Country." Sometimes, when he could stay at Coldingham, Alice would journey to the city and enjoy herself with her female friends. Her daughters were charged with taking care of their father.[47]

The Colden children, especially when young, must have relished farm life. Sandie and Bettie had their own colts, and all the children enjoyed the animals. They chose interesting (and colorful) names for the cows—Strawberry, Cherry, Whity, Blossie, and (for some reason) Molly and Hannah, among others. As the boys matured, each in turn relieved their mother of many of her agricultural duties.[48]

Coldingham had another major drawback for its proprietor although the Hudson was a major transportation hub. Rather large and comfortable sloops sailed back and forth between Albany and New York City and were complimented by tourists. Service was usually very good except during the winter. John Fontaine described the problem well: "The river is frozen in the winter, sometimes all over and such abundance of ice comes down that it often cuts the cables of the ships." In such conditions travel by sloop was far too dangerous, creating a situation in which, as Colden observed in February 1729 from Coldingham, "in this place . . . I am frozen up from all the Rest of the world."[49]

With river travel stymied by ice, only the hardiest souls tried journeying by land. Colden was stuck in Coldingham. He became very afraid of the cold, a fear that worsened as he got older. He explained to a governor, "My age, the cold season, bad roads and bad lodging makes me much averse to traveling by land." West of the Hudson, roads often did not exist. Coldingham was truly isolated: "I am at present by the season of the year entirely ignorant at present of what passes in the world."[50]

Since Colden was "almost entirely shut up within doors," he occupied himself as best he could. He would do scientific experiments and write letters—very long letters. These missives were so extensive that "I don't doubt," he assured his correspondent, that "you'll join with me in wishing for warm weather that you may not have the trouble of reading so much at one time."[51]

Though Coldingham served as a retreat for Colden, he could not totally forget his political functions. Because he was a councilor, he formed part of the legal system of the colony as a justice of the peace. At times his neighbors would complain about some troublemaker and Colden saw to it that justice took its course. Yet no doubt exists about his happiness in September 1728. He arrived at Coldingham from the sickly city, relieved to see "the healthy clear countenances of the children" that were "so very different" from what he had encountered in the city. Despite the "inconveniences in the Country" the satisfied father remarked, "what can be compared with health." All the difficulties involved in the trek to Ulster seemed worthwhile.[52]

Feeling "like a bird that has escaped from a gilded cage into the woods," Colden continued to make improvements to Coldingham. One project created some historical confusion: "As early as 1724," according to a modern historian, "Cadwallader Colden had proposed that a canal be built through the great opening that the Mohawk River and Wood Creek cut in the Appalachian chain," which implies that Colden first suggested the future Erie Canal. He did not.[53]

Colden's report of 1724 on the fur trade never used the word canal. Rather, he, in his report, described a mostly water route across the future state of New York that accommodated the lightweight commodity in demand—furs. In 1724 the westernmost part of the route, unknown to the British, had to be surmised, and Colden guessed wrong. After the details became known, Colden did not hesitate to repeat his belief in the great value for commerce of that convenient passage. Although Colden may have thought that a canal would be beneficial there (canal building had been often suggested in Pennsylvania years before), the first advocacy of making travel easier on the Mohawk was in 1768 by Sir Henry Moore, a governor Colden had little to do with. The first actual suggestion of the future Erie Canal was made after the American Revolution.[54]

What seems to have inspired the Colden-Erie Canal assertion is that he did build a canal on his Coldingham estate. About 1750 Colden took advantage of a brook on his property to construct a small canal. First, using stones to stop drainage, he created a pond which increased the height of the brook; the brook could then be used by boats. The motive, it appears, was to exploit a good supply of peat, which easily paid all the expenses. This canal, the first in New York, also made the transportation of heavy materials much simpler. In 1864 an author pondered why Colden would go to such lengths for peat. Why not just cut down and burn the trees? That would have ruined the whole lifestyle of Coldingham. Nature and plant life remained important to Colden, both for aesthetic and scientific reasons.[55]

Because Coldingham was well inland, some eight miles from the Hudson, Colden knew having a landing on the river would greatly enhance the value of the property. He located a landowner willing to sell some 250 acres with a landing. But Colden could not afford the price. Then others, including John Alsop, also sought to purchase it. Colden added some partners. When they did not produce the cash they had promised, James Alexander stepped in and bought it for Colden. Alsop tried offering more money but the deal had already been finalized, leaving Alsop "very much out of Humour." A store that Colden and his partners built on Colden's landing soon grew into a community called Newburgh, a Scottish town name. For this and other help Alexander provided, Colden thanked his friend. Indeed, Colden could not possibly repay Alexander's many favors to him.[56]

The two friends' political alliance stayed strong during the changed political atmosphere of New York after the death of George I in 1727. The new king, George II, wished to honor those who had served him well, one of whom, Colonel Montgomerie, had been a loyal member of his household. Offered a position in Britain or in the colonies, Montgomerie chose the governorship of New York. Far healthier than his other colonial alternative,

Jamaica, New York seemed "the most lucrative and attended with the least trouble," as he later explained to Colden.[57]

Displaced by this royal whim, Burnet, when he heard of his removal, "could not avoid entertaining some resentment." It was galling, Colden commented, that Burnet had been "turned out to make room for one who had only private merit in personal services to give him a preference." Transferred to Massachusetts, Burnet would flounder on the same "rocks" his predecessor there had—the governor's salary. Burnet "loved an argument" Colden insisted, and the governor continued to battle the Massachusetts assembly over that issue "and made it vexatious and disagreeable to himself." A friend of Colden's on the scene had described that assembly's attitude to be erratic before Burnet's arrival: "I find that in all our Colonys their House of Representatives require a taught rein." The argument ended when Burnet "died of a fever without receiving any salary."[58]

Colden had been very nervous about the new governor of New York. The contentious issues in Burnet's time in New York remained on hold until Montgomerie's appearance. Colden, feeling that his stands had been misrepresented to London by Clarke, was "sensible enough of the risk that I run from the resentment" of his opponents. Colden's concern was justified. All royal commissions, including his as surveyor-general, had been voided by the death of the king. Would Governor Montgomerie allow him to keep what he had?[59]

When Montgomerie took over New York's administration on April 15, 1728, Colden could not have been happy at what he witnessed. "As we were walking in formality to publish Col. Montgomerie's commission, I overheard him say to Mr. Clarke that he would absolutely trust to his advice." Although he did so, Colden discovered that Montgomerie was not really a danger to him. The governor did drink too much and was "the most diffident of himself of any man I ever knew," but Montgomerie's lack of assertion worked in Colden's favor. The governor wanted to make as much money as he could "with as little trouble to himself as possible." Replacing an official such as Colden, who was known in London as a staunch supporter of the prerogative, would be troublesome and Montgomerie knew that. The governor sought "a peaceful, uninterrupted, stream," and firing prominent officials in New York was not the way to bring that about.[60]

Montgomerie's early actions seemed mixed at best to Colden. According to Alexander's news in May, "Mr. Montgomerie carries it very Civil to Everybody, he spoke to me as to you, but is closely attended by Mr. Clarke, Philipse etc." By November the governor still showered Colden with an "abundance of Civility" along with promises "week after week to renew my Commissions." At the same time, however, Colden learned that a New Yorker, Stephen Bayard, planned to seek the post of surveyor-general from London, bypassing the governor. Colden could not be certain Montgomerie opposed Bayard; the governor might have preferred British officials do the deed for him. Adolph Philipse, reportedly, planned to write the Lords of Trade or perhaps officials much closer to the king. At last in January 1729 Montgomerie told Alexander that he would "renew Colden's Commission and mine which to me Seems a pretty bold Step in him considering who have been chiefly About him." The governor had decided that the attacks on them were "only malice." In March the grateful Colden asked that Alexander pass on to the governor his "proper acknowledgements for me on his renewing my Commissions." Although Alexander was superseded in London, Colden was not.[61]

The malice flying about had been generated by Philipse, still angry over his defeats in the chancery court, which he tried to use "to make a party." The Philipse supporters may have pushed too far, Alexander believed. "The Lengths they have already gone has Exasperated many." Colden warned that "Truth and Justice will always prevail where they are evident but the Enemies to truth and Justice are indefatigable in hood winking the People that they cannot see it."[62]

By June 1728 the Philipse party in the Assembly talked openly of impeaching Colden from the surveyor-generalship. "The Impeachment is a jest to me," Colden retorted, calling it a trick to divert attention "while some other unpopular things must be attempted." And from where did the Assembly obtain the power to impeach a royal official, something never even suggested in the American colonies. "I believe a Parliament must suffer no other authority besides themselves to exercise such an authority." If the assemblymen tried to impeach him for, say, excessive fees, attention would be drawn to the fees charged by New York's secretary, Clarke. Talk of impeachment went nowhere.[63]

Even the Council was dripping with malice masterminded by Clarke. In August the governor gave Colden permission to rejoin his family at Coldingham. Stalled by contrary winds for awhile, just as he could finally leave Colden received a Council order to turn over all depositions the council committee had taken concerning Philipse's manipulation of the Assembly regarding the chancery court. None of the committee members were aware of this order pushed by Clarke, who was in league with Philipse. The witnesses had been promised that their names would be kept secret; Philipse wanted to know who they were.[64]

Colden was in a bind. His family was ill so he returned to Coldingham, leaving the desired documents with Alexander and Lewis Morris Jr. In carefully chosen legal language, Alexander accused Clarke with conspiring with Philipse, making a mockery of his councilor's oath. The assemblymen had bragged "that if they could not get a sight of our minutes that way they would find another." Already some councilors had been slandered "probably with a view to incense the mob . . . against us to pull us to pieces." Everything the

Assembly had been doing would "open a plain gate for the Independence of this Colony." This latest assault failed, just like the impeachment. Meanwhile, Colden, safe from the furor, expressed his sympathy to his friend and assured him that "I often think of the state I left you in."[65]

While still at Coldingham, Colden in November availed himself of Governor Montgomerie's invitation "to write as often as I should think . . . it necessary." Taking advantage of Montgomerie's hope that a bill to partition the joint tenant grants be passed, Colden seemed to welcome the idea. The easiest way to make property secure, Colden assured the well-meaning governor, was to carefully survey all the boundaries so that every property could be held safely. If this was done, Colden explained, his time as governor would produce "more Honour and advantage to your Self then any of your Predecessors" had. Colden still thought Montgomerie could be won over to the cause of land reform.[66]

Despite all the fury stirred up by the Philipse party, Colden believed that, given the circumstances, he and his friends had done surprisingly well. He advised Alexander that "we ought to show no Jealousy of his Excellency" though they should "neglect no means for our own Security." It was obvious "that our adversaries' strength lies only on false play and in little tricks and we must guard against them."[67]

Nonetheless another little trick worked even better than the Philipse forces could have imagined. In 1729 Colden and Alexander did not like what the Assembly had done with the warrants to pay the salaries of royal officials; their pay was lessened. Montgomerie did not like it either, but he did not want to initiate a quarrel with the Assembly. Alexander, knowing by then how Montgomerie preferred to act, suggested to him that he bring the issue to the attention of the Lords of Trade. Although the officials would lose some pay, the possibility existed that the Lords would overrule the Assembly. Colden could not attend the upcoming Council meetings on the pay warrants because of his family's illness (and he became ill too) but, confidentially, sent the governor a personal letter of the chief justice to give him foreknowledge of how the meeting would probably go.[68]

Colden guessed wrong. The big issue, the pay warrant for Chief Justice Morris, lowered his salary by £50. Morris saw the pay cut as a personal slight, which it was (Colden quipped that "When an assembly act merely from humor they act like children"). To Lewis Morris Jr.'s surprise, the Council meeting of June 12, 1729 involved the immediate signing of the warrants; the governor wanted his own salary. The younger Morris "coloured," then erupted in fury and demanded that none of the warrants be accepted. Heated debate ensued, and the governor ordered him out of the meeting, but after an apology he was allowed back in. At the next day's meeting—the ill Colden missed all the June meetings—the fury continued. Morris ridiculed two of the Dutch councilors for not knowing enough English to understand the warrants. His behavior shocked everyone. During the June 26, 1729 meeting, after Morris read aloud "a scandalous paper," Montgomerie suspended him; the Lords of Trade agreed and expelled him from the Council. As the Morris era seemed to be ending, another began. On the same day Morris was suspended, Stephen DeLancey's son, James, replaced a dead councilor.[69]

When Alexander informed his absent friend about the mess young Morris had conjured up, Colden was not surprised. Thinking that the younger Morris was pleased by his improper behavior, Colden questioned the Morrises' political skills. "I think it the fault of the Morris Family that they exhaust the subject they treat upon." Using "small arguments" only "weakens the Cause." Furthermore, "Every thing might have been said that was necessary without using any hard word and any disrespect shown to the Governour." Considering himself "very lucky in being out of the squabble," Colden would try "to continue so."[70]

Colden's suspicion that the bizarre event would push the resentful Montgomerie closer to Clarke and Philipse would be confirmed by Alexander in August 1729. Colden recommended that they both begin to separate themselves from their close relations with both Morrises so that the governor would not think that they were in collusion with them. Alexander, fearing that the angered Montgomerie might fire Colden from his offices, even suggested they should avoid each other. Rejecting that suggestion, Colden pointed out that he and his friend had not planned to do anything except to disapprove of the pay warrants.[71]

Montgomerie, no doubt remembering Colden's secretive revelation of Morris's letter, did not blame him at all for what had transpired. After Colden at last came to the city, the governor showed him "copies of all that passed and declared Mr. Morris had forced him to do a thing much against his inclination." Earlier, the governor had been willing to seek London's assistance in restoring the chief justice's pay cut. By September 1729 Montgomerie assured his superiors that the Assembly action had been justified. Clarke and his allies had won. "Our Constitution is very sickly" Colden lamented in June.[72]

Despite that political disaster, Colden and Montgomerie still could work with each other, and in 1730–1731 they settled a lingering problem —creating a mutually agreed upon border with Connecticut. In 1683 the two colonies tried to settle their confused border. Although New York was supposed to extend twenty miles east of the Hudson, Connecticut already had encroached in that area. Connecticut surrendered some territory to its neighbor, but kept a strip of land along Long Island Sound. To compensate New York for its loss, Connecticut agreed to turn over some 61,440 "equivalent" acres, forming a rectangle eventually called the Oblong, but Connecticut then stalled for several decades.[73]

Finally, in January 1724 the attempt to resolve the issue resumed. Colden, as surveyor-general of New York, was named, with two others, to meet with their Connecticut counterparts. Modestly, Colden would write that "I had a considerable share" in producing the eventual deal. In reality, he was the driving force behind it.[74]

From the beginning things did not go well. Governor Burnet complained that the Connecticut commissioners had not been given as extensive powers as the New Yorkers—a common technique practiced by New Englanders that allowed Connecticut to ignore the proceedings if they did not work out in its favor.[75]

At the first meeting, the Connecticut men delved into history, complaining about the political atmosphere of the 1680s. Under the Stuarts, Connecticut suffered "threats and Compulsion" by "Arbitrary" kings who sought to destroy their government, so Connecticut had refused to accept the old agreement. Nor did the other meetings Colden attended get anywhere; he thought the Connecticut commissioners were deliberately doing everything possible "to perplex the matter" to prevent any survey.[76]

During what seemed to be the final meeting of the border commissioners, their discussion was as useless as before and they resolved to drink "a parting glass." At that point, Colden decided to privately approach one of the Connecticut commissioners, probably Roger Wolcott whom he had befriended. Asking that Wolcott "be free with" him, Colden asked for the real reason for Connecticut's obstructionism and, promising to "make no bad use of what he should tell me," Colden suggested that a remedy could be found. Then came the revelation. Ridgefield, Connecticut, had much land within the Oblong, which it feared losing to some New York manor lord. That explained why the Connecticut members had advocated the supposed "Dukes tree" (for whose existence no documentary evidence could be found) for the easternmost spot of the border, which would have kept Ridgefield in Connecticut. The New Yorkers preferred the more eastward "Great Stone."[77]

Once Colden understood the problem, he surveyed some angles that left a large part of Ridgefield in Connecticut. As for the rest, the New Yorkers promised that the Ridgefield inhabitants now in New York would receive a New York grant for their land; they happily agreed to become New Yorkers and pay quitrents. The Connecticut commissioners accepted "the great rock." Colden and the other New Yorkers issued a report (masterminded by Colden) to Governor Burnet that approved the boundary line compromise. It had been best to "Yield" to satisfy "those people who had Spent their Substance and their labour of the best part of their life in Improving those lands."[78]

However, the money appropriated by New York for the survey ran out in 1725 before it could be finished. Once again, the New York Assembly, controlled by Philipse, injected itself. The Oblong bordered Philipse's huge estate and he wanted as much of the Oblong as he could grab. Acting to benefit their speaker, the Assembly cut off all funds to complete the New York-Connecticut border, ending the process before others could be confirmed as landowners in the Oblong. The Assembly's delaying tactics continued until 1730.[79]

The Assembly, Colden believed, would have gotten its way except for the determined sturdy yeomen of Ridgefield. Writing to Governor Montgomerie, they urged that private money be collected to finish the survey in return for land. Montgomerie and Clarke agreed, and New Yorkers such as Alexander and Kennedy joined in the deal as did the Ridgefield farmers. Colden agreed to a share of the land in lieu of his significant fees and surveying costs; he knew the Assembly would not compensate him. Late in September 1730 the commissioners of both colonies, including Colden, worked out the details.[80]

Colden could not complete the survey before a "Severe winter" hit, making his aunt Elizabeth very distressed. The remaining lines were laid out "in the Spring" of 1731 and the commissioners approved the final border. In June the Ridgefield farmers received their grants and those to the New Yorkers were clearing the legal hurdles slowly but surely. Despite Governor Montgomerie's death in July 1731, the grant process continued, which Colden had thought unlikely, under the president of the Council, Rip Van Dam, who was also involved in the Oblong.[81]

Before August Colden learned of the governor's death and that the tale of the Oblong had taken a surprising turn. While the finishing touches were being made on the Oblong, "great men" in Britain secured a grant there for the entire territory. The Oblong, a major political issue when Montgomerie's successor arrived in the colony, would be just one of the disputes that arose between Colden, his friends, and New York's most notorious governor, William Cosby.[82]

NOTES

1. William Smith, Jr., "Information to Farmers and Mechanics intending to remove from Europe to America," c. 1774, *SM*, vol. 1, 200.

2. W. Smith, Jr., "Information to Farmers," *SM*, vol. 1, 201; James Logan, "A Quaker Imperialist's View of the British Colonies in America: 1732," ed. Joseph E. Johnson, *Pennsylvania Magazine of History and Biography* 60, no. 2 (1936): 123; William Livingston and others, *The Independent Reflector or Weekly Essays on Sundry Important Subjects More particularly adapted to the Province of New York*, ed. Milton M. Klein (Cambridge, MA: Harvard University Press, 1963), 107–8. Smith did not mention where the lands were until his third paragraph, and talked about leasing in the eighth paragraph.

3. Anne Grant, *Memoirs of an American Lady with Sketches of Manners and Scenery in America as They Existed Previous to the Revolution* (London: Longman, Hurst, Rees, and Orme, 1808; repr. New York: Research Reprints, 1970), vol. 1, 13; Cynthia A. Kierner, *Traders and Gentlefolk: The Livingstons of New York, 1675–1790* (Ithaca, NY: Cornell University Press, 1992), 90; Georgina C. Nammack, *Fraud, Politics, and the Dispossession of the Indians: The Iroquois Land Frontier in the Colonial Period* (Norman: University of Oklahoma Press, 1969), 100.

4. Nammack, *Fraud*, 20; Sung Bok Kim, *Landlord and Tenant in Colonial New York: Manorial Society, 1664–1775* (Chapel Hill: University of North Carolina Press, 1978), 236; Brooke Hindle, "A Colonial Governor's Family: The Coldens of Coldengham," *New York Historical Society Quarterly* 45, no. 3 (1961): 236.

5. CC, "The State of the Lands in the Province of New York, In 1732," in *The Documentary History of the State of New-York; Arranged Under Direction of the Hon. Christopher Morgan, Secretary of State*, ed. Edmund B. O'Callaghan (Albany, NY: Weed, Parsons, 1849), vol. 1, 378–80; CC to George Clarke, December 6, 1731, George Hyde Clarke Papers, box 30, f. 2, Carl A. Kroch Library, Cornell University, Ithaca, NY; Armand La Potin, "The Minisink Grant: Partnerships, Patents, and Processing Fees in Eighteenth Century New York," *New York History* 56, no. 1 (1975): 33.

6. CC, "State of the Lands," 380–82; Stanley Nider Katz, *Newcastle's New York: Anglo-American Politics, 1732–1753* (Cambridge, MA: Harvard University Press, 1968), 145; Irving Mark, *Agrarian Conflicts in Colonial New York, 1711–1775* (New York: Columbia University Press, 1940), 27; La Potin, "Minisink Grant," 33, 48.

7. CC, "State of the Lands," 380–84.

8. CC, "State of the Lands," 384–85; Patricia U. Bonomi, *A Factious People: Politics and Society in Colonial New York* (New York: Columbia University Press, 1971), 205–6; Carole Shammas, "Cadwallader Colden and the Role of the King's Prerogative," *New York Historical Society Quarterly* 53, no. 2 (1969): 108; CC, Representation to Burnet on Joint Tenancy, November 1721, *CP*, vol. 8, 164.

9. J. Craggs to Hunter, February 2, 1720, PRO *Cal.*, vol. 31, 328; Hunter to CC, February 18, 1719/20, *CP*, vol. 1, 100–101; Peter Schuyler to Lords of Trade, October 31, 1719, April 27, 1720, *NYCD*, vol. 5, 532, 537; Petition of Allane Jarratt to Council, [September 1719], in New Jersey Colony, *Documents Relating to the Colonial History of the State of New Jersey*, ed. William A. Whitehead (Newark, NJ: Daily Advertiser Printing House, 1880–1886), vol. 4, 403–406; Council's Report, September 24, 1719, New Jersey Colony, *Documents Relating to the Colonial History of the State of New Jersey*, ed. Whitehead, 406–8; Petition of Cornelius Cozyn and others to Schuyler, c. November 20, 1719, C05/1052/ff. 111–114, LC transcript; New York Colony, *Calendar of New York Colonial Commissions, 1680–1770*, comp. E. B. O'Callaghan (New York: New York Historical Society, 1929), 18; New York Colony, Council, *Calendar of Council Minutes, 1668–1783*, comp. Berthold Fernow (Albany: University of the State of New York, 1902; repr. Harrison, NY: Harbor Hill Books, 1987), 279.

10. CC, "Interpretation of the governor's power of granting land," n.d., CPU, reel 2; CC's notebook for 1721–1726, CPU, reel 2; CC to R. Hill, December 10, 1720, *CP*, vol. 1, 49–50; CC to Kennedy, [September 1722?], *CP*, vol. 8, 169; Burnet to Lords of Trade, June 2, 1726, *NYCD*, vol. 5, 777; Raymond Phineas Stearns, *Science in the British Colonies of America* (Urbana: University of Illinois Press, 1970), 563; Alexander C. Flick, *History of the State of New York* (New York: Columbia University Press, 1933–1937), vol. 3, 154–55; Walter Klinefelter, "Lewis Evans and His Maps," American Philosophical Society, *Transactions*, n.s., 61, no. 7 (1971): 16; Matt Bushnell Jones, *Vermont in the Making, 1750–1777* (Cambridge, MA: Harvard University Press, 1939), 92. Handwritten copies of the books are in Colden Family Papers, box 12, NYHS.

11. Burnet to CC, August 25, 1727, Rutherfurd Papers (microfilm), New York Historical Society, New York City (hereafer cited RP), vol. 1, 39; New York City, *Minutes of The Common Council of the City of New York, 1675–1776* (New York: Dodd, Mead, 1905), vol. 3, 359; vol. 4, 24; "By his Excellency William Burnet . . . To Cadwallader Colden Esqr. Surveyor General of the Province of New York," December 21, 1722, Real Estate Collection, Museum of the City of New York.

12. Arthur Pound, "Charles Clinton: The First of the American Clintons," *Quarterly Journal of the New York State Historical Association* 12, no. 4 (1931): 382–83; E. Wilder Spaulding, *His Excellency George Clinton: Critic of the Constitution* (New York: Macmillan, 1938), 6; Thomas Jones, *History of New York during the Revolutionary War*, ed. Edward F. DeLancey (New York: New York Historical Society, 1879; repr. Cranbury, NJ: Scholar's Bookshelf, 2006), vol. 2, 325; CC to _____, June 11, 1725, Ch A2. 90, Boston Public Library, Boston, MA.

13. Problems with the Wappingers started again when the old sachem died. Catharyna Brett to Sir William Johnson, August 26, 1762, in William Johnson, *The Papers of Sir William Johnson*, ed. James Sullivan et al. (Albany: University of the State of New York, 1921–1965), vol. 10, 493–94 (hereafter cited *JP*); New York State, *Calendar of N.Y. Colonial Manuscripts Indorsed Land Papers in the Office of the Secretary of State of New York, 1643–1803*, comp. E. B. O'Callaghan (Albany, NY: Weed, Parsons, 1864; repr. Harrison, NY: Harbor-Hill Books, 1987), 150–51.

14. CC to Mrs. CC, September 6, 1722, *CP*, vol. 8, 165; CC to Kalm, February 1751, *CP*, vol. 4, 260.

15. Representations of the Lords, September 26, 1722, *NYCD*, vol. 5, 651; CC Jr. to _____, April 27, 1796, in Samuel W. Eager, *An Outline History of Orange County* (Newburgh, NY: S. T. Callahan, 1846–1847), 237; Flick, *History*, vol. 3, 156; E. M. Ruttenber and L. H. Clark, *History of Orange County, New York* (Philadelphia: Everts & Peck, 1881), 16; Alice Mapelsden Keys, *Cadwallader Colden: A Representative Eighteenth-Century Official* (New York: Columbia University Press, 1906; repr. New York: AMS Press, 1967), 32; CC, "Vindication of Burnet," n.d., RP, vol. 1, 47.

16. CC, "Vindication of Burnet," n.d., RP, vol. 1, 47; CC to Kennedy, n.d., *CP*, vol. 8, 166–69.

17. La Potin, "Minisink Grant," 30–31, 37–40; Burnet to Lords of Trade, November 30, 1721, *NYCD*, vol. 5, 644.

18. Burnet to Lords of Trade, November 30, 1721, *NYCD*, vol. 5, 644 and PRO *Cal.*, vol. 32, 492; Memorial of CC to Burnet, July 19, 1721, PRO *Cal.*, vol. 32, 492–93; CC, Representation, November 1721, *CP*, vol. 8, 161; New York Colony, *Journal of the Legislative Council of the Colony of New York, Began the 9th day of April, 1691; and ended the [3d of April, 1775]* (Albany, NY: Weed, Parsons, 1861), vol. 1, 473.

19. Burnet to Lords of Trade, November 30, 1721, *NYCD*, vol. 5, 644; Lords of Trade to Burnet, June 6, 1722, *NYCD*, vol. 5, 648; CC, Memorial, July 19, 1721, PRO *Cal.*, vol. 32, 492–93; New York Colony, *Journal of the Votes and Proceedings of the General Assembly of the Colony of New York, 1691–1765* (New York: Hugh Gaine, 1764–1766), vol. 1, 467–69.

20. New York Colony, *Journal of the Legislative Council of the Colony*, vol. 1, 544–45, 547; CC to Kennedy, [1727–8?], *CP*, vol. 8, 188–89; New York Colony, *An Act for the Easier Partition of Lands held in Common*, Evans no. 2787 (New York: William Bradford, 1726), 21–27.

21. CC, Memorial against the Act for the Partition of Lands held in Common, December 4, 1726, *NYCD*, vol. 5, 807.

22. Burnet to Lords of Trade, December 20, 1726, *NYCD*, vol. 5, 812; New York Colony, *Journal of the Votes and Proceedings of the General Assembly*, vol. 1, 556.

23. CC to JA, June 30, 1728, RP, vol. 1, 53; John Montgomerie to Lords of Trade, September 8, 1727, *NYCD*, vol. 5, 832.

24. CC to Popple, December 4, 1726, *NYCD*, vol. 5, 805–6.

25. CC to Popple, December 15, 1727, *NYCD*, vol. 5, 844–45; CC to JA, June 30, 1728, RP, vol. 1, 53; New York Colony, *Journal of the Votes and Proceedings of the General Assembly*, vol. 1, 582–83.

26. Robert Livingston to [Burnet?], November 17, 1724, *CP*, vol. 8, 175–77; Robert R. Livingston, "Mr. Robert R. Livingston's Reasons against a Land Tax," ed. Beverly McAnear, *Journal of Political Economy* 48, no. 1 (1940): 88.

27. "Copy of a Letter from D. B. to C. C.," *General Magazine and Historical Chronicle*, 1, no. 3 (March 1741): 200.

28. CC to Kennedy, [1727–8?], *CP*, vol. 8, 187–88; CC, "State of the Lands," 385; Flick, *History*, vol. 3, 157; M. B. Jones, *Vermont*, 91; Kim, *Landlord*, 350–52; Milton M. Klein, "Archibald Kennedy: Imperial Pamphleteer," in *The Colonial Legacy*, ed. Lawrence H. Leder (New York: Harper & Row, 1971), vol. 2, 82–83.

29. Edith M. Fox, *Land Speculation in the Mohawk Country* (Ithaca, NY: Cornell University Press, 1949), 6–7; La Potin, "Minisink Grant," 36.

30. E. M. Fox, *Land Speculation*, 4, 6, 10–11, 49–50; Beverly McAnear, *The Income of the Colonial Governors of British North America* (New York: Pageant Press, 1967), 32–33, 129;

SM, vol. 3, 567; certificate about agreement with CC for 1,000 Acres, *CP*, vol. 8, 246; Clarke to CC, June 27, 1735, *CP*, vol. 8, 224; CC to Clarke, December 6, 1731, Clarke Papers, box 30, f. 2.

31. CC to Clarke, May 18, 1732, Clarke Papers, box 30, f. 3; CC, Indenture with Benjamin Johns, March 10, 1749/50, Ms. Acc. 1315, Manuscript Collection, Boston Public Library; CC to Henry Clinton, June 6, 1765, Sir Henry Clinton Papers, vol. 2: 14, Clements Library, Ann Arbor, Michigan (hereafter cited CL); Joseph Kastner, *A Species of Eternity* (New York: Knopf, 1977), 6; Peter Wilson Coldham, *American Loyalist Claims Abstracted from the Public Record Office*, ed. Sally Lou Mick Haight (Washington, DC: National Genealogical Society, 1980), vol. 1, 95. For CC selling land in Ulster in 1751, see *New-York Gazette, or The Weekly Post-Boy* (Parker), August 12, 1751.

32. Grant, *Memoirs*, vol. 2, 47; E. M. Fox, *Land Speculation*, 10; McAnear, *Income*, 32–33, 73.

33. CC to JA, March 5, 1731/2, James Alexander Papers, box 3, f. 1, NYHS; Patrick M'Robert, *A Tour Through Part of the North Provinces of America* (Edinburgh: Printed for the Author, 1776; repr. ed. Carl Bridenbaugh. New York: New York Times, 1968), 36; E. M. Fox, *Land Speculation*, 48; Nammack, *Fraud*, 20.

34. CC to JA, August 31, 1743, RP, vol. 3, 9; CC to Collinson, May 1742, *CP*, vol. 2, 261–63; McAnear, *Income*, 129; Markus Hünemörder, *The Society of the Cincinnati: Conspiracy and Distrust in Early America* (New York: Berghahn Books, 2006), 172.

35. William Allen, *An American Biographical and Historical Dictionary* (Cambridge, MA: William Hilliard, 1809), 199; John P. Kaminski, *George Clinton: Yeoman Politician of the New Republic* (Madison: University of Wisconsin Press, 1993), 12; Eugene R. Fingerhut, *Survivor: Cadwallader Colden II in Revolutionary America* (Washington, DC: University Press of America, 1983), 3; Roy N. Lokken, "Cadwallader Colden's Attempt to Advance Natural Philosophy Beyond the Eighteenth-Century Mechanistic Paradigm," American Philosophical Society, *Proceedings* 122, no. 6 (December 1978): 366; CC to Mitchell, November [1751?], *CP*, vol. 9, 108–9.

36. CC to Kalm, February 1751, *CP*, vol. 4, 260; CC to JA, May 27, 1729, RP, vol. 1, 119; New York State, *Calendar of N.Y. Colonial Manuscripts Indorsed Land Papers*, comp. O'Callaghan, 123, 128–29; New York Colony, *Calendar of Council Minutes*, comp. Fernow, 269.

37. New York State, *Calendar of N.Y. Colonial Manuscripts Indorsed Land Papers*, comp. O'Callaghan, 131; E. M. Fox, *Land Speculation*, ix, 9; Kim, *Landlord*, 136.

38. Allen, *American Biographical and Historical Dictionary*, 199.

39. New York Colony, *Calendar of New York Colonial Commissions*, comp. O'Callaghan, 17; CC to Dr. Home, December 7, 1721, *CP*, vol. 1, 51; Edgar J. McManus, *Black Bondage in the North* (Syracuse, NY: Syracuse University Press, 1973), 32–34.

40. CC to E. Hill, June 1, 1724, *CP*, vol. 8, 173–74; E. Hill to CC, April 29, 1726, *CP*, vol. 8, 182.

41. CC to Kalm, February 1751, *CP*, vol. 4, 260; CC to Collinson, May 1742, *CP*, vol. 2, 261–63; CC, "Farming on the Hudson Valley Frontier: Cadwallader Colden's Farm Journal, 1727–1736," ed. Jaquetta M. Haley, *Hudson Valley Regional Review* 6, no. 1 (March 1989): 10; Purple, "Notes," 162.

42. CC, "Farming on the Hudson Valley Frontier," 11, 13–14, 23.

43. CC, "Farming on the Hudson Valley Frontier," 7, 16; CC to JA, June 21, 1728, RP, vol. 1, 50–51.

44. CC, "Farming on the Hudson Valley Frontier," 10–11, 13–18, 20, 22–23, 27; CC to Kalm, February 1751, *CP*, vol. 4, 260. For tobacco as a medicine, see Marcy Norton, *Sacred Gifts, Profane Pleasures: A History of Tobacco and Chocolate in the Atlantic World* (Ithaca, NY: Cornell University Press, 2008), 41, 142–44. When CC and his political foes were not trying to defeat each other, they could be surprisingly civil. James DeLancey gave CC apple seeds for Coldingham, for example. In 1721, CC vowed to bring a cheese from Rhode Island, a delicacy apparently, to, of all people, George Clarke. CC, "Farming on the Hudson Valley Frontier," 21; Isaac Bobin, *Letters of Isaac Bobin, Esq., Private Secretary of Hon. George*

Clarke, Secretary of the Province of New York, 1718–1730 (Albany, NY: J. Munsell, 1872), 104.

45. CC to Peter Templeman, February 6, 1761, Guard Books, Royal Society of the Arts, London; CC's Observations on the bite of a rattle snake, c. 1743, *CP*, vol. 3, 66–68.

46. CC to JA, July 12, 1735, RP, vol. 2, 79; CC to [Douglass], c. September 1728, *CP*, vol. 1, 271–72; CC to Collinson, July 7, 1749, *CP*, vol. 4, 114–15.

47. CC to Mrs. CC, May 6, 1736, *CP*, vol. 8, 240–41; CC to Mrs. CC, June 19, 1746, *CP*, vol. 3, 214–15; *SM*, vol. 2, 30; Hindle, "Colonial Governor's Family," 238–39.

48. CC, "Farming on the Hudson Valley Frontier," 15–16, 18, 25, 28, 32.

49. Francis W. Halsey, ed., *A Tour of Four Great Rivers: The Hudson, Mohawk, Susquehanna and Delaware in 1769, Being the Journal of Richard Smith* (Port Washington, NY: I. J. Friedman, 1964), 4; Andrew Burnaby, *Travels Through the Middle Settlements in North America in the Years 1759 and 1760 With Observations upon the State of the Colonies* (London: T. Payne, 1775; repr. New York: Kelley, 1970), 113–14; James Birket, *Some Cursory Remarks Made by James Birket in his Voyage to North America, 1750–1751* (New Haven, CT: Yale University Press, 1916; repr. Freeport, NY: Books for Libraries Press, 1971), 43; John Fontaine, *The Journal of John Fontaine: An Irish Huguenot Son in Spain and Virginia, 1710–1719*, ed. Edward Porter Alexander (Williamsburg: Colonial Williamsburg Foundation, University Press of Virginia, 1972), 115; CC to JA, February 4, 1728/9, RP, vol. 1, 109.

50. CC to Admiral George Clinton (hereafter cited GC), January 29, 1747/8, February 20, 1750/1, *CP*, vol. 4, 6–10, 263; CC to Clarke, December 6, 1731, Clarke Papers, box 30, f. 2.

51. CC to John Rutherfurd, [1750?], CPU, reel 2.

52. CC to Gilbert Livingston, April 7, 1736, HM9836, Benedict Coll., Huntington Library, San Marino, CA; CC to JA, September 6, 1728, RP, vol. 1, 81; CC to Johnson, May 3, 1762, Etting Collection, HSP.

53. CC to JA, September 6, 1728, RP, vol. 1, 81; Edward Countryman, "From Revolution to Statehood (1776–1825)," in *The Empire State: A History of New York* (Ithaca, NY: Cornell University Press, 2001), ed. Milton M. Klein, 268; "Notes on the Erie Canal," *Bulletin of the Business Historical Society*, 6, no. 5 (1932): 6; Peter L. Bernstein, *Wedding of the Waters: The Erie Canal and the Making of a Great Nation* (New York: W. W. Norton, 2005), 77; Margaret V. S. Wallace, "'Big' Little Britain: Cadwallader Colden and His Canal," *Orange County Post*, February 20, 1967.

54. CC to Clarke, February 14, 1737/8, PRO *Cal.*, vol. 44, 130–34; CC, "Observations on the Situation, Soil, Climate, Water Communications, Boundaries etc. of the Province of New York . . . 1738," in *DH*, vol. 4, 173–74; Noble E. Whitford, *History of the Canal System of the State of New York, together with Brief Histories of the Canals of the United States and Canada* (Albany, NY: State Engineer and Surveyor, 1906), vol. 1, 16–17; S. H. Sweet, *Documentary Sketch of the New York State Canals* (Albany, NY: Van Benthuysen, 1863), 90–91; P. L. Bernstein, *Wedding*, 52; A. Barton Hepburn, *Artificial Waterways of the World* (New York: Macmillan, 1914), 34–35; Gerard Koeppel, *Bond of Union: Building the Erie Canal and the American Empire* (Cambridge, MA: Da Capo Press, 2009), 19–21; Alvin F. Harlow, *Old Towpaths: The Story of the American Canal Era* (New York: D. Appleton, 1926; repr. Port Washington, NY: Kennikat Press, 1964), 7; Deborah Epstein Popper, "Poor Christopher Colles: An Innovator's Obstacles in Early America," *Journal of American Culture* 28, no. 2 (2005): 178.

55. Wallace, "'Big' Little Britain;" John M. Eager, "An Early Canal," *Historical Magazine* 8, no. 3 (March 1864): 114–15; Whitford, *Canal System*, vol. 1, 7; Harlow, *Old Towpaths*, 12; Ulysses Prentiss Hedrick, *A History of Agriculture in the State of New York* (Albany, NY: New York State Agricultural Society, 1933; repr. New York: Hill and Wang, 1966), 242.

56. CC to JA, October 3, 1729, Alexander Papers, box 2, f. 7, NYHS; CC to JA, December 15, 1729, Alexander Papers, box 2, f. 7, NYHS; CC to JA, February 21, 1729/30, Alexander Papers, box 3, f. 1, NYHS; JA to CC, December 21, 1729, Alexander Papers, box 1, f. 1, NYHS; Jeffrey Amherst, *The Journal of Jeffrey Amherst Recording the Military Career of General Amherst in America from 1758 to 1763*, ed. Clarence Webster (Toronto: Ryerson Press, 1931), 271; Fingerhut, *Survivor*, 3; CC to JA, December 12, 1729, *CP*, vol. 7, 319–20.

57. CC to his son, December 31, 1759, CC, "Letters on Smith," 217.

58. CC, "Letters on Smith," 217–19; William Douglass to CC, November 20, 1727, January 1, 1727/8, *CP*, vol. 1, 238–39, 246–47.

59. CC to Popple, December 15, 1727, *NYCD*, vol. 5, 845; Rex Maurice Naylor, "The Royal Prerogative in New York, 1691–1775," *Quarterly Journal of the New York State Historical Association* 5, no. 3 (1924): 226.

60. CC to his son, January 31, 1760, CC, "Letters on Smith," 220; William Smith, Jr., *The History of the Province of New York*, ed. Michael Kammen (Cambridge, MA: Belknap Press of Harvard University Press, 1972), vol. 1, 187–88.

61. CC to [Burnet?], November 19, 1728, *CP*, vol. 1, 273–74; JA to CC, May 5, 1728, *CP*, vol. 1, 259–61; JA to Burnet, January 27, 1728/9, in New Jersey Colony, *Documents Relating to the Colonial History of the State of New Jersey*, ed.Whitehead, ed., vol. 5, 230–33; CC to JA, March 4, 1728/9, RP, vol. 1, 109. In April 1729, Montgomerie consulted CC on the advisability of shutting down the government because of a measles epidemic. New York Colony, *Calendar of Council Minutes*, comp. Fernow, 307.

62. JA to Morris, [ante April 15, 1728], in Lewis Morris, *The Papers of Lewis Morris*, ed. Eugene R. Sheridan (Newark, NJ: New Jersey Historical Society, 1991–1993), vol. 1, 329–30; CC to JA, June 21, 1728, RP, vol. 1, 50, 51.

63. CC to JA, June 21, 1728, RP, vol. 1, 50, 51.

64. "May it please your Excellency," RP, vol. 1, 63; JA, "Concerning the Court of Chancery," September 1, 1728, *CP*, vol. 1, 263–69.

65. JA, "Concerning the Court," *CP*, vol. 1, 263–69; CC to JA, September 6, 1728, RP, vol. 1, 81; "May it Please your Excellency," RP, vol. 1, 63.

66. CC to JA, November 19, 1728, RP, vol. 1, 93; CC to Montgomerie, November 8, 1728, RP, vol. 1, 92.

67. CC to JA, November 19, 1728, RP, vol. 1, 93.

68. [CC to Montgomerie, March 28, 1729], RP, vol. 1, 111; JA to CC, June 18, 1729, RP, vol. 1, 123; JA to CC, March 14, 1728/9, *CP*, vol. 1, 275–76.

69. CC to his son, January 31, 1760, CC, "Letters on Smith," 221–23; JA to CC, June 18, 28, 1729, *CP*, vol. 1, 280–89; JA to CC, June 18, 1729, RP, vol. 1, 123; New York Colony, *Calendar of Council Minutes*, comp. Fernow, 307–8; W. Smith, Jr., *History*, vol. 1, 193.

70. CC to JA, July 13, 1729, RP, vol. 1, 127; CC to JA, July 23, 1729, *CP*, vol. 1, 289–90.

71. JA to CC, August 12, 1729, *CP*, vol. 1, 291–94; CC to JA, August 29, 1729, RP, vol. 1, 131.

72. CC to his son, January 31, 1760, CC, "Letters on Smith," 222–23; JA to CC, September 11, 1729, *CP*, vol. 1, 295–300; CC to JA, June 22, 1729, RP, vol. 1, 124; Bonomi, *Factious People*, 100.

73. CC to Micajah Perry, n.d., *CP*, vol. 2, 26–30; CC to Douglass, January 21, 1739/40, CPU, reel 2; Philip J. Schwarz, *The Jarring Interests: New York's Boundary Makers, 1664–1776* (Albany: State University of New York Press, 1979), 33.

74. Bobin to Clarke, January 7, 1723/4, in Bobin, *Letters of Isaac Bobin*, 174–75; CC to Perry, n.d., *CP*, vol. 2, 26–30; JA to CC, December 23, 1731, *CP*, vol. 2, 39–41.

75. Burnet to Deputy Gov. Jonathan Law, February 1, 1724/5, in Joseph Talcott, *The Talcott Papers*, ed. Mary Kingsbury Talcott, Connecticut Historical Society, *Collections* 4 (1892): 45–46. For New England obstructionism, see Philip Ranlet, *Enemies of the Bay Colony: Puritan Massachusetts and Its Foes*, 2nd ed. (Lanham, MD: University Press of America, 2006), passim.

76. CC to Perry, n. d., *CP*, vol. 2, 26–30; CC to his son, January 31, 1760, CC, "Letters on Smith," 223–24.

77. CC to his son, January 31, 1760, CC, "Letters on Smith," 223–24; CC to Major Woolcot, March 6, 1731/2, *CP*, vol. 2, 54–58; New York commissioners to Connecticut commissioners, April 14, 1724, *CP*, vol. 1, 162–63; CC and others, May 19, 1725, in New York State, *Report of the Regents of the University on the Boundaries of the State of New York*, ed. Daniel J. Pratt (Albany, NY: Argus, 1884), vol. 2, 345–46; "Agreement between the Comrs of New York and Connecticut of part of the lines," November 21, 1730, NYHS, New York and Connecticut Boundary: Oblong or Equivalent Lands, box 1; Connecticut Colony, *The Public*

Records of the Colony of Connecticut, ed. J. Hammond Trumbull (Hartford: University of Connecticut, 1850–1890), vol. 6, 57, 422, 496; vol. 7, 296.

78. New York commissioners to Conn. commissioners, April 14, 1724, *CP*, vol. 1, 163–64; CC to Perry, n. d., *CP*, vol. 2, 26–30; CC and others to Burnet, May 19, 1725, New York State, *Report of the Regents*, ed. Pratt, vol. 2, 345; Schwarz, *Jarring*, 67–68.

79. CC to his son, January 31, 1760, CC, "Letters on Smith," 223–24; CC to Perry, n.d., *CP*, vol. 2, 26–30; Schwarz, *Jarring*, 68.

80. CC to his son, January 31, 1760, CC, "Letters on Smith," 224–25; Montgomerie to Gov. Joseph Talcott, September 3, 1730, in Talcott, *Talcott Papers*, vol. 4, 205–8; CC to Perry, n.d., *CP*, vol. 2, 26–30; JA to CC, July 25, 1730, *CP*, vol. 2, 16–17; Schwarz, *Jarring*, 68–70.

81. Montgomerie to Talcott, September 3, 1730, in Talcott, *Talcott Papers*, vol. 4, 205–6; JA to CC, June 23, July 3, 1731, *CP*, vol. 2, 20–23; CC to Perry, n.d., *CP*, vol. 2, 26–30; CC to Mrs. CC, August 11, 1731, *CP*, vol. 2, 35; E. Hill to CC, March 31, 1731, *CP*, vol. 8, 196–97; Rip Van Dam to Lords of Trade, July 1, 1731, *NYCD*, vol. 5, 921; W. Smith, Jr., *History*, vol. 1, 192; Schwarz, *Jarring*, 68–71.

82. JA to CC, July 3, 1731, *CP*, vol. 2, 23; CC to Perry, n.d., *CP*, vol. 2, 26–30.

Chapter Four

Tyrant

In 1737 Cadwallader Colden reflected on the political battles he and his allies had fought since the arrival of Governor William Cosby five years before. "Men that boldly stand up in Defence of the Liberty and Privileges of their Country in Opposition to the Violence and Oppression of men in Power, deservedly gain Honour and are esteemed by their Fellow Citizens." But Colden insisted on a caveat. Such opposition to a governor should take place only due to "apparent unavoidable necessity" that occurred when a governor distorted his powers to hurt the ruled and became "violent, obstinate, stupid or incorrible" in the pursuit of "Wicked Measures." Colden believed that summed up Cosby well, the only governor in this period whom he could not support.[1]

The battle that epitomized the Cosby administration actually started while Governor John Montgomerie still lived, because of scheming by Francis Harison, a lawyer and councilor who became one of the slimiest figures in the history of New York. Harison displayed so much "stupid criminality" that he has never had a defender among historians. As early as 1720 James Logan called him "that little creature Harison." In 1729 Harison tried to stop Colden from getting his landing, making him, Colden sarcastically declared, "just as much beloved here as at New York." And Colden even opposed Harison being picked as a local road commissioner for Ulster County, probably because Harison sought to aid one resident, "very busy in raising clamours," who was angry that Colden had received an Ulster land grant.[2]

Harison had been an ally of Governor Robert Hunter and had been recommended to him by the Lords of Trade. In fact, Harison would say that those recommendations "are the only support I have." And he would knock "these stupid Americans" who failed to understand "how great a man the Queen has sent 'em." Along with Colden, Harison switched his allegiance to Governor

William Burnet after Hunter's departure. Unlike Colden, however, news of Burnet's transfer to Massachusetts convinced Harison to join the forces of Adolph Philipse. Angry, Burnet did not recommend him to Montgomerie, who at first did not assign him a grant in the Oblong despite his membership on the boundary commission. Montgomerie did relent but Harison's slice was not enough for him, which spelled trouble for the future.[3]

In the middle of 1730 Harison wrote to a nobleman, James Brydges, the naive Duke of Chandos, whom he had known since at least 1724, and convinced him that the Oblong was the eighteenth-century version of the cities of gold that had enthralled many explorers. Not only was the Oblong a center of mineral wealth (Harison had sent samples of iron and copper from its nonexistent mines), it had a thriving fur trade. Although it did have much "good Land," it was portrayed as a veritable cornucopia of useful naval stores such as hemp and tar. Actually, there was doubt that there were any pine trees, the source of tar, in the Oblong. Chandos had a history of falling for spiels about investments—including the South Sea Bubble in which he tossed in £50,000—given by shady characters. Harison fit that description well. Accepting Harison's fantasies as truth, the gullible Chandos used his court connections—created by bribing important people—to obtain a royal grant for himself, other prominent British figures, Harison, and his factional allies such as his old friend Adolph Philipse. Some London merchants fronted for the duke. The amazed Colden knew there had been no such grant of New York land since the original gifting of the colony to the Duke of York in the 1660s. The Chandos grant had been completed shortly before that of Colden and his comrades in New York, which Harison had predicted. Flushed with success, Harison even expected to become the colony's attorney-general.[4]

James Alexander told Colden they needed to counter Harison's scheming. Believing that the speedy English grant smacked "of Fraud"—a baron had gotten the king's signature, that of various bureaucrats, and the proper seals within a few hours in one day—Colden eagerly wanted to help in any way he could. He would write to an old friend of his in Britain, Micajah Perry, one of the British grantees, whom he had known when they were traders in Philadelphia. Colden, trying to lessen the expectations of the Chandos grantees, explained the realities of the Oblong. Distant landholders had little chance of making a fortune from the Oblong, Colden emphasized—though those on the scene might earn something from it—and he and his partners would not simply give up their claim. As for Harison, any New Yorker in the mother country could explain all about Harison's reputation, "for he is generally known here."[5]

Perry, though, provided little or no help, and Harison seemed to be outmaneuvering his rivals. Quickly, Harison had signed up Oblong squatters as his tenants (squatters were commonplace in any unsettled area). Although the yeomen farmers of Ridgefield stuck with Colden and his allies, their sons went over to Harison. No matter who won the legal dispute, the Ridgefield farmers would get their land. The only good news centered on George Clarke, whom Harison had tried to recruit by having him included in the Chandos grant. But Clarke wanted nothing to do with Harison. A relieved Colden observed that he was "well pleased to find Mr. Clarke so hearty for he may be of considerable use in England." Unknown to Colden, Clarke convinced Chandos that he backed him.[6]

Colden did not think one man like Harison could possibly be "more diligent" than all his foes put together. It was true, as Colden later wrote, that Harison now confronted "men of Spirit that would not yield their right while there was any means of Supporting it." Yet this did not change the basic facts—the king had the right to grant lands in New York and the Chandos grant pre-dated the New York grant. Alexander knew very well that Harison, Chandos and their partners "would have the Law on their Side" despite Harison, an inept surveyor to be sure, giving Chandos a wrong location for the Oblong which had been inserted into their grant. Colden and Alexander had no way of knowing that their odds would become even worse. Harison easily brought the new governor, Cosby, as corrupt as Harison, over to his side.[7]

The fog over the identity of Montgomerie's successor began to lift in February 1732. Reports reached New York that Colonel William Cosby had won the position. The news became definite in April. All accounts emphasized his fitness to govern the colony—he had married well. His connections were, indeed, impressive in the context of eighteenth-century Britain. His wife, Grace Montague, belonged to the upper crust of the nobility. Her brother, Lord Halifax, and her cousin, the Duke of Newcastle, gave Cosby great influence. Newcastle, especially, had great power over the American colonies during his many decades of officeholding. Despite his importance, "slow-witted" Newcastle, according to historians, only cared about patronage. Another doubts that anyone can prove "that Newcastle made a single positive contribution to the welfare of the colonies or to the strength of the imperial connection." The appointment of Cosby strengthens such assertions.[8]

The Cosbys were a team. Grace Cosby came to be nicknamed "The Governess" by newcomer Daniel Horsmanden (who became both Colden's friend and bitter enemy). She "had the entire management of that weak madman her husband," Lewis Morris asserted. Mrs. Cosby became a major figure during her husband's tenure as governor.[9]

Mrs. Cosby's relatives had earlier put her husband in charge at an English possession in the Mediterranean, the island of Minorca. There his arbitrary governing and blatant corruption had forced his recall and impoverishment due to all the cash he had to surrender to the government. Needing money, he had been given another position, governor of a colony in America, the Leeward Islands. Montgomerie's death spared that colony as Cosby was then switched to New York where more riches seemed available to a needy governor. Colden later wondered "How such a man after such a flagrant Instance of Tyranny and Robbery came to be entrusted with the Government of an English Colony."[10]

Cosby himself supplied part of the answer to Colden's question. In New York, when told one of his actions violated a law, Cosby waved off that complaint by saying "How gentlemen, do you think I mind that, alas! I have a great interest in England." And Cosby knew how to flatter and win the support of British government officials. As an example, he wrote in 1732 to an under-secretary:

> I am extremely pleased with your Nephew he is a very pretty fellow and we are very well together, and he is a great favourite with us, I am to do something essential for him and his sister Phanney in giving them some tracts of Land, which I will do very cheerfully, and with a great deal of pleasure.[11]

Cosby's past and corrupt character did not become known to Colden for some time after the governor's arrival in the colony on August 1, 1732. In contrast, everything Colden learned about Cosby seemed very positive and augured an administration where the doctor would be very influential. Alured Popple, the secretary of the Board of Trade, had recommended Colden to Cosby as a valuable ally knowledgeable of the people and government of New York.[12]

Even Colden's father reported good news for his son's career. Cadwallader Colden's Scottish connections had spent much time convincing Cosby of his importance. Lord Jedburgh, now the marquess of Lothian, had passed on to Rev. Colden that Lord Ilay and his brother, the Duke of Argyle, had talked with Cosby and, apparently more important, to his "lady friend." Mrs. Cosby was told Colden "might be very useful to the Col. he being a stranger to . . . New York." The marquess had gotten still another ally to push the prospects of his old friend, Colden. He had written the marquess to ask for his aid, but the results had to have been more than he had hoped for.[13]

Because of the nature of Colden's office, he depended upon his correspondents for news of the governor. From what Colden learned, practically everyone was enthralled with Cosby and his family. Archibald Kennedy reported that he and his family had socialized several times with the Cosbys during the Christmas holidays. "It is an agreeable family," he assured Colden. Another acquaintance, told by the governor he wanted to give him a land grant, informed Colden that he had personally introduced Alice and young Bettie "to Mrs. Cosby at the Fort where they were received very handsomely and kindly." But the Cosbys' glittering social scene was an illusion. Harison had quickly latched on to Cosby as a like-minded individual and became the governor's political "hatchetman," who would deal with enemies of the administration as they appeared.[14]

Alexander learned the truth about Cosby and experienced "the first appearance of his madness (the most charitable name I can give to his Conduct here)." The governor of New York commanded some regular troops stationed in the colony, and he arranged with Alexander to pay the men until he reached New York; the agreeable councilor spent a hefty sum doing so. After Cosby arrived he gave Alexander a note for £500 that was rejected and then stalled him for three months. Finally, Alexander sued Cosby which "put him in a Rage and Storm in which he threatened terribly." At last the governor paid most of what he owed Alexander, who signed a receipt. Only later did he realize that the receipt specified that all the debt had been handed over. In December 1732 Governor Cosby blasted the "very obnoxious" and "dishonest" Alexander, calling him a Jacobite who was "the only man that has given me an uneasiness since my arrival." Such a man should be dismissed from all offices, the governor urged his British connections.[15]

As Alexander fell out of favor with the governor, Colden stayed in his good graces and had been asked by him for a formal report about the colony's land system for London. Having experienced the oddities of that quagmire for many years, Colden submitted it along with a batch of papers for Cosby's perusal.[16]

Colden admitted that he had thought his extensive work on the lands of New York would win him favor with his superiors. Instead, he had "suffered by looking into secrets which so nearly concern the Interest of many powerful men." He knew that he would continue to have their "utmost resentment to struggle with." Realizing the ministers in far-off London were busy men, their "attention to such remote affairs" could only be gained with "constant application." While "a poor Officer at the Distance America is" would be forgotten in London, "the people here who may imagine that they have received an Injury will never forget" it. Though somewhat reluctant to endure such hostility, Colden promised Cosby that, because of the governor's pledge of his "Patronage and encouragement," he had resolved "to do my Duty as far as my Capacity enables me."[17]

Along with the land report, Colden promised to send Cosby a "Plan" which he had forgotten about but which he now vowed to finish. This plan, likely the draft entitled "Comments on government in general" still in Colden's papers, would have created a radically different New York. The unbalanced nature of colonial governments would likely cause them to resist the mother country. In order to stop that dangerous prospect, Colden recommended that there be "a perpetual Revenue," and governmental salaries set by the king paid for by quitrents. Each colony should have a hereditary senate like the House of Lords. These senators would be granted an estate of, say, 40,000 acres which could not be alienated. (Colden's senate was probably inspired by the colonial nobility established in the charter of Carolina written by John Locke in the seventeenth century.) Non-senators could hold up to 3,000 acres. In New York, the great landlords would be made senators, gratifying their egos as compensation for losing land while similar owners would pay less for quitrents than they currently did in taxes. Overall, the power of colonial assemblies would be balanced with the other branches of the government.[18]

More down to earth, Colden related to the governor the news he had of potential mines in Albany County, some of which "the Indians have [not] as yet discovered them to any Christian." Such mines were avidly sought after, even to the point of breaking up families. Colden himself was one of nine partners in a lead mine, which, like other mines in New York, produced little, if any, profit.[19]

More wealth could come from good land, Colden knew, and he filled Governor Cosby in on his latest observations. Because of the unsettled border between the counties of Albany and Ulster, some good land seemed to be available. This long uncertain border had apparently been decided by one of Colden's surveys, which eliminated the claim of Kingston in Ulster to territory it had claimed, now in Albany. This fine land, presently with no owner, appeared ripe for the taking and Colden requested Cosby grant him a 4,000 acre slice from it. Colden advised the governor to insert the name of one of his farm workers of Coldengham, Andrew McDowal, instead of his own, the common technique of New Yorkers to avoid the legal acreage limit and make the grant seem less "extraordinary." Here, Colden is much more grasping than usual.[20]

Cosby responded to Colden that he had gotten the papers, and had read some of them. The governor promised to ready the 4,000 acre grant Colden had requested. By August 1733 Cosby and Colden still remained on good terms.[21]

Despite what Colden must have been expecting, no grant to Andrew McDowal appears until 1738, well after Cosby's death, when McDowal is listed along with Patrick McClaghry, another Colden worker. This grant may have actually been for the two men. Colden did not receive the grant from Cosby.[22]

Why did Governor Cosby ignore Colden's request? Cosby, temperamental to say the least, once banned a man from any land grant in the colony because he had not appeared grateful enough. But Colden probably was frustrated because a host of the governor's acolytes in New York City also wanted grants from the same area—they were on the scene and Colden was not.[23]

In 1752 Colden still had not gotten over this disappointment. Thinking that the governor had not read his report on New York lands, Colden believed he had just given it to Harison who "had no inclination to forward the purposes of it." But Cosby had read the report, using it to instruct himself on ways to take advantage of the trickery endemic in New York's land system. And Cosby learned well.[24]

An example of the governor's newfound expertise involved one of the most infamous land swindles in New York, the notorious Albany patent. In 1730 Albany purchased some 1,000 acres from the Mohawks, insisting that it had a right to buy the land. Soon, the Indians complained that the town had defrauded them. In spite of the complaints, Albany continued to hold the deed until Governor Cosby came to the town, and gave it to the Indians who then destroyed it. Quietly, Cosby then granted the area to himself and a host of partners including Harison, Clarke, Kennedy, and James DeLancey. Thanks to Colden's unintended tutelage, Cosby made a mockery of the rule that the governors were not allowed to accept land grants. Using other names, Cosby became a major landholder in New York, gaining, for example, the 42,000 acres of "Cosby Manor" along with much other real estate. By January 1734 Cosby had amassed enough land, even for him, and announced that he would now accept only cash for his fees.[25]

While Colden had been busy with land issues, events had transpired at a rapid rate in the colony's capital. The first political crisis stirred up by Cosby had its beginning with Montgomerie's death. The senior councilor, Rip Van Dam, as president of the Council, took charge as acting governor. But how much should he be paid? According to a proclamation issued by William III in the 1690s, the king would receive one half of the salary after a governor's death and the king could dispose of the money as he chose. When a new governor received his commission, he received one half of the salary until he arrived at the colony, when he earned all of it.[26]

But King William was long dead, and the custom in New York changed over time. The Council, with Colden wintering in Coldengham, had debated the question. Van Dam obtained Chief Justice Morris's opinion, which Alexander accepted and expanded on. Then the Council decided that, without any written instruction otherwise, Van Dam should receive the whole salary; Montgomerie's instructions had specified that an absent governor got one half the salary but did not mention what rule to follow when a governor died. Clarke agreed with Morris but DeLancey strongly dissented as did Kennedy who also missed the meeting. The Assembly remained silent on the matter.[27]

Then Governor Cosby assumed his office and rejected all that reasoning. He had been given an order from the king's privy council entitling him to one half of the salary from Montgomerie's death. Although Van Dam refused to surrender the money, he did make a substantial loan to Cosby, a common enough courtesy to a newly-arrived governor. In his *Arguments* Van Dam wrote that "the Governour . . . acknowledges the Obligation, and promises gratefully to pay me; but has not thought fit to do it." This was Cosby after all. Not only did the governor refuse to pay back the loan, he sued Van Dam.[28]

Cosby had some legal options he could pursue. A jury trial, composed of New Yorkers, would likely favor Van Dam, not the stranger who had only recently come to New York. The chancery court could deal with such a case, but even Cosby shrank from being the judge in his own suit. However, "a rather vague tradition" existed that the Supreme Court of New York, presided over by Morris, could sit as still another type of court, an exchequer court, which could also handle Cosby's case. This court had fallen into disuse and Morris rejected the suggestion. A trial by jury found for Van Dam. Though the governor did not accept that result as final, it created a precedent that, years later, would benefit Cadwallader Colden.[29]

Governor Cosby wanted the money Van Dam had received and he would not let Chief Justice Morris stop him. In August 1733 Cosby summoned Colden to New York City, supposedly about land matters. When Colden came to Cosby's residence, he hugged him, saying "my Dear Colden I am glad to see you." Then, for several days, the entire Cosby family "caressed" him. Just before a scheduled Council meeting, Cosby, Colden related, sat with him "upon the Couch . . . and seemed to entertain me in the most friendly manner" but said nothing about the agenda of the meeting.[30]

The reason behind the governor's silence about the business to be done soon became evident. When the Council met, Cosby announced that he had formally removed Chief Justice Morris and "thought this the most proper place to give the first notice of it," in blatant violation of proper procedure. The governor was supposed to seek the advice of the councilors before acting on an important matter; firing the chief justice certainly qualified. Stunned by the governor's announcement, Colden asked: "Then your Excellency only tells us what you have already done?" Cosby said yes, causing Colden to say: "It is what I could not have advised." In response the animated governor stated "I do not seek your advice." Because Colden had objected, he later wrote, the governor "never forgave me."[31]

Replacing Morris, Cosby picked DeLancey, who had been the second judge after Morris, as chief justice. Morris believed that the Council would never have agreed to his dismissal "being pretty well assured," he wrote soon after the meeting, "that neither Colden, who well knows the state of the province, nor Kennedy the Collector, nor I believe DeLancey himself would have advised the doing of any such thing." Cosby filled DeLancey's place with Frederick Philipse, formerly the third judge. According to Colden, Philipse, whose "weak" mind was marked by "Ignorance," had no "pretence to any skill or knowledge in the law."[32]

Morris may have been well informed about DeLancey's opinion. Although DeLancey had been studying law, he had never practiced as a lawyer. He had been a young boy when Morris became chief justice; Alexander had been practicing law longer than DeLancey had been alive. No doubt, DeLancey, knowing his lack of experience—Montgomerie had appointed him and Philipse to the bench in 1731—was embarrassed by his rapid rise and tried to explain why he had accepted the position. He "excused" the act, Colden learned, because if he had turned the governor down, Cosby would have made Harison chief justice.[33]

Whatever Chief Justice DeLancey may have thought privately, he did Cosby's bidding along with Philipse. Cosby's suit against Van Dam would be continued in an exchequer court, but it generated "a paper war" which the governor insisted "prostituted" the prerogative "to the censure of the mob." Van Dam's *Heads of Articles of Complaint*, produced by New York printer John Peter Zenger, declared that he had "been condemned unheard." "Restless minds" really wrote it for Van Dam, Cosby's men on the Council declared, and "in reality he is no other than the Instrument and the work of their hands."[34]

"Those turbulent spirits" behind Van Dam, including Colden, founded a newspaper, published by Zenger—"a good and nimble printer"—to continue the assault on Cosby. In contrast, Harison dreamed up "ridiculous flatteries" that filled up William Bradford's Cosby-controlled *Gazette*, Alexander informed Brigadier Hunter. Van Dam's friends revealed nothing about the authors who filled up Zenger's *New York Weekly Journal*—the articles were all anonymous to save their authors from jail. Colden was one of these secret wits. No stranger to anonymous tracts, Colden delighted in anonymity and used words people would not expect from him to conceal his identity. He enjoyed hearing people try to guess who had written his pieces.[35]

By January 1734 Colden, once again spending the winter at Coldengham, explained to Aunt Elizabeth that the news she had heard at Philadelphia was all "too true." New Yorkers felt uneasy because of the conduct of their governor. "However, the distance I am [from] New York frees me from a good deal of uneasiness that could not be avoided were I there at this time." He wanted "to maintain the Character of an honest man," a difficult task indeed while Cosby governed New York. "You sit still by your Country fire, enjoying yourself and family with the utmost peace and Satisfaction," an envious Horsmanden told Colden, "while we are in the midst of party flames, and where things will End I'm not prophet enough to foretell."[36]

What Colden did to stay an honest man is clear. On December 17, 1733, the Council wrote to the Duke of Newcastle to defend the governor at his request, as they were the "nearest witnessed to his actions." Colden had not been at the meeting where the letter was composed as he was not in the city. However, as the governor charged later, Colden "prevailed" on a clerk to copy it for him. Then Colden gave it to Morris who would use it in a new version of Van Dam's *Articles of Complaints*, printed in Boston where Cosby had no power. The pamphlet included a Van Dam letter from December 15,

1733, the Council's letter to Newcastle, and a reply to that letter. The Council's letter was published before Newcastle had responded.[37]

Exactly when Colden became the "spy" of Cosby's foes, through what is the first media leak in New York, is not certain. It might have occurred in December 1733, but perhaps not till after April 1734 when Horsmanden repeated an ominous warning from a year before. "I am credibly informed," Colden was told, "That there are designs upon your place of Surveyor as well as Councilship." Horsmanden could only explain why Colden's Council membership had been targeted—"the pretence of Living out of Town at a Great Distance has been hinted to myself." Colden's prolonged absences had to have convinced Cosby by June 1734 that Colden had joined with the "tyrant" Morris, whose "adherents," the governor insisted, "amount to no more than two or three Scotsmen and I am very sorry to say it hold employments under the King."[38]

In light of Colden's vulnerability, who wanted to be the colony's new surveyor-general? In 1731 DeLancey campaigned hard, through his powerful in-laws, the Heathcotes, to be made surveyor-general for the "Northern district of America," based in Boston, if nobody else had already been appointed. The incumbent had died on the voyage from Britain. DeLancey planned to spend a huge sum in his campaign. "You will know how to apply the money properly" he noted to his correspondent, hoping to duplicate his father's success with the Lords of Trade. But the campaign failed. There is no evidence that in 1734 DeLancey, at this stage of his career, wanted to try to unseat a living officeholder. More likely, Harison fancied himself in Colden's office. Having served on the commission that determined the Connecticut border would seem like a qualification. Harison's incompetence at surveying would not have dissuaded Governor Cosby from appointing him.[39]

In any case, Colden's action was only discovered during November 1734, when he told Horsmanden that he was thinking of traveling to Great Britain. Van Dam's Boston pamphlet had reached New York and Colden knew he was in trouble. Apparently, he had been the only councilor who had asked for a copy of the letter—the identity of the leaker seemed obvious. On December 10, 1734, Cosby wrote to the Duke of Newcastle, telling him what Colden had done. "I will further trouble your Grace with this observation on the General behaviour of Mr. Colden, that it is inconsistent with, and unworthy of the Character of a Councilor." How could the Council still function if its "most secret consultations and resolutions" were leaked, the governor inquired. Aware of Colden's noble friends, Cosby preferred to have London fire his foe rather than do it himself.[40]

Meanwhile, Colden had become publicly enmeshed in the governor's campaign to try Zenger for seditious libel, and Colden was not even in the city. On November 2, 1734 the Council ordered that Zenger's paper be publicly burned; Colden was listed in the printed account as being at the meeting. But Colden had been no where near it. Some ninety miles away in the town of Esopus in Ulster, Colden had been dealing with some personal business. "When the Minutes both of Council and Assembly thus appear contrary to fact, what must the people think of it" Alexander wondered.[41]

During 1735 the proceedings against Zenger, whose lawyers were Alexander and William Smith, Sr., began to proceed under the supervision of Chief Justice James DeLancey. Earlier, Smith had already attacked DeLancey's unsuccessful charge to the grand jury. "I was in some Pain for poor Zenger," Smith wrote, "his Judge having, previous to any Presentment, declared His Opinion." DeLancey's bias continued to show. In a startling act he disbarred the printer's two lawyers. That move "surprised" Colden, "for it seems to me it must be a very notorious crime that would make a Judge Silence a Lawyer for offering anything he thought necessary for the Defense of his Client because of the dangerous Consequences of too free an exercise of such Power." Colden admitted that he was "the least Capable of any of you to write" on such complex legal matters. Nonetheless, he continued to do so, just telling Alexander to make any necessary changes.[42]

Zenger's case continued and he was tried in August 1735; eventually a lawyer was brought in from Pennsylvania. Despite the chief justice's partiality, the jury cleared Zenger of the crime of seditious libel, a substantial defeat for the governor's forces. Although the disbarred Alexander could not speak in the courtroom, his legal reasoning had saved Zenger. When the not guilty verdict was announced, Colden related, "the numerous audience expressed their joy in three loud Huzzas."[43]

One item in Zenger's newspaper soon demonstrated to Colden that he could not escape a tyrant's reach even at Coldengham. A friend of his, Vincent Matthews, an assemblyman from Orange County, had attacked Harison on the floor of that house and Zenger printed a letter from some Orange voters thanking him. Governor Cosby then fired Matthews from his appointed offices in the county including a judgeship. Harison sent two of his allies, Edward Blagg and John Alsop, to deal with those men who had so publicly thanked their assemblyman; those among them who held an office were also summarily dismissed.[44]

Colden knew Harison's agents well, especially Alsop, his neighbor disgruntled by his failure to get the Colden landing. "You know what Blagg is capable of," Colden told Alexander. "Alsop is no way inferiour to him." Alsop, in particular, was not doing well financially and Colden suspected he would "take desperate Courses" to improve his prospects. Both Blagg and Alsop, dubbed "Harison's Scholars" by Colden, "Value themselves upon their Skill in his Political or rather deceitful wicked Principles." If such principles continued, Colden warned, "We shall become a Society of Rogues and Robbers," but he hoped that "every honest man will be as Industrious in preserving the Virtue of the Society where they live as Some others are to destroy it."[45]

Harison's scholars, meanwhile, tried to destroy Matthews's support in the county and solicited voters to sign a public letter thanking Cosby for firing Matthews and the others. Most of the signers were misled about the letter's true purpose. At militia meetings, Matthews's support became apparent. Most of the signers, now aware of how Alsop and Blagg had misled them, wanted their names crossed out. Colden did everything he could to rally support for the beleaguered assemblyman. In early April 1735 Horsmanden learned that letters addressed to both Matthews and Colden had been opened and read.[46]

Because Cosby's minions had not succeeded in destroying Matthews, they intensified the attack. Suddenly, those who had thanked Matthews discovered that "Subpoenas are issued out of Chancery against them for their Quitrents," a blatant "attempt against the Liberties and Freedom of the People in their Representative Capacities." These local farmers had gotten their land from the town of Goshen and so were responsible for part of Goshen's tiny quitrent; their share of the town's quitrent totaled less than "one half penny a piece." When the sheriff gave each men a subpoena, he demanded a fee of £3. These "people are so poor and so terribly afraid of charges they must do any thing." They could not afford the sheriff's fee, and the exorbitant charges of the chancery court would utterly destroy them. Other, richer landholders who had not incurred the wrath of Governor Cosby, despite also failing to pay quitrents, were ignored. Colden complained to Alexander: "By this you see for what use the Powers of Chancery in the Governor's hands are employed." He urged his friend to employ his considerable talents to help Cosby's latest targets.[47]

When Matthews returned to the city to attend the Assembly, he tried to rally support against such abuses. On October 21, 1735, in a speech written by Colden, Matthews blasted Cosby and his minions: "They have so many ways of oppressing and terrifying private men that few in a private condition dare oppose them." Blasting the lawyers Blagg and Alsop, whom Cosby had made an attorney, Matthews wondered "what name to call such Creatures." Dismissing Matthews's "long Speech," the Assembly silenced him. The Assembly, controlled by Adolph Philipse, would not help Cosby's targets because Philipse still wanted a share of the Oblong and would tolerate anything to get it.[48]

Cosby's machinations continued to haunt Matthews and his friends. In December 1735 Colden learned that Cosby had another ally in Orange— Thomas Smith, the brother of William Smith Sr., the colleague of Alexander in the legal battles with Cosby. According to some of Matthews's allies in Goshen, Thomas Smith did everything he could to convince a grand jury to indict Matthews on a trumped up charge. Once again Alsop and his partner

Blagg lurked in the shadows. Enough individuals, however, defended Matthews before the grand jury to prevent it.[49]

Disturbing as that was to Colden, he uncovered more perplexing information about the Smith family. "What shocks people most," Colden alerted Alexander, was that the Smiths stated that "they do nothing without Mr. William Smith's advice" and that his father "openly" said so. "I am told of many other things which make people generally believe" that the Smiths were "in a concerted design" with Alsop, Blagg and other Cosby men. The behavior of William Smith Sr.'s family, Colden insisted, was "frequently the subject of Discourse" outside of the city.[50]

Matthews, who seems to have had an agreeable personality, was "entirely satisfied in Mr. William Smith's Friendship and stifles Resentments." Nonetheless, plenty of New Yorkers, including Clarke and Horsmanden, did their best to be on both sides at once, and it would not surprise that William Smith, Sr. might have been doing the same. In any case, Cadwallader Colden never was close to Smith or his family.[51]

No one could mistake on which side Alsop stood. In Matthews's speech Colden accused Alsop of forgery. Earlier, Colden publicly suggested that his neighbor had engaged in other criminal conduct, but Alsop had no fear what the councilor Colden thought of him. To begin with, Governor Cosby controlled the courts and Harison was also there to protect him. Rather cocky, Alsop, in front of witnesses, taunted Colden for not also saying, the lawyer mocked, that he "was a vile rogue and a knave and that I would have him the said Alsop indicted." Such bravado suggests that he expected to replace Colden on the Council. Whatever Alsop may have dreamed, the Cosby regime began to suffer reversals. For example, few of the Goshen farmers were dragged before the Chancery court—Cosby had so many targets it was difficult to deal with all of them quickly. And, though the colony had not yet been milked dry, Cosby ran into problems with his wealth-gathering too, especially with the Oblong.[52]

The Oblong seemed like a ripe plum for Cosby to pluck, and the Duke of Chandos bribed the governor with a chunk of it. "Poor Creatures," Cosby called the New Yorkers who claimed the Oblong. "What can they do in Opposition to such great men in England." What, indeed.[53]

Harison would lead the charge against his rivals for the Oblong, but he and Adolph Philipse "were constantly together privately" when the initial plans were laid down. Harison and Philipse, who had a mutual friend in Britain, had known each other since at least 1710. They realized that a proceeding in a regular court of law—with a jury—did not favor them. To get what they wanted, a chancery action had to be conducted. Governor Cosby could then steer the trial in the proper direction. Having the governor vacate a land grant in that fashion disturbed the councilor and manor lord Philip Livingston who feared the effect on other huge grants.[54]

Meanwhile, Colden had been getting information from Horsmanden, then writing a draft of the legal charge. He warned him that the language used in such a legal document, including one for a chancery court, contained rather offensive "Epithets" that Horsmanden found "odious" himself. Knowing that Colden had been thinking of going to Britain, he promised to delay handing over his draft until Colden left the colony; the delay would prevent a legal order, a *Ne exeat*, preventing those accused in a charge from leaving a jurisdiction, which Horsmanden knew Harison was contemplating. Colden stayed home.[55]

Horsmanden at last gave his draft to Richard Bradley, the New York attorney-general, who wasted no time working on the final document. He dropped a suggestion that Colden had undertaken "an unfair unequal and partial Survey" of the Oblong: Colden's reputation made that passage unbelievable. It did, however, state that the border commission had conducted "Arbitrary and Illegal proceedings" that were intended "To Alienate . . . the Lands of the Crown" and those of the Duke of Chandos and his partners, to whom the king had granted the land of the Oblong. Even the Ridgefield yeomen were attacked. Overall, the charge implied that all the participants had been engaged in what Colden dismissed as "feigned frauds."[56]

By February 4, 1735 Alexander knew that the battle was about to begin. The subpoenas went out in March; Colden, on March 20, got his, ordering him to appear for a hearing in the chancery court. As the legal maneuverings progressed, the New York grantees vowed "to Defend against the attorney general's bill to the Last." But before the first hearing, in June 1735, the cast of characters had changed suddenly.[57]

Late on February 1, 1734 a strange letter was discovered near the entrance of the Alexander home. An attempt to intimidate Mrs. Alexander into paying money to some criminal, her husband quickly identified the writing as "Frank Harison's." Although there were others who witnessed the discovery, the Council did its best to exonerate Harison, smeared by his "Blood-Thirsty-Enemies;" a Council committee believed "that he is incapable of being Guilty of so foul a Deed." Cosby's minions then began setting the stage for an indictment of James Alexander for forgery or, at least, try to trick him into perjury; William Smith, Sr., who had not even been at the house, was another potential target. Did the letter indicate that Harison needed cash? In May 1735 he had to flee the colony for misrepresenting himself as the agent of a debtor's creditor. Safe in Britain, Harison convinced the ever-gullible Chandos that he had been "victimized" by the noble's foes in New York, and Harison was awarded a batch of slaves he could sell as compensation for his troubles.[58]

As Colden discovered, Harison's departure led to problems in the Cosby administration's plan to seize the Oblong. "Mrs. C could not be diverted from that Scheme," he explained to Alexander, and saw to it that Adolph

Philipse "succeeded" Harison "in the Ministerial Office and carrys on the same Scheme." But Clarke was not happy at Philipse's increase in power in the Cosby regime. Colden had been told by Governor Montgomerie that "G[eorge] C[larke] likes A[dolph] P[hilipse] as little as you do." Nor could Clarke have liked that Harison's accomplices, Alsop and Blagg, since his escape "went constantly, apply to and receive their Instructions from A. P."[59]

Because of the Oblong prosecution, Colden had to come up with an answer to the charges. Cadwallader Colden knew more about the Oblong than anyone else. He had plenty of documents involving the territory and transmitted them to Alexander, along with a long draft of a reply in which he blasted the now-absent Harison's role in stirring up the British grant and even specified what should be added to a map of the area that would be submitted. Colden did his best to be as clear as possible.[60]

The chancery hearing seemed mild, without even "a harsh word," compared to what had been feared, which Colden attributed to Clarke's influence. Apparently, the governor, disagreeing with his wife, by June 1735 leaned once again on Clarke as his chief advisor, promising "to preserve friendship with him." According to Alexander, Clarke blamed "Harison and others for the past violent acts." With Harison "gone all these things will be at an End," the happy Clarke assured everyone he talked with. As part of the governor's new image, he hosted a barbecue. Even Cosby's judges tried to be charming. Still, during chancery proceedings, Alexander had asked for a delay of "three months time" to work on their defense; Cosby granted but one.[61]

The charm offensive, which had been suggested by Cosby's British allies, did not last long. The governor's intense enmity to his enemies such as the Morrises could never be put aside. The continuing prosecution of Zenger proved that. Colden thought that Cosby had "so little Capacity" he could not conceal his true character.[62]

Alexander, Colden, and their partners' weak case pushed them to take surprising steps —attacking the chancery court itself and asking the New York Assembly to aid them. In October 1735 some fifty petitioners begged the assemblymen to save their liberty and Morris gave "a long Speech" in support. On November 6, 1735 the Assembly responded with another in a long line of meaningless resolutions condemning chancery courts. These resolutions had never stopped New York governors from hearing cases in chancery, nor would this one, as Adolph Philipse knew very well. Just what the petitioners hoped to gain from their repudiating old beliefs is not clear, but this strategy did not help. Colden did not learn that Philipse was in cahoots with Cosby until after this debacle had played out.[63]

Although the petition to the Assembly was signed by an assortment of Alexanders, Smiths, and others interested in the Oblong, the name of Cadwallader Colden does not appear. Colden, however, did sign a sixty-seven page attack on chancery courts that was sent to London. Attacking any aspect of the royal prerogative made Colden uncomfortable. Admittedly, powers granted by the prerogative, including a chancery court, could be abused by an over-bearing governor. Yet the same powers wielded by a faithful royal servant acting "upon good grounds" could only be beneficial to a colony.[64]

Given Colden's serious concerns about both the fate of the prerogative and the Oblong, it was not surprising that on November 29, 1735, when he was safely ensconced in Coldengham, he wrote Alexander: "I long to hear what proceedings have been held in Chancery." Far away in Ulster, Colden could not have guessed that the chancery proceedings would suddenly halt, leaving him and his partners in control of the territory. Nor could he have thought that Cosby would be departing from the governorship. Nor could he have imagined that Cosby's departure would not happen the way Colden and his friends had been planning it—as a result of pressure applied to London officials.[65]

Attacks upon Cosby flowed to London. In 1733, for example, Alexander warned Popple that he had feared that Cosby could have provoked violence from normally tranquil New Yorkers. Gossip about Governor Cosby increased to the point where Perry assured Colden, "the disturbances in your Government makes a good deal of noise here," mostly hostile to Cosby. And Popple bemoaned that Cosby had not taken his advice to be guided by Colden: "I am well assured you would have led him into no Scrape." Despite such reports, information received from Britain indicated that Morris had almost no change of being restored as chief justice.[66]

Because of such news, Morris decided to present his own case in London. As the Philipse-dominated Assembly refused to make Morris its agent, he needed some sort of authorization. Petitions from the people, it was thought, would remedy that problem. A large group signed in New York City. Colden, who was "well pleased" with the "very useful" petition, agreed to have his name on it, and was seconded by Livingston though he insisted his support must be kept secret in the colony itself. Livingston told Alexander: "It's very shocking that your letters have been intercepted." What else could be "expected . . . from such Vile Varlets who are guilty of such a Felony." Both Colden and Livingston wanted it impressed upon Morris to make the protection of "their offices" an important part of his mission. For safety reasons, that petition went to London from Philadelphia.[67]

In London, Morris learned surprising information about Cosby. At last New Yorkers learned about their governor's shady activities in Minorca, which amazed Colden. It was apparent, Colden believed, that Cosby had gotten away from his misdeeds there only through "the Connivance of some great men."[68]

Still more would be discovered as Morris kept digging. As he wrote to Alexander, who must have been astonished:

when I am more Master of the affair you Shall know all I can discovery of the great and worthy character of Your great man [Cosby] who was once a handsome person of a man and the meanes of his rise known to every body Acquainted with Lord Stanhope and almost to Every body Else.[69]

Sexual charges directed at New York politicians have to be taken with the proverbial grain of salt. A famous charge levelled at a New York governor is the supposed transvestism of Lord Cornbury, who reportedly wore women's clothing. In reality, Cornbury was sporting a silky garment fashionable with the nobility called a morning gown, not a dress.[70]

The charge against Cosby, however, is surprisingly specific. Morris was suggesting that Cosby had engaged in homosexuality or, in the language of the day, Cosby was a sodomite. His reputed lover, Lord Stanhope, a prominent general and politician in the early eighteenth century, had been Cosby's commanding officer. Earlier, Stanhope had gained "the intimacy" of William III, another sodomite, and rose rapidly. When, in 1710, Stanhope ran for election to Parliament, a mob accused him of sodomy and of "having profanely defiled the altars;" he lost.[71]

If Morris was correct, given the libertinism common among the British aristocracy of the day, Cosby may have had a much wider network of connections than the nobles related to his wife. Cosby did brag about his powerful connections in the mother country. Morris's charge helps give new meaning to a seemingly innocuous passage in Colden's history about Cosby and, apparently, its author cleaned things up again. Cosby "bought a small Equipage and went into the Army in Spain under the Command of General Stanhope and gained a Commission. But it is most probable that his rise was chiefly owing to his Marrying the Earl of Halifax's sister."[72]

However Cosby gained his governmental connections, Morris soon discovered that the governor had solid support in the British government. When Morris reached London, he learned that an English printer had been jailed under circumstances much like that of Zenger. The British government did not care about the fate of a German printer in a colony. Despite Cosby's "most extravagant Behaviour," the Lords of Trade backed him and knocked Morris for "appealing to the Country" in print.[73]

Morris's son, Robert Hunter Morris, continued to lobby in the imperial capital after his father left for home. Young Morris met naval captain George Clinton, an heir to the Duke of Newcastle's title. "We drank Verry Hard till 10 at night," Morris noted in his diary, "when Capt. Clinton began to open, and, speaking of Cosby, He said the Duke of Newcastle Had given Him up and at the same time said He believed He Had gone too far." Nonetheless, future events would demonstrate that Clinton was as gullible as the Duke of Chandos, especially after drinking. What Clinton had been thinking of came out soon after. The plan involved just moving Cosby to Barbados, which panicked all the Barbadians in London. It is doubtful that even a transfer would have happened as the merchants from Barbados opposed it.[74]

Meanwhile, Colden had to be surprised by what happened as a result of his letter-writing campaign against Governor Cosby. Colden had written to his friend Popple, the secretary to the Lords of Trade. In February 1736 Colden complained to Alexander about how Popple had responded: "he chides me for not answering his Expectation in renewing friendship with the Govr and blames me for excepting to the Court of Chancery." Popple, upset with Colden, had complained that "Upon this Occasion I cannot help being Surprized that you who was so strenuous for it"—the Chancery court—"as appears by the Minutes of Council of the 5th of December 1727, should now oppose the holding that Court."[75]

Popple also predicted to Colden that London would back the governor's holding the chancery court, and he was correct. In December 1735 the *New York Gazette* reported that the governor had, indeed, been vindicated on that point. Then the newspaper connected Cosby with the wise King Solomon by quoting one of his proverbs: "When it goes well with the righteous the City Rejoyceth."[76]

At least Colden had received some good news. While Morris was still lobbying in London, he sought to find out if Cosby could successfully remove Colden from his offices. He planned to talk with Colden's noble friends, but it quickly became apparent, as Morris explained to Alexander, that he did "not apprehend the Doctor" to be "in much danger." Cosby's powerful interest did have some limits.[77]

Morris, though, consulted with both the Marquess of Lothian and the Duke of Argyle. The marquess remained firmly behind his old friend, but admitted he had little influence with the government. To stir him to do what he could, Morris presented a long letter to him full of facts that could be used to help Colden, whom Morris stated had feared he would be "displaced." Colden's fears were "too well Grounded," Morris asserted, when he knew Cosby really had little chance of removing Colden. To further enliven the noble, Morris insisted that Colden had been branded a Jacobite, a charge certain to inflame a man who knew the truth, and which seems to have been an invention on Morris's part. Finally, Morris wrote that Colden had not leaked the Council's letter to him, another blatant untruth.[78]

The Marquess urged Morris to meet with the far more politically influential Duke of Argyle, and he did so. The Duke, Morris related to Colden, "professed a great friendship for Your father whom he knew to be an honest worthy man and said he would do You all the Service in his power." And that included meeting with the Duke of Newcastle himself if need be. Colden appeared safe "unless the whole ministry Should Join in Cosby's favour," an unlikely prospect in Morris's view.[79]

By all indications, Cosby, though stuck with Colden, seemed certain to remain governor of New York for many more years. But circumstances changed. In late November 1735 the governor became ill. All chancery proceedings about the Oblong stopped and were never completed. Colden referred to the governor's illness as "a Violent Peri pneumony;" the *Gazette* said Cosby had "a Cough, and is Consumptive;" a historian has suggested tuberculosis. In any case, it was a very severe lung infection recognized as a "Dangerous Indisposition." The governor's doctors did not consult Colden, but he was kept informed about the governor's health by letters from Horsmanden and Kennedy.[80]

Cosby may have had this illness before, as his family soon realized that he was in serious trouble. Apparently, his wife pushed the doctors to use much bloodletting, rousing him enough so he could talk again. On November 24, 1735 the Council gathered around the governor's bed and heard him suspend Van Dam, thus making Clarke, the next in line, his successor. According to Kennedy, that dismissal "created a most terrible outcry" in the city.[81]

As the governor's condition worsened, Clarke saw where it was all leading. He began distancing himself from the Cosbys, infuriating Mrs. Cosby. One of her friends, Horsmanden wrote Colden, declared "That he looks on Mr. Clarke to be the greatest Enemy The Govr. has. This he joins with the Women in proclaiming to all who come near them." Clarke, meanwhile, prayed for the governor's recovery, but Mrs. Cosby wanted nothing to do with him.[82]

Cosby lingered into January 1736, in an "almost Desperate Condition," sometimes delirious, sometimes coherent. Mrs. Cosby "peeped" into official correspondence, then claimed that London had accepted the firing of Van Dam and Alexander, who had also been suspended; she opened a dispatch in front of her husband. Despite what Mrs. Cosby said, the British government, so far, had not yet backed either suspension.[83]

By late February Colden knew that Cosby's demise was near when an express messenger appeared at Coldengham to speed up the delivery of paperwork for land grants to the governor's children. "I dont in the least doubt of your ready compliance," Colden was told, "and it will be a particular favour done to Mrs. Cosby and the Family."[84]

William Cosby died on March 10, 1736, or as one English observer described it, "the Tyrant marched off." No one could say the governor failed to provide for his family. According to one historian, when Mrs. Cosby sailed away from New York, "she took with her in excess of 1,000 pounds in property and silver plate." In fact, on the very warship in which she left the colony, she sold a huge tract of land along the Mohawk to the ship's captain, Peter Warren, who had married a DeLancey. Warren now needed someone to oversee his large estate in New York.[85]

Years later, Colden would look back at the Cosby administration and realized how the man had hurt the British Empire. When Rip Van Dam was acting governor, it was learned that the French had encroached on New York's territory and would build a fort, Crown Point, on the shore of Lake Champlain. The Council met to discuss the problem—then Cosby became governor. Confronting the French did not seem to be a good source of wealth to him and Colden did not know if Cosby ever thought of dealing with that serious problem. Colden would lament "that nothing relating to the safety or prosperity of the Province ever entered his thoughts or if any thing did it never gave him any concern but so far as the thought he could get or lose money by it." The colony of New York suffered because of Cosby's inattention to its basic security.[86]

Many observers tried to assess Cosby. Kennedy believed that Bradford, the governor's kept printer, had "Blundered out" something true about his master. Every man, the newspaper essay went on, "should maintain a Modest Opinion of himself." Otherwise, "he will be apt to over-look his own Misgovernment."[87]

Colden, much more brutal, observed that "Despotick and arbitrary power is always hated in a free country," but sometimes a tyrant managed to die a natural death, "the common way of other men." Nonetheless, when tyrants die "they leave behind them a putrid fame which stinks in the nostrils of the latest posterity and their memory is had in detestation."[88]

Perhaps Zenger's *Journal* was pithier. Cosby, the newspaper commented, "was a Man of no Education, not capable of Writing a common Letter; he spoke little but when he was angry, and the most he then could utter were Oaths." (His favorite appears to have been "God Dam ye.") "To be short with his Abilities," the paper continued, "there have been better Men, but never any so bad."[89]

NOTES

1. CC, "A Letter about Governors," in *The Letters and Papers of Cadwallader Colden* (New York: New York Historical Society, 1937), vol. 9, 242–43.

2. Logan to [Hunter], October 1, 1720, James Logan Papers, Logan Letter Books, vol. 2, 226–28, HSP; CC to JA, October 3, 1729, James Alexander Papers, box 2, f. 7, NYHS; CC to Gilbert Livingston, September 12, 1732, Livingston Family Correspondence Coll., Adriance Memorial Library, Poughkeepsie, NY; CC to Clarke, May 18, 1732, George Hyde Clarke Papers, box 30, f. 31, Cornell University, Ithaca, NY; Vincent Buranelli, "Governor Cosby's Hatchet-Man," *New York History* 37, no. 4 (1956): 27–28; Buranelli, ed., *The Trial of Peter Zenger* (New York: New York University Press, 1957), 17.

3. Francis Harison to Lords of Trade, March 13, 1712, CO 5 / 1085 / no. 10, LC transcript; Harison to John Champante, October 5, 1710, Rawlinson Mss., A272, f. 255, Bodlein Library, Oxford, Library of Congress Foreign Reproductions, Washington, DC; CC to his son, January 31, 1760, in CC, "The Colden Letters on Smith's History," New York Historical Society, *Collections* 1 (1868): 225.

4. CC to his son, January 31, 1760, in CC, "Letters on Smith," 225–26; CC, "Cadwallader Colden's History of William Cosby's Administration as Governor of the Province of New York and of Lieutenant-Governor George Clarke's Administration Through 1737," in *The Letters and Papers of Cadwallader Colden* (New York: New York Historical Society, 1937), vol. 9, 308–9; Great Britain, *Calendar of Treasury Books and Papers, 1731–1734*, ed. William A. Shaw (London: H. M. S. O., 1898), vol. 2, 52; William Smith, Jr., *The History of the Province of New York*, ed. Michael Kammen (Cambridge, MA: Belknap Press of Harvard University Press, 1972), vol. 1, 192–93; Philip J. Schwarz, *The Jarring Interests: New York's Boundary Makers, 1664–1776* (Albany: State University of New York Press, 1979), 70–73, 260n30; John M. Beattie, *The English Court in the Reign of George I* (Cambridge: Cambridge University Press, 1967), 163; Joan Johnson, *Princely Chandos: James Brydges, 1674–1744* (Gloucester: Sutton, 1984), 61; C. H. Collins Baker and Muriel I. Baker, *The Life and Circumstances of James Brydges, First Duke of Chandos, Patron of the Liberal Arts* (Oxford: Clarendon Press, 1949), 349–50, 352; B. R. Crick and Miriam Alman, eds., *A Guide to Manuscripts Relating to America in Great Britain and Ireland* (London: British Association for American Studies, Oxford University Press, 1961), 380; *Oxford DNB* s.v. Brydges, James; JA to CC, n.d., *CP*, vol. 2, 24–26; CC to JA, December 6, 1731, Alexander Papers, box 2, f. 7, NYHS; JA to CC, July 25, 1730, *CP*, vol. 2, 16–17.

5. JA to CC, July 3, November 22, 1731, n.d., *CP*, vol. 2, 23, 35–38; CC to Perry, n.d., *CP*, vol. 2, 26–31; Perry to CC, December 27, 1731, *CP*, vol. 2, 45–48; CC to JA, October 6, 1731, Alexander Papers, box 2, f. 7, NYHS; CC, "Cadwallader Colden's History of William Cosby's Administration," 310–11; Elizabeth Donnan, "Eighteenth-Century English Merchants: Micajah Perry," *Journal of Economic and Business History* 4, no. 1 (1931–1932): 71, 73, 84–85, 96–98; Baker and Baker, *Life*, 350.

6. CC to JA, November 9, December 6, 1731, Alexander Papers, box 2, f. 7, NYHS; JA to CC, March 23, 1731/2, *CP*, vol. 2, 59–60; JA to CC, April 30, 1732, *CP*, vol. 2, 60–61; Baker and Baker, *Life*, 352.

7. CC, "Cadwallader Colden's History of William Cosby's Administration," 308–10; JA to CC, July 3, 1731, *CP*, vol. 2, 23; CC to JA, April 18, 1732, Alexander Papers, box 3, f. 1, NYHS; Buranelli, ed., *Trial*, 17–18.

8. JA to CC, February 21, 1731/2, April 24, 1732, *CP*, vol. 2, 48–51, 61–62; Stanley Nider Katz, "Newcastle's New York Governors: Imperial Patronage During the Era of 'Salutary Neglect,'" *New York Historical Society Quarterly* 51, no. 1 (1967): 9; Katz, *Newcastle's New York: Anglo-American Politics, 1732–1753* (Cambridge, MA: Harvard University Press, 1968), 23–24; James A. Henretta, *"Salutary Neglect": Colonial Administration Under the Duke of Newcastle* (Princeton, NJ: Princeton University Press, 1972), 271n100; Theodore Draper, *A Struggle for Power: The American Revolution* (New York: Times Books, 1996), 93.

9. Daniel Horsmanden to CC, January 16, 1735/6, *CP*, vol. 2, 144–45; Lewis Morris to Sir Charles Wager, October 12, 1739, in Lewis Morris, *The Papers of Lewis Morris*, ed. Eugene R. Sheridan (Newark, NJ: New Jersey Historical Society, 1991–1993), vol. 3, 47.

10. CC, "Cadwallader Colden's History of William Cosby's Administration," 286; W. Smith, Jr., *History*, vol. 2, 3.

11. W. Smith, Jr., *History*, vol. 2, 23; Cosby to De La Faye, December 18, 1732, *NYCD*, vol. 5, 942.

12. Alured Popple to CC, November 1, 1734, *CP*, vol. 2, 114–15; CC to E. Hill, May 2, 1732, *CP*, vol. 8, 200; W. Smith, Jr., *History*, vol. 1, 195–96.

13. Rev. A. Colden to CC, August 5, 1732, *CP*, vol. 2, 72–73.

14. Kennedy to CC, January 20, 1732/3, *CP*, vol. 2, 86; J. Warrell to CC, March 20, 1732/3, *CP*, vol. 2, 89–90; CC, "Cadwallader Colden's History of William Cosby's Administration," 309; Buranelli, ed., *Trial*, 10, 18.

15. JA to Collinson, June 4, 1739, New Jersey Colony, *Documents Relating to the Colonial History of the State of New Jersey*, ed. William A. Whitehead (Newark, NJ: Daily Advertiser Printing House, 1880–1886), vol. 6, 71–77; Cosby to Newcastle, December 18, 1732, New Jersey Colony, *Documents Relating to the Colonial History of the State of New Jersey*, ed. Whitehead, vol. 5, 323–25; Cosby to De La Faye, December 18, 1732, New Jersey Colony,

Documents Relating to the Colonial History of the State of New Jersey, ed. Whitehead, vol. 5, 326.

16. CC, "The State of the Lands in the Province of New York, In 1732," in *The Documentary History of the State of New-York; Arranged Under Direction of the Hon. Christopher Morgan, Secretary of State*, ed. Edmund B. O'Callaghan (Albany, NY: Weed, Parsons, 1849), vol. 1, 377–89.

17. CC to [Cosby], [November 30, 1732?], Cadwallader Colden Papers, NYHS.

18. "Comments on government in general," n.d., CPU, reel 2; Wesley Frank Craven, *The Colonies in Transition, 1660–1713* (New York: Harper & Row, 1968), 99–100.

19. CC to [Cosby], [November 30, 1732?], Colden Papers, NYHS; CC to JA, June 21, 30, 1728, RP, vol. 1, 53; JA to CC, June 5, 1730, *CP*, vol. 2, 15; Cosby to Board of Trade, December 6, 1734, *DH*, vol. 1, 724; CC, "Observations on the Situation, Soil, Climate, Water Communications, Boundaries etc. of the Province of New York . . . 1738," in *DH*, vol. 4, 174.

20. CC to [Cosby], [November 30, 1732?], Colden Papers, NYHS; CC, "Farming on the Hudson Valley Frontier: Cadwallader Colden's Farm Journal, 1727–1736," ed. Jaquetta M. Haley, *Hudson Valley Regional Review* 6, no. 1 (March 1989): 7–8; Warrell to CC, March 20, 1732/3, *CP*, vol. 2, 89–90.

21. Cosby to CC, December 1, 1732, March 19, 1732/3, August 3, 1733, *CP*, vol. 8, 203, 207; vol. 2, 86.

22. New York State, *Calendar of N.Y. Colonial Manuscripts Indorsed Land Papers in the Office of the Secretary of State of New York, 1643–1803*, comp. E. B. O'Callaghan (Albany, NY: Weed, Parsons, 1864; repr. Harrison, NY: Harbor-Hill Books, 1987), 235; CC, "Farming on the Hudson Valley Frontier," 7–8.

23. Warrell to CC, March 20, 1732/3, *CP*, vol. 2, 89–90; Frederick Morris to CC, October 27, 1733, *CP*, vol. 8, 210.

24. CC, "State of the Lands," 388–89.

25. Council to Newcastle, December 17, 1733, *NYCD*, vol. 5, 983; Horsmanden to CC, January 8, 1733/4, *CP*, vol. 2, 99; Eric Hinderaker, *The Two Hendricks: Unraveling a Mohawk Mystery* (Cambridge, MA: Harvard University Press, 2010), 128–30; Robert Hunter Morris, "An American in London, 1735–1736," ed. Beverly McAnear, *Pennsylvania Magazine of History and Biography* 64, nos. 2–3 (1940): 173–74; Beverly McAnear, *The Income of the Colonial Governors of British North America* (New York: Pageant Press, 1967), 31; Edith M. Fox, *Land Speculation in the Mohawk Country* (Ithaca, NY: Cornell University Press, 1949), 9.

26. McAnear, *Income*, 34.

27. JA to CC, February 21, 1731/2, Alexander Papers, box 1, f. 1, NYHS; James Alexander, *A Brief Narrative of the Case and Trial of John Peter Zenger*, ed. Stanley Nider Katz (1736; rept. Cambridge, MA: Belknap Press, 1963), 3.

28. Vincent Buranelli, "Governor Cosby and His Enemies (1732–36)," *New York History* 37, no. 4 (1956): 369; Rip Van Dam, *The Arguments of the Council for the Defendant, In Support of A Plea to the Jurisdiction* (New York: John Peter Zenger, 1733), 3; McAnear, *Income*, 34–35.

29. Herbert A. Johnson, "The Rule of Law in the Realm and the Province of New York: Prelude to the American Revolution," *History* 91, no. 1(301) (2006): 11–12; Stanley Nider Katz, "The Politics of Law in Colonial America: Controversies over Chancery Courts and Equity Law in the Eighteenth Century," *Perspectives in American History* 5 (1971): 278–79; Buranelli, ed., *Trial*, 11–12; Alexander, *Brief Narrative*, ed. Katz, 3–4.

30. CC, "Cadwallader Colden's History of William Cosby's Administration," 298.

31. CC, "Cadwallader Colden's History of William Cosby's Administration," 298.

32. CC, "Cadwallader Colden's History of William Cosby's Administration," 298, 293, 303; Morris to Lords of Trade, August 27, 1733, *NYCD*, vol. 5, 951–52.

33. Rip Van Dam and others, *Heads of Articles of Complaint by Rip Van Dam, Esq.; Against His Excellency William Cosby, Esq.* (Boston: John Peter Zenger, 1734), 16; JA and William Smith, Sr., *The Complaint of James Alexander and William Smith to the Committee of the General Assembly of the Colony of New York* [New York: John Peter Zenger, 1735?], 12; William Livingston, *A Review of the Military Operations in North-America* (London, 1757), 18, 26–27; CC, "Cadwallader Colden's History of William Cosby's Administration," 298–99;

New York Colony, *Calendar of New York Colonial Commissions, 1680–1770*, comp. E. B. O'Callaghan (New York: New York Historical Society, 1929), 22.

34. Rip Van Dam and others, *Heads of Articles of Complaint made . . . on Thursday, the 30th of May, 1734 to the Committee of Grievances* (New York?, 1734) 69; Cosby to Newcastle, December 17, 1733, PRO *Cal.*, vol. 40, 262–63; Council to Newcastle, December 17, 1733, *NYCD*, vol. 5, 979, 984; Buranelli, ed., *Trial*, 12.

35. JA to Hunter, November 8, 1733, New Jersey Colony, *Documents Relating to the Colonial History of the State of New Jersey*, ed. Whitehead, vol. 5, 359–60; Council to Newcastle, December 17, 1733, *NYCD*, vol. 5, 981; CC to JA, December 1729, *CP*, vol. 7, 324–25; JA to CC, January 9, 1729/30, *CP*, vol. 7, 329–30; Leonard W. Levy, *Emergence of a Free Press* (New York: Oxford University Press, 1985), 39; Buranelli, "Governor Cosby and His Enemies," 365; Eugene R. Sheridan, *Lewis Morris, 1671–1746: A Study in Early American Politics* (Syracuse, NY: Syracuse University Press, 1981), 157–58.

36. CC to E. Hill, January 19, 1733/4, *CP*, vol. 2, 101–3; Horsmanden to CC, January 24, 1733/4, *CP*, vol. 2, 103–4.

37. Council to Newcastle, December 17, 1733, *NYCD*, vol. 5, 981; Cosby to Newcastle, December 10, 1734, *NYCD*, vol. 6, 26–27. For the Van Dam pamphlet, see n33 above.

38. Cosby to Newcastle, December 10, 1734, *NYCD*, vol. 6, 26–27; Horsmanden to CC, April 1, 1733, *CP*, vol. 2, 91; Horsmanden to CC, April 26, 1734, Gratz Coll., HSP; Cosby to Newcastle, June 19, 1734, British Museum Additional Manuscript 32689, LC transcript; Katz, *Newcastle's New York*, 79–80.

39. James DeLancey to John Heathcote, June 21, 1731, Letters of James DeLancey to the Heathcotes, Lincolnshire Archives, Lincoln, England; DeLancey to Sir Gilbert Heathcote, June 21, 1731, Letters of James DeLancey; DeLancey to John Heathcote, December 30, 1731, Letters of James DeLancey; DeLancey to Sir Gilbert Heathcote, December 30, 1731, Letters of James DeLancey.

40. Horsmanden to CC, November 28, 1734, HM22355, Huntington Library, San Marino, CA; Cosby to Newcastle, December 10, 1734, *NYCD*, vol. 6, 26–27; Horsmanden to CC, November 11, 1734, *CP*, vol. 2, 116–17.

41. "Article Proposed in Journal concerning Colden's Name Being used in Council When Not Present," December 1734, James Alexander Papers, John Peter Zenger Trial Coll., NYPL; "Article proposed," n.d., James Alexander Papers, John Peter Zenger Trial Coll., NYPL; JA to Morris, December 30, 1734, Morris, *Papers of Lewis Morris*, ed. Sheridan, vol. 2, 125; Alexander, *Brief Narrative*, ed. Katz, 44–45.

42. CC to JA, April 23, 1735, Livingston Rutherfurd, *Family Records and Events: Compiled Principally from the Original Manuscripts in the Rutherfurd Collection* (New York: De Vinne Press, 1894), 13–14; CC to JA, March 12, 1734/5, *RP*, vol. 2, 111; Alexander, *Brief Narrative*, ed. Katz, 19–21; Eben Moglen, "Considering *Zenger*: Partisan Politics and the Legal Profession in Provincial New York," *Columbia Law Review* 94, no. 5 (1994): 1515; William Smith, Sr., *Some Observations on the Charge given by the Honourable James DeLancey, Esq.; Chief Justice of the Province of New-York, to the Grand Jury* (New York: J. Peter Zenger, 1733/4), 1–2.

43. CC, "Cadwallader Colden's History of William Cosby's Administration," 339; Leonard W. Levy, "Did the Zenger Case Really Matter? Freedom of the Press in Colonial New York," *William and Mary Quarterly*, 3rd ser., 17 (1960): 43; Moglen, "Considering *Zenger*," 1519.

44. Buranelli, ed., *Trial*, 35–36; Buranelli, "Governor Cosby's Hatchet-Man," 30; Alexander, *Brief Narrative*, ed. Katz, 223n25.

45. CC to JA, March 12, 1734/5, *RP*, vol. 2, 111.

46. CC to JA, March 4, 1734/5, *RP*, vol. 2, 107; Horsmanden to CC, April 2, 1735, *CP*, vol. 2, 132–33.

47. CC to JA, August 1, 20, 1735, *RP*, vol. 2, 125, 129.

48. "Speech of Vincent Matthews," October 21, 1735, *CP*, vol. 8, 229, 233, 238; *New York Gazette* (Bradford), November 10–17, 1735.

49. CC to JA, December 27, 1735, *RP*, vol. 2, 87.

50. CC to JA, December 27, 1735, *RP*, vol. 2, 87.

51. CC to JA, January 16, 1735/6, *RP*, vol. 2, 175.

52. Matthews's speech, October 21, 1735, *CP*, vol. 8, 229; "Memorandum about John Alsop and CC," March 18, 1734/5, *CP*, vol. 8, 221; Katz, "Politics of Law," 279–80. William Smith's son, William Smith, Jr. saw Alsop as being victimized by CC. See *SM*, vol. 2, 32–33.

53. CC, "Cadwallader Colden's History of William Cosby's Administration," 309–10; Schwarz, *Jarring*, 71–72.

54. Harison to Champante, October 5, 1710, Rawlinson Mss., Bodlein Library, LC transcript; CC to JA, December 27, 1735, RP, vol. 2, 149; CC, "Cadwallader Colden's History of William Cosby's Administration," 310; Milton M. Klein, "Democracy and Politics in Colonial New York," *New York History* 40, no. 3 (1959): 226.

55. Horsmanden to CC, November 19, 27, 1734, *CP*, vol. 2, 121–23; *Black's Law Dictionary With Pronunciations*, 5th ed., ed. Henry Campbell Black (St. Paul, MN: West Publishing, 1979), 929.

56. Horsmanden to CC, November 27, 1734, *CP*, vol. 2, 123; Richard Bradley, "To His Excellency William Cosby, Esqr.," n.d., BV Oblong Tract, NYHS; CC, "Cadwallader Colden's History of William Cosby's Administration," 310.

57. JA to Morris, February 4, 1735, Morris, *Papers of Lewis Morris*, ed. Sheridan, vol. 2, 131; CC to JA, March 27, April 8, 1735, *CP*, vol. 2, 128–29, 134–35; Schwarz, *Jarring*, 72–73.

58. Francis Harison, *To the Right Worshipful, the Mayor, Aldermen and Commonalty of the City of New York* (New York: William Bradford, 1734), 9; *The Report of the Committee of His Majesty's council, to whom it was Referred, to examine and make enquiry, touching a letter found and in the house of Mr. Alexander in New-York, on Friday the first day of February, 1733/4* (New York: William Bradford, 1734), 11; James Alexander and William Smith, *The Vindication of James Alexander . . . and of William Smith* (New York: John Peter Zenger, 1734), 1, 5–6; Memorandum by John Hamilton, n.d., Alexander Papers, Zenger Trial, NYPL; John Hamilton's certificate, April 26, 1734, Alexander Papers, Zenger Trial, NYPL; W. Smith, Jr., *History*, vol. 2, 9, 11; Buranelli, ed., *Trial*, 19–20; Baker and Baker, *Life*, 351–52, 352n1.

59. CC to JA, December 27, 1735, RP, vol. 2, 149.

60. CC to JA, July 1, 12, August 20, 1735, RP, vol. 2, 79, 127; CC, "Materials for Answer," n.d., Connecticut and New York Boundary Papers relating to the Oblong, 1733, box 1, NYHS; Schwarz, *Jarring*, 73.

61. CC, "Cadwallader Colden's History of William Cosby's Administration," 312; JA to Morris, June 16, 1735, Morris, *Papers of Lewis Morris*, ed. Sheridan, vol. 2, 177–78; "Answer of The Proprietors of the Equivalent Lands," n.d., Connecticut and New York Boundary Papers relating to the Oblong, 1733, box 1, NYHS.

62. CC, "Cadwallader Colden's History of William Cosby's Administration," 297–98; Horsmanden to CC, March 25, 1734, *CP*, vol. 2, 106–8.

63. *New York Gazette* (Bradford), November 10–17, 1735; *New York Weekly Journal* (Zenger), November 24, 1735; Katz, "Politics of Law," 277–78.

64. *New York Weekly Journal* (Zenger), November 24, 1735; Exceptions offered against the constitution of the Court of Chancery in New York, n.d., PRO *Cal.*, vol. 41, 454; CC to JA, December 3, 1735, RP, vol. 2, 85; CC, "Cadwallader Colden's History of William Cosby's Administration," 305–6.

65. CC to JA, November 29, 1735, RP, vol. 2, 81; Katz, "Politics of Law," 281; Schwarz, *Jarring*, 72–73.

66. JA to Popple, December 4, 1733, New Jersey Colony, *Documents Relating to the Colonial History of the State of New Jersey*, ed. Whitehead, vol. 5, 360–64; Perry to CC, August 30, 1734, *CP*, vol. 2, 111–12; Popple to CC, November 1, 1734, *CP*, vol. 2, 114–15; Horsmanden to CC, November 11, 1734, *CP*, vol. 2, 118–20.

67. JA to Morris, December 30, 1734, January 17, 1734/5, Morris, *Papers of Lewis Morris*, ed. Sheridan, vol. 2, 124, 129; Philip Livingston to JA, January 7, 1734/5, Rutherfurd, *Family Records*, 17–18; Will Allen to JA, February 7, 1734/5, RP, vol. 2, 105; Klein, "Democracy and Politics," 227; CC to JA, January 1, 1734/5, RP, vol. 2, 101.

68. CC, "Cadwallader Colden's History of William Cosby's Administration," 283, 285.

69. Morris to JA, March 31, 1735, Morris, *Papers of Lewis Morris*, ed. Sheridan, vol. 2, 151.

70. On Cornbury see W. Smith, Jr., *History*, vol. 1, 130; and Patricia U. Bonomi, "New York: The Royal Colony," *New York History* 82, no. 1 (2001), 10–11. Before Cornbury came to New York, the English upper classes had taken to wearing such a gown (called a *banyan* in India). Men even wore them outside the home. The fad did not become established in the American colonies until much later. Amelia Peck, ed., *Interwoven Globe: The Worldwide Textile Trade, 1500–1800*, Exhibition catalogue, Metropolitan Museum of Art, New York, September 16, 2013–January 5, 2014 (New Haven, CT: Yale University Press, 2013), 263–65.

71. Basil Williams, *Stanhope: A Study in Eighteenth Century War and Diplomacy* (Oxford: Clarendon Press, 1932; repr. Oxford: Oxford University Press, 1968), 16–18, 125–27; William Thomas Morgan, "An Eighteenth-Century Election in England," *Political Science Quarterly* 37, no. 4 (1922), 595; CC, "Cadwallader Colden's History of William Cosby's Administration," 283; Morris, *Papers of Lewis Morris*, ed. Sheridan, vol. 2, 152–153n10.

72. CC, "Cadwallader Colden's History of William Cosby's Administration," 283.

73. Morris to JA, March 31, 1735, Morris, *Papers of Lewis Morris*, ed. Sheridan, vol. 2, 151–52; Matthew Norris to Morris, January 28, 1734, Morris, *Papers of Lewis Morris*, ed. Sheridan, vol. 2, 84; Robert Hunter Morris to JA, October 16, 1735, New Jersey Colony, *Documents Relating to the Colonial History of the State of New Jersey*, ed. Whitehead, vol. 5, 432–33; Collinson to JA, March 8, 1735, Rutherfurd, *Family Records*, 24–25; Stanley Nider Katz, "Between Scylla and Charybdis: James DeLancey and Anglo-American Politics in Early Eighteenth-Century New York," in *Anglo-American Political Relations, 1675–1775*, ed. Alison Gilbert Olson and Richard Maxwell Brown (New Brunswick, NJ: Rutgers University Press, 1970), 97.

74. R. H. Morris, "American in London," ed. McAnear, 392–93.

75. CC to JA, February 5, 1735/6, RP, vol. 2, 175; Popple to CC, September 16, 1735, *CP*, vol. 2, 140–41.

76. Popple to CC, September 16, 1735, *CP*, vol. 2, 140–41; *New York Gazette* (Bradford), December 23–30, 1735.

77. Morris to JA, February 8, 1734/5, Morris, *Papers of Lewis Morris*, ed. Sheridan, vol. 2, 133.

78. Morris to Lothian, March 26, 1735, *CP*, vol. 2, 124–28.

79. Morris to JA, February 8, 1734/5, Morris, *Papers of Lewis Morris*, ed. Sheridan, vol. 2, 133; Morris to CC, April 11, 1735, *CP*, vol. 2, 136–38.

80. CC, "Cadwallader Colden's History of William Cosby's Administration," 312, 345–46; *New York Gazette* (Bradford), December 30, 1735–January 6, 1735/6, January 6–13, 1735/6; Katz, *Newcastle's New York*, 133.

81. CC, "Cadwallader Colden's History of William Cosby's Administration," 345–46; New York Colony, Council, *Calendar of Council Minutes, 1668–1783*, comp. Berthold Fernow (Albany: University of the State of New York, 1902; repr. Harrison, NY: Harbor Hill Books, 1987), 325; Kennedy to CC, December 22, 1735, *CP*, vol. 2, 143.

82. Kennedy to CC, December 22, 1735, *CP*, vol. 2, 143; Horsmanden to CC, December 19, 1735, *CP*, vol. 2, 141–42.

83. Horsmanden to CC, January 16, 1735/6, *CP*, vol. 2, 144–45.

84. Charles Williams to CC, February 27, 1735/6, *CP*, vol. 2, 147–48; CC to JA, February 22, 1735/6, RP, vol. 2, 87.

85. H. A. Johnson, "Rule of Law," 11n27; Hinderaker, *Two Hendricks*, 156; New York Colony, *Calendar of Council Minutes*, comp. Fernow, 325; Collinson to JA, August 28, 1736, RP, vol. 4, 57.

86. New York Colony, *Calendar of Council Minutes*, comp. Fernow, 316; CC to John Rutherfurd, 1750?, CPU, reel 2.

87. Kennedy to CC, January 17, 1735/6, *CP*, vol. 2, 145; "Of Human Virtues which belong to a Man," *New York Gazette* (Bradford), January 13–20, 1735/6.

88. CC, "Affairs of New York and New Jersey, Under the Joint Governors," New Jersey Historical Society, *Proceedings* 9 (1860–1864): 92–93.

89. *New York Weekly Journal* (Zenger), July 5, 1736; Lewis Morris Jr. to CC, January 17, 1734, *CP*, vol. 2, 100–1.

Chapter Five

Enlightenment

By 1700 it had become commonplace for the curious to peer into a microscope and see all the funny-looking creatures swimming about. Soon microscopes became rather boring as new, exciting fields of learning appeared. The eighteenth century, dubbed "an age of Wonders" by a Colden friend, truly was a time of enlightenment.[1]

A key participant in this enlightenment, Cadwallader Colden, became an international figure and all but established science in New York. Historian Dixon Ryan Fox has written: "Colden merits a statue in a pantheon, which we may imagine and perhaps sometime secure, devoted to the civilizers of New York." Indeed, the province of New York benefited by his presence. According to Colden's old Scottish friend, Dr. William Douglass, living in Boston was like living in "a factory." As for Philadelphia, before the emergence of Benjamin Franklin, James Logan still bemoaned the loss of his intellectual friend. In 1720 Logan felt "very dull." Wondering if truth could actually be discovered, he even questioned whether people had any "Organs fitted for the Discovery."[2]

In one way, New York seemed perfect for the spread of knowledge— there was encouragement at the top. Robert Hunter urged Colden to investigate "the natural history of that Country." William Burnet numbered among those seeking truth. John Montgomerie had a library of over a thousand books, helping explain why he and Colden got along so well. And, despite James Alexander's legal practice in two colonies, he still saved time for the pursuit of learning.[3]

However, the man most responsible for spreading Colden's intellectual musings lived in England. The Quaker Peter Collinson managed to combine a career in trade along with membership in the Royal Society. His many friends around the world sent him seeds for his garden, which blossomed in every season. When he looked at his flourishing plants they reminded him of his far-flung correspondents. During his contemplation of the thriving larch and spruce trees in his garden, he thought of Colden who had provided the seeds. Collinson also had one of the best collections of fossils in Great Britain. One of the "Virtuosi" in Britain, Collinson spread his infectious love of nature to everyone he met.[4]

Colden valued his friendship with Collinson "as one of the happy incidents in my life." The New Yorker had wished for someone with "my own taste" with whom he could discuss the natural world "for we scarcely have a man in this country that takes any pleasure in such kind of Speculations." Just as impressed with Colden, Collinson called him "a very Ingenious Intelligent Man" and sent Colden's gathered data about nature in America to such luminaries of the day as the great Dutch botanist Johann Friedrich Gronovius and the even greater Swede Carolus Linnaeus, who systematized the study of plants.[5]

Although Colden first made a name for himself in botany, his early delvings into nature did not seem propitious. When his botany professor at the University of Edinburgh, Dr. Charles Preston, learned that Colden was going to Pennsylvania—its botany was unknown—he pressed Colden to send back plants and he agreed. Preston then referred him to James Petiver, a fellow of the Royal Society. Petiver instructed him on the fine points of preparing samples. The botanists also hoped for other things from Colden—shells, insects, even fossils. The young man assured Petiver that "I think [it] my duty to give you all the Assistance in my power. You may assure yourself I will omit no opportunities of doing it." That was the last time either Preston or Petiver heard from him.[6]

Despite Colden's youthful confidence, when he arrived in America he discovered the enormity of the task ahead of him. As a Swedish immigrant to Pennsylvania remarked in 1714, "Here are so many strange and different plants that it is impossible to describe all of them." The books Colden consulted were practically useless for the task and he grew "discouraged."[7]

Although Colden had abandoned the pursuit of botany as a science, he remained interested in the medicinal use of plants and, after he moved to New York, their economic and political value as well. In 1725 he sent seeds to Lord Ilay, the brother and heir of the Duke of Argyle. He thought Ilay would be instrumental in seeding America with plants from the Old World which could not grow in Britain; the Dutch had recently started growing coffee in one of their American colonies. Why not follow their example? The best candidate for transplanting, Colden thought, was the Asian plant rhubarb, which "has been of late very dear and is always in great demand."[8]

A sudden discovery decades later would restore Colden's enthusiasm for uncovering the secrets of botany. In 1735 Linnaeus published his first book describing his method of classifying plants based on their sexual organs.

When, in 1742, a visiting student of the University of Leiden in Holland gave Colden one of Linnaeus's books to read, "It excited my curiosity to examine the plants which grew about my house," Colden later explained. By 1743 he had his own copy.[9]

As Colden produced his "characters"—descriptions—of the plants inhabiting his property, he learned the fine points of the Linnaean system. Despite some initial errors, Colden soon produced excellent work, which he sent to Collinson who would comment that "I was surprised with his proficiency in the Linnaean system." Gronovius, whom Colden thought would correct his errors, also received characters from him. Collinson reported to Colden that "my Valuable Friend Doctor Gronovius Let Me know what a fine present you have made Him the Good Man is in Raptures" and added that "I doubt not but Doctor Linnaeus had heard of it Long before this."[10]

Gronovius did send Colden's characters to Linnaeus, who was just as thrilled, offered to publish his work, and named a plant "Coldenia" after him. In fact, Linnaeus wanted to see all of Colden's work. One of Linnaeus's students, Peter Kalm, assured Colden that "there are few persons he sets such value upon as upon you." Somewhat astonished by such reactions, he insisted he knew little about botany but Collinson told him "your skill in that Science was Self Evident." Colden even received an invitation to suggest improvements to the Linnaean system. After getting letters from Linnaeus, Colden told him "I can no way deserve the praises you are pleased to bestow on the little performances I have made," assuming the compliments came about from "your willingness to encourage every attempt to promote knowledge."[11]

Linnaeus kept his promise about publishing Colden's characters; they all finally reached scholars in 1749 and 1751. Written in Latin—still the language of the scholarly world in Europe—and published in two parts in Sweden, the "Plantae Coldenghamiae In Provincia Noveboracensi"—the plants of Coldengham in New York—described the varied plant life there. Digitalis, flowers such as impatiens and azaleas, and hundreds of others were described. Colden stated that another plant, the water dock, helped treat scurvy. Linnaeus, writing to the Scot Dr. James Lind, who studied scurvy, informed him about the virtues of the water dock "which I have introduced on the recommendation of your countryman Colden, who was taught its use by the Country people of New York." Colden—called "Summus perfectus" by Linnaeus—and his observations made a huge impact on the European audience and inspired other British colonists to follow his example.[12]

And Americans did need encouragement. In 1742 Colden observed that "Few in America have any taste of Botany and still fewer if any of these have ability to form and keep a Botanical Garden without which it is impracticable to give compleat Characters of Plants." Of Americans, Colden lamented, "not one" had "both the power and the will for such a performance." He also believed that botanical work should be written in English because few Americans knew Latin.[13]

One of those colonials ignorant of Latin, the Quaker John Bartram of Pennsylvania, "a wonderful Natural Genius" and "a great teacher unto Nature" according to Collinson, soon became a major figure in botany with some assistance from Colden. Despite Bartram's eagerness to investigate plant life, he had "the lowest Education"—Colden translated "the Latin parts" in letters Bartram received. Directed to Colden by Collinson in 1741, Bartram traveled to Ulster but missed him. At last catching the doctor of Coldengham, Bartram was impressed by him and saw, for the first time, the work of Linnaeus which provided Bartram with "the greatest knowledge in Botany of any" book he had read. Colden recommended that Bartram investigate the far away Iroquois lands, an expedition that proved very successful.[14]

Their friendship stayed strong over the years. In 1753, for example, Bartram brought his son William, a future botanist, along on a trip to Coldengham. Missing Colden again, his family took care of the Bartrams, who busied themselves gathering seeds in the area. Colden, the elder Bartram declared, "is one of the most facetious, agreeable gentlemen I ever met with."[15]

One of the things that most intrigued Bartram about Coldengham—aside from Colden himself—were the numerous fossils there, especially "petrified shells," as fossils were described at the time. Bartram carried off "a considerable piece" from Coldengham. Colden believed that such finds proved the site had, at one time, been underwater, but they did "not prove that the face of the Earth" then was "the same it is now." Such drastic change, he thought, "probably has happened by great and general Earthquakes." He knew well "the shock" and power of earthquakes. On November 18, 1755, in the early morning, his bed and house shook "in such a manner as to alarm me greatly." Nor was that the only "remarkable earthquake" Colden experienced in New York.[16]

Those fossilized seashells revealed more than a puzzle of ancient times. They demonstrated a basic difference between the two men. Colden believed in opening up land to yeomen farmers who would put it to good use. Bartram had become concerned about the impact of development upon wildlife. In 1755 Bartram told Collinson about the location of a "stone, composed of sand and cockle shells" located closer to the Highlands than Coldengham was. Bartram believed that Colden could still find it but doubted he could because "there is now great alteration since I was there; and very like, the woods in which I found it may now be cornfields" which would disorient him.[17]

In 1772 Bartram seemed even more pessimistic about the fate of American animals. All the discoveries of giant bones, he felt, could be evidence that creatures such as unicorns and dragons might have once lived but disappeared. "Our Buffaloes, beavers and rattlesnakes" are likely "to be destroyed." "If they are so continuously destroyed for a Century to come as they have been for the last 50 years there will be but few left." Legends of their existence might then be thought as fanciful as the stories of dragons. The prospects for the animals he mentioned were not good. Each year some 50,000 beaver skins were sold in Britain; the eastern buffalo Bartram knew did go extinct.[18]

In 1754, the year before Bartram's lament about the burgeoning cornfields in New York, another botanist, Dr. Alexander Garden, a Scot, also entered into Colden's orbit. In 1754 Garden, living in South Carolina, became sick and needed to travel to a cooler climate to regain his health. Traveling to New York, he asked for directions to "Coldenhamia." Realizing whom he wanted to see, New Yorkers directed him to Ulster where he met Colden and examined the plants at Coldengham. Suddenly, Bartram appeared at the estate as well, delighting Garden, who also read Linnaeus's works there for the first time. "How happy should I be to pass my life with men so distinguished by genius, acuteness, and liberality, as well as by eminent botanical learning and experience!" Garden exulted. He got along well with all of the Colden family, especially Jane Colden, another devotee of Linnaeus. Nine years later, Garden, for whom the gardenia is named, fondly recalled "the happy and cheerful Days which I used to pass at York after being lucky enough to attain their acquaintance."[19]

Swedish botanist Kalm also met Cadwallader Colden. Having been recommended by Linnaeus, Collinson, Dr. John Mitchell, and another friend, Benjamin Franklin, Colden welcomed Kalm to Coldengham and New York City. Dispatched across the Atlantic in the 1740s to write a "Natural History of the most Northern parts of America," Colden helped him get to French Canada safely. Colden and everyone else Kalm talked with were impressed by the Swedish visitor—until 1772 when extracts of an English translation of his book at last reached America. Kalm presented hosts of stories which he attributed to Colden, Franklin and others; they all insisted that these stories had not come from them. Colden could not comprehend why the Swede had done that. Why Kalm misrepresented his sources has never been explained.[20]

Colden once had a fleeting opportunity to write a natural history that would have been far more memorable than Kalm's. Governor Robert Hunter arranged for Colden to be paid to write a book detailing the flora and fauna he saw while surveying around the entire colony of New York. When the promised money did not materialize, the book died with it. Therefore, the "Plantae Coldenghamiae" would be his longest work in natural history. Nonetheless, Colden made significant contributions to the field in shorter writings involving meteorology and climate. He figured out, for example, that waterspouts actually formed because of wind conditions in clouds.[21]

In 1723 Colden, acting upon a request from the Lords of Trade to Governor Burnet, produced a document entitled "An Account of the Climate of New

York." This report reflects the belief of the time that "local weather patterns determined the general state of health of the populace."[22]

As Colden had only been in New York a few years, he had to have talked with some of the older Dutch settlers, for he provided historical information. During the summer months, he related, "when the Country was first settled" winds from the northwest created gusts that "were very frequent hardly a day in the hot seasons passing without them;" these winds brought "heavy showers of rain and thunder claps." In a word, these early summers were "sultry," almost semi-tropical.[23]

Colden did not need help describing the New York winter, which ran from "the middle of November to March," but "the violent Frosts" usually hit "about Christmas and then to the middle of February" and stayed "extremely cold." Albany experienced far worse winters than the city. The Hudson River froze during these cold months and "horses and Sleds pass daily upon it." Although the southern part of the river nearest to New York City did not freeze each year "there is often so much Ice floating that it is not safe for Vessels to go to sea or come in."[24]

New York's fall and spring made up for the icy winter. Fall in New York went from September to mid-November. Colden described it: "The weather being mild and dry. The Sky always serene, and the People healthy." Spring was late, however. Only in very late April did it manifest itself; "March is generally cold and windy, tho for the most part the latter end of February be mild and warm."[25]

In 1723 summer heat arrived only at "the end of May," with July and August "the most sultry months and very often rainy." The humidity in July and August was very high; New York's air then was "always full of moisture, so much that the Doors and windows" were "more swelled than at any other time of the year and Iron rusts so much that it is difficult to keep any time."[26]

New York's weather was very changeable Colden noted. The heat sometimes seemed like that of the tropics, while the cold could be just as bad as that of the arctic parts of Europe. Still, Colden preferred New York's climate to England's especially as New York's weather appeared to be moderating and it grew "every day better." He believed that resulted from the New Yorkers' penchant for chopping down trees, a common belief of the time. As the trees disappeared, New York became "more healthy as all the people that have lived long here, testify." But even he had noticed the change despite his short time in the colony. "I therefore doubt not," he predicted, that New York would possess "in time . . . one of the most agreeable and healthy Climates on the face of the Earth."[27]

The climate of New York was moderating but not because trees were disappearing. Colonists thought it was for a simple reason. When trees declined in numbers there was less pollen in the air, resulting in fewer allergies caused by it. With fewer allergic reactions, New Yorkers felt healthier and attributed it to an improving climate. By 1776, with even fewer trees about, Colden's friend Thomas Pownall called New Yorkers "an hospitable cheerful social people," and mentioned that the Hudson "is seldom frozen up in Winter," a great change from Colden's report in 1723.[28]

The cause for the moderation of New York's climate was something far beyond the comprehension of enlightened observers of Colden's day. The world had been in the midst of a harsh cold period, the Little Ice Age, which started in, perhaps 1550 AD and ended in 1900 AD, assuming that it has ended. This Little Ice Age was not uniformly cold, and there were periods when the climate began to moderate. One of these warmer periods began about 1664, when England conquered Dutch New Netherland, and extended throughout Colden's entire lifetime. It would have surprised someone watching ice float by Newburgh to know that these bitter winters also represented a moderating trend from the far worse winters of centuries before. Near the end of the American Revolution, the moderating stopped and the Little Ice Age resumed its ferocity. During the brutal winter of 1779–1780, for example, the huge harbor of New York City froze over completely, the first time on record.[29]

Colden, in his report, took readings of the temperatures in New York but, despite having one of the best thermometers of the day—made by John Patrick—the information is of little value. According to Colden, he endured a bitter January when the temperature reached 103 and a hot summer when the heat hit 15. The Patrick temperature scale gave high numbers to cold temperatures and low ones to hot temperatures. The number for "Extreme Hott"— zero—is probably equal to 96 degrees Fahrenheit.[30]

Another problem exists in comparing Colden's readings to data compiled by other observers of the eighteenth century. Scientific instruments such as thermometers and barometers were built by men who knew little about science. Patrick had been trained to build cabinets and the wood casing cost far more than the apparatus it held. These devices were really meant to be admired, not used. Because Patrick's expertise was in woodmaking, his temperature scale was idiosyncratic and differed from that of other instrument makers. Colden's data, therefore, can only be compared to readings from other Patrick thermometers. Scientific data of this period had definite limitations.[31]

Limits also affected medicine of the Enlightenment and the medical research that Colden relished. He retained a belief in humors, a medical idea from ancient times. Nonetheless, doctors had to deal in more than just old theories. As he pointed out, he and other doctors could not "determine scientifically the Virtues of any Plant or Drugs, otherwise than by Experience of its Use and Effects." A doctor would keep trying different remedies until a patient got better or died.[32]

To better the odds during these "repeated Experiments," Colden and other doctors spent much energy in "Observations of the Vulgar," home remedies. This strategy resulted in the "Discovery of the Virtues of the most valuable Medicines, now in use" Colden wrote in 1745. Such observations by "a prudent Physician" would enable him to "frequently discover thereby Things, which by all his Skill he could not have otherwise done." Many of the most important drugs of Colden's time had originally been discovered by American Indians—quinine for example.[33]

Sometimes, though, the experiments were too close to home. On May 28, 1729, at Coldengham, the Colden family increased with the birth of a boy, John. Suddenly, on May 29 the Coldens's youngest daughter, "poor little Sarah," came down "with a Violent fever" and suffered "the most Violent Convulsions I ever saw," Colden remarked. Never regaining consciousness, she died on June 3. Her mother fell deep in the throes of grief "at a dangerous time for her health." Alice's condition gave her husband "great Anxiety" that prevented sleep.[34]

Both parents took ill as well. Alice became sick almost as soon as Sarah did. Colden blamed his own condition on his lack of sleep. He came down with "a violent headache" which "never entirely ceased" until mid-June. After feeling better, he "had a relapse . . . with very odd symptoms." "I have large patches upon my Skin of a deep red colour like the Rose but without any pain, swelling or itching." This disaster was the reason Colden was not present when Lewis Morris, Jr. made a fool of himself.[35]

A scary time for the Coldens, the widespread sickness was "the first time that our Solitaryness" at Coldengham "became truly uneasy to both of us." Even their best neighbor, Jacobus Bruyn, was away. The frightened parents "had apprehensions that we kept from each other." Luckily, all except Sarah survived including baby John.[36]

Dr. Colden had no idea what had hit his family. The reddish rash and the headaches suggest a disease now called scarlet fever was the villain. Only in the 1730s did the name "throat distemper" appear and, in the 1750s, Colden stated that he had seen throat distemper "only in my own family, and in a few neighbours." What happened in 1729 had to have been the Colden family's first brush with the throat distemper.[37]

Colden had only learned about throat distemper in 1739 when his old friend William Douglass, whom he had met at the University of Edinburgh, wrote him about it and gave his permission to publish the data if he chose. Realizing the importance of Douglass's considerable experience with the contagion, Colden urged Alexander to have it printed in Zenger's newspaper but not to associate his name with the letter to avoid "an opportunity for some ill natured sneer." When throat distemper reappeared in New York, Colden "followed Dr. Douglass's Sentiments" regarding treatment. "I have done this," he reported to Alexander, "with so much success that not one has hitherto died of those who followed my advice," in sharp contrast to those who listened to "meddling women."[38]

In 1753, years after Douglass's death, Peter Collinson urged Colden to write to a friend of his, Dr. John Fothergill, a prominent English physician, about throat distemper. Colden did so, emphasizing he was relaying Douglass's data, and pointing out that "it did not spread in the same manner contagious distempers usually do." Fothergill, thrilled by Colden's analysis, "could not forbear" getting it into print. Delighted by Fothergill's reaction, Colden insisted that the important thing "in all publications of this sort is the use they may be." And the letter of "the ingenious Cadwallader Colden, Esq." received a good, if critical, review in a British journal.[39]

Of course, much has been learned about the dreaded throat distemper. This contagion turned out to be two different diseases, diphtheria and scarlet fever, both of which break out in epidemics usually targeting children. Colden believed that throat distemper was less deadly if a rash appeared (as in his own case); that meant the disease was scarlet fever. Indeed, in outbreaks of scarlet fever the death rate hovered around three percent. The rash-less diphtheria, on the other hand, killed far more of its victims.[40]

A possibility exists that another illness had mixed in with the twin killers, diphtheria and scarlet fever. When medical observers such as Colden tried to describe the outbreak and progress of a disease, they wrote in complete ignorance of the actual causes of disease. Until the next century, no one connected the funny creatures seen under a microscope with illness. Colden, therefore, sought to record every curious fact that seemed connected to the illness he was seeing. Often, such things were mere coincidences and later students of disease ignored them as wrong-headed ideas of an earlier day.

Colden, however, may have picked up a clue pointing to a very dangerous contagion. In his letter to Fothergill about throat distemper, Colden noted: "It seems as if some seeds, or leaven, or secret cause remains wherever it goes." He pointed out that

> The poorer sort of people were more liable to have this disease than those who lived well, with all the conveniences of life. It has been more fatal in the country than in great towns. People of a scorbutic habit were most subject to it, and they who fed on pork, or lived on wet and low grounds.[41]

Among all the false leads, there is an important fact. People who kept pigs seemed especially hard hit by throat distemper; Coldengham had pigs. Diseases can jump from animals (including pigs) to humans. Combined with the other killers, it appears, was what in later centuries would become known as swine flu.

Throat distemper was but one illness that attracted the attention of Dr. Colden. A deadly disease, usually thought to be yellow fever, arrived in New

York City in 1741 "but it never spread" very far. Everyone agreed that it had been brought by a ship from the Caribbean. Another outbreak hit the city the next year but, again, stayed confined. "In the summer of the year 1743 the yellow fever became first Epidemical in New York," Colden would explain to his friend, Dr. John Mitchell, who had investigated the disease in Virginia.[42]

Several hundred New Yorkers died from yellow fever, distressing Colden. "No Man who has any Share of Humanity, or Regard for the Welfare of the Society wherein he lives, can with Indifference observe or hear of the Mortality" without wanting to do something about it. He knew that the easternmost shore of the city, the location of the docks, was a dumping ground for "all the filth and nastiness of the town" so that, during the summer months, there was "constantly a most offensive abominable smell." He also knew that the section of town next to the docks, to which the fever spread, although then built up, had originally been a swamp.[43]

Medical researchers of later days would have impressive devices to aid their work, but Colden had nothing of the sort. Instead, Colden had books, and he searched through history for an answer. He consulted a book published in Italy during 1717, written by Giovanni Maria Lancisi, the doctor of Pope Clement XI. It was "a rare Book, and perhaps not another Copy of it" existed "in this Part of the World, besides that which I have." In it, Colden found what he was looking for.[44]

New Yorkers, Colden believed, had paid little attention to "the ill Effects of stagnating Waters" because they lived in a colder climate. In Rome, however, the problems generated by stagnant water were more obvious. A sickly place, swampy Rome had plenty of stagnant water. In the city's glory days canals and sewers drained it making Rome usually healthy. Then, as the empire weakened, barbarians destroyed that infrastructure and sickness returned. Finally, in the sixteenth century the popes who then ruled Rome drained off the stagnant water and removed smelly garbage dumps and dead animals decaying in the streets. Draining the city and keeping it clean restored health to Rome's population.[45]

A "prudent Pope" had already done much to protect Rome from "Slime and Filth," but Lancisi knew more had to be done. When the Tiber overflowed its banks, stagnant water contaminated wells and cellars of buildings. These problems had to be dealt with as well. When other Italian cities were hit by fever, he could guess the problem: they had "neglected their Drains" or had become careless about "Filth and stagnating Waters." When mistakes had been rectified, fevers disappeared.[46]

Discovering that all medical observers confirmed what Lancisi had written, Colden stated that "stagnating Waters have been infamous from all Antiquity for their noxious Quality, and for that Reason were by the ancient

Figure 5.1. *Cadwallader Colden*, by an unknown artist based on an original by Matthew Pratt. Colden as a philosopher of the Enlightenment. Oil on canvas. ID 1878. *Collection of the New-York Historical Society.*

Poets described under the Representation of the Hydra throwing out a poisonous deadly Breath."[47]

In December 1743 Colden notified Alexander about his discoveries in Lancisi's book and alerted him about his sending extracts for examination by the city's magistrates but had gotten no response. Sending a copy to Alexander for his perusal, Colden declared that "I am much perswaded that the method there proposed will be effectual in New York."[48]

Not only was Alexander enthused about Colden's research, the magistrates were too. Most of them resolved to finally start enforcing laws about cleaning streets and vowed to improve the smelly situation at the docks. Alexander thought they might actually move the city's tanners and skinners, two trades that produced much pollution, to more appropriate areas. To Colden's surprise, his long essay would be printed in both of the city's newspapers and in Franklin's *Pennsylvania Gazette*; all of the transcriptions had numerous errors. Franklin had already made similar suggestions about tanners in his city.[49]

The strong, favorable reactions to Colden's cleanliness campaign came partly because he went beyond Italian history and would "apply some of preceeding Observations to New York in particular." The yellow fever ravaged neighbourhood, befitting its earlier status as a swamp, was "flat and the Water not easily drained from thence," creating a perfect reservoir for stagnant water. Practically every cellar there had water coming in. The docks, with their "filthy Smell," had been polluted with garbage by "an intolerable Carelessness." Nor did the rotting garbage float away. Instead it fermented; "it appears as it were boiling to the Eye of the Spectators." Drains were never cleaned nor were cellars cleansed of "corrupted Slime." Was there any doubt why terrible fevers appeared in New York City? Colden realized that the city magistrates would have problems cleaning up the city because "some People are so wretchedly stupid, that rather than take some Trouble for a few Days, will risk their own Health and even the Destruction of the whole Community."[50]

The magistrates did a good job following Colden's ideas and the next year New York City was a healthy place. Colden had come upon a solid way to wipe out yellow fever. The disease spreads by mosquitoes which breed in stagnant water. When stagnant water disappeared, fewer mosquitoes could breed and then infect people. Although mosquitoes could still fly off ships, the incidence of yellow fever would still be much less. Malaria was probably mixed in with the yellow fever epidemics, but as malaria also spreads by mosquitoes, the elimination of stagnant water would lessen the impact of that contagion as well.[51]

In December 1744 Colden pressured the magistrates to continue their campaign against stagnant water. During "party disputes many pretended to a great concern for the . . . publick benefit," he reminded one alderman. Now was the time to act, or did some politicians really not care about the public after all?[52]

It turned out that much of the public did not care about the public benefit. Colden's warning about stupid people proved more prescient than he could have imagined. The cost of adding drains and new laws caused "inconveniences to several private persons" who "raised such a clamour amongst the poorer people" that plans were made to throw out all the magistrates. The cleaning stopped and in June 1745 yellow fever returned in the city.[53]

Colden's relationship with Mitchell lasted longer than the plan to cleanse New York City. During 1745 they exchanged comments on yellow fever. Colden, who had never encountered yellow fever, explained that his critique of Mitchell's work was "mere speculations" done "only by the way of amusement, to fill up a vacant hour in a solitary part of the country" and "to make your performance more perfect." Dr. Colden deferred to Mitchell, who had dealt with numerous cases of the disease. Ironically, some scholars doubt that Mitchell actually saw what became known later as yellow fever.[54]

In 1745 the two medical researchers also discussed one of the perplexing disputes of the eighteenth—and later—centuries: the origin of syphilis or "French Pox" as Colden called it. Identified by many names, syphilis became identified with the French because a French army had introduced the disease into Italy during 1494. All of Colden's information suggested that syphilis was an American disease. Another venereal disease, yaws, originated in Africa although he thought the American Indians themselves could not be certain about the origin of yaws. Regarding the treatment of those diseases, Colden noted that, despite their similarity, each disease required "different Methods of cure." In 1757, at Collinson's request, Colden passed along information, acquired from Kalm, about a plant whose root the Iroquois—who kept it a secret from the French—used to treat venereal disease. Colden had listed it in his "Plantae Coldenghamiae." His letter about this plant was published without his permission.[55]

Mitchell had a role in propagating more information provided by Colden, this time about an American plant called pokeweed. Writing to Collinson, Colden told him about the good effect pokeweed juice had on cancerous tumors. Impressed, Collinson sent Colden's essay to Mitchell who dispatched it to the *Gentleman's Magazine* which printed it. Pokeweed was another cure "discovered by the experience of the vulgar," Colden wrote, and correctly saw a connection between swellings on plants caused by insects and the swelling caused by cancer, which he speculated might be the result of insect eggs or "seed of some parasitic vegetable," very fanciful ideas. In 1752 Colden relayed data that pokeweed had cured a woman of breast cancer, but he also learned that sometimes pokeweed had no effect.[56]

Mitchell and Colden did have a disagreement about one of the most bizarre medical fads of the period, tar water, about which Colden became a major advocate though Mitchell had his doubts. Tar water had been pushed by the Anglican bishop, George Berkeley, one of the most prominent philosophers of the period. While serving in New England, Berkeley became aware of tar water, a common folk remedy. He became not only its publicist but also an indulger in it. He drunk "above a gallon" of the "vulgar juice" within just "a few hours" and cured himself of a fever.[57]

The bishop asserted the healing function of tar had been known since ancient times. During the eighteenth century, leaves and "tender tops" of trees such as fir and pine were turned into "diet drinks." The essential "spirit of those evergreens" were believed encased in tar and so easily available. Tar water was produced by inserting tar into water, stirring and shaking, until the soaked tar released its medicinal nutrients into the water. Then, the concoction was left standing about two days. Finally, the "Clear Water" was "poured off and kept for use." In America tar water was believed to ward off smallpox and Berkeley thought it had proven its use in "Bites of venomous Creatures," dropsy, and indigestion.[58]

Impressed by Berkeley's account, Colden would reprint an extract from the bishop's work on tar water and his own thoughts upon it, first in a newspaper and soon as a separate pamphlet. He extracted "the more historical Part" of Berkeley's book but left out his arguments. Colden ended his account "with some Reasoning more adapted to common Understandings than the Bishop's are" to demonstrate tar water's "Virtues." Admitting that Berkeley might have gotten carried away, Colden was "fully persuaded that he has thereby made a valuable Present to the Publick" which medical authors had ignored.[59]

Colden believed that tar water was "generally useful in all chronical Diseases," but, in acute cases "it requires a good Deal of Skill, Care and Attention." One disease he thought tar water was perfect for was scurvy. Practically every mouth he had examined in America "too plainly show the Scurvy almost every where." He lamented, "How many fine Mouths has this barbarous Disease ruined?" Scurvy, at least partially, explained the epidemic of "bad teeth" in the American colonies.[60]

The prevalence of scurvy on land—not at sea where it usually dwelled—had much to do with the colonial diet. According to one scholar, Americans normally boiled "meat and vegetables together, destroying any sources of vitamin C," a vital nutrient that protects against scurvy. Making matters worse, many colonists thought that eating fruit, a major source of the vitamin, caused fevers. In reality, fruit happened to ripen during the sickly months of summer; the connection between fruit and illness was just a coincidence. New Yorkers, braver than most, devoured watermelons (and some other fruits), but, as the name implies, watermelon is mostly water.[61]

By the 1740s Colden had realized that people who avoided fruit were not protected from the fevers, so the illnesses "must be attributed to some other Cause." And Colden's remedy for scurvy, tar water, did have a beneficial effect as there was some vitamin C in it. The plants from which tar was made could cure scurvy. In 1535, for example, the French explorer Jacques Cartier recovered from scurvy after drinking a brew created from tree leaves and sap by a kindly Indian. Granted, the production of tar destroyed much of the vitamin, but the traces left constituted a significant increase of vitamin C ingested by Americans, especially given the large amount of tar water usually drunk.[62][2]

Colden recommended tar water for his daughter Alice's upset stomach, but Alexander too became enamored of the vulgar juice. Not in the best of health, Alexander was very overweight and sedentary—his profession kept him at his desk "reading and writing." Earlier in his life, he had had a metabolic problem—very "sweaty feet" that smelled badly. Upon gaining weight, Alexander came down with gout, which at least stopped the excessive sweating.[63]

Then Alexander read Berkeley's book on tar water and tried the concoction. His "appetite and Digestion" improved, probably because of the traces of vitamin C in tar water. Amazingly, his gout went away as well. Alexander attributed gout's disappearance to tar water although Colden insisted it was too early to be certain of the cause. Alas, the sweating problem returned but Alexander could afford the numerous stockings required to deal with that annoyance. Colden's suggestion was correct. Vitamin C can not cure gout. What happened is simple. Alexander filled his stomach with so much tar water that he drank less wine; large amounts of certain wines trigger an attack of gout, so when he cut down his wine consumption gout disappeared.[64]

Yet such analysis could not be imagined in the eighteenth century. When two of Alexander's children became ill, he was convinced that tar water aided their recoveries. He informed Colden of other remarkable cures of toothache, female "hystericks," and rheumatism. "If all this be true" then tar water "bids far to be the universal medicine." All the Alexanders drank it at bedtime. Not surprisingly, Alexander shepherded Colden's praise of tar water into print.[65]

In April 1745 Colden's "little book upon tar water" had reached Bartram, who knew that the juice had been used 30 years earlier to treat smallpox, and relayed the news that it had not helped two of the advocates who succumbed to smallpox. Nor had it helped stop a case of stomach pain. As for Berkeley, Bartram had just read one of his books. While liking parts of it, he got lost towards its end where the bishop "hath dipped into such Confounded abstruse enquiries that I can hardly understand what he means and perhaps he doth not know himself."[66]

Another of Colden's friends, the Rev. Samuel Johnson of Connecticut, an Anglican, had known Berkeley in America and sent him a copy of Colden's tar water pamphlet. In 1752 Berkeley mentioned its existence and added that in North America "much use" of tar water had been made "particularly by those who possess great numbers of slaves."[67]

Colden's pamphlet, aside from its historical approach to tar water, also sheds light on Colden's thoughts about cold. "Nothing deserves more Attention, than to prevent catching of Cold," he insisted. The throat distemper, he believed, "has shewn how dangerous Cold is." One excellent way "to keep out Cold" was to make use of a superb new invention, the Pennsylvania fireplace—a stove. So impressive was this device that Colden sent news of it to Europe. The Pennsylvania fireplace was the handiwork of another enlightened friend of Colden's, Franklin.[68]

Oddly enough, the two men met in Connecticut "by our accidental Meeting on the Road." Colden, who had been picked as part of a royal commission to investigate the land claims of the Mohegan Indians against the colony of Connecticut, had been traveling to fulfill his duty; Franklin had been heading back to Philadelphia. They had much in common. Both had risen to prominence from humble beginnings and both had a great interest in the pursuit of knowledge. Their first "Conversation . . . tho very short" convinced Colden to start "a Correspondence" with the Philadelphia printer. And Franklin's frequent visits to New York cemented their friendship.[69]

Over their several decades of friendship, Colden and Franklin discussed many different topics ranging from human anatomy to comets. But, logically enough, their first subject involved printing. Colden had come up with an idea for a new style of printing, since named stereotype, useful in producing many copies of a book, such as a Bible, that there would be much demand for over a long period. Franklin liked the idea, but Colden discovered his innovation was already being employed in Britain.[70]

Within a few years, the two friends' attention would be drawn, along with the "Vertuosi of Europe," to the wonders of electricity, and especially to Franklin's "Electrical Kite." All of Colden's friends, it seemed, were astonished by the "Electrical Fire." Getting shocked by an electric current was all the rage in Europe and America. As Collinson tried to explain the latest fad, "there is no describing the Electrical power unless a person feels it himself." Having watched an electric experiment—which was really a public shocking—Bartram could not contain his amazement how "the fire" went through a man's finger and shocked someone else. "I take this to be the most Surprising Phenomena that we have met with and is wholly incomprehensible to thy friend" he assured Colden.[71]

Colden was curious enough to want to experience the electric fire himself. Getting a "Glass Tube," the instrument used to dispense a shock, from Franklin Colden also received his detailed instructions how to produce the necessary electricity. Colden did not record his reaction, but in August 1747 he did relay the request of assorted New Yorkers about having the electric "Apparatus" constructed in Philadelphia "and what may be the price."[72]

Franklin hoped that Colden would take up electricity as a subject of inquiry. Colden's "Skill and Expertness in Mathematical Computations"—

not Franklin's forte—would give his friend a great advantage. Despite Colden's obtaining the necessary equipment and trying to experiment, he got nowhere. "My Notions on Electricity are confused and indigested," he admitted to Franklin. "I know not wherein consists the difference between an Electric body per se and a non-electric," making it "very difficult if not impossible to account for the Phenomena or to understand any reasoning on the Phenomena." Although he kept trying, he produced nothing worth mentioning. Despite this failure, he rejoiced at Franklin's success with his kite experiment, famed throughout the world, which his friend greatly appreciated. However, Colden's youngest child, David, did have some real success with electricity.[73]

As for another mysterious force, magnetism, Colden does not seem to have been tempted by it despite a great advance. Collinson informed him that steel had been successfully magnetized for the first time and proved to be more powerful than natural loadstones. Colden did spread the news in the American colonies.[74]

Although Colden had long service as a conduit for the spreading of scientific knowledge, he hoped for a more systemic way for scholars to communicate with their comrades. In 1728 Colden wanted to establish a group dedicated to "the advancing of Knowledge," by which he meant natural history; nothing came from that. William Douglass did create a "Medical Society," based at Boston, which did not last.[75]

Franklin had somewhat more success. In 1744 he founded a society in Philadelphia and Colden was soon recruited into it by Bartram who hoped "this undertaking may be of publick benefit to our american Colonies." Indeed, Colden had as high hopes for Franklin's creation as did Bartram. Franklin had been the one who initiated the correspondence between Mitchell and Colden on yellow fever. New Yorkers such as Alexander, Daniel Horsmanden, and James DeLancey were interested in joining.[76]

Their hopes were soon dashed. "We make at present but a poor progress in our Philosophical Society," Bartram complained to Colden in 1745. Franklin seemed just as disappointed: "The Members of our Society here are very idle Gentlemen." Colden dismissed most of the members as "lazy" or "officious." Eventually, the Philadelphia group evolved into the American Philosophical Society.[77]

No one could call Colden lazy. He and Bartram were "the most active members in our Society." Colden did have a restless mind. In 1755 he announced to Gronovius that "I am now entirely wrapped up in philosophical amusements" which bordered on metaphysics. Still, he never abandoned natural history. As late as 1768, in his eighties, he looked into "the Powers producing the Phaenomena of Needles swimming in Water." Despite the crises swirling around him then, Cadwallader Colden remained committed to scientific inquiry.[78]

NOTES

1. Collinson to CC, March 30, 1745, *CP*, vol. 3, 109–10; Druin Burch, "Death Beds," *Natural History* 117, no. 10 (November 2008), 17.
2. Douglass to CC, February 20, 1720/1, *CP*, vol. 1, 11^#–16; Logan to CC, July 14, 1720, *CP*, vol. 1, 102–3; Alexander C. Flick, *History of the State of New York* (New York: Columbia University Press, 1933–1937), vol. 9, 96–97.
3. Hunter to CC, February 5, 1721/2, *CP*, vol. 1, 140; Austin Baxter Keep, *History of the New York Society Library* (New York: De Vinne Press, 908), 122.
4. The trees contributed by CC were still thriving in the early part of the twentieth century. R. Hingston Fox, *Dr. John Fothergill and His Friends: Chapters in Eighteenth Century Life* (London: Macmillan, 1919), 173–74, 173n–174n; Collinson to CC, May 19, 1756, February 25, 1764, *CP*, vol. 5, 80–81; vol. 6, 288–90; Dr. John Fothergill to Dr. Charles Alston, February 19, 1740/1, in John Fothergill, *Chain of Friendship: Selected Letters of Dr. John Fothergill of London, 1735–1780*, ed. Betty C. Corner and Christopher C. Booth (Cambridge, MA: Harvard University Press, 1971), 54; Fothergill to Linnaeus, April 4, 1777, Fothergill, *Chain of Friendship*, 409; James Delbourgo, *A Most Amazing Scene of Wonders: Electricity and Enlightenment in Early America* (Cambridge, MA: Harvard University Press, 2006), 29.
5. CC to Collinson, May 1742, *CP*, vol. 2, 261–63; Collinson to John Bartram, February 3, 1741/2, in John Bartram, *The Correspondence of John Bartram, 1734–1777*, ed. Edmund Berkeley and Dorothy Smith Berkeley (Gainesville: University Press of Florida, 1992), 181; Joseph Kastner, *A Species of Eternity* (New York: Knopf, 1977), 18–19.
6. CC to Kalm, n. d., *CP*, vol. 4, 258–59; Charles Preston to James Petiver, September 24, 1708, in Raymond Phineas Stearns, *Science in the British Colonies of America* (Urbana: University of Illinois Press, 1970), 483; Petiver to CC, October 27, 1709, Stearns, *Science*, 493–94; CC to Petiver, October 17, 1709, Stearns, *Science*, 494; Petiver to Preston, 1711, Stearns, *Science*, 494; Stearns, *Science*, 102.
7. Hesselius to his mother, June 26, 1714, Gustavus Hesselius, "'With God's Blessings on Both Land and Sea': Gustavus Hesselius Describes the New World to the Old in a Letter from Philadelphia in 1714," trans. Carin K. Arnborg, *American Art Journal* 21, no. 3 (1989): 7; CC to Kalm, n. d., *CP*, vol. 4, 259.
8. "An Account of some plants the seeds of which were sent to Brigadier Hunter at his desire for the Earl of Islay," October 1725, CPU, reel 2. On rhubarb, see Alan W. Armstrong, ed., *"Forget not Mee and My Garden...": Selected Letters, 1725–1768 of Peter Collinson, F.R.S.* (Philadelphia: American Philosophical Society, 2002), 63n1.
9. CC to [Dr. Whytte?], February 15, 1758, *CP*, vol. 5, 216–17; CC to Kalm, n.d., *CP*, vol. 4, 260; Bartram to Collinson, June 11, 1743, Bartram, *Correspondence of John Bartram*, ed. Berkeley and Berkeley, 216; Buckner Hollingsworth, *Her Garden Was Her Delight* (New York: Macmillan, 1962), 30; Stearns, *Science*, 527.
10. CC to [Whytte?], February 15, 1758, *CP*, vol. 5, 216–17; Collinson to CC, March 9, 1743/4, *CP*, vol. 3, 50–52; Collinson to Bartram, March 10, 1743/4, in John Bartram, *Memorials of John Bartram and Humphry Marshall, with Notices of Their Botanical Contemporaries*, ed. William Darlington (Philadelphia: Lindsay & Blakiston, 1849), 171.
11. J. F. Gronovius to CC, April 3, 1744, *CP*, vol. 3, 58; CC to Collinson, June 1744, *CP*, vol. 3, 60–61; Collinson to CC, August 23, 1744, November 1, 1747, *CP*, vol. 3, 68–69, 428; CC to Gronovius, [December 1744], *CP*, vol. 3, 83–91; Kalm to CC, January 4, 1751, *CP*, vol. 4, 250–51; CC to [Whytte?], February 15, 1758, *CP*, vol. 5, 216–17; CC to Gronovius, n.d., October 29, 1745, in CC, *Selections from the Scientific Correspondence of Cadwallader Colden with Gronovius, Linnaeus, Collinson, and Other Naturalists*, ed. Asa Gray (New Haven, [CT]: B. L. Hamlen, 1843), 14–16; CC to Linnaeus, February 9, 1748/9, Colden Family Papers, LC; Stearns, *Science*, 528, 565; Brooke Hindle, *The Pursuit of Science in Revolutionary America, 1735–1789* (Chapel Hill: University of North Carolina Press, 1956), 41.
12. CC, "Plantae Coldenghamiae in Provincia Noveboracensi Americes sponte crescentes, quas ad methodum Cl. Linnaei Serualem, anno 1742. ets. Observavit and descripfit," *Acta Societatis Regiae Scientiarum Upsaliensis* 4 (1743/1749), 92–93; CC, "Plantae Coldenghamiae In Provincia Nove boracensi Americes sponte crescentes Pars Secunda," *Acta Societatis Regiae*

Scientiarum Upsaliensis 5 (1744/1751), 52, 70; Linnaeus to Dr. James Lind, n.d., in Linnaeus, *A Selection of the Correspondence of Linnaeus and Other Naturalists, from the Original Manuscripts*, ed. Sir James Edward Smith (London: Longman, Hurst, Rees, Orme, and Brown, 1821), vol. 2, 476; Saul Jarcho, "Biographical and Bibliographical Notes on Cadwallader Colden," *Bulletin of the History of Medicine* 32, no. 4 (1958): 327; Kastner, *Species of Eternity*, 7; William H. Welch, "The Interdependence of Medicine and Other Sciences of Nature," *Science*, n.s., 27, no. 680 (January 10, 1908): 59; George E. Gifford, Jr., "Botanic Remedies in Colonial Massachusetts, 1620–1820," in *Medicine in Colonial Massachusetts, 1620–1820*, Colonial Society of Massachusetts, *Publications* 57 (1980): 283–84.

13. CC to Collinson, November 13, 1742, *CP*, vol. 2, 280–82.

14. Collinson to Bartram, February 25, 1740/1, June 6, 1741, Bartram, *Memorials*, ed. Darlington, 142; Bartram to Collinson, December 18, 1742, June 11, 1743, [c. 1743/4], Bartram, *Memorials*, ed. Darlington, 161–62, 164, 169; Bartram to Collinson, [c. 1741], Bartram, *Correspondence of John Bartram*, ed. Berkeley and Berkeley, 165; Collinson to CC, March 5, 1740/1, March 7, 1741/2, *CP*, vol. 2, 207–8, 245–57; CC to Gronovius, May 30, 1746, *CP*, vol. 3, 209–11; Brooke Hindle, "The Quaker Background and Science in Colonial Philadelphia," *Isis* 46, no. 3 (1955): 249.

15. Bartram to Collinson, September 5, 1742, December 1744, in Bartram, *Memorials*, ed. Darlington, 160–61, 173; "A Journey to the Katskill Mountains, with Billy," 1753, in Bartram, *Memorials*, ed. Darlington, 195; William Bartram, "Travels in Georgia and Florida, 1773–74, A Report to Dr. John Fothergill," ed. Francis Harper, American Philosophical Society. *Transactions*, n.s., 33, no. 2 (November 1943): 129.

16. CC to Collinson, [October 1755?], *CP*, vol. 5, 38–39; CC to Collinson, December 9, 1755, "An Account of the Earthquake felt in New York, Novem. 18, 1755, in a Letter from Cadwallader Colden, Esq.; to Mr. Peter Collinson, F.R.S.," Royal Society, *Philosophical Transactions* 49, part 1 (1755): 443; Hindle, *Pursuit of Science*, 94; Norman G. Brett-James, *The Life of Peter Collinson, F.R.S., F.S.A.* (London: E. G. Dunstan, 1925), 159; Stearns, *Science*, 574. CC sent items to the Royal Society that were not published. See Jarcho, "Biographical," 323.

17. Bartram to Collinson, September 28, 1755, Bartram, *Memorials*, ed. Darlington, 200–201.

18. Michael Collinson to Bartram, March 6, 1772, Bartram, *Correspondence of John Bartram*, ed. Berkeley and Berkeley, 748; Bartram to M. Collinson, November 11, 1772, Letters to Peter Collinson, 1725–1790, British Museum Additional Manuscript, 28727, 120, LC transcript. There are references to this extinct buffalo in Thomas Jefferson, *Notes on the State of Virginia*, ed. William Peden ([Paris], 1785; rept. Chapel Hill: University of North Carolina Press, 1954), 50, 54.

19. Alexander Garden to Linnaeus, March 15, 1755, Linnaeus, *Correspondence*, ed. J. E. Smith, vol. 1, 286; Garden to John Ellis, March 25, 1755, Linnaeus, *Correspondence*, ed. J. E. Smith, vol. 1, 343; Garden to David Colden, February 1, 1764, *CP*, vol. 6, 282; Louis B. Wright, *The Cultural Life of the American Colonies, 1607–1763* (New York: Harper & Row, 1962), 230–31; Edmund Berkeley and Dorothy Smith Berkeley, *Dr. Alexander Garden of Charles Town* (Chapel Hill: University of North Carolina Press, 1969), 40–41; Kastner, *Species of Eternity*, 3–4.

20. Collinson to CC, June 20, 1748, *CP*, vol. 8, 353; Kalm to CC, September 29, 1748, *CP*, vol. 4, 77; CC to Linnaeus, February 1, 1750/1, *CP*, vol. 4, 255–56; D. Colden to BF, November 30, 1772, *CP*, vol. 7, 184, *FP*, vol. 3, 319, 300n9; BF to D. Colden, March 5, 1773, *FP*, vol. 20, 95–97; CC to Johnson, May 27, 1749, *JP*, vol. 1, 228. For the supposed information provided by CC, see Peter Kalm, *The America of 1750: Peter Kalm's Travels In North America, The English Version of 1770*, ed. Adolph B. Benson (New York: Wilson-Erickson, 1937), vol. 1, 216, 256–57, 298–99; vol. 2, 467, 620.

21. Anna Murray Vail, "Jane Colden, An Early New York Botanist," *Torreya: A Monthly Journal of Botanical Notes and News* 7, no. 2 (1907): 22; Kastner, *Species of Eternity*, 22.

22. Burnet to Council of Trade, June 25, 1723, PRO *Cal.*, vol. 33, 290; Susan E. Klepp, ed., *"The Swift Progress of Population": A Documentary and Bibliographic Study of Philadelphia's Growth, 1642–1859* (Philadelphia: American Philosophical Society, 1991), 11–12.

23. CC, "An Account of the Climate of New York," in *Documents Relative to the Colonial History of the State of New-York*, ed. Edmund B. O'Callaghan and Berthold Fernow (Albany, NY: Weed, Parsons, 1853–1857), vol. 5, 691–92.

24. CC, "Account of the Climate of New York," 692.

25. CC, "Account of the Climate of New York," 691–92.

26. CC, "Account of the Climate of New York," 691.

27. CC, "Account of the Climate of New York," 690, 692; Jan Golinski, *British Weather and the Climate of Enlightenment* (Chicago: University of Chicago Press, 2007), 190, 198. See also Thomas Pownall, *A Topographical Description of the Dominions of the United States of America* (Rev. ed. of London: J. Almon, 1776; Pittsburgh: University of Pittsburgh Press, 1949), 148–49.

28. Pownall, *Topographical*, 45.

29. Philip Ranlet, *The New York Loyalists*, 2nd ed. (Lanham, MD: University Press of America, 2002), 74; John A. Matthews and Keith R. Briffa, "The 'Little Ice Age': Re-Evaluation of an Evolving Concept," *Geografiska Annaler Series A: Physical Geography* 87, no. 1 (March 2005): 19, 31; H. H. Lamb, *Climate, History and the Modern World* (New York: Methuen, 1982), 202, 308. Whether the Little Ice Age ended is impossible to tell. Given the great age of the planet, the time since 1900 is the equivalent of a blink of an eye for the Earth. H. H. Lamb theorized that the Little Ice Age may have been "interrupted" by human pollution (361). Extending Lamb's thinking, if mankind's pollution significantly declined, its impact on the climate might lessen, causing the Little Ice Age to resume where it left off.

30. CC, "Account of the Climate of New York," 691–92; W. E. Knowles Middleton, *A History of the Thermometer and Its Use in Meteorology* (Baltimore: Johns Hopkins University Press, 1966), 60–61. I would like to thank David Ranlet for his computation of the equivalent Fahrenheit reading.

31. Golinski, *British Weather*, 122–24, 127; Middleton, *History of the Thermometer*, 61.

32. CC, *An Abstract from Dr. Berkley's Treatise on Tar-Water with some Reflections Thereon, Adapted to Diseases Frequent in America* (New York: J. Parker, 1745), 10; Saul Jarcho, "Cadwallader Colden as a Student of Infectious Diseases," *Bulletin of the History of Medicine* 29, no. 2 (1955): 104.

33. CC, *Abstract from Dr. Berkley's Treatise on Tar-Water*, 10; CC, "Sir, According to my Promise," *Pennsylvania Gazette*, Part 2, January 26, 1743/4.

34. CC to JA, June 14, 1729, RP, vol. 1, 121; Edwin R. Purple, "Notes, Biographical and Genealogical, of the Colden Family, and of Some of Its Collateral Branches in America," *New York Genealogical and Biographical Record* 4 (1873): 170.

35. CC to JA, June 14, 22, 1729, RP, vol. 1, 121, 124.

36. CC to JA, June 14, 1729, RP, vol. 1, 121.

37. CC, "Extract of a letter from Cadwallader Colden, esq. to Dr. Fothergill, concerning the throat distemper," *American Museum* 3 (January 1788), 53–59; Anne Hardy, "Scarlet Fever," in *The Cambridge World History of Human Disease*, ed. Kenneth F. Kiple (Cambridge: Cambridge University Press, 1993), 991.

38. CC to JA, January 21, 1739/40, *CP*, vol. 7, 337–38; CC to JA, November 4, 1741, RP, vol. 2, 201; CC to Douglass, January 21, 1739/40, CPU, reel 2; Alfred R. Hoermann, *Cadwallader Colden: A Figure of the American Enlightenment* (Westport, CT: Greenwood Press, 2002), 17, 54–55; George H. Weaver, "Life and Writings of William Douglass, M.D. (1691–1752)," *Bulletin of the Society of Medical History of Chicago* 2, no. 4 (1921), 230–31, 237.

39. Fothergill to CC, October 23, 1755, Gratz Coll., HSP; CC to [Fothergill], January 8, 1756, *CP*, vol. 5, 63–65; *Monthly Review* 16 (1757), 553–54; R. H. Fox, *Dr. John Fothergill*, 174.

40. Ernest A. Caulfield, *A True History of the Terrible Epidemic Vulgarly Called The Throat Distemper Which Occurred in His Majesty's New England Colonies Between the Years 1735 and 1740*, in *Disease and Society In Provincial Massachusetts: Collected Accounts, 1736–1739* (1939; rept. New York: Arno Press, 1972), 42–46, 92, 100.

41. CC, "Extract of a letter . . . concerning the throat distemper," 53–59.

42. CC, "Sir, According to my Promise," *Pennsylvania Gazette*, Part 1, January 11, 1743/4; CC to Mitchell, November 7, 1745, *CP*, vol. 8, 328–32; Mitchell to CC, March 25, 1749, John Mitchell, "A Letter form John Mitchell to Cadwallader Colden," ed. Theodore Hornberger *Huntington Library Quarterly* 10, no. 4 (1947): 412–14; George William Edwards, *New York as an Eighteenth Century Municipality, 1731–1776* (New York: Columbia University Press, 1917; repr. New York: AMS Press, 1968), 170.

43. CC to Mitchell, November 7, 1745, *CP*, vol. 8, 328–32; CC, "Sir, According to my Promise," *Pennsylvania Gazette*, Part 1, January 11, 1743/4; Packard, *Medicine*, vol. 1, 114.

44. Jarcho, "Cadwallader Colden as a Student of Infectious Diseases," 103; CC, "Sir, According to my Promise," *Pennsylvania Gazette*, Part 1, January 11, 1743/4.

45. CC, "Sir, According to my Promise," *Pennsylvania Gazette*, Part 1, January 11, 1743/4.

46. CC, "Sir, According to my Promise," *Pennsylvania Gazette*, Part 2, January 26, 1743/4.

47. CC, "Sir, According to my Promise," *Pennsylvania Gazette*, Part 2, January 26, 1743/4.

48. CC to JA, December 5, 15, 1743, RP, vol. 3, 11.

49. JA to CC, January 22, 1743/4, *CP*, vol. 3, 46, 48; CC to Mitchell, November 7, 1745, *CP*, vol. 8, 328–32; J. A. Leo Lemay, *The Life of Benjamin Franklin, Printer and Publisher, 1730–1747* (Philadelphia: University of Pennsylvania Press, 2006), vol. 2, 462.

50. CC, "Sir, According to my Promise," *Pennsylvania Gazette*, Part 3, February 2, 1743/4.

51. CC to Mitchell, November 7, 1745, *CP*, vol. 8, 328–32; John B. Blake, "Yellow Fever in Eighteenth Century America," *Bulletin of the New York Academy of Medicine*, 44, no. 6 (1968): 673; Jarcho, "Biographical," 328; Edmund Berkeley and Dorothy Smith Berkeley, *Dr. John Mitchell: The Man Who Made the Map of North America* (Chapel Hill: University of North Carolina Press, 1974), 75–76.

52. CC to Alderman Johnson, December 1744, *CP*, vol. 3, 95–96.

53. CC to Mitchell, November 7, 1745, *CP*, vol. 8, 328–32. Regarding yellow fever, CC also commented that it "has been many Times observed in Camps, Towns besieged, Prisons, Ships crowded with People, where sufficient Care has not been taken to keep them clean." That disease is actually typhus, rare in colonial America. But CC correctly noted the importance of cleanliness, which lessens the incidence of lice which spread typhus, as well as when he stated that "Air filled with Corruption" nourished the disease. Typhus does spread through air too. CC, "Sir, According to my Promise," *Pennsylvania Gazette*, Part 3, February 2, 1743/4. On typhus see Philip Ranlet, "Typhus and American Prisoners in the War of Independence," *Mariner's Mirror* 96, no. 4 (2010): 443–54.

54. CC, "Observations on the Yellow Fever of Virginia, with some Remarks on Dr. John Mitchell's Account of the Disease," *American Medical and Philosophical Register* 4 (1814): 378–79; Jarcho, "Cadwallader Colden as a Student of Infectious Diseases," 106; Blake, "Yellow Fever," 673; Berkeley and Berkeley, *Dr. John Mitchell*, 73–74, 79–80; Hindle, *Pursuit of Science*, 47–48.

55. CC to Mitchell, November 7, 1745, *CP*, vol. 8, 334–35; CC, "Extract of a Letter from an eminent Physician of the Province of New York, concerning an Indian Remedy for the Venereal Disease," *Gentleman's Magazine* 27 (September 1757): 405–6; CC to Robert Whytt, 1758, in CC, *The Philosophical Writings of Cadwallader Colden*, ed. Scott L. Pratt and John Ryder (Amherst, NY: Humanity Books, 2002), 227–29; Alfred W. Crosby, Jr., *The Columbian Exchange: Biological and Cultural Consequences of 1492* (Westport, CT: Greenwood Press, 1972), 124–25, 149. George Croghan, a Pennsylvanian who worked with Indians, remained unsure about the origin of syphilis, but commented on the skill of Indian doctors in treating it. See Croghan, "The Opinions of George Croghan on the American Indian," ed. Nicholas B. Wainwright, *Pennsylvania Magazine of History and Biography* 71, no. 2 (1947): 155. Cotton Mather thought that believing in an American origin of syphilis was "doubtless a Mistake!" See Mather, *The Angel of Bethesda*, ed. Gordon W. Jones (Barre, MA: American Antiquarian Society, 1972), 117.

56. CC, "The Cure of Cancers, From an eminent physician at New-York," *Gentleman's Magazine* 21 (July 1751): 305–8; CC, "Farther account of the Phytolacca," *Gentleman's Magazine* 22 (July 1752): 302; Samuel Johnson to CC, February 19, 1753, in *Samuel Johnson, President of King's College: His Career and Writings*, ed. Herbert Schneider and Carol Schneider (New York: Columbia University Press, 1929), vol. 2, 305; Berkeley and Berkeley, *Dr.*

John Mitchell, 164–65; Jarcho, "Cadwallader Colden as a Student of Infectious Diseases," 110; Thomas Hallock, "Male Pleasure and the Genders of Eighteenth-Century Botanic Exchange: A Garden Tour," *William and Mary Quarterly*, 3rd ser., 62 (2005):706.

57. George Berkeley, "Farther Thoughts," in *The Works of George Berkeley, Bishop of Cloyne*, ed. A. A. Luce and T. E. Jessop (London: Nelson, 1953), vol. 5, 217; Berkeley, "On Tar" (1744), in *Works*, ed. Luce and Jessop, vol. 5, 225; Saul Jarcho, "The Therapeutic Use of Resin and of Tar Water by Bishop George Berkeley and Cadwallader Colden," *New York State Journal of Medicine* 55, no. 6 (1955): 834, 837; Berkeley and Berkeley, *Mitchell*, 73–74.

58. Berkeley, *Sirus* (1744), in *Works*, ed. Luce and Jessop, vol. 5, 34–35; CC, *Abstract from Dr. Berkley's Treatise on Tar-Water*, 1–2. Tar was better known in ancient history as one of the materials referred to as bitumen, an essential part of incendiary weapons, perhaps including the most famous of those times, Greek fire. See Adrienne Mayor, *Greek Fire, Poison Arrows and Scorpion Bombs: Biological and Chemical Warfare in the Ancient World* (Woodstock, NY: Overlook Duckworth, 2003), 213, 221, 240.

59. CC, *Abstract from Dr. Berkley's Treatise on Tar-Water*, preface, 10.

60. CC, *Abstract from Dr. Berkley's Treatise on Tar-Water*, 13, 19; CC to Fothergill, October 18, 1757, *CP*, vol. 5, 204.

61. Helen Brock, "North America, a Western Outpost of European Medicine," in *The Medical Enlightenment of the Eighteenth Century*, ed. Andrew Cunningham and Roger French (Cambridge and New York: Cambridge University Press, 1990), 210–11; CC, "Account of the Climate of New York," 692.

62. CC, "Sir, According to my Promise," *Pennsylvania Gazette*, Part 3, February 2, 1743/4; Stephen R. Bown, *Scurvy: How a Surgeon, a Mariner, and a Gentleman Solved the Greatest Medical Mystery of the Age of Sail* (Chichester, UK: Summersdale, 2003), 38–42.

63. CC to Mrs. CC, August 3, 1747, *CP*, vol. 3, 413; CC to Mitchell, November 7, 1745, *CP*, vol. 8, 335–36.

64. CC to Mitchell, November 7, 1745, *CP*, vol. 8, 335–36; CC to Gronovius, 1744/5, *CP*, vol. 3, 97–98.

65. JA to CC, February 10, March 18, 1744/5, September 22, October 6, 1745, *CP*, vol. 3, 102–3, 107–9, 154–55, 164–65.

66. Bartram to CC, April 7, 1745, Ch A 4.82, Boston Public Library.

67. Johnson to CC, October 5, 1745, *CP*, vol. 3, 160; Berkeley, "Farther Thoughts on Tar-Water" (1752), in *Works*, vol. 5, 211.

68. CC, *Abstract from Dr. Berkley's Treatise on Tar-Water*, 15–16; BF, *An Account of the New Invented Pennsylvanian Fire-Places* (1744), in *FP*, vol. 2, 420. Other medical works have been attributed to CC, but either they never existed or were written by someone else. See Jarcho, "Biographical," *passim*.

69. CC to BF, [October 1743], *FP*, vol. 2, 385–87; BF to Jane Mecom, [June? 1748], *FP*, vol. 3, 302; Carl Van Doren, "The Beginnings of the American Philosophical Society," American Philosophical Society, *Proceedings* 87, no. 3 (1943): 280–81.

70. BF to CC, November 4, 1743, *FP*, vol. 2, 387–88; Collinson to CC, March 2, 1742/3, *CP*, vol. 3, 10–11; CC to William Strahan, November 1743, *CP*, vol. 3, 37–39; Strahan to CC, May 9, 1744, *CP*, vol. 3, 58–59; CC, "An original paper of the late Lieut. Gov. Colden, on a new method of Printing discovered by him," *American Medical and Philosophical Register* 1 (April 1811), 439–46; Van Doren, "Beginnings," 281; Hoermann, *Cadwallader Colden*, 79; Walter Isaacson, *Benjamin Franklin: An American Life* (New York: Simon & Schuster, 2003), 133; Lemay, *Life of Benjamin Franklin*, vol. 2, 460–61.

71. Collinson to CC, March 30, 1745, *CP*, vol. 3, 109–10; Bartram to CC, March 6, 1746/7, *CP*, vol. 3, 362–63; Collinson to BF, April 12, 1747, *CP*, vol. 3, 371–72; CC to BF, October 24, 1752, *FP*, vol. 4, 376; Delbourgo, *A Most Amazing Scene of Wonders*, 88.

72. BF to CC, June 5, 1747, *FP*, vol. 3, 142–43; CC to BF, August 3, 1747, *FP*, vol. 3, 167–68; Collinson to CC, March 30, 1745, *CP*, vol. 3, 109–10.

73. CC to BF, October 28, 1751, March 16, October 24, 1752, *FP*, vol. 4, 200, 278–81, 373–76; BF to Collinson, [October 1752], *FP*, vol. 4, 377; BF to CC, February 28, 1753, *FP*, vol. 4, 448; CC to BF, [August 12, 1756], *CP*, vol. 5, 88–89.

74. Collinson to CC, April 26, 1745, *CP*, vol. 3, 113–14; Bartram to CC, October 4, 1745, *CP*, vol. 3, 159; Patricia Fara, "'A Treasure of Hidden Vertues': The Attraction of Magnetic Marketing," *British Journal for the History of Science* 28, no. 1 (1995), 17–18.

75. CC to Douglass, [c. September 1728], *CP*, vol. 1, 271–72; Douglass to CC, March 31, 1729, February 17, 1735/6, *CP*, vol. 8, 190–91, vol. 2, 146–47.

76. Bartram to CC, March 27, 1744, Spec. Mss. Coll., Typographic Library, Columbia University, New York City; CC to JA, November 9, 1744, RP, vol. 3, 14; JA to CC, November 12, 1744, *CP*, vol. 3, 82–83; Isaacson, *Benjamin Franklin*, 122–23; Van Doren, "Beginnings," 281.

77. Bartram to CC, April 7, 1745, ChA 4.82, Boston Public Library; BF to CC, August 15, 1745, *FP*, vol. 3, 33–36; CC to Bartram, November 7, 1745, Bartram, *Memorials*, ed. Darlington, 330; Joyce E. Chaplin, *The First Scientific American: Benjamin Franklin and the Pursuit of Genius* (New York: Basic Books, 2006), 96; Hindle, "Quaker Background," 246.

78. Bartram to CC, April 7, 1745, Ch A 4.82, Boston Public Library; CC to Gronovius, October 1, 1755, in CC, *Selections from the Scientific Correspondence*, ed. Gray, 21; "An Inquiry into the Powers producing. . . . Needles swimming in Water," August 1768, CPU, reel 1. On his experiment with needles, CC states that he was 81, demonstrating that he calculated his age from the Julian year 1687. Old habits were truly hard to break for those born under the old calendar. George Washington, for example, celebrated his birthday on February 11, not February 22. In 1768 CC was a mere 80 years old.

Chapter Six

Revolts

Luckily for Cadwallader Colden, his forays into the natural world as well as his sylvan retreat helped to steel him for the vicious cockpit of New York politics. The death of Governor William Cosby made the "publick Spectacles" in the colony even worse. Bitter as the battles of George Clarke's administration were—and they verged on civil war—the colony's slaves stirred up New York far more.[1]

In 1736, either before or just after Cosby's demise, Colden fixed upon the idea of translating part of a relevant letter of Cicero, a foe of tyrants who threatened the Roman Republic. Cosby's tyrannical government seemed to conjure up the dangers that Cicero had warned against.[2]

Cicero had a large audience of receptive Americans and he was a particular favorite of James Logan. Colden, like many others, would freely drop some astute saying of the ancient Roman into his letters. Unlike Colden and other classically-trained colonists, however, most Americans wanted to read the great orator of Rome in English, not the original Latin. The 1740s saw a boom in English renditions of Cicero, a trend Colden anticipated by a few years.[3]

To help out, James Alexander sent Colden a French version of the letter his friend had picked. But Colden rejected the Frenchman's work "because he has taken a latitude which I could not allow my self." What attracted Colden to Cicero—his "Manner" and clever word placement—had been weakened by the foreigner; Colden wanted to stay "as close" to Cicero's actual words "as I could." When Alexander expressed his strong approval of Colden's effort, he asked Alexander to study both translations and his introduction to correct any errors. And Colden requested he draft William Smith, Sr., an adept student of French and Latin, to look them over as well as Colden's introduction to his translation.[4]

Colden intended his translation and the introduction to have "a close application to the present times and persons" but not "accompanied with so much bitterness" or create "so much resentment and for that reason may perhaps do much good" than some other approach. But he did warn that it had to be printed "before the New Governor's arrival" because "the Introduction may be thought to have some Design that may not please him." Before its publication, he cautioned Alexander, he had "to consider how seasonable" the introduction would be "at this time."[5]

This translation of Cicero would not be published in the New York newspapers. However seasonable Alexander might think Colden's handiwork might be, the political crisis caused by Cosby's death rapidly spiraled out of control. Colden's literary effort became dated very quickly.[6]

In fact, a battle to succeed the dead governor began just a few hours after his death on March 10. When Rip Van Dam learned that Cosby had died he rushed to Fort George but its gates had been "shut against him." Not leaving, Van Dam insisted on talking with Mrs. Cosby whom a guard insisted was "indisposed." Mrs. Cosby, whose coup had created the mess that would follow, had already sent her husband's official documents and the provincial seal off to New York's Council, of which Clarke had become the senior member after Van Dam's suspension.[7]

Van Dam did not know that the Council had already met and had agreed that Clarke was acting governor, confirming the coup. At last, Clarke's secretary reminded the angry Dutchman that Cosby had removed him from the Council which did not calm Van Dam. He refused to accept the Council's decision, insisting that Cosby had been "delirious and non compos mentis" when he suspended him. That legal argument, along with several others, proved to Van Dam that he should be in charge, not Clarke.[8]

The legal reasoning had come from Alexander, of course, not Van Dam. Alexander had also been suspended in the coup, but Clarke chose to ignore that to weaken Van Dam's support. President Clarke had summoned Alexander to the March 10 meeting and to many others in the coming months, an obvious sign to Alexander that Clarke had restored his membership. Still, Alexander refused to attend, which would have been a tacit acceptance of Clarke's authority.[9]

Instead of taking the easy way out and abandoning Van Dam, Alexander became his champion. He issued a broadside in late March denying that he had "consented" to Clarke's usurpation of power and would not allow "his Silence" to be construed as acceptance. Clarke had no right to perform "any Act of Government whatsoever, as President."[10]

Meanwhile, Colden had been at Coldengham but returned on the day Cosby died, arriving soon after the governor's demise. Shocked by the rapid escalation of rhetoric, Colden's "thoughts and time both were fully employed and hurried." As the party lines hardened, he hastened out of the city to "avoid entering into new Disputes in which my friends were taking opposite sides." Coldengham, he hoped, would once again be a safe asylum.[11]

Colden's instinct for political survival had served him well. Both Van Dam and Clarke acted as president. Both of them appointed men to the various offices. Two different governments tried to function in the colony. For once, even the New York Assembly was speechless. It kept insisting that Clarke prorogue it—that is, to suspend its meeting until a future date. The Assembly refused to meet until someone had uncontested authority to serve as acting governor. One assemblyman commented that it was "not Safe to Act." So many members stayed away that a quorum might not have been obtained anyway.[12]

The colony of New York was in turmoil, the inevitable result of the departure of a tyrant. At Coldengham, Colden heard many rumors as they swirled about New York. And these rumors told of forthcoming violence. The followers of Van Dam, the reports suggested, planned to kill Clarke or James DeLancey (perhaps both) or seize them. "At this time," Colden recorded, "we had all the appearance of a civil War which had it happened must have been accompanied with much cruelty." Passions kept mounting "as almost every man was exasperated against his Neighbour . . . resentment and Anger was burning in every man's breast."[13]

Colden did everything he could to calm the colony before it imploded. Because he had connections in both camps, his actions may have been essential in keeping the peace. Advising Clarke, who seemed "prudent" in avoiding "tumults," not to meet the Assembly, Colden also did his best to use his friendship with Alexander to quiet the angry supporters of Van Dam. Colden, criticizing the strident actions of some pro-Van Dam assemblymen, suggested to his old friend that perhaps their arguments had just not penetrated his own "thick Skull." Such arguments, Colden suggested, "are like undisciplined Horse [troops] in any army that if you once disorder them they do more hurt to their friends than to their foes." But if their foes fled, "they may do more execution than good Soldiers."[14]

Yet Colden could not be seen as too close to the Van Dam faction. As surveyor-general Colden continued to fulfill the duties of his office. During June 1736, for example, he came to the capital and presented Clarke with official documents about a requested land grant. To Colden, Clarke was president of the Council. In September 1736 Colden, by then "for some time in the woods surveying," wrote the president:

> Your prudence and patience in the conduct of the public affairs gives me much pleasure. Your persevering in the same method I think cannot fail of success unless prevented by foreign accidents which a wise man cannot guard against. May you receive your reward in the good effects of restoring peace and con-

tent to the inhabitants of this province, and I shall for the promoting of this good purpose do everything in [my] power.[15]

Early in the crisis, when Clarke fell ill and was "dispirited," he left for his distant home in eastern Queens County, thereby putting "the entire conduct of the publick affairs" in the charge of the next most senior councilor. That was Colden. He could guess that London would back Clarke, with his substantial connections, over Van Dam, who had little if any influence in Britain; Van Dam's position would not even be considered there.[16]

Colden, however, had not planned to return to the city until about mid-October. By that time, Clarke's prudence had evaporated. He could no longer stand the pounding he constantly received from Alexander and various other authors in John Peter Zenger's newspaper. On October 7, 1736 he announced to the Council of Trade that he was sending it a batch of the worst issues and broadsides. He accused Alexander, Lewis Morris, Jr., and Smith of being the authors. Since the president had "no regular proof" he could not send the culprits to Britain for trial, but if "the authors of those papers with their printer Zenger were sent home it would at once put an end to the Faction." Suspecting that Zenger was the weakest link, Clarke urged the government to dangle a pardon in front of him to get the necessary proof against the others. Colden never knew, by design, that the crisis was on the verge of a giant explosion.[17] His friendship with Alexander caused Clarke to keep this plan secret from him.

Would the king have agreed to the greatest trial in colonial history? The answer will never be known because, less than a week after Clarke's letter, news finally arrived from London accepting Clarke as the acting governor and soon he would be made lieutenant governor. To Colden's great relief, the disturbance in the colony of New York ended at once. Unfortunately for Alexander, he was dropped from the Council but both he and Smith, partly by Colden's lobbying, were allowed to rejoin the New York bar.[18]

The contentions from Cosby's era had, without question, gone. Even Zenger's newspaper became silent about politics. Clarke, meanwhile, had also dropped his plan to destroy his enemies, preferring now to forget the abuse he had received and calm the populace.[19]

While Colden shared the desire for some tranquility, that did not mean that he had forgotten what had happened. His reaction can be guessed when he received a letter from his once bitter antagonist, John Alsop, who referred to "The Unhappy Misunderstanding that had been between us." Calling the harassment inflicted by Alsop a misunderstanding was laughable. His new "innocent and reconciled behaviour," caused by the tyrant's death, did not fool his old target. In August 1737 Colden wrote of "The Parasites and Flatterers and Tools of a C[osb]y" who then were trying to portray themselves as "Patriots," a stance so blatantly ridiculous "it turns people's Stomachs." At least, Colden realized, Alsop no longer had the power or influence to injure any more of his neighbors.[20]

Revenge against Cosby's tools had no value to Colden. Instead, even during the tumultuous early period of Clarke's administration, Colden would use his influence with Clarke to initiate a major reform in the handling of land purchases from the Indians.

Prominent New Yorkers had swindled Indians out of their land for so long that a few more frauds seemed almost normal. Peter Van Brugh Livingston and his agent in Britain, Samuel Storke, employed the trick Francis Harison had used with the Oblong: they humbly petitioned the Board of Trade for a grant of good land owned by the Mohawks that they had not yet bothered to buy from the Indians. The Lords of Trade then sent the request to Clarke for his comments and he, unhappy that the British government had once again interfered with a local affair, notified Colden about the matter. "It will Chagrin the Indians to See their Lands granted before they are purchased," Clarke complained, "and discourage people from applying for Grants here," fearing that London might have given the land away already.[21]

Colden went to the Mohawk country to investigate. Supposedly, Livingston and Storke had assured the Lords of Trade that they were asking for only six square miles, a small grant, but Colden suspected something was wrong. Much of the land the two said they wanted had already been given to others; the rest did not seem worth the huge cost of getting a grant from the British government. Suspicious, Colden examined the specified borders closer. He realized that the phrase "Northmost Spring" was a trick. The grant would not be six square miles, Colden discovered, but "a vast Tract" that would be "Six miles in Breadth and to extend the whole length of the Mohawks River upwards to its head," some 130 miles long, an intolerable grant for both New Yorkers and the Indians. Clarke lost no time in alerting the Board of Trade how it had been tricked, killing the grant.[22]

Colden would soon uncover more swindles involving Indian land. During August and September 1736 Colden again traveled to the Mohawk country assuming that this trip, at least, would be straightforward. He planned to survey some land already sold by the Indians, but things did not go as simply as he expected. The Mohawks refused to let Colden do the surveys. Not surprisingly, he wanted to know why. Colden did not understand Indian languages so he needed translators—picked by the Albany Indian commissioners led by the Livingstons—but Colden soon gathered that the translators were distorting what had been said. As Colden later wrote, "I found the Indians had the same suspicions for they several times, by signs, expressed their earnest wish that we could understand each other."[23]

Step by step, Colden slowly unraveled the web of deceit inflicted on the natives: "some persons had fraudulently obtained a conveyance from them, of the very lands on which they lived and planted." He could not then find out "the particulars" because of "the unwillingness . . . of the Interpreters to have the fraud discovered." But he soon learned the truth. The Indians thought they were selling only enough land for a few farms, but none of the Mohawks could read the land deed in English and the interpreters misled them. Nor did the Indians understand the compass readings or "English measures" mentioned in deeds. Such "pretended Purchases" made them "highly exasperated."[24]

The surveyor-general seems to have been just as exasperated. He knew that similar tricks had caused serious unrest in Maine. To "quiet their minds," he promised to bring their complaints to Clarke's attention and on November 3, 1736, he did so. Colden laid out new "Regulations" designed to stop such frauds. Before deeds were approved, the Indian land in question had to be surveyed while the Indians watched. Someone with official status had to certify that a deed and the survey results agreed. That official should see that the natives were "fairly paid" and that they understood the terms of the deed.[25]

Disturbed by Colden's information, Clarke informed him of the dismay he felt at the lack of cooperation he had gotten from "the Gentlemen who were concerned" in that land grant. Clarke accepted Colden's advice and the Council approved the new rules, which ended Indian complaints about land sales dating from that time. The strict regulations actually discouraged people from buying land from the Indians, finding purchases from other colonists much simpler.[26]

Colden's success in reforming the mess involving Indian land sales had been engineered with surprisingly little trouble. Despite what had to be Colden's finest moment in the new administration, he knew, as he informed his father, that "the differences" in New York were "far from being over." In 1737 Colden admitted to his wife: "Our party Disputes are as high as ever while some are endeavoring to widen the vent others are endeavoring to patch it up," of whom he was one. Colden did what he could to keep the political turmoil out of his personal affairs. But Clarke desperately needed Colden's presence in the capital to deal with the "great Confusions," forcing him to spend less time with his family at Coldengham.[27]

Making things difficult for Clarke was the lackadaisical attitude of the noble picked to succeed Cosby, Lord De la Ware. At times he seemed ready to leave for New York, sometimes not. New Yorkers, unsure how long Clarke would be in power, did not know how seriously to take him. Finally, it became obvious that De la Ware had little intention of living in the colony, which left Clarke in charge.[28]

Clarke also had a host of problems with the Assembly elected in 1737. Alexander, one of the victorious assemblymen, still had no affection for him nor did the Morrises, also elected in what was a strong rejection of the old

Cosby faction. The Morrises now targeted all of their enemies, a move that backfired.[29]

Adolph Philipse had been defeated in the election, but, because of the death of a New York City member, Philipse ran for that seat. According to Colden, "The sick the lame and the blind were all carried to vote, they were carried out of Prison and out of the poor house to vote—such a struggle I never saw." With that effort, the imaginative handling of the election by the sheriff, Governor Cosby's namesake son, and "A few bloody noses," Philipse won by fourteen votes. Philipse's successful return to New York politics gave Clarke even more headaches; Philipse had not lost his skill in controlling what Colden called the "ignorant part of that house," with predictable results.[30]

In 1739 Clarke had to agree to accept a yearly salary decided by the Assembly; no earlier governor had fallen to such a degree. Clarke's son believed "that an unruly Spirit of Independency and dissatisfaction had at last got to Such a height" in New York that his father "found the weight and authority of a Lieutenant Governor though Managed in the best Manner would not be able to Subdue it." Ten years after Clarke's surrender, a future governor advised by Colden stated that the one year salary and Clarke's allowing the Assembly to spend "the publick money without warrant from the Governor" were "the foundation" of its "Power." Royal government could not be strengthened without destroying such usurpations of the Assembly.[31]

Despite the implications for the future, in 1737 at least, Colden had to put his personal affairs in order. Never flush with cash, Colden suddenly needed it. His wharf, his landing and his store there were in a precarious position. In October the wharf needed immediate work or the first flood on the Hudson would wash it away. If that was not pressing enough, debt incurred in the defense of the Oblong had to be paid. Lawyer Joseph Murray had lent Colden and his partners a substantial sum in 1732 and, five years later, not even the interest had been paid, embarrassing everyone involved. Alexander and Smith had to warn the debtors, one of whom was Colden, that, if necessary, they would have to take them to court after March 10, 1738 to pay Murray.[32]

Colden apologized for his "negligence," blamed the press of business, and felt "ashamed" that Murray had not been compensated. Colden vowed to pay his share but asked for a delay which stretched longer and longer. Finally, in December 1739, Murray sued the partners and won. Although Alexander and Smith did not really want to sue Archibald Kennedy, Vincent Matthews, or Colden, they would have to but agreed to settle any dispute about what each owed. That got Colden moving and, giving more excuses, agreed to go over his account. In May 1742 he handed over a deed and received credit for services he performed such as his travel to the Oblong in October 1740 to check on squatters—a trip cut short by a "Sudden" cold snap. The payment ended this embarrassing episode for all concerned, demonstrating again that New York land speculation did not necessarily bring sudden riches.[33]

One legitimate excuse Colden gave in December 1741 for his slowness in paying was his travel throughout New England. He had just written to the Duke of Newcastle enclosing the report of one of his assignments, the border dispute between Rhode Island and Massachusetts. Colden had learned of his appointment to that commission in December 1740. Earlier, in 1737, he had been named to investigate another contentious border dispute, that between Massachusetts and New Hampshire. Colden "presided" over and was "Principally intrusted" in each.[34]

Massachusetts lost the argument with both its adversaries, but the loss to Rhode Island rankled the most, at least with Thomas Hutchinson. In his *History of the Colony and Province of Massachusetts-Bay* Hutchinson complained about "A gentleman of the council of New York" who "had great influence at the board of commissioners." Whenever land, deeds, or the like were being discussed, Colden is the logical candidate for this man of influence who favored Rhode Island. Massachusetts lost because it had inherited Plymouth's old land claim to the area. Plymouth colony had no royal charter; Rhode Island did. Such basic logic points to Colden. Hutchinson's suggestion that this reasoning represented a plot to aid the territorial ambitions of New York over Massachusetts is quite a stretch. As Colden assured Newcastle, the commissioners took "all possible care to make the whole Evidence appear clearly and impartially for his Majesty's Judgment." And the king accepted the commission's decision.[35]

In Rhode Island, Colden was lauded and its agents in Britain "applaud your Judgment," he was told. Rhode Islanders saw Colden as a fair man because of this "upright Judgment," as he called it. These circumstances explain why a minister in Rhode Island would soon be writing him about an event in New York. During Colden's absence in Rhode Island, April-June 1741, a conspiracy—supposedly a slave revolt—erupted in New York that even touched the household of his eldest daughter.[36]

Colden's attitudes about slavery were in the mainstream of his time. His Scottish friend James Cheape participated in the African slave trade. As has been related, Colden owned slaves in Philadelphia and owned some slaves who worked to get Coldengham into shape as a viable farm; Alice wanted a female slave to be a nanny for her small children. He sold a slave whom he thought was a bad influence on his "Negro Wench." Colden probably had the most slaves of anyone in Ulster County, but far fewer than many gentlemen in the southern colonies. In 1732, some years after the move to Coldengham, he had six slaves.[37]

Simply put, Colden supported the institution of slavery and opposed any tax on such labor. He wrote in 1726 that "the Want of Hands and the Dearness of the Wages of hired Servants, makes Slaves at this Time necessary,... nothing that is necessary is to be discouraged."[38]

Nor did Colden mellow on the subject as he aged. In 1754 he and John Bartram read their mutual friend Benjamin Franklin's essay on human population growth. Neither objected to his desire that there were more whites and fewer blacks to keep the British colonies whiter. They only objected that Franklin's statement should not be near the essay's conclusion.[39]

By 1741 New York City and its environs had a substantial slave population, which privateers added to. Britain and Spain had gone to war in 1739, which made Spanish ships open to attack by British privateers. Part of the loot they seized were slaves, or at least people thought to be slaves. The privateers had taken Spanish sailors, including those of mixed race. When no evidence existed of their status as free men, British courts ruled they were slaves and they were sold, over their bitter protest and that of Spanish officials who knew the truth, to eager buyers. Quickly, the New York slave population grew. The newcomers were Roman Catholics who owed allegiance to George II's enemy, the king of Spain. All of these captives realized that their only chance for freedom rested on a successful Spanish attack on New York. They surely told other slaves of this potential path to freedom. Adding to the volatile mix were other imported African slaves who had converted to Catholicism before their arrival in the British domain.[40]

The presence of so many bitter, Spanish Catholics provided a fertile breeding ground for the so-called New York slave revolt of 1741. The presence of a large number of whites involved in this slave revolt has puzzled historians, especially as there are no similar cases. Rebellious slaves proved to be more likely to kill whites rather than plot with them. They all could have been criminals using fires to conceal thefts, as has been suggested.[41]

Although goods might have been stolen, the presence of one white in particular, a reputed Catholic priest, suggests an entirely different motive. This individual, John Ury, was probably the instigator of much of what happened in New York. Catholic priests in Protestant territories served the interest of the Catholic world powers, France and Spain. Priests had been closely involved with the French colonial empire for many decades, so clerical spies were a familiar concern especially while the British were at war with Catholic Spain. In May 1741 General James Oglethorpe warned Lieutenant Governor Clarke to be wary of Catholic priests sent by the Spanish as part of a scheme to set fire to gunpowder stockpiles "and considerable towns in ... English North America" to disrupt the war effort.[42]

The only problem linking Ury with being a priestly spy is that he was not a Catholic priest. Historian Thomas J. Davis found evidence that Ury had not taken communion or confessed his sins. Although Catholic priests cannot hear their own confessions, every priest during a Catholic mass partakes of a communion host. Accordingly, Ury was not an ordained Catholic priest.[43]

Most likely, Ury was a deacon, the lowest Catholic order of priesthood. A deacon has limited authority and cannot perform any of the sacraments. That helps to explain why Ury went to a confectioner in New York City to try to get communion wafers, something such tradesmen did not carry. These wafers were baked in molds made by a different artisan, a joiner. A Catholic priest would have known such a basic detail.[44]

Ury's probable status as a deacon suggests why he was so concerned about confession; masquerading as an ordained priest is considered a great sin among Catholics, requiring confession and a suitable penance. Ury might have been denied ordination because of his poor education and no doubt still desired ordination, which would explain why he was not seeking a wife.[45] He must have assumed the priesthood would be his if he did something spectacular—such as lead a Jacobite rebellion. This revolt was not primarily a slave revolt, although many of the participants were slaves. It must not be forgotten that many of the participants were Catholics, a group drawn to opposition to the Protestant Hanoverian dynasty.

As William Smith, Jr. wrote in his *History of the Province of New York*, "No man . . . doubted of the reality of a plot, but for what end was only conjecture." After a serious fire at Fort George in March 1741, Clarke believed that the blaze had been accidental. Then more fires hit the city, so many that they called attention to themselves, hardly a way to conceal burglaries. Another serious case of arson in Newark, New Jersey, had been instigated by slaves. When Clarke determined that New York's fires had been started by slaves, he assumed it was a slave rebellion, though he eventually concluded that it had been a Jacobite conspiracy, an idea that Colden supported. There was no doubt where Daniel Horsmanden stood. On August 7, 1741 he alerted Colden that "tho' the Mystery of Iniquity has been unfolding by very Small and Slow Degrees, it has at length been discovered that popery was at the Bottom."[46]

Shocked by the turn of events in New York City, Colden had to be extremely disturbed that his daughter Bettie, who had married a DeLancey, might have been in danger. She explained to her father in June that some of the DeLancey slaves, "ours in particular," planned to "set fire to the house and to have destroyed us but there is no certain proof yet of it." Colden's description "of the horrid Plot" stirred his brother-in-law in Scotland "enough to make one tremble that reads it." Andrew Chrystie warned him that "if either You or Your Daughter DeLancey take these Negroes in their Service from that time they will be to Blame."[47]

As to the plot's cause, Colden leaned to Jacobitism, a very real concern to all Scots. Four years after the events in New York, Scotland suffered through another Jacobite invasion and his brother endured an occupation by "our merciless enemies." The "panic" that swept through Scotland, James Colden related, was "universal."[48]

Cadwallader Colden, always alert to foes of the Hanoverians, had learned about a curious Irish fellow, Luke Barrington, who settled in Ulster during 1740 and started a school. Given the scarcity of educated men in the countryside, when a new one appeared Colden wanted to meet him. Adept at languages and reportedly an able scholar, Barrington seemed like an interesting dinner companion. Colden sent several invitations to him but was greeted with silence, a very unusual result in itself. The newcomer preferred the company of Irish Catholic servants. Eventually Colden discovered why. When Barrington attended a fair, he got drunk and responded to a toast for the king of England with one to the king of Spain, adding that if the Spanish invaded, he would join them and "knock all the English on the head." Upsetting to all but the Catholic Irish there, an argument ensued. Fleeing the area, Barrington then claimed to be a Protestant minister as a cover. Colden knew that Catholic agents were sent to blend into Protestant countries and so notified the justices of the peace in both Dutchess and Ulster counties and the governor. Barrington was imprisoned and admitted to being a Catholic. Giving what he insisted was his real name, Villars Roche, he denied being a papal spy and was a poor son of a noble. He used aliases because he was an absconded indentured servant. Rather than stay in jail, he begged to be allowed to fulfill his indenture. The disposition of the case is unknown.[49]

Curious as the Barrington story is, Colden is better known for his involvement with another odd incident—an anonymous letter he received comparing New York's harsh treatment of the plotters to the Salem Witchcraft trials of 1692.

On August 8, 1741 Bettie sent her father a letter that purported to have come from New England; she lived in Westchester through which ran the Boston Post Road. The letter urged a stop to the executions of "the poor Negroes and the Whites too." The author could not accept that "the whites should join with the Blacks"—although they did—or that the slaves "should attempt the Destruction of a City"—although they set many fires in a mostly wooden city. Nor should the confessions be taken seriously, he believed; confessions can be extorted. Among the dozens of confessions of witchcraft at Salem, none was "worth a Straw." "Let Justice be done to your own people," he urged Colden, "whatever Treatment the People of the Massachusetts may meet with when you sit in Judicature about their affairs."[50]

Colden did not need a lecture about the dangers caused by a popular frenzy, whether it involved tulips in Holland, "the oddest enthusiasm," or witchcraft in Salem, "put a stop to . . . by an immediate application to the crown." Colden compared the government of New York, even at its worst, to that of Massachusetts under "genuine independent republicans." If not "restrained by the King's Authority," they would have "gone near to have unpeopled the Country, by the numerous prosecutions and Executions on pretense of Witch Craft." He knew that "Reason has no force with enthusiasts."[51]

The letter seemed suspicious to Colden. Not only was it unsigned, but he thought the author had tried to disguise his handwriting. Who would do that? Could an undiscovered Jacobite in New York be trying to save his fellow plotters? Yet Colden did not treat it as if it were an annoying letter written by a crank. He brought it to the attention of Lieutenant Governor Clarke and urged an investigation to identify the author, part of which would entail determining if it had actually come in the mail from New England or if his daughter had been tricked. At that point, Colden admitted, he could only "conjecture." Perhaps someone might recognize the handwriting, "the Seal or the paper." It sounded as if Colden thought this was a criminal matter.[52]

The other possibility, as Colden knew, was that the letter was merely expressing its author's beliefs about the conspiracy trials and executions. But was this person trying to influence public opinion? Colden urged that it was best to publish Ury's trial along with "other Material Evidences of the Plot" to stop any such campaign.[53]

Clarke took the letter seriously as well and showed it to James DeLancey. Both knew learning the author's identity would be hard. Since Colden would be returning to Providence, Rhode Island soon, Clarke suggested that the doctor might learn about the author there. "It seems to be wrote by an angry man," Clarke surmised, "and it may be in your Examinations you may have wrung a Conscience too close."[54]

Jill Lepore believed that a Massachusetts commissioner in the Rhode Island border dispute wrote the missive and also fingered James Alexander as a possible suspect. (Alexander would have just told Colden what he thought.) Those suspects were innocent, but Clarke's guess about Providence turned out to be right. The letter's author was not angry so much as cranky.[55]

Rev. Josiah Cotton, who served a Congregational church in Providence from 1741–1747, wrote the letter. He would have a long history of battling his church members and had to move about over the years. His disputes became legendary in New England. Cotton wrote a version of the letter to Colden in his personal diary where he says he authored it. On September 29, 1741 Cotton published the letter in the *New England Weekly Journal*. In his diary Cotton explained his motive for the letter. Concerned about the executions, he believed it best two murderers go free rather than one innocent suffer the death penalty. He was not angry about the Massachusetts-Rhode Island border dispute.[56]

Perhaps Colden saw that newspaper with Cotton's letter in it while away in New England or upon his return to New York. A Jacobite would not have published his letter in a newspaper, thus ending Colden's concern on that score. If Colden seems unduly paranoid about the letter, his fear for his daughter's safety had caused it. Nor should it be forgotten he had come up against Jacobites in Scotland.

One thing does appear to have come about because of Colden's letter to Clarke. It was decided to publish an account of the trials, which would be written by Horsmanden who saw the plot as the "most horrible and Detestable piece of Villany a Scheme which must have been brooded in a Conclave of Devils, and hatched in the Cabinet of Hell." Horsmanden's strong belief that the episode was a Catholic conspiracy must have moved him to change his intended title from the "Negro Conspiracy," the way he must have described it to Colden, to one in which "White People" were mentioned first.[57]

In the book Horsmanden discussed Catholic conspiracies in England to answer the complaint that the chief plotter, Ury, failed to publicly confess his role, insisting he was innocent. "You do not conceive," Horsmanden observed, "that people who have hardened their courage a long while before, for an enterprize, the most hazardous in the world, should have resolution to keep, till death, a secret."[58]

Lepore attacks Horsmanden repeatedly, and mentions his early life in an apparent attempt to discredit him. Granted, Horsmanden was not a saintly man. His cousin, William Byrd II of Virginia, detailed their visits to English bordellos and other sexual trysts.[59]

Trained as a lawyer, Horsmanden nonetheless ran up huge debts he could not pay. A friend of Micajah Perry, he recommended him to Colden, the Duke of Newcastle, and to Governor Cosby of New York, where he settled. Only when the Morris family broke with Horsmanden, thinking he wanted to usurp the chief justiceship, did Cosby appoint him the recorder of the city, making him its chief lawyer. Horsmanden settled his debts by marrying a rich widow. Eventually, he broke with Colden and allied himself with the DeLanceys.[60]

While Horsmanden was not a nice man, as Colden learned to his dismay, that does not mean that he faked his account of the plot. Everything seems to point to Horsmanden doing his best "to be objective, complete and fair-minded."[61]

Cotton's letter and its reference to Salem has been used many times to attack both the trials and Horsmanden. It should be noted that slaves, including those in New England, who were convicted of major crimes suffered hideous fates. Nine years after the New York conspiracy, two slaves in Massachusetts murdered their owner. A female slave was "burned at the stake," a traditional punishment for witchcraft in Europe if not in England and its colonies. Her male accessory was executed. His chained body was publicly displayed for decades, reminiscent of the fate of the defeated Indian leader, King Philip.[62]

While the trials of the conspirators were taking place, Clarke learned that he would be superseded by a new governor, Captain George Clinton. In

August 1741 Clarke told Colden that Clinton was expected in a few weeks, but he would not show up in New York until 1743.[63]

Colden kept busy while the colony waited for Clinton. Back in the 1720s he had amassed more information of Indian relations to be used in an expanded version of his Indian history. But he was swamped with public business and averaged some nine months away from home each year. Earlier he had hoped to learn more about the Indians by living with them as a modern anthropologist would do, but with no flair for learning the natives' languages, he would have needed an interpreter, a prohibitive expense. So the data gathered dust until Peter Collinson urged him to bring out a new edition. During the winter of 1741–1742 Colden finished it, even though he had done some new research. His "chief view," he told Collinson, was "to do you a pleasure."[64]

Colden had other reasons for revising his Indian history. First, he wanted to make money. Colden needed the cash and hoped to spend it on books for himself or his children. And he hoped there would be a good profit. Only 500 of the first edition had reached the public, and copies of it had been unavailable for years, a fact he assumed would attract a publisher.[65]

Second, Colden expected the revamped book to "be of advantage to the publick." By the end of 1743 he expected a peace treaty with France, almost certainly rekindling the clandestine fur trade between Albany and French Canada as well as French "Incroachments" on British colonial territory. He wanted to add his old report on the fur trade as well as other illustrative documents. "I should hope that I have been of some use to my Country," a concern that had to be weighing on his mind. In 1743 he told Collinson "I am grown old and begin to be infirm." Then in his mid-fifties, Colden must have been contemplating his own mortality and wanted to strengthen his legacy to his country.[66]

Although the second edition of the book extended to 1699, perhaps the things Colden left out of it are even more interesting. These "facts," he explained to Collinson, were "not proper by any means to be made publick." The earliest Dutch traders had such a "Scandalous attachment . . . to the getting of Money" that occasionally, to stop an Indian from selling his furs to another dealer, some of the Dutch "would suffer the Indian to turn into bed to their wives." Colden had been told many times that it was true and that "strong proofs remain still in being in their families." And another disturbing example of trade, Colden insisted, happened during one of the Dutch wars when Esopus Indians had besieged a town. Dutch merchants traveled to the warring tribes and sold them "all kind of ammunition" that enabled them to kill the Dutchmen's "own Countrymen."[67]

More recent history produced still another case of a Dutchman's greed. One merchant, whom Colden identified in 1751 as Nicholas Schuyler, sold a large quantity of rum to naive Indians who had never encountered Dutch merchants before. When the natives finally opened the barrels, hundreds of miles away, they "found them filled with nothing but Water." Outrageous even for Dutch Indian traders, the authorities planned to bring him to justice. But, because of the king's death in 1727, the Assembly was dissolved and Schenectady elected Schuyler as its representative. He used the political influence he now had to stop any legal proceedings against him. This sort of thing, Colden explained to Dr. Mitchell, made the Indians "have more confidence in the English and in the Germans, than in the low dutch, whom they heartily despise."[68]

During the spring of 1742 Colden sent off the last of the revised manuscript to Collinson, who had been delegated to find a good English publisher for the second edition. That task would take some time.[69]

In the meantime, during 1742, Colden had to deal with still another time-consuming royal commission, this one dealing with an old land dispute between the Mohegan Indians and Connecticut. Colden took the side of the colony, insisting that the Mohegans were not a sovereign people. On August 15, 1743 Colden and a majority of the commissioners found in favor of Connecticut, nullifying an earlier decision in 1705. However, this dispute endured for some more decades.[70]

Four years later, Colden's revised Indian history at last appeared in England. A printer in London, Thomas Osborne, had decided to publish the book without any kind of subsidy, accepting the manuscript because he knew of Colden's "great good character" and hopes he would aid the sale of Osborne's various titles in America. Flushed with prospects of more profit, he invited Colden to expand the book, in yet another edition, with "some of your Neighbouring Nations." From March through June 1747 the history was in production.[71]

When Franklin saw the revised book he wanted to sell copies. Assuming that the added documents had been inserted by Osborne "to puff up the Book" to raise the price, Franklin called it "a common Trick of Booksellers." Osborne, who had a history of exasperating authors, this time was innocent, as the added documents were Colden's idea.[72]

Apparently, the only one not happy with the second edition was Colden. Dr. Mitchell had written a new title page that included a very long blurb intended to sell the book, which Colden never would have approved. The revised title itself put the Iroquois in French Canada, a mistake with serious political implications. Mitchell also changed the dedication to honor James Oglethorpe, whom Colden had never met or communicated with. Colden had wanted to keep the old dedication to William Burnet, his deceased friend, to honor his memory. At least General Oglethorpe "Approved" the book "very much."[73]

The long delay in publishing the Indian history had made it available during still another war with the French, which had to have boosted sales.

When Osborne announced he had sold or "sent Abroad" 500 copies, half of the press run, Colden, a savvy author, knew that the printer had made back all his costs. All further sales represented profit. Informing his publisher that he expected a share of the profit in books, Colden received a surprising response. Osborne sold the remaining copies to someone else. Within a few years, there would be two more printings of the history in England, including another by Osborne.[74] But Colden had little time to dwell on eccentric booksellers. During 1747 Colden would be deeply involved in a fierce battle with his political foes in New York.

Yet, before the 1740s, Colden had to have been dwelling on the passage of time and what havoc it was wreaking in Scotland. As one of his Scottish nephews would remind him: "you know our Scotch temper, and how anxious we generally are about the welfare of absent friends."[75]

Although Alice's mother died in 1719, their surviving parents remained in reasonable health. They were happy at their children's success in New York, but Alice's brother was not quite sure just what a surveyor-general did.[76]

Letters kept the scattered relatives together. "All your letters are refreshing to us," Rev. Colden assured his son, who would be instructed not to miss any "opportunity of writing to me." They would remember their grandchildren in their prayers and Cadwallader's mother asked him for medical advice concerning her injured hand.[77]

Sometimes the letters did not sooth fears. In 1723 the Chrysties and Cadwallader's brother James traveled together to Kelso where they were told by the residents that they had been told that Alice had died. Shocked, they rushed to Oxnam where the Coldens informed them that they had received a letter from their son who had forgotten to mention his wife. That convinced her father that "she is certainly gone." When the Coldens tried to calm him, pointing out that Cadwallader had written "We are all well," that only made Chrystie believe his son-in-law meant the children, not Alice, and was keeping the news from him. Luckily, he soon realized that she was, indeed, alive. He would reprimand his daughter: "I hope it will be a lesson to you for the future."[78]

Letters were, of course, a poor substitute for an actual visit to Scotland. In 1724 James Colden tried to coax his brother to journey to his native land: "I am sure it would give you a great deal of pleasure to see our father so healthy and vigorous as he is." Six years later, Alice's brother tried his luck. Reminding his sister that she had written that she would have "a great deal of uneasyness, if she thought she was never to see her Father again," he pointed out that they could not put off a visit if they wished to see their surviving parents: "they are all of them now in an advanced Age . . . according to the Course of Nature, If you expect to see them, That must be [done] without much longer delay." Could not his aunt Elizabeth (who was elderly herself and unlikely to be up to the task) take care of the younger children? Could not deputies handle Colden's offices for a while? The answer that came, after such suggestions, was that a trip was "impracticable." It must have been hard for Colden when he learned his mother died in 1731.[79]

By 1737 Colden's father did have one hope. Perhaps his grandson Sandie might become a merchant and could visit Scotland. Nonetheless, Rev. Colden could not recommend it because by the time Sandie reached Britain, both of his grandfathers might be dead. All they would ever see of Sandie Colden was his portrait.[80]

Alice's father had been at the Heriot Hospital for many years. Finally by 1736 his health had declined so much he had to leave Edinburgh and live with his minister son James. David Chrystie died in the early months of 1738. James, Cadwallader's old college friend, followed about a year later.[81]

Rev. Alexander Colden had kept performing his duties as a minister. In October 1737 he sent a religious tract to his son for his Quaker sister-in-law, no doubt hoping to save her soul. Then in December "the greatest half of his church fell" down. James Colden begged his father to "stay with me till his church was rebuilt, at least till the weather should be warmer but to no purpose." Nothing could deter Alexander Colden from preaching the Word of God "as long as he had strength and did preach" in his ruined church "some very stormy days with wind and rain and some times snow in his face." He was never the same. After a pastoral visit to a parishioner, Rev. Colden fell off his horse but was not hurt, or so it seemed. Yet a week later, in June 1738, he died at the age of 84.[82]

One of Alexander Colden's parishioners wrote an elegy praising him as he "did not lay Aside his Master's Work, until that he Was but a few Steps from Eternitie." Rev. Colden "blaz'd like a Star of the first Magnitude." Noting that Colden had two sons living, James was honored for showing "his Father . . . a due Respect;" the other son was in America. In 1796, some 58 years after the death of Rev. Alexander Colden, his grandson Cad observed that visiting Scots "spoke so highly . . . and with the highest veneration" of his grandfather whom he had never met.[83]

Although the older generation was passing on, Cadwallader and Alice had a host of children who formed a new, American generation of the Colden family.

NOTES

1. CC to JA, December 6, 1729, James Alexander Papers, box 2, f. 7, NYHS.

2. CC to JA, [1736], RP, vol. 2, 89; Eben Moglen, "Considering *Zenger*: Partisan Politics and the Legal Profession in Provincial New York," *Columbia Law Review* 94, no. 5 (1994): 1523; Stephen Botein, ed., *"'Mr. Zenger's Malice and Falshood': Six Issues of the New-York Weekly Journal, 1733–34"* (Worcester, MA: American Antiquarian Society, 1985), 48.

3. Frederick B. Tolles, *Meeting House and Counting House: The Quaker Merchants of Colonial Philadelphia, 1682–1763* (Chapel Hill: University of North Carolina Press, 1948), 194; Stephen Botein, "Cicero as Role Model for Early American Lawyers: A Case Study in Classical 'Influence,'" *Classical Journal* 73, no. 4 (1978): 314–15.

4. CC to JA, [1736], RP, vol. 2, 89; CC to JA, May 25, 1736, RP, vol. 2, 183.

5. CC to JA, [1736], RP, vol. 2, 89; CC to JA, May 25, 1736, RP, vol. 2, 183.

6. When CC's papers were still in his grandson's hands, a copy of CC's translation and introduction was still among them. But the work is not in the papers held by the NYHS. Apparently, the papers were divided among relatives after Cadwallader D. Colden's death and before the deposit of the papers there. The Cicero work and some other important items may still exist in some private collection. See C. D. Colden to Dr. Mitchell, September 25, 1809, in Cadwallader D. Colden, "For the Port Folio," *Port Folio*, n.s., 3rd ser., 3 (January 1810): 33–34.

7. "Protestation of Rip Van Dam, Esq.," March 11, 1736, PRO *Cal.*, vol. 42, 168–70.

8. "Protestation of Rip Van Dam, Esq.," March 11, 1736, PRO *Cal.*, vol. 42, 168–70; George Clarke, proclamation of March 10, 1736, PRO *Cal.*, vol. 42, 168.

9. Clarke to Council of Trade, October 7, 1736, PRO *Cal.*, vol. 42, 296.

10. JA, *Whereas on the 13th day of this Instant March*, March 24, 1735/6, Evans no. 3980.

11. CC to E. Hill, July 12, 1736, *CP*, vol. 8, 242–43.

12. Clarke to Popple, October 7, 1736, PRO *Cal.*, vol. 42, 295; JA to CC, April 30, 1736, *CP*, vol. 2, 148–49; Moglen, "Considering *Zenger*," 1521.

13. CC, "Cadwallader Colden's History of William Cosby's Administration as Governor of the Province of New York and of Lieutenant-Governor George Clarke's Administration Through 1737," in *The Letters and Papers of Cadwallader Colden* (New York: New York Historical Society, 1937), vol. 9, 348–50.

14. CC, "Cadwallader Colden's History of William Cosby's Administration," 348–50; CC to Duke of Bedford, November 22, 1748, *NYCD*, vol. 6, 469; CC to JA, April 6, 1736, RP, vol. 2, 89; CC to JA, May 25, 1736, RP, vol. 2, 183.

15. Clarke to Popple, June 18, 1736, *NYCD*, vol. 6, 67; Clarke to Popple, October 7, 1736, PRO *Cal.*, vol. 42, 295.

16. CC to Bedford, November 22, 1748, *NYCD*, vol. 6, 469; CC, "Cadwallader Colden's History of William Cosby's Administration," 347; William Smith, Jr., *The History of the Province of New York*, ed. Michael Kammen (Cambridge, MA: Belknap Press of Harvard University Press, 1972), vol. 2, 28–29.

17. Clarke to Popple, October 7, 1736, PRO *Cal.*, vol. 42, 295; Clarke to Council of Trade, October 7, 1736, PRO *Cal.*, vol. 42, 298; Joseph Henry Smith and Leo Hershkowitz, "Courts of Equity in the Province of New York: The Cosby Controversy, 1732–1736," *American Journal of Legal History* 16, no. 1 (1972): 47.

18. CC, "Cadwallader Colden's History of William Cosby's Administration," 348–50, 353–54; Council of Trade to king, April 14, 1738, *PRO Cal.*, vol. 44, 66; Patricia U. Bonomi, *A Factious People: Politics and Society in Colonial New* York (New York: Columbia University Press, 1971), 132–33; Edith M. Fox, *Land Speculation in the Mohawk Country* (Ithaca, NY: Cornell University Press, 1949), 5–6; Smith and Hershkowitz, "Courts of Equity," 48.

19. Horsmanden to CC, *CP*, vol. 2, 164–65; William Sharpas to CC, December 24, 1736, *CP*, vol. 2, 166.

20. John Alsop to CC, December 12, 1736, *CP*, vol. 2, 160; CC, "A Letter about Governors," in *The Letters and Papers of Cadwallader Colden* (New York: New York Historical Society, 1937), vol. 9, 241–42.

21. Clarke to CC, May 10, 1736, *CP*, vol. 2, 150; Georgiana C. Nammack, *Fraud, Politics, and the Dispossession of the Indians: The Iroquois Land Frontier in the Colonial Period* (Norman: University of Oklahoma Press, 1969), 25.

22. CC to Clarke, June 9, 1736, *NYCD*, vol. 6, 68–69; Clarke to Popple, June 18, 1736, *NYCD*, vol. 6, 67; Nammack, *Fraud*, 26–27.

23. CC to Lords of Trade, March 1, 1762, *NYCD*, vol. 7, 492–93; Alfred R. Hoermann, "A Savant in the Wilderness: Cadwallader Colden of New York," *New York Historical Society Quarterly* 62, no. 4 (1978): 284; Nammack, *Fraud*, 28.

24. CC to Lords of Trade, March 1, 1762, *NYCD*, vol. 7, 492–93; CC, "To the Honourable George Clarke," November 3, 1736, CO 5 / 284 / no. 77, LC transcript and *CP*, vol. 2, 158–60; Nammack, *Fraud*, 28.

25. CC to Lords of Trade, March 1, 1762, *NYCD*, vol. 7, 492–93; CC, "To the Honorable George Clarke," November 3, 1736, CO 5 / 284 / no. 77, LC transcript and *CP*, vol. 2, 158–60; Nammack, *Fraud*, 28.

26. Clarke to CC, September 13, 1736, *CP*, vol. 8, 245–46; CC to Lords of Trade, March 1, 1762, *NYCD*, vol. 7, 492–93 and *CLB*, vol. 1, 176–82; CC to Mitchell, August 17, 1751, *CP*, vol. 9, 106–7; Don R. Gerlach, *Philip Schuyler and the American Revolution in New York, 1733–1777* (Lincoln: University of Nebraska Press, 1964), 77.

27. Rev. A. Colden to CC, March 9, 1737, *CP*, vol. 2, 168–71; CC to Mrs. CC, September 27, 1737, *CP*, vol. 2, 180–81; JA to CC, April 6, 1739, *CP*, vol. 2, 194; CC to Mrs. CC, November 10, 1737, *CP*, vol. 8, 255–56.

28. CC to Mrs. CC, September 11, 17, 1737, *CP*, vol. 2, 179, vol. 8, 250.

29. Philip L. White, *The Beekmans of New York in Politics and Commerce, 1647–1877* (New York: New York Historical Society, 1956), 179–80.

30. CC to Mrs. CC, September 11, 1737, *CP*, vol. 2, 179; CC, "Cadwallader Colden's History of William Cosby's Administration," 354–55; Jill Lepore, *New York Burning: Liberty, Slavery, and Conspiracy in Eighteenth-Century Manhattan* (New York: Knopf, 2005), 139.

31. George Clarke, Jr. to Lord Delaware, June 20, 1740, George Chalmers Coll., vol.1, no. 69, NYPL; [GC to Duke of Bedford], February 24, 1749, George Clinton Papers, vol. 9, CL; Bonomi, *Factious People*, 135.

32. CC to Mrs. CC, October 10, 1737, *CP*, vol. 8, 252–53; Smith to CC, December 31, 1737, *CP*, vol. 2, 185–86; JA and Smith to Debtors of Equivalent Comp., December 31, 1737, *CP*, vol. 2, 187.

33. Joseph Murray to Equivalent Land Proprietors, December 20, 1739, *CP*, vol. 2, 203; CC to JA and Smith, January 22, 1739/40, *CP*, vol. 2, 203–4; JA and Smith to CC, December 1741, *CP*, vol. 2, 232–34; CC to JA, December 14, 1741, May 1, 1742, *CP*, vol. 2, 236–37, 256–57; CC to JA, October 20, 1740, Alexander Papers, box 3, f. 3, NYHS.

34. CC to JA, December 14, 1741, *CP*, vol. 2, 236–37; CC to Newcastle, November 26, 1741, Newcastle Papers, British Museum Additional Manuscript, 23698, f. 383, LC transcript; Clarke to CC, December 15, 1740, *CP*, vol. 2, 205–6; Commission for settling the Boundary between Massachusetts and New Hampshire, April 9, 1737, *CP*, vol. 2, 172–75; CC to Bedford, November 22, 1748, *NYCD*, vol. 6, 469.

35. Thomas Hutchinson, *The History of the Colony and Province of Massachusetts-Bay*, ed. Lawrence Shaw Mayo (London, 1768; repr. Cambridge, MA: Harvard University Press, 1936), vol. 2, 304–5; CC to Newcastle, November 26, 1741, Newcastle Papers, British Museum Additional Manuscript, 32698, f. 383, LC transcript.

36. Peter Bours to CC, December 8, 1743, *CP*, vol. 3, 40–41; CC to Bours, January 25, 1743/4, *CP*, vol. 3, 41–42; Lepore, *New York Burning*, 205–6.

37. James Cheape to CC, August 1, 1718, *CP*, vol. 1, 92–93; CC to Home, December 7, 1721, *CP*, vol. 1, 51; CC to Van Pelt, December 17, 1726, *CP*, vol. 1, 59; Mrs. CC to E. Hill, September 8, 1732, *CP*, vol. 8, 201–2; Joyce D. Goodfriend, *Before the Melting Pot: Society and Culture in Colonial New York City, 1664–1730* (Princeton, NJ: Princeton University Press, 1992), 118; Eugene R. Fingerhut, *Survivor: Cadwallader Colden II in Revolutionary America* (Washington, DC: University Press of America, 1983), 5.

38. CC, *The Interest of the Country In Laying Duties: Or A Discourse, showing how Duties on some Sorts of Merchandize may make the Province of New-York richer than it would be without them* (New York: J. Peter Zenger, 1726), 31–33.

39. CC to BF, February 13, 1754, *FP*, vol. 5, 197, 197n2.

40. Harry Bernstein, *Origins of Inter-American Interest, 1700–1812* (Philadelphia: University of Pennsylvania Press, 1945), 73; Leopold S. Launitz-Schürer, Jr., "Slave Resistance in Colonial New York: An Interpretation of Daniel Horsmanden's New York Conspiracy," *Phylon* 41, no. 2 (1980): 138, 145–46; Peter Charles Hoffer, *The Great New York Conspiracy of 1741: Slavery, Crime, and Colonial Law* (Lawrence: University Press of Kansas, 2003), 122; Lepore, *New York Burning*, 183.

41. Ferenc M. Szasz, "The New York Slave Revolt of 1741: A Re-Examination," *New York History* 48, no. 3 (1967): 226–27.

42. James Oglethorpe to Clarke, May 16, 1741, repr. Thomas J. Davis, *A Rumor of Revolt: The "Great Negro Plot" in Colonial New York* (New York: Free Press, 1985), 211–12; Serena R. Zabin, *Dangerous Economies: Status and Commerce in Imperial New York* (Philadelphia: University of Pennsylvania Press, 2009), 147–48. For the role of French priests, see Philip Ranlet, *Enemies of the Bay Colony: Puritan Massachusetts and Its Foes*, 2nd ed. (Lanham, MD: University Press of America, 2006), passim.

43. Davis, *Rumor of Revolt*, 194–95; D. N. Power, "Priesthood in Christian Tradition," in *New Catholic Encyclopedia*, 2nd ed. (New York: Detroit: Thomson/Gale, 2003), vol. 11, 700, 704.

44. J. J. O'Rourke and others, "Deacon," in *New Catholic Encyclopedia*, 2nd ed. (New York: Detroit: Thomson/Gale, 2003), vol. 4, 551; Davis, *Rumor of Revolt*, 197, 214; Hoffer, *Great New York Conspiracy*, 140.

45. Daniel A. Horsmanden, *The New York Conspiracy* (New York: James Parker, 1744; repr. ed. Thomas J. Davis, Boston: Beacon Press, 1971), 381–83; Davis, *Rumor of Revolt*, 162.

46. W. Smith, Jr., *History*, vol. 2, 52–53; Clarke to Lords of Trade, June 20, 1741, *NYCD*, vol. 6, 197–98; Serena R. Zabin, introduction to Clarke letter, in *The New York Conspiracy Trials of 1741: Daniel Horsmanden's Journal of the Proceedings with Related Documents*, by Daniel Horsmanden, ed. Zabin (Boston: Bedford/St. Martin's, 2004), 168; Horsmanden to CC, August 7, 1741, *CP*, vol. 2, 224–28.

47. Elizabeth DeLancey to CC, June 1, 1741, *CP*, vol. 8, 265; Andrew Chrystie to CC, April 10, 1742, *CP*, vol. 2, 253; Davis, *Rumor of Revolt*, 79, 135, 145, 225.

48. James Colden to CC, October 15, 1746, *CP*, vol. 8, 151–52.

49. CC to Horsmanden, July 29, 1742, *CP*, vol. 8, 288–89; CC to Clarke, August 24, 1742, *CP*, vol. 2, 266; CC to Peter Mullender, c. August 1742, *CP*, vol. 2, 265; affidavit of James McClaghry, *CP*, vol. 2, 264; Villars Roche to CC, August 25, 1742, *CP*, vol. 2, 268–70; Zabin, *Dangerous*, 148–49.

50. "Anonymous Letter to CC about the Negro Plot in New York, 1741," *CP*, vol. 8, 269–72; David C. Humphrey, "Urban Manners and Rural Morals: The Controversy Over the Location of King's College," *New York History* 54, no. 1 (1973): 12–13. CC's copy is in Colden Family Papers, box 12, NYHS.

51. CC, "Account of the Government of the New England Colonies," *CP*, vol. 9, 245–46; CC to his son, July 5, 1759, in CC, "Letter on Smith's History," New York Historical Society, *Collections* 2 (1869): 208–9; CC, "The Reading of an Elaborate Treatise on the Eye, by the Learned and Ingenious Dr. Porterfield Is the Occasion of the Following Reflections," in *The Philosophical Writings of Cadwallader Colden*, ed. Scott L. Pratt and John Ryder (Amherst, NY: Humanity Books, 2002), 140.

52. Letter to CC, 1741, *CP*, vol. 8, 269; CC to Clarke, [August 1741], *CP*, vol. 8, 272–73.

53. CC to Clarke, [August 1741], *CP*, vol. 8, 272–73; T. Wood Clarke, "The Negro Plot of 1741," *New York History* 25, no. 2 (1944): 181.

54. Clarke to CC, August 18, 1741, *CP*, vol. 8, 273–74.

55. Lepore, *New York Burning*, 206–8, 304–305n12.

56. Josiah Cotton's History of the Cotton Family, 320–24, Hyde Coll., Ms. Am. 1165, Houghton Library, Harvard University, Cambridge, MA; *New England Weekly Journal*, September 29, 1741; Clifford K. Shipton, *Biographical Sketches of Those Who Attended Harvard College in the Classes 1722–1725* (Boston: Massachusetts Historical Society, 1945), vol. 7, 50–56.

57. The slaves did not get top billing until an edition of 1810. Horsmanden to CC, August 7, 1741, *CP*, vol. 2, 224–28; CC to Horsmanden, July 29, 1742, *CP*, vol. 8, 288–89; Horsmanden, *New York Conspiracy*, xxi, xxx–xxxi.

58. Horsmanden, *New York Conspiracy*, 426.

59. William Byrd, *The London Diary (1717–1721) and Other Writings*, eds. Louis B. Wright and Marion Tinling (New York: Oxford University Press, 1958), 112, 140, 156, 206, 289; Pierre Marambaud, *William Byrd of Westover, 1674–1744* (Charlottesville: University Press of Virginia, 1971), 67. The tone of Lepore's book suggests she tried to strengthen the

case for reparations for slavery, which she worked into her book. See Lepore, *New York Burning*, 18–21, 230.

60. W. Smith, Jr., *History*, vol. 2, 101; Perry to CC, December 27, 1731, *CP*, vol. 2, 47; Horsmanden to CC, August 27, 1734, *CP*, vol. 2, 109–10; Cosby to Newcastle, December 18, 1732, *NYCD*, vol. 5, 940; Alice Mapelsden Keys, *Cadwallader Colden: A Representative Eighteenth-Century Official* (New York: Columbia University Press, 1906; repr. New York: AMS Press, 1967), 124; George William Edwards, *New York as an Eighteenth Century Municipality, 1731–1776*. (New York: Columbia University Press, 1917; repr. New York: AMS Press, 1968), 25–26.

61. Hoffer, *Great New York Conspiracy*, 175.

62. Eric W. Plaag, "New York's 1741 Slave Conspiracy in a Climate of Fear and Anxiety," *New York History* 84, no. 3 (2003): 275–76; Jill Lepore, "How Longfellow Woke the Dead," *American Scholar* 80, no. 2 (2011): 43; Ranlet, *Enemies*, 104.

63. Clarke to CC, August 18, 1741, *CP*, vol. 8, 273–74.

64. Collinson to CC, March 5, 1740/1, March 7, 1741/2, *CP*, vol. 2, 207–8, 245–47; CC to Collinson, [May?] 1741, April 9, May 1742, *CP*, vol. 2, 210–11, 250–51, 257–61; Lawrence C. Wroth, *An American Bookshelf, 1755* (London: Oxford University Press, 1934; repr. New York: Arno Press, New York Times, 1969), 91–92.

65. CC to Collinson, April 9, 1742, December 1743, *CP*, vol. 2, 250–51, vol. 3, 43–45.

66. CC to Collinson, April 9, 1742, December 1743, *CP*, vol. 2, 250–51, vol. 3, 43–45.; CC to Collinson, n. d. [1743], *CP*, vol. 3, 12–13.

67. CC to Collinson, May 1742, *CP*, vol. 2, 257–61.

68. CC to Collinson, May 1742, *CP*, vol. 2, 257–61; CC to Mitchell, August 17, 1751, *CP*, vol. 9, 103–6; Bonomi, *Factious People*, 303–4.

69. CC to Collinson, April 9, May 1742, *CP*, vol. 2, 250–51, 257–61; Collinson to CC, September 3, 1742, *CP*, vol. 2, 271–72.

70. CC and others, *Governor and Company of Connecticut, and Moheagan Indians, By Their Guardians, Certified Copy of Book of Proceedings Before Commissions of Review, MDCCXLIII* (London: W. and J. Richardson, 1769), 137, 140, 143; CC to Bartram, c. 1743, *CP*, vol. 3, 25–26; Joseph Henry Smith, *Appeals to the Privy Council from the American Plantations* (New York: Columbia University Press, 1950), 434–35; Ranlet, *Enemies*, 197–98.

71. Collinson to CC, March 27, 1746/7, June 1, 1747, *CP*, vol. 3, 367–69, 394; Thomas Osborne to CC, June 12, 1747, *CP*, vol. 3, 402–3.

72. BF to CC, October 1, 1747, *FP*, vol. 3, 178–79; Wroth, *American Bookshelf*, 92.

73. Collinson to CC, March 27, 1746/7, *CP*, vol. 3, 367–69; Osborne to CC, June 12, 1747, *CP*, vol. 3, 402–3; CC to Mitchell, July 6, 1749, *CP*, vol. 9, 18–19; CC, *The History of the Five Indian Nations of Canada. . .* 2nd ed. (London: John Whiston, 1747), title page, iii; Wroth, *American Bookshelf*, 92. Oglethorpe and Colden supported different sides during the American Revolution. See William Smith, Jr., *The Diary and Selected Papers of Chief Justice William Smith, 1784–1793*, ed. L. F. S. Upton (Toronto: Champlain Society, 1963), vol. 1, 38.

74. Osborne to CC, June 6, 1748, *CP*, vol. 4, 64–65; CC to Osborne, [1748?], *CP*, vol. 7, 344; Alfred R. Hoermann, *Cadwallader Colden: A Figure of the American Enlightenment* (Westport, CT: Greenwood Press, 2002), 166.

75. Alexander Colden to CC, September 5, 1754, *CP*, vol. 4, 464.

76. David Chrystie to CC, January 30, 1720, *CP*, vol. 1, 108; James Chrystie to CC, September 9, 1720, *CP*, vol. 8, 55.

77. Rev. A. Colden to CC, February 19, 1725, January 24, 1726, March 9, 1737, *CP*, vol. 1, 184–88; vol. 8, 113; vol. 2, 168–71.

78. David Chrystie to Mrs. CC, December 18, 1723, *CP*, vol. 8, 87–88.

79. James Colden to CC, September 22, 1724, June 14, 1743, *CP*, vol. 8, 99, 145–46; James Chrystie to CC and Mrs. CC, February 9, 1730, *CP*, vol. 8, 128–30; James Chrystie to CC, March 1, 1731, *CP*, vol. 8, 131–32; Andrew Chrystie to CC, July 12, 1725, *CP*, vol. 1, 177–80.

80. Rev. A. Colden to CC, March 9, 1737, *CP*, vol. 2, 168–71; David Chrystie to CC, January 30, 1720/1, *CP*, vol. 1, 108.

81. James Colden to CC, August 23, 1736, March 23, 1739, *CP*, vol. 8, 136–37; vol. 2, 191–92; James Chrystie to Mrs. CC, September 1, 1738, *CP*, vol. 8, 138, 140–41.

82. Rev. A. Colden to CC, October 13, 1737, *CP*, vol. 2, 181–85; James Colden to CC, July 7, 1739, June 14, 1743, *CP*, vol. 8, 142–46.

83. George Robson, *An Elegy Upon The Death of that Godly, Pious and Painful Minister, Mr. Alexander Colden Late Minister of the Gospel at Oxname* (Edinburgh: Thomas Lumisden and John Robertson for the Author, 1739), iii, 22–23; C. Colden to _____, April 27, 1796, in Samuel W. Eager, *An Outline History of Orange County* (Newburgh, NY: S. T. Callahan, 1846–1847), 248.

Chapter Seven

Jennie and Davie

Cadwallader and Alice Colden's "Deare Little family," as it was called in 1727, would grow into a brood of eight who survived infancy. Of those eight, two of them—Jane, nicknamed Jennie, and the youngest, David—followed their father in making a significant impact on science. The education of the Colden children, a matter of great importance to both parents, demonstrates "the best attributes of the favored home of the period."[1]

In 1729 Cadwallader Colden sharply criticized education in New York. He complained to James Alexander, "the advancing of Learning . . . has been hitherto more neglected in this Province than any where else in the King's Dominions." Education was essential Colden thought because "Religion" and "Liberty of Learning go hand in hand so that Slavery and Superstition could never be introduced absolutely when Learning flourished."[2]

The Coldengham area had nothing resembling a public school when the Colden children were young. Though at first Colden feared they would not receive a proper education, he soon realized that was not the case. In fact, he mistrusted "the common methods of teaching" in such schools which served "only to fill young people's heads with useless notions and prejudices, which unfit them for the acquiring of real and useful knowledge." Education was even worse where Catholic priests controlled the schools, Colden declared: "They know well how easy it is to instill strong prejudices into young minds, and of what force these prejudices are in the whole course of life."[3]

Instead, the Coldens taught their own children. According to Brooke Hindle, "The vigorous personality of their father was recognizably stamped upon them but so was the warmth and practicality of their mother." Overall, individuality was stressed along with "unusual concentration upon the values cultivated within the home." The children's education would be boosted too by the many, varied visitors Colden welcomed to his retreat. Talking with intelligent people broadened the children's knowledge far more than would be the case by depending on books alone.[4]

Both Coldens schooled their offspring. Although Scottish women did not receive much formal education, Alice's father, a teacher, must have given his daughter a thorough education. Alice taught her children all the basics while her husband handled the more advanced subjects. Cad, who showed little interest in anything except farming, received his education mostly from his mother and his brother Alexander—Sandie—probably did also. In contrast, their younger brother David spent much time with his father.[5]

Colden tried to steer his sons into complementary occupations thus lessening sibling rivalry. As he suggested to his daughter Elizabeth—Bettie—about her own family: "You should endeavour to educate your children to different kinds of business, for . . . they will thereby become more useful to each other by promoting their mutual benefits and advantage."[6]

Because Bettie was not very intellectual herself, her father recommended that her children study under a schoolmaster who would curtail "any unruly appetites" his grandchildren might have. One of them, though, Peter DeLancey appeared to him to have intellectual capacities and volunteered to help him "in making a further progress than is commonly made in this country."[7]

Colden intended to be a factor in his grandchildren's lives long after his death by writing instructional essays for them. He had done the same for his children years before.[8] His accumulated knowledge had been gained by decades of child rearing.

It all started with Sandie and Bettie, the oldest. Their parents were helped by the presence of a relative in America. Although Elizabeth Hill was cantankerous, especially in trade, she was fond of her only family within reach and rewarded the children with gifts to reinforce good behavior. When, in 1726, six year old Bettie sent her aunt a pincushion she had made herself, Hill showed it off to her friends, all of whom were impressed. Pleased by the little girl's effort, she sent her a guinea, a huge sum of money for a child, and directed her mother to use it for things Bettie wanted. "I hope she will be a help to her Mother in her sewing," the generous aunt wrote. In 1731 Bettie thanked her aunt for still another cash gift "for it has made me so rich I know not what to do with all my money."[9]

By all appearances, the Coldens were indulgent parents but took every opportunity to educate their children. When little Sandie and Bettie saw their Dutch friends playing at being merchants, they wanted to play too. Colden wrote all the way to London for suitable goods. Knowing that Mrs. Alexander had a store, Colden thought that this play would introduce both of his children to potential livings. Sandie would be drawn to trade but his sister was not.[10]

Eventually, Sandie and Bettie needed to have their education broadened somewhat, requiring their exposure to the city which would "rub off some of that country awkwardness." They would be learning penmanship and how to dance, vital knowledge for young people wanting to advance in society. In 1732, when Sandie was 16 years old and his sister 12 years, they were sent to New York City for a few months. Sandie stayed in his aunt's New York house, while his sister boarded with people of "good character." But their aunt did not approve of the expense. Hill, a Quaker, had also been displeased when a minister had tutored Sandie in Latin. To a Quaker, learning Latin suggested a career as a priest. Quickly, Colden explained to his aunt the benefits of dancing and that Latin remained essential for a boy to enter practically all occupations, not just the Church of England, which seems to have calmed her.[11]

The expedition of the Colden children to the big city did not end the way their father had hoped. In November 1732 Sandie had booked passage for himself and his sister onboard a sloop and stored their baggage including their winter clothes. Before the scheduled departure, with the boat's master and the Coldens not yet aboard, three passengers broke into his liquor supply, got very drunk, and sailed the sloop to their destination.[12]

When Colden met the boat at the landing, he was shocked to discover that his children were not aboard but their bags were. He panicked, fearing what might happen now that his children were exposed to the cold and blamed "the Insolence of the Mob." Their mother, even more frightened, became sick with fear. Colden rushed off a letter to James Alexander—"you know what it is to be a Parent"—he told his friend and asked him for news of the children. Needless to say, Sandie and Bettie survived their curious adventure.[13]

Meanwhile, Aunt Elizabeth had been suffering "the infirmities of old age" and the Coldens were too far away to help. Since the 1720s they had been trying to convince her to live with them; the children were just as eager as their parents to have their aunt with them. Hill kept refusing until 1737 when she at last gave in, to the delight of the Colden children. With his aunt increasingly frail, her nephew rejoiced in 1737 when she was well enough "to walk over the Farm" and see that her family had "not been idle and lazy whatever else she may dislike." They did "every thing to make her present state of Life agreeable to her." She resided at Coldengham until May 1744 when she died just as her nephew was about to turn her in her bed. She had requested a plain Quaker burial so Colden conferred with the two Quakers in the area and followed their suggestions. Hill was buried in the Coldengham orchard where, Colden said, "I hope to be laid myself."[14]

Aunt Elizabeth surely had been pleased at Bettie's wedding. In 1732 Colden had alerted his aunt that Bettie, while in New York City, "is taken much notice of by the best families in the Town." Her father could not have been more astute. Shortly before her eighteenth birthday, in 1738 she married Peter DeLancey, the brother of the chief justice. While it has the air of a dynastic marriage—Colden called it "an alliance"—nothing suggests that it had been arranged by the families. Her father certainly hoped it would boost his family's status. In 1741 in Rhode Island, the pleased father observed: "The Chief Justice is here he behaves to me like a kind relation." But it did not last. Although a few years later the brothers had a bitter fight over their inheritance, Colden and James DeLancey stayed friendly until New York's politics exploded in 1746.[15]

Reflecting on the marriage after Bettie's death, her brother Cad remarked that she "soon became the mother of a fine family of sons and daughters; and, as a wife and mother, was held in high esteem by all her acquaintance, though she was not very happy in a husband." Cad also said Peter DeLancey had died "not much regretted," perhaps because of a DeLancey family trait—a "violent overbearing temper" according to one DeLancey enemy. Both the chief justice and Peter had vile tempers. The same enemy listed Peter as one of the DeLancey "Bullies" who intimidated voters in a 1750 election. Yet nothing suggests that Peter DeLancey was anything but a dutiful son-in-law to Cadwallader Colden, who had advised his daughter in 1737 to always provide "comfort" to her husband and to defend his "honour" at all times. Her father urged Bettie to seek the counsel of her mother-in-law, who knew how to deal with the male DeLanceys.[16]

What did Bettie think of her husband? In the 1740s she was upset that her newborn son had not been named Cadwallader "after my own Father." She confessed to him that "I had no vote in it." Soon, she was bitterly angry that her new daughter had not been christened Alice. "I promised obedience," she reminded her parents. None of her sons bore the name Cadwallader, but in 1746 there would be an Alice DeLancey, whom everyone called Aly.[17]

One wonders what Bettie thought when Peter DeLancey was the only family member who did not attend her aunt's funeral, although her father excused DeLancey's absence as he was too far away to send for. Except for these points, there is no evidence that it was an unhappy marriage though letters with such information would have been prime candidates for destruction by descendents. Whatever the truth, Bettie was a dutiful wife to her husband.[18]

As for Sandie, he became a successful merchant and greatly helped in the development of Newburgh into a town, convincing many people to settle there. He would assist his father with his surveying duties and succeeded him as surveyor-general. Without a doubt, his father assumed that his eldest son would advance to his political position in the colony of New York.[19]

Sibling rivalry seemed to be a dominant factor with Sandie's brother Cad. The more the eldest succeeded, whether with his Newburgh store and mill and even with ferries, Cad simmered. His father gave him 500 acres of the Coldengham estate, but that was not enough. The first son likely would have received the bulk of the land upon his father's death. Worst of all, Cad believed his father preferred Sandie, which might have been the case. Bettie alerted her mother about Cad's whining.[20]

One of Benjamin Franklin's humorous essays, the "Advice to a Young Man on the Choice of a Mistress," written about 1745, was intended for Cad, then in his early twenties. Franklin's recommendation of an older woman as a mistress, with a basket over her head if necessary, did not sway Cad who married soon after.[21]

Oddly enough, Bettie revealed some early problems in Cad's marriage. He grumbled that his father-in-law had not provided the sort of financial support he had expected. However rocky the marriage might have been at the start, it became solid and lasted for many decades. Although Cad held local offices in Ulster and was a pillar of the Anglican church in Newburgh, his only attempt for a seat in the Assembly failed in 1768.[22]

The least known of Cadwallader Colden's sons is John, born in the midst of the scarlet fever outbreak of 1729, hardly a fortuitous entrance into the world. In 1744, when John was 15 years old, his father took him to the city and was pleased to inform John's mother that he was "very useful to me and more careful than expected."[23]

John had talent, and in 1748 his father saw him as a good candidate to be a bookseller. But Governor George Clinton, wishing to reward his faithful advisor, appointed his son John Colden in that year as the keeper of military stores in the city. Then the death of the Albany clerk created an interesting opening for John. Once again, in 1749, Clinton, acting on his own suggestion, rewarded the father again by appointing John to the position, although Cadwallader Colden was to receive the salary until his death—which he had to have believed was not all that far off.[24]

In late March 1749 John Colden left for Albany where he knew no one. His father expected John to need his advice, which he offered freely, especially regarding strengthening contacts with individuals with links to nobles, who could help further his prospects (just as nobles had helped his father's career). John, no doubt missing his distant family, must have been disappointed when, in late December 1749, he learned from his father that his mother was ill and "I am afraid of the Cold" so "you cannot expect to see either of us at Albany."[25]

One of the friends John made at Albany, the Rev. John Ogilvie, the town's Church of England minister, also preached to the Mohawks. In August 1750 John traveled with the minister on one of his trips to the Indians. On August 16 Ogilvie recorded in his diary that "Mr. Colden is taken ill with a Fever and sore Throat." Two days later John Colden "departed this Life with Hopes full of Immortality" at the age of 21 years.[26]

Ogilvie notified John's shocked parents of his sudden death, emphasizing comforting thoughts of everlasting life. As Alice told her daughter, she was consoled by John's "Resignation to the will of God in his sickness." When

John became ill, he "seemed" to realize his fate. "At the last moment he was heard by a Loud Ejaculation to the Almighty to desire him to receive his departing Spirit." Rev. Ogilvie even came to visit her giving her "the greatest comfort and satisfaction that could be desired in my present distress."[27]

Bettie, shocked by her brother's death, quickly became concerned by her mother's "overflow of Tears." She warned her distressed father: "I am very fearful that this affliction will affect my Mother's health." A mother herself, Bettie took action to distract Alice's attention by first emphasizing the saintly aspects of John's death. Then she told her mother about her namesake granddaughter, little Aly DeLancey, who had come down with a slight illness worrying her grandmother still more. "What would her dear grandmama say if she knew she was so sick" the child observed. "I believe," Bettie wrote to her mother, "she has as sensible a tenderness for you as one of her years can have and I hope will never be otherwise."[28]

Nor did Bettie neglect her father who was in the city. Cadwallader Colden visited the DeLancey homestead twice and told her "he felt better then he had done in Town." Both of her parents survived the ordeal of John's death. Although Elizabeth was neither an intellectual nor a beauty, she had an inner strength that proved valuable in this and in future crises.[29]

Much less is known about two of Bettie's younger sisters, Alice and Catherine. Alice, born in 1725, married a widower, William Willett, who, though "almost sixty" on their wedding day, would survive her. They had four children.[30]

Catherine, the youngest daughter, seems to have been the liveliest. Sandie teased her about "her Wild Giddy humours." Her father may have disapproved somewhat as he complained about "airs of levity" in women. After her death at 31 years old in 1763, an obituary praised her "wholly inoffensive" life and called her "eminently possessed of every social, every domestic virtue."[31]

In sharp contrast, Alice and Catherine's older sister Jane is the most famous of the Colden siblings. Usually called Jennie within the family or sometimes Jean, she was the next oldest daughter after Bettie. Only a little girl when the family moved to Coldengham, she had plenty of space to play amid all the undisturbed plants and trees on the estate. Her father, as part of his educational efforts with his children, assigned them "research," which sometimes involved local plants. He noticed as well that Jane took to reading and was far more serious about learning than her sisters.[32]

Given Jennie's demeanor, her father thought that botany would be perfect for her. "As the Ladies take a particular pleasure in flowers and Gardens," he wrote to his daughter, "and have a natural curiosity about plants," sorting out one plant from another and figuring out its name would "be an agreeable amusement" and useful. Elaborating on his thinking later to Gronovius, Colden also considered that "the pleasure" women "take in the beauty and variety of dress seems to fit them" for botanical studies. What could be more beautiful than the world of plants? The rest of Colden's longish letter to Jane saw him attempt to inform her about everything she needed to know about botany.[33]

Only Cadwallader Colden would have attempted to sum up an entire science in one letter, but his basic strategy was sound. Treatises on botany were almost always done in Latin; women did not learn classical languages. What had been written in English was inadequate. So he summarized the Linnaean system in basic English and disposed of as much of the scientific jargon—which made understanding the subject "so tiresome and disagreeable"—and Jane was absorbed by "natural History." "She eagerly swallowed the bait" her happy father told Dr. Fothergill. With her father's explanation at hand, she "now understands in some degree Linnaeus's characters" without having learned Latin.[34]

Once Jennie started investigating plants, it became a passion. She even learned some Latin. "You cannot imagine with what pleasure she has passed many an hour which otherwise might have been very dull and heavy" in the countryside. Her father bought books with illustrations of plants to broaden her knowledge. Inspired by his daughter, Colden hoped that other women, endowed with "their natural curiosity and the accuracy and quickness of their Sensations," would take up botany in their spare time. With numerous undiscovered plants in America, there was plenty of work to be done.[35]

By 1755 Jane Colden had amassed hundreds of plant descriptions and her proud father sent examples of her work to his botanical colleagues. Jane added that she hoped any errors in her work would be corrected. Linnaeus was pleased with what he saw. So were Gronovius, Collinson, John Bartram, John Ellis, and Alexander Garden. Collinson predicted that "the More She practices the more She Will Improve."[36]

Garden, unmarried, became so enthusiastic that he got a bit carried away. Jane was only a few years older than him and he, "innocently," wrote "some expressions that insensibly dropt from my pen as archetypes of what my heart dictated," which upset both Jane and her father. What was so disturbing to them in the proper eighteenth century is not known (Garden had called her "lovely" in a surviving letter), but Garden had to have hoped he had found a wife. Cadwallader Colden had cautioned young ladies to raise "a secure guard against any unbecoming liberties which men may take," and he gave Garden the benefit of his "observations on the Sexes." The South Carolinian was properly chastened and the incident soon forgotten.[37]

What was behind such enthusiasm? Granted, none of these botanists had ever heard of a woman working with Linnaeus's classification scheme, but there has to be more behind the excitement. Nor were Jane's drawings particularly good as art. She had had no skilled artist available to teach her the fine points of drawing, and the reproductions of leaves are probably tracings. In other cases, the plant was covered with ink and then pressed onto paper.[38]

The secret behind Jennie Colden's acclaim can be discovered in her "Cheese Book," a record she kept detailing her campaign to make good cheese. Starting with her sister Alice's cheese recipe, Jennie went to work, adding here, changing there, while carefully recording what went right or wrong. The result was, as a happy consumer noted, that "She makes the best cheese I ever ate in America." She sold 348 pounds of cheese in just one year. Jane Colden was a perfectionist.[39]

Jennie's predilection to seek perfection produced superb botanical work. She recorded everything she saw—her descriptions were "extremely accurate," Garden informed her father. Her ecstatic father himself noted that "she is more curious and accurate than I could have been her descriptions are more perfect and I believe few or none exceed them." As one scholar, Elizabeth C. Hall, has commented, "one marvels at her ability to observe and evaluate the minutest details of the plant that she is studying." That fact is what most impressed her botanical colleagues, not her sex.[40]

Despite all the gushing praise Jennie received from her fellow botanists, she still felt like an amateur, especially considering the decades many of her colleagues had spent in the field. Responding to a Scot who wanted to publish her work that he had received, she wrote him that "I must beg as a favour of you, that you will not make any thing publick from me, till (at least) I have gained more knowledge of Plants, and then perhaps I shall be able to make some amendments to my Descriptions." After all, Jane realized she had been investigating plants for only a few years. Perfectionists tend to think that their work is never perfect enough. Her request was denied and her plant description was published in Edinburgh.[41]

Jane produced a hefty "Botanic Manuscript" incorporating 340 plant descriptions, but only a chunk of the manuscript survived. What remained would only be printed in the twentieth century. But the surviving examples of her "style" display "a delightful freshness and spontaneity" which made her a better botanist than her father.[42]

In March 1759 Jennie married Dr. William Farquhar, called by Cad "an old widower, but a very worthy good Scotchman." Garden transmitted his congratulations. Farquhar, one of the "top" doctors in New York, also happened to be the nephew of a major intellectual figure in Scotland, Dr. William Porterfield. Farquhar seems to have been a younger version of her father. The newlyweds loved each other very much. A few months after the wedding, however, Jane seemed too serious for Dr. Farquhar. To lighten her mood, he lifted her up, then tried turning her, badly wrenching his thigh in the process. Her husband's pain brought forth a flood of affection from Jennie.[43]

Cadwallader Colden believed it likely that Jane's marriage would stop "her botanical amusements." Being a wife in the eighteenth century did entail many time consuming duties, but Jane, by the time of her marriage, had largely taken over the domestic management of Coldengham from her mother while also busily examining plant life.[44]

What Colden probably thought to be a major impediment for Jane was her moving from Coldengham, where the natural setting still was largely intact, to the site of Farquhar's practice, New York City. Its native plant life had been destroyed long before. Much of the rest of the island was farmland, also a disaster for native plants. If, as has been suggested, the Farquhars had a home on Long Island, the story remained the same. The original environment of the westernmost part of the island had been plowed over before Jennie had been born.[45]

One suspects that Mrs. Farquhar would have returned to botany, which she enjoyed so much, given time. Yet it was not to be. Jane had married in her thirties and had given birth to her first child in her forties, a risky situation for any woman and especially so in the eighteenth century. In 1766 both she and the baby died.[46]

Although Jane has been renowned for scientific proclivities, the significant role played by her youngest sibling, David, has been largely forgotten. Davie, born in 1733, appeared to be a typical boy, thin, "lively," and "well shaped" until about 1747 when he was a young teenager. Suddenly, his life changed dramatically. For no apparent reason, his body slowly deformed. Within a few years his spine took "the shape of an S, one Shoulder became prominent and the other depressed." Because of his twisted backbone, his chest cavity became constricted and restricted the movement of his lungs, lessening his air supply. Often hit by chest pains, he coughed frequently and wheezed constantly. Any exercise caused shortness of breath. His blood circulation was so poor that either of his hands might appear "to all appearance to be dead." He could only tolerate a dosage of medicine suitable for a young child.[47]

For the rest of Davie's life, he had to confront the difficulties caused by his deformed body. When he looked healthier than usual, it was a source of comment in the family. His puzzled father thought his son had been hit by some sort of disease which could have been cured, if he could have only figured out what it was. He discovered that other doctors disagreed with his diagnosis. The condition seemed to have been fairly common, Dr. Colden revealed, for "many instances of the like kind with my Son's have happened."[48]

Davie's precarious health forced his father to re-think his long held view about inoculation for smallpox. Puritan minister Cotton Mather called inoculation "a New and a Right Method of treating the Small-Pox" but many doctors dissented including Colden and his friend in Boston, Dr. William Douglass.[49]

As a young doctor in Philadelphia, Colden received a personal lesson in dealing with smallpox. Shortly after Sandie's birth in 1716, the disease hit the city and the Colden home. All the slaves became infected as did Sandie. Because Alice was still weak from the delivery, Dr. Colden hired a cook "by the hour" to feed the household. Meanwhile, his services were needed so much "that I was fatigued off my legs and seldom had one night without being called up." He first suggested bleeding to deal with the malady but, realizing most people were reluctant to try that, he fell back on his "cool regimen," a drug to combat fever, and drinking of some liquor. Spermaceti oil cut down facial scarring. He did not lose a single patient to smallpox.[50]

What happened in Boston during 1721 is far more famous. A smallpox epidemic caused Mather, Benjamin Colman and other ministers to call for inoculation which Dr. Douglass opposed. He knew very well about the scientific literature on inoculation that the "credulous vain" Mather had seen and that the procedure had been gaining popularity in Britain. Douglass suspected that Mather's real motive was to get published by the Royal Society again; the minister had grumbled that his submissions had been rejected. Despite the poor recording of the causes of death during the epidemic, Douglass "candidly" informed his fellow doctor, who had opposed inoculation, that it killed fewer people than "the natural way" of getting smallpox did. Douglass took up inoculation himself in due course.[51]

During 1731–1732 inoculation had spread throughout New York, especially in Westchester County, with the Dutch on Long Island, and in New Jersey as well. After James Alexander lost a son to smallpox, he became a strong advocate of inoculation, impressed by its overwhelming success. Alexander urged Colden to inoculate his family because of its proven record. Bettie would be inoculated in 1739, but that was after her marriage. Although Alexander kept trying to convince Dr. Colden of its worth, he still did not favor the technique (and his brother James in Scotland opposed it for religious reasons). In 1746 the colony's governor observed, "There is not one family in New York but what has had or has the smallpox in their houses." Despite that disaster, in 1747 inoculation was banned in New York City.[52]

Colden's aversion to inoculation had lessened by October 1753. He related to Dr. Fothergill a talk he had with some of his slaves, whom he had owned for a long time, that inoculation was standard procedure in their homeland. When smallpox appeared, the younger generation would be inoculated the same way it was done in the British domains. During the course of inoculation, the Africans abstained from meat and drank lime juice mixed with water. Colden commented that "This, perhaps, may be worth observation." He was amazed by this information, new to him, and complained that "we seldom converse with our negroes, especially with those who are not born among us."[53]

In 1757 smallpox hit New York again and Sandie inoculated one of his children because of "the Success that has attended Inoculation." The inoculation succeeded. Dr. Colden now was increasingly alone in his opposition. When Davie, with his fragile health, announced that he wanted to be inoculated, his father was "uneasy." Still, he realized that his son was "in great danger" of getting smallpox, and inoculation, which was supposed to give a patient a weaker case of the disease, gave him a better chance of survival than "the natural way." He gave in. Davie was no longer a child and knew the risks. And inoculation was a risk. In 1757 Dr. Colden's friend, Dr. John Bard, had a son inoculated. He died from it.[54]

Though Colden would not do the inoculation himself, he would set the parameters of the procedure and hovered about while Davie was inoculated and quarantined. No one with his health problems had ever been inoculated before. His father forbade the use of mercury. The doctors, knowing that his father was uneasy about bleeding, decided against it. In fact, Dr. Colden had prepared his son for some time before the procedure by giving him a concoction of quinine "mixed with Rhubarb," no surprise knowing Colden. The treatment worked because Davie was in good health before the inoculation.[55]

Once the doctors inoculated Davie, they continued to rely on his father's advice. After all, he understood his son's health better than anyone. And it was a difficult case. Although Davie had no problem breathing, he came down with bizarre "visions" that disappeared when he opened his eyes. So he could not sleep. The atmosphere was kept as cool as possible. Slowly, with the ingestion of various medicines and another dose of quinine with rhubarb, Davie survived.[56]

The "ingenious" David Colden, as Franklin called him, is remarkable not only because of his battle with his crippled body or for surviving inoculation. Davie made his mark in science, specifically in electricity, a field his father could not master.[57]

In 1752 Franklin learned about David's proclivity to experiment from his father. During 1753 Davie had performed his experiments which showed Franklin's electrical ideas to be correct and a French critic wrong. An impressed Franklin wanted to have young Colden's "judiciously made" observations published right away, but Davie was reluctant. Modestly, much like Jennie, Davie thought "there is nothing new in it to deserve publishing." Disagreeing with his son, Colden sided with Franklin who had Davie's work included in one of his books published in England. An English review declared that David Colden's experiment in electricity showed the Frenchman "has related his own experiments in a very partial manner."[58]

Davie could not make a living with experiments, however. His father thought that a career in trade might work for him, but, apparently, a trial run of Davie as a merchant did not succeed. Instead, Dr. Colden trained his son to be a doctor; his chief patient would be himself. Most of the time, Davie assisted on the farm. While heavy labor was out of the question, David did a good job managing a farm. He even constructed a new style of "Drill Plough." Once again impressed, Franklin called Davie's plow "ingeniously contrived." Franklin and "a great connoisseur in such Matters" urged that it be sent to British agricultural experts for their opinions.[59]

In later years David Colden served as his father's secretary, a task at which he was very good. Of all Cadwallader Colden's sons, he seems the best candidate for a college education. (Jennie, like all women of the day, could not attend a college, which were all male.) Unlike their college-educated father, none of the Colden boys went to college, in America or Europe. The Coldens did not have the money required for a European college, and the American colleges primarily trained prospective ministers, a job that none of the younger generation of Coldens had any interest in.

Although none of Cadwallader Colden's sons attended a college, that did not mean that he had no opinions on what a college should be like. Unlike most New Yorkers, he did and freely expressed them. According to one of his friends, he had it "very much at heart" though it was also true that "He had a superlative Contempt for American Learning," at least some of it.[60]

Harvard and Yale did seem useless to Colden. As he wrote, those institutions "were Established by the Independents"—that is, Puritans—and "they are under all the Restrictions and Prejudices which arise from the Narrow Principles of men bigotted to those Sects." Not surprisingly, "none of their Masters have gained any Reputation in any one Branch of Learning."[61]

Regarding Virginia's William and Mary, governed by Anglicans, Colden commented: "I Suppose" it was "on a better Foundation." It still was lacking. Why that college "has in no Shape Distinguished it Self I know not." But the climate of Virginia was so sickly, parents in other colonies feared "Sending their Children Thither."[62]

On the other hand, New York would be a perfect site for a college. It was the wealthiest colony in the north, but little attention had been paid there to education. Without good education, both religion and "Civil Government" were endangered. New York's Assembly, Colden knew, because of "the low method of thinking which prevails among the Members could never be induced to give any proper Incouragement for This Purpose." The Assembly leaders' "Selfish Views" and "the Narrow thoughts of all of them" would doom any college created by them.[63]

The best place in New York for a college, Colden believed, was near his abode, the town of Newburgh, about halfway between Albany and New York City, situated on the river that served as the colony's main thoroughfare. However, the area was populated by a batch of different nationalities and faiths, with few ministers, an essential part of Colden's plan. He hoped to interest Anglican charities such as the Society for the Propagation of the Gospel to support and fund his college. Creating an important Church of England institution inevitably would spread Anglican doctrines and influence throughout central New York. This "Seminary for Learning" would be a far better investment than pumping more money into the already wealthy Trinity Church in New York City.[64]

Colden, no doubt, thought of the intellectual excitement a college would create in his area, a backwater except for Coldengham. But he had another argument for Church of England officials. New York, a royal colony, was more dependent on the king than, say, a nearby proprietary colony such as Pennsylvania. New York's good climate would attract students from other areas.[65]

The best argument of all, however, was some 500 acres of land that lay unused "within the Bounds" of Newburgh's Anglican church. This land, granted to a long-gone Lutheran congregation, had already been given by the present owners to the Church of England for its Newburgh mission. The land would serve as a very nice campus for this college.[66]

Colden's hopes for what this college would be like can be seen in his comments about education with Franklin. Colden insisted it should teach agriculture, which he had instructed his own sons in, an occupation that could "be made as much a Science as any of those that are not purely Mathematical." Farming was the bedrock of a country's "Wealth and welfare" and so there should be one professor at the school in touch with the best farmers around. Instruction in farming would be another reason to pick the Newburgh site.[67]

A country site would also protect the college students from the distractions from learning that a city provided. In the countryside they would be "freed from many temptations to idleness and some worse vices that they must meet with in" an urban setting. Although students in a rural area would lack the polish gained from mixing in genteel society, the school could compensate by teaching them "good manners" suitable for gentlemen. One way to do that was to teach dancing, which Colden had made sure his children learned. Declamation and debate and even acting could all be employed to give the proper polish expected of a gentleman.[68]

One major difference between Colden's hoped for college and his own alma mater, the University of Edinburgh, would involve Latin and Greek. While part of the curriculum, not all students would have to learn them. Practically all classical literature could be read in English anyway. Students who took up trade, for example, had little need for Latin or Greek. Instead, "English Authors both in prose and verse" should be taught to demonstrate "the beauties and energy of our own language." French should also be taught, something potential merchants would find useful.[69]

In 1752 the tract in Newburgh had been formally given to the Church of England, but Trinity Church triumphed. Trinity donated land in New York City for the college and it was located there, not Newburgh. To get to King's College, as it became known, students had to pass by dens of prostitution, hardly the atmosphere Colden had hoped for. Years later, his bright grandson Peter DeLancey journeyed to London to study law, and there contracted a sexually-transmitted disease. One can guess that Cadwallader Colden was glad his sons never pursued higher education in a den of iniquity.[70]

Anglican King's College became a major political issue in New York. Presbyterians, calling the college an "unrighteous Scheme," saw it as "an Encroachment" on their "Rights and Priviledges." Although King's College admitted students who were not Anglican, it still had "Enemies in Attendance" throughout "the Continent."[71]

Cadwallader Colden had little role in these later disputes over King's College. But he would be very busy indeed during the turbulent administration of George Clinton.

NOTES

1. Mrs. Martha Heathcote to Mrs. CC, August 1727, *CP*, vol. 8, 184; Brooke Hindle, "A Colonial Governor's Family: The Coldens of Coldengham," *New York Historical Society Quarterly* 45, no. 3 (1961): 233.

2. CC to JA, May 20, 1729, RP, vol. 1, 119.

3. CC, "An Introduction to the Study of Phylosophy Wrote In America for the Use of a Young Gentleman," in *American Philosophical Addresses, 1700–1900*, ed. Joseph L. Blau (New York: Columbia University Press, 1946), 289–90, 292; CC to E. Hill, June 1, 1724, *CP*, vol. 8, 173–74; Alexander C. Flick, *History of the State of New York* (New York: Columbia University Press, 1933–1937), vol. 3, 73.

4. CC, "An Introduction to the Study of Phylosophy," 311; Hindle, "Colonial Governor's Family," 234, 238.

5. C. Colden to _____, April 27, 1796, Samuel W. Eager, *An Outline History of Orange County* (Newburgh, NY: S. T. Callahan, 1846–1847), 245; Hindle, "Colonial Governor's Family," 239, 243; Amelia Peck, "The Verplanck Room: Coldenham, New York, 1767," in *The Period Rooms in The Metropolitan Museum of Art*, ed. Peck et al. (New York: Metropolitan Museum of Art, 1996), 206.

6. CC to Elizabeth DeLancey, n. d., *CP*, vol. 4, 339–40.

7. CC to Elizabeth DeLancey, n. d., *CP*, vol. 4, 339–40.

8. CC, "An Introduction to the Study of Phylosophy," 289; CC to his children, February 29, 1739/40, *CP*, vol. 1, i–ii; Alfred R. Hoermann, *Cadwallader Colden: A Figure of the American Enlightenment* (Westport, CT: Greenwood Press, 2002), 144.

9. E. Hill to CC, October 28, 1726, *CP*, vol. 1, 193–94; E. Colden to E. Hill, June 29, 1731, *CP*, vol. 8, 199; CC to E. Hill, January 19, 1733/4, *CP*, vol. 2, 101–3.

10. CC to Falconer, May 4, 1724, *CP*, vol. 1, 51–53; Serena R. Zabin, *Dangerous Economies: Status and Commerce in Imperial New York* (Philadelphia: University of Pennsylvania Press, 2009), 32; Esther Singleton, *Social New York under the Georges, 1714–1776* (New York: D. Appleton, 1902), 76.

11. CC to E. Hill, October 23, 1732, *CP*, vol. 2, 84–85; Mrs. CC to E. Hill, September 8, 1732, *CP*, vol. 8, 201–2.

12. CC to JA, November 22, 1732, RP, vol. 1, 157.

13. CC to JA, November 22, 1732, RP, vol. 1, 157.

14. CC to E. Hill, October 23, 1732, *CP*, vol. 2, 84–85; E. Hill to CC, n. d., *CP*, vol. 2, 92–93; CC to Mrs. CC, September 27, 1737, *CP*, vol. 2, 180–81; Rev. A. Colden to CC, January 24, 1726, February 6, 1727, *CP*, vol. 8, 109, 120–21; CC to E. Hill, March 27, 1737, *CP*, vol. 8, 248; CC to Mrs. CC, September 17, 1737, *CP*, vol. 8, 250; CC to John Armitt, May 28, 1744, *CP*, vol. 8, 303–4; CC to Mrs. CC, September 17, 1737, *CP*, vol. 8, 250; CC, E. Colden, and AC to E. Hill, June 18, 1733, *CP*, vol. 8, 204–6; E. Hill to CC, August 4, 1736, *CP*, vol. 8, 244–45

15. CC to E. Hill, October 23, 1732, *CP*, vol. 2, 84–85; CC to Mrs. CC, May 22, 1741, *CP*, vol. 2, 222–23; JA to CC, November 12, 1744, n.d., *CP*, vol. 3, 80–82, 100; CC to Duke of Bedford, November 22, 1748, *NYCD*, vol. 6, 469.

16. C. Colden to _____, April 27, 1796, Eager, *Outline History of Orange County*, 246–47; GC to Bedford, June 28, 1749, *NYCD*, vol. 6, 513–14; GC to Robert Hunter Morris, August 29, 1750, Robert Hunter Morris Papers, New Jersey Historical Society, Newark, NJ; CC to Elizabeth DeLancey, 1737, DeLancey Papers, Museum of the City of New York.

17. E. DeLancey to Mrs. CC, November 9, 1742, DeLancey Papers, Museum of the City of New York; E. DeLancey to CC, [March 24, 1743?], *CP*, vol. 8, 292; CC to James Colden, c. June 19, 1746, *CP*, vol. 3, 224–26; Edwin R. Purple, "Notes, Biographical and Genealogical, of the Colden Family, and of Some of Its Collateral Branches in America," *New York Genealogical and Biographical Record* 4 (1873): 172.

18. CC to Armitt, May 28, 1744, *CP*, vol. 8, 303–4; E. DeLancey to CC, July 20, 1742, DeLancey Papers, Museum of the City of New York.

19. Eager, *Outline History of Orange County*, 236; E. M. Ruttenber, *History of the Town of Newburgh* (Newburgh, NY: E. M. Ruttenber, 1859), 264; Eugene R. Fingerhut, *Survivor: Cadwallader Colden II in Revolutionary America* (Washington, DC: University Press of America, 1983), 8.

20. Fingerhut, *Survivor*, 8, 148; E. DeLancey to Mrs. CC, n. d., *CP*, vol. 5, 409–10; C. Colden to _____, April 27, 1796, Eager, *Outline History of Orange County*, 247.

21. BF, "Advice to a Young Man on the Choice of a Mistress," c. June 25, 1745, *FP*, vol. 3, 30–31, 30n1; Purple, "Notes," 174–75.

22. E. DeLancey to Mrs. CC, n. d., *CP*, vol. 5, 409–10; Joseph Bragdon, "Cadwallader Colden, Second: An Ulster County Tory," *New York History* 14, no. 4 (1933): 415–16.

23. CC to Mrs. CC, September 8, 1744, *CP*, vol. 3, 74–75.

24. GC to CC, April 25, 1748, *CP*, vol. 4, 61; Osborne to CC, June 6, 1748, *CP*, vol. 4, 64–65; John Colden to Maynard Guerin, November 19, 1748, *CP*, vol. 4, 80; John Colden's affidavit, March 22, 1748/9, *CP*, vol. 4, 108–9; CC to GC, February 9, 1748/9, Bancroft Coll., Colden Papers, vol. 1, 95–96, NYPL.

25. CC to Johnson, March 30, 1749, *JP*, vol. 1, 220; CC to John Colden, October 13, December 25, 1749, *CP*, vol. 9, 43, 57; CC to John Colden, April 8, 1749, in *Treaties* 16393, Rare Books, Huntington Library, San Marino, CA.

26. John Ogilvie, "The Diary of the Reverend John Ogilvie, 1750–1759," ed. Milton W. Hamilton, *Bulletin of the Fort Ticonderoga Museum* 10, no. 5 (1961): 339; William M. Beauchamp, *The Life of Conrad Weiser* (Syracuse, NY: Onondaga Historical Association, 1925), 95. The possibility exists that, as a baby, John Colden contracted scarlet fever which did internal damage not apparent until 1750. Ogilvie gave so few details any explanation is just speculation. See Anne Hardy, "Scarlet Fever," in *The Cambridge World History of Human Disease*, ed. Kenneth F. Kiple (Cambridge: Cambridge University Press, 1993), 990–92.

27. Mrs. CC to E. DeLancey, [August 1750], Colden Family Papers, box 11, f. 71, NYHS.

28. Mrs. CC to E. DeLancey, [August 1750], Colden Family Papers, box 11, f. 71, NYHS; E. DeLancey to CC, September 2, 1750, *CP*, vol. 9, 74–75; E. DeLancey to Mrs. CC, October 4, 1750, *CP*, vol. 9, 80–81.

29. E. DeLancey to Mrs. CC, October 4, 1750, *CP*, vol. 9, 80–81.

30. C. Colden to _____, April 27, 1796, Eager, *Outline History of Orange County*, 246–47; Wadsworth, "A Sketch," 1819, Gordon Lester Ford Coll., NYPL; Purple, "Notes," 178.

31. AC to Catherine Colden, April 25, 1759, *CP*, vol. 9, 174; CC to his granddaughters, n.d., *CP*, vol. 7, 305–8; *New York Mercury* (Gaine), May 24, 1762; Hindle, "Colonial Governor's Family," 245.

32. CC to Fothergill, October 18, 1757, *CP*, vol. 5, 203–4; CC to Gronovius, October 1, 1755, *CP*, vol. 5, 29–31; Hindle, "Colonial Governor's Family," 247–48; Buckner Hollingsworth, *Her Garden Was Her Delight* (New York: Macmillan, 1962), 27.

33. CC to Jane Colden, n.d., Ms Am 76, Boston Public Library; CC to Gronovius, October 1, 1755, *CP*, vol. 5, 29–31.

34. CC to Gronovius, October 1, 1755, *CP*, vol. 5, 29–31; CC to Fothergill, October 18, 1757, *CP*, vol. 5, 203–4; CC to J. Colden, n.d., Ms Am 76, Boston Public Library.

35. CC to Fothergill, October 18, 1757, *CP*, vol. 5, 203–4; CC to Collinson, [October 1755?], *CP*, vol. 5, 37–38; CC to Collinson, November 13, 1742, *CP*, vol. 2, 280–82.

36. CC to Gronovius, October 1, 1755, American Science and Medicine, box 1, CL; "Botanical Observations by Mistress Colden of New York," September 30, 1755, American Science and Medicine, box 1, CL; Collinson to CC, September 1, 1753, *CP*, vol. 4, 405–6; Garden to CC, December 17, 1754, *CP*, vol. 4, 475; CC to Collinson, [October 1755?], *CP*, vol. 5, 37–39; Collinson to CC, October 5, 1757, *CP*, vol. 5, 190–91; John Ellis to Linnaeus, April 25, July 21, 1758, in Linnaeus, *A Selection of the Correspondence of Linnaeus and Other Naturalists, from the Original Manuscripts*, ed. Sir James Edward Smith (London: Longman, Hurst, Rees, Orme, and Brown, 1821), vol. 1, 94–95, 98; Bartram to J. Colden, January 24, 1757, John Bartram, *Memorials of John Bartram and Humphry Marshall, with Notices of Their Botanical Contemporaries*, ed. William Darlington. (Philadelphia: Lindsay & Blakiston, 1849), 400–1; John C. Dann, ed., *One Hundred and One Treasures From the Collections of The William L. Clements Library: A Celebration of Seventy-five Years, 1923–1998* (Ann Arbor: Clements Library, University of Michigan, 1998), 59; Andrea Wulf, *The Brother Gardeners: Botany, Empire and the Birth of an Obsession* (London: W. Heinemann, 2008), 121.

37. Garden to CC, May 23, 1755, *CP*, vol. 5, 10–11; Garden to Ellis, March 25, 1755, Linnaeus, *Selection of the Correspondence of Linnaeus*, vol. 1, 343; CC to his granddaughters, n.d., *CP*, vol. 7, 305–8; Edmund Berkeley and Dorothy Smith Berkeley, *Dr. Alexander Garden of Charles Town* (Chapel Hill: University of North Carolina Press, 1969), 42–43; Margaret Denny, "Naming the Gardenia," *Scientific Monthly* 67, no. 1 (1948): 18–19.

38. Collinson to Bartram, January 20, 1756, Bartram, *Memorials*, 202; Collinson to Linnaeus, May 12, 1756, April 30, 1758, Linnaeus, *Selection of the Correspondence of Linnaeus*, vol. 1, 39, 45; CC to Fothergill, October 18, 1757, *CP*, vol. 5, 203–4; CC to Gronovius, October 1, 1755, *CP*, vol. 5, 29–31; Hollingsworth, *Her Garden*, 30–31. See the impressions contained with her "Botanical Observations" of 1755 in American Science and Medicine, box 1, CL.

39. Jane Colden, "Memorandum of Cheese made 1756," *CP*, vol. 5, 55–63; Walter Rutherfurd to _____, n.d., in Livingston Rutherfurd, *Family Records and Events: Compiled Principally from the Original Manuscripts in the Rutherfurd Collection* (New York: De Vinne Press, 1894), 13n1; Hindle, "Colonial Governor's Family," 247–48.

40. Garden to CC, December 17, 1754, *CP*, vol. 4, 475; Elizabeth C. Hall, "The Gentlewoman, Jane Colden, and Her Manuscript on New York Native Plants," in Jane Colden, *Botanic Manuscript of Jane Colden, 1724–1766*, ed. H. W. Rickett and Elizabeth C. Hall (New York: Garden Club of Orange and Dutchess Counties, 1963), 20; CC to [Dr. Whytte?], February 15, 1758, *CP*, vol. 5, 216–17; Flick, *History*, vol. 4, 288.

41. Jane Colden to Dr. Charles Alston, May 1, 1756, in William Martin Smallwood, *Natural History and the American Mind* (New York: Columbia University Press, 1941; repr. New York: AMS Press, 1967), 92–93; Garden to Ellis, January 13, 1756, in Linnaeus, *Correspondence of Linnaeus*, vol. 1, 366; Collinson to Linnaeus, April 1, 1757, in Linnaeus, *Correspondence of Linnaeus*, vol. 1, 40.

42. Hall, "Gentlewoman," 17, 21; Susan Scott Parrish, *American Curiosity: Cultures of Natural History in the Colonial British Atlantic World* (Chapel Hill: University of North Carolina Press, 2006), 196; Diana Lipscomb, "Women in Systematics," *Annual Review of Ecology and Systematics* 26 (1995): 327–28; Smallwood, *Natural History*, 92; Dann, ed., *One Hundred and One Treasures*, 58–59. For pokeweed, a plant of interest to her father, see J. Colden, *Botanic Manuscript*, 83.

43. C. Colden to _____, April 27, 1796, Eager, *Outline History of Orange County*, 246–47; CC to Robert Whytt, 1758, in CC, *The Philosophical Writings of Cadwallader Colden*, ed.

Scott L. Pratt and John Ryder (Amherst, NY: Humanity Books, 2002), 229; CC to Dr. William Porterfield, May 19, 1760, CPU, reel 2; Jane Farquhar to Katherine Colden, May 16, 1759, *CP*, vol. 9, 175; Garden to CC, March 31, 1759, *CP*, vol. 5, 300.

44. CC to Whytt, 1758, in CC, *Philosophical Writings*, 229; AC to K. Colden, April 25, 1759, *CP*, vol. 9, 174.

45. Ulysses Prentiss Hedrick, *A History of Horticulture in America To 1860* (New York: Oxford University Press, 1950), 72; Hollingsworth, *Her Garden*, 33–34; John Fontaine, *The Journal of John Fontaine: An Irish Huguenot Son in Spain and Virginia, 1710–1719*, ed. Edward Porter Alexander (Williamsburg: Colonial Williamsburg Foundation, University Press of Virginia, 1972), 114.

46. Hindle, "Colonial Governor's Family," 249; Hollingsworth, *Her Garden*, 32–33.

47. CC to Dr. John Bard, July 5, 1758, *CP*, vol. 5, 234–35, 238–39.

48. CC to Dr. John Bard, July 5, 1758, *CP*, vol. 5, 234–35, 238–39; E. DeLancey to CC, March 7, 1755, *CP*, vol. 9, 151. David Colden likely had a condition called scoliosis.

49. Cotton Mather, *The Angel of Bethesda*, Edited by Gordon W. Jones (Barre, MA: American Antiquarian Society, 1972), 98.

50. CC to JA, March 1, 1729, RP, vol. 1, 107; CC to Graham, October 1716, CC and Hugh Graham, "The Correspondence of Cadwallader Colden and Hugh Graham on Infectious Fevers (1716–1719)," ed. Saul Jarcho, *Bulletin of the History of Medicine* 30, no. 3 (May–June 1956): 205–6.

51. Douglass to CC, May 1, July 25, 1722, *CP*, vol. 1, 141–45; Maxine Van De Wetering, "A Reconsideration of the Inoculation Controversy," *New England Quarterly* 58, no. 1 (1985): 47, 50, 53; George H. Weaver, "Life and Writings of William Douglass, M.D. (1691–1752)," *Bulletin of the Society of Medical History of Chicago* 2, no. 4 (1921): 235–36; Brooke Hindle, *The Pursuit of Science in Revolutionary America, 1735–1789* (Chapel Hill: University of North Carolina Press, 1956), 50; Claude E. Heaton, "Medicine in New York during the English Colonial Period," *Bulletin of the History of Medicine* 17, no. 1 (1945): 22; Philip Ranlet, *Enemies of the Bay Colony: Puritan Massachusetts and Its Foes*, 2nd ed. (Lanham, MD: University Press of America, 2006), 223–24.

52. JA to CC, n. d., December 23, 1731, March 23, 1731/2, *CP*, vol. 2, 24, 42, 59–60; James Colden to CC, April 27, 1732, *CP*, vol. 2, 63–65; Peter DeLancey to CC, January 25, 1738/9, *CP*, vol. 8, 260–61; JA to CC, January 20, 1745/6, *CP*, vol. 3, 190–91; GC to Peter Warren, April 24–27, 1746, Peter Warren, *The Royal Navy and North America: The Warren Papers, 1736–1752*, ed. Julian Gwyn (London: Navy Records Society, 1975), 235; Heaton, "Medicine," 23–25.

53. CC to Fothergill, October 1, 1753, in CC, "Extract of a Letter from Cadwallader Colden, esq. to Dr. Fothergill, concerning the throat distemper," *American Museum* 3 (January 1788): 53–59. For Africa see Eugenia W. Herbert, "Smallpox Inoculation in Africa," *Journal of African History* 16, no. 4 (1975): 539–59.

54. AC to George Harison, March 2, 1757, Richard Harison Papers, box 2, NYHS; Dr. John Bard to CC, April 2, 1757, *CP*, vol. 5, 136–37; CC to Bard, July 5, 1758, *CP*, vol. 5, 234, 236–37; AC to CC, March 18, 1757, *CP*, vol. 5, 127.

55. CC to Bard, July 5, 1758, *CP*, vol. 5, 236–39.

56. CC to Bard, July 5, 1758, *CP*, vol. 5, 237–39. For a positive view of inoculation by a survivor see Joyce D. Goodfriend, ed., "New York City in 1772: The Journal of Solomon Drowne, Junior," *New York History* 82, no. 1 (2001): 25–52.

57. DF to AC, February 2, 1773, *FP*, vol. 20, 33.

58. CC to BF, October 24, 1752, *FP*, vol. 4, 373–76; BF to CC, January 1, 1753/4, *FP*, vol. 5, 185–86; CC to BF, February 13, 1754, *FP*, vol. 5, 198; *Monthly Review* 11 (December 1754), 420–421.

59. BF to David Colden, March 5, 1773, *FP*, vol. 20, 95–97; vol. 5, 135n7; CC to Collinson, October 28, 1749, *CP*, vol. 4, 147. David Colden also married into the Willett family and fathered a son, Cadwallader David Colden, and four daughters who survived infancy. All of these girls died young of consumption. Purple, "Notes," 178–79; Wadsworth, "Sketch," 7–8, Gordon Lester Ford Coll., NYPL.

60. Samuel Johnson to CC, April 15, 1747, in *Samuel Johnson, President of King's College: His Career and Writings*, ed. Herbert Schneider and Carol Schneider (New York: Columbia University Press, 1929), vol. 2, 296; Ezra Stiles, *The Literary Diary of Ezra Stiles, D. D., LL. D., President of Yale College*, ed. Franklin Bowditch Dexter (New York: C. Scribner, 1901), vol. 2, 77–78; Singleton, *Social*, 314–15.

61. CC to Hezekiah Watkins, December 12, 1748, Society of the Propagation of the Gospel Papers, Series B, vol. 20, 202–14, LC transcript.

62. CC to Hezekiah Watkins, December 12, 1748, Society of the Propagation of the Gospel Papers, Series B, vol. 20, 202–14, LC transcript.

63. CC to Hezekiah Watkins, December 12, 1748, Society of the Propagation of the Gospel Papers, Series B, vol. 20, 202–14, LC transcript.

64. CC to Hezekiah Watkins, December 12, 1748, Society of the Propagation of the Gospel Papers, Series B, vol. 20, 202–14, LC transcript.

65. CC to Hezekiah Watkins, December 12, 1748, Society of the Propagation of the Gospel Papers, Series B, vol. 20, 202–14, LC transcript.

66. CC to Hezekiah Watkins, December 12, 1748, Society of the Propagation of the Gospel Papers, Series B, vol. 20, 202–14, LC transcript. Much of CC's letter is reprinted in George H. Moore, *Collegium Regale Novi Eboraci: The Origin and Early History of Columbia College* (New York: G. H. Moore, 1890), 37–43.

67. CC to BF, [November 1749], *FP*, vol. 3, 431.

68. CC to BF, [November 1749], *FP*, vol. 3, 431.

69. CC to BF, [November 1749], *FP*, vol. 3, 432; Margaret Barton Korty, "Benjamin Franklin and Eighteenth-Century Libraries," American Philosophical Society. *Transactions*, n.s., 55, part 9 (1965): 32; Hoermann, *Cadwallader Colden*, 76; Meyer Reinhold, "Opponents of Classical Learning in America during the Revolutionary Period," American Philosophical Society, *Proceedings* 112, no. 4 (August 15, 1968): 222–24.

70. David C. Humphrey, "Urban Manners and Rural Morals: The Controversy Over the Location of King's College," *New York History* 54, no. 1 (1973): 11–12, 22; M. Ruttenber and L. H. Clark, *History of Orange County, New York* (Philadelphia: Everts & Peck, 1881), 129; Julie Flavell, *When London Was Capital of America* (New Haven, CT: Yale University Press, 2010), 137.

71. William Livingston to Henry Livingston, n.d., in "A Packet of Old Letters (found in old Poughkeepsie Court House; Livingston, Beekman families; 1732–1755)," Dutchess County Historical Society, *Year Book* 6 (1921): 52–53; Myles Cooper to Jonathan Boucher, March 22, 1773, in George Washington, *The Papers of George Washington, Colonial Series*, ed. W. W. Abbot (Charlottesville: University Press of Virginia, 1983–1995), vol. 9, 213–214n2.

Chapter Eight

The Empire Calls

Cadwallader Colden's time in New York saw frequent clashes between European empires for many reasons, including the desire of monarchs to expand their colonial holdings. Colden, an ardent imperialist himself, had worked hard against French interests in America, but he also encouraged the British to resist the Russian movement into Alaska.[1] Colden's vigorous support of the British Empire will propel him, to his shock, into a political struggle that rivaled the tempests of the William Cosby era.

The catalyst who sparked the newest political turmoil in New York turned out to be George Clarke's successor at the helm of the colony of New York, George Clinton. A naval man, Captain Clinton owed his rank only to his birth, not merit—assuming he had any. The Royal Navy tried to find places to send him where he could do the least damage. The Duke of Newcastle's ardent desire to give his kinsman a job as a royal governor served the navy's agenda well. The British Admiralty preferred that Clinton cause damage in New York rather than at sea.[2]

Debt pushed Captain Clinton, concerned about being sued, to America. Owing over £5,000, he was drawn to New York which had a reputation as a colony where a governor could rake in cash. In Clinton's day New York had even more appeal than Virginia for a debtor with political connections with the British ministry. And Clinton, like all New York governors, did his best to maximize his income while running the colony.[3]

A political neophyte, Clinton needed help to handle the governorship of New York. Such assistance had always been standard practice—and greatly needed—when a new governor had no administrative experience. In England, Clinton had been given advice as to whom he should consult on the scene in New York and the suggestions centered upon the two chief office holders under the governor himself. Clarke, as lieutenant governor, had extensive political experience that would be of great help to any newcomer. The second was the province's chief justice, James DeLancey.[4]

When Clinton arrived in New York in 1743, Colden realized which man the governor had picked as his advisor. "I observed," the canny Scot noted, "that pains had been taken to infuse prejudices against all persons that the Chief Justice Imagined would not be subservient to the purposes he had in view." Governor Clinton, acting as if Colden "was not worthy his Least Notice," ignored him. Therefore, Colden "never intermeddled" in these early days of the new administration.[5]

Clarke, who had tried to buy the governorship from Clinton, also found himself ignored. Too proud to act only as a councilor again after running the colony since Cosby's death, Clarke soon left New York for England only to be captured by a French privateer—King George's War (1740–1748) was underway. In 1745 Clarke formally resigned from the Council because of "his infirmities."[6]

Initially, DeLancey's personality had attracted the governor away from Clarke. Even a political enemy acknowledged the chief justice's "uncommon vivacity, with the semblance of affability and ease, his adroitness at a jest, with a shew of condescension to his inferiors, wonderfully facilitated his progress." But the presence of Peter Warren, another naval officer who had befriended Clinton, had helped to undermine Clarke; Warren was DeLancey's brother-in-law.[7]

Now without a serious rival, DeLancey could consolidate his power. Colden realized how the chief justice could manipulate Clinton. DeLancey, Colden observed, had the advantages of "his office and his being of the Council but principally by his Disposition to good fellowship which suited with the Governor's humour." Here, Colden is saying, as nicely as he could, that Governor Clinton drank too much and that DeLancey knew it.[8]

DeLancey introduced the newcomer to the drinking life in New York City, which centered around an "infamous" drinking society, "the Hungarian Club," based at a tavern. Aside from DeLancey, its "bawdy" members included Adolph Philipse and Daniel Horsmanden. According to a tourist, its members were "all bumper men," and the best way "for a stranger to recommend himself" with the club's adherents was "To drink stoutly . . . and a sett among them are very fond of making a stranger drunk." The tourist noted in 1744 that Governor Clinton "himself is a jolly toaper and gives good example and, for that one quality, is esteemed among these dons." Unlike the tourist, who tired of "excessive drinking," Clinton did not.[9]

Cadwallader Colden liked his ale, and had fond memories of sharing a bottle of wine with James Alexander. When Colden was with his friends, he could be rather ribald too. He has even been credited with inspiring the creation of a rum industry in New York. But Colden never got drunk for the sake of being drunk, the sole purpose of the Hungarian Club.[10]

Not surprisingly, Clinton preferred the company of his drinking buddies and foolishly believed they had his best interests at heart. Taking advantage of the gullible governor, DeLancey convinced him to give him a commission for his office, allowing him to hold it as long as he practiced "good behavior." No judge had ever been granted such a commission in the history of the province, because it gave the officeholder practically a lifetime tenure. Earlier, commissions had specified that the recipient could be removed at "the king's pleasure" giving a governor the power to replace any official who went against the wishes of the Crown. Now that Chief Justice DeLancey was all but invulnerable, he could act against the foolish governor at any time of his choosing.[11]

Clinton fell entirely into DeLancey's hands and always followed his advice. The governor appointed DeLancey's allies to open seats in the Council, giving the chief justice control. Again at DeLancey's urging, Clinton called a new assembly election which would wipe out opposition to the chief justice there too. Then DeLancey created "a powerful Faction in the Assembly," Colden later explained, "by perswading the Govr. to make such concessions," in violation of his own instructions, that made all government officials "entirely dependent on the Chief Justice and his Faction in the Assembly" for both their nomination to office and salaries, with devastating impact upon the royal prerogative. Colden remarked that "in effect the Govr. had inadvertently put the whole executive powers into their hands."[12]

While DeLancey had been indulging his "passion for power," the military situation in New York declined rapidly. Colden received firsthand accounts of the problems from a recent arrival in the colony, the Scot John Rutherfurd. The Colden and Rutherfurd families had been close in Scotland, literally. The Rutherfurds lived in nearby Jedburgh. John Rutherfurd, the only New York friend of Colden's from "the spot" where he grew up, would be "the only one I ever saw in America." Rutherfurd had done well for himself, serving as a member of Parliament from Roxburghshire during 1734–1742. But on December 31, 1741 he had been appointed a captain in one of the regular army companies based in New York, explaining his move to America. He would be based in Albany where, like Colden, he entertained himself with "Mathematics, Philosophy, Politicks, etc." Rutherfurd was, Colden wrote, a man of "universal knowledge."[13]

Before Clinton's arrival, Captain Rutherfurd was distressed over the security of New York. He could not understand how Cosby could have permitted the French to fortify Crown Point "from whence in a Week's time they can plunder Boston or Albany." For that matter, Rutherfurd saw no hope of holding Oswego—if the French chose to seize it. He also believed that the French could just as easily detach two of the members of the Iroquois Confederacy, the Onondagas and Senecas, away from the British. Not only would that mean the fall of Oswego but the collapse of the fur trade and the loss "of the friendship of all the Indians" as well. How strange it would seem, Rutherfurd lamented, if "the French have the pleasure of affronting and plundering us from Crown Point at the same time they are overpowered every where in Europe."[14]

In 1745 Governor Clinton tried to follow his instructions about defending the province but he did not yet realize that someone else was actually in charge. Rutherfurd, who had been named to the Council, had gone to New York City and, although "always in A Hurry," he realized that the Assembly had done nothing "showing no less indifference about providing for their own defence than in assisting their Neighbours." The assemblymen had even refused to let the governor appoint men to meet with other colonies. New York's forts had almost no stockpiles of gunpowder or even food. A fort in Saratoga was so useless Indians considered it "a great Joke."[15]

On May 14, 1745 Governor Clinton had tired of the Assembly's inaction on his requests which were "immediately related to his Majesty's Service, and the Interest and Security of the Province" and dissolved the Assembly. The voters appeared not to care as they re-elected almost all of the assemblymen who had ignored the governor. Philipse, though, undercut by DeLancey, lost, finally removing Ape from politics. Meanwhile, Rutherfurd, who had taken part in the Council, discovered that he was "reckoned as odd and singular at New York for insisting upon a proper defence for Albany." Colden's presence in the Council, Rutherfurd thought in June 1745, "will be extremely wanted" there along with his "Knowledge and experience in affairs" which would "be thoroughly tried in getting things done . . . in so Critical a Juncture." But on August 7, 1745 Colden explained his reluctance to attend the Council. Cad's wedding had been expensive, so his father had "to mind my private business" and "avoid all the extraordinary expence I can" unless serious security matters were on the agenda.[16]

Conditions continued to deteriorate. Seeing the inaction of the British, the Iroquois sought to protect themselves by backing away from them and taking a non-belligerent stance with the French. The governor wanted the Iroquois "to draw blood," believing that, if they stayed neutral, "The Enemy will be emboldened to committ Ravage daily in the Frontiers." But his meeting with the Iroquois in October 1745—his long speech had been written by Horsmanden—has been termed a "debacle" by one scholar. Colden had not been there.[17]

Nor did the Dutch in Albany seem motivated for defense. Another Colden friend, Dr. Alexander Colhoun, a military doctor, told him in January 1746 about his troubles. Ordered by the governor to establish a hospital at Albany, Colhoun discovered that the inhabitants "made many promises" but did nothing. Even more troublesome, the people of Albany refused to quarter troops in their homes and instead converted some public buildings for the purpose. Colhoun realized that the quarters were "so very insufficient and cold, the men so crowded together that the Sick will probably perish (in spite of Art)."[18]

Given such circumstances, Governor Clinton's desire to be anywhere but New York can be understood. And the problems had all been stirred up by DeLancey. As a cynic observed, DeLancey had "continually fomented the quarrel he himself excited." Colden believed that the chief justice had "formed a scheme to make Mr. Clinton so uneasy in his Govt. as to make him willing to come to an easy [compensation] for it."[19]

It was no secret that Clinton had come to New York to make money, a common enough motive for colonial governors. Governorships were bought and sold as a commodity. New York lawyer Joseph Murray, for example, wanted to buy the office but Clinton did not take him seriously. The best deal, Clinton believed, would come from his naval comrade, Warren, whose wife, a DeLancey and a New Yorker, must have wanted to settle down among her relatives. Before Clinton had left for America, Warren had expressed interest in the post. When Governor Clinton had gotten to New York, he discovered he did not like the place, "it being the worst climate I ever was in."[20]

Warren and Clinton kept negotiating over the proposed deal, but, apparently, Warren had no real desire to be a governor. A suggestion that he run New Jersey while waiting for New York to be available went nowhere, because he wanted to stay on active duty at sea while holding that office. His early wish to be named to New York's Council demonstrates that he desired the prestige that came with political office or, perhaps, that his wife wanted it.[21]

In all likelihood, a Governor Warren of New York would have spent most of his time on his land, living as a country squire, but going to the capital for balls, banquets and other social events where his wife could bask in the prestige of being the governor's spouse. But who would be running the province? The answer is James DeLancey.[22]

As the distress generated by the chief justice's political machine exasperated Governor Clinton, his good friend Warren sent his condolences. "I am sorry to hear the Indians are dissatisfied and that you find so much trouble with your assembly," all problems caused by the machinations of Warren's in-law, Chief Justice DeLancey, to make Warren governor.[23]

When Warren succeeded in the "Bold undertaking" of seizing the powerful French fortress, Louisbourg, DeLancey's calculations became even more personal. Colden analyzed the chief justice's motivation: "when A[dmiral] W[arren's] good fortune before L[ouisbourg] raised his hopes above the Govt. of New York.... Mr. C[hief] J[ustice] succeeded him in the design on the Govt." of New York. If Warren received something more important, DeLancey would have the reins of power directly in his own hands rather than as a mere fill-in.[24]

Then, suddenly, everything seemed to fall apart. Warren's influence in Britain was not as strong as he had imagined. Far worse, he and Clinton could not come to a deal. Clinton wanted more than Warren was willing to pay. The chief justice's scheming had not prevailed, at least not yet.[25]

At last DeLancey decided that he could obtain nothing of value anymore from Clinton, and concluded that it was time for him to go, whether he wanted to or not. The specifics are unclear but, according to William Smith Jr.'s *History of the Province of New York*, "on a certain occasion," Clinton, who had finally realized he had given DeLancey too much power, "expressed with some tartness his resolution to maintain the dignity of his station." Then, in what appears to have been bad theatrics, "DeLancey left the table"—perhaps during a session of the Hungarian Club—and uttered "an oath of revenge." Colden described DeLancey's acting as "pretended disgust."[26]

Just when the governor and DeLancey had their falling out, Clinton received orders from London to organize a military invasion of French Canada. Part of the preparations involved convincing the Iroquois to participate, thus ending their neutrality. DeLancey and his minions refused to aid Governor Clinton in any way, knowing that, if the project failed, Clinton would be disgraced. He would have two choices: wait to be recalled or sell the governorship to Warren at his price. And recruiting the Iroquois appeared to be an impossible task. DeLancey understood that by sabotaging the war effort, he could gain the political dominance he craved. His betrayal, a disgusted New Yorker commented, "did the province more injury than he will ever be able to repair."[27]

The DeLancey-controlled Council, following his lead, refused to journey to Albany. Let Colden go with you they told the governor, but only because they were sure Colden would not go. The last trip he had made on Council business had forced him to spend £30, making him very grumpy about the expense. In fact, Colden had not undertaken Indian diplomacy in some time. DeLancey's forces assumed he would stay at home in Coldengham spending his time pursuing philosophical amusements which they did not value. During 1748 one Delanceyite mocked "the little Chap" —Colden— who preferred "Starr-gazing" and displaying his "Excess of Folly and Vanity" in his "Conceit" that he had the ability to make "further Improvements upon Sr. Isaac Newton's Phylosophy."[28]

While all the backstabbing was underway, Colden had, once again, insulated himself from all that by staying in Coldengham. He had written the governor with some suggestions about the province's defense. Making observations about how the Assembly had usurped the governor's authority, Colden called it "destructive of Good Govt. and of his Majesties Authority in this Province." Most of all, he feared that Britain might impose "a more Despotick Government if the Conduct of Assemblymen" gave London "any Jealousy of an Inclination in the People here to free themselves" from "Dependence on their Mother Country."[29]

In early June 1746 Colden at Coldengham received a summons from the governor, "by advice of the Council," that his "attendance upon the publick Business of the Province is required and expected at New York." Colden could never have guessed that, by answering the call, his blissful retirement would suddenly end.[30]

The summons was about the governor's planned trip to Albany to bring the Indians into the Canadian invasion force. In order to validate an Indian treaty, the governor had to have the deal approved by the Council and three was its quorum; Rutherfurd and Philip Livingston were already in Albany. Colden would be the needed third—if he went. If Colden stayed home, there would be no treaty.[31]

Having been away for some time, Colden had not taken a public stand for or against the expedition. When he arrived in the city, "no gains were omitted" by DeLancey's "cabal" of councilors "to bring him over to their measures." He noticed "these unusual and unprecedented methods of proceeding" and "was surprised to find that all the Govrs friends had left him." The cabal made its formal demand that Colden go to Albany at a meeting held while he was visiting Bettie in Westchester.[32]

Colden had traveled to see his daughter for a specific reason. At the end of June Rutherfurd begged him to come to Albany with Clinton for "'tis necessary for the publick good." But Colden was aware of the "great deal of Jealousy" directed at him for "being in town at this time." Seeing a political explosion already simmering, he visited Bettie "that I might be as little concerned in the conduct of affairs as possible." Still, the excursion was just a delaying tactic—he could not be "unconcerned" for too long without endangering "the success of the Expedition and for the success of which I think no man living in this Country can be indifferent." Despite his decades of political combat, Colden did not yet realize how wrong he would prove to be.[33]

On July 4, 1746 Colden attended the Council meeting and "we had a strong debate" over who should join Clinton in Albany. "Every one" was "for my going," Colden informed his wife, "not withstanding all the opposition I could make to it." He suspected "it will fall to my lot tho' I still use all my endeavours to avoid it."[34]

When Colden had arrived in New York and met with Clinton, "I was surprised at the state in which I found him." Even before Colden's visit with Bettie, the governor "desired me with some concern to go with him to Albany but I with a great deal of earnestness declined it." The governor grew increasingly desperate. Ever since he had received his orders about the Canadian invasion, he had encountered "a most vile and insolent Treatment" from both the Assembly and Council. No one else but Colden remained who could

Figure 8.1. *Cadwallader Colden*, c. 1749-52 by John Wollaston (c. 1710-c. 1767). Colden about 1750. Oil on canvas, 30 x 25 in. Bequest of Grace Wilkes, 1922 (22.45.6) ART463380. *The Metropolitan Museum of Art. Image copyright © The Metropolitan Museum of Art. Image source: Art Resource, New York.*

provide him with the support and advice he needed to carry out his directions from Britain.[35]

Clinton tried a second time, after the Council meeting, to change Colden's mind. He saw it "as a particular hardship on me to be singled out." Finally, the governor's "earnest desire" won him over.[36]

In the end, Colden could not refuse to help the governor of New York battle the French. In May 1746 Colden had already called King George's War "a most barbarous war with Indians, Popish converts, set on by accursed Priests to murder innocent People in their beds or at their daily labour." This conflict with France was no ordinary war he believed. "Good God what a Religion must that be that incites men to such cruelties." He had even warned Gronovius that Holland did not appear "sufficiently apprehensive of being again subjects of such a bloody cruel tyranny." No wonder the thrifty Scotsman had forgotten about the cost of a trip to Albany.[37]

Once Colden had committed himself, he would give his all. And this conference, which seemed ill-fated from the start, required his constant attention. Clinton left New York City with "such Persons as, by the best Information he could receive, had Influence among the Six Nations." Colden, of course, was one of these people as he had been adopted by the Mohawks and had received an Indian name, Cayenderongue. They reached Albany on July 21, 1746, a day after the original suggested meeting date. But Albany was ravaged by two different epidemics of smallpox and yellow fever.[38]

Given that Albany was riven with disease, it should not surprise that most of the Indians did not arrive until the following month. A few had come and presented the governor with some French scalps, an indication that these early arrivals—an Oneida accompanied by two Onondagas—represented the war party among the Indians. One of the militants sought a new name from Clinton, who dubbed him "Path-opener," greatly pleasing the man. Colden had to have taught a quick course on Indian diplomacy for Governor Clinton while journeying on the Hudson.[39]

Because of the collapse of British-Iroquois relations, that any Indians at all had come is surprising. Even the war party, Colden revealed, had told New York's leaders that the Mohawks' "friendship" with the British "was more in their lips than in their hearts." Colden knew, as did everyone else, that Albany's "ill usage" had alienated many of the Indians, making them "dissatisfied and wavering in their Fidelity to the British Crown." Nor had the French been lax. Their diplomats had availed themselves of the opportunity the British had provided them to sow the seeds of distrust. This disastrous scenario had come about, Colden wrote, because of "some Neglects or Misconduct of those . . . entrusted by . . . New-York with the Management of the Indian Affairs." On July 24, 1746 those responsible for the mess, the Indian Commissioners based at Albany, told Governor Clinton that the task he had come to perform there—recruiting the Indians for an attack upon Canada—was impossible, and reminded him that they had told him so many times before.[40]

While waiting for the still-absent Indians to appear, Colden kept himself busy meeting with the representatives of other colonies, especially those from Massachusetts. He apologized to Alice for the shortness of his letters, offering in his defense that "there is something almost every hour to take up my time." By early August, with the Indians still not there, he added that "We are constantly employed about something or other but it will be hard to say what we have done." These meetings took place in a tense atmosphere. Colden could not wander about looking for new plants. As he explained to John Bartram, "We durst not go without the fortifications without a guard, for fear of having our scalps taken."[41]

When the Mohawks finally converged on Albany, they were far more militant than anyone could have imagined—for which a newcomer to New York, William Johnson, was responsible. Johnson, Warren's nephew, had come to the colony to oversee his uncle's landholdings and had joined with the governor to bring the Mohawks back into agreement with the British. The Iroquois had learned that they could trust Johnson, unlike the officials they had encountered in Albany, men whom Johnson had no tie with. His fur trading was honest, very different from that conducted at Albany, making him popular with the Indians.[42]

Johnson's success with the Mohawks—and how he did it—had to have surprised not just the Albany officials but Colden too. As he recounted the scene,

> Mr. William Johnson was indefatigable among the Mohawks; he dressed himself after the Indian Manner, made frequent Dances, according to their Custom when they excite to War, and used all the Means he could think of, at a considerable Expence, (which his Excellency had promised to repay him) in order to engage them heartily in the War against Canada.[43]

Colden would never have considered dressing up like an Iroquois "War Captain." Besides, he was a bit old for war paint or for the war dances, which must have been much more vigorous than a jig. Although Johnson had totally won over the young warriors, Colden still had important roles to play. Two of the older sachems remained unconvinced, thinking that neutrality remained the best course for their confederacy. Having these elders on the British side seemed essential, so Colden had "a private Conference" with these reluctant sachems, whom he had known for many years. No stranger to Indian diplomacy, Colden employed his considerable experience and "After this Conference these Sachems appeared as hearty as any of the others."[44]

Despite the great success with the Mohawks, problems remained. The ill governor of Virginia, designated as the invasion's commander, declined the job throwing more responsibility upon Clinton's shoulders. Then he became ill himself, not surprising given all the contagions rampaging through Albany. Typhoid had levelled Governor Clinton. Colden recommended "the use of old generous Madeira wine" for that disease, a much more pleasant medicine than usually prescribed in those times. By all accounts, the drinking of wine, which had been prescribed since ancient times, worked well with the sick in Albany. Colden, though, did not handle Clinton's treatment. Dr. Colhoun kept an eye on him for several days until the "very ill" patient recovered.[45]

Clinton's incapacitation came at a bad time as the conference had come to the pivotal point, the actual ceremony about a new treaty. Because, the Indians were told, the governor did not want "to detain them without Necessity," he inquired, "if they desired it," whether they would be willing to have "Mr. Colden to speak to them in his Name, what he designed to say." The Indians "answered, that they would be well pleased to hear it from Mr. Colden's Mouth."[46]

On August 19, 1746 the Indians got their wish. With his fellow councilors, Rutherfurd and Livingston (who doubled as the colony's Indian secretary) in attendance, Colden explained to the assembled Indians that the governor, too ill to be in public, had delegated him, "(being the next Person to him in the Administration) to speak to you in his Name." And the words Colden spoke, which he had written, went over very well. He condemned the French for not fighting "in a manly manner" as they persisted in "Murdering private People, by Sculking Indians." Reminding the Iroquois of their promise that, if that continued, they would fight against the French, Colden added that the British king had promised great aid to seize Canada. Why, the Iroquois' dead ancestors would be overjoyed to see "revenge" taken against all the ancient crimes against them by the "deceitful" and treacherous French. When the Iroquois responded in a few days, all doubt had vanished. "They accepted the Hatchet," they declared, and also demanded that Johnson be their commander, which Clinton accepted without question.[47]

On August 20, the day after Colden's performance, he believed that the governor had "recovered" but that turned out to be somewhat premature. Colden had to give Clinton an emetic—"I made the Govr. lose his Dinner today" the doctor noted—and so he was asked by Governor Clinton again to fill in for him at a conference with another group of New York Indians, the River Indians. On August 21, 1746 Colden stood in for a second time. His speech was just as successful as his earlier effort and the River Indians joined the effort against the French.[48]

Despite Colden's assurance about how the British monarch would help, affairs in Europe pushed the British government to back away from its pledge and the promised assistance never left for America. "If the Fleet had arrived in time I doubt not every thing had succeeded" Colden believed.[49]

The possibility that the planned expedition against Canada would not happen in 1746 had already been considered in July by both Governor William Shirley of Massachusetts and Warren. They suggested to Clinton a much easier alternative that could be seized without British help—Crown Point, only 90 miles from Albany. Johnson discovered that the French fort was poorly defended. Changing the target did not faze the Indians, as Crown Point was also an immediate threat to them as well as to the colonists.[50]

But could the New York Assembly and James DeLancey be won over to the war effort? In August 1746 Clinton wrote to the chief justice explaining that both Shirley and Warren had recommended Crown Point be attacked. The governor of New York felt that he could not dismiss the assembled troops without a direct order from the Crown. The soldiers were needed to protect the colony's frontiers anyway and, unless there was some "vigorous attempt" against the French, the dispirited Indians would drift back into the French orbit. An offensive against Crown Point would end "all intercourse" between the Indians and the enemy.[51]

Clinton then offered DeLancey command of the army, which has to be Colden's most clever idea in this period. The proffering of what, in DeLancey's words, was "a command above my expectations," had to have surprised him. The chief justice thanked the governor but turned him down, partly for political reasons. DeLancey had "several objections" to the campaign "in general." But he had "personal" reasons as well. Having never studied military matters, the chief justice believed he was not qualified for the job. Even more relevant, DeLancey explained, was his "own indisposition being at this time, as I usually am at this season of the year, troubled with my old disorder the Asthma."[52]

Governor Clinton had not been totally honest with the chief justice when he stated that the councilors in Albany supported attacking Crown Point. Colden did (although he cautioned about being "too sanguine" in war) and Rutherfurd did, but Livingston did not, especially as fall approached. He had wanted the Canadian attack to start in the spring, fearing a winter campaign against Crown Point had too many problems confronting it—getting heavy cannons to the French fort would be hard at any time and even more so in winter weather.[53]

Livingston's patriotic feelings towards the British Empire can not be doubted. On January 14, 1746 he declared: "I acknowledge our assembly have not done their duty to his majesty nor their Neighbours on the frontier in not providing for their defence." He did not welcome DeLancey's machinations against the war, and in June Livingston remained distressed about the "miserable Condition the County of Albany is Reduced to by the Skulking parties of the French and Indians without any assistance of Defence."[54]

Nor was Livingston motivated by what Albany leaders were still moved by—protecting the smuggling trade with French Canada. Livingston's hopes for the campaign against Canada were as expansive as Colden's. "If we be determined to Conquer Canada we must have our Eyes on quebeck take that then we have all and all the Rest of that Country must soon Submit," which did happen in a future war. He would resent the "false Stories" going around that he opposed conquering French Canada. The source of these stories, he believed, were "the faithless Creatures about our Govr." To drive home his point Livingston remarked: "D[r]. C[olden] and R[utherfurd] are most dangerous men."[55]

Livingston's problems with the Crown Point attack were largely generated by personal dislike and jealousy. A great landlord, Livingston had to have been uncomfortable working with a man who wanted to reform New York's land system which had brought great wealth to the Livingston family. And Colden had more influence with the Indians than Livingston did. On September 18, 1746, after the successful Indian diplomacy, Livingston moaned: "I never Spent a Summer more Idle and to less Purpose Since I came to years of maturity." He went on blasting the "Strange and most Surprising management which is to be imputed to a company of vile flatterers," Colden and Rutherfurd. Livingston's mood only worsened as time passed. The next year he again complained of "vile management." Why, "D[r]. C[olden] . . . ought to be turned off or Sent back to his own place." Livingston directed his rage at Colden, whom one historian, when discussing the conference, had called "shrewd."[56]

William Johnson's meteoric rise could not have helped Livingston's ego either. A young man, only in the colony a few years, had shown he had more influence with the Iroquois than New York's Indian secretary. A man of Johnson's gifts stirred up jealousy, a fact that continued to be evident. Years later, a writer noted that Johnson's "Enemies . . . envy his rising Merit." Livingston's bitterness pushed him into DeLancey's corner, forcing the governor to ask London to fire him from his post, a request that failed. Livingston's opposition continued to strengthen. On December 21, 1747, he moaned: "there is no hopes that our Govr will dismiss his darling the Doctor."[57]

Not surprisingly, Colden would have had his fill of dealing with Livingston at Albany. For that matter, Colden was tired of being in Albany, threatened by both disease and "sculking parties of the French Indians." When he at last left that town and was back in the capital, he urged Clinton "to regain if possible the assistance of his former friends." In Colden's mind, his duty had been done. The Iroquois had been won over, once again, to the British Empire and now he could return, once again, to blissful Coldengham and his philosophical pursuits. That was a forlorn hope. The governor's overtures to the DeLancey faction failed and Clinton encountered "Sessions of Assembly where a popular party in opposition to the Govr. appeared with more intollerable insolence than was ever known (in this Province at least)." Clinton needed Colden more than ever.[58]

During November 1746 the Assembly turned its ire upon Clinton and Colden, using provisions for the army around Albany as the cudgel. In October the commissioners in charge of the provisions—Assembly appointees—refused to send supplies to the army. Technically, the Assembly had not voted funds to move the supplies. The commander of the New York forces, John Roberts, armed with an impressment from the governor, had the storehouse with the goods broken into and the supplies taken. Colden knew nothing about this impressment as he and the governor had already left Albany. Calling this action "arbitrary and illegal," the Assembly zeroed in on one individual "in particular," Colden, who, earlier, had "made such Demand, and even threatened that if they did not undertake to transport the Provision with the Army, they would take them out of their Hands, and appoint other Commissioners in their Stead." Colden had committed "a high Misdemeanor" an Assembly committee insisted, and demanded that he be prosecuted. The governor, of course, refused.[59]

Colden saw the Assembly's attack for what it was. "It is impossible to act in the Station I am in without meeting with ill natured returns for actions which perhaps are most deserving." He had been targeted because he had helped the governor. To be accused of a crime for only reminding the commissioners that Clinton had to replace them if they did not do their jobs—an obvious fact—seemed "silly" (as Rutherfurd dismissed the Assembly's complaint). The governor had sent Colden to the commissioners to deliver that very message. Colden warned his wife not to worry about what she read in the newspapers regarding this strange behavior of his "Enemies."[60]

On October 18, 1746 Governor Clinton had reminded the Council "that if the Provisions for the Army be put into Persons Hands independent of the General. . ., all his Designs may at any time be frustrated ." But DeLancey and his Assembly allies thought they had a good issue anyway. A letter, supposedly from a Dutch farmer near Albany, complained that soldiers had impressed everything from his farm, including his cow. It was "barbarous and inhuman." Were not Albany's farmers "intitled to Magna Charta?" Did he "run the risk of having my Neck broke for publishing this Account?" DeLancey's forces stopped at nothing to discredit the governor and his advisor.[61]

Another assault upon Colden totally surprised him. He had written a small book describing the Indian conference in Albany, emphasizing its great success to counteract "the most malicious and base slanders of the Governor among the People" regarding the Indian alliance. None of the councilors had complained about the book, which they all knew he had written.[62]

On December 4, 1746 Colden attended a meeting of the Council where it was supposed to function as part of the colonial legislature and debate proposed bills without the governor. Recent Council meetings had been sparsely attended; the quorum had not been attained. Imagine Colden's surprise when he walked in and discovered that everyone was there including Livingston. The three lawyer members, DeLancey, Horsmanden, and Joseph Murray, all had prepared speeches in front of them. DeLancey announced that there was no legislative business left to do, so the Council would conduct an investigation of the treaty book which had been available for some weeks.[63]

DeLancey read out a single paragraph in the book which stated that all but three members had refused to go to Albany for the conference. This paragraph, the chief justice went on, contained "a Misrepresentation of Facts, and an invidious reflection upon such as the members of his Majesty's Council as did not attend his Excellency to Albany" and asked that the printer be summoned to find out who the author was, which they already knew. Horsmanden urged that the paragraph be "censured." He spoke so "warmly" that Colden insisted he respect "the Decency" of correct Council proceedings. They denied his request that the Council reconvene as a privy council which Governor Clinton could attend.[64]

Colden, astonished at what was happening, hesitated for a few seconds before admitting his authorship of the book. The councilors called this a confession when the minutes were drawn up, giving the impression Colden had been guilty of a crime. In these circumstances, he delayed briefly, trying to avoid "a direct answer." Within seconds, though, he admitted that he had told the printer to publish it with Governor Clinton's "approbation." Colden offered to correct any factual error, but DeLancey and his allies had no interest in that. The censure passed and was published in New York (although it would not be included in the Council minutes sent to London).[65]

Why DeLancey plotted this set-up by men who had no "regard to truth or decency" seemed clear. First, they hoped to discredit Colden's account of the Albany conference by attacking it. Second, by harassing the senior councilor they assumed that "all others will have dread to oppose them." But the set-up of Colden had several effects that DeLancey had not expected. Clinton soon urged the British government to remove Horsmanden from the Council to "check" the influence "of that faction" and replace him with James Alexander, whom DeLancey could not frighten.[66]

Another Colden friend rejoiced that he was in the city where he "might put a Stop to all the folly that was going on there." But the governor had even more praise for Cadwallader Colden. Without him, Clinton assured his superiors, he would not have been able to organize the planned Canadian expedition. On December 9, 1746 he recommended that Colden be appointed lieutenant governor of New York as his expertise with the Indians would be very useful. Clinton's regard for his advisor soon grew into friendship.[67]

DeLancey, however, had not yet finished blasting Colden, whom the allies of the chief justice insisted was to blame for all the disputes. Waiting until he had left for Coldengham to spend the winter months, usually a quiet time, with his family, some of his foes went to the governor to plot against the absent advisor. Insisting there was "resentment . . . only at Mr. Colden," they promised that if Clinton "would no longer follow Mr. Colden's advice every thing should be made easy" in his government. Livingston and other councilors presented a "Humble Representation" to Clinton attacking Colden, an "Artfull and Designing" man, who "has Told the World in Print of his being the Next person to your Excellency in the Administration." That seemingly innocent remark, the plotters suggested, meant that Colden planned "to Embroil" the government to aid "his getting the Reins of Government into his own hands."[68]

When Colden learned of the "low artifice" his enemies had resorted to while he "was cut off" from the city, he had just gotten back to "the innocent amusements I enjoy in my retirement" when he had to deal with "this disagreeable subject." Most exasperating to Colden was the insinuation that he had been scheming to seize control of the government. Everyone in New York had to know that, with no lieutenant governor, Colden was next in line. While "vanity" was "a weed which is observed to grow luxuriantly in an American soil," being president of the Council could not increase his vanity very much. He had mentioned his position to explain to the Indians why the governor had selected him to speak to them. When Colden contemplated recent events, he concluded that a message from the Assembly to the governor "seems to be a claim of Independency."[69]

Having already been deceived by DeLancey and his allies, Clinton did not fall for their latest gambit. The governor assured Colden that "as you entered voluntarily with me and took my part against a Haughty Insolent set of people . . . I will never drop you." The latest scheme failed, but it set a pattern among the governor's foes who, when they sought something from Clinton, would only broach the idea to the governor if Colden had left for Coldengham.[70]

Despite all the political grief, the Crown Point attack had remained an option, because of the continued enthusiasm for it among the New Englanders. But when a French fleet appeared off Nova Scotia, the Massachusetts soldiers had to withdraw to guard against a potential attack upon their own colony. Meanwhile, Governor Clinton had finally given in to Livingston's belief that attacking Crown Point was impossible during the winter months; even Colden at last agreed. John Rutherfurd, though, complained that "The Winter proved extremely favourable for such an attempt."[71]

With the approach of the spring of 1747, hopes for an attack against Crown Point rose again. Governor Clinton asked the Assembly for financial support, which would only be forthcoming, Assembly leaders insisted, if all assemblymen were told "the whole design and plan of Operations" to enable them to "Judge" if the campaign had been "well concerted." Now the Assembly was attempting to usurp another executive power, control over an army's operations. Both the governor and Colden realized if this new demand was accepted, the secret details of the campaign "must have become the next day the common subject of discourse of the whole town" and would have become known by the French. Even the Council rejected the idea. An attempted compromise, informing some select assemblymen of the details, did not move the Assembly from its dogmatic stand. There would be no supplies or pay for New York's soldiers, preventing any action at all.[72]

An unpaid army is a dangerous thing to have about and tension slowly built. During April 1747 in New York City a rumor spread of a slave rebellion but nothing developed. What did occur was bad enough. By the start of May a true report reached the governor that the army stationed near Albany had mutinied.[73]

Very quickly, the governor became concerned about the extent of the "disorders." He had hoped the men "would have borne with Patience the Want of their pay," but that obviously was not going to happen. Some of them had refused "to do any duty" and left their posts. Calming for a while, the soldiers exploded when they learned that their comrades from New Jersey had just gotten all the money they had been owed. The angry New York soldiers, a shocked Colden wrote, vowed "to plunder the Country if they have not their whole pay," a threat he took seriously. Not only could Colden not leave the governor in this crisis, he warned his wife he might have "to send for you and the Children" to come to New York City.[74]

On June 7, 1747 Colden's anxiety level increased a great deal. By that time he had decided to return to Coldengham along with his daughters Jennie and Alice who had stayed with him in the city. When he told Clinton his plan of sending the sisters home, the governor "immediately answered that He thought it very wrong in me to send them in the way of the Mutineers" until it was certain that the mutiny had ended; they stayed in the city. Earlier, Colden had insisted that his wife and children leave for Sandie's home in Newburgh, but now he instructed her to leave Coldengham with the rest of the family if she heard "any account of the Mutineers marching downwards" and come to the capital "for they have openly threatened to take their pay in plunder wherever they go and if once they begin such kind of work none can tell what other outrages they may be guilty of." Colden cautioned his wife not to talk about this; the panic it would have caused is self-evident.[75]

Governor Clinton planned to stop the mutiny by forwarding some money for the soldiers. Since the Assembly would contribute nothing, Clinton had to use "my own Fortune" to cover this expense. He had already, by January 1747, floated bills of almost £40,000. Not only did this latest round of payments expand his personal debt, he would never be compensated for them.[76]

Clinton's personal sacrifice did little good. When he ordered New York City's militia to gather in November 1747 so their officers could draft ten percent of their men to create a force to rush to help the frontier, the men, claiming the order to be "Despotic and Tyrannical," refused to obey. These militiamen, with their minds already poisoned by the Assembly, insisted that their assemblymen had to approve the governor's order. The assemblymen remained furious that the governor had tried to use the militia without their approval. The continuing frenzy created so much "uneasiness" in Ulster that Alice, as she informed her husband in November, was more worried about rebellious soldiers than earlier. She rushed "4 Trunks and 2 Chests" filled with money, plate, bonds and assorted valuables along with his account books to her husband in the city for safekeeping. Even the final cancellation of the Canadian expedition in October 1747 had not calmed the riled province as the men had not received all of their pay.[77]

The New York Assembly's "ridiculous farce," as the governor called it, did not go over well in other colonies. Watching from Pennsylvania, Benjamin Franklin complained to Colden: "The violent Party Spirit that appears in all the Votes etc. of your Assembly, seems to me extremely unseasonable as well as unjust, and to threaten Mischief not only to your selves but to your Neighbours." Franklin feared that the French in Canada "may reap great Advantages from your divisions." All he could hope was that "God grant they be as blind to their own Interest, and as negligent of it, as the English are of theirs." Franklin's request was granted as the enemy made no attempt to move against the chaotic colony of New York.[78]

Clinton did what he could do against his enemies. Tired of waiting for London to act, on September 12, 1747 the governor fired Horsmanden from all his offices, calling him the "principal actor in the opposition." Even DeLancey, it was claimed, had tried to convince Horsmanden to lessen his public "Insolence" toward Clinton. Horsmanden, though, blamed his dismissal on "the ill Offices of Mr. Colden."[79]

Nor did the Assembly fail to target the governor's advisor. On October 9, 1747, the Assembly blasted Colden for recounting the success of the Indian conference of 1746, claiming that the supposed success there "never had other Existence, than in the wicked Imagination and Invention of his own Brain." It was truly unfortunate, the assemblymen declared, that "in this Time of eminent Danger," the governor would "depend solely upon the Advice and Caprice of a Man so obnoxious."[80]

Although Clinton could ignore such silly comments, in wartime he could not reject all objectionable bills the legislature had passed. Some he had to accept, but Colden voiced substantive objections to bad legislation at Council meetings, thus putting them into the minutes and so, hopefully, protecting the governor from the ire of London.[81]

With no reason to keep this exasperating Assembly in existence any longer, Governor Clinton, in a speech written by Colden, would dissolve it. The speech complained of the Assembly's "grasping at Power, both Civil and Military" and criticized its members for the "little Regard you have to those who have been willing to expose their Lives, in the Service of their Country" just as they exposed "the Lives and Estates of the people you represent" to the enemy. Convinced that most New Yorkers had opposed the

Assembly's actions, Clinton gave the people a chance to prove their loyalty in an election for a new assembly.[82]

But would the people do so? Colden tried his hand at electioneering as did Horsmanden. Soon after Colden finally left for Coldengham, Horsmanden published a tirade against Clinton's administration. It savaged Johnson, but the chief target remained Colden whom he blamed for his dismissal. Colden's "First Motive," Horsmanden asserted, was "a firm Principle of Disloyalty"—he was a Jacobite—"notwithstanding his outward Shew and Pretences, since the Troubles in Britain" in 1745. After the failed Jacobite revolt, Scots had become unpopular in England and charges of Jacobitism against them had become common. That Horsmanden would try to import the tactic to New York should not surprise nor should Colden's reaction when he learned about it. Angry at what Horsmanden had "dared to belch out," Colden branded him a "vile hackney scribbler."[83]

Colden's own frontal assault in the *Weekly Post-Boy* ran on January 18, 1748, a few days before the Assembly election in New York City. Supposedly from a New York freeholder, Colden's "Address" gave vent over his "grief" at the "publick dissentions" in New York while the colony was locked in conflict with a "barbarous" foe which had "laid waste" much of it. All "impartial" observers "wished that our Representatives . . . had rather exerted their Bowels and compassion for the sufferings of the innocent" rather than having "all their passions employed in Dissentions and contention with their Governor."[84]

Colden made sure to mention "a piece of Insolence," which he thought "cannot be believed in any other part of the world," but had been verified by reliable witnesses. During a parade of the militia "past the Govrs house," Clinton and his daughter were at a window. As a militia unit commanded by an assemblyman marched by, "a fellow in one of the ranks turned round on his heel faced the window took his gun from his shoulder presented it towards the Window and fired." All the assemblyman did was laugh.[85]

The storm that Colden's "Address," which a critic termed "the Excrements of his Brain," stirred up turned out to be greatly increased by the fact that the essay was not as anonymous as he thought. The great length of the piece gave away the author's identity. Printed by James Parker, the official printer, it filled three pages of his regular issue; he had to add a supplement and the essay filled almost another page of that. No other author except Colden would have been allotted such space.[86]

"The expected Paper of Advice, to the Electors, is at length arrived from the Highlands" and "it has been well known who it was to come from," declared one anonymous Colden foe. The "Old Dog," the "little Man," had made up the tale of the crazed militiaman. Colden was "a Lying Minister" asserted another. Still another writer attacked "Dr. Littlecraft": "all will detest the Memory of thy Ministry, Thy Actions, Thy Manners, Thy Face, and even the very Name of Littlecraft." And the insults kept coming: "no Man was ever universally contemptible, or ridiculous without deserving it."[87]

Four militia officers gave depositions that were also printed, attempting to disprove Colden's statement that the governor had been shot at. The incident had supposedly occurred in November 1747 before the New York County militia was to draft some of its members as the governor had ordered. All agreed that no one had been at the window. Three of the officers claimed not to have heard any gun being fired, but one, Brandt Schuyler, swore that "he did hear a Gun discharged by one of the Men and was very much displeased at it." Because of the great racket created by the discharge of a firearm of this time, it is highly improbable that three of the officers could not hear it. Colden's sources—two of whom had to be Governor Clinton himself and his daughter—were more reliable but the cover-up of the incident succeeded.[88]

One attack on Colden, the essay entitled "Fellow Citizens," had been written by Daniel Horsmanden, who included in it a slur against Colden that would reappear. "What is a Drum or a Trumpet without an Artist to play upon them," Horsmanden asked. Colden, he wrote, had referred to

> Warlike instruments, to which he had been accustomed, and to his talking only of a Drum and being silent as to a Drummer, we know he is an artful designing Man, and therefore suspect he left that Vacancy with a private View to supply it himself, having, as 'tis said, been bred up to that Profession and is a great proficient in it; we remember to have heard him acknowledge that at the Time of the Rebellion in North Brittain in King George the First's Time he was in a large Company . . . upon the March, whether to join the Royalists or the contrary party, we chuse to leave as a Matter for conjecture, that every one may judge as they see Cause.[89]

Colden had told Horsmanden about his exploits during the Jacobite rebellion of 1715 when he had stayed as his guest at Coldengham in 1733. At that time, Horsmanden had been in financial trouble so Colden let him stay for weeks. At the end of the prolonged visit, Horsmanden noted how their friendship had grown so quickly. Of course, Horsmanden had given a "malicious turn" to Colden's story and he never forgave him. The enraged Scot, who had learned from experience, would observe "that a wise Foe would always pretend Friendship when he meant to give his Adversary the deepest Thrust." Horsmanden's hint that Colden had been a "Rebell Drummer" would not disappear from the public's memory.[90]

Despite the "great snows" that blanketed the province, DeLancey supporters from New York City were "indefatigable" in traveling about campaigning for their faction's allies. Colden's essay campaign, in contrast, did little to help the governor's friends. His candidates in Westchester got almost no votes, but still did better than the Clinton forces in New York City which experienced a huge turnout and no support at all for the governor. It was claimed that Colden's "Address" was responsible for the "Wonderful" result. In many races across the colony the DeLancey candidates were declared elected; there was no need for a formal vote count.[91]

Ulster was one of the few places where the Clinton men did not suffer a crushing defeat. When Colden had returned to Coldengham, he had discovered that stories "even viler" than Horsmanden had belched had "spread every where" in the county. Colden, however, told his friends the truth and the word spread. Office holders loyal to the Assembly had been the source of the twisted information. When "the very officers of the Government"—subordinated to DeLancey and his faction—"are principally employed in this dirty work what can be expected from the people" Colden lamented.[92]

The hatred stirred up at Governor Clinton extended to his son and daughter, who found themselves snubbed by high society. The young Clintons spent their time with youthful military officers and others of their generation who were not interested in political vendettas.[93]

Even Clinton began to adjust to the hate-filled atmosphere. Eventually, a new club formed with the governor joined by James Alexander, Archibald Kennedy, and both John Rutherfurd and Colden when they were in town. Far more sedate than the Hungarian Club, their wives and families accompanied the men. In 1750, when Colden was away, Alexander informed him about what had transpired during the festivities. "You have been [the governor's] toast every one of those three times that I have been in Company with him," but, at the last session "Mrs. [Anne] Clinton found fault with his toasting of you for that you were her Constant toast."[94]

In the midst of the chaotic political mess in New York, Colden observed "that many things have happened which I did not expect." He knew very well that most of the unexpected events had happened because of James DeLancey, including the plotting at what the governor called "the Jacobati House," which must have been the home of the chief justice. Nonetheless, no stratagem Colden came up with would succeed in stopping the DeLancey juggernaut.[95]

NOTES

1. Norman G. Brett-James, *The Life of Peter Collinson, F.R.S., F.S.A.* (London: E. G. Dunstan, 1925), 159.

2. *ANB*, s.v. Clinton, George (d. 1761).

3. Stanley Nider Katz, "Newcastle's New York Governors: Imperial Patronage during the Era of 'Salutary Neglect,'" *New York Historical Society Quarterly* 51, no. 1 (1967): 14; Beverly McAnear, *The Income of the Colonial Governors of British North America* (New York: Pageant Press, 1967), 4, 10, 54, 56, 74–75.

4. Stanley Nider Katz, *Newcastle's New York: Anglo-American Politics, 1732–1753* (Cambridge, MA: Harvard University Press, 1968), 165.

5. CC to William Shirley, [1749?], CPU, reel 2; Collinson to CC, August 3, 1747, *CP*, vol. 3, 410–12.

6. GC to Warren, [July] 1746, Peter Warren, *The Royal Navy and North America: The Warren Papers, 1736–1752*, ed. Julian Gwyn (London: Navy Records Society, 1975), 297–98; Great Britain, *Acts of the Privy Council, Colonial Series*, ed. William L. Grant and James Munroe (London: H. M. S. O., 1908–1912), vol. 4, 792; Edith M. Fox, *Land Speculation in the Mohawk Country* (Ithaca, NY: Cornell University Press, 1949), 46; Katz, *Newcastle's New York*, 159.

7. William Livingston, *A Review of the Military Operations in North America* (London: R. and J. Dodsley, 1757), 18; Katz, *Newcastle's New York*, 165; Julian Gwyn, *An Admiral for America: Sir Peter Warren, Vice Admiral of the Red, 1703–1752* (Gainesville: University Press of Florida, 2004), 48.

8. CC to Mitchell, July 6, 1749, *CP*, vol. 9, 20.

9. Alexander Hamilton, *Gentleman's Progress: The Itinerarium of Dr. Alexander Hamilton, 1744*, ed. Carl Bridenbaugh (Chapel Hill: University of North Carolina Press, 1948), 42, 88–89, 173–75; Milton M. Klein, "The Cultural Tyros of Colonial New York," *South Atlantic Quarterly* 66, no. 2 (1967): 226.

10. Logan to CC, January 24, 1720/1, James Logan Papers, Logan Letter Books, vol. 3, 2, HSP; CC to JA, December 6, 1729, James Alexander Papers, box 2, f. 7, NYHS; *SM*, vol. 2, 30; Justin DiVirgilio, "Rum Punch and Cultural Revolution: The Impact of the Seven Years' War in Albany," *New York History* 86, no. 4 (2005): 440–41.

11. CC to William Pitt, September 24, 1761, *CLB*, vol. 1, 116–17.

12. CC, "The Rise and Progress of the Publick Dissensions of New York," CPU, reel 2; CC to Mitchell, July 6, 1749, *CP*, vol. 9, 20–21.

13. CC, "Rise and Progress," CPU, reel 2; CC to JA, November 2, 1742, RP, vol. 2, 83; John Rutherfurd to CC, January 10, 1743, *CP*, vol. 3, 1–3; CC to [Collinson], n.d., *CP*, vol. 3, 16–17; Rutherfurd to CC, September 1, 1743, *CP*, vol. 8, 297–98; Gerrit P. Judd, *Members of Parliament, 1734–1832* (New Haven, CT: Yale University Press, 1955), 324; Worthington Chauncey Ford, ed., *British Officers Serving in America, 1754–1774, Compiled from the "Army Lists"* (Boston: D. Clapp, 1894), 88.

14. Rutherfurd to CC, January 10, March 2, 1742/3, *CP*, vol. 3, 1–3, 6–7.

15. Rutherfurd to CC, April 22, 1745, January 25, 1745/6, *CP*, vol. 3, 112–13, 192–93.

16. Rutherfurd to CC, n.d., June 20, 1745, *CP*, vol. 3, 105–7, 115–17; CC to _____, August 7, 1745, *CP*, vol. 3, 136–39; GC to Assembly, May 14, 1745, New York Colony, Council, *Journal of the Legislative Council of the Colony of New York, Began the 9th day of April, 1691; and ended the [3d of April, 1775]* (Albany, NY: Weed, Parsons, 1861), vol. 2, 885; Alan Tully, *Forming American Politics: Ideals, Interests, and Institutions in Colonial New York and Pennsylvania* (Baltimore: Johns Hopkins University Press, 1994), 128.

17. Isaac Norris, "The Journal of Isaac Norris During a Trip to Albany in 1745, and an Account of a Treaty Held There in October of that Year," *Pennsylvania Magazine of History and Biography* 27, no. 1 (1903): 24; GC to Major Glen, March 10, 1745/6, George Clinton Papers, Misc. Mss., NYHS; "Propositions made by his Excellency," October 10, 1745, *CP*, vol. 3, 166; Richard Haan, "The Problem of Iroquois Neutrality: Suggestions for Revision," *Ethnohistory* 27, no. 4 (1980): 325; Eric Hinderaker, *The Two Hendricks: Unraveling a Mohawk Mystery* (Cambridge, MA: Harvard University Press, 2010), 173.

18. Dr. Alexander Colhoun to CC, January 25, 1745/6, *CP*, vol. 3, 193–94; John Bartram, *Memorials of John Bartram and Humphry Marshall, with Notices of Their Botanical Contemporaries*, ed. William Darlington (Philadelphia: Lindsay & Blakiston, 1849), 318n.

19. W. Livingston, *Review*, 126; CC, "Rise and Progress," CPU, reel 2.

20. GC to Warren, April 24–27, 1746, Warren, *Warren Papers*, ed. Gwyn, 236–37; Gwyn, *Admiral for America*, 45.

21. Warren to GC, August 22, 1742, October 11, 1745, Warren, *Warren Papers*, ed. Gwyn, 29, 178; Warren to George Anson, October 2, 1745, Warren, *Warren Papers*, ed. Gwyn, 168; Warren to Newcastle, June 18, 1745, June 7, 1746, Warren, *Warren Papers*, ed. Gwyn, 126, 277–78; Gwyn, *Admiral for America*, 44, 122–25.

22. Gwyn, *Admiral for America*, 44.

23. Warren to GC, September 14, 1745, Warren, *Warren Papers*, ed. Gwyn, 163; CC to Collinson, October 4, 1754, *CP*, vol. 4, 465–67.
24. CC, "Rise and Progress," CPU, reel 2; JA to CC, March 18, 1744/5, *CP*, vol. 3, 107–9.
25. CC, "Rise and Progress," CPU, reel 2; Warren to GC, August 28, 1745, Warren, *Warren Papers*, ed. Gwyn, 156; Gwyn, *Admiral for America*, 125.
26. William Smith, Jr., *The History of the Province of New York*, ed. Michael Kammen (Cambridge, MA: Belknap Press of Harvard University Press, 1972), vol. 2, 73; CC to Mitchell, July 6, 1749, *CP*, vol. 9, 20–21; W. Livingston, *Review*, 18–19.
27. CC, "Rise and Progress," CPU, reel 2; CC to Mitchell, July 6, 1749, *CP*, vol. 9, 20–22; W. Livingston, *Review*, 20.
28. "The Humble Representation of the Underwritten Members of his Majestys Council for the Said Province," December 16, 1746, *CP*, vol. 3, 296; "A. Z.," *New York Evening Post* (DeForeest), February 8, 1747/8.
29. CC, "Colden's Observations on the Balance of Power in Government," *CP*, vol. 9, 256–57; CC, "Memoranda," *CP*, vol. 3, 183–84.
30. John Catherwood to CC, June 6, 1746, George Clinton Papers, vol. 3, CL.
31. CC to Mitchell, July 6, 1749, *CP*, vol. 9, 21–22; CC to GC, January 19, 1746/7, *CP*, vol. 3, 341.`
32. CC, "Rise and Progress," CPU, reel 2; CC to Clarke, November 26, 1746, *CP*, vol. 3, 290–91; CC to GC, January 19, 1746/7, *CP*, vol. 3, 340–41; CC to Mitchell, July 6, 1749, *CP*, vol. 9, 20.
33. Rutherfurd to CC, June 26, 1746, *CP*, vol. 3, 218–19; CC to Mrs. CC, [end of June 1746], July 3, 1746, *CP*, vol. 3, 220–22; CC to GC, January 19, 1746/7, *CP*, vol. 3, 337–39.
34. CC to Mrs. CC, July 3–4, 1746, *CP*, vol. 3, 221–22.
35. CC to Mrs. CC, [end of June 1746], *CP*, vol. 3, 220; CC to Clarke, November 26, 1746, *CP*, vol. 3, 290–91; CC to Mitchell, July 6, 1749, *CP*, vol. 9, 21–22; GC to Andrew Stone, September 1747, Newcastle Papers, British Museum Additional Manuscript 32713, f. 185, LC transcript.
36. CC to GC, January 19, 1746/7, *CP*, vol. 3, 337–41.
37. CC to Gronovius, May 30, 1746, *CP*, vol. 3, 209–11.
38. CC, *A Treaty between His Excellency The Honourable George Clinton, . . . And The Six United Indian Nations, and other Indian Nations depending on the Province of New York* (New York: James Parker, 1746), 3; Katz, *Newcastle's New York*, 180; John Duffy, *Epidemics in Colonial America* (Baton Rouge: Louisiana State University Press, 1953), 226; Joseph Kastner, *Species of Eternity* (New York: Knopf, 1977), 20.
39. CC, *Treaty*, 4.
40. CC to JA, July 23, 1746, *CP*, vol. 3, 227–28; commissioners' answer, July 24, 1746, *CP*, vol. 3, 230–31; CC, *Treaty*, 3; GC, "A Short Account of Governor Clinton's Conduct," September 27, 1747, *NYCD*, vol. 6, 399.
41. CC to Mrs. CC, July 24, 29, August 4, 1746, *CP*, vol. 3, 229–30, 232–33, 238–39; CC to Bartram, January 27, 1746/7, John Bartram, *The Correspondence of John Bartram, 1734–1777*, ed. Edmund Berkeley and Dorothy Smith Berkeley (Gainesville: University Press of Florida, 1992), 284.
42. "Memorandum of Col. Daniel Claus," n.d., *JP*, vol. 13, 723; Katz, *Newcastle's New York*, 179–80.
43. CC, *Treaty*, 7.
44. CC, *Treaty*, 7–8.
45. CC to Mitchell, July 6, 1749, *CP*, vol. 9, 22; Warren to Newcastle and Shirley, October 16, 1746, Warren, *Warren Papers*, ed. Gwyn, 354–55; CC, "Farther account of the Phytolacca," *Gentleman's Magazine* 22 (July 1752): 302; CC to Bartram, January 27, 1746/7, Etting Coll., HSP; Colhoun to GC, July 7, 1751, George Clinton Papers, vol. 11, CL; Duffy, *Epidemics*, 157–58; Alfred R. Hoermann, *Cadwallader Colden: A Figure of the American Enlightenment* (Westport, CT: Greenwood Press, 2002), 56.
46. CC, *Treaty*, 9.
47. CC, *Treaty*, 9; "Copy of his Excr. the Honble George Clinton's Speech," August 19, 1746, *CP*, vol. 3, 247–53; Conference between Governor Clinton and the Indians at Albany the

19th August 1746, *NYCD*, vol. 6, 317; CC, *The History of the Five Indian Nations of Canada . . .*, 2nd ed. (London: John Whiston, 1747), 153–96; Peter Wraxall, *An Abridgment of the Indian Affairs Contained in Four Folio Volumes, Transacted in the Colony of New York, From the Year 1678 to the Year 1751*, ed. Charles Howard McIlwain (Cambridge, MA: Harvard University Press, 1915; repr. New York: Benjamin Blom, 1968), 248; Hinderaker, *Two Hendricks*, 179–80; Victor Hugo Paltsits, "A Scheme for the Conquest of Canada in 1746," American Antiquarian Society, *Proceedings*, n.s., 17 (1905–1906): 87.

48. CC to Mrs. CC, August 20, 1746, *CP*, vol. 3, 259–60; CC, *History* (1747), 182.

49. CC to Mrs. CC, August 28, 1746, *CP*, vol. 3, 266; Arthur H. Buffington, "The Canada Expedition of 1746: Its Relation to British Politics," *American Historical Review* 45, no. 4 (1940): 574–75, 578.

50. Shirley and Warren to GC and Council, July 9, 1746, Warren, *Warren Papers*, ed. Gwyn, 289; Gwyn, *Admiral for America*, 118; Hinderaker, *Two Hendricks*, 188.

51. GC to James DeLancey, August 24, 1746, George Clinton Papers, vol. 4, CL.

52. GC to James DeLancey, August 24, 1746, George Clinton Papers, vol. 4, CL; DeLancey to GC, August 30, 1746, George Clinton Papers, vol. 4, CL.

53. GC to DeLancey, August 24, 1746, George Clinton Papers, vol. 4, CL; CC, "Observations on the Plan of Operations," n.d., *CP*, vol. 3, 215–16; Philip Livingston to Jacob Wendell, January 14, 1745/6, Livingston Papers, Philip Livingston Boxes, Museum of the City of New York.

54. Livingston to Wendell, January 14, 1745/6, June 2, 1746, Livingston Papers, Museum of the City of New York.

55. Livingston to Wendell, January 14, 1745/6, June 2, 1746, Livingston Papers, Museum of the City of New York; Livingston to Wendell, December 13, 1746, Livingston Papers; GC to Stone, September 1747, Newcastle Papers, British Museum Additional Manuscript 32713, f. 185, LC transcript.

56. Livingston to Wendell, September 18, 1746, October 19, 1747, Livingston Papers, Museum of the City of New York; Peter H. Bryce, "Sir William Johnson, Bart., The Great Diplomat of the British-French Frontier," *Quarterly Journal of the New York State Historical Association* 8, no. 4 (1926): 360; Patricia U. Bonomi, *A Factious People: Politics and Society in Colonial New York* (New York: Columbia University Press, 1971), 154–55.

57. New York City, "A Defence of New York Against the Slanders of New England," February 23, 1756, in *Manual of the Corporation of the City of New York* (New York: New York Common Council, 1870), 892; Livingston to Wendell, November 9, December 8, 21, 1747, Livingston Papers, Museum of the City of New York; Bonomi, *Factious People*, 154–55; Katz, *Newcastle's New York*, 181.

58. CC to Collinson, October 4, 1754, *CP*, vol. 4, 467; CC to Bartram, January 27, 1746/7, Etting Coll., HSP.

59. *Assembly Journal*, vol. 2, 134; CC, "An account of Gov. Clinton's administration," n.d., CPU, reel 2; CC to Mitchell, July 6, 1749, *CP*, vol. 9, 26–27; Draft of GC's speech, November 24, 1746, *CP*, vol. 3, 287–88.

60. CC to Mrs. CC, November 9, 11, 18, 1746, *CP*, vol. 3, 278–81; Rutherfurd to CC, November 19, 1746, *CP*, vol. 3, 284; Draft of GC's speech, November 24, 1746, *CP*, vol. 3, 287; CC to Mitchell, July 6, 1749, *CP*, vol. 9, 26–27.

61. GC to Council, October 18, 1746, George Clinton Papers, vol. 4, CL; "Nickus Roolefse" to James Parker, November 10, 1746, *New York Gazette, or the Weekly Post-Boy* (Parker), December 29, 1746.

62. Memorandum in CC's handwriting, n.d., *CP*, vol. 3, 306–7; CC to GC, January 19, 1746/7, *CP*, vol. 3, 341–42; CC to Mitchell, July 6, 1749, *CP*, vol. 9, 25–26; GC to Lords of Trade, n.d., *NYCD*, vol. 6, 328–29.

63. New York Colony, Council, *Journal of the Legislative Council of the Colony of New York*, vol. 2, 957–58; Memorandum in CC's handwriting, n.d., *CP*, vol. 3, 306–7.

64. Memorandum in CC's handwriting, n.d., *CP*, vol. 3, 306–7; CC to GC, January 19, 1746/7, *CP*, vol. 3, 341–43; GC to Lords of Trade, n.d., *NYCD*, vol. 6, 328–29; "Abstract of the Evidence in the Books of the Lords of Trade relating to New-York," c. April 2, 1751, *NYCD*,

vol. 6, 659; New York Colony, Council, *Journal of the Legislative Council of the Colony of New York*, vol. 2, 957–58.

65. "Abstract of the Evidence in the Books of the Lords of Trade relating to New-York," c. April 2, 1751, *NYCD*, vol. 6, 659; *New York Gazette, or the Weekly Post-Boy* (Parker), December 8, 1746; New York Colony, Council, *Journal of the Legislative Council of New York*, vol. 2, 957–58; memorandum in CC's handwriting; n.d., *CP*, vol. 3, 306–7; GC to Lords of Trade, n.d., *NYCD*, vol. 6, 328–29; CC to GC, Jan. 19, 1746/7, *CP*, vol. 3, 341–43.

66. CC, "Clinton's administration," CPU, reel 2; Memorandum in CC's handwriting, n.d., *CP*, vol. 3, 306–7; CC to GC, January 5, 1746/7, *CP*, vol. 3, 328–30; GC to Newcastle, December 9, 1746, *NYCD*, vol. 6, 312–14; GC to Lords of Trade, n.d., *NYCD*, vol. 6, 328–29.

67. GC to Newcastle, December 9, 1746, *NYCD*, vol. 6, 312–14; Eleanor Rutherfurd to CC, December 9, 1746, *CP*, vol. 3, 292; CC to Henry Clinton, June 6, 1765, Sir Henry Clinton Papers, vol. 2: 14, CL.

68. CC, "Clinton's administration," CPU, reel 2; Livingston, DeLancey, and others, "Humble Representation," December 16, 1746, *CP*, vol. 3, 304–5.

69. CC, "Clinton's administration," CPU, reel 2; CC to GC, January 5, 19, 1746/7, *CP*, vol. 3, 328–30, 337–39, 353–55.

70. GC to CC, January 22, 1746/7, *CP*, vol. 3, 356–57; Henry Beekman to Henry Livingston, November 26, 1747, "A Packet of Old Letters (found in old Poughkeepsie Court House; Livingston, Beekman families; 1732–1755)," Dutchess County Historical Society, *Year Book* 6 (1921): 33.

71. GC to CC, December 17, 1746, *CP*, vol. 3, 308; CC to Clarke, January 18, 1746/7, *CP*, vol. 3, 336–37; Kennedy to CC, January 23, 1746/7, *CP*, vol. 3, 357–58; Rutherfurd to CC, March 17, 1747, *CP*, vol. 3, 365; CC to Mitchell, July 6, 1749, *CP*, vol. 9, 22–23.

72. CC to Mitchell, July 6, 1749, *CP*, vol. 9, 28–30.

73. CC to Mitchell, July 6, 1749, *CP*, vol. 9, 30–31; CC to Mrs. CC, April 18, May 2, 1747, *CP*, vol. 8, 345; vol. 3, 378.

74. GC to commanding officers, May 3, 1747, George Clinton Misc. Mss., f. 2, NYHS; CC to Mrs. CC, May 2, 1747, *CP*, vol. 3, 378; Peter Wraxall to CC, May 15, 1747, *CP*, vol. 3, 385–86; CC to Mrs. CC, June 2, 1747, *CP*, vol. 3, 394–95; GC to Newcastle, May 11, 1747, *CP*, vol. 3, 381–84.

75. CC to Mrs. CC, May 6, June 7, 1747, *CP*, vol. 3, 380, 400–2.

76. GC to Newcastle, May 11, 1747, *CP*, vol. 3, 381–84; GC to Major Glen, January 16, 1746/7, George Clinton Misc. Mss., f. 2, NYHS; GC to Stone, July 24, 1747, *NYCD*, vol. 6, 377.

77. CC to Mitchell, July 6, 1749, *CP*, vol. 9, 30–31; Henry Beekman to Henry Livingston, November 24, 1747, Beekman Family Papers, box 1, f. 15, NYHS; Mrs. CC to CC, November 22, 1747, *CP*, vol. 3, 429–30; GC to Lords of Trade, November 30, 1747, *NYCD*, vol. 6, 413; Bonomi, *Factious People*, 156–57; Paltsits, "Scheme," 92.

78. BF to CC, November 27, 1747, *FP*, vol. 3, 212; CC, "Address to The Freeholders and Freemen of the Cities and Counties of the Province of New York On Occasion of the ensueing Elections for Representatives in General Assembly," January 18, 1747/8, *CP*, vol. 3, 318.

79. GC to Newcastle, September 27, 1747, *NYCD*, vol. 6, 395–96; Horsmanden to Lords of Trade, Sept. 29, 1747, *NYCD*, vol. 6, 404–5; John Ayscough to CC, *CP*, vol. 4, 208–10.

80. Remonstrance of General Assembly, October 9, 1747, *NYCD*, vol. 6, 618, 621.

81. GC to Lords of Trade, November 30, 1747, *NYCD*, vol. 6, 413; New York Colony, Council, *Journal of the Legislative Council of the Colony of New York*, vol. 2, 992–94, 998–99; "Abstract of the Evidence," April 2, 1751, New York Colony, Council, *Journal of the Legislative Council of the Colony of New York*, vol. 2, 680.

82. GC to Assembly, November 25, 1747, New York Colony, Council, *Journal of the Legislative Council of the Colony of New York*, vol. 2, 999–1002; *CP*, vol. 3, 431.

83. Daniel Horsmanden, *A Letter from Some of the Representatives in the Late General Assembly of the Colony of New-York to His Excellency Governor C———n* (New York: James Parker, 1747), 16; CC to GC, January 29, 1747/8, *CP*, vol. 4, 6–10; *SM*, vol. 2, 32–33; G. J. Bryant, "Scots in India in the Eighteenth Century," *Scottish Historical Review* 64, no. 177 (1985): 29.

84. CC, "An Address to The Freeholders," January 18, 1747/8, *CP*, vol. 3, 312–13; GC to CC, January 14, 1747, *CP*, vol. 3, 332–34.

85. CC, "An Address to The Freeholders," January 18, 1747/8, *CP*, vol. 3, 319.

86. *New-York Gazette, Revived In the Weekly Post-Boy* (Parker), January 18, 1747/8; "A. Z..," *New York Evening Post* (DeForeest), February 8, 1747/8.

87. "Fellow Citizens," January 20, 1747/8, *New York Evening Post* (DeForeest), January 25, 1747/8; "Philalethes," *New York Evening Post* (DeForeest), February 1, 1747/8; "Decipherer," January 28, 1747/8, *New York Evening Post* (DeForeest), February 8, 1747/8; "The Nature and Effects," *New York Evening Post* (DeForeest), February 22, 1747/8.

88. Depositions of Paul Richard, Brandt Schuyler, Garret Van Horne, and Abraham Lott, Jr., January 20, 1747, *New York Evening Post* (DeForeest), January 25, 1747/8.

89. Horsmanden, "Fellow Citizens," January 20, 1747/8, *New York Evening Post* (DeForeest), January 25, 1747/8.

90. "A Narrative of some facts," c. December 1765, *CLB*, vol. 2, 63–64; Horsmanden to CC, December 30, 1733, *CP*, vol. 2, 95–97; *SM*, vol. 2, 32–33.

91. "Z. D.," January 16, 1747/8, *New York Gazette, or the Weekly Post-Boy* (Parker), January 18, 1747/8; "To C. C. Esqr. in Answer to his Address," *New York Evening Post* (DeForeest), January 25, 1747/8; CC to Catherwood, January 3, 1747/8, George Clinton Papers, vol. 7, CL.

92. CC to GC, January 29, 1747/8, *CP*, vol. 4, 6–10.

93. GC to Shirley, April 1748, George Clinton Papers, vol. 7, CL; Kennedy to CC, February 9, 1746/7, *CP*, vol. 3, 358–59.

94. GC to CC, March 11, 1747, *CP*, vol. 3, 363–65; JA to CC, December 10, 1750, *CP*, vol. 4, 240.

95. GC to CC, January 14, 1747, *CP*, vol. 3, 332–34; CC to Warren, September 26, 1747, *CP*, vol. 3, 425–26.

Chapter Nine

The Ottoman Family

On March 29, 1748, James Alexander wrote to Cadwallader Colden, then at Coldengham recovering from the election debacle of the previous January. Alexander assured his friend that "I would rather chuse your present State with a very moderate Subsistence than the fatigues you underwent for a year before with a thousand [pounds] a year Laid in the Scale with them."[1]

By any standard it had been a trying year for the sage of Coldengham, who had just turned 60 years old. And more was to come, courtesy of "the Ottoman Family," as an enemy called the DeLanceys. Aside from James DeLancey, who so far had tried to at least remain civil, Governor George Clinton and Colden had to keep a watchful eye on the chief justice's younger brother, Oliver DeLancey, who failed to hide his true self. This DeLancey, "to shew his resentment against Mr. Clinton and his adherents, assaulted the mayor; whipped the sheriff; damned the Governor; and stabbed his physician." A DeLancey foe truthfully remarked that New York "became the sport and contempt of our neighbours."[2]

Oliver DeLancey tossed threats about with abandon. Late in 1747, the governor reported, Oliver had promised in public "that the Faction would hang three or four people and set up a Government of their own." Given that, it is not exaggerating to suggest that Colden had to be cautious. For his transgression of writing the speech with which Clinton had dissolved the Assembly, Colden had been branded "an Enemy to the Colony," "an Enemy to the general Assembly" and also an enemy of the "People of this Province." Zealous DeLancey supporters considered all those charges as hanging offenses. Undeterred, Colden did not give up the fight while Clinton remained governor of New York.[3]

Nonetheless, by the time Colden received Alexander's letter another blow had been delivered to the governor and his primary advisor. Clinton had desperately wanted permission to return to England for health reasons but also to secure repayment for the money he had advanced for the abortive Canadian invasion. The leave had been approved, but James DeLancey had been commissioned to be lieutenant governor, putting him in control of the province when Clinton left. This news had arrived during the Assembly election. The "unexpected promotion" produced shock waves through the colony as "messengers were immediately dispatched throughout the Province," and "damped" the enthusiasm of the governor's friends who now dreaded "the exorbitant power and resentment of this man," the presumptive lieutenant governor. Colden knew of one case where the news changed some thirty votes, thus electing the chief justice's candidates.[4]

Both Colden and Clinton had underestimated DeLancey's influence. The chief justice had once plainly told the governor that the DeLancey connections in Britain were far better than his (even though the Duke of Newcastle was related to Clinton). Despite DeLancey's powerful friends (and the DeLancey money that flowed to various other important people), Peter Warren's presence in the imperial capital had won the lieutenant governorship for the chief justice. Sir Peter declared his belief that the appointment "will contribute to the settling all the uneasiness that have so unhappily subsisted for some time past." He assured the governor that he had written to DeLancey "and I dare say you will find he will do everything to your satisfaction that can be consistent with honour."[5]

Clinton was flabbergasted that his naval buddy had betrayed him in so serious a fashion. The governor's candidate for the position, Cadwallader Colden, had been shunted aside while the man who had betrayed his trust, James DeLancey, had been promoted. The governor believed that his critical reports about DeLancey had "been intercepted [or] misconstrued" to Newcastle "by Sir Peter who I find stiks at nothing for the sake of his own Interest." Furthermore, Clinton thought that some of his supposed friends "are bribed by Sir Peter." This charge refers to Robert Charles, Warren's secretary, whom the governor had picked as one of his agents. Clinton had helped Charles by recommending him to his noble nephew. To reward this betrayal, the New York Assembly made Charles its agent.[6]

On the other hand, Colden took his rejection for the post surprisingly well. "I knew the chances that attended the Game." He actually defended the Duke of Newcastle. A man of such importance had to be preoccupied "in affairs of greatest importance." In comparison, an appointment in a distant colony seemed minor, especially with Warren assuring the duke that favoring DeLancey would calm the turbulence in New York, cutting down the duke's workload. Colden, though, had to have been pleased when the governor assured him that "none but Partys in opposition to all good Government could find fault with the Measures that were taken by your advice."[7]

What Colden did fear, he told Clinton, was what else the duke might have agreed to do. Far worse to Colden was the duke's "restoring the infamous scribbler to any power of exerting his Malice otherwise than by his vile pen which must soon want ink if your Excellency do not enable him to go on." How galling it would be for Colden if Daniel Horsmanden, who had betrayed his trust with "scandalous printed libels," regained his offices. The governor vowed never to restore Horsmanden no matter what orders came from London.[8]

Colden, eventually, learned what strategy had been used against him in London. "Dr. Colden is not well spoke of here," the governor heard from Peter Wraxall, a New Yorker whom he had also delegated to help him in the mother country. Colden had been portrayed as "a person disagreeable to both the Council and Assembly" and so not the best man to calm the disputes in New York. The governor called this attack upon his advisor "a Defamation."[9]

The governor urged Colden to counter the lies told about him in Great Britain by writing to the Duke of Newcastle "to blacken your vile Accusers," promising the aid of his own connections. Eager to expose "the vile Slanders which have been thrown and industriously spread against me," Colden wrote to the duke on March 21, 1748 to defend himself, if a bit apologetically. Realizing Newcastle was a busy man, Colden laid out his side of the story pointing out that the New York assemblymen were "of the lowest rank of mankind easily deluded and led away with popular pretences." The people themselves "greedily swallow" anything that lessens the stature of "their Superiors." The faction's "appeals to the People . . . are dangerous" especially "in a dependant Government." For good measure, Colden explained that he had not been a Jacobite in 1715 and referred the duke to the marquess of Lothian who knew the truth.[10]

Governor Clinton kept his word to his chief advisor. Writing to both the duke and his powerful brother, Henry Pelham, the governor explained that Colden, because he had aided him and the British Empire, "drew upon himself the rage of a violent Faction." Most telling, however, Colden's foes had failed to produce any specifics against him; all they said was "He was obnoxious to us," that is, he backed the governor. Therefore, Clinton recommended that Colden be made lieutenant governor because of "his long service." Already president of New York's Council, Colden "may have some pretence to expect" the promotion.[11]

Colden wrote the governor's letter and also presented another attack upon DeLancey, this one constitutional. Suggesting that the governor consult lawyers, Colden asked how could one man, if he employed his commission of lieutenant governor, be the governor, the chief justice, and also the chancellor of the colony "at the same time?" Did not the governor's instructions specify that he could hold no other office? Could this be a clever scheme to have Horsmanden serve as a temporary chief justice while DeLancey acted as governor?[12]

The only positive thing about DeLancey's appointment was that the governor had been ordered to present the commission to him before returning to Britain on his granted leave of absence. So Clinton, informing Colden "that I intend Staying as long as possibly I can," gave his embattled advisor another promise: "nor will I leave the Province before I see you in some way or other Secured from the Resentment of your Enemies." After consulting with Alexander, the governor learned that he could make Colden surveyor-general "for life" and sought a salary for the post too.[13]

The governor realized that the war had wiped out the income from Colden's office of surveyor-general—"I have not got ten pounds by it" Colden complained. As partial compensation, the governor appointed John Colden to some jobs and often consulted with his chief advisor about the most deserving candidates for offices still controlled by the executive. Cad, for example, became a militia captain in Ulster while his sisters received land grants.[14]

Nor did Clinton's campaign to stop DeLancey from succeeding him upon his departure end. The push for Colden continued. If he could not be lieutenant governor, an alternative plan was hatched. Deny DeLancey his commission, Clinton suggested, then Colden could be "left President in my absence for his faithful services." Allowing his advisor to be in charge as president of the Council would also protect him from "the exorbitant power and resentment" of the chief justice.[15]

In case Colden's being left in charge of New York could not be sold to London, another scenario came about. If DeLancey kept his lieutenant governor commission, the governor would insist he surrender his salary as chief justice. With that money, Clinton would appoint "Phi___," presumably Philip Livingston, so bringing him back to the governor's side. With two other new judges aiding the new senior jurist, a break would be put upon DeLancey's power on the bench. Livingston's death in 1749 ended that idea.[16]

A modified version, however, evolved a few years later. Another member of the influential Livingston family, Robert Livingston, suggested that, in return for his support, Clinton place his son, Robert R. Livingston, on the bench. Alexander supported the move, and Clinton asked Colden for his opinion of "King Robert's Son." Colden had asked young Livingston to read his manuscript on gravitation, but hesitated to endorse him for the court. "I have heard a good Character of him but this was only in private life." Nor did he know anything about his legal skills. "It has frequently happened," Colden observed, "that a man who has gained an esteem in private life after he has been invested with power has appeared in a very different light." However, the chief justice learned about this plan and manipulated Livingston into backing away from it. Colden's scepticism proved justified. Years later, Robert R. Livingston created his own political machine that rivaled that of the DeLanceys.[17]

Even the petering out of King George's War did not end the political infighting. During the closing days of the war the Assembly had "acted a bad part" the governor explained to William Shirley, the governor of Massachusetts. And Colden stayed a target of Clinton's foes. In August 1748 he revealed to London that Colden "has had to struggle with the most violent attempt of an insolent faction, who have endeavoured to expose his person to the mob, throwing out the vilest slanders upon him, and even threatened with death." Clinton, pleased to report that "they have not been able to effect their wicked designs," again urged that Colden's effort be rewarded.[18]

In October 1748 the Council finally exploded. On October 8 it met to consider Clinton's response to a letter of the French governor of Canada. The meeting started cordially, with DeLancey praising the draft of Clinton's response, but urged that it be restructured to be more like each paragraph responding to a specific paragraph of the Frenchman's missive. Clinton then had the Council secretary read the draft, paragraph by paragraph, so the necessary alterations could be made.[19]

Everything went well until the reading of a paragraph involving the exchange of prisoners of war, which mentioned that the Indians were reluctant to surrender those prisoners that had "been given up to particular families and adopted." Sometimes, American Indians took captives to replace family members who had been killed.[20]

After hearing the paragraph DeLancey "kept silent for some time." Asked what he thought, the chief justice said "it was not English, and that he could not understand the meaning of it" and suggested it be made clearer. Colden took a stab at revising it but DeLancey insisted it remained a puzzle to him. Colden recommended that the paragraph should be marked "not intelligible" and worked on later.[21]

Suddenly, what the governor called "DeLancey's insolent revengeful temper" flared up. Interrupting Colden, DeLancey "said we must guard against misrepresentations." Not following what he meant, Colden asked for an explanation and the chief justice stated, "Mr. Colden discovered the other day a most Iniquitous Flagitious and wicked mind in Council" when he had criticized a commissioner of provisions' response to a recent "Message" from Clinton. Colden demanded that DeLancey's explanation "be taken down" in the Council minutes, and the chief justice "with a loud and threatening voice repeated them . . . or others as injurious" and promised to write them down.[22]

Still raging, DeLancey "called for a Bible" that the Council's clerk could be "examined upon Oath, as to what passed that day in Council." Colden promptly "objected, as not being the proper business of that Committee" nor were witnesses supposed to be sworn during a Council meeting about what happened at a different meeting. Colden promised to use "a proper method." Then "the Committee broke up," apparently in some disorder.[23]

For the governor's benefit, Colden explained the meaning of DeLancey's "injurious reflections." There had been some question as to whether or not the commissioners of provisions had been willing to supply the soldiers still defending the frontier. Colden had asked that part of the "circumstantial account" should be placed in the minutes. DeLancey then moved that all of the story be recorded; Colden did not object. No one at this earlier meeting had complained about Colden's comments, nor did he "in the least imagine they were liable to any."[24]

DeLancey tried to defend his behavior, in a letter to the governor, by resorting to legal technicalities and that he had more pressing duties than responding to Colden's written attack, as he "seems to be very fond of writing a great deal." Besides, the chief justice declared "that by Law no Man is bound to accuse himself, so that had I uttered any words of which advantage could be taken against me, I am not by Law obliged to disclose them to my own prejudice." The "procedure" Colden had put forth was very "unfair" DeLancey suggested. Why take down only a part of a conversation, which would seem different when taken in context? "I have a very mean opinion of Mr. Colden," he explained to Clinton, "and as Mr. Colden's character is notorious, I imagined the attempt then made to proceed from the Depravity of his heart ." So it was all Colden's fault.[25]

Colden wrote even more on the subject, which he read in the Council on November 8, 1748. Replying to DeLancey's letter to the governor, Colden pointed out that "One half" of it "is employed in things foreign to the Matter in Question." Having examined the Council records, he insisted: "I have not found or heard of the like Misdemeanor, committed before this by any Councillor." What had he done to make him notorious in DeLancey's eyes? Thinking of Horsmanden, Colden referred to "some notorious Calumnies, which have been published in this place" that "perhaps" DeLancey had been referring to. Anyone who had read DeLancey's letter "can doubt of his willingness to blacken my Character" especially given "what a Slight occasion he has in this case made use of for that purpose." Why, "People unacquainted with the affairs of this Government, may think it impossible that such rancour and malice, as has appeared against me, should be raised without some prior cause on my part."[26]

DeLancey's tirade in the Council, Colden declared, had been "premeditated," but that is unlikely. The paragraph of Clinton's draft that caused DeLancey's outburst may not have been written by Colden although in that case he would have critiqued it. However, the reference to Indian adoption made DeLancey assume it was Colden's handiwork, causing the angry explosion.[27]

Plenty of reasons existed for DeLancey to resent Colden, who blocked his rise to power. The chief justice still did not have his lieutenant governor commission, and he likely suspected that Clinton's campaign against him in Britain might work. Anyone in the imperial government capable of reading a map could see that Crown Point "seems very dangerous and threatening to New York, and may one day enable France from thence to push thro' our Northern Colonies to the Sea." Imperial officials had "Expected" that the colonists would seize the fort without any British help, and everyone who knew about the mess in New York realized that James DeLancey had been responsible for the failure to take Crown Point.[28]

Chief Justice DeLancey had ample reason to be concerned about his political well-being, which worsened because of his nasty temper. Governor Clinton, seeking to take full advantage of his foe's blunder, sent to London copies of the Council minutes "relating to the insult offered to Mr. Colden" and urged that the king issue "orders . . . to preserve the dignity of His Council." These minutes, "the strongest evidence that can be given of the good character of the person calumniated," and the "Malice" of the chief justice, demonstrated the necessity of his removal. The Lords of Trade could "judge of the characters of both of them."[29]

James DeLancey, however, when compared to his younger brother Oliver, seemed like a paragon of self-control. On February 2, 1750, for example, Oliver and some accomplices, "with their faces black'd and otherwise disguised," forced their way into the home of a Jewish couple by smashing the door and windows. The gang "pulled and tore every thing to pieces, and then swore they would lie with the woman," frightening the victims. Oliver then piped up that "she was like Mrs. Clinton, and as he could not have her, he would have her likeness." Afterward, the husband consulted three top lawyers, Joseph Murray, John Chambers, and William Smith Sr., all of whom declined to act, recommending compromise as the thugs "were related to the principal People of the Town." Chambers remarked, "he would be ruined if he proceeded against them." DeLancey money apparently quieted the harassed couple. This disturbing thuggery explains why the governor, in December 1748, feared what might happen to his wife if he died in New York.[30]

About the same time as the attack upon the Jews, "Oliver met a poor man on the road . . . and bid him stop, and because he did not immediately comply with his orders, he broke his head." Despite this victim's complaint, "nothing" was "done, so that the man was obliged to go home, and sit down quietly with his broken head," probably wondering what sort of place he lived in.[31]

Oliver DeLancey's reign of terror included other outrages. In January 1749, according to the governor, Oliver, coming into his own, had already been "insolent," but much more was to come. By early February 1749, Edward Holland, whom Clinton had named New York City's mayor, was already so "frightened" of Oliver that he was hesitant to leave his home. On March 11 DeLancey hit new heights. He rode by Holland spewing "Scurrilous Language," telling the mayor "were it not for your Post . . . I would lay my Horse whip over Your back and whip you as Long as I Could Stand over you." Then he called Holland "a Dirty nasty Scoundrill." The mayor's attempt to have him indicted failed.[32]

Not satisfied with threatening the mayor of New York, Oliver DeLancey, possessed of "an unquiet, turbulent, factious and Seditious Disposition," in June 1749, beat and stabbed Dr. Alexander Colhoun; the angle of the knife wound indicated that Colhoun was already on the ground when DeLancey knifed him. Oliver also wounded another doctor, Richard Shuckburgh. Most of the witnesses to DeLancey's violence fled the scene as did Oliver.[33]

Before Oliver's disappearance, he wanted the governor to know what he thought of him. "Damn the Governour and all them that take his part." Colden had not been forgotten either. Not only was George Clinton a "Scrub" and a "villain," "all the People about him are a pack of damned Scoundrels." For good measure, DeLancey told witnesses "go and tell the Governor" what he had called him.[34]

Though Colden avoided a physical assault at the hands of Oliver DeLancey, the doctor did not mince words on the attack upon Colhoun, describing it as "Such a shameful Action as no man of the least honour or courage could be guilty of." The melee "too plainly shews what some people are capable of." Colhoun, seemingly near death, survived.[35]

On July 1, 1749, Governor Clinton presented depositions detailing what Oliver DeLancey had said about him. A case could be made that he had committed sedition, a serious crime. When Oliver's brother, the chief justice, heard what he had said, he "declared his abhorrence of such words, and desired leave to withdraw." Yet Oliver escaped an indictment for sedition, and escaped punishment for attacking the doctors. In spite of James DeLancey's public repudiation of his brother, Clinton declared: "No man can imagine that any one durst go such lengths, that did not think himself protected by the Chief Justice and by a Brother."[36]

Even the influence of Chief Justice DeLancey had its limits. In Britain the allies of George Clinton "were exceedingly irritated" after learning what Oliver DeLancey had done to Dr. Colhoun. When Sir Peter Warren heard of the assault on Colhoun, the admiral "Shrugged up his Shoulder Swearing a great oath he thought they had been mad enough before but that now he thought they were grown desperate." The antics of his DeLancey in-laws had greatly harmed his own political prospects. As a gleeful Clinton announced to Colden, the governor had received word from London that he "should have put [Oliver] in Irons" while others informed him that he "should have Sent him home in Irons." More news from the imperial capital had it that James DeLancey had "received letters from S[i]r P[eter] which galls him much and certain hints to him that he will be turned out of all" his offices.[37]

Colden, whose prospects of running New York as lieutenant governor were suddenly brighter than ever, advised Governor Clinton that, by firing DeLancey himself, he would make London's imperial bureaucrats happier. Backing him up rather than having to dismiss DeLancey themselves would be "easier" for them. Colden admitted that firing the chief justice could "create disorders" in New York—as had happened at the end of Governor William Cosby's administration—but recent events "will humble" the faction in the colony. Colden thought the gamble of getting rid of DeLancey was worth taking, especially as the powerful official Lord Halifax seemed to be hinting that Clinton should deal with DeLancey. The governor, though, decided to remain cautious, at least for now.[38]

Warren's sensing that his New York in-laws had gotten desperate is borne out by the strange antics of the New York Assembly, controlled by the DeLanceys, in 1749 while Oliver DeLancey engaged in his rampage. With the war over, Clinton sought to regain the executive powers he had surrendered—with no success.[39]

On August 4, 1749 Governor Clinton, using Colden's language, would lambast the assemblymen: "I am truly sorry that this Session of the General Assembly must end without producing any one Thing for the Benefit of the People you represent." It was truly remarkable, the governor believed, "that you met together, not to proceed on Business, but to prevent every Thing that might be proposed for removing the Differences" that so riled the colony. Most incredible, "not one Bill was read," even one to provide funds to help exchange prisoners of war. Far more interesting to the Assembly were old disputes such as the movement of provisions from their storehouse back in 1746.[40]

The exasperated governor defended his role in a lawsuit, which the Assembly continued to harp on. Some militia deserters had actually "sued their Captain for their Pay." Assuming that a jury in the countryside would not know about the relevant law of New York, Clinton wrote to the local court which ended the charade. Finally, "as you have already continued twelve Days (since your Resolution to go on no Business) without entering upon any" the governor ended the session because "your Constituents" had been "put to an useless Expense."[41]

Although Colden kept complaining about his age, his pen still possessed a fiery spirit. However, to demonstrate the governor's "moderation," he would have Alexander and William Smith, Sr. write his speeches. Their styles were quite different from the "incautious, luxuriant compositions and high principles" of Colden's efforts (as William Smith, Jr. described them). The change in speechwriters did not change the Assembly's behavior.[42]

The Assembly did not moderate because James DeLancey did not moderate. He controlled the Assembly, down to "preparing all business which was to pass through the Assembly before it was brought into the House." In one case DeLancey and his "junto," according to the governor, sent a "Remonstrance (ready ingrossed) into it, which was read and hurried through without debate, voted and sent to me at my house, in half an hour after it was first brought in." The governor's allies in the Assembly would have no warning at all about bills being voted on.[43]

Under these circumstances, and the political problems afflicting New York, in 1749 the DeLanceys wrongly expected the governor to call for a new general Assembly election. Despite the terrible cold of February 1749 Oliver DeLancey went on a campaign swing through the colony, bringing "all the songs and faction papers with him." According to Colden, DeLancey's stop at an Ulster tavern did not win any votes for his candidates.[44]

The year 1750, however, did see an election that focused on Westchester County, where Lewis Morris Jr. had backed the governor. The chief justice led a parade into the town of Eastchester, and his forces neglected "no Trick, Stratagem, Allurement, Promise or even Threats" needed "to carry their Point." With good reason, DeLancey believed his candidates could win every single contest, or so Governor Clinton moaned. Colden's son-in-law Peter DeLancey won the election for the borough town of Westchester, ousting Morris, no victory for DeLancey's father-in-law.[45]

At least in 1750 Colden was no longer isolated in the Council or the only man Clinton could totally trust. Alexander, lessening the burden on his old friend, had begun helping the governor, who strongly supported his return to the Council. London bureaucrats, preferring to ignore how Alexander had lost his seat, pretended he had been left off the list of councilors through an accident. On November 26, 1750 Alexander took the oath and rejoined Colden. James DeLancey remarked that "he was sorry for it, but it could not be helped." Other appointments had strengthened the Clinton forces; everyone could "plainly see what difference there is in the proceedings of Council men from what it was."[46]

Yet the chief justice had not lost his flair for creating political problems for George Clinton. His daughter had eloped and married Robert Roddam, captain of the warship *HMS Greyhound*. In June 1750 a sailor on board that ship fired a gun that accidently killed a civilian. The naval culprit was arrested and convicted of manslaughter in a civilian court, all of which had been done with DeLancey's approval. However, the prerogative had specified that nothing that happened on a naval ship came within the purview of civil law.[47]

Chief Justice DeLancey knew very well what the governor's instructions said about warships. DeLancey also knew that the *Greyhound*'s captain was the governor's son-in-law; this incident served perfectly as still another cudgel to bludgeon Clinton with. Colden learned that James DeLancey and his associates had met at their usual tavern "and spent the whole night together in drinking;" the Hungarian Club had not changed. Colden gathered that the drinkers had consulted "how to make the best use of this incident for increasing and confirming their popularity" in the 1750 Assembly election, where it worked very well. Eventually, the governor procured the sailor's release.[48]

While perfect for domestic political consumption, the *Greyhound* incident and other positions DeLancey had taken by June 1750 "much pleased" Alexander, who knew they were "in direct opposition to the Governor's Commission." All that had to be done, Alexander believed, was to produce "a proper Representation of the Facts" to be sent to London, an assignment given to Colden. Alexander had no doubt that the chief justice had violated the good behavior required of him. A well-done account of DeLancey's actions "may be a finishing stroke to him" Alexander predicted.[49]

By June 1750 obvious confidence surged among the governor's friends. Practically all intelligence received from Britain had suggested that, as Clinton told Colden, "I shall be vigorously Supported." The good news continued as the year progressed; Clinton had "a fair Prospect" of winning his battle with James DeLancey, despite his control of the Assembly. In December Clinton remained "very cheerful." The governor had predicted earlier in the year that "there can be no likelyness of a DeLancey succeeding [me] in any Shape." Clinton wrote Colden, "I thought it proper to let you know this and keep up your Spirits and hope every thing will turn out [to] your Satisfaction."[50]

With Colden's ascension to the post of lieutenant governor seemingly only a matter of time, he did face a problem. Because a lieutenant governor could not hold another executive office at the same time, he could no longer be surveyor-general. He wanted his eldest son to succeed him. Although Colden continued to talk about a blissful retirement musing upon nature, being in charge of New York would be anything but quiet, "perhaps with more trouble than profit," while in London Clinton sorted out his financial affairs. In all likelihood Colden, "far advanced in years," assumed he would die soon. In 1750 he had turned 62 years old, making him one of the "old people" by the standards of the time. Some arrangement had to be made insuring that his eldest son Sandie Colden succeeded him in any event.[51]

Since 1748 Alexander had been working on how to solve his friend's problem. Various possibilities were discussed. At first Colden wanted to hand over the office in a "Deed of Trust" which he had discovered in a legal text. But Alexander reminded him that, in such a situation, if Sandie died young before his father, the office would be lost to the family. Instead, the lawyer came up with another idea—that Colden hold the office together with his son. This practice, a joint commission, common in Britain, seemed perfect as long as Governor Clinton agreed to it.[52]

Alexander, accompanied by Sandie, brought the question of his father's office to the governor's attention. The death of Clinton's daughter stopped everything. Her fate apparently convinced both Alexander and Sandie to abandon the deed of trust in favor of the joint commission.[53]

When the governor's mourning ended, he accepted the joint commission but hesitated because Dr. Colden wanted the commission to be for good behavior. Having given DeLancey such a commission and been betrayed, Clinton did not want a repetition. Alexander convinced him that history would not repeat itself. Colden got his wish; his son was in no danger of being replaced if, by some chance, DeLancey bested Clinton.[54]

The chief justice learned, in February 1751, that the Coldens had gotten a commission "during good behaviours," and was convinced that the governor would soon be traveling to the mother country. DeLancey assumed wrong as Clinton would not leave until Colden was in charge of New York. That matter could only be settled in Britain where the governor had sent agents to accomplish a victory over DeLancey.[55]

The most prominent of these agents, Governor William Shirley of Massachusetts, had been recruited by Colden. By all appearances, Colden and Shirley had become friends during Indian diplomacy and the New Yorker filled the governor in on what the DeLancey faction had done. Eager to help, Shirley actually wrote a speech for Clinton to give before the New York Assembly; it had no effect. When Shirley had been allowed to return to Britain, he vowed to support Clinton in London as well as straighten out any misconceptions about Colden that had been believed by powerful officials. Colden did caution the governor of Massachusetts that "There are some in this Province capable of every thing that Caesar Borgia was And therefore I must beg that nothing of this appears as from me in the public offices." Shirley's short stay in New York had to have convinced him of Colden's justified concern.[56]

However promising Shirley's advocacy seemed in September 1750, rumors reached both Boston and New York City that Shirley sought to leave Massachusetts to be governor of New York and New Jersey. "I can't hardly think him So base, but I have Seen So much of it Since I have been here, that I don't know what to think" the puzzled Clinton wrote. When a second report reached Clinton at the end of September, Colden thought the source might be in league with DeLancey.[57]

Though hard to believe, the reports were true. To Shirley's credit, he emphasized to the Duke of Newcastle that he had been assured that Clinton was in line to receive something better. And if both colonies could not be under one governor, then Shirley would settle for just New York. Despite his hopes, he did not receive either colony, blaming New York merchants angry over how Shirley had settled their wartime bills. Lord Halifax had someone else in mind anyway.[58]

Unlike Shirley, Colden's old friend Peter Collinson was one of the few in London involved with the lobbying over New York seeking nothing for himself. Doing his best to protect the interests of Cadwallader Colden, Collinson assured him of his wish that Clinton would prevail over his enemies yet noted "there is great pushing against him." DeLancey's weakened position had not destroyed the influence of his still potent allies.[59]

Luckily, Clinton had not depended solely upon Shirley. New York's beleaguered governor had dispatched his secretary to Britain. In 1749 John Catherwood presented Clinton's memorial complaining about DeLancey and requested that Colden replace him as lieutenant governor, but Clinton had his agent suggest an alternative. "If Mr. Colden is not thought deserving of that appointment," Catherwood observed, the governor would be pleased if John Rutherfurd received it. Colden had to have known about that option. Apparently, he did not object to Rutherfurd's promotion. The soldier's candidacy, however, did not cause any excitement in London and disappeared. Though Rutherfurd did return to Britain, there is no evidence that he sought the job.[60]

Catherwood, who had never lobbied government officials before, did what he could. To help him overcome a weapon used against Clinton, the Assembly's not renewing the colony's customs duties—which the agent did not explain—Colden provided extensive points of argument. Ultimately, he remarked to Catherwood, no one could expect "that any Assembly would willingly give up powers they are so fond of." He also denied to Catherwood that Governor Clinton had lost faith in him, which was not true.[61]

Because Chief Justice Robert Hunter Morris of New Jersey had decided to travel to London to settle some New Jersey business, Clinton added him to his lobbyists. Colden had soured on the Morris family long before; he knew them too well. His attitude probably had not changed. If so, he would not have been shocked at what transpired. When Morris reached London, he pursued his own agenda which included restoring his brother to the Council seat he had lost so many years before, exasperating the governor who had nominated William Smith Sr. instead.[62]

In 1750 Governor Clinton instructed Morris to ensure that London replaced DeLancey, saving the governor from the political problems that would ensue if he did it himself. But Clinton added more to his instructions to Morris, a matter "which nobody knows any thing of but our Selves and Mrs. Clinton." This secret was that the new lieutenant governor should be Robert Hunter Morris; the governor told him "to Sollicit" for the position. Perhaps out of guilt Clinton, late in 1751, ordered Morris "to push for Doctor Colden" as lieutenant governor or allowing him to govern as the Council president. By that time Colden was already out of the running. George Clinton's first priority had been "to Crush the Chief Justice here." If that meant abandoning Colden, then Colden would be abandoned.[63]

John Rutherfurd informed his old friend what had happened. On August 16, 1751, Rutherfurd explained that "Chief Justice Morris had a Commission made out for being Lt. Govr. having been recommended failing of you by

Govr. Clinton." Morris himself had told Rutherfurd the news. According to Rutherfurd, the ministers had "bad impressions" of Colden, the reason he had been passed over. In June 1752 Rutherfurd noted that, oddly, after the first report, the whole subject of Morris as lieutenant governor of New York had disappeared, the explanation of which became known only later.[64]

Being blamed for Clinton's miscues exasperated Colden, because the governor sometimes had ignored his advice. Not really surprised though, Colden had stated "that any application to a Governor or to Ministers however usefull however necessary would be disregarded if it were not attended with a profusion of Money." That was how DeLancey became lieutenant governor and, apparently, Morris received his commission the same way.[65]

When Collinson learned of Colden's defeat is not clear, but Colden had also expressed his desire for another office, that of postmaster for the northern colonies. Really the best job for him, Colden said "it is attended with little trouble and will leave me at liberty to pursue the speculations I take delight in." His long career, he thought, would be an advantage in winning the position. However, Franklin won the contest.[66]

Determined to help Colden obtain a major post in either government or the post office, Collinson did his best. He presented copies of Colden's Indian history to one minister "new in his office and perhaps in American History"—and also the introduction to Colden's book on gravitation; no one in the government would have understood the rest. Collinson observed that "the promises of Courtiers are words of Course." And that is what they proved to be—only words. Collinson's effort to give the office of surveyor-general a salary, which Colden had always desired, failed as well.[67]

Eventually, Colden learned more specifics over why Lord Halifax and the Board of Trade had rejected him for lieutenant governor. Halifax suggested to him that "if a man of Quality" such as Clinton "could not, with the assistance of Mr. Colden bring the Assembly to terms, how could Mr. Colden expect to do it in his absence"? What was needed in New York was "a Man of Weight" dispatched from the mother country. The Board of Trade, in a formal letter to the governor, denied that any complaint about Colden had been brought before it, which is possible only as an item of its formal business agenda. With Colden only a transitional figure, and DeLancey displaced to allow that to happen, Clinton's enemies would be riled even more causing "still greater confusion."[68]

All the transatlantic scheming did not end the necessity of dealing with the subject of Indian relations, still essential to New York despite the return of peace. By the fall of 1750 the French, once again, had tried to reassert their influence among the Iroquois because of scheduled talks in Europe over the border between the French and British empires. Claiming Iroquois lands as part of the French empire was high on their agenda.[69]

Because Colden knew more about the geography of the region than anyone else, it fell to him to collect evidence backing the British claim to Iroquois territory. Colden collected and sent off to William Shirley, Sr., one of the border negotiators, documents bolstering the rights of the British Empire. According to Colden, the Iroquois had submitted their lands south of Lakes Ontario and Erie, along with their conquests, to the British with the proviso that only the Iroquois could use the area.[70]

Despite the death of Philip Livingston, which left the colony with no Indian agent, Indian relations had gone well because of William Johnson. In 1748 Colden had been thrilled that Johnson would be helping the governor sort out the various problems with the Indians, one less task for him. Warren tried to muddy the waters by ordering Johnson to stop helping the governor and concentrate on watching Warren's land. Johnson resisted his uncle's directive, but the New York Assembly continued its refusal to compensate Clinton's Indian agent for the huge sums he had spent handling Indian diplomacy. No one could suffer such financial losses forever. Finally, in 1751 Johnson informed the governor he had to stop his work with the Indians, who wanted him to continue, and declined the post of Indian secretary as well.[71]

In such a case, who else could the governor turn to other than Colden? In 1746 Clinton had recommended changing the office of lieutenant governor. He should have a salary, Clinton suggested, and live at Albany to deal with Indian relations, thus allowing the governor to spend more time in the capital. With the lieutenant governorship transformed in that fashion, "Mr. Colden may be of more use than another, as it is known that he has particularly applied his thoughts to the Indian Affairs." Although an interesting suggestion, London did not accept it.[72]

The office of Indian secretary did come with a salary, paid by the British government. A friendly British secretary told Catherwood that Colden would be a fine Indian secretary and would push for him "tho' he did think it incompatible with" Colden's "present station." Colden had not given that official, who had probably read his Indian history, "the least hint from me that I was desirous of that office."[73]

Clinton held the post open for Colden, but he had little interest in it after the death of his son John who would have been his father's deputy. Indian diplomacy, both time-consuming and difficult, had new problems popping up all the time. In 1751, for example, Christian Indians were inflamed. One had left his son with "a Villain" as a "pawn"—a hostage—in order to briefly leave to get money to pay a debt. "Immediately," before the father could possibly return, the colonist tried to sell the boy in Albany. Colden declined the job, using the uncertain salary as a convenient excuse.[74]

The governor did ask Colden to prepare a report on Indian relations for the Board of Trade, which he finished during the summer of 1751, and, like so much of Colden's writings, ran to "great length." It would also be influential. In his "The Present State of the Indian Affairs" Colden presented a review of the past, attacking the Indian commissioners at Albany who wanted no outsiders involved with the Indians. The commissioners' "resentment was increased," Colden declared, by Clinton's putting Indian relations "into the hands of an Englishman," Johnson, "whom the Dutch look on as intruders into their patrimony."[75]

Colden presented other suggestions, including a recommendation that a British sloop be stationed at Oswego on Lake Ontario to counteract French forces, an idea he had also broached to George Clarke. But the most important proposal involved the creation of an intercolonial Indian superintendent appointed by London, perhaps inspired by the earlier, abandoned idea of expanding the authority of the lieutenant governor of New York. Colden was not the only one to suggest a royally-appointed superintendent; Kennedy did so too. Everyone knew that Johnson would be the superintendent. In Colden's essay he wrote that Johnson had "made a greater figure, and gained more influence among the Indians than any person before him. . .," including himself.[76]

Governor Clinton also had a more mundane task for the old surveyor-general of New York. Clinton had told him earlier to watch for good land that the governor could obtain for himself, and Mrs. Clinton asked that Colden keep an eye out for her as well. Since the Clintons knew that his governorship would be ending, hopefully in the near future, the governor requested Colden explain how the couple could take advantage of the colony's often abused granting of land. He did so. In 1750 one land grant of 4,000 acres supposedly went to Jacobus Bruyn and George Murray but they conveyed it to John Ayscough, the governor's secretary, who then conveyed it to the governor. Among those who witnessed the deed were William Smith Sr. and Colden. Colden did try to convince the governor to stop the auctioning off of offices but with no success.[77]

At least Clinton received some land and money; the rest of his administration seemed like a heavy burden to him. His health declined and in May 1751 the governor insisted he would fire DeLancey but did not. When the governor called new Assembly elections for February 1752, the results would be depressingly similar. DeLancey crushed the governor's allies again. As one enthused foe of the governor remarked, Clinton's party "is still universally despised, nor has been able to gain a single Proselyte to their desperate Cause." In July Clinton all but begged his agents to get him out of New York.[78]

Each succeeding blow pushed George Clinton into a deepening paranoia, made worse by drinking. But sometimes the betrayals were real. While abroad Wraxall got himself appointed New York's Indian secretary despite the governor's wishes and had also misrepresented Colden to London. Clinton, furious at Wraxall, "a little dirty dog," would explode at Colden when some of his relatives—presumably Bettie and her husband—had Wraxall stay with them. That congeniality, the governor told Colden in 1753, was "a countenance I never shewed to any professed Enemy of yours."[79]

When Dr. Colhoun asked the governor for payment for medical supplies provided to the military back in 1746, Clinton exploded when he received his letter. Colhoun wrote back, insisting that the governor had read too much into his comments, which did not help. In 1752 the governor wrote a brusque letter to Colden, calling Colhoun his "Agent" when in Britain, probably because Colhoun had mentioned the Duke of Argyle in the offending letter, and suggested they had conspired to rig the accounts. Colden had not done any mercantile activity for decades; Dr. Shuckburgh had partnered with Colhoun. Colden's response is unknown, but surviving evidence suggests that he had trusted only two men to speak for him in Britain, John Mitchell and Collinson. Any lobbying Colhoun had done for Colden abroad had to have been minor.[80]

Well before 1752 both Colden and Alexander had been astonished how Clinton could discover insolence and hostility even in letters Colden had written. After Colden had returned to Coldengham, in early January 1751, Alexander alerted his friend that the governor had been "displeased" by what he had stated. Colden rushed off an apology but asked Alexander, once again, for his help. Colden had looked over his drafts and had no idea what had been so displeasing. Could Alexander find out what the problem was?[81]

As usual, Alexander rushed to help Colden. Contacting Ayscough, Alexander perused the offending letter "again and again" and could find nothing offensive in it; Ayscough agreed. Yet the problem developed again in 1752 when Alexander went through the same process over two more totally innocent letters. Alexander "wondered how his Excellency could so misapprehend." The whole situation, the lawyer suggested, had happened because of the governor's "Lowness of Spirits by his being there alone without Cheerful Company."[82]

More paranoia became evident. Clinton had supped with some unidentified persons, who insinuated that Colden had been deliberately delaying the issuing of land grants so he could receive higher fees when he headed the government; the governor believed these people. One can only guess how much he had been drinking while he dined—he reportedly "rested" the entire evening. Alexander, again, assisted in calming Clinton. The exasperated Colden had hoped "from the long knowledge his Excellency has had on me and in difficult times that he could not have entertained any Jealousies" that he was secretly hurting the governor to help himself.[83]

Unfortunately for Colden, Clinton's paranoia could not be quieted. Another letter disturbed him. Colden's statement of his fear of "travelling in the Cold" convinced the governor that his chief advisor was trying to excuse himself from assisting him, suggesting that "what he had before, had been only with a prospect of Lucre." Then, in early 1753, Colden was accused of misleading the governor about some land. Exasperated, Colden told Clinton once again: "none can be more faithful than I have been."[84]

As if the governor was not paranoid enough, during his daughter's final illness, Sandie, who did not have his father's political instincts, sued Clinton for a debt. The bill of exchange the governor had given him as payment had been rejected. Reminding Colden how his son had profited during the preceding years, Clinton commented "that Suit (at his own Expense) would have been as well let alone." Apparently, Colden had a talk with Sandie as the lawsuit disappeared from sight.[85]

Clinton also began to realize that his contest with James DeLancey seemed to be ending, and not the way it had been expected. Suddenly, during March 1753 Clinton received a strict order, written in November, not to fire DeLancey as lieutenant governor. The puzzled Clinton wrote, "The very great change in the Board of Trade, against all their former Opinions of the necessity of Suspending the Chief Justice at any rate vastly surprises me to guess what should occasion so sudden a Turn." It was not because of the 1751 Board of Trade examination of the problems in New York, which has been proffered as the reason.[86]

Whenever James DeLancey and an inexplicable event in the corridors of power in London are connected, one must assume that large amounts of DeLancey money was responsible for the change, making it suddenly understandable. Robert Hunter Morris had money—far more than Colden had—but DeLancey had much more than either, explaining why Morris had been shoved aside along with Colden, who knew all about DeLancey's "love of money." The chief justice loved money because it brought him what he loved even more, power.[87]

With Warren in eclipse, DeLancey's focus had shifted to keeping the office of lieutenant governor. Meanwhile, everyone in the British government realized that "Clinton will not, nor indeed should not, stay at New York." He had to be replaced by a great man from Britain, who would restore the battered royal prerogative in New York. As long as a governor resided in the colony, a lieutenant governor had no power from his office. So, keeping DeLancey in the office seemed to present no obstacle to reform, and the London bureaucrats could make a nice profit by allowing DeLancey to keep a powerless post. To make sure DeLancey could do no further harm, Clinton had been ordered to delay his departure until his replacement came, which the governor thought was part of "some clandestine dealings." For once his paranoia had alerted him to the truth. It seemed like a good plan. Now all the Duke of Newcastle had to do was to find something to keep Clinton busy when he returned so his lobbying would not drive his relatives batty.[88]

Governor Clinton, meanwhile, in July 1753 received a letter from Lord Halifax for Colden. Halifax tried to dispel Colden's fear based on "an ill-founded supposition of your standing ill in the opinion" of the king's ministers because he would not be allowed to take over when the governor left. No one had questioned Colden's "character." The reason, Halifax insisted, was that DeLancey had a commission as lieutenant governor (technically, Clinton still had not handed it over). Firing DeLancey "would create discord and dissention" and was also "impolitic." Nor could a salary be affixed to the position of surveyor-general; the quitrents were too meager to pay for it. Halifax assured him that "I am very sensible of your Abilities" and well knew his role in defending the prerogative. His lordship assumed that "The same zeal and Loyalty" Colden had displayed with Clinton would also be exerted in aid of his successor.[89]

Colden was nothing if not persistent. Thrilled that his lordship had responded with such a long missive, unusual for a high government official, the doctor sent another letter to Collinson to prove that the amount of New York quitrents was more than Halifax realized. And Colden had every intention of supporting the new governor, Sir Danvers Osborn, a member of Parliament from Bedfordshire since 1747. His chief qualification was his marriage to Halifax's sister. As events transpired, Colden could not demonstrate his zeal to Osborn, or for that matter, even meet him.[90]

On October 7, 1753 Sir Danvers Osborn arrived in New York. On October 10 Clinton presented DeLancey with his lieutenant governor commission; Osborn took his oath as governor. Then the festivities started and soon got out of hand: "the huzzas of the mob were scarce intermitted for a moment." Clinton, after "some indecent expressions respecting himself," left the scene but not before Osborn told him he expected that, sooner or later, he would share his fate as governor of New York. Osborn's face displayed "melancholy gloom," while the festivities became a "Bacchanalian frolic" with "every excess of riot."[91]

The next day Governor Osborn met with the Council. He had been given strict instructions to rollback the Assembly's usurpations of the Clinton years, and demanded a permanent salary for the governor. Osborn had been told, wrote one cynical observer, before he had sailed to New York, "that Mr. DeLancey, by means of his great popularity, would enable him to carry it into execution." But that was before DeLancey had gotten his commission. A New Yorker, perhaps Alexander, warned the governor "that those promises were by no means to be depended on." At the Council meeting Osborn discovered that the prediction was true; there would be no permanent salary. "What then am I come hither for?" the "uneasy" baronet stated. Later that day, Osborn told DeLancey, "I shall soon leave you the government. I find myself unable to support the burden of it."[92]

Colden did not attend the swearing in of Sir Danvers Osborn. Colden had been at such ceremonies before and, besides, he probably expected the debacle it became. Instead, he stayed in Ulster taking care of personal matters. There would be plenty of time to meet the new governor.[93]

On October 12, 1753, as the sloop carrying Colden approached the outskirts of New York City, the boat was hailed by Richard Nicholls, the New York postmaster (and also Sandie's father-in-law). He asked Colden to come ashore immediately, then informed him that the governor had committed suicide by hanging himself. A "most surprising end" Colden thought. He would be a pallbearer at the funeral. An inquest discovered, thanks to the testimony of Thomas Pownall, Osborn's secretary, that Osborn was insane. After the death of his wife, Osborn had been depressed and had tried to kill himself. Making him governor of New York, Halifax hoped, would restore his spirits. It did not.[94]

Osborn's sudden exit had created a very unusual scenario. Two stunned observers in New York exclaimed: "in less than 48 hours we have had three Governours." James DeLancey had gained the power he had fought so long for and paid so much for. The day after becoming acting governor DeLancey went to see Colden. Missing him, DeLancey then "sent to desire my Company at the Fort." When they talked, Colden informed Alice, "Nothing but mutual civilities passed between us." On October 13, after Colden had renewed his oath at the Council meeting, the two former rivals talked again. Lieutenant Governor DeLancey wished that Colden would not leave the city quickly "because he wanted to advise with me on some affairs of Consequence. He shews as much regard to me as to any of the Council and takes every opportunity to do it." It was as if everything that had happened since 1746 had not happened. DeLancey could afford to be magnanimous; he had won.[95]

DeLancey even reached out to George Clinton, who was staying in Flushing on Long Island before he left New York never to return. DeLancey sent a friend to win over the ex-governor, hoping to add him to the substantial DeLancey forces in Great Britain. And Clinton seemed willing to be won over; no record exists of how much liquor Clinton had consumed. But Mrs. Clinton, at least, was not ready to forget what James DeLancey had done to her husband. She aimed at DeLancey's "plenipotentiary such a volley of invective against his constituent, as rendered all future overtures, entirely hopeless."[96]

Mrs. Clinton responded very differently when two other visitors journeyed to Flushing to visit her husband. Colden and Alexander wished to bid farewell to George Clinton. Their conversation, though not recorded, seems obvious. No doubt they enjoyed some laughs at the expense of the imperial officials who had insisted that Colden was not a great enough man to govern the colony. The man of weight they sent over did not last a week in New York.[97]

The irony aside, the ascension of James DeLancey meant that in 1753 the long political career of Colden had ended. He assured Alice: "Now My dear my mind will be free of some anxieties which I formerly could not avoid and I hope we shall seldom for the future be from each other. . .," something that she must have enjoyed hearing. Colden had to be realistic. He was 65 years old; James DeLancey was almost fifteen years younger than him. Outliving him seemed improbable. A New Yorker, DeLancey would not be going to Britain on leave so Colden could not take over from him as president of the Council. Nor would London replace the new, clever lieutenant governor. At the end of October 1753, for example, he blasted the Assembly for its "contempt" and "unwarrantable proceedings." Why, he thundered, "by our excellent constitution the executive power is lodged in the Crown." Imperial officials in Britain would relish such words and, if not, there still remained plenty of DeLancey money about.[98]

Colden was really retired this time. The day had arrived for him to return to Coldengham and spend his remaining years pursuing philosophical amusements. Unbeknown to Colden, however, Coldengham would soon not be the safe asylum from the cares of the world it had been for decades.

NOTES

1. JA to CC, March 29, 1748, *CP*, vol. 4, 30.

2. "Watchman," no. 2, February 17, 1770, *New York Journal* (Holt), April 12, 1770; William Livingston, *A Review of the Military Operations in North America* (London: R. and J. Dodsley, 1757), 20.

3. GC to Lords of Trade, November 30, 1747, November 15, 1748, *NYCD*, vol. 6, 413, 468; "Abstract of the Evidence," c. April 2, 1751, *NYCD*, vol. 6, 674.

4. Wraxall to GC, October 27, 1747, George Clinton Papers, CL; CC to GC, December 29, 1748, George Clinton Papers, vol. 8, CL; GC to Duke of Newcastle, February 13, 1747/8, *NYCD*, vol. 6, 416–18.

5. Warren to GC, December 1747, *CP*, vol. 3, 432; Warren to GC, October 18, 1747, in Peter Warren, *The Royal Navy and North America: The Warren Papers, 1736–1752*, ed. Julian Gwyn (London: Navy Records Society, 1975), 393; Fintan O'Toole, *White Savage: William Johnson and the Invention of America* (New York: Farrar, Straus, and Giroux, 2005), 91; Stanley Nider Katz, "Between Scylla and Charybdis: James DeLancey and Anglo-American Politics in Early Eighteenth-Century New York," in *Anglo-American Political Relations, 1675–1775*, ed. Alison Gilbert Olson and Richard Maxwell Brown (New Brunswick, NJ: Rutgers University Press, 1970), 100, 106.

6. GC to CC, March 11, 1747/8, April 1, May 16, 1748, *CP*, vol. 3, 363–65, vol. 4, 32–34, 62–64; Nicholas Varga, "Robert Charles: New York Agent, 1748–1770," *William and Mary Quarterly*, 3rd ser., 18 (1961):213; Katz, "Between Schylla," 102.

7. CC to GC, February 14, 1747/8, *CP*, vol. 4, 13–14; CC to Richard Nicholls, February 14, 1747/8, *CP*, vol. 4, 14–15; GC to CC, March 11, 1747/8, George Clinton Papers, vol. 7, CL.

8. CC to GC, February 14, 1747/8, January 12, 1748/9, *CP*, vol. 4, 13–14, 88–89; GC to CC, April 1, 1748, *CP*, vol. 4, 32–34.

9. Wraxall to GC, October 27, 1747, George Clinton Papers, CL; CC's memo on Warren to GC, December 1747, *CP*, vol. 3, 433; Stanley Nider Katz, *Newcastle's New York: Anglo-American Politics, 1732–1753* (Cambridge, MA: Harvard University Press, 1968), 236–237n140; GC to CC, January 31, 1747/8, *CP*, vol. 4, 10–11.

10. GC to CC, March 11, 1747/8, George Clinton Papers, vol. 7, CL; CC to Shirley, [1749?], CPU, reel 2; CC to Newcastle, March 21, 1747/8, *CP*, vol. 4, 21–25.
11. GC to Henry Pelham and Newcastle, October 11, 1748, George Clinton Papers, vol. 8, CL.
12. GC to Henry Pelham and Newcastle, October 11, 1748, George Clinton Papers, vol. 8, CL; CC to GC, March 21, 1747/8, *CP*, vol. 4, 25–27.
13. GC to Newcastle, February 13, 1747/8, *NYCD*, vol. 6, 416–18; GC to CC, January 31, 1747/8, April 25, May 16, 1748, *CP*, vol. 4, 10–11, 61–64; GC to Pelham, August 15, 1748, *CP*, vol. 8, 353–55.
14. CC to Catherwood, January 29, 1747/8, George Clinton Papers, vol. 7, CL; GC to CC, December 13, 1748, George Clinton Papers, vol. 8, CL; CC to GC, September 29, 1749, George Clinton Papers, vol. 9, CL; CC to Lady Clinton, [1749?], Bancroft Coll., Colden Papers, 1722–1775, vol. 1, 99–100, NYPL; GC to Duke of Bedford, May 23, 1751, C05/1096/206, LC transcript; CC to GC, *CP*, vol. 4, 44–45; GC to CC, April 25, 1748, *CP*, vol. 4, 61.
15. GC to Newcastle, February 13, 1747/8, *NYCD*, vol. 6, 416–18.
16. GC to CC, March 29, 1748, *CP*, vol. 4, 28–29; Milton M. Klein, "Democracy and Politics in Colonial New York," *New York History* 40, no. 3 (1959): 227.
17. JA to CC, December 5, 1751, *CP*, vol. 4, 303–4; GC to CC, January 6, 1752, *CP*, vol. 4, 306–7; Robert R. Livingston to CC, March 16, 1743/4, Robert R. Livingston Papers, reel 1, NYHS; CC to GC, n.d., CPU, reel 2; "Watchman," no. 3, March 10, 1770, *New York Journal* (Holt), April 19, 1770; Cynthia A. Kierner, *Traders and Gentlefolk: The Livingstons of New York, 1675–1790* (Ithaca, NY: Cornell University Press, 1992), 171–72; Patricia U. Bonomi, *A Factious People: Politics and Society in Colonial New York* (New York: Columbia University Press, 1971), 163–64.
18. GC to Shirley, April 1748, George Clinton Papers, vol. 7, CL; GC to Bedford, August 15, 1748, *NYCD*, vol. 6, 431.
19. CC, "The Humble Memorial of Cadwallader Colden, Esq.," October 10, 1748, C05/1062/90–93, reel 16, NYHS.
20. CC, "Humble Memorial."
21. CC, "Humble Memorial."
22. CC, "Humble Memorial"; GC to Bedford, February 24, 1748/9, *NYCD*, vol. 6, 475–76.
23. CC, "Humble Memorial."
24. CC, "Humble Memorial."
25. James DeLancey to GC, October 19, 1748, C05/1062/93–95, reel 16, NYHS.
26. CC, "The Replication of Cadwallader Colden Esq. to the Answer of Mr. Chief Justice DeLancey," November 3, 1748, C05/1062/95–97, reel 16, NYHS.
27. CC, "Republication"; CC to GC, n.d. [1749?], CPU, reel 2.
28. Hardwicke to Newcastle, May 15, 1752, Newcastle Papers, British Museum Additional Manuscripts 32727, f. 181, LC transcript; Nicholls to CC, December 22, 1746, GLC08014.04, Gilder Lehrman Coll., Gilder Institute of American History, New York City.
29. GC to Lords of Trade, October 30, November 15, 1748, *NYCD*, vol. 6, 459, 468; GC to Bedford, February 24, 1748/9, *NYCD*, vol. 6, 475–76.
30. GC to Catherwood, February 17, 1749/50, *NYCD*, vol. 6, 471; GC to CC, February 9, 1749/50, *CP*, vol. 4, 188–91; GC to CC, December 15, 1748, *CP*, vol. 4, 82–83.
31. GC to Catherwood, February 17, 1749/50, *NYCD*, vol. 6, 471.
32. GC to CC, January 3, February 3, 1748/9, *CP*, vol. 4, 84–85, 90–91; "Memorial of Edward Holland," May 1, 1749, C05/1062/26, LC transcript.
33. GC to Bedford, June 28, 1749, *NYCD*, vol. 6, 513–14; copy of the complaint The King vs. Oliver DeLancey, July 1749, *CP*, vol. 4, 116–19; affidavit of Richard Shuckburgh, June 23, 1749, George Clinton Papers, vol. 9, CL.
34. Copy of the complaint The King vs. Oliver DeLancey, July 1749, *CP*, vol. 4, 116–19.
35. CC to John Colden, June 28, 1749, *CP*, vol. 9, 14.
36. "Abstract of the Evidence," c. April 2, 1751, *NYCD*, vol. 6, 693–94; GC to Bedford, July 7, 1749, *NYCD*, vol. 6, 514–15.
37. CC to JA, November 21, 1749, Rutherfurd Family Coll., box 8, f. 1, NYHS; AC to CC, November 7, 1749, *CP*, vol. 9, 49; GC to CC, November 6, 1749, *CP*, vol. 4, 148–50; Julian

Gwyn, *An Admiral for America: Sir Peter Warren, Vice Admiral of the Red, 1703–1752* (Gainesville: University Press of Florida, 2004), 125.

38. GC to CC, November 6, 1749, *CP*, vol. 4, 148–50; CC to GC, [November 9, 1749], *CP*, vol. 4, 150–51.

39. Oliver Morton Dickerson, *American Colonial Government, 1696–1765: A Study of the British Board of Trade in Its Relation to the American Colonies, Political, Industrial, Administrative* (Cleveland, OH: A. H. Clark, 1912), 165.

40. GC to Lords of Trade, August 7, 1749, *NYCD*, vol. 6, 523–24; GC to Assembly and Council, August 4, 1749, New York Colony, Council, *Journal of the Legislative Council of the Colony of New York, Began the 9th day of April, 1691; and ended the [3d of April, 1775]* (Albany, NY: Weed, Parsons, 1861), vol. 2, 1039–41.

41. GC to Assembly and Council, August 4, 1749, New York Colony, Council, *Council of the Colony of New York*, vol. 2, 1039–41.

42. CC to GC, February 9, 1748/9, *CP*, vol. 4, 91–95; GC to Lord Holderness, November 25, 1751, George Clinton Papers, vol. 22, CL; William Smith, Jr., *The History of the Province of New York*, ed. Michael Kammen (Cambridge, MA: Belknap Press of Harvard University Press, 1972), vol. 2, 123.

43. GC to Newcastle, September 30, 1748, Newcastle Papers, British Museum Additional Manuscripts 32716, f. 399–402, LC transcript.

44. CC to GC, February 19, 1748/9, *CP*, vol. 4, 102.

45. GC to Robert Hunter Morris, August 29, 1750, Robert Hunter Morris Papers, New Jersey Historical Society, Newark, NJ; Bonomi, *Factious People*, 307.

46. GC to CC, November 27, 1750, *CP*, vol. 4, 237; JA to CC, September 17, 1751, *CP*, vol. 4, 297; GC to Holderness, November 25, 1751, George Clinton Papers, vol. 22, CL; Great Britain, *Acts of the Privy Council, Colonial Series*, ed. William L. Grant and James Munroe (London: H. M. S. O., 1908–1912), vol. 4, 792.

47. Ayscough to CC, May 9, 1749, Bancroft Coll., Colden Papers, vol. 1, 101, NYPL; CC's thoughts on *Greyhound* case, June 1750, *CP*, vol. 4, 214–18; Ayscough to CC, August 8, December 11, 1750, *CP*, vol. 4, 222–23, 242; CC to GC, June 19, 1750, *CP*, vol. 4, 213–14; Douglas Edward Leach, *Roots of Conflict: British Armed Forces and Colonial Americans, 1677–1763* (Chapel Hill: University of North Carolina Press, 1986), 141–44.

48. Ayscough to CC, May 9, 1749, Bancroft Coll., Colden Papers, vol. 1, 101, NYPL; CC's thoughts on *Greyhound* case, June 1750, *CP*, vol. 4, 214–18; Ayscough to CC, August 8, December 11, 1750, *CP*, vol. 4, 222–23, 242; CC to GC, June 19, 1750, *CP*, vol.4, 213–14; Leach, *Roots of Conflict*, 141–44.

49. Ayscough to CC, June 18, 1750, *CP*, vol. 4, 212–13.

50. GC to CC, February 5, [c. March–April 1749/50], *CP*, vol. 4, 198, 201–2; Ayscough to CC, November 19, 1750, *CP*, vol. 4, 232–33; JA to CC, December 10, 1750, *CP*, vol. 4, 240; GC to Halifax, April 9, 1750, George Clinton Papers, vol. 10, CL; Collinson to CC, July 27, 1750, Emmet Coll., no. 3203, NYPL.

51. CC to JA, December 15, 1750, *CP*, vol. 4, 242–43; CC to Mitchell, July 18, 1751, *CP*, vol. 9, 98–102; CC to GC, February 26, 1748/9, George Clinton Papers, vol. 22, CL.

52. JA to CC, April 17, 1748, December 10, 15, 1750, *CP*, vol. 4, 47–48, 240, 242–43.

53. JA to CC, January 2, 1750/1, *CP*, vol. 4, 245–50; CC to JA, December 15, 1750, *CP*, vol. 4, 242–43.

54. JA to CC, January 2, 1750/1, *CP*, vol. 4, 245–50.

55. Ayscough, "Memorandum What C. J. said to me," February 19, 1750/1, George Clinton Papers, vol. 11, CL.

56. CC to Shirley, August 22, 1748, July 25, 1749, *CP*, vol. 4, 73–74, 124; CC to Collinson, July 7, 1749, October 4, 1754, *CP*, vol. 4, 114–15, 467–68; Shirley to CC, [June 26, 1749], *CP*, vol. 9, 13; George Arthur Wood, *William Shirley, Governor of Massachusetts, 1741–1756: A History* (New York: Columbia University Press, 1920), 389–90.

57. GC to R. H. Morris, September 8, 1750, Robert Hunter Morris Papers, New Jersey Historical Society; CC to R. H. Morris, October 1, 1750, Robert Hunter Morris Papers.

58. Shirley to Newcastle, September 1, 1750, Newcastle Papers, British Museum Additional Manuscripts 32422, f. 212–13, LC transcript; Shirley to Newcastle, January 23, 1753, British

Museum Additional Manuscripts 32731, f. 100–101; John A. Schutz, *William Shirley, King's Governor of Massachusetts* (Chapel Hill: University of North Carolina Press, 1961), 166.

59. Collinson to CC, October 3, 1750, *CP*, vol. 9, 78–79; Katz, "Between Scylla," 106.

60. Catherwood to Bedford, April 20, 1749, CO5/1096/74, LC transcript; Rutherfurd to CC, August 16, 1751, *CP*, vol. 4, 287; Katz, *Newcastle's New York*, 236–37.

61. CC to Catherwood, November 22, 1750, Robert Hunter Morris Papers, New Jersey Historical Society; Katz, *Newcastle's New York*, 203–4.

62. [JA or Rutherfurd] to CC, August 30, 1749, Rutherfurd Family Coll., box 11, f. 22, NYHS; GC to R. H. Morris, April 16, 1753, Robert Hunter Morris Papers, New Jersey Historical Society; JA to CC, September 25, 1749, *CP*, vol. 4, 144; CC to GC, January 29, 1747/8, *CP*, vol. 4, 7; Katz, *Newcastle's New York*, 204–5.

63. GC to R. H. Morris, September 5, 8, 1750, December 10, 1751, Robert Hunter Morris Papers, New Jersey Historical Society.

64. Rutherfurd to CC, August 16, 1751, June 8, 1752, *CP*, vol. 4, 287, 334.

65. CC to Collinson, May 28, 1754, *CP*, vol. 4, 448; CC to Rutherfurd, [1750?], CPU, reel 2.

66. CC to Collinson, June 12–14, 1751, *CP*, vol. 9, 95–97.

67. Collinson to CC, January 15, [1752], *CP*, vol. 9, 110–11; CC to Collinson, July 28, 1752, *CP*, vol. 9, 116–18; Collinson to Holderness, February 10, 1752, *CP*, vol. 4, 314; Collinson to CC, March 4, 1752, *CP*, vol. 4, 312–13; CC to Collinson, September 6, 1753, New Netherlands, oldest New York, and the colonial government, 1655–1774, microfilm, NYHS.

68. Extract from Mr. Catherwood's Letter to GC, n.d., *CP*, vol. 4, 304–6; Lords of Trade to GC, November 29, 1752, *NYCD*, vol. 6, 770.

69. GC to Board of Trade, September 8, 1750, George Clinton Papers, vol. 22, CL; BF to CC, October 11, 1750, *FP*, vol. 4, 67–68; GC to Lords of Trade, December 13, 1750, *NYCD*, vol. 6, 603.

70. GC to Lords of Trade, July 30, 1750, *NYCD*, vol. 6, 576–77; CC to James Hamilton, March 31, 1750, GLCO7901, Gilder Lehrman Coll., Gilder Lehrman Institute of American History.

71. CC to GC, May 26, 1748, George Clinton Papers, vol. 7, CL; CC to Shirley, July 25, 1749, *JP*, vol. 9, 43–45; GC's speech to Council and Assembly, October 8, 1751, New York Colony, Council, *Council of the Colony of New York*, vol. 2, 1074; GC to Bedford, May 23, 1751, CO5/1096/206, LC transcript; James Thomas Flexner, *Lord of the Mohawks: A Biography of Sir William Johnson*, 2nd ed. (Boston: Little, Brown, 1979), 109; O'Toole, *White Savage*, 94–95.

72. GC to Newcastle, December 9, 1746, *NYCD*, vol. 6, 313–14.

73. CC to GC, February 12, 1750, George Clinton Papers, vol. 10, CL.

74. CC to GC, February 12, 1750, George Clinton Papers, vol. 10, CL.; CC to GC, February 9, 1748/9, *CP*, vol. 4, 91–95; JA to CC, January 2, 1750/1, *CP*, vol. 4, 245–50; CC to JA, January 17, 1750/1, *CP*, vol. 4, 253–54; GC to R. H. Morris, August 18, 1751, Robert Hunter Morris Papers, New Jersey Historical Society; JA to CC, January 23, 1750/1, *CP*, vol. 4, 255.

75. CC to Mitchell, July 18, August 17, 1751, *CP*, vol. 9, 98–106; CC, "The Present State of the Indian Affairs with the British and French Colonies in North America," August 8, 1751, *CP*, vol. 4, 272–73; Eric Hinderaker, *The Two Hendricks: Unraveling a Mohawk Mystery* (Cambridge, MA: Harvard University Press, 2010), 223.

76. CC, "Present State," August 8, 1751, *CP*, vol. 4, 272; *NYCD*, vol. 6, 745; Alan Rogers, *Empire and Liberty: American Resistance to British Authority, 1755–1763* (Berkeley: University of California Press, 1974), 23; John R. Alden, "The Albany Congress and the Creation of the Indian Superintendencies," *Mississippi Valley Historical Review* 27, no. 2 (1940): 196–97; Edith M. Fox, *Land Speculation in the Mohawk Country* (Ithaca, NY: Cornell University Press, 1949), 47.

77. CC to Lady Clinton, [1749?], Bancroft Coll., Colden Papers, vol. 1, 99–100, NYPL; CC to JA, August 24, 1749, Rutherfurd Family Coll., box 8, f. 1, NYHS; George Murray and Jacobus Bruyn to Ayscough, October 12, 1750, George Clinton Papers, vol. 22, CL; declaration of trust, July 26, 1750, George Clinton Papers, vol. 22, CL; conveyance of land, October 4, 1750, George Clinton Papers, vol. 22, CL; receipt by Ayscough, June 29, 1752, George Clinton

Papers, vol. 22, CL; GC to CC, July 28, 1752, *CP*, vol. 4, 342; CC to Collinson, October 4, 1754, *CP*, vol. 4, 468; Katz, *Newcastle's New York*, 232.

78. JA to CC, February 18, 1752, *CP*, vol. 4, 311–12; *New York Gazette, or the Weekly Post–Boy* (Parker), February 24, 1752; GC to R. H. Morris, May 19, 1751, July 26, 1752, Robert Hunter Morris Papers, New Jersey Historical Society.

79. GC to R. H. Morris, November 26, 1751, Robert Hunter Morris Papers, New Jersey Historical Society; JA to CC, May 17, 1751, *CP*, vol. 4, 266–67; GC to CC, March 2, 1753, *CP*, vol. 9, 122–24.

80. Dr. Alexander Colhoun to GC, June 24, August 12, 1751, George Clinton Papers, vol. 11, CL; GC to CC, June 12, 1752, GC Letterbook, 60, CL.

81. CC to GC, January 11, 1750/1, *CP*, vol. 4, 252–53; CC to JA, January 17, 1750/1, *CP*, vol. 4, 253–54.

82. JA to CC, January 24, 1750/1, June 13, 1752, *CP*, vol. 4, 255, 335–36.

83. JA to CC, May 22, 1752, *CP*, vol. 4, 330–31; CC to JA, [1752?], CPU, reel 2.

84. GC to JA, October 7, 1752, *CP*, vol. 4, 345; CC to GC, January 19, 1753, *CP*, vol. 4, 361–62.

85. GC to CC, March 2, 1753, *CP*, vol. 9, 122–24.

86. GC to R. H. Morris, April 16, 1753, Robert Hunter Morris Papers, New Jersey Historical Society; Katz, *Newcastle's New York*, 237–38, 240.

87. CC, "Remarks on the Subject Matter of the papers sent me by his Excellency," April 5, 1748, *CP*, vol. 4, 34.

88. Newcastle to Pelham, October 13, 1752, Newcastle Papers, British Museum Additional Manuscripts 32730, f. 112, LC transcript; GC to R. H. Morris, July 26, 1752, Robert Hunter Morris Papers, New Jersey Historical Society; Beverly McAnear, *The Income of the Colonial Governors of British North America* (New York: Pageant Press, 1967), 107.

89. JA to CC, July 30, 1753, *CP*, vol. 4, 401–2; Earl of Halifax to CC, May 17, 1753, *CP*, vol. 4, 389–91.

90. CC to Collinson, September 6, 1753, New Netherlands Coll., NYHS; Gerrit P. Judd, *Members of Parliament, 1734–1832* (New Haven: CT: Yale University Press, 1955), 294.

91. Livingston, *Review*, 92–93, 122–23; W. Smith, Jr., *History*, vol. 2, 133; New York Colony, Council, *Calendar of Council Minutes, 1668–1783*, comp. Berthold Fernow (Albany: University of the State of New York, 1902; repr. Harrison, NY: Harbor Hill Books, 1987), 389.

92. Livingston, *Review*, 91, 123–24; W. Smith, Jr., *History*, vol. 2, 133, 135–37; "Extracts of his Majesty's Instructions directed to the late Sir Danvers Osborn," August 13, 1753, New York Colony, Council, *Council of the Colony of New York*, vol. 2, 1127–28.

93. CC to Mrs. CC, October 14, 1753, *CP*, vol. 4, 407–8.

94. CC to Mrs. CC, October 14, 1753, *CP*, vol. 4, 407–8; W. Smith, Jr., *History*, vol. 2, 134–35; John A. Schutz, *Thomas Pownall, British Defender of American Liberty: A Study of Anglo–American Relations in the Eighteenth Century* (Glendale, CA: Arthur H. Clark, 1951), 15–16.

95. Robert and Richard Ray to Robert Sanders, October 13, 1753, Wayne Andrews, ed., "In Flocks, Like Ill–Boding Ravens: Being an Account of the Tragic End of Sir Danvers Osborne, Bart.," *New York Historical Society Quarterly* 35, no. 4 (1951): 406–7; CC to Mrs. CC, October 14, 1753, *CP*, vol. 4, 407–8; New York Colony, Council, *Calendar of Council Minutes, 1668–1783*, comp. Fernow, 390.

96. Livingston, *Review*, 21; W. Smith, Jr., *History*, vol. 2, 137–38; CC to Mrs. CC, October 14, 1753, *CP*, vol. 4, 407–8.

97. CC to Mrs. CC, October 14, 1753, *CP*, vol. 4, 407–8.

98. CC to Mrs. CC, October 14, 1753, *CP*, vol. 4, 407–8; DeLancey to Council and General Assembly, October 31, 1753, New York Colony, *State of New York: Messages from the Governors, Vol. 1, 1683–1776 Colonial Period*, ed. Charles Z. Lincoln (Albany, NY: J. B. Lyon, 1909), 528; CC to General Amherst, August 4, 1760, *CLB*, vol. 1, 1; CC to Thomas Pownall, August 22, 1760, *CLB*, vol. 1, 12–13; *ANB*, s.v. DeLancey, James (b. 1703).

Chapter Ten

Coldengham Under Siege

"Politics—for I know from experience—is much easier to keep out of . . . than to get out" Cadwallader Colden explained to Peter Collinson in 1753. Although happily retired from the political fray, events conspired against Colden's wishes. Another major war between Britain and France ignited a new round of Indian warfare that threatened Ulster and Orange counties. Colden's neighbors turned to the councilor who lived among them (and who also happened to be an authority on Indians) for leadership.[1]

In retirement, Colden complained to his correspondents about his diminishing faculties. His memory seemed to be failing along with his mental acuity. His weakening eyesight made it harder to examine the tiny parts of plants. Despite his ageing, Colden continued to take every opportunity to advance the prospects of his sons. If anything, these signs of his own mortality spurred him to action. "I am so far advanced in years that I can be of use to my children only for a little time," he pointed out to Collinson.[2]

Encouraged by Lord Halifax's positive letter to him, along with news that Halifax had publicly praised him, Colden asked Collinson to continue to lobby his lordship about affixing a salary to the surveyor-general office of New York. A salary would help Sandie, who was doing practically all of the job by now. Collinson's determined efforts produced plenty of praise— "courtier Like"—for Colden but no salary. "So my Dear friend I See no hopes of prevailing" Collinson assured the frustrated father. Undaunted, Colden had Collinson try again, this time to help Davie, whose "weak constitution" made him unsuited for most work, receive a post in the colonial customs to replace a senile official. That campaign also failed. These rebuffs strengthened Colden's belief that he had been neglected.[3]

At least Sandie remained secure as surveyor-general, although he had become a target for Indians who felt mistreated over land grants. In 1753 the

Mohawk Hendrick, called King Hendrick by the colonists, knocked Sandie for surveying land for a grantee that the incited Indians believed was still theirs. They aired their complaints at a Council meeting in June 1753 which Colden did not attend. Finally, Hendrick proclaimed: "We don't lay the blame so much on Mr. Colden as on those persons who employed him." In November 1753 his father had to be greatly relieved when Sandie assured him: "The Liet. Govr. received me very civilly when I waited on him."[4]

Though Sandie and James DeLancey appeared to get along well, Colden stayed retired. He did not appear at a meeting of the Council when it served as a legislative body until January 1756, well into the administration of the new governor, Sir Charles Hardy. A naval man, Hardy was out of his league as a colonial governor and he knew it. He sought no fight with DeLancey and allowed him to serve as chief justice again as well as a councilor. Colden's determination to remain retired had to have strengthened when he learned that Hardy's commission had restored Daniel Horsmanden to his Council seat.[5]

The retired Colden did not attend one of the most well known events of this period, the Albany Congress of 1754, but he did give some "short hints" about "uniting the Northern colonies" to Benjamin Franklin who did. Colden revealed that the British government, as long ago as the 1720s, had thought of appointing a governor-general to handle the defense of the northernmost American colonies. But the idea languished because no one believed the colonies would provide adequate finances for such an office. Warning that a "Grand Council"—a legislature for this colonial union—presented problems, Colden explained that if its members served a brief term, nothing long-lasting could be done. On the other hand, if these officials had a lengthy term and could not be fired by London "they may become dangerous." He emphasized "that England will keep their Colonies as far as they can dependent on them." No British monarch would pursue any other policy.[6]

On July 14, 1754, after the Albany Congress had concluded, Franklin and some colleagues arrived at the Colden landing to give Colden the news that the Plan of Union had been created by the Congress—though his hints and James Alexander's had arrived too late to be of much help. Unable to procure transportation to Coldengham, the visitors had to be content with a letter and sailed away. In the end, it did not matter; the Plan of Union had little support and went nowhere.[7]

These talks at Albany had acquired a sense of urgency because, a few months before, Virginia and the French had clashed over the construction of a fort at the beginning of the Ohio River. This early suggestion of renewed warfare gave even more importance to talks with the Iroquois that also took place at Albany, which Lieutenant Governor DeLancey led (Hardy did not arrive in the colony until September 1755).[8]

Thoroughly disgruntled, the Iroquois insisted that they wanted to deal with William Johnson, not the Albany commissioners. Learning of this, Johnson came to Albany and assisted DeLancey. But on July 2, 1754 King Hendrick did not hide his disgust from the lieutenant governor and the commissioners: "Tis your fault Brethren that we are not strengthened by conquest, for we would have gone and taken Crown Point, but you hindered us." Although the Iroquois willingly renewed their ties to New York, another observer wrote, they "Laid the faults to the English or rather N York Government whom they had no Interview for 3 years; upbraided them with folly and Cowardise in neglecting their fortifications, in not taking Crown point etc. . .." During Hendrick's visit of 1755 to Philadelphia, he spread the word to other colonists: "The Government of New York does not use Us well."[9]

DeLancey knew that he could not make the memory of his resistance to taking Crown Point disappear, but now he was in charge of New York. He had to have been dismayed by another dismissive comment Hendrick made at the Albany Congress. "Look about your Country," he suggested, "and see you have no Fortifications about you, no, not even to this City." Given its closeness to Canada, "the French may easily come and turn you out of your doors." So, on February 4, 1755 DeLancey called for the Assembly to provide funds to upgrade the defenses of New York City, which had twice been conquered by a foreign fleet. And Albany needed new defenses too, he insisted, "for if that be taken, I do not see what could stop an Enemy from passing on the West Side of Hudson's River, through Ulster and Orange, even into Jersey or Pennsylvania." Recall that the Coldens had known and feared that nothing could have stopped New York's own mutinous army from leaving Albany and rampaging through the neighborhood of Coldengham.[10]

The lieutenant governor knew that his proposal of a strong fort on the Hudson and scouts to watch for the French enemy would be expensive, but "Security cannot be purchased at too high a Rate." He assured the assemblymen: "I flatter myself, you will not risk losing your all, by an ill-timed Parsimony." It was essential to raise funds, DeLancey declared, "for your own Preservation and the Continuance of the Blessings we now enjoy." The assembly responded with taxes, including a stamp tax, which the lieutenant governor stated "will be so diffused as to be in a Manner insensible."[11]

DeLancey had crafted a defense plan that he thought would work well. Traditionally, there were two ways that the colony had been attacked: from the north, by the French, who traversed Lake Champlain or overland via Indian trails from Canada; and from the sea, by European navies, against the colonial capital. DeLancey did not comprehend that the North American chessboard, upon which the imperial powers made their moves, had altered significantly. The French movement into the Ohio River valley meant that they and their Indian allies would no longer be blocked by Iroquois territory from attacking New York. Instead, the enemy could approach the colony from the west. DeLancey had mentioned the counties of Ulster and Orange only once in his February speech to the Assembly—and that in the context of an attack from the north. Both counties would be soon defenseless from a western attack. And it was in Ulster that Colden was spending his blissful retirement.[12]

A military disaster made the new, dangerous situation obvious. Virginia's problems with the French over the Ohio River had caused the British government to send an army to deal with the foreign interlopers. Its commander, Sir Edward Braddock, brought with him a commission for Johnson putting him in charge of Indian affairs under the general.[13]

On July 9, 1755 Braddock, who had no experience of American conditions, blundered into a bloody ambush when he led forces against the French. With the general killed and his army devastated, George Washington, who had been at Braddock's defeat, wrote that "I Tremble at the consequences that this defeat may have upon our back settlers, who I suppose will all leave their habitations unless there are proper measures taken for their security," prophetic words indeed.[14]

In Pennsylvania, the Quakers at first thought the report of Braddock's defeat was just a lie. The colony fell into "utmost Confusion." Indians soon attacked the Pennsylvania frontier, and there "put numbers to death without asking their Religion." Virginians in the backcountry, attacked as well, fled leaving counties all but deserted as was western Maryland. In December 1755 Robert Hunter Morris, now the governor of Pennsylvania, felt amazed that the Indians "in this Short Space of time" had laid "waste a Considerable Tract of Country, extending a Vast Length from beyond the Appalachian Hills in Virginia." More was to come, he thought: "it may be expected that they will next fall on Jersey, and perhaps New York, as they follow the chain of Mountains."[15]

When New Yorkers learned for sure about Braddock's disaster, they expressed "Concern and amazement" and fear what effect it would have on New York's Indians. Immediately, Lieutenant Governor DeLancey forbade any of the printers in the city from publishing anything mentioning what had befallen Braddock and his men, which Sandie heartily endorsed, wishing that no one in any of the English colonies print the news to prevent Indians from learning about the disaster. However, there was no way Braddock's misfortune could be covered up.[16]

As it turned out, Sandie was extremely well-informed about "the most shameful defeat that ever stained the English annals"—his report came directly from Benjamin Franklin. On August 1, 1755 Sandie wrote his father, giving him all the gory details. Before that date, 1755 had been a rather uneventful year for Colden. He had spent some time trying to settle a border dispute between Ulster and Orange. Nor did a curious story spreading among

New York's slaves escape his attention—somehow the slaves had come to believe that Sir Danvers Osborn had been instructed by the king to liberate all slaves in New York but, after his death, DeLancey had suppressed the king's orders. Colden had also speculated that the tensions between Britain and France might lead to the French being driven away from the Mississippi. France's control of the Great Lakes, the tributaries of the Mississippi, and the river's mouth made the French dangerous not only to British territory but also to the rich Spanish possession of Mexico. Perhaps, Colden hoped, Spain and Britain might have a common cause against France.[17]

Sandie's letter jolted Colden away from such speculation. This "Melancholy account" of Braddock's fate "must employ the thoughts of every man who has any public Spirit on what may be the consequences." Sandie continued to keep his father informed about events in the capital relating to "the Shameful defeat near the Ohio" including the need to stop the sale of any supplies to French Canada and that Governor Hardy had hurried to Albany as the capital was "so far from the seat of action."[18]

While there was plenty of action in northern New York, Colden and his family at Coldengham could not avoid a feeling of "uneasyness" as they learned the details of the Indian attacks in the backcountry of the English colonies. Morris made clear that the attacks had all been "on the North side of that Chain of Hills, which is called the endless Mountains"—the Appalachians—"that take their Rise in New England." Nor did it take a genius to realize that the "Ravages" would follow the mountains into both New Jersey and New York.[19]

In New York's Ulster and Orange counties, the Appalachians were called the Highlands—a tourist could not help but state they "indeed are extremely high." Thomas Pownall described the topography of the Highlands, which stretched "about 12 Miles across" but had a natural pass through it. Coldengham was but three miles away from the eastern end of this pass, creating a direct passage for any attacking force heading for Coldengham. John Bartram sadly noted that he could not go to North Carolina. "No traveling, now, to Doctor Colden's, nor to the back parts of Pennsylvania, Maryland, nor Virginia."[20]

Various tribes of Indians participated in these attacks. Most startling to New Yorkers, however, was that two members of the Iroquois Confederacy, the Senecas and Cayugas, joined in with the French. King Hendrick had "blamed" Lieutenant Governor DeLancey to his face as being responsible for the deterioration of relations between New York and the Iroquois, warning him that "the French were drawing the Five Nations away."[21]

In Ulster, Colden saw, first hand, the results of this defection. To avoid confronting the still pro-British Iroquois, the Seneca attacked Ulster, well to the south of Mohawk lands. A number of Iroquois war parties, each led by a Frenchman, struck at isolated homes; one of the French leaders was captured just fifteen miles from Coldengham. Sheer panic overcame residents who fled their farms, moving the frontier of settlement in 1757 to a mere six miles from Coldengham. The shocked Colden received local intelligence that "cunning French spies are everywhere among the inhabitants of our frontiers," attempting to convince the settlers "that they would be more secure under a French Government and that they cannot be safe from the Indians otherwise." Early on in the fighting, Colden hoped "our cruel barbarian enemies, I mean the French, for the Indians are only their tools, will be made sensible of their wickedness by their punishment." The French had dreamed of conquering the colony and port of New York since the seventeenth century.[22]

Because Coldengham lay close to the Delaware River, Colden could learn much about "these barbarous cruelties" of which there were plenty. For some sixty miles along the Delaware, there was little but desolation. Most of this had been perpetrated by the Delawares, the Susquehannas, and the Shawnees. That the Delawares had joined the French demonstrated how weakened the Iroquois had become. The Delawares, conquered by them, had been a subject people or, as Colden put it using Indian terminology, the Iroquois had "put Petticoats on them." Then the French contacted the Delawares, promising them if they switched sides "they would restore them to their ancient Lands independent of the Five Nations." Colden related what message the Iroquois received from their former vassals: "We are Men."[23]

Very concerned about the defense of both Ulster and Orange, Colden was astonished "by the English prints" that glorified "the Martial spirit of the Americans." How could anybody expect much "from people brought up to the plow or to handycrafts and who have lived in peace from their cradles." Many years had passed since warfare had plagued that part of New York. To a militia officer nervous about his lack of experience, Colden reminded him that no one else had more than him. All poor farmers wanted was a good enough chunk of land so that they could prosper eventually, while merchants cared only about making a profit. However brave the amateur soldiers might be, Colden believed, "it is certain that nothing will be done effectually without a sufficient force of old troops to cooperate with them." "We want the Sinews of War," he insisted, "Arms Ammunition Money and experienced officers." An English journal soon agreed with him and complained about their "confused . . . News-writers."[24]

Nor was Colden the only one who realized how unprepared Ulster was. A minister observed that the Indians "understand the Woods better than we." Most of the colonists, he continued, being farmers, "live scattered" and "are exceedingly exposed to the Enemy." Even their fields "are surrounded with bushes," giving Indians cover to approach working farmers without being seen. The Ulster militiamen were also poor shots, because they had "but very few which deserve the Name of a Gun." In fact, the minister thought, "I believe One-half of the Militia" in both Ulster and Orange "have not Guns any ways near so good as the Law require." Most of the settlers were too poor to buy a firearm. Nor did the men have anything like military discipline. They shot their guns off for no reason, causing panic that sometimes spread thirty miles away.[25]

While New Yorkers watched the militia march on roads, they sometimes "behaved shamefully, the officers worse than the Men." Sandie declared to his father that "Every one cries out and few think there is any Safety in the Province." He told his father that the New York militia "answer the Opinion you have long entertained of them." The situation was so bad, Colden believed, that William Johnson's victory at the Battle of Lake George on September 8, 1755 saved James DeLancey's New York from conquest by the French.[26]

Colden, a magistrate as well as a councilor, concerned himself with the safety of Ulster. In December 1755, when he learned that Indians had appeared who had been near hostiles, he ordered that they be questioned and held if necessary. He also thought it best that River Indians who dwelt in "the Woods or Unsettled or thinly settled parts . . . make their Wigwams" in "well settled Towns" where they could be watched. If these Indians objected, he thought it wise that they be "secured" to calm those residents fearful of attack. "All prudent precautions ought to be taken against any ill designs of the Indians among us." Colden's idea to have peaceful Indians live right by frightened colonists would backfire in a way he never expected.[27]

At the same time Governor Hardy decided in late December to seek the expertise of Colden, whom he had not yet met. Asking for his comments on recommendations for local offices, the governor also sought his ideas about "any other points relative to the future Security of your Frontiers." Colden, pleading "Infirmities," had not intended to visit the capital until spring arrived. That all changed when he read Hardy's letter and realized that the governor would be receptive to his advice. Braving the cold, on January 8, 1756 Colden appeared at his first Council meeting in years.[28]

Colden had ideas on just about everything including martial matters. Dr. Colden—botanist, philosopher, historian—now became a military strategist. Right away, he recommended that blockhouses be built to protect the people of Ulster and Orange. Blockhouses were hardly a new idea, but Colden suggested a change in their positioning. Blockhouses had always been placed in a town or at its border. Instead, Colden suggested that blockhouses be situated at some distance from a community, especially on roads. Indian warriors always wanted an unobstructed escape route. With that prevented by a blockhouse, Indians would be reluctant to attack in the first place, giving the settlers more security. He also recommended his old colleague from his surveying days, Charles Clinton, not only for a high rank in the militia but also as the right man to decide the location of the blockhouses.[29]

Hardy accepted Colden's ideas, including having the River Indians live among the colonists. The problem was to get the Assembly to move on them. In December 1755 the governor ordered militiamen from Ulster and Orange to act to protect the ravaged frontiers there and so stop the flight of the inhabitants from danger. But would the militia be paid or supplied? Hardy reminded the assemblymen that "This Duty will fall very unequally on the People, by being confined to the Militia of those two Counties." Far worse, many of them could not afford to buy supplies, even ammunition. The Assembly, after wisely urging that there be cooperation with the militia of northern New Jersey (which bordered Orange and Ulster), voted to make "reasonable allowance" for supplies for the embattled militia and rangers who had been recruited. Curiously, this Assembly resolution did not mention the Indians.[30]

Then, the next day, January 13, 1756, Governor Hardy made a mistake. He alerted the Assembly that he had received a petition from Orange County asking for protection from the enemy, "for want of which Numbers are daily moving off, and the rest, is to be feared, may soon follow." The solution, Hardy announced, was to construct blockhouses "at some Distance from the Settlements." Blockhouses appeared successful in New Jersey the governor added. He urged that the Assembly fund the building of this defensive line of blockhouses and pay their garrisons. The error occurred when Hardy sent not only the petition, but also included "a Sketch of the Country and Settlements, in Orange and Ulster."[31]

Everyone in the Assembly knew that only one man would have the knowledge to write a historical account of two counties—Cadwallader Colden. If blockhouses had appeared to be Hardy's idea, the Assembly might have accepted it. If the suggestion had seemed to be inspired by New Jersey's experience, perhaps the Assembly would have approved it. But, as it had to have been dreamed up by the hated Colden, the Assembly would reject it. On January 23, 1756 the Assembly refused to fund the building of blockhouses by a vote of fifteen to five. Of the five supporting the motion, four were from Ulster and Orange; the other hailed from Dutchess County, across the Hudson from Ulster. The defeated motion had also included sending guns to the two embattled counties. If Colden had been killed in an Indian raid, few tears would have been shed in the Assembly chamber.[32]

With Colden being seen as Hardy's military advisor, the Assembly wanted to punish Ulster and Orange because Colden lived there. On February 25, 1756 an assemblyman from Orange moved that, because the two counties had recruited sixty rangers to patrol their frontier, that number be credited toward their allotment for a planned attack on Crown Point, a reasonable request. The motion received only four votes, all from Orange and Ulster.[33]

In February 1756 the Assembly's ire against Colden had been raised by his opposition to what was dubbed "the debt bill." His assertion that he still remained retired except for military matters was not totally true. DeLancey's hold on his office of chief justice had been confirmed in this bill when the Assembly gave him a salary for it; Horsmanden benefited too. Overall, it did not specify for what these debts were for. And some of Sir William Johnson's old expenses still went unpaid; he and other creditors were not mentioned. Alexander and William Smith, Sr. joined in Colden's dissent, but, after some compromise, the debt bill became law.[34]

When on March 2, 1756, Hardy wrote to the Assembly, noting more attacks in Ulster, the Assembly tried to dodge the issue. The governor asked that a large force be authorized to follow and hit the Indians so hard they would, at last, want peace. He was certain that New Jersey, also threatened, would join with its neighbor in this campaign. Instead, the next day the Assembly authorized a thousand man New York force, but it had to work with both New Jersey and the Quaker colony of Pennsylvania. Pennsylvania's cooperation seemed uncertain at best. On March 5 a communication from the militia colonels of Ulster and Orange was referred to a committee.[35]

Then the Assembly really had its ire stirred when James Parker and his partner, William Weyman, published an essay attacking the assemblymen, which they assumed Colden had written, over their failure to protect Ulster. "W." insisted that "Tho' repeated Application has been made to the Guardians of our Country," that is, the assemblymen, "yet we have been most cruelly neglected, to almost the Ruin of this Part of the Province." The angry author continued:

> If they are . . . lost to all Compassion, we will beg Leave to bring some of the Men who are next murdered by the Indians, and lay the mangled Bodies at their Feet; hoping that . . . the dead Bodies of our Countrymen, with their gasping Wounds, may . . . induce them to take into consideration, the distressing Condition of his Majesty's good Subjects in this Part of the Province, before it is too late.[36]

That essay certainly seemed lively enough to be by Colden. The Assembly lost no time in jailing both printers to force them to divulge the obvious identity of the author. To the Assembly's chagrin, Colden was not the culprit. Instead, it was Rev. Hezekiah Watkins, a Church of England missionary at Newburgh. The Colden family worshipped at his services. Close, but not close enough. Suddenly, the Assembly lost interest in the matter, waiting until late October 1756 to give the erring and briefly jailed minister "a Reprimand from Mr. Speaker." The Assembly would have wanted Colden drawn and quartered.[37]

The assemblymen, however, being politicians, were concerned about their popularity. The day after the attack was printed, the Assembly voted for another 715 soldiers, 400 of whom were specifically intended for "an offensive War against the Indians, who almost daily ravage the Western Frontiers of this Colony," a bill the Assembly had been stalling. But complaints kept being voiced in Ulster. The people of Ulster had paid heavy taxes used to fortify the capital against an attack from the sea which would not happen as long as the British navy dominated the Atlantic. Nor did they fail to notice that New Jersey, with its blockhouses, had become relatively secure. "Shall we . . . be despised and neglected because we are poor when the money that is necessary for our defence would be no more felt by the rich than a drop of water is in the Sea," the common people complained to Colden. Their bitter words exasperated Colden. He had nothing to do with DeLancey's defensive plans, his taxes, or the Assembly's antics.[38]

Colden had seen for himself the deteriorating conditions. Although he had wanted to influence the governor, his departure from Coldengham had been fueled by more than that—Ulster was a war zone—and a very dangerous one. Many of the River Indians had disappeared and some were identified as having participated in attacks upon the settlers. According to Sandie, the River Indians had been "admitted into the People's Houses with the same freedom they would admit one another." Now settlers, he revealed, "are made very uneasy especially as they have Several of these vile dogs living amongst them." Some of the dead settlers had been killed "by Indians who they were well acquainted with." (Sandie never used such language when writing to his father.) This turn of events made Sandie concerned about his father and the rest of the family at Coldengham as "there was a Number of Indians about him and Constantly at his House." Alexander had already voiced his concern about the Indian visitors at Coldengham.[39]

What Sandie envisioned as a threat—the presence of Indians at Coldengham—his father saw as a boon. The friendly Indians, in effect, served as a protective shield against an enemy attack. The trees had long since lost their leaves, making an Indian war party more likely to be seen before they arrived at their target. A "slight snow," making it easier to track a war party, also would discourage an attack. Judging from Colden's later behavior, he did not think it necessary to leave Coldengham (though he probably was the only one who thought that). Still, he knew very well that "my name is known among all our Indians." It was "prudent" to leave he realized. When Governor Hardy sent his letter asking for his advice, that convinced him. Colden, Alice, their daughters Jennie and Cathy (along with some female slaves), arrived at Sandie's home in New York City on Christmas, December 25, 1755. Davie stayed behind, with the male slaves, to watch over Coldengham.[40]

Sandie had expressed the fear that if nearby Minisink fell to the Indians, then the neighborhood of Coldengham could be easily "cut off." In January 1756 a substantial number of hostile Indians, about sixty in all, attacked Minisink. However, some twenty-seven militiamen from New Jersey, camped nearby, rushed to its aid and "beat the Indians off." The threat to

Coldengham had been thwarted. With no further attack upon Minisink, Sandie, relieved, wrote that "the People in the Highlands begin to be more Easy then they were," but "they apprehend when the Leaves come out and the Woods grow thick they may be in greater danger from the Indians then any time yet."[41]

By the end of February 1756, the Coldens were thinking of going to Coldengham; the Hudson was navigable again. Their plans changed suddenly. In January 1756 Colden revealed what the frontiersmen now felt about the "barbarous cruelties . . . committed by the Indians living among the people in professed friendship." Their betrayal "gives me and all my neighbours Jealousies of the Indians who live among us." Some of the settlers' emotions had gone far beyond concern and anger. Hatred, growing in Ulster, soon exploded.[42]

A proclamation by Governor Hardy detailed what had happened in Ulster on March 2–3, 1756:

> A Party of armed men, headed by one Samuel Slaughter, came on the 2nd Instant, to the House of Charles Stephenson, at Wilemanton, in Ulster County, and killed an Indian and his Squaw, whom they found there: And early the next Morning went to a Wigwam, or Indian Settlement [nearby] and there killed and scalped three Indian Men, two Squaws, and two Indian Children. And whereas such Proceedings if not immediately put a Stop to, or the Authors of those already committed be suffered to escape with Impunity, may not only draw upon us the Resentment of all the Settlement Indians, as yet our Friends, of whom it is not doubted there are many, but give great Disgust to other Nations in Friendship with the English.[43]

Hurriedly, Hardy had surviving River Indians from both Orange and Ulster escorted to the capital "under a proper Guard of white Men, to protect them from the Insults of the enraged Populace." Other River Indians found shelter with still pro-British Iroquois. The governor also directed local sheriffs to arrest the aptly-named Slaughter and the other murderers. Having the River Indians live by the colonists had not provided the comfort Colden had assumed it would.[44]

Despite Hardy's intentions of bringing the miscreants to justice, they escaped punishment. According to William Smith, Sr., the common people in Ulster "prevented an Inquisition concerning that Indian Blood that was shed." Slaughter, Smith confided to Colden, had been "too much countenanced by some in the County." Colden could not have doubted that.[45]

Though murders of innocent Indians had stopped in Ulster, the following year a sudden attack by Indians near Coldengham had been instigated, Smith believed, "more by private Revenge than the Publick Quarrel." And hatred of Indians remained strong throughout the threatened counties. One of Colden's correspondents told him: "You See how we are Destroyed by those Indians who are Called our friend Indians for they Come Down on our frontiers and Murder us." The writer added: "to this pass is our poor province Brought and these Frontiers have no assistance from the province." The Assembly, maintaining its claim to control the militia, had done little to help the western frontier, Ulster and Orange.[46]

Because of Slaughter's Massacre, Colden delayed his return to Coldengham. When he "heard of the late Mischiefs" in Ulster, he left Westchester (where he had been visiting Elizabeth) to go to New York City "to give what assistance is in my power." Fearful that the Indians would set forest fires to destroy the settlers, he advised that Hardy direct that the forest undergrowth be carefully burned as quickly as possible to prevent the Indians from using flaming woodlands as a weapon. It would also stop some accidental fire from spreading more panic which Ulster and Orange already had plenty of. This tactic worked. After Hardy gave the order, the inhabitants calmed; some refugees even returned to their homes.[47]

Defense matters crowded the agenda of the Council. Alexander, despite having a bad outbreak of gout, attended one of these meetings because he knew how important the defense of Ulster and Orange was to Colden. On top of his gout, Alexander caught a chill which developed into pneumonia. He died on April 2, 1756. "It adds to my grief," Colden lamented, "that his friendship to me was the occasion of his exposing himself to the cold at that time." Having now lost "all my old friends" from his early days in America, Colden's anxiety for his family members outside of the capital—still endangered by the war—never left his mind. He hoped that the enemy would soon leave the western frontier ending any danger from returning to Coldengham.[48]

Very little changed, however. Colden could not understand why the Assembly refused to back the building of blockhouses which had won the support of practically everyone on the Ulster-Orange frontier. Nor did the Assembly agree to pay the hard-pressed militiamen; officers had to guarantee their pay before anyone agreed to do anything. Some young men fought in nearby counties to escape the constant service in Orange and Ulster. Perhaps most assemblymen were ignorant of the poverty of the farmers on the western frontier. The only concession the Assembly made, after another appeal by the governor, was to exempt Ulster and Orange from drafts for service elsewhere—and that was only until their frontier quieted.[49]

The only good news for Colden was that the hatred directed at him since he joined George Clinton seemed to be abating. In early June 1756 Alice, who stayed in the city longer than her husband, reported that "I have had all the respect shewed to me that I could desire or expect." Before her husband left for Coldengham in May 1756, Peter DeLancey came to visit them. The "very agreeable" DeLancey made a point of meeting with his father-in-law, which "we were pleased with" Alice wrote.[50]

When Colden arrived at Coldengham, everything seemed secure. When Alice returned, she brought her young granddaughter, Aly DeLancey, with her to Coldengham. The Coldens assumed the worst was over. They were wrong.[51]

There would, however, be a new man at the top. The Scot, Lord Loudoun, had been placed in command in North America. Sandie enthused that at the general's "arrival we shall see a great change of affairs in America." Surely, Crown Point would soon fall.[52]

What Loudoun needed was maps done "with the utmost care and ability" and he believed that Cadwallader Colden had them, a logical assumption, as Colden's mapmaking had started when William Burnet was governor of New York. Everyone, including the English, had accepted the veracity of French maps of North America, which included as part of their empire large swaths "of what is actually settled by the Inhabitants of New York." Burnet ordered Colden, as surveyor-general of New York, to produce an accurate map of the colony.[53]

Colden's predecessor as surveyor-general had left him little of value, but Colden plowed ahead. Finished in late 1723, the new map corrected the wild French claims. Published in 1724, it was included in his Indian history. Decades later, Colden (and Alexander) gave invaluable help to Lewis Evans, whose excellent map of the New York-Pennsylvania region would be published in 1749.[54]

Given Colden's record, Loudoun had been expecting a great deal, embarrassing Colden, who had given most of his maps to Sandie, now really the surveyor-general. However, he did have some local maps of Orange and Ulster, which he sent. For the army's benefit, Colden dispatched a new chart of the two counties. The big obstacle to mapmaking in New York, he explained, the great manors on the east side of the Hudson, had never been surveyed. "I was once so vain," he admitted, "as to entertain hopes of obtaining encouragement from the Crown to form a general Map of the Northern Colonies" done in cooperation with surveying officials elsewhere. With a host of surveys, Colden, using astronomy, could have brought all the scattered data together. At first he tried to handle all the expenses himself, but that could not last very long. He believed he was "too inconsiderable" to convince the British government of the value of such a map.[55]

Colden went on to explain that the office of surveyor-general had no salary attached to it. Lord Halifax had done his best but the British Treasury had rejected the request. "The reason of failing I can only guess." As it turned out, Sandie went to Loudoun to deliver the maps sent from Coldengham. In Sandie's presence, the general read his father's letter in front of other high-ranking officers. When the commander-in-chief reached the part about the Treasury's refusal, he spoke: "Oh . . . I know the reason they don't care to part with Money." Because the government had not paid him, Colden "was right not to take any further trouble" about the map project. Then the general praised all the maps Colden had dispatched. The two Scotsmen had bonded before they had met.[56]

Colden also made a pitch to Loudoun to quarter some regular soldiers on the embattled western frontier of New York. He informed the general that "very lately some persons have been murdered and houses burnt about 16 miles in a straight line from my house" while the local militia had become exhausted "by almost continual military duty without any assistance from the other parts of the province."[57]

Governor Hardy had already convinced Loudoun about the need of the embattled counties and, after they settled a jurisdictional dispute, Loudoun ordered some New York provincial soldiers—raised by the colony—to Kingston. The general, though, who had not yet seen Colden's chart, did not realize that Kingston was a very long march from the more southerly area where they were needed. The governor told Colden to send a message to alert the troops to get off their transport well before Kingston. Thrilled at the prospect of help for the frontier, Colden eagerly complied.[58]

But something else happened that made life very difficult for the Coldens. By the middle of February 1757, Alice had broken her thigh. Unlike the case with other bones, doctors of that time found it difficult to put a restraining bandage that would do any good around a broken thigh, resulting in the thigh bone not healing properly. One leg became shorter than the other producing, at best, a limp. She would not be very mobile for some time. If a sudden emergency happened, such as an Indian raid near Coldengham, evacuating her quickly would be difficult.[59]

And, by June 1757, the area around Coldengham had, once again, become very dangerous. The prospects seemed so bad that William Smith, Sr. advised Colden to leave and ignore "the Clamour" that might follow an evacuation.[60]

In the midst of the increasing danger, another change happened at the top. Governor Hardy had asked to be relieved from the difficult job of running wartime New York. On July 2, 1757 he sailed away resuming his naval career. Lieutenant Governor DeLancey again took charge of the colony. No new governor would be named, probably because the imperial bureaucrats were resigned to the fact that anyone they sent from Britain would just be bedeviled by the Assembly.[61]

If, by some chance, the Coldens did not realize one of DeLancey's shortcomings, they learned of it in September 1757. Sandie brought him one of his father's letters concerning the western frontier, a subject, Sandie stated, that the lieutenant governor thought "so little about." DeLancey did not seem to grasp the importance of the information. When, the next month, Sandie brought a letter from Johnson with correct intelligence about a planned Seneca attack on Ulster, the "alarmed" DeLancey's reaction was to get out his carriage and drive Sandie directly to Lord Loudoun. Colden praised DeLancey when he did anything to bolster the defenses of the frontier. DeLancey meant well but he was reluctant to do anything that the Assembly might not approve. Though DeLancey had great legal talent, he just was not cut out to be a war governor.[62]

Meanwhile, Lord Loudoun, realizing how panicky the western frontier was, promised Sandie that he would send soldiers to safeguard the frightened inhabitants. However, Loudoun, taking Oliver DeLancey's advice as to where the soldiers should be based, ordered them to a town, far from the frontier, where they served no purpose.[63]

When Colden realized what had happened, he wrote to the commander-in-chief and the lieutenant governor to explain that "a high ridge of mountains" separated the post from the frontier preventing the men from assisting "on any emergency." Even worse, Loudoun's orders superseded a letter to Colden from DeLancey authorizing him "to advise and assist" the officer in charge regarding the stationing of his soldiers "to the best advantage" to protect the area. The mistake especially rattled the frontiersmen because so many of their sons had left to engage in "lucrative" privateering, leaving only their fathers to defend their families. Nor was confidence raised by the knowledge that the Indians closely watched the movement of the local guards. As soon as these men moved from a neighborhood, the Indians attacked the now defenseless inhabitants. Sandie actually pointed out to Loudoun on a map where soldiers "should be Posted."[64]

Colden knew how bad things were. Because so many scared people were fleeing, "I know not what part of this Country will be a frontier next." His concerned children feared for their parents' safety and Sandie voiced their distress. Intelligence from a captured Indian—that his comrades had planned to split up and attack several targets at the same time—escalated the fright of Sandie and his siblings. "It's very Plain the Enemy lie not far from you," Sandie pleaded with his father. "It would be a very great Satisfaction to every one of us your children," he implored, "who are absent from you to have you out of a Country where none of us can think you can remain in Safety." He made the same request frequently without the desired effect. His mother was as determined to stay at Coldengham as her husband.[65]

Sandie's father did his best to calm him. "If proper resolutions be taken," Colden insisted, he had "no Inclination to move and will not." His resolve had to have been strengthened when Lord Loudoun corrected the earlier blunder of the posting of the soldiers. The general now specified that the troops set up their base near Coldengham.[66]

During Sandie's campaign to influence his parents, he even tried to enlist Lieutenant Governor DeLancey, but he was not much help. As Sandie told his father, DeLancey said that "he would advise your moving your family but that such advice would not be proper for him to give on account of Alarming the Country." In other words, if Colden was seen as fleeing from the Indians, a mass panic would break out leading to the depopulation of both Ulster and Orange.[67]

Nor could Colden have forgotten what happened the last time he had left Ulster—frightened people filled with hate had massacred innocents. Ulster and Orange had "become the Theater of a cruel war."[68] The only way to assure that the frontiersmen felt secure was to insure that a proper defense had been arranged for the besieged counties before he could possibly give in to the wishes of his children. Colden still believed that blockhouses remained the only way to protect the western frontier.

On October 16, 1757 Colden wrote to the lieutenant governor about still more dismal news about still another Indian attack. A house, equipped with loopholes for shooting, barely managed to hold out because its door had been closed just in front of attacking Indians. Despite that fortunate circumstance, the enemy, who took losses, shot their guns at the door, killing two of the occupants. Everyone in the area wished, Colden assured DeLancey, that he urge the lieutenant governor to consider building blockhouses. In a dramatic ending, Colden passed on the intelligence that the night before the sound of gunfire had been heard coming from the frontier, wherever it was at the moment. No more time could be lost.[69]

Colden continued to press for blockhouses, utilizing the positioning of the soldiers Loudoun had ordered to the frontier. Formed into two units, one located at Goshen in Orange County, and the other near Coldengham, the soldiers were separated by some 20 miles. The officers had been directed to confer at Coldengham about the placement of the troops, but had neglected to tell Colden they were coming. The surprised Colden met with them happily and steered the meeting to one conclusion. The officers knew that hostile Indians could easily pass by them in the huge gap between the posts and had already done so. All of them agreed with Colden that blockhouses be constructed somewhat away from the settlements. Militiamen would be thrilled to build them which would take, at most, a week. He informed both DeLancey and Loudoun that, if these fortifications were constructed, the "present uneasiness of the inhabitants" would "be removed."[70]

Colden did recommend that some changes be made from the original planned sites. Upon closer examination, it had been realized that the blockhouses would have been endangered by higher ground near them. Colden had determined a safer defensive line for the buildings. If the construction did not happen quickly Colden warned, then the officers might lose control of the situation on the frontier, causing turmoil. Everyone knew that dangerous possibility had to be avoided at all costs; there had already been one massacre and another must be prevented.[71]

On November 3, 1757 Lieutenant Governor DeLancey received still another letter from Colden pushing for a system of blockhouses, emphasizing the value of the new, projected route. Also enclosed was a new, helpful, map of the affected area. DeLancey presented both items to the Council which resolved that he should "give directions for building a number of blockhouses on the Line proposed by Mr. Colden."[72]

DeLancey then authorized Colden to have these defenses constructed. The lieutenant governor had earlier cautioned him "that these blockhouses could not be built without my Lord Loudouns approbation as it depended on him to place men in them to cover the Country." Immediately after the councilors acted, DeLancey heard from the general. If these blockhouses were thought "absolutely necessary" and were more useful than his own suggestions, the commander-in-chief gave his "directions" to build them. Notified of Loudoun's letter by the lieutenant governor, Colden reiterated the reasons why the structures were absolutely necessary, adding that many frontiersmen were getting rid of their animals to start an exodus from the distressed borderland. Some planned to go to New Jersey, already well protected by its blockhouses. Acting upon the authority of Loudoun, the lieutenant governor, and the Council, Colden directed the militia to build the structures "about two miles" away from "the Settlements." Upon Colden's request, Loudoun sent regular soldiers to garrison the blockhouses. No one had consulted the Assembly.[73]

With a good defense in place, Colden took the female members of the family out of the war zone. Sandie had been looking for a house for them for some time. The Coldens finally decided upon the town of Flushing in Queens County, a place especially favored by well-off New York City merchants wanting a place in the country. Though Flushing tended to be rocky, the soil was fertile and experienced farmers such as Colden and Davie could do well with it. Colden had first experienced life in Flushing when he visited George Clinton at his country home there, and Sandie might have been able to rent the same home. Now much nearer to the capital than when at Coldengham, Colden assured the lieutenant governor that "When at Flushing I shall be nearer to receive your honours commands and to give any information that may be expected."[74]

DeLancey probably appreciated having Colden closer because the war dragged on. The French constructed a much more powerful fort than Crown Point on Lake Champlain—even closer to Albany—that the British colonists called Ticonderoga. In 1758, during a failed attack to seize the bastion, Colden's old friend John Rutherfurd was killed while at the head of his soldiers. "I am really so much afflicted that company would be uneasy to me" Colden revealed. One can only guess how future events might have played out if Rutherfurd had been by Colden's side in the Council.[75]

As for the Ulster-Orange frontier, Minisink saw another outburst against the Indians. In 1761, a British general related, "the inhabitants of Minisink had been warned by the Indians and were afraid of being attacked. They had killed two Indians who had behaved ill to them."[76]

While the French and Indian War continued, a war of words broke out among historians. Colden now had a competitor who presented his own view of New York's past. In 1757 William Smith Jr. published his *The History of the Province of New York*.

Colden's first run-in with William Smith Jr.—and there would be many—came shortly before Smith and another young lawyer, William Livingston, published in 1752 a compendium of the laws of New York, a significant work. The two editors had checked the earlier printed version of each law with the original text. Whenever the original could not be located, a note was to be added. Then they could not find the original version of a 1699 law that vacated the Evans Patent. Both of them realized the seriousness of the matter. Not finding the original could call into question the legitimacy of the claims of the present occupants of the Evans Patent. The editors, who never doubted that the law had been "regularly passed," talked with other lawyers including the senior Smith, Alexander and Chief Justice DeLancey. All agreed with the editors' decision to note the absence of the original.[77]

When Colden arrived in the city from Coldengham, he learned what had transpired. At first he "urged strenuously for our leaving out the Note, and would listen to no Argument against his Importunity," Smith insisted. The next time Colden talked to them he exploded and "flew into a Rage, and swore if we persisted" he would make sure that Governor Clinton would never agree to their being paid for their labor. The two young men "told him that he and the Money might go to the Devil" and left. Afterward, Colden calmed and referred to the matter "in soothing Terms."[78]

Unlike much of what Smith wrote about Colden, there is no reason to doubt that story. Throughout Colden's long career, he had shown a remarkable ability to control his temper, even when under blistering attack. But these exchanges came during the Clinton administration which has been detailed. Under intense pressure, Colden was clearly affected by it. In 1749 Colden believed that his mail had "been intercepted by some villanous people here." The obvious threat to the legal title to Coldengham was too much pressure and he snapped.[79]

The only surprise relating to this editorial dispute was how long it took for a legal challenge about the Evans Patent to finally appear. In 1764 the holders of the Minisink Patent disputed the borders of the Evans Patent. They did not go after the titles of the important men with land there. Instead, the Minisink patentees targeted smaller farmers, whom they thought could not defend themselves. The "rich and powerful Men" of Minisink would be surprised. Their targets went to someone who had been their neighbor for many years, Cadwallader Colden, then the acting governor, who had, in 1722, been involved in settling part of the borders of the Evans Patent.[80]

Calling the sued men "really poor industrious Farmers" who "by their labour rendered a Country useful to the Community," Colden sought royal aid for them. Ordering the New York attorney-general, John Tabor Kempe, to enter the case, Colden wrote a thorough account for him detailing all the twists and turns of the Evans Patent's history, going back to Evans's purchase of it from the Esopus Indians and another group, the Murder Creek Indians. Truly, as Gary B. Nash has written, Colden was "the upper-class tribune for laboring people who suffered at the hands of wealthy exploiters" of whom there were plenty in New York.[81]

Smith would not be interested in such things unless, of course, he had received a retainer. He insisted that Colden's "Acts and Threats" over the missing original law was the reason he and William Livingston "maintained our Opinions" of him.[82]

But was this "righteousness of youth," as Milton Klein dubbed it, the actual reason behind Smith's distaste for Colden? Certainly, the distaste did not stop William Livingston from writing to Colden in 1760 asking that he pick a friend of his brother, Robert Livingston, Jr., as Albany's sheriff.[83]

Something else seems to have motivated Smith. In 1763 Smith wrote mocking Colden, comparing him unfavorably to the present governor: "Colden unable for want of Purse, ten thousand times now so for want of spirit, to install the dignity of his Government, lives cheap and retired at Flushing." To Smith, Colden did not possess enough money to justify his holding a high post in the government of New York. The son of a rich man, Smith disliked seeing the son of a poor man, such as Colden, having authority. This explains the inevitable string of insults Smith seems addicted to when he comments on Colden.[84]

In one respect Smith was similar to another foe of Colden's, James DeLancey, in that both had great personal popularity. DeLancey's character was more like that of a convivial party guest. Smith, however, displayed the elegance of a perfect gentleman. Yet Smith kept a side of himself hidden. At one point, early in the 1760s, Colden dined with, among others, Governor Henry Ellis of Georgia who thoroughly praised Smith's *History* while Colden differed. Ellis told him "Your Honor does not know Mr. Smith." Later, Colden tried to explain to the visitor that he did not really know the real William Smith, but Ellis refused to believe him. To prevent any further argument, Colden conjured up a story that their "Bickering" wives were responsible for the problems between the Coldens and the Smiths. When Smith learned of that he called it "Falsehood and Cowardice." Colden knew that when the elegance was stripped aside, the real William Smith was haughty and arrogant, which is obvious from his famed *History of New York*.[85]

One scholar has thoroughly castigated Smith's *History*, which dominated the retelling of New York's history for many years. According to Roger

Wines, Smith's "book, though wider in scope, is inferior in scholarship to Colden's earlier account of the Indian Nations in New York." Furthermore, Smith's epic had "several serious errors of fact." Overall, "The whole work is . . . colored with a strong bias which sometimes stretches the fact;" the bias favors the Livingstons, Smith's in-laws. All of these comments suggest why Colden insisted that "It is not fit that Mr. Smith's history should pass for a chronicle of the province of New York."[86]

Colden attacked Smith's very competence as a writer of history. And the best evidence showing Smith's poor historical judgment appears in his own private diary amid a passage that lambasts Colden after his death. Smith resurrected the charge that Colden had been a Jacobite drummer in 1715. A source told Smith that Colden's gait and his height convinced everyone that he had been a drummer boy. This story had been given out by Governor Montgomerie, the source said. As Smith recorded this, he suddenly remembered that Colden was in his late twenties then and could not have been a drummer boy. Colden in the 1760s may well have referred to himself as a boy in 1715, but only in the sense of an old man thinking of his youthful self as boyish. Smith's source for this confused account, Horsmanden, had spread the slander in the first place.[87]

When William Smith thought he had a credible source such as Horsmanden, he saw no need to check original documents. If something fit with his biased opinion, then it had to be true and no further research was needed. Smith's history recorded a story—impugning Colden by implication—that even the author admitted came from "a Party interested."[88]

In 1759 Colden finally got his hands on Smith's book and was disturbed. Although it was supposed to stop at the start of Cosby's administration, Smith's history "made a large stride" to discuss a failed attempt by a Scottish immigrant, Laughlin Campbell, to obtain a very large land grant during Clarke's administration. Remembering what had happened when he argued with Smith over the lost law, Colden decided to write Smith and even tried to employ the elder Smith as an intermediary. Aside from delivering the letter and urging his son to respond, the senior Smith did not want to get involved—his son's "resentment" at the letter was obvious. The elder Smith advised Colden not to dwell on the matter because his name had not been mentioned in the Campbell story.[89]

Colden, though, had no intention of letting the subject drop. He realized that Smith's book, because it was "the first and only History of this Province," would likely become "a foundation for future History" and Smith's totally wrong version of what happened to Campbell would be repeated by future historians many times. It would be seen as factual because of numerous repetition. And Colden knew the failure to mention his name was meaningless. Anyone who heard about a land grant in New York immediately thought that Cadwallader Colden had been closely involved with it. Inevitably, future generations would believe he had helped to swindle Campbell.[90]

In Colden's letter of January 15, 1759, he urged the younger Smith to correct the account of Campbell's attempt to receive land. Campbell did not have the financial resources to start a large settlement, Colden explained. Most of the people who sailed with Campbell did not realize they were meant to be his tenants and refused to exchange one landlord for another. Governor Clarke had made sure of their opinion by interviewing them. Nor did the Assembly support Campbell. His request was rejected and no one in New York was blamed for it. The sob story that Smith printed spread only after Campbell's death. Colden attributed Smith's publishing the story to his mistaken "credulity" in believing a falsehood and his "indignation" over what seemed mistreatment. Colden assumed that the author would correct his error thus confirming the opinion of Smith's "sincerity and integrity" which Colden had "hitherto entertained."[91]

Smith's biographer has called his response "surly." Insisting that "the Facts are notoriously true," Smith seemed most concerned, as he told Colden, about the fate of his papers which "may after your Decease, fall into such Hands, as may make a bad use of that Letter." Though Smith admitted he had gotten the details from the Campbell family, he had also talked about the incident with James Alexander. Furthermore, the publication of the story had made Campbell's widow very happy, pleasing the author.[92]

Writing back to Smith, Colden commented that he had only sought a retraction of "a vile aspersion." He explained to Smith that he had checked the Council records which supported his memory of the Campbell incident. He also reminded Smith that James Alexander had not been on the Council when the events transpired. After two decades, he had to have forgotten the specifics of something he had not been involved in. Once again, Colden requested that Smith display the "candour and love of truth, the most distinguishing qualifications of an Historian." However, Smith never retracted his account of Campbell's spiel to get a land grant. In fact, Smith, in a second volume of the *History* only published in the nineteenth century, repeated his allegations and turned the story into a diatribe against Cadwallader Colden, who had had the effrontery to question his accuracy.[93]

Probably thinking that Smith would try to influence future scholars in such a manner, Colden placed copies of the relevant documents in his papers; Smith had worried that Colden's papers would cast in doubt the veracity of the Campbell story. Colden's forethought would win most writers to his side. A comparison of the copies of what remains of the originals has only confirmed what Colden stated about Lachlan Campbell.[94]

Colden's concern over Smith Jr.'s *History* and its future reception pushed him to pen memoirs meant for his children. Written as letters to Sandie, Colden did his best to comment calmly and objectively about events he had participated in. These memoirs became another counterweight to Smith's work; Colden made sure to discuss the Campbell episode. These memoirs correct Smith's interpretation in many other details, which had to be done because of his rival's "stubborn temper of mind."[95]

For example, Colden commented that "When a man of candour finds a gentlemans character aspersed with such odious epithets as Arbitrary Tyrant, Sycophantic tool etc." as Smith doled out "without proof to support them he cannot avoid to have his indignation raised." "Popular republican writers" such as Smith "know the use of Epithets, with Superficial Readers, and never neglect the use of them."[96]

Regarding Smith's attacks on various New York governors, Colden informed Sandie, "even supposing them as bad as Mr. Smith represents them," none of them did as much damage to the colony as Leisler's Rebellion of 1689, whose participants lacked "any real concern for the good of their country." Then Colden continued giving his analysis of the historical record:

> This is too generally the case in all popular commotions, under the plausible outcry for Liberty. How cautious then ought every one to be in contributing anything towards the weakening of the legal powers of Government, or to do any thing which may give power to a disorderly Mob. A Mob can never be directed by reason; but is hurried into the worst extremes, by prejudice and passion. . . . Every attempt to put power in the mob ought to be crushed in the bud, especially in mixed governments.[97]

While Colden had busied himself answering Smith, the war waged on and Lieutenant Governor DeLancey had to deal with it. In 1759 he urged both the Council and Assembly to squeeze even more money out of New York's stamp tax; Colden was not there to hear his speech. Colden, who had turned 71 in 1759, once again declared to a correspondent: "I am now retired from the world in old age."[98]

Colden's retirement did not stop him from urging reform in the British Empire when peace finally arrived. He recommended that the British government buy Indian land in New York and then pay all the costs of subdividing and surveying the land so allowing poorer farmers, who could not afford the expenses, to settle and develop the colony. All a prospective settler would have to pay was a minimal sum, £5 per hundred acres, thus bringing the dream of landownership within reach of many more people. Newly-available purchased Indian land constituted one of the few sources of real estate for smaller farmers. Even in the New York of the 1750s, Milton Klein declared, "One million acres were owned by eighteen manor lords." Colden even urged the abolition of some fees as well as the creation of a brief, printed form simplifying the process still more. Such changes would also lessen the appeal of land speculation, something he himself indulged in. Under his plan poorer people could get land directly from the government instead of dickering with a wealthy man who could handle the heavy expense of the current system.[99]

The retired Colden advised other reforms such as a uniform quitrent for all New Yorkers to fund the government. He also suggested that purchasing a commission for a government office be made a crime. And he recommended his sons for positions needed to bring his plans to fruition.[100]

Colden hoped for the reform of all the American colonies, making them of greater benefit to Great Britain. There was a problem on the horizon he thought. "I am much afraid of the Popularity, which for some time has been pursued to serve private Purposes." The cry for liberty had been employed by people who sought power or profit for themselves. And "it may at last introduce a general Licentiousness and Disregard of every Law and Authority" leading ultimately to "both public and private Mischiefs."[101]

In 1757, a few years before Colden wrote about his proposed reforms and his forebodings, he took advantage of the location of his new Flushing residence to easily journey to New York City. At last, Colden met Lord Loudoun and spent a pleasant time with him and other senior army officers who wanted to meet him. But Colden did not want to spend much time socializing. Instead he soon returned to Flushing. Cadwallader Colden, since the 1740s, had been engaged in still another philosophical project, the most ambitious yet. He intended to unlock the mysteries of the cosmos.[102]

NOTES

1. CC to Collinson, December 5, 1753, *CP*, vol. 4, 418–19.
2. CC to Samuel Pike, 1755, in *The Philosophical Writings of Cadwallader Colden*, ed. Scott L. Pratt and John Ryder (Amherst, NY: Humanity Books, 2002), 214–16; CC to Gronovius, October 1, 1755, *CP*, vol. 5, 29; CC to Collinson, June 3, 1755, *CP*, vol. 5, 12–14.
3. CC to BF, February 13, 1754, *FP*, vol. 5, 196–97; CC to Collinson, December 5, 1753, November 19, 1754, June 3, 1755, [October 1755?], *CP*, vol. 4, 420, 473–74, vol. 5, 12–14, 36–37; Collinson to CC, July 30, 1754, March 13, 1755, *CP*, vol. 4, 461–62, vol. 5, 6–7.
4. Council meeting, June 12, 1753, *NYCD*, vol. 6, 783; conference minutes, June 16, 1753, *NYCD*, vol. 6, 786; AC to CC, November 7, 1753, *CP*, vol. 9, 129–34; CC to Abraham Douw, November 19, 1753, *CP*, vol. 9, 135–36.
5. New York Colony, Council, *Journal of the Legislative Council of the Colony of New York, Began the 9th day of April, 1691; and ended the [3d of April, 1775]* (Albany, NY: Weed, Parsons, 1861), vol. 2, 1231; William Livingston, *A Review of the Military Operations in North America* (London: R. and J. Dodsley, 1757), 113–17; JA to CC, September 23, 1755, *CP*, vol. 5, 24; James Grant Wilson, "Sir Danvers Osborne and Sir Charles Hardy, 1753–61," in *The Memorial History of the City of New-York From Its First Settlement to the Year 1892*, ed. Wilson (New York: New York History, 1892), 299–300.
6. CC to BF, June 20, 1754, *FP*, vol. 5, 353–54.
7. BF to CC, July 14, 1754, *FP*, vol. 5, 392–93.
8. *DH*, vol. 4, 1053.
9. Meeting of Albany Congress, July 2, 1754, *NYCD*, vol. 6, 870; JA to CC, July 26, 1754, *CP*, vol. 4, 460–61; Thomas Pownall to [Halifax?], July 23, 1754, Beverly McAnear, ed., "Personal Accounts of the Albany Congress of 1754," *Mississippi Valley Historical Review* 39, no. 4 (1953): 740, 736–37; ; William M. Beauchamp, *The Life of Conrad Weiser* (Syracuse,

NY: Onondaga Historical Association, 1925), 106; Eric Hinderaker, *The Two Hendricks: Unraveling a Mohawk Mystery* (Cambridge, MA: Harvard University Press, 2010), 242–43.

10. Meeting of the Albany Congress, July 2, 1754, *NYCD*, vol. 6, 870; DeLancey to Assembly, February 4, 1755, in New York Colony, Assembly, *Journal of the Votes and Proceedings of the General Assembly of the Colony of New York, 1691–1765* (New York: Hugh Gaine, 1764–1766), vol. 2, 433–34.

11. Meeting of the Albany Congress, July 2, 1754, *NYCD*, vol. 6, 870; DeLancey to Assembly, February 4, 1755, in New York Colony, Assembly, *Journal of the Votes and Proceedings of the General Assembly of the Colony of New York, 1691–1765*, vol. 2, 433–34; DeLancey to Assembly, August 6, 1755, in New York Colony, Assembly, *Journal of the Votes and Proceedings of the General Assembly of the Colony of New York, 1691–1765*, vol. 2, 453; Mack Thompson, "Massachusetts and New York Stamp Acts," *William and Mary Quarterly*, 3rd ser., 26 (1969): 252–55, 257.

12. Meeting of the Albany Congress, July 2, 1754, *NYCD*, vol. 6, 870; DeLancey to Assembly, February 4, 1755, in New York Colony, Assembly, *Journal of the Votes and Proceedings of the General Assembly of the Colony of New York, 1691–1765*, vol. 2, 433–34.

13. John R. Alden, "The Albany Congress and the Creation of the Indian Superintendencies," *Mississippi Valley Historical Review* 27, no. 2 (1940): 208–9.

14. George Washington to Robert Dinwiddie, July 18, 1755, in George Washington, *The Papers of George Washington, Colonial Series*, ed. W. W. Abbot (Charlottesville: University Press of Virginia, 1983–1995), vol. 1, 340.

15. AC to Johnson, July 26, 1755, Quaker Coll., CL; Adam Stephen to Washington, December 3, 1755, Washington, Papers, *Colonial*, vol. 2, 197; Washington to Dinwiddie, April 24, 27, 1756, Washington, Papers, *Colonial*, vol. 3, 45, 59; Council of War, July 10, 1756, Washington, Papers, *Colonial*, vol. 3, 243; Washington to Stephen, August 5, 1756, Washington, Papers, *Colonial*, vol. 3, 337; Washington to Lord Fairfax, August 29, 1756, Washington, Papers, *Colonial*, vol. 3, 380; R. H. Morris to Shirley, December 3, 1755, *JP*, vol. 2, 368–69; Philip Otterness, *Becoming German: The 1709 Palatine Migration to New York* (Ithaca, NY: Cornell University Press, 2004), 158.

16. Goldsbrow Banyar to Johnson, July 25, 1755, *JP*, vol. 1, 767; AC to James Parker, July 28, 1755, *FP*, vol. 6, 114.

17. AC to Johnson, July 26, 1755, Quaker Coll., CL; AC to CC, August 1, 1755, Bancroft Coll., (Colden), vol. 2, 48, NYPL; CC to JA, February 23, 1755, Alexander Papers, box 10, f. 32, Princeton University Libraries, Princeton, NJ.

18. AC to CC, August 27, 1755, Bancroft Coll., Colden Papers, vol. 2, 52, NYPL; AC to CC, September 22, 1755, Bancroft Coll., Colden Papers, vol. 2, 43–44; CC to Kennedy, August 7, 1755, *CP*, vol. 5, 19–20; CC to Collinson, [October 1755], *JP*, vol. 9, 292–93.

19. JA to CC, December 11, 1755, *CP*, vol. 5, 48–49; R. H. Morris to Johnson, November 15, 1755, *JP*, vol. 9, 309–10.

20. John Lees, "Journal of J. L. of Quebec Merchant," 1768, British Museum Additional Manuscript 28605, LC transcript; Isaac Norris, "The Journal of Isaac Norris, During a Trip to Albany in 1745, and an Account of a Treaty Held There in October of That Year," *Pennsylvania Magazine of History and Biography* 27, no. 1 (1903): 27; Thomas Pownall, *A Topographical Description of the Dominions of the United States of America*, rev. ed. of London: J. Almon, 1776 (Pittsburgh: University of Pittsburgh Press, 1949), 38–39; Bartram to Garden, March 14, 1756, Darlington, ed., *Memorials*, 394.

21. Shirley to Johnson, May 16, 1756, *JP*, vol. 9, 452; Council meeting at Albany, June 28, 1754, *NYCD*, vol. 6, 867.

22. CC to [Fothergill], January 8, 1756, *CP*, vol. 5, 63–65; CC to Collinson, December 31, 1757, *CP*, vol. 5, 211–14; John Mitchell, *The Contest in America between Great Britain and France with Its Consequences and Importance* (London: A. Millar, 1757; repr. New York: Johnson, 1965), 82–83.

23. CC to Halifax, March 10, 1764, *JP*, vol. 4, 361–62; Shirley to Johnson, May 16, 1756, *JP*, vol. 9, 451; Pownall to Johnson, December 21, 1755, *JP*, vol. 13, 76–77; Corporation of Kingston to Johnson, January 17, 1756, *JP*, vol. 2, 418–19; Sir Charles Hardy to Johnson, November 30, 1755, *JP*, vol. 2, 359; CC to [Fothergill], January 8, 1756, *CP*, vol. 5, 63–65;

Amand La Potin, "The Minisink Grant: Partnerships, Patents, and Processing Fees in Eighteenth Century New York," *New York History* 56, no. 1 (1975): 48.

24. CC to Collinson, April 23, 1756, Ayer Manuscripts, Newberry Library, Chicago; CC to [Beamsley Glazier], March 4, 1756, Emmet Coll., no. 2605, NYPL; CC to [Fothergill], January 8, 1756, *CP*, vol. 5, 63–65; *Monthly Review* 16 (1757): 524.

25. Hezekiah Watkins, "Observations on the Circumstances and Conduct of the People in the Counties of Ulster and Orange, in the Province of New-York," *New York Gazette or Weekly Post-Boy* (Parker), March 15, 1756.

26. AC to CC, August 22, 1757, *CP*, vol. 5, 176–78; CC to [Fothergill], January 8, 1756, *CP*, vol. 5, 63–65.

27. [CC] to Capt. Johannis Newkerk, December 20, 1755, *CP*, vol. 5, 51–52; CC to Johnson, May 3, 1762, Etting Coll., HSP.

28. Hardy to CC, December 22, 1755, *CP*, vol. 5, 53–54; New York Colony, Council, *Journal of the Legislative Council of the Colony of New York, Began the 9th day of April, 1691; and ended the [3d of April, 1775]*, vol. 2, 1231.

29. CC to Hardy, [summer 1756?], *CP*, vol. 5, 105–7; CC to Hardy, [1756 or 7?], *CP*, vol. 5, 110; E. Wilder Spaulding, *His Excellency George Clinton: Critic of the Constitution* (New York: Macmillan, 1938), 14.

30. Hardy to Assembly, December 16, 1755, in New York Colony, Assembly, *Journal of the Votes and Proceedings of the General Assembly of the Colony of New York, 1691–1765*, vol. 2, 467; resolution, December 18, 1755, in New York Colony, Assembly, *Journal of the Votes and Proceedings of the General Assembly of the Colony of New York, 1691–1765*, vol. 2, 468; Hardy to Assembly, January 10, 1756, New York Colony, Assembly, *Journal of the Votes and Proceedings of the General Assembly of the Colony of New York, 1691–1765*, vol. 2, 471–72; resolution, January 12, 1756, in New York Colony, Assembly, *Journal of the Votes and Proceedings of the General Assembly of the Colony of New York, 1691–1765*, vol. 2, 472.

31. Hardy to Assembly, January 13, 1756, in New York Colony, Assembly, *Journal of the Votes and Proceedings of the General Assembly of the Colony of New York, 1691–1765*, vol. 2, 472. CC's sketch has not been located. Perhaps he penned it himself. If Hardy sent the original to the Assembly, the handwriting would have made CC's authorship apparent.

32. Motion, January 23, 1756, in New York Colony, Assembly, *Journal of the Votes and Proceedings of the General Assembly of the Colony of New York, 1691–1765*, vol. 2, 474.

33. Motion, February 25, 1756, in New York Colony, Assembly, *Journal of the Votes and Proceedings of the General Assembly of the Colony of New York, 1691–1765*, vol. 2, 485.

34. CC to Collinson, April 23, 1756, Ayer Manuscripts, Newberry Library; New York Colony, Council, *Journal of the Legislative Council of the Colony of New York, Began the 9th day of April, 1691; and ended the [3d of April, 1775]*, vol. 2, 1242; CC, JA, and William Smith, February 10, 1756, in New York Colony, Council, *Journal of the Legislative Council of the Colony of New York, Began the 9th day of April, 1691; and ended the [3d of April, 1775]*, vol. 2, 1243–44; William Smith, Jr., *The History of the Province of New York*, ed. Michael Kammen (Cambridge, MA: Belknap Press of Harvard University Press, 1972), vol. 2, 199, 201–2; Livingston, *Review*, 113–17.

35. Hardy to Assembly, March 2, 1756, in New York Colony, Assembly, *Journal of the Votes and Proceedings of the General Assembly of the Colony of New York, 1691–1765*, vol. 2, 485, 485–86; CC to [Glazier], March 4, 1756, Emmet Coll., no. 2605, NYPL.

36. W[atkins], "Observations on the Circumstances," *New York Gazette, or the Weekly Post-Boy* (Parker), March 15, 1756.

37. New York Colony, Assembly, *Journal of the Votes and Proceedings of the General Assembly of the Colony of New York, 1691–1765*, vol. 2, 487–89, 510–11; W. Smith, Jr., *History*, vol. 2, 201–2; Leonard W. Levy, "Did the Zenger Case Really Matter? Freedom of the Press in Colonial New York," *William and Mary Quarterly*, 3rd ser., 17 (1960): 41.

38. New York Colony, Assembly, *Journal of the Votes and Proceedings of the General Assembly of the Colony of New York, 1691–1765*, vol. 2, 486; CC to Kennedy, November 17, 1756, *CP*, vol. 9, 165–67; W. Smith, Jr., *History*, vol. 2, 201.

39. AC to George Harison, January 24, 1765, Richard Harison Papers, box 2, NYHS; JA to CC, December 11, 1755, *CP*, vol. 5, 51.

40. AC to George Harison, January 24, 1765, Richard Harison Papers, box 2, NYHS; JA to CC, December 11, 1755, *CP*, vol. 5, 51; CC to Hardy, [May 11, 1756?], *CP*, vol. 5, 74–76; CC to Collinson, December 31, 1757, *CP*, vol. 5, 211–14.

41. AC to Harison, January 24, February 23, 1756, Richard Harison Papers, box 2, NYHS.

42. CC to [Fothergill], January 8, 1756, *CP*, vol. 5, 63–65; AC to Richard Harison, February 23, 1756, Richard Harison Papers, box 2, NYHS.

43. Hardy, proclamation, March 8, 1756, *New York Gazette, or the Weekly Post-Boy* (Parker), March 15, 1756.

44. Hardy, proclamation, March 8, 1756, *New York Gazette, or the Weekly Post-Boy* (Parker), March 15, 1756; Indian Congress, May 28, 1756, *JP*, vol. 9, 465.

45. Smith to CC, June 14, 1757, *CP*, vol. 5, 150–51.

46. Smith to CC, June 14, 1757, *CP*, vol. 5, 150–51; Vincent Mathews to CC, March 12, 1757, *CP*, vol. 5, 129.

47. CC to [Glazier], March 4, 1756, Emmet Coll., no. 2605, NYPL; CC to Hardy, [May 11, 1756?], *CP*, vol. 5, 74–76.

48. CC to Collinson, April 23, 1756, Ayer Manuscripts, Newberry Libary.

49. CC to Hardy, [May 11, 1756?], *CP*, vol. 5, 74–76; CC to Hardy, [1756 or 7?], *CP*, vol. 5, 110–11; AC to CC, May 18, 1756, *CP*, vol. 5, 78; CC to Hardy, [summer 1756?], *CP*, vol. 5, 105–7; petition to DeLancey, [1757], *CP*, vol. 5, 108; address of officers to Hardy, [1756 or 7?], *CP*, vol. 5, 109; Hardy to Assembly, April 29, 1756, in New York Colony, Assembly, *Journal of the Votes and Proceedings of the General Assembly of the Colony of New York, 1691–1765*, vol. 2, 490–91.

50. Mrs. CC to John Colden, June 4, 1756, *CP*, vol. 5, 86.

51. Mrs. CC to John Colden, June 4, 1756, *CP*, vol. 5, 86; CC to Hardy, [May 11, 1756?], *CP*, vol. 5, 74–76.

52. AC to Harison, May 21, 1756, Richard Harison Papers, box 2, NYHS; AC to CC, June 19, 1756, Bancroft Coll., (Colden), vol. 2, 62, NYPL.

53. Capt. James Cunningham to CC, November 13, 1756, *CP*, vol. 9, 161–62; CC, "Observations on the Situation, Soil, Climate, Water Communications, Boundaries etc. of the Province of New York . . . 1738," in *The Documentary History of the State of New-York; Arranged Under Direction of the Hon. Christopher Morgan, Secretary of State*, ed. Edmund B. O'Callaghan (Albany, NY: Weed, Parsons, 1851), vol. 4, 178; Burnet to Lord Carteret, June 25, 1723, PRO *Cal.*, vol. 33, 290; Gregory H. Nobles, "Straight Lines and Stability: Mapping the Political Order of the Anglo-American Frontier," *Journal of American History* 80, no. 1 (1993): 17.

54. Burnet to [Lord Carteret?], December 16, 1723, PRO *Cal.*, vol. 33, 396; Burnet to Lords of Trade, June 2, 1726, *NYCD*, vol. 5, 777; Lawrence Henry Gipson, *Lewis Evans* (Philadelphia: Historical Society of Pennsylvania, 1939), 13, 17–18, 21–23; Edmund Berkeley and Dorothy Smith Berkeley, *Dr. John Mitchell: The Man Who Made the Map of North America* (Chapel Hill: University of North Carolina Press, 1974), 191–92; Walter Klinefelter, "Lewis Evans and His Maps," American Philosophical Society, *Transactions*, n.s., 61, no. 7 (1971): 16, 22. For CC's map of the New York area, see CC, *The History of the Five Indian Nations Depending on the Province of New-York in America* (1727, Part 1; 1747, Part 2) (New York: T. H. Morrell, 1866; repr. Ithaca, NY: Great Seal Books, 1958), xviii–xix.

55. CC to Cunningham, December 6, 1756, *CP*, vol. 5, 100–103.

56. CC to Cunningham, December 6, 1756, *CP*, vol. 5, 100–103; AC to CC, [December 14, 1756], *CP*, vol. 9, 162–64.

57. CC to Cunningham, December 6, 1756, *CP*, vol. 5, 100–103.

58. Hardy to CC, December 3, 1756, *CP*, vol. 5, 98–99; CC to Hardy, December 5, 1756, *CP*, vol. 5, 100; Stanley McCrory Pargellis, *Lord Loudoun in North America* (New Haven, CT: Yale University Press, 1933), 263–64.

59. AC to CC, February 16, 1757, *CP*, vol. 5, 117; Dr. J. Bard to CC, April 2, 1757, *CP*, vol. 5, 137–38.

60. Smith, Sr. to CC, June 14, 1757, *CP*, vol. 5, 150–51.

61. DeLancey to Council and Assembly, September 2, 1757, New York Colony, Council, *Journal of the Legislative Council of the Colony of New York, Began the 9th day of April, 1691; and ended the [3d of April, 1775]*, vol. 2, 1304; W. Smith, Jr., *History*, vol. 2, 214.

62. CC to DeLancey, September 16, 1757, *CP*, vol. 5, 183; AC to CC, September 23, 1757, *CP*, vol. 5, 187–89; AC to CC, October 13, 1757, *CP*, vol. 5, 198–200.

63. CC and others to DeLancey, October 10, 1757, Loudoun Papers, LO 4623, Huntington Library, San Marino, CA; CC to Loudoun, October 11, 1757, *CP*, vol. 5, 200–202; AC to CC, October 13, 1757, *CP*, vol. 5, 198–200.

64. AC to CC, October 13, 1757, *CP*, vol. 5, 198–200; CC to AC, October 3, 1757, Loudoun Papers, Huntington Library, LO 4577, Huntington; CC to DeLancey, October 21, 1757, Loudoun Papers, LO 4685; CC and others to DeLancey, October 10, 1757, Loudoun Papers, LO 4623; CC to Loudoun, October 11, 1757, *CP*, vol. 5, 200–2; AC to CC, October 6, 1757, *CP*, vol. 5, 193–97; James G. Lydon, "The Great Capture of 1744," *New York Historical Society Quarterly* 52, no. 3 (1968): 255.

65. CC to AC, October 3, 1757, Loudoun Papers, Huntington Library, LO 4577, Huntington; CC and others to DeLancey, October 10, 1757, Loudoun Papers, LO 4623; AC to CC, September 23, 1757, *CP*, vol. 5, 187–89; AC to CC, October 6, 1757, *CP*, vol. 5, 193–97.

66. AC to CC, October 6, 1757, *CP*, vol. 5, 193–97; AC to CC, October 11, 1757, *CP*, vol. 5, 197.

67. AC to CC, October 13, 1757, *CP*, vol. 5, 198–200.

68. CC to Fothergill, October 18, 1757, *CP*, vol. 5, 204–5.

69. CC to DeLancey, October 16, 1757, Loudoun Papers, Huntington Library, LO 4644, Huntington.

70. CC to DeLancey, October 21, 1757, Loudoun Papers, Huntington Library, LO 4685; CC to Loudoun, October 21, 1757, *CP*, vol. 5, 205–6.

71. CC to DeLancey, October 21, 1757, Loudoun Papers, Huntington Library, LO 4685; CC to Loudoun, October 21, 1757, *CP*, vol. 5, 205–6.

72. DeLancey to CC, November 4, 1757, *CP*, vol. 9, 172; Council minutes, November 4, 1757, *CP*, vol. 5, 208–9.

73. DeLancey to CC, November 4, 1757, *CP*, vol. 9, 172; CC to DeLancey, [November 1757?], *CP*, vol. 5, 209–11; CC to Collinson, December 31, 1757, *CP*, vol. 5, 211–14.

74. CC to DeLancey, [November 1757?], *CP*, vol. 5, 209–11; AC to CC, August 29, September 1, 1757, *CP*, vol. 5, 179–82; CC to Collinson, December 31, 1757, *CP*, vol. 5, 211–14; G. Taylor, *A Voyage to North America Perform'd by G. Taylor of Sheffield in the Years 1768, and 1769* (Nottingham, UK: S. Creswell for the Author, 1771), 70.

75. CC to Collinson, August 23, 1758, *CP*, vol. 5, 251; CC to Kennedy, July 17, 1758, *CP*, vol. 9, 173.

76. Jeffrey Amherst, *The Journal of Jeffrey Amherst Recording the Military Career of General Amherst in America from 1758 to 1763*, ed. J. Clarence Webster (Toronto: Ryerson Press, 1931), 271.

77. *SM*, vol. 2, 31; Milton M. Klein, *The American Whig: William Livingston of New York* (New York: Garland, 1990), 401; Klein, "Prelude to Revolution in New York: Jury Trials and Judicial Tenure," *William and Mary Quarterly*, 3rd ser., 17, no. 4 (1960): 445; L. F. S. Upton, *The Loyal Whig: William Smith of New York and Quebec* (Toronto: University of Toronto Press, 1969), 18–19.

78. *SM*, vol. 2, 31.

79. CC to Collinson, July 7, 1749, *CP*, vol. 4, 114.

80. CC to Board of Trade, November 1764, *CLB*, vol. 1, 403; CC, "Heads of Some Arguements to Prove that the Lands in Question are Really Contained within the Bounds of the Lands granted to Captn John Evans," n.d., Orange County, NY—Minisink, NYHS; "At a Committee of the Council," July 21, 1722, Orange County, NY, file 1700–1730, NYHS.

81. CC to Board of Trade, November 1764, *CLB*, vol. 1, 403; "Heads of Some Arguements," n.d., Orange County, NY—Minisink, NYHS; Gary B. Nash, *The Urban Crucible: Social Change, Political Consciousness, and the Origins of the American Revolution* (Cambridge, MA: Harvard University Press, 1979), 301.

82. *SM*, vol. 2, 31.

83. Robert Livingston, Jr., to Abraham Yates, September 9, 1760, Abraham Yates Jr. Papers, reel 1, NYPL; Michael Kammen, "William Smith's History of New York: Its Qualities, Sources and Critics," in W. Smith, Jr., *History*, vol. 1, lxviii.

84. William Smith, Jr. to Horatio Gates, November 22, 1763, Horatio Gates Papers, reel 1, NYHS.

85. *SM*, vol. 2, 32.

86. CC to AC, n.d., *CP*, vol. 5, 313–19; Roger Andrew Wines, "William Smith, the Historian of New York," *New York History* 40, no. 1 (1959): 3, 9–10, 12.

87. Paul Hamlin, ed., "'He Is Gone and Peace to His Shade': William Smith, Historian, Posthumously Boils Lieutenant Governor Cadwallader Colden In Oil," *New York Historical Society Quarterly* 36, no. 2 (1952): 164; *SM*, vol. 2, 31.

88. Smith, Jr. to CC, February 5, 1759, *CP*, vol. 5, 289–91.

89. CC to Smith, Sr., January 15, February 19, 1759, *CP*, vol. 5, 286–87, 295; Smith, Sr. to CC, January 31, 1759, *CP*, vol. 5, 287–88; W. Smith, Jr., *History*, vol. 1, 195; CC to AC, February 21, 1760, CC, "The Colden Letters on Smith's History," New York Historical Society, *Collections* 1 (1868): 227.

90. CC to AC, June 15, 1759, CC, "Letters on Smith," 181.

91. CC to Smith, Jr., January 15, 1759, *CP*, vol. 5, 183–86.

92. Smith, Jr. to CC, February 5, 1759, *CP*, vol. 5, 289–92; Upton, *Loyal Whig*, 39.

93. CC to Smith, Jr., February 17, 1759, *CP*, vol. 5, 293–95; W. Smith, Jr., *History*, vol. 2, 44.

94. For the most important documents, a draft and the Council committee report written by Horsmanden, see *CP*, vol. 2, 218–22. Historians who back CC include Kammen, "William Smith's History," in W. Smith, Jr., *History*, vol. 1, lxix–lxxi; Wines, "William Smith," 12; George S. Pryde, "Scottish Colonization in the Province of New York," *New York History* 16, no. 2 (1935): 147–51; Ian Charles Cargill Graham, *Colonists from Scotland: Emigration to North America, 1707–1783* (Ithaca, NY: Cornell University Press, 1956), 80. Curiously, Thomas Jones, who detested Smith, accepted his version of the Campbell story. See Thomas Jones, *History of New York during the Revolutionary War*, ed. Edward Floyd De Lancey (New York: New York Historical Society, 1879; repr. Cranbury, NJ: Scholar's Bookshelf, 2006), vol. 2, 352–53. For other Smith supporters, see Edith M. Fox, *Land Speculation in the Mohawk Country* (Ithaca, NY: Cornell University Press, 1949), 30; Frederick B. Richards, "The Black Watch at Ticonderoga," New York State Historical Association, *Proceedings* 10 (1911): 419–20.

95. CC to AC, June 15, 1759, CC, "Letters on Smith," 181; CC to AC, July 5, 1759, CC, "Letter on Smith," 207; CC to AC, March 1, 1760, *CP*, vol. 5, 309. For CC on Campbell, see CC to AC, February 21, 1760, CC, "Letters on Smith," 227–28, 230–35.

96. CC to AC, June 25, 1759, CC, "Letters on Smith," 190; CC to AC, July 5, 1759, CC, "Letter on Smith," 206.

97. CC to AC, July 5, 1759, CC, "Letter on Smith," 203–4.

98. DeLancey to Council and Assembly, December 6, 1759, New York Colony, Council, *Journal of the Legislative Council of the Colony of New York, Began the 9th day of April, 1691; and ended the [3d of April, 1775]*, vol. 2, 1379; CC to Whytt, July 21, 1759, in CC, *Philosophical Writings*, ed. Pratt and Ryder, 232–33.

99. CC to Halifax, August 25, 1759, Dartmouth Manuscripts, Staffordshire Record Office, Stafford, UK; Milton M. Klein, "The Cultural Tyros of Colonial New York," *South Atlantic Quarterly* 66, no. 2 (1967): 222–23.

100. CC to Halifax, August 25, 1759, Dartmouth Manuscripts, Staffordshire Record Office.

101. CC to Halifax, August 25, 1759, Dartmouth Manuscripts, Staffordshire Record Office.

102. CC to Collinson, December 31, 1757, *CP*, vol. 5, 211–14.

Chapter Eleven

The Intelligent Being

On September 17, 1744 Cadwallader Colden alerted his friend Benjamin Franklin that "I have opened to myself a large Prospect either into Nature or into Fairyland." This speculation constituted a novel "way of thinking" about the workings of the universe, and involved going beyond the theorizing of Sir Isaac Newton. Most scholars are convinced that Colden did invent a bizarre fairy tale. His forays into physics are puzzling and seem to show him stumbling badly. Nonetheless, he seems to have been stumbling in the right direction.[1]

In order to understand why Colden speculated as he did, his religious faith has to be explained. Colden was a deist, a common belief system during the Enlightenment. Deists believed in God—"the infinite intelligent Being or Mind of the Universe" as Colden called Him—but disliked reliance on "amazing Absurdities" pushed by "the Oracles of God." Colden disapproved of churches that placed "Religion in the opposition to Reason and Morality," a stand, he remained convinced, that was "the invention and imposture of Popery." Faiths that rejected "any speculation in philosophy from principles of religion" did not benefit their acolytes. "Nothing has been a greater injury to true religion than the pretenses . . . that religion is not the object of the understanding but is merely founded on authority." To Colden, God, "the supreme Governour of his Creatures," was "the Great Architect and Contriver of nature."[2]

Colden did not reject everything expounded by "the inspired writers" in the Scriptures. He thought that "the universe must have been framed by a wise or intelligent agent" but this truth "can not be discovered by reason. This is only to be learned by revelation." After reading a Colden essay, his pleased friend Samuel Johnson, a Church of England minister in Connecticut, noted that the writing "made such an easy, gradual, and natural progress from physics to metaphysics, and from thence to morality, as is very pleasing to the mind." Colden believed that "immorality is an absurdity, a contradiction to pleasure and an egregious folly."[3]

William Smith Jr. insisted in his diary that Colden detested ministers, even "their Profession itself." Biased against Colden, Smith wildly exaggerated his foe's religious feelings. No one can doubt that Colden respected his father and, in Scotland, all the ministers who knew him liked him. Cadwallader Colden was not a revolutionary in everyday life—his "radical" scientific speculation was something else again. He realized a "philosopher performs the duties of worship without in the least suffering his philosophical opinions to be affected thereby." He knew that "So many of the most renowned priests and philosophers of old did, and I make no doubt many at this time do."[4]

Colden asserted that "Philosophy is entirely distinct from religion, they have not the same object." "A wise philosopher," he reasoned, "as such never opposes the religion of his country, but conforms to it so far as required by a good subject." He did not start any religious disputes in Scotland or, for that matter, in America.[5]

However, Colden's deism did first take root in Scotland, most likely while he attended the University of Edinburgh. When he left his homeland after his marriage, his mother made a "parting request" to Alice "with tears" which made a great "impression" on her. His mother, who knew her son well, asked his wife "to set up family worship" and pray together and also be "encouraging to the presbyterian minister." Mrs. Jane Colden did not forget to remind her daughter-in-law about her promise to do so. Alice fulfilled her mother-in-law's desire; none of her grandchildren ever displayed any trace of deism.[6]

In America, though, Colden and his family did not worship as Presbyterians. The established church in Scotland, Presbyterianism in America had been strongly influenced by New England Puritanism. Colden could not stand the unending doctrinal arguments stirred up by New Englanders. He detested anyone who fell "into the most dangerous sin of enthusiasm." Such ministers easily created "false notions" of God as "an arbitrary or tyrannical Being." His friendship with Samuel Johnson had to have been boosted by what he endured when he abandoned Puritanism for the Church of England. According to Colden, the New Englanders, who hated Johnson, "put such constructions on Gods revealed Will as sets it in opposition to his Will declared in every man's heart." When Johnson commented that "the Jersey College"—Presbyterian-leaning Princeton—"will be a fountain of Nonsense." Colden did not contradict him.[7]

Instead of Presbyterianism, Colden and his family were drawn to Anglicanism. It has been thought that Colden, because of his deism, gravitated to the Church of England which tolerated it. Perhaps so, but Colden's remark about supporting the country's religion should be remembered. Anglicanism was the established church in four counties of New York including New York City where Colden lived before his move to Ulster. Both of his mentors, Robert Hunter and William Burnet, were also Anglicans.[8]

James Alexander, another Anglican, probably had the greatest influence on his friend. The two Scots must have frequently talked about religion. In 1730, for example, Colden sent to Alexander a now lost newspaper essay on the value of obtaining virtue which noted "the Little Effect our Saviours Doctrine . . . had on great nations heretofore," and asked Alexander to make any changes he saw fit before seeking publication. Alexander feared that some readers might interpret Colden's observation "as a Slur" on "our Saviours Doctrine" but did not change the passage because it was obviously "true and notorious."[9]

Only in 1724, some years after Colden's arrival in New York, did he officially join Anglican Trinity Church in New York City. He bought half a pew there, enough for his family. His sons Sandie and Cad, prominent Anglicans, became vestrymen of Trinity and the Newburgh church respectively. Their father did not call attention to his deism and only those who knew him well were aware of his theological divergences from Christian dogma. The loyalist historian Thomas Jones, not close to Colden, declared him to be "a strict, honest, rigid Churchman," that is Anglican; he was not.[10]

Colden's belief in a reasonable, rational God had to be the driving force behind his attempt to go beyond Sir Isaac Newton's physics. Colden felt that he could prove the existence of God—the Intelligent Being—by extension from "the design and harmony of the universe."[11]

Newton, the greatest scientific figure of his age, would be Colden's starting point. Newton's theories had displaced the ideas of the French philosopher René Descartes, who had himself replaced the ancient theories of the Greek philosopher Aristotle. In 1705 Colden had been introduced to Newtonian physics at the University of Edinburgh and had accepted its validity. During the 1740s, however, Colden became convinced that he could "explain the Cause of Gravitation, a point which has hitherto puzzled the ablest Philosophers."[12]

According to a more recent philosopher, "Colden rushed in where others feared to tread." Even Newton had hesitated about gravity. Though he had figured out how gravity functioned on this planet—inspired by the famed apple—he could not explain how gravity operated beyond the bounds of Earth. Vague as to the actual cause of the force, Newton resorted to mysterious "occult" explanations for it. If Colden could supply what Newton could not, a place in the pantheon of philosophy for him would be assured.[13]

By all appearances, Colden had been inspired by speculative parts in Newton's *Principia* and his *Opticks*. But the "Queries" section of *Opticks* attracted Colden the most. There, as Brooke Hindle wrote, "Newton tended to let his imagination roam far and wide." No evidence was given for what

Raymond P. Stearns called "daring speculations." In fact, Newton called upon other thinkers to flesh in the details of his queries. Colden accepted the challenge. Despite the "esteem" he felt for his predecessor's "knowledge and performances," he knew "That man never existed who never err'd." He knew that applied to him too.[14]

To explain gravitation, Colden postulated three "forces;" their interaction created gravity. One was a "resisting" force, Newton's *vis inertiae*—inertia. Despite what Newton theorized about inertia, Colden believed it to be "active," not passive. "Force without action is a Contradiction of Terms" he insisted. This force only had a comparatively small part in his system—it kept the planets in their orbits.[15]

Another Newtonian subject, light, was the second, the "moving" force. Light from the sun moved the planets along their way in their orbits. The speed of their movement varied by each planet's distance from the principal source of the moving force, the sun. Colden later observed that "the motion of the planets seems to put it beyond dispute, that their motion proceeds from the light of the sun." This force also caused each planetary body to rotate as it went on its journey. Light produced most motion, and every solid object gave off at least some light.[16]

Colden's third force, "aether," or, to give it its modern spelling, ether, was "elastic." The most important of Colden's powers, it "occupies all the space not filled with other Matter, and permeates all the Interstices or Passages which are in or between Bodies." The ether, if pushed into motion by "Light from the Sun, Planets, and Stars," would be "stronger on one Side of a Body at rest" thus moving the body, creating gravity. To Colden, ether was matter.[17]

A modern reader might be the most puzzled by ether, whose most common meaning has evolved from when Colden wrote. In the nineteenth century the word became affixed to the first anesthesia. The adjective form, ethereal, is much closer to how philosophers of Colden's century thought of ether—it was celestial.[18]

Newton had interjected ether into his physics in *Opticks*, but he mentioned it as one of his queries; the basic idea of this "elusive substance" had originated with Descartes. Therefore part of Newtonian physics, Newton left ether rather vague and mysterious explaining why the "strange medium" had been all but ignored until about the time Colden became intrigued by the subject. He was not the first in his day to be curious about Newton's ether nor did it become something that held only antiquarian interest later. The nineteenth century remained fascinated by it, and Albert Einstein's theory of "general" relativity is chock-full of ether. In 1920 he proclaimed: "the endeavour toward a unified view of the nature of forces leads to the hypothesis of an ether."[19]

Given the revolutionary nature of Colden's thinking about gravitation, he, logically, sought advice from his friends in America and abroad. In Pennsylvania, he solicited the comments of James Logan and Franklin, who offered to publish the final result. Colden's book "must excite the Curiosity of all the Learned," and Franklin predicted, optimistically, that it could "hardly fail of bearing its own expense." In Connecticut, Colden sought the opinion of Samuel Johnson who urged him to write to Anglican bishop George Berkeley, himself a prominent philosopher who was a vigorous critic of Newton. Colden had embraced the bishop's ideas about tar water but rejected his attack on Newton. As for Johnson himself, he doubted he knew enough to criticize Colden's theory of gravitation but thought he would "learn something from it."[20]

Colden alerted his friends across the Atlantic about his work "on a subject which has puzzled philosophers in all ages." He asked Johann Fredrich Gronovius to solicit Dutch mathematicians to read his work. Peter Collinson, whose membership in the Royal Society seemed advantageous, was informed by his friend how his work might help determine longitude, a major goal in that century, or at least "will make the future discovery more easy."[21]

And Colden counted on two nearby friends, one of whom was John Rutherfurd. An unusual army officer, Rutherfurd was well-versed in science. He remarked that "I am firmly persuaded The Great Author of Nature at the Creation of all possible Worlds chused the best or more perfect and always maintains it so." He respected Newton's scientific work, but Rutherfurd maintained that Newton really was a throwback to the Middle Ages nor could he "ever envy a Man or call him truly Great who never enjoyed any pleasure in Society, died a Virgin, and wrote upon the Revelations." Of course Colden did not share such sentiments about Newton.[22]

Most of all, Colden counted upon his best friend, James Alexander. He knew Alexander's breadth of intellect. After Colden revealed to him what he had done, Alexander commented: "The Discovery of the cause of Gravity is what I did not So much as hope for in my days." He did raise a serious objection to Colden's system but in 1746 Alexander told his friend that "I am everyday more and more reconciled to it." Needless to say, Colden was very grateful for all the time his friend spent contemplating his philosophizing.[23]

Once Colden's friends had made their suggestions, he needed to reach out to others, especially to scientists in Europe. Making handwritten copies in the quantity he wanted would be quite a chore, so having them printed made sense. James Parker, a business partner of Franklin's in New York, did the work. In no way was this printing meant for public consumption. This publication was similar to what scholars in the twentieth century did to secure copies for expert readers. Instead of a printing press, carbon paper or a xerographic machine provided duplicates. On Colden's title page, Parker put the year 1745, the year he started producing the proofs. Colden did not distribute copies of the work until 1746 after Alexander completed proofreading Parker's printing. Alexander had often proofed and copyedited Colden's essays whose author was usually far away at Coldengham. Alexander knew what he was doing, but with a subject so complex Colden should have checked it himself; an author always knows his work best. But he saw this merely as a preliminary stage, not the finished product others would see it as. Colden had no idea that when he sent copies to England, a bookseller there got his hands on one and published an unauthorized edition.[24]

Colden began his *An Explication of the First Causes of Action in Matter, and, of the Cause of Gravitation* with a lengthy dedication to Alexander, who had helped the author so much with his incisive comments that resulted in many changes to the original text. It was "difficult," Colden admitted, "to convey new Conceptions of Things to others, with that Conciseness I at first intended." To understand gravity his readers will "require a Method of thinking entirely different from that which . . . has become habitual to them." The author eschewed bombarding readers with higher mathematics. Instead he sought to "lead the Mind of the Reader, step by step, into the same conceptions I have."[25]

These ideas were "new Principles in Physics, different from those of all Writers before me," Colden explained. These principles were not easy: "To attempt to explain the Cause of Gravitation, after all the great Men in Philosophy have failed, and after Sir Isaac Newton stopt short, as at an Enquiry not surmountable by his Sagacity which has discovered so many wonders" was a difficult task indeed.[26]

Colden feared that his *Explication* would be seen "not only . . . as bold and rash" but "so vain and foolish as not to deserve a Reading, or any Consideration." He hoped that "the Force of the Evidence on my Mind is as strong as that of Day-Light after the Sun is up in cloudy Weather." The author foresaw "a Prospect of great Improvement in all the useful Sciences in human Life" from his work, which he suggested would "serve as Hints to others of much greater Abilities than I can pretend to."[27]

The author intended "printing only so many copies . . . as may be sufficient to submit my Thoughts to the Examination of the Learned, and without any Design of troubling the World any further on this Subject, but according to the Reception these Sheets shall have with proper Judges." If his ideas had "any Merit to preserve themselves from oblivion," it would preserve "the Memory of the Friendship that has for many Years subsisted between" him and Alexander.[28]

Now all Colden had to do was wait for the reactions of the learned. In America, Franklin could not understand Colden's treatise, nor could "Seven or eight" scholarly men (including Logan) he showed it to. Most blamed the "Abstruseness of the subject," not Colden's writing. Johnson liked Colden's "Elastic Ether," but admitted that it was mostly beyond his abilities.[29]

Meanwhile, Collinson distributed copies of the *Explication* among Europeans, and attributed the pirated British printing to the "demand" for the work despite its being in English, not Latin. The initial reaction boosted the author's hopes. "It is much admired by Some," Collinson announced, "and those of most abilities have told me that it was no trifling affair but required great Consideration." One mathematician, whom Collinson dismissed as "a Little touched" in the head, insisted that the whole thing had been plagiarized from a book published in Europe—American authors tended to be dismissed by Europeans. Alexander, calling Colden "an open hearted man," dismissed the charge with scorn.[30]

Eventually, Collinson received comments from scholars to whom he had sent copies. There was nothing good to report. As he confided to Alexander, "I don't hear of any one that can comprehend his system." Originally, the readers remarked, "they thought they understood his Principles but as they advanced, he grew more and more obscure until at last they gave it up, and could not come to any Conclusion." Some of the experts declared "it is Descartes revived" yet these men were a definite minority. One British reader's remarks were both brief and pithy: "Mr. Colden is Mistaken in every part of his Conjectures."[31]

Two Germans became Colden's most vociferous critics. Leonhard Euler blasted the *Explication*, but, apparently, did not comprehend what the author was trying to say. Abraham Kastner, who published a German version of the *Explication*, tried to be kind but found nothing redeeming in the book. Generally, Collinson informed Colden, Germans liked his work "as far as page 34 but afterwards they are at a loss to comprehend it." When Colden, some years later, finally found someone—" a German minister"—to translate the "remarks" added to his work, he had to be astonished. The original translator had insisted that the discussion of ether had been written in Pennsylvania, not in the colony of New York. Colden gathered that "as there are many Germans in Pennsylvania it seems the Translator has a mind to lay in a Claim for his Nation to this discovery."[32]

The hostile reaction of Euler and Kastner may have been so heated because Colden's text showed that he had not read any of their work. In fact, Euler then was working on a project similar to Colden's. Colden disliked academics in general, dismissing them as pedants, "Conceited, Peevish" men "hating Contradiction or advice," and "troublesome Neighbours" to boot. They "miscarry in their private affairs whereby they become poor and needy without being pitied." Moreover, they complain about the "world as not knowing how to Value their Merit." Why should Colden value the opinion of men who display "Their Ignorance"?[33]

Though Colden had vowed to drop his metaphysical musings if experts did not accept them, he plowed ahead anyway despite pedantic complaints. He thought he was right and just had not expressed himself as clearly as necessary. "Such kind of work as mine never meets with so much encouragement as a Tale of a Tub," a literary piece by Jonathan Swift. Colden found such philosophical problems fascinating. Besides, the *Explication* contained only two chapters; he had many more ideas that he wished to share with the world, including a foray into higher mathematics.[34]

The early years of the eighteenth century have been dubbed "the calculus wars," a time when higher mathematics inflamed passions among its devotees. Newton had first created calculus, which he called "fluxions," in the 1660s while a college student. However, he only used it privately. Some years later, a German mathematician, Gottfried Leibnitz, also developed it and revealed it to the public. Because he had seen some of Newton's earlier work, a charge that he had stolen the Briton's idea arose. Then Leibnitz's allies accused Newton of stealing it from the German and the dispute raged on.[35]

Perhaps the only clear thing about fluxions, as this "Arithmetic of Infinities" was generally called, was that it was not clear. Bishop Berkeley, in one of his writings, lambasted Newton's "defective" elaboration of calculus "and that he (Sir Isaac) was not quite pleased with it himself." This is where Colden enters the story. As one of the estimated dozen men in the British colonies who could at least follow Newton's invention, he still had problems with fluxions, which he "attributed to the weakness of my own imagination and judgment." Realizing that someone such as Berkeley, after much study, had problems with fluxions too, Colden understood that "the difficulties . . . were really in the subject, or in the method the authors had taken to convey their conceptions." He decided to try to clarify the subject for those "who are not much conversant in these matters." Colden never suggested he had made any new mathematical discovery—he just wanted to clear up the mystery. Though not meant to be part of his book, Colden included his fluxions essay anyway.[36]

Once again Colden solicited the opinion of his friends on his discussion of fluxions. An enthused Alexander wrote that Colden's fluxions essay had placed the obtuse subject "in such a clear light as I never Saw it before" which would put "the world" in his debt. Rutherfurd "was much entertained" by his friend's effort: "I find it helps the imagination prodigiously, which is of great use in things where we are apt so soon to lose ourselves." He acknowledged that "I begin now to think fluxions more founded in Nature than I've done hitherto."[37]

Things did not go as well in Pennsylvania. Franklin, not much help regarding math, passed it on to Logan, an accomplished mathematician far better than Colden. Logan insisted that Colden had made mistakes—Franklin tried to be diplomatic, calling them "Slips of the pen." Later, Logan referred to Colden's fluxions chapter as "intolerably tedious." Despite Logan's dislike of the piece, Franklin quoted him as saying that Colden was "the ablest Thinker . . . in this part of the World."[38]

At least the reaction in Connecticut was somewhat better. Johnson was most happy to read Colden's "very ingenious performance on Fluxions," According to Johnson that essay "has set them in a more Advantageous Light to me than any thing I had before Seen." He hoped Colden's work would be published to aid those who wished to learn about the complex subject. As Colden continued to elaborate his ideas, however, the minister had to admit that he had no real preparation to understand "your Calculations and mathematical Reasonings" and "am soon overwhelmed." He therefore "must be content to take things on trust."[39]

Though Johnson did not fully understand Colden's math, he did feel competent to comment on his friend's ideas about the Intelligent Being, God. Colden's "materialistic" system of gravitation did not have God immediately determining each movement. The minister objected to Colden's "Metaphysical Thoughts," particularly his "Ascribing Action to Matter, which I ever took to be a mere passive thing." Instead "the principle of action must also be the principle of Conscious Design and wise contrivance." That is, the action Colden attributed to matter itself "must be the Actions of Mind"—God. This "Agent" was the cause of it and matter "can be no more than a mere passive tool." Johnson, very direct, referred to "that intelligent self-active Being who is the Cause of Gravity."[40]

An individual at Yale, who Johnson showed his friend's work to, suspected Colden of atheism. Medical doctors tended to be branded as atheists in the eighteenth century to begin with. Colden's system, where God was not all that active, seemed to confirm it. Johnson did not believe that of Colden, who himself criticized those who did not believe in spiritual beings. Colden reasoned:

> The duration of God must be infinitely greater than any other infinite duration that can be supposed. It is then a most erroneous method of arguing, to say that any thing or being does not exist, because we can form no idea of that thing in our mind: for we may be most evidently convinced from reason, of the existence of things, of which we can form no idea, as I think I have evidently shewn.[41]

Being accused of atheism disturbed Colden and he responded directly to the charge. "This is a misfortune which has happened to all new Discoveries" he reminded Johnson. "So Copernicus So Galileo DesCartes Leibnitz etc. have all been branded." People who called such philosophers atheists had "very weak minds." Truly, God was, in the end, responsible for action but He was not "the immediate cause of all motion." "All allow that when God created matter he gave it some essential Properties. . . ." What were these properties? "God gave at the Creation to different kinds of matter different and distinct kinds of Action." What Colden was trying to understand were the principles relating to gravity that God had established at the beginning of time.[42]

If anything, Colden believed that God's principles were so finely crafted that they could reset everything if necessary—without Him having to act, only supervise. The Intelligent Being "has ordered so, . . . since the several individual systems must in time fail, from their natural constitution." If the sun's light ceased, gravity would be disturbed and "chaos" would ensue. Then a "confused mixture" of all matter in the solar system "must ensue." The "infinite intelligent Archeus"—God—would then oversee the formation of "a new solar system, and a new heaven" and even, possibly, "a new earth." This process had, clearly, already been "confirmed by the appearing of new stars, and reappearing of some which before had disappeared." The cosmos, an extraordinary place, followed the principles created by God.[43]

Roy Lokken has summed up Colden's ideas succinctly: "The intelligent agent operates within a functioning material system and gives it such direction as will serve its purpose." Another scholar has pointed out that Colden's beliefs "exhibit a principle of design which could only be ascribed" to God. Not surprisingly, Johnson accepted that Colden's system did not include atheism.[44]

Because Colden sought to explain the motion of objects in the solar system, he needed to delve into astronomy. A true son of the Enlightenment, he had been interested in the field and made observations on the bodies that could be seen through a telescope. Such observations were needed to calculate longitude, a very difficult task during Colden's lifetime. Nonetheless, he admitted that "Astronomy was never properly my study any further than as an amusement."[45]

Colden had been amusing himself for many years. After he settled in New York, he assisted Governor William Burnet, an enthusiastic amateur astronomer, to study an eclipse of a Jovian moon to guess New York's longitude. Both men, along with James Alexander, made the astronomical observations; Colden did the necessary mathematics. Their estimate would be somewhat off.[46]

Whenever some stellar event could be seen, Colden would be interested in it, whether a comet in 1744 or a total eclipse of Earth's moon in 1740. Also a part of an international effort to observe the 1753 transit of Mercury across the disk of the sun (as seen from Earth), Colden and his associates hoped that careful readings would aid in finding the longitude of various American cities. With sightings from around the world, including French Canada, astronomers could determine how far the Earth was from the sun. Alas, clouds covered the sky in eastern North America; only one observation could be made, on the Caribbean island of Antigua.[47]

Colden, after working for years to further his celestial observations to improve his explorations in physics, had to have been pleasantly surprised when, in 1749, Alexander received a totally unexpected letter from Oxford. The Rev. Dr. Joseph Betts, a fellow at University College and a mathematician with a keen interest in comets, had reasoned that Alexander was the man to whom Colden had dedicated his *Explication*. Dr. Betts complained that in the book Colden had given "very little Encouragement to the learned World to expect that he would compleat his Design." Four years had gone by since the *Explication* had appeared, dismaying Betts. "I really thought a Person of his Philosophic Turn could not stop short in the midst of such useful and pleasing Speculations for a few Inconveniences." He had hoped, especially, that Colden would theorize more about the moon, a subject "which everyone knows the Value of, that is not quite a Stranger to Astronomy." Urging Alexander to convince Colden "to finish his Design," Betts added his certainty that its completion "would be thankfully received by the learned World." That letter would be the first response Colden received from Britain about his principles.[48]

Betts's reaction would have encouraged anyone; it was obviously much better than that from the Germans. In order to proceed, Colden needed "a close application of thought," which had to be draining, and confessed "that it will not be easy for me to bring my mind to reconsider that subject." He had originally planned to prove his theories by duplicating Newton's *Opticks*, but how much more "leisure" could he possibly have, or for that matter, would he live long enough to perform such a task? At last, in 1751 Colden decided to publish his *The Principles of Action in Matter*.[49]

Colden had been advised to publish his book in Britain to protect it from unscrupulous printers there who would otherwise print unauthorized versions. He had already suffered that annoyance with *Explication*. Rutherfurd would safely convey the text to London, where Collinson would handle the publication process. The author directed that his book be given the best appearance possible—large print and high quality paper.[50]

Dedicated to the Earl of Macclesfield, a prominent British astronomer who collected Newton's correspondence, whom Collinson had picked for the honor, Colden explained in his preface that his *Explication* had been only a work in progress. He had corrected mistakes in the two chapters printed in *Explication* and had added six more. He admitted that he sometimes disagreed with Newton but "no man can have a greater opinion of Sir Isaac's wonderful sagacity and accuracy in discovering the most hidden truths, than the author has."[51]

Collinson's connections meant that Colden's *Principles* attracted the attention of the leading popular magazines of the day. In December 1752, the *London Magazine* heralded "An Account of a new System of Philosophy" and printed his preface. The *Gentleman's Magazine*, calling Colden's ideas "entirely new," promised to print extracts from *Principles*. The selections, starting in November 1752, continued until February 1753 where "to be continued" appeared at the end of the extract. But it was not continued, an ill omen.[52]

Another important journal, the *Monthly Review*, published an anonymous review of Colden's *Principles*. To explain to its readers what Colden had theorized, the reviewer first summarized the book. He praised the author's defense of fluxions from Berkeley's attack and made note of Colden's chapter on God:

> Here the ingenious author observes, that the beauty and propriety of the several parts of the universe sufficiently demonstrate, that the whole was formed by some intelligent being: that some intelligent being governs it, and directs each particular part in such a manner, as is most conducive to the well-being of every individual, and of the universal system of nature.[53]

Ether did not fare as well. The reviewer attacked it.

> Whether what Mr. Colden has advanced be sufficient to satisfy the Newtonians, we shall not pretend to say: but it may be observed, that the very existence of this aether is questioned, and, consequently, whatever theory is built upon it, must be subject to infinite disputes.[54]

Colden's universe was a very complicated one, too complicated for most readers to understand, too complicated to accept. Making matters worse, in 1753 Macclesfield sent him his latest astronomical observations which showed that Colden's beliefs about planetary motion had been wrong. Lokken explained Colden's reaction: "The more he reviewed his own work, the more aware he was of his mistakes."[55]

Such disappointments would have discouraged most men but not Colden. Still convinced that he was right, he refused to abandon his basic ideas. "I have from the beginning been aware of the difficulties an obscure person living in an obscure corner of the Earth must meet with on so great an attempt as to establish new principles" in physics. He recalled that when Newton first revealed his principles they "were received at first with great prejudice because contradictory to DesCartes." But Newton was an academic which aided their reception; Colden was not. Furthermore, he had discovered that "English gentlemen" believed that Newton had brought "natural Philosophy to the outmost stretch of human knowledge" so they were prejudiced against "everything . . . that looks like an attempt to go farther." Such "a path not trod in before" was all but certain to be greeted "with censure." Indeed, anyone who criticized Newton would be attacked or ignored.[56]

None of that meant that Colden did not realize his book was riddled with errors. He had discovered that he was wrong about some things, and the typographical errors were "numerous." Some of these typos were very serious and "entirely destroy the sense" of the passage they marred. These were good reasons to work on a new edition of *Principles*.[57]

Colden made a point of alerting Macclesfield of the typos in *Principles* and thanked him for the observations he had sent. In addition, Colden sent some revisions of the book to the astronomer which, according to Collinson, appeared to please him.[58]

Both James Alexander and Samuel Johnson read Colden's revised work. Alexander made some objections. Johnson praised Colden's revised "very ingenious performance," but admitted that he remained puzzled by ether. Johnson, however, had found someone more qualified than himself to evaluate Colden's scientific foray—Thomas Clap, the president of Yale. One of the most prominent scientific figures in the American colonies, Clap examined the "curious Thoughts" found in *Principles* that had "entertained my Mind with much Pleasure and Satisfaction." Colden's astronomical observations were most interesting Clap thought. He also agreed with Colden's thinking about the Intelligent Being, but emphasized that he needed more time to fully understand Colden's other theories. Ultimately, Clap rejected Colden's system of the universe.[59]

Although the reactions to the revised *Principles* were mixed at best, Colden learned that he had a group of fans he had not expected. From South Carolina, Alexander Garden informed Colden that the only one there who had a copy of *Explication* happened to be a minster who had picked up a copy in Britain. The reverend "expressed a great desire to see the Second Edition the plan of which he likes so much."[60]

The "most unexpected" response to *Principles*, Colden stated, came from a minister in London, Samuel Pike, who praised the "penetrating author" of *Principles*. When finishing his own book, Pike had discovered the work of the "ingenious and laborious" Colden, whose principles "are exactly accounted for from revelation." The minister had seen Colden's first edition which, he insisted, clarified some mysterious biblical passages, but the second, enlarged, book had "really approached nearer to the truth of Revelation than any former enquiries." No doubt existed, Pike proclaimed, that Colden had "come nearer to the divine standard than any other ever did, who never looked into the sacred oracles for information in this point."[61]

Proving the truth of the scriptures was not what the deist Colden had been trying to do. He nevertheless thanked Pike for his kind comments. Admitting that he had not sought inspiration for his ideas from the Bible as he saw it only as a moral guide, Colden did mention that he had thought that God's "manner" in sorting out the universe could be gathered from the biblical books of Moses. But lacking knowledge of their original language, Hebrew, he abandoned that train of thought. Their correspondence continued for a few years.[62]

Colden had to have been happy to have received praise for his work from anyone. Euler's attack on *Principles* just about ended any interest academics in Britain had for Colden's theories. Collinson, though, did find another astronomer who agreed to peruse Colden's revisions, Dr. John Bevis. A medical doctor by profession, Bevis had pursued philosophical amusements as Colden had. Unlike Colden, Bevis limited his attention to astronomy and had become prominent in that field and a member of the Royal Society. "Dr. Bevis," Colden stated, was "so much a Philosopher, that he will take pleasure in the trouble which the examination of any new Discovery may give him" and would help anyone who had "err'd in a sincere search after truth." After all, Bevis was not a pedantic academic.[63]

As Colden finished making his revisions, they were sent off to London for Bevis's perusal. In 1755 the astronomer told Collinson that "I had difficulties" with Colden's work "that I could not well reconcile" even after reading it a second time, and decided to call for the advice of a friend, Dr. Bradley—presumably James Bradley, a major astronomer of the time—who knew more about higher mathematics than he did. Perhaps Bradley could comprehend it better, but Bevis believed that Colden's principles were "irreconcilable." While Colden's science appeared puzzling, he was "everywhere master of the true style of the Philosopher; modest, concise, strong, and rational." Bevis thought Colden should continue to try to clear up the confusion rather than abandon his book.[64]

Bevis's critique was both friendly and meant to be helpful. By 1755 even Colden was getting discouraged. After reading the comments of another scholar, Colden thought that his ideas "may die in obscurity in America with its author." Bevis's initial remarks had to have made the author gloomier about the fate of *Principles*.[65]

In 1756 Bevis still had not given his final thoughts about *Principles*. He believed that "every new hypothesis should be examined with a mind void of prejudice and prepossession." And he insisted that "unless he were sure his mind was thus prepared, he should look upon himself as an improper judge."[66]

By the next year Colden felt "ashamed" of sending more revisions to Bevis and wasting his time anymore. But the next batch of revisions actually impressed the reader. Colden had been doing additional astronomical observations and noticed something peculiar. As the Earth turned on its axis from the winter solstice to the summer solstice, the planet wobbled and slanted slightly on its axis. When he told Franklin about his finding, his enthused friend wrote: "I congratulate you on your discovery of a new Motion in the Earth's Axis. You will, I see, render your name immortal." Colden informed Macclesfield of this adding that *Principles* "may excite Astronomers to a more accurate observation of the position of the Axis of the Earth in several parts of its orbit."[67]

Macclesfield must have been as surprised as Bevis was. Colden was alerted that Bevis "had found some very surprising things in your last papers" relating to "a phenomenon which has puzzled all our Philosophers, the variation of the solstitial altitudes." Some French astronomers had written about the wobble, and both Bevis and Bradley had seen it too. Both of them had dismissed the wobble as a measuring error. That Colden, in far-off America, had detected it too proved that the wobble was a natural phenomenon, not a mistake. It is now called "precession of the equinoxes."[68]

Despite that discovery, in 1759 Bevis and Bradley informed Colden that they could not "comprehend" his theories "especially as to us they seem incompatible with principles established upon the most certain foundations." Graciously, Bevis remarked that perhaps they just did not understand "the Ideas of a Philosophy that is quite new." Others might understand Colden's ideas, so if he wanted to have his revisions published in London, Bevis volunteered to proofread the final version for him. Colden, however, did not want to impose on him; instead he hoped to remove all of Bevis's objections. Colden failed at that.[69]

Meanwhile, Colden believed that electricity could prove his ideas and hoped that Franklin could do it. Franklin never pursued such experiments. Instead, David Colden, who had given his father the idea in the first place, stepped into the breach to assist his father. In 1757 the Coldens had collaborated and were convinced that their electrical experiments proved the principles. Hoping to have these results published in Britain, David sent them off across the Atlantic. In 1761 Collinson sent him bad news. An expert on electricity had tried to duplicate these experiments but "could not verify" them "because he could not understand your father's principles."[70]

Electricity and gravitation, Cadwallader Colden conjectured, were not the only forces governed by his principles. He began to apply them to "the most general phenomena of nature." The movement of fluids in bodies and life itself was controlled by them he reasoned. Perspiration, the movement of blood, and digestion were all the result of "fermentation" created by the interaction of his principles. Colden postulated such things in an early work, "The Animal Oeconomy," which aimed at improving medicine. Later, in the 1760s he penned another essay, "An Inquiry into The Principles of Vital Motion." As Colden explained, because of microscopes scientists had learned that sperm was "full of little Animalilis, in shape like Tadpoles and in continual Motion." The creation of such "Secretions" proved "the direction of an Intelligent being." How else could they "remain regularly the same"? Lokken asserted that Colden's insistence on the existence of fermentation in bodies provided "an insight that pointed in the direction of modern biochemistry."[71]

Colden's extensions of his theories demonstrate that, after all the criticisms, he had not lost faith in them. To respond to the attacks on them he resolved to write a letter to the *Monthly Review*. Flustered that he had not yet received Bevis's definitive remarks, in 1759 he asked the journal's editors for advice as to whether his revised *Principles* should ever see the light of day and to print a letter he meant for publication. The *Monthly Review* seemed to be the best venue for his letter, he explained to the editors: "The men of learning among the English have sometimes been charged with want of politeness to Strangers—if there be any ground for this reflexion. I think you are an exception to it."[72]

The journal did publish the letter "from the ingenious and industrious" Colden. In the missive, he wrote of his plan to have a revised version of *Principles*. His book, though "thought to be contradictory to what Sir Isaac Newton has demonstrated," really was not. The conception "arises from a mistake, and want of attention." Then he tried to demonstrate why such criticism was mistaken. This letter proved to be the author's most clear discussion of what his book was all about.[73]

Colden's letter did obtain a response, but not the sort he had hoped for. "W. K." complained that Colden like "many other physical Writers," had "set out on imaginary principles, and builds his whole system on a metaphysical plan." Although he thought "Mr. Colden has gone a little out of his way, he has, in my opinion, proceeded much farther toward the explanation of the phenomena of Gravitation, and the Motion of the Planets, than any other physical Writer." "W. K." did complain about such authors that they kept "running into chimeras."[74]

Not happy at all, Colden wrote back, once again defending his work, insisting that "no body knows how Light acts" and that he was trying to explain "some of the most difficult phenomena in nature." When "W. K." explained celestial motion, "he shall be at liberty to laugh at the Author of the *Principles of Action*."[75]

The *Monthly Review*'s editors jumped in immediately with a note that they thought Colden was mistaken—"W. K." was not laughing at him and had praised him in his letter. Right after Colden's response, they published another letter from "W. K." where he stated "I should not take the liberty to laugh at anyone, by whose assistance, I must confess myself so much obliged, as by that of Mr. Colden." Then he agreed with Colden's criticism of the original review. The long battle over his principles had made Colden very exasperated.[76]

The fate of *Principles* would finally be decided at Colden's old school, the University of Edinburgh. A professor there, Dr. Robert Whytt, a doctor of medicine whose field was medical theory, would be Colden's chief contact at the college. In 1757 Garden, who knew both of then, brought them together. Whytt, especially intrigued to correspond with Colden, shared similar views with him about two of the pressing issues of medical theory of the time—

what were the natures of the mind and the soul. Whytt also complained of "rigid and literal Newtonians" which had to have pleased Colden.[77]

To Colden, "The mind is not confined to any particular part of the body; for nothing can act where it is not." Yet a person was "only conscious of those sensations which are communicated, by the nerves, to the common sensorium," that is, the mind. The mind was the center of thinking and imagination, and dreaming was part of imagination. Dogs clearly dreamed; probably all animals did but humans could not prove it. In the mind ideas accumulated and could only be changed "with great difficulty," which Colden knew from experience. For example, Colden, the son of a minister, pointed to "our childhood ideas of ghosts that go about in the dark or haunt church yards." When children grew up, they still thought of ghosts whenever they "are in the dark or in a churchyard" and will continue until such "connections of ideas" are broken. Such "errors" often reappear "when their judgment fails by sickness or age." He wondered about the soul as well.[78]

Whytt and "That learned Philosopher" got along well, and it did not take Colden long to confide in him about the fate of the revisions of *Principles*. "I have sometimes thoughts of ordering them to be committed to the flames," Colden admitted, and other times considered depositing them at the University of Edinburgh "where I had my education in hopes of a future resurrection."[79]

Urging Colden not to destroy his work, Whytt reminded him that even though "it may not be altogether Convincing," it could inspire useful work in the future. Yet Whytt was realistic about his contemporaries. "The taste of the present age is so little for metaphysical disquisitions" and thus a shorter book would likely be better received. He had discovered that London doctors "begin to despise reasoning too much, and to trust what they call experience and observation alone," but he believed the two approaches had to be used together.[80]

When Whytt pointed out a serious flaw in the revised *Principles* Colden had to revise his work again. Overall, however, *Principles* was "too deep" for Whytt and so he could not say whether it should be published or not; Scotland might be more receptive than England had been. So Whytt convinced philosopher Adam Ferguson, also of the University of Edinburgh, to examine it. He concluded that Colden's manuscript had "many Ingenious thoughts" and "Subtle reasoning" and "might very well merit publication." He foresaw a problem—"Newtonian Doctrine is so universally prevalent in Britain," Ferguson doubted the book "would meet with a favorable reception."[81]

Given that verdict, Whytt checked to see if the university would accept Colden's manuscript as a donation, which Colden himself had suggested. The decision lay with the school's principal, William Robertson, a prominent Scottish historian, who was "much obliged . . . for Such a present." The revised *Principles* remains at the University of Edinburgh, still awaiting the resurrection the author hoped for.[82]

Historians tend to enjoy dismissing Colden's foray explaining gravitation, but they should remember that "Colden did not solve the problem of the cause of gravitation, but . . . neither did any European scientist in the eighteenth century." Even then Colden's *Principles* had devoted admirers, including a vigorous defender of Newton, the French scientist the Count de Buffon. He had received a copy of the *Explication* and had been "so charmed" that he had it published in a French translation. His English copy had gotten lost, which bothered him so much that he "made repeated trials to have it found in England." Finally, in the 1780s he appealed to Thomas Jefferson, then the American minister in Paris, for his aid.[83]

Buffon was not alone. A number of scholars have stated that Colden's theories have a definite "modern" feel to them and are "very suggestive."[84] It should also be mentioned that modern science has made Colden seem less laughable.

Take, for example, what appears to be one of Colden's more humorous assertions, that the planet Jupiter gave off light. In the 1970s an American space mission, Pioneer 10, confirmed that, indeed, Jupiter is a source of light. Nor should Colden's inability to explain his theories be considered as a terrible flaw. Such a problem is endemic in the field of physics. Einstein could not explain his ideas either; he "was not a natural popularizer." Relativity "had to be explained to the world (and even to physicists) mainly by others with a gift for communication."[85]

Perhaps the strangest of all of Colden's principles—that light was one of the forces affecting gravity—has to be understood in the context of the eighteenth century. Colden wrote about physics in what really was "the Newtonian conception of the universe;" it dominated the era. There is no surprise, then, that he used Newton's physics to advance beyond Newton—those were the tools available to him—and light was an important part of Newton's physics. Describing something new in words suggestive of something older—the existing "toolbox"—is not unusual. Early automobiles were at first called horseless carriages. If Colden had seen a light bulb powered by electricity, he might well have dubbed it "a candle without a flame."[86]

When Colden talked about light, he "was groping towards a modern conception of energy—rest-mass energy and internal energy. . . . Colden could not have known of the modern energy concept." Only in 1807, long after Colden's death, did Dr. Thomas Young "use the term energy in its modern scientific sense." With that step, the progression of science would lead to the end of Newton's way of explaining the universe, despite the fact that, as Einstein noted, "Newton's followers . . . were entirely under the spell of his doctrine."[87]

Regarding Colden's insistence upon the existence of ether, later times demonstrated that he was not spreading a fairy tale. Visible matter is but part of the matter in the cosmos. The discovery of the so-called "dark matter" meant that ether actually exists. Dark matter, along with the even more mysterious "dark energy," have been shown to affect gravitation which Colden and many others believed.[88]

Although Colden never doubted that his principles were right, the deposit of his manuscript at the University of Edinburgh in 1764 ended his attempt to revise Newtonian physics. Off-and-on, he had devoted some twenty years to the task. But by 1764 his life had changed in a way he had never theorized.[89]

NOTES

1. CC to BF, September 17, 1744, *FP*, vol. 2, 416.

2. CC to Samuel Johnson, April 12, 1746, *CP*, vol. 3, 202–3; Johnson to CC, April 22, 1746, April 15, 1747, *CP*, vol. 3, 205–6, 372–75; Garden to CC, February 1, 1764, *CP*, vol. 6, 284–85; CC to Johnson, January 27, 1746/7, in Samuel Johnson, *Samuel Johnson, President of King's College: His Career and Writings*, ed. Herbert Schneider and Carol Schneider (New York: Columbia University Press, 1929), vol. 2, 293–94; CC, "The Reading of an Elaborate Treatise on the Eye, by the Learned and Ingenious Dr. Porterfield Is the Occasion of the Following Reflections," in *The Philosophical Writings of Cadwallader Colden*, ed. Scott L. Pratt and John Ryder (Amherst, NY: Humanity Books, 2002), 144–45; CC, "Of the First Principles of Morality or the Actions of Intelligent Beings," in *Philosophical Writings*, ed. Pratt and Ryder, 111; Joseph L. Blau, *Men and Movements in American Philosophy* (New York: Prentice-Hall, 1952), 34.

3. CC, "First Principles," 114–15, 117; Johnson to CC, April 15, 1747, Johnson, *Samuel Johnson*, ed. Schneiders, vol. 2, 294; Robert H. Hurlbutt III, *Hume, Newton, and The Design Argument*, rev. ed., 2nd Landmark ed. (Lincoln: University of Nebraska Press, 1965), 87.

4. *SM*, vol. 2, 30; James Colden to CC, October 3, 1721, *CP*, vol. 8, 63–64; CC, "Reading of an Elaborate Treatise on the Eye," 149; Max Savelle, *Seeds of Liberty: The Genesis of the American Mind* (New York: Knopf, 1948), 45.

5. CC, "Reading of an Elaborate Treatise on the Eye," 144–45.

6. Mrs. Jane Colden to Mrs. CC, n.d., February 5, 1717, *CP*, vol. 8, 19–20.

7. CC, "First Principles," 113; Johnson to CC, April 15, 1747, *CP*, vol. 3, 372–75; CC to Johnson, April 12, 1746, *CP*, vol. 3, 202–3; Louis Leonard Gitin, "Cadwallader Colden as Scientist and Philosopher," *New York History* 16, no. 2 (1935): 176; Theodore Hornberger, "Samuel Johnson of Yale and King's College: A Note on the Relation of Science and Religion in Provincial America," *New England Quarterly* 8, no. 3 (1935): 378; Savalle, *Seeds of Liberty*, 67.

8. Alfred R. Hoermann, "A Savant in the Wilderness: Cadwallader Colden of New York," *New York Historical Society Quarterly* 62, no. 4 (1978): 277; Alison Gilbert Olson, "Governor Robert Hunter and the Anglican Church in New York," in *Statesmen, Scholars and Merchants: Essays in Eighteenth-Century History presented to Dame Lucy Sutherland*, ed. Anne Whiteman et al. (Oxford: Clarendon Press, 1973), 45; CC, "Reading of an Elaborate Treatise on the Eye," 144–45.

9. JA to CC, January 9, 1729/30, James Alexander Papers, box 1, f. 1, NYHS; Alan Valentine, *Lord Stirling* (New York: Oxford University Press, 1969), 31.

10. Eugene R. Fingerhut, *Survivor: Cadwallader Colden II in Revolutionary* America (Washington, DC: University Press of America, 1983), 8–9; M. Ruttenber and L. H. Clark, *History of Orange County, New York* (Philadelphia: Events & Peck, 1881), 253; Petition for a charter for the Newburgh Mission, November 17, 1769, in New York Colony, *Ecclesiastical Records State of New York*, ed. Hugh Hastings (Albany, NY: J. B. Lyon, State Printer,

1901–1916), vol. 6, 4172; Thomas Jones, *History of New York during the Revolutionary War*, ed. Edward Floyd De Lancey (New York: New York Historical Society, 1879; repr. Cranbury, NJ: Scholar's Bookshelf, 2006), vol. 1, 19; Morgan Dix, *A History of the Parish of Trinity Church in the City of New York, To the Close of the Rectorship of Dr. Inglis, A.D. 1783* (New York: G. P. Putnam,, 1898), vol. 1, 389; Edward P. Alexander, *A Revolutionary Conservative: James Duane of New York* (New York: Columbia University Press, 1938), 10.

11. Blau, *Men and Movements*, 34.

12. CC to Collinson, June 20, 1745, *CP*, vol. 3, 117–19; Brooke Hindle, "Cadwallader Colden's Extension of the Newtonian Principles," *William and Mary Quarterly*, 3rd ser., 13 (1956): 462; Michael Hunter, *Boyle: Between God and Science* (New Haven, CT: Yale University Press, 2009), 3; William R. Brock and C. Helen Brock, *Scotus Americanus: A Survey of the Sources for Links between Scotland and America in the Eighteenth Century* (Edinburgh: Edinburgh University Press, 1982), 212.

13. I. Woodbridge Riley, *American Philosophy: The Early Schools* (New York: Russell & Russell, 1958), 352; Sara S. Gronim, "At the Sign of Newton's Head: Astronomy and Cosmology in British Colonial New York," *Pennsylvania History* 66, supp. (1999): 59–60; Roy N. Lokken, "Cadwallader Colden's Attempt to Advance Natural Philosophy Beyond the Eighteenth-Century Mechanistic Paradigm," American Philosophical Society, *Proceedings* 122, no. 6 (December 1978): 375; Hindle, "Cadwallader Colden's Extension," 459; Brooke Hindle, *The Pursuit of Science in Revolutionary America, 1735–1789* (Chapel Hill: University of North Carolina Press, 1956), 43; Blau, *Men and Movements*, 29.

14. CC to Johnson, June 2, 1746, *CP*, vol. 3, 212; Hindle, "Cadwallader Colden's Extension," 463; Raymond Phineas Stearns, *Science in the British Colonies of America* (Urbana: University of Illinois Press, 1970), 569.

15. CC, *An Explication of the First Causes of Action in Matter, and, of the Cause of Gravitation* (New York: James Parker, 1745 [sic 1746]), 3; Herbert W. Schneider, *A History of American Philosophy* (New York, 1946), 24; Lokken, "Cadwallader Colden's Attempt to Advance Natural Philosophy," 370; Hindle, "Cadwallader Colden's Extension," 466; Adam Leroy Jones, *Early American Philosophers* (New York: Macmillan, 1898; repr. New York: F. Ungar), 17–18; Blau, *Men and Movements*, 29–30; Riley, *American Philosophy*, 333.

16. Schneider, *History*, 24; Lokken, "Cadwallader Colden's Attempt to Advance Natural Philosophy," 370; Hindle, "Cadwallader Colden's Extension," 466–67; CC, "An Introduction to the Study of Phylosophy Wrote In America for the Use of a Young Gentleman," in *American Philosophical Addresses, 1700–1900*, ed. Joseph L. Blau (New York: Columbia University Press, 1946), 304.

17. CC, *Explication*, 18, 25; Lokken, "Cadwallader Colden's Attempt to Advance Natural Philosophy," 371–72; Joyce E. Chaplin, *The First Scientific American: Benjamin Franklin and the Pursuit of Genius* (New York: Basic Books, 2006), 97; Schneider, *History*, 24; Jones, *Early American Philosophers*, 18; Louis Leonard Tucker, "President Thomas Clap of Yale College: Another Founding Father of American Science," *Isis* 52, no. 1 (1961): 60; Hindle, "Cadwallader Colden's Extension," 463–64.

18. *Oxford English Dictionary*, s.v. "ether," "ethereal."

19. Einstein, "Ether and the Theory of Relativity," in *The Collected Papers of Albert Einstein, The Berlin Years, 1918–1921*, trans. Alfred Engel (Princeton, NJ: Princeton University Press, 2002), vol. 7, 163; Walter Isaacson, *Einstein: His Life and Universe* (New York: Simon & Schuster, 2007), 111, 318; Jurgen Neffe, *Einstein: A Biography*, trans. Shelley Frisch (New York, 2007), 133, 230; Hindle, "Cadwallader Colden's Extension," 463–65; P. M. Heimann, "Ether and imponderables," in *Conceptions of Ether: Studies in the History of Ether Theories, 1740–1900*, ed. G. N. Cantor and M. J. S. Hodge (Cambridge: Cambridge University Press, 1981), 62, 64; Frank Wilczek, *The Lightness of Being: Mass, Ether, and the Unification of Forces* (New York: Basic Books, 2008), 76–77, 82.

20. BF to CC, November 28, 1745, *FP*, vol. 3, 46–48; Johnson to CC, June 26, October 5, 1745, *CP*, vol. 3, 120–21, 162–63; CC to Johnson, March 26, 1744, in Johnson, *Samuel Johnson*, ed. Schneiders, vol. 2, 287; CC, "Introduction to the Study of Phylosophy," 298–99; Marina Benjamin, "Medicine, Morality and the Politics of Berkeley's Tar-water," in *The Medical Enlightenment of the Eighteenth Century*, ed. Andrew Cunningham and Roger French

(Cambridge and New York: Cambridge University Press, 1990), 186; Lokken, "Cadwallader Colden's Attempt to Advance Natural Philosophy," 369; Roy N. Lokken and James Logan, "The Scientific Papers of James Logan," American Philosophical Society, *Transactions*, n.s., 62, no. 6 (1972): 9; James Delbourgo, *A Most Amazing Scene of Wonders: Electricity and Enlightenment in Early America* (Cambridge, MA: Harvard University Press, 2006), 218–19.

21. CC to Gronovius, May 30, 1746, *CP*, vol. 3, 209–11; CC to Collinson, June 20, 1745, *CP*, vol. 3, 117–19.

22. Rutherfurd to CC, April 19, 1743, *CP*, vol. 3, 17–21; Hindle, "Cadwallader Colden's Extension," 462–63.

23. JA to CC, February 15, 1743/4, February 23, 1745/6, *CP*, vol. 3, 48–50, 198–99; CC to JA, June 2, 1744, James Alexander Papers, box 5, f. 1, NYHS; Hindle, "Cadwallader Colden's Extension," 470.

24. JA to CC, January 30, 1745/6, *CP*, vol. 3, 194–95; CC to Collinson, July 8, 1746, *CP*, vol. 3, 222–24; CC to Gronovius, May 30, 1746, *CP*, vol. 3, 209–11; CC to Mitchell, November 7, [1745], *CP*, vol. 8, 336–37; Carl Van Doren, "The Beginnings of the American Philosophical Society," American Philosophical Society, *Proceedings* 87, no. 3 (1943): 287; Hindle, *Pursuit of Science*, 45.

25. CC, *Explication*, iii–vi.
26. CC, *Explication*, iii–vi.
27. CC, *Explication*, iii–vi.
28. CC, *Explication*, iii–vi.

29. BF to CC, July 10, October 16, 1746, August 6, 1747, *FP*, vol. 3, 80–81, 89–92, 169; Johnson to CC, October 31, 1746, Gratz Coll., HSP; Stearns, *Science*, 570.

30. Collinson to BF, April 12, 1747, *CP*, vol. 3, 371–72; Collinson to CC, August 3, 1747, *CP*, vol. 3, 410–12; Collinson to Linnaeus, October 26, 1747, in Linnaeus, *A Selection of the Correspondence of Linnaeus and Other Naturalists, from the Original Manuscripts*, ed. Sir James Edward Smith (London: Longman, Hurst, Rees, Orme, and Brown, 1821), vol. 1, 19–20; JA to Collinson, July 20, 1747, RP, vol. 4, 79, NYHS; Lokken, "Cadwallader Colden's Attempt to Advance Natural Philosophy," 369; Norman S. Fiering, "Early American Philosophy vs. Philosophy in Early America," Charles S. Peirce Society, *Transactions* 13, no. 3 (Summer 1977): 227; Susan Scott Parrish, *American Curiosity: Cultures of Natural History in the Colonial British Atlantic World* (Chapel Hill: University of North Carolina Press, 2006), 128–29.

31. Collinson to Alexander, October 14, 1747, RP, vol. 4, 81, NYHS; Collinson to CC, August 3, 1747, *CP*, vol. 3, 410–12.

32. Collinson to CC, June 20, 1748, *CP*, vol. 4, 67; CC to Collinson, July 28, 1752, *CP*, vol. 9, 118–19; Lokken, "Cadwallader Colden's Attempt to Advance Natural Philosophy," 374; Hindle, "Cadwallader Colden's Extension," 470–71; Joseph Kastner, *A Species of Eternity* (New York: Knopf, 1977), 21.

33. CC to BF, November 29, 1753, *FP*, vol. 5, 122–23; CC, "Essay on the Art of Right Living," CPU, reel 2; Hindle, "Cadwallader Colden's Extension," 469, 471.

34. CC to Collinson, July 28, 1752, *CP*, vol. 9, 118–19; Hindle, "Cadwallader Colden's Extension," 461.

35. Jason Socrates Bardi, *The Calculus Wars: Newton, Leibniz, and the Greatest Mathematical Clash of All Time* (New York: Thunder's Mouth Press, 2006), v–viii, 155–57.

36. CC, *The Principles of Action in Matter, The Gravitation of Bodies, and the Motion of the Planets, explained from those Principles* (London: R. Dodsley, 1751), preface, 191–93; CC to Johnson, December 31, 1744, Samuel Johnson Papers, vol. 6, Columbia University, New York City; Frederick E. Brasch, "The Newtonian Epoch in the American Colonies (1680–1783)," American Antiquarian Society, *Proceedings* 49 (1939): 323.

37. JA to CC, June 10, 1744, *CP*, vol. 3, 62–63; Rutherfurd to CC, March 2, 1742/3, April 19, 1743, *CP*, vol. 3, 6–7, 17–21.

38. BF to CC, October 25, 1744, *FP*, vol. 2, 417–18; CC to BF, December 1744, *FP*, vol. 2, 446–47; BF to CC, August 15, 1745, *FP*, vol. 3, 33–36; Logan to BF, July 19, 1747, *FP*, vol. 3, 152–53; Frederick B. Tolles, *James Logan and the Culture of Provincial America* (Boston: Little, Brown, 1957), 205–6; Lokken and Logan, "Scientific Papers of James Logan," 61.

39. Johnson to CC, February 25, July 10, 1745, *CP*, vol. 3, 104, 127; Johnson to CC, October 31, 1746, Gratz Coll., HSP.

40. Johnson to CC, April 22, 1746, January 12, 1746/7, *CP*, vol. 3, 207, 330–31; Lokken, "Cadwallader Colden's Attempt to Advance Natural Philosophy," 373; Riley, *American Philosophy*, 356.

41. CC, *Principles*, 214; Blau, *Men and Movements*, 31; M. Benjamin, "Medicine," in *Medical Enlightenment*, ed. Cunningham and French, 166; Hoermann, "Savant," 276.

42. CC, *Principles*, 37; CC to Johnson, November 19, 1746, *CP*, vol. 3, 282–83; Hoermann, *Cadwallader Colden: A Figure of the American Enlightenment* (Westport, CT: Greenwood Press, 2002), 109.

43. CC, *Principles*, 167; John C. Greene, "Some Aspects of American Astronomy, 1750–1815," *Isis* 45, no. 4 (1954): 355.

44. Johnson to CC, January 12, 1746/7, *CP*, vol. 3, 330–31; Lokken, "Cadwallader Colden's Attempt to Advance Natural Philosophy," 373; Alfred R. Hoermann, "Cadwallader Colden and the Mind-Body Problem," *Bulletin of the History of Medicine* 50, no. 3 (1976): 395.

45. CC to Dr. Betts, April 25, 1750, *CP*, vol. 4, 204–7.

46. Thomas Robie to [Burnet?], November 9, 1723, *CP*, vol. 1, 157; William Burnet, "Observations of the Eclipses of the First Satellite of Jupiter, Communicated by His Excellency William Burnet, Esq.; Governor of New York, F.R.S.," Royal Society, *Philosophical Transactions* 33 (1724–1725): 162; Thomas Pownall, *A Topographical Description of the Dominions of the United States of America*, Rev. ed. of London: J. Almon, 1776 (Pittsburgh: University of Pittsburgh Press, 1949), 14.

47. CC to Douglass, January 21, 1739/40, CPU, reel 2; CC to Johnson, March 20, 1753, William Samuel Johnson Papers, box 1, Columbia University, New York City; JA to CC, January 22, 1743/4, *CP*, vol. 3, 46; La Galissoniere to CC, October 10, 1752, *CP*, vol. 4, 346–47; Collinson to CC, March 6, 1754, *CP*, vol. 4, 433; Collinson to BF, August 12, 1753, *FP*, vol. 5, 20.

48. Joseph Betts, "A Letter from the Rev. Mr. Joseph Betts, M. A. and Fellow of University College, Oxon to Martin Folkes, Esq.," Royal Society, *Philosophical Transactions* 43 (1744–1745): 91; Dr. Joseph Betts to JA, September 7, 1749, *CP*, vol. 4, 137–38; CC to Betts, April 25, 1750, *CP*, vol. 4, 204–7.

49. CC to Mitchell, July 18, 1751, *CP*, vol. 9, 102; CC, *Principles*, 149.

50. Joseph Davidson to CC, January 26, 1749/50, *CP*, vol. 4, 195–96; CC to Collinson, June 15, 1751, HM8255, Huntington Library, San Marino, CA.

51. CC, *Principles*, preface; Collinson to CC, December 11, 1751, *CP*, vol. 9, 109; *Oxford DNB*, s.v. Parker, George.

52. *London Magazine* 21 (December 1752): 560–62; *Gentleman's Magazine* 22–23 (1752–1753): 498–500, 570–71, 589–90, 65–66.

53. *Monthly Review* 63 (December 1752): 465, 467.

54. *Monthly Review* 63 (December 1752): 463.

55. Lokken, "Cadwallader Colden's Attempt to Advance Natural Philosophy," 375.

56. CC to BF, May 20, 1752, *FP*, vol. 4, 314–15; CC to Collinson, December 5, 1753, May 28, November 19, 1754, *CP*, vol. 4, 418–19, 447, 473–74, *CP*, vol. 9, 144–48; Collinson to CC, March 13, 1755, *CP*, vol. 5, 6–7; CC to Samuel Pike, 1755, in CC, *Philosophical Writings*, ed. Pratt and Ryder, 214–16; Andrew Robinson, *The Last Man Who Knew Everything: Thomas Young, the Anonymous Genius Who Proved Newton Wrong and Deciphered the Rosetta Stone, Among Other Surprising Feats* (New York: Plume, 2006), 95.

57. CC to BF, May 20, 1752, *FP*, vol. 4, 314–15; CC to Johnson, December 20, 1752, in Johnson, *Samuel Johnson*, ed. Schneiders, vol. 2, 299–300; CC to Pike, 1753, in CC, *Philosophical Writings*, ed. Pratt and Ryder, 210–13.

58. CC to Macclesfield, 1753, CPU, reel 1; CC to Macclesfield, February 16, 1753, *CP*, vol. 4, 370–71; Collinson to CC, June 2, 1753, *CP*, vol. 4, 391–92; CC to Collinson, July 7, 1753, *CP*, vol. 4, 395–96.

59. JA to CC, March 4, 1753, *CP*, vol. 4, 374; Johnson to CC, February 19, [1753], in Johnson, *Samuel Johnson*, ed. Schneiders, vol. 2, 302–3; Thomas Clap to CC, July 1, 1753, Gratz Coll., HSP; Louis Leonard Tucker, *Puritan Protagonist: President Thomas Clap of Yale*

College (Chapel Hill: University of North Carolina Press, 1962), 100–1; Hindle, "Cadwallader Colden's Extension," 470.

60. Garden to CC, November 22, 1755, *CP*, vol. 5, 41–42.

61. Samuel Pike, *Philosophia Sacra: Or, the Principles of Natural Philosophy, Extracted from Divine Revelation* (London: Printed for the Author, 1753), 133, 138; Pike to CC, July 10, 1753, *CP*, vol. 4, 396–99; *Oxford DNB*, s.v. Pike, Samuel; CC to BF, November 29, 1753, *FP*, vol. 5, 121–24.

62. CC to BF, November 29, 1753, *FP*, vol. 5, 121–24; CC to Pike, 1753, in CC, *Philosophical Writings*, ed. Pratt and Ryder, 210–13; CC to Pike, May 12, 1755, *CP*, vol. 5, 7–9; CC to Pike, June 1755, CPU, reel 1; Pike to CC, September 9, 1755, Gratz Coll., HSP.

63. Collinson to CC, March 7, 1753, *CP*, vol. 4, 355–57; Collinson to CC, September 26, 1755, *CP*, vol. 5, 28; CC to Alexander Colden, December 20, 1756, CPU, reel 2; *Oxford DNB*, s.v. Bevis, John.

64. John Bevis to Collinson, [May 15, 1755], August 10, 1755, *CP*, vol. 5, 10, 22–24; *Oxford DNB*, s.v. Bradley, James.

65. CC to Garden, 1755, in CC, *Philosophical Writings*, ed. Pratt and Ryder, 216–23; Hindle, "Cadwallader Colden's Extension," 470.

66. Alexander Colden to CC, September 20, 1756, *CP*, vol. 5, 92–94.

67. BF to CC, February 28, 1753, *FP*, vol. 4, 448; CC to Macclesfield, April 2, 1753, *CP*, vol. 4, 379–81; CC to Alexander Colden, c. May 1757, *CP*, vol. 5, 147–48.

68. Alexander Colden to CC, May 20, 1757, *CP*, vol. 5, 143–44; Alexander Colden to CC, March 28, 1759, *CP*, vol. 5, 299; Joe Rao, "The Southern Cross," *Natural History* 105 (May 1996): 67; Donald Goldsmith, "Turn, Turn, Turn," *Natural History* 115 (December 2006–January 2007): 22, 24–26.

69. Bevis to Alexander Colden, June 9, 1759, *CP*, vol. 5, 302–3; CC to Bevis, September 12, 1759, CPU, reel 2.

70. CC to BF, October 24, 1752, *FP*, vol. 4, 373–76; D. Colden to BF, September 18, 1757, *FP*, vol. 7, 263; D. Colden to Alexander Colden, September 23, 1757, *CP*, vol. 5, 185–87; Collinson to D. Colden, May 7, 1761, *CP*, vol. 6, 31; D. Colden to Sir William Johnson, December 19, 1763, *CP*, vol. 6, 265; Stearns, *Science*, 573–74.

71. CC, "The Animal Oeconomy," CPU, reel 1; CC, "An Inquiry into the Principles of Vital Motion," March 13, 1763, CPU, reel 2; BF to CC, August 15, 1745, *FP*, vol. 3, 33–36; CC to BF, March 16, 1752, *FP*, vol. 4, 278–81; CC to Bard, July 5, 1758, *CP*, vol. 5, 240; Lokken, "Cadwallader Colden's Attempt to Advance Natural Philosophy," 368–69, 376; Chaplin, *First Scientific American*, 97–98; Stearns, *Science*, 574; Roger K. French, "Ether and Physiology," in *Conceptions of Ether: Studies in the History of Ether Theories, 1740–1900*, ed. G. N. Cantor and M. J. S. Hodge (Cambridge: Cambridge University Press, 1981), 111.

72. CC to William Popple, September 2, 1762, *CP*, vol. 6, 193–97; CC, "To the Authors of the *Monthly Review*," August 6, 1759, CPU, reel 2.

73. CC, "Colden's Letter on the Principles, etc.," *Monthly Review* 21 (November 1759): 397–403.

74. "W. K.," "A Letter to the Authors of the *Monthly Review*," *Monthly Review* 21 (December 1759): 500–12.

75. CC, "To the Authors of the *Monthly Review*," July 7, 1760, *Monthly Review* 23 (November 1760), 380–87.

76. CC, "To the Authors of the *Monthly Review*," 384; "W. K.", "To the Authors of the *Monthly Review*," n.d., *Monthly Review* 23 (November 1760): 387–89.

77. Garden to CC, April 15, 1757, March 14, 1758, *CP*, vol. 5, 142–43, 227–28; Hoermann, "Cadwallader Colden and the Mind-Body Problem," 396, 398; French, "Ether and Physiology," 113–14.

78. CC to Whytt, April 15, 1760, in Robert Whytt, *Physiological Essays* (Edinburgh: Hamilton, Balfour and Neill, 1761), 260–62; CC, "Reading of an Elaborate Treatise on the Eye," 127–28, 130–31, 136. For Whytt's ideas, see Roger K. French, *Robert Whytt, the Soul, and Medicine* (London: Wellcome Institute, 1969), 145–64.

79. Whytt, *Physiological Essays*, 260–62; CC to Whytt, 1758, in CC, *Philosophical Writings*, ed. Pratt and Ryder, 227–29.

80. Whytt to CC, October 20, 1760, *CP*, vol. 5, 356.

81. CC to Whytt, July 21, 1759, in CC, *Philosophical Writings*, ed. Pratt and Ryder, 231; CC to Whytt, February 25, 1762, *CLB*, vol. 1, 166–70; Whytt to CC, October 30, 1762, *CP*, vol. 6, 197–98; CC to Whytt, March 7, 1763, CPU, reel 2; Whytt to CC, May 16, September 3, 1763, *CP*, vol. 6, 217–19, 272–74; Whytt to CC, April 16, 1764, Gratz Coll., HSP; *Oxford DNB*, s.v. Ferguson, Adam.

82. CC to Whytt, September 3, 1763, *CP*, vol. 6, 272–74; Whytt to CC, April 16, 1764, Gratz Coll., HSP; Colin G. Calloway, *White People, Indians, and Highlanders: Tribal Peoples and Colonial Encounters in Scotland and America* (New York: Oxford University Press, 2008), 78; Lawrence Henry Gipson, *The British Empire Before the American Revolution* (Caldwell, ID: Caxton Printers; New York: A. A. Knopf, 1936–1970), vol. 15, 353. The NYHS also has a copy.

83. Thomas Jefferson to Francis Hopkinson, January 3, [1786], Thomas Jefferson, *The Papers of Thomas Jefferson, November 1785–June 1786*, ed. Julian P. Boyd (Princeton: NJ: Princeton University Press, 1954), vol. 9, 148; Hopkinson to Jefferson, June 28, 1786; and *June 1786–December 1786*, vol. 10, 78; Lokken and Logan, "Scientific Papers of James Logan," 9; Florian Cajori, *A History of the Conceptions of Limits and Fluxions in Great Britain from Newton to Woodhouse* (Chicago: Open Court, 1919), 203–4; J. B. Shank, *The Newton Wars and the Beginning of the French Enlightenment* (Chicago: University of Chicago Press, 2008), 407–8; Michael Kraus, "Scientific Relations between Europe and America in the Eighteenth Century," *Scientific Monthly* 55, no. 3 (1942): 268.

84. Riley, *American Philosophy*, 335; Savelle, *Seeds of Liberty*, 97; Lokken, "Cadwallader Colden's Attempt to Advance Natural Philosophy," 371n37.

85. Lokken, "Cadwallader Colden's Attempt to Advance Natural Philosophy," 372, 372n47; Robinson, *Last Man*, 86.

86. Tucker, *Thomas Clap*, 99–100; Neil de Grasse Tyson, "Galactic Engines," *Natural History* 106 (May 1997): 66–67.

87. Lokken, "Cadwallader Colden's Attempt to Advance Natural Philosophy," 371; Robinson, *Last Man*, 125; Einstein, "Ether and the Theory of Relativity," 163.

88. Wilczek, *Lightness*, 22; Richard Panek, "Probing the Biggest Mystery in the Universe," *Smithsonian* 41 (April 2010): 31–32; Donald Goldsmith, "Dark Energy Crisis," *Natural History* 117, no. 10 (December 2008–January 2009): 30.

89. William Allen, *An American Biographical and Historical Dictionary* (Cambridge, MA: William Hilliard, 1809), 202.

Chapter Twelve

Phoenix

In 1759 Cadwallader Colden once again reminded his son Alexander that "by my age" he had "become unfit for action and retired." Yet in 1760 when the philosopher was even older, 72 years, his retirement suddenly ended, and he remained at or near the center of events for the rest of his life.[1]

July 30, 1760 dawned just like any other day for Lieutenant Governor James DeLancey. Soon after, though, he felt a pain in his chest and died of a heart attack. His long bout with asthma, which he may have had since childhood, could have damaged his heart. All those sessions of the Hungarian Club could not have helped either.[2]

With DeLancey's demise, Colden, as president of the Council, took command of the government. He had outlived the younger man after all. "I am under great concern least his Majesties Service may suffer by the loss of a person of Mr. DeLancey's abilities and experience in the present situation of affairs," Colden asserted in an official notice to London. (The war with France had not ended.) DeLancey's funeral would be unparalleled as the procession of mourners stretched out of sight.[3]

All the signs of mourning and respect given to the deceased politician did not obscure a basic reality—much had changed since DeLancey had become lieutenant governor. Colden explained the matter to Lord Halifax: "Lt. Governor DeLancey's Interest was on the Decline before he died." The colony of New York's economy was "flourishing," an astute tourist noticed in 1760, because of the huge outlays of money that flowed from the extensive presence of the British military. But, the visitor realized, New York, heavily in debt, was "burthened with taxes." DeLancey's taxes were truly a burden, and the Assembly refused to renew his unpopular stamp tax in 1760.[4]

The heavy taxes had not only destroyed the lieutenant governor's popularity but that of his family as well. When Oliver DeLancey had been appointed to the Council, he had delayed resigning from the Assembly to engineer a deal to have his brother's namesake eldest son take the seat. The maneuverings failed. When young James DeLancey ran for the Assembly in 1761, he was crushed, coming in dead last. "Thus was the Son of the man," a cynical observer pointed out, "who used to give law to this province and settled elections at a beer-house with his companions by sending out his minions" thoroughly defeated, "very mortifying" to the once-dominating family.[5]

New York's political scene had changed dramatically and Colden's political career had been restored from the ashes of defeat. All signs seemed positive. The Assembly acted graciously and, after a short time, Colden concluded that New Yorkers "will be as much united in their Zeal for his Majesties Service as ever they were in any time," but their zeal would be for a new monarch. Some time after DeLancey "made his exit to the world of spirits," George II died and had been succeeded by "our young patriot King," George III. To the New York legislature, Colden declared how lucky the British Empire was to be ruled by "a Sovereign, who considers the Love of his People, as the greatest and most permanent Security of his Throne." Despite Colden's heady optimism, the days of his being called "old Grey Head" and a despot would arrive soon. The new king, in time, would fare no better.[6]

Colden, of course, could not know what the future would bring, but he already knew that he had many expenses to bear. A certain type of lifestyle was expected of the head of the colony and even for a councilor. In 1750 he, distressed by the lack of funds coming in, commented to his wife that the purchase of a ring created a need for economy. Such economy would not have won any sympathy on the frontier, yet anyone who lived in the expensive city would have understood. To keep up appearances in the capital, families tended to splurge on a funeral and then to try to weasel out of paying the costs of the actual burial. Even John Tabor Kempe, the attorney-general, who had a salary of £150, official fees of £500, and a law practice worth about £500 (perhaps more) still felt he needed additional income. He was not alone.[7]

Alexander Colden did not fare as well as his father in such a spendthrift atmosphere. In 1756 he dissolved a partnership that profited from lucrative contracting with the British army "having a Number of Offices to attend." Entering the customs service while continuing mercantile activity presented an "impossible" conflict of interest. His appointment had come about because London knew who his father was. New York merchants, discovering that Coldens did not take bribes, tried to retaliate. One office seeker appears to have made an improper offer to Alexander to influence his father which the son dutifully reported. This customs job was in addition to his work as surveyor-general.[8]

The additional £60 Alexander gained working for the customs service was not enough; he needed more income. By 1753 he had taken over the post office in New York and moved it near his home. Dispensing with a clerk, he had a daughter help him instead. A visitor from South Carolina, Henry Laurens, was pleased with the "indulgent" postmaster after a meeting. Colden had "said every Thing affable and obliging that could be expected from a Gentleman and a good Officer." Mostly he dealt with complaints. A furious Governor Francis Bernard of Massachusetts fumed at him because a private business letter took almost two months to be delivered while an official document arrived after only sixteen days. The governor of Nova Scotia complained to Colden about the poor service given in Boston, and London protested that official letters for other colonies that went to New York's post office took too long to reach their destinations.[9]

Grumbles about slow mail are commonplace. What had to have concerned Alexander's father were reports of Alexander's job performance. At times, he appeared "unready" and even botched his accounts. Given his working at multiple jobs, Alexander Colden could have been too busy to properly attend to them all.[10]

All the work did not save Alexander from debt. If he had taken bribes, his finances would not have been so precarious. By 1765 he owed much money to his brother-in-law George Harison. Capable of making only a partial payment, Alexander's failure to square the debt forced Harison to obtain a loan from Cadwallader Colden. The problem ended only when Alexander's father, as he seems to have done with his extended family, sent him a large sum of money which he never repaid. However, Alexander did procure a country house on the shorefront of Long Island with a splendid view of the city and harbor. Such prime real estate, far beyond his means, had to have been secured mostly for prestige.[11]

After Cadwallader Colden finally became lieutenant governor, he would never be in bad economic straits again. That did not mean he did not fear it might happen anew. When he took over from DeLancey, it had caused Colden "so much expense" that if he did not stay in charge for a least a year, it would "be a prejudice to my private fortune than of advantage." In 1760 he informed Halifax that "The price of provisions and of all the necessaries of life has increased for several years . . . to three times the value they formerly were." That inflation had destroyed the value of the usual salary and fees an acting governor received. Therefore, the heavy expenses of both a governor and his family meant that they could not "live in any degree suitable to his Rank." Wealthy merchants in the city lived in an opulence for beyond the reach of a governor. A few years later, when the Council delayed approving the act for his salary, Colden, "with some emotion," asked the councilors: "Do you intend to distress me?"[12]

And Colden employed a story that Governor William Burnet told him in an attempt to obtain more of a governor's perquisites while he commanded the colony. During 1720, Colden recalled, Burnet stated that an imperial clerk, acting under no order, added the word "of" to the governor's instructions. In context that word cut the acting governor's share of perquisites to half the value instead of all of them. After a diligent search in London, however, no evidence could be found in the files that backed up Colden's memory. Colden's long campaign to give a New York lieutenant governor a salary, perhaps derived from the military budget, also came to naught.[13]

Colden did have some luck on the financial side. Soon after he commenced his administration of the province, Montreal fell, causing, at long last, the surrender of Canada. With New Yorkers finally safe from attack, a long pent-up demand for farm land on the frontier burst onto the scene. DeLancey, not known for his work ethic, had left a good number of land grants unsigned, which also benefited Colden. The fees from land grants enriched any governor and the sudden boom in settlement brought in a substantial sum.[14]

This manna from heaven enabled Colden to upgrade his living accommodations. As acting governor, he had to be closer to the capital than he was at Coldengham. He gave that property to Cad, who wanted it; Alexander no longer had any interest in farming. Their father, flush with cash, purchased 120 acres in Flushing from the Willett family and proceeded to build a dwelling on the land, Spring Hill. According to someone who lived in it well over a century later, "the building was of exceptionally strong construction. The floor contained heavy oak beams surrounded by cement and the woodwork was of mahogany." Unlike Coldengham, Spring Hill was a mansion, complete with "spacious" rooms "with high ceilings," suitable enough for the acting governor of New York. The family moved in on June 19, 1762 although Spring Hill was not completely finished until 1763. All told, Colden spent over £2,775 creating both the house and garden. Some additional land would be bought.[15]

By the time Spring Hill was finally complete, it would be a much lonelier place than Colden had imagined. Throughout his papers, there are numerous references to family illnesses, some minor, others far more serious. Each and every time, Colden had managed to pull his kin through safely. The only exceptions so far were two infants and his son John, who had moved far away. Eventually, a time came when Dr. Colden could not cheat death.

In August 1760 Colden's wife Alice, who had been in "much pain" for years, had been badly ill and he felt it best to move his entire family to the governor's house inside Fort George, still the main defense of New York City. Colden himself became sick of what he called "a dangerous illness"—a lung infection—in April 1761, so ill that a concerned General Jeffrey Amherst, now the commander-in-chief of British forces, believed that he was

Figure 12.1. Spring Hill. The front view of Colden's mansion as it appeared in the 1920s shortly before it was torn down. Photo by A. J. Wall. PR 020 (Geographic File) Queens. ID87250d. *Collection of the New-York Historical Society.*

"not out of danger." Although incapacitated for six weeks, Cadwallader Colden "perfectly recovered."[16]

Alice, however, was near her end. Her husband did not give any specifics about her illness but, from later family history and what her daughter Catherine caught, she suffered from a "Hectic" fever. This condition, closely connected to the deadly disease then called consumption, is now named tuberculosis. Mrs. Alice Colden died, "vastly beloved," within the fort on January 16, 1762, ending their fruitful marriage of 46 years. She was 72 years old. When Sir William Johnson learned the sad news, he tried to console his friend about the loss "of an Amiable Consort." Such a "great trial of human patience" fell upon "a Gentleman" who knew "the Accidents to which human nature is liable." That truth, along with "the certainty of the happiness" Alice, "as a good Christian must now enjoy," would "enable him to bear up" under such an "affliction."[17]

But more misfortune arrived. The very infectious tuberculosis struck at two more Colden ladies. Mrs. Alice Willett caught the disease, probably from visiting her mother, and died at the end of April or early May 1762. Her sister Catherine had become "dangerously ill" as she had been nursing her mother. "Naturally delicate and infirm," her father had probably warned her against the strenuous task of taking care of her mother. If so, she provided "assiduous care" anyway. Cathy lingered quite a while but finally succumbed on May 19.[18]

The "melancholy accidents" had a serious impact on Colden, so disturbed that he "could not fix my attention to any subject." He wrote to Johnson "that these repeated losses of those who were the dearest to me must be very hard to bear at my age," which Benjamin Franklin understood. He wrote to console his friend about "the grievous Breaches" in his family. "Loss of Friends and near and dear Relations, is one of the Taxes we pay for the Advantage of long Life, and a heavy Tax indeed it is!"[19]

Unhappy though Colden was, he had his duty to perform. Being acting governor was an important job and he could not neglect it. He mourned for his lost loved ones but he had to return to the affairs of New York. He learned that other governors welcomed his ascension though they regretted DeLancey's passing. The governor of Virginia declared that New York's "affairs" had come into the hands of "a Gentleman who has on many occasions shewn his ability to undertake them," while Pennsylvania's executive told Colden he was pleased that New Yorkers' new leader was "a Gentleman so able, and from long experience, so perfectly acquainted with their publick affairs ." South Carolina's lieutenant governor, William Bull, was especially happy to see Colden elevated; the two had met and been friends since Colden's return voyage from the West Indies so many decades before.[20]

After a few weeks in charge, Colden was upbeat. "I am still of opinion that my administration will be easy to me," he assured his wife who probably had doubts having seen New York politics up close for too long. By November 1760 his confidence about a peaceful administration remained strong. Even at the end of January 1761, Colden bubbled over with "pleasure." As he informed William Shirley, now the governor of the Bahamas, "everything in this Government since I took the administration upon me, has passed as much to my satisfaction as I could wish." Especially satisfying to him, the Assembly kept his salary the same as DeLancey's.[21]

Not surprisingly, Colden wanted even more. Having attained his old goal of running New York, Colden asked that he be kept in command for an extended period so he could recoup his expenses. He also requested the office of lieutenant governor, an obvious sign of the king's favor, as both "a reward to my past services" and to encourage others to champion the prerogatives of the Crown. Nor did Colden forget to lobby for his family. He recommended that his eldest, Alexander, be placed on the Council to fill DeLancey's old seat. Despite there being two members of the DeLancey extended family on the Council, Halifax rejected Alexander. One of Halifax's own kin, whose son had married a DeLancey relative, was pushing for a Council seat for him; his lordship thought it best that the new governor should make the decision. But Alexander did receive a commission as surveyor-general in his own name.[22]

According to Franklin, at least the prospects looked good for Colden staying in office for a good while. The government, pleased he had taken over the province, was not in a rush to supersede him. Colden obtained the same news from the influential John Pownall, the secretary of the Board of Trade and the brother of Thomas Pownall, a former governor of Massachusetts. Thomas Pownall, a friend of Colden's, now held considerable influence in London and had told him to keep in touch.[23]

Meanwhile, the New York Assembly, bereft of DeLancey's leadership, was still "unformed" and uncertain. Some of the assemblymen wanted to dismiss their agent, Robert Charles, a DeLancey holdover who was not very effective or liked. As Colden explained, some of the assemblymen thought John Pownall might be a good agent for them though some complained that his brother's running Massachusetts would be a conflict of interest. Because that was no longer the case, Colden asked the secretary, who would have been an influential agent for the colony, if he would be interested causing a historian to lambast Colden's "venal intrigue." It appeared that he was trying to swap that job for a commission as lieutenant governor. Such a tactic is not unusual; if anything it was standard practice. Both Pownalls knew, of course, that Colden had no power to pick the Assembly's agent or even an agent for the colony itself—all he could do was make a recommendation. This incident suggests that Colden was trying to be useful to his patrons—and he saw both Pownalls that way—just as he made similar remarks to anyone in Britain who helped him with some matter.[24]

John Pownall did not want the job but he recommended someone else, thinking that the agency was already vacant. Talking with Charles, he discovered that was not the case; Pownall then wrote Colden telling him he did not want Charles fired because of his recommendation. Armed with the news, Charles used it to inflame the Assembly against Colden's "great presumption," thus stopping Colden from talking to assemblymen about the agency. Pownall's candidate would not have gotten the position anyway because no one in New York had ever heard of him.[25]

These machinations had no impact on who would be the next lieutenant governor of New York. Colden seems fortunate that there was no other serious rival for the position. No New Yorker had any better claim than Colden did and no one tried to outbid him. No one in Britain of any importance wanted to be New York's lieutenant governor, which had no salary affixed to it. The incumbent could only earn income in the absence of a governor. Nor did anyone of importance seek the job for some ally. As early as January 1761 John Pownall was rather confident that Colden would triumph.[26]

Colden had, quickly, informed Peter Collinson of DeLancey's death and of his desire to succeed him. Being lieutenant governor would give him "more influence" to serve the king's interests. When Collinson wrote Halifax, he discovered that his lordship "was well pleased" that Colden had taken over for DeLancey. Halifax had not forgotten Colden's "experience, publick

Services and Integrity." The earl's only doubt centered on Colden's age; he wondered if Colden would be physically overwhelmed by the burdens a lieutenant governor had to face when in command of a province. However, Halifax had just gotten "a very Sensible and prudent Letter" from him "by which he appears to me Equally willing and capable of Undertaking the Trust." Whatever advice the Pownalls gave, Colden was later "convinced," as he declared to Halifax, "that by your Lordship's favor only I was appointed Lieutenant Governor of this Province." At long last, Cadwallader Colden received his reward for aiding George Clinton.[27]

On April 14, 1761, Colden's commission as lieutenant governor was formally approved and he received it on August 7. He saw the appointment as "a mark of his Majesties approbation of my past conduct in the administration." He held the commission for the rest of his life. Cadwallader Colden would be, by far, the oldest man ever to serve as a lieutenant governor or governor in the British colonies.[28]

Well before Colden received the commission, however, in May 1761 word had reached New York that a governor for the colony had been appointed. It was not Colden's dream candidate, Thomas Pownall, who wanted nothing to do with New York's "arduous" administration. A soldier, General Robert Monckton, would take over from Colden. Monckton, picked by William Pitt, gained the position because Johnson turned it down. The news that Colden would soon be out of power promptly lessened his influence. In June Collinson confirmed Monckton's appointment, adding that he knew nothing about the general. In July John Pownall sent his regrets that political changes in London had "accelerated" the naming of the new governor. Colden's influence with the Assembly had just about evaporated by January 1762.[29]

Lieutenant Governor Colden knew much more about Monckton than Collinson did. During the campaign against the French stronghold of Quebec, the future governor of New York had served as General James Wolfe's second in command. In 1759, during the decisive British victory on the Plains of Abraham, he was hit by "a musket ball in his lungs, which obliged him to quit the field." The wound was "dangerous," but he survived and in October of that year he was dispatched to New York City to recuperate. There Colden met him, learned about his noble connections and how popular Monckton was with his fellow army officers, who hoped he would become New York's governor.[30]

That ambition was fulfilled, but Monckton remains one of the most obscure governors the colony ever had. A colonial governor was expected to write numerous letters discussing affairs in the colony he was charged with. Perhaps no one explained that to him as the London files that are jammed with reports from other governors have nothing from him at all. Even Edmund O'Callaghan, the assiduous compiler of gubernatorial correspondence, printed only one letter from Monckton in his massive compilation. Apparently, Monckton's earlier appointment as lieutenant governor of Nova Scotia was mostly a patronage job.[31]

Monckton's conduct after he arrived in New York in late October 1761 to assume the governorship suggests that he had little understanding of civil administration. Although Monckton made his commission as governor public, he concealed the fact that he still lacked his instructions, which established the Council and listed its membership. If the governor left New York and the lieutenant governor died (recall that Colden was elderly by the standards of 1761), then the senior councilor could not take over, because, without Monckton's instructions, legally there was no eldest councilor or a Council. The governor, who had not mentioned the missing instructions to anyone, dismissed Colden's request for them by saying "that he had none, and hoped never to have any, that he might be at liberty to copy after the example of his royal master," a nonsensical remark which dismissed all precedent. The instructions arrived, finally, in January 1762.[32]

Moreover, Colden and others noticed that Monckton seemed under the influence of his secretary and military aide-de-camp, Major Horatio Gates. The loyalist historian Thomas Jones dismissed the future rebel Gates as "a man of mean capacity, trifling intellect, little understanding, and no learning." Yet Monckton did everything Gates advised. A "republican cabal," Jones related, had descended upon the new governor who "was coaxed, caroused, flattered, and entertained," not all that different from how James DeLancey had tricked Clinton. Colden must have preferred Gates over the man who soon replaced him in the governor's esteem.[33]

In a few days Colden learned that the lawyer William Smith Jr. had "insinuated himself" into Monckton's circle, and influenced the soldier to have "some disgust" of Colden. Monckton publicly attacked Colden for refusing to give New York's judges "commissions during good behaviour" which Colden had been instructed not to do. Giving a judge such a commission would soon be considered in London a firing offense for any governor.[34]

Smith had more in store for Colden. The lawyer provoked another dispute, inflaming Monckton over what he would gain from his salary if he left the province, not an unexpected development for a military man during a war. Monckton asked Colden to agree in writing to the division of salary and other income as specified in Governor Hardy's instructions. However, as Colden knew, the wording regarding such things sometimes changed from one set of instructions to the next. Besides, Colden could recall no case where a written agreement had been made in ignorance of the actual content of a governor's instructions. At a Council meeting Colden said that "I would yield obedience to the Instructions," whatever they said, when he knew what they said, and would be happy to have his declaration put into the minutes. Monckton, "in a violent passion," then "broke up the Council."[35]

Colden hoped that the new instructions—when at last read—might be more favorable to him than Hardy's—at least regarding the land grant fees. Because Monckton seemed determined to prevent that, Colden, seeking someone to broker a compromise, sought out a councilor on good terms with the governor, the merchant John Watts. He recommended that the two officials work out a written agreement on dividing the income. After Colden consented, he received "a paper in the handwriting of Smith the younger," deliberately insulting, that provided a huge financial penalty for Colden if he violated the agreement. Colden responded: "whatever the consequences be of my refusal, I will not sign that paper or any paper similar to it as it is a thing unworthy to be offered to any gentleman or to one in my Station." Quickly, Smith penned another paper even more insulting that required, not only a hefty bond of £2,000, but, "security that I should account upon oath." Watts, no friend of Colden's, insisted that the "security" was not needed —he himself would advance "double that sum" to the lieutenant governor—and "that the words upon oath could only serve to irritate" him, leading to the rejection of the paper. Even John Watts told Monckton that he would "advise" Colden not to sign it. The merchant's advice calmed the governor and the oath was deleted. Colden did sign a new agreement in which he promised to provide a more reasonable bond pegged to the amount of a half of the salary and fees if the new instructions reiterated the wording of Hardy's. This struggle, engineered by William Smith, Jr., finally ended.[36]

Why did Smith do all this? He sought to provoke Colden, to anger him, in an attempt to echo his fury at Smith over the missing law affecting the Evans Patent. Smith assumed that Monckton would then dismiss Colden as lieutenant governor, which a governor could do, or suspend him and let London fire him. Smith, not as clever as he thought he was, had misjudged his target. Colden would never had been disrespectful to a governor (as Lewis Morris Jr. had been to Governor Montgomerie so many years before). In this petty dispute, Colden acted with caution and restraint befitting his many years of political experience. In the future Smith lied to his diary that he had never sought "any Opportunity" to "Harm" Colden. This episode would be repeated by others—though Smith usually covered his tracks better.[37]

Monckton was bluffing when he told Smith that he would be happy "to suspend" Colden if he failed to sign an agreement. With no instructions and thus no Council, there was nobody else to succeed him. And Colden realized that if Monckton named another lieutenant governor, there was no certainty that a lieutenant governor, appointed solely by a governor, had the legal authority to take command of the province in the governor's absence. Any action taken by such an appointee would likely provoke many lawsuits and many complaints to London. Monckton must have come to understand that reality.[38]

The reason why Monckton willingly caused legal confusion by assuming his office without instructions became readily apparent on November 13, 1761. He announced to the Council that, by the king's order, he would command a British expedition to conquer the French island of Martinique in the Caribbean and had been given a leave of absence from his duties as New York's governor. Smith's assertion that Monckton knew nothing about that command beforehand is a blatant falsehood. A friend of the general's congratulated him on his new military command in September 1761 (and he probably was aware of it long before that). Amherst had received the formal order for Monckton on October 8, 1761, well before Monckton assumed the governorship. The only reason he ignored his lack of instructions was to secure one-half of the governor's income while also receiving his military salary at the same time. To Monckton, it was all about money.[39]

It had been a bizarre eighteen days for Cadwallader Colden. Monckton returned the official seals to him and he was acting governor once more by virtue of his commission. Colden wished the general success in his campaign against the French. Above all, Colden remained a militant patriot of the British Empire nor did he doubt Monckton's military abilities. In February 1762 this "glorious expedition" resulted in the surrender of Martinique. When the news reached London, Monckton's friends there rejoiced at the "Joyfull News."[40]

On June 12, 1762 Governor Monckton returned to New York; he had almost been captured by a French warship on the way. The two officials settled their financial matters. Colden paid off the final sum in September 1762, asking for his bond back (plus a receipt). He could not help but mention: "Your Excellency would have received the same benefits had no such bond been given." He could not resist writing that he was in his seventies "and this is the first bond I had ever given." When Monckton assumed his duties again, Colden journeyed back to Flushing to repose at Spring Hill. Once again, Colden believed he was retired.[41]

Monckton, however, was disgruntled at his situation as governor of New York. Whatever he thought his income would be—and he must have thought it would be splendid—he discovered he had been wrong. During the tug of war he had played with Colden, his lieutenant governor had bluntly informed him that the salary and most of the fees that went with the job "have not done more than defrayed the expenses of my family tho' conducted with all the saving economy I could." The fees from land grants, the only exception, could be "considerable." Likely, this explains why Thomas Jones insisted that Monckton became friendly with Colden despite Smith's influence; Colden's assessment of income coming to New York's governor proved to be true.[42]

General Monckton would explain to his eventual successor as governor "that the salary and common Fees would not pay my expenses" in New York.

And the general wanted to see greener pastures. On November 29, 1762, he wrote his brother: "I hope that things will so turn out that I shall not Remain in this part of the World much longer as I have had my share of it."[43]

Nor was Monckton healthy. His wound received at Quebec, portrayed as "not dangerous" at first, seems not to have healed. He informed his brother about it but apparently no one else outside his own household. Nonetheless, word leaked out and Colden received some accurate gossip as early as March 1763: "General Monckton for some time past has been indisposed and it is said that he intends to return to England for his health." The governor assumed that taking the waters at Bath in England would help his old wound.[44]

By April 1763 Monckton had received permission to leave his government and journey to England. Dispatching his family there immediately, he delayed his departure primarily to settle his affairs. However, he told no New Yorkers that he was seeking some better-paying position elsewhere. His confidant, William Smith, Jr., did not learn the governor was leaving until June. Watts, who would administer Monckton's estate in the colony, knew earlier but had to guess if he would ever come back.[45]

Monckton left New York on June 28, leaving his supporters distraught. Watts called him "much regretted and much wished for again." The sale of his left-behind furniture and other property did not diminish their hopes. Smith kept pining for Monckton's return, begging Gates for news: "Is that wound now promising?" By March 1764 Smith complained of "this long-long Silence" from the general. In contrast, Colden saw the sale as an opportunity and bought Monckton's chariot, a type of carriage. Only in 1765 did Smith learn that Monckton had received a good military posting in Britain.[46]

Smith's disappointment had been made worse because Monckton's sailing away from New York meant that Cadwallader Colden—still healthy despite his age— became acting governor for the third time, which he called unexpected. "The Old Man of course succeeds again as he seems to be immortal" Watts lamented. Months later he still had not recovered from the shock. "The Grey Headed Gentleman . . . is fortune's favourite in his old days."[47]

Although Monckton had been governor only briefly, the political roster had changed significantly. Archibald Kennedy had retired from the Council because of his age and died in 1763. Monckton had wanted to appoint William Smith, Jr. as chief justice but he declined because of his youth and his wish not to lose the substantial wealth generated from his law practice, over £1,000 a year. Instead, the disappointed governor felt he had no choice but to appoint, reluctantly, Daniel Horsmanden to the post, a result that must have disturbed Colden greatly. For that matter, by this time Colden avoided socializing with the Council members, most of whom had little desire to see him anyway. Another Monckton appointee to the court, Robert R. Livingston, would soon cause Colden much additional grief.[48]

The Council, in the 1760s, gave plenty of signs of being totally dysfunctional. Johnson, swamped with his duties with the Indians, almost never appeared. George Clarke's namesake son had been named to the Council decades before but had never showed up in New York. His name finally disappeared from the Council by January 1768. With such absences, the Council had trouble reaching a quorum.[49]

Colden did make recommendations to fill Council vacancies, which went nowhere. Once again he recommended his son Alexander as a suitable councilor because he was surveyor-general. As Colden knew, his son's candidacy "seems not agreeable." So he made another of a Scot who had replaced Kennedy as collector of the port, Andrew Elliot. Colden had an eye for talent. Elliot eventually replaced him as lieutenant governor, but in the 1760s Elliot would be passed over for the Council.[50]

Among the two who did join the Council was William Alexander, the son of Colden's old friend James Alexander. The son claimed to be the heir to a vacant title, the earl of Stirling. Lord Stirling, as he was usually called in America, proves that great abilities are not necessarily passed down from father to son (just like Colden's son Alexander). Another new councilor, Charles Ward Apthorpe, caused a small storm when his "Mandamus," giving him the office, sank in an unlucky mail packet. Apthorpe received a copy, certified by a clerk Colden had never heard of. The lieutenant governor, backed by Attorney-General Kempe, believed the document not good enough to accept. Stirling "warmly" disagreed and Apthorpe took Colden's refusal as an insult. Though such copies had been considered official elsewhere, London accepted Colden's objections and sent a new mandamus signed by the king.[51]

A grumpy Council made Colden's administration more difficult. Because of Monckton's escape from New York, Colden was in charge until near the end of 1765. The lieutenant governor correctly remarked to Halifax that "my administration of government was attended with unusual variety and multiplicity of business."[52]

First of all, Colden had to deal with "this expensive Conflict" with the French. Alexander Garden astutely wrote to his old friend that "it must . . . give great joy to your Own Heart to see that period of the reduction of Canada fall out under your Administration." Especially as he "had so long ago and so earnestly wished for" such a result for the welfare of the British Empire. "No Man had a Clearer Idea of the Danger attending the growing power of the French" than Colden, nor had anyone else "ever painted the consequences that must naturally have attended their encroachments, in more lively colours to the Ministry" than him.[53]

Indeed, no one had desired the fall of Canada more than Cadwallader Colden, but he had to struggle with New Yorkers and a political institution, the Assembly, that mostly had little or no interest in opposing the French. At first everything seemed easy for him. In September 1760 the lieutenant governor issued a proclamation urging New York merchants to raise foodstuffs both for the occupying army in Canada and the people there, who had suddenly come under the sway of George II. The journey there was not all that difficult for "adventurers" who would discover that "the whole Communication will be as safe and secure as any Road in the other Colonies." Despite the furor created by the impressments of sailors by British captains in New York harbor, in 1760 the Assembly passed every war measure that Colden had asked for. Patriotism —and profit— was still in vogue as demonstrated by the veritable host of privateers.[54]

Eventually, it did dawn on the Assembly that the immediate threat to New York from the French had disappeared. As Colden himself said when he addressed the colony's legislature, New York had been "Freed from the Calamities which so lately surrounded us."[55]

In 1761 the Assembly acted differently. When Amherst requested more troops, early in that year, the Assembly refused to authorize conscription in case enough volunteers did not step forward, believing that a draft was uncalled for in an unimportant mission. Though Colden continued to praise the assemblymen's loyalty, they grumbled that the army had been slow in paying for their provisions. In September 1761 the Assembly did agree to support the number of troops then asked for, but even Amherst admitted that these soldiers might not actually be needed.[56]

When, in April 1762, Amherst again asked for troops for a top-secret mission (which turned out to be an attack on Spanish Cuba), the Assembly became even less cooperative. Colden kept cajoling the assemblymen to act, but all they would do was provide an enlistment bounty far less than the previous year. Nor was conscription authorized. Colden explained to London that the New York Assembly was "strongly averse to Recruiting the Regulars" because everyone expected that British soldiers would now be based in America "in times of peace." Therefore, the Assembly feared it would set a "precedent" requiring them to fund recruitment of British Army soldiers after the war ended. The best Colden could say to London was that "this Province has done more in proportion than any other of the colonies."[57]

Albany, however, produced the most serious problems Colden had to confront. The British army had moved its headquarters to that town, much closer to Canada. Friction developed when a British officer was jailed over a civil property dispute. By the end of 1760 orders requiring the quartering of both soldiers and officers had riled the people of Albany. Quartering constituted a major difficulty for Albany, a small community. A visitor described it as "a dirty, ill-built Dutch town, of about 300 houses." Colden tried to interject himself between the military and angry civilians. He reminded General Amherst that "arbitrary quartering" was just as unpopular in Britain as in Albany and urged him to use his influence "to prevent any just complaint of this kind." If more incidents added to the civilians' hostile attitude, "it will be not in my power to put a stop to public clamor."[58]

Colden also made sure to stay on good terms with Amherst, who would be a powerful ally for him in Britain. When the position of Albany sheriff opened in 1761, Amherst pushed the candidacy of Harmanus Schuyler, an assistant alderman of Albany and a personal friend of Albany's quartermaster, Colonel John Bradstreet. Then General Monckton, not yet governor, visited Colden to add his support of Schuyler. With such strong backing from the military—and with the war still on—Colden felt he had no choice but to appoint Schuyler, upsetting both Johnson and the Albany assemblymen who had not backed him. Amherst appreciated Colden's gesture, believing that Schuyler as sheriff would "greatly conduce to the general benefit of the inhabitants . . . and the Troops who may be quartered here."[59]

Colden's concession to the military did not end the "constant" problems in Albany. If anything, they worsened in 1762 as the war wound down. In May farmers around Albany refused to surrender fifteen wagons, along with horses, despite a requisition order from the army. The horses, they explained, had had a rough winter, nor was there enough feed to supply them either. The farmers insisted that only if the Assembly specified that it be done would they agree. And "the troops in garrison here are not able to take them against their inclinations."[60]

Albany's mayor and one of its assemblymen visited Colden to alert him about "abuses" committed by soldiers unsupervised by officers. Hearing the officials' complaints, Colden had to observe to Amherst that "If what they told me be true, it is no wonder that the people are disgusted, and that the service meets with opposition." He warned Amherst it was best not to pursue the matter in the Assembly. "I am afraid," Colden cautioned, "that if the power of impressing come before the Assembly, I may receive a remonstrance on that head." Knowing how the New York Assembly worked, Colden knew it would turn the dispute from a political problem to a constitutional one, with potentially serious consequences.[61]

The crisis in Albany soon intensified anyway. At the end of May the magistrates refused to help officers requisition wagons they wanted and actually "do every thing in their power to hinder and obstruct it" by telling the farmers to ignore the demands—unsupported by any law passed by the Assembly. The mayor, attempting to intimidate the military, issued a warning that, as soon as troops returning from Canada left the area, he would "order the constables to take up and put into jail the first . . . troops that should impress horses or carriages." He also insisted that Colden had "misapprehended us"—they had never agreed, as Colden stated, that they would help get the items wanted if officers would only "apply" to them. (The lieutenant governor heard them correctly despite this new assertion.) Colonel Bradstreet, on the scene, bluntly asked if the mayor still intended to jail solders "that I may know how to govern myself with respect to it." However, the mayor wisely restrained himself from sending the angry quartermaster a written version of the threat.[62]

Colden must have breathed a sigh of relief when the French and Indian War finally ended in 1763. Peace with France, however, did not end the danger from Indians who had backed the French. In July 1763 official news of the peace treaty reached New York, but Colden had not given up his hope that hostile Indians be punished in some way. Former Indian attackers of New York, he believed, "will at all times be ready to plunder when not restrained by fear." That included the Senecas who had attacked Ulster. Johnson thought differently and his plan would be implemented.[63]

Yet the peace provided by the French treaty proved to be an illusion. In May 1763 Indian tribes to the west resumed fighting in a conflict called Pontiac's Rebellion. By July 1763 Colden was troubled: "what I hear of the Indians gives me great concern." Soon Johnson confirmed his fears, relating that the Senecas, joining the revolt, had captured a fort. Watts thought that an officer who had departed from Oswego had probably "lost the Skin off his head, among the mysterious and savage Race of Vermin." To Watts, the Indians were "ungrateful Vermin."[64]

"Timidity will certainly bring greater Mischiefs on the Frontiers," Colden assured a militia officer, adding that "Destruction will certainly fall on those cruel treacherous Barbarians, and proper measures are taken for that purpose." The lieutenant governor predicted to Cad, now a major in the Ulster militia, that this conflict would not last very long; if the people remained alert and watchful the Indians could do little. Cadwallader Colden had the New York militia in readiness to fend off attacks. "Much Depends on the Spirit and Firmness of the Militia," he emphasized to another Ulster officer, "who I hope will not be wanting in a cause in which their own Safety is immediately involved."[65]

The Assembly agreed to enlistment of more men to watch New York's frontiers and Colden promptly issued warrants to bring it about. A group of volunteers wanted to rush out to confront some hostile Indians reportedly on the New York-Pennsylvania border northeast of the Susquehanna River. These Indians had "done the most mischief" to the New York frontier. Though he suspected the expedition would not be successful, he granted his permission. Their ardor soon dimmed, but he had not thought it "proper" to oppose the effort. Although the "Rogues" on the Susquehanna had attacked Pennsylvania, this time no New Yorkers were killed. "Indians seldom attack those who are on their Guard," the pleased lieutenant governor would note.[66]

Amherst's successor, General Thomas Gage, also called upon Colden's expertise. Gage and Colden "frequently" talked about "Indian affairs, and I never fail to give him all the information I can" Colden reported to Halifax. There is no evidence that Amherst or Gage ever told the lieutenant governor about an attempt to spread smallpox among hostile Indians besieging Fort Pitt, something that would have shocked Colden despite his anger at the natives at this time.[67] What Colden did do was write to Halifax and the Board of Trade about his idea to punish the Seneca, a failed attempt to get around Johnson's opposition. Colden also made a point of reporting to London that, as far as he knew, Pontiac's Rebellion had not been caused by some "ill usage or any just reason of offence." Nor had it been provoked "by the Indians having been cheated of the Lands by the English" despite what British newspapers reported.[68]

Colden's expertise on the Indians seemed more valuable than ever to the Board of Trade. It consulted him on its plan to reform how the British dealt with them. He recommended that Indians have "an easy method of obtaining Justice" for their complaints. Knowing how highly they valued honesty, he urged the "absolute necessity of allowing Indian Evidence" in any court proceedings. Because Indian traders, as a group, were disreputable, the trade with distant Indians should be limited to specified outposts. Rum was too valuable and desired by the Indians to ban, yet their drinking it should not be allowed at trading posts—only at their homes. Furthermore, he advised the Board that New York's system regulating Indian land sales be extended to all the colonies. Later, he advised the British government to stop "setting one Indian nation against another" which pushed them to fight against their rivals. With less provocation, the Indians would calm down, devote themselves to peaceful activities, and "become most useful."[69]

While Colden made sensible recommendations for the postwar world, he had to deal with the aftereffects of the brutality of both the war and Pontiac's Rebellion. In December 1763 some of the "back Inhabitants" of Pennsylvania brutally killed Christian Indians who had lived in peace and had nothing to do with any attacks in either the war or the rebellion. The survivors, still in danger from the frontiersmen, wished to join Indians under the protection of Johnson in New York. On January 5, 1764, Governor John Penn of Pennsylvania wrote to Colden asking that the 140 survivors be allowed to enter New York to reach Johnson's domain.[70]

Colden had been given no warning about Pennsylvania's plan to transfer its problem to him. The refugees were waiting at Perth Amboy in New Jersey for permission to cross over to Staten Island; New Jersey had been untroubled by their transit through it. New York responded differently and the Indians' arrival became a major crisis requiring all of Colden's time.[71]

As soon as the lieutenant governor received Penn's letter, he summoned the Council to ask its advice. The five councilors who attended —including Horsmanden, Watts, Stirling and William Smith Sr.— were shocked that Penn did not consult with New York's government beforehand. Convinced that the Indians' passage through New York "can not but excite the greatest uneasiness at this time among the Inhabitants," the Council called the Indians' entrance "unadviseable." It would increase the population of hostile Indians "from whom" New Yorkers "have already suffered so much, that this Government are Rather disposed to attack and punish, than to Support and protect them, whom they still consider as their Enemy." The Indians whom the refugees wanted to live with were the same natives on the Susquehanna who had proven to be hostile to New York. No one dissented from advising Colden to keep them out of the colony. He issued the necessary orders to the authorities on Staten Island.[72]

Even Johnson urged caution. These refugee Indians were related to the Iroquois and attacks on them might spark a new war, a chilling prospect. Colden's answer to Penn is unusually hostile for him. The refugees would be going to an area where the natives had been targeted enemies not long before. Colden knew that the refugees needed an armed escort because "The minds of the people are so generally irritated" at the Indians there. Not stated by Colden was a scary possibility—that the New Yorkers guarding the refugees might kill them, creating another vicious massacre. Colden did offer Penn something: permission would be granted for two of the refugees, along with a chaperone, to enter New York and confer with Johnson. That was all Colden offered.[73]

Pennsylvania, however, did not give up. These Indians remained in danger there and Penn repeated his request, without consulting Colden, via Johnson. The Council again advised against having the refugees travel in New York, and were joined by both Gage and Colonel Henry Bouquet. Colden, annoyed, once again said no to his counterpart in Pennsylvania. Eventually, when that colony calmed, the refugees were dispatched by a different route, far from those who detested them.[74]

Meanwhile, London had, finally, tired of Indian complaints about land sales. In 1761 a new instruction was sent to Monckton banning any granting of Indian land without permission from London. Any governor who violated that order would be dismissed. Colden had already vowed that no Indians would "be deceived in any purchases of Lands made while I have the administration." When the royal ban arrived, Colden lost the power to grant such land. Ironically, the first and most prominent victim of the new policy would be Sir William Johnson, whom the Indians had given a huge gift of land. The Council refused to confirm Johnson's 40,000 acre present, the size of which violated established New York limits. The royal ban prevented Johnson from seeking redress in the courts.[75]

London had also received complaints that Colden and the New York Council had been enriching both themselves and their relatives by granting Indian land to themselves. On March 1, 1762, Colden responded to the "general accusation" by demanding that the Board of Trade's source "give any one Instance wherein I am interested in any Purchase from the Indians, or License to Purchase or in any Grant of Lands in any shape whatsoever."

Truly, there had been an unusually large number of grants during his time in charge—fifty-five (excluding military grants)—but all but thirteen were old grants originating before he ascended to command of the province. The old grantees had delayed their land acquisition because the war made new settlement too dangerous.[76]

As for the claim that his family had profited as well, Colden declared:

> I must observe to your Lordships that my children have been grown up to the State of Men and Women for some years past. Some of them have children of full age of Maturity. They are not under my direction, and I know no reason to debar them from any priviledge or benefit which his Majesty's other subjects in this Province have; but at the same time I declare that I do not know that any of them have been interested in the Purchase of Lands from the Indians since I have had the administration of government.[77]

Later, in 1764, Colden again defended himself from the charge of giving huge amounts of land to relatives. By then he had some thirty surviving children or grandchildren. Only three had received a grant from him, all in 1761. Goldsbrow Banyar, the colony's deputy secretary, and "Mr. Colden"—this must be Alexander—sought a land patent, but their request had originated in 1755. In 1761 Cad and David received a grant for some land in Ulster—specifically in the Evans Patent which had been bought from the Indians decades before—near both Coldengham and property owned by Kennedy. The lieutenant governor himself would write:

> I solemnly declare to your lordships that I am in no shape interested in any Purchase of Lands from the Indians, or in any License to Purchase, or in any Grant of Lands, in any share or part either great or small, or by any person in trust for me at any time since the administration of Government has been in my hands. Nor have I had so much as an inclination to be interested in any Purchase of the Indians, or Grants of Lands whatsoever.[78]

Colden's denial was about as specific as any denial could be. In 1762 he alerted Governor Monckton to what the Board of Trade had said and asked him to investigate. The allegations disappeared.[79]

Watts could not help being amused by London's indignation about prominent New Yorkers getting land grants. "They are so bountiful at Home that tho' our Governors were condemned for swallowing Gnats, they themselves swallow Camels, immense Orders [land grants] are duffused every where to wipe off all kinds of Scores."[80]

The sudden generosity of the British government began with General Amherst. During the war, after Crown Point had been seized, he began to strengthen it. Colden suspected that the General planned to have the area split off from New York and formed into a new colony, populated by retired soldiers, to be a bulwark against French Canada. With the cession of Canada, the circumstances had changed and Amherst received a huge grant in New York as vaguely worded as the patents of the Hudson manors. He also secured a grant, just as vague, for Major Philip Skene, a favorite of Amherst's with a distinguished record in the war.[81]

London had assumed from the maps of New York it had—including Colden's—that the northern reaches of the colony were totally unsettled, which was no longer the case in the 1760s. Other New York grants had recently been given. Skene's grant was especially troubling: New York's Council had voted to give him 25,000 acres; then came a decree from London that limited grants to 20,000. Skene, however, expected the full 25,000 acres which New York now could not give him. To make matters worse, part of his claim had already been promised to artillery officers. Though Skene had somewhat improved the land at Wood Creek, Colden believed the improvements Skene had done there could not possibly have cost as much as he claimed. Colden, politely, requested that Skene provide "a more particular description" of his improved land and its "exact distance and bearing from Fort Edward" so it would not be mistakenly given to someone else.[82]

The line of people favored by London to gain huge tracts of land included Lieutenant Donald Campbell, the son of Laughlin Campbell—the heroic victim of William Smith, Jr.'s history. The king had signed an order granting him 30,000 acres. The order was sent not to Colden, but to Lieutenant Campbell's agent, William Smith, Jr. Colden realized that this grant came about because of Smith's sympathetic account of Campbell's father in his book.[83]

Colden tried to explain to his London superiors that young Campbell had just been given 10,000 acres for himself and his siblings and was due another chunk of land for his military service. In addition, Colden related that before Campbell left the colony,

> I had granted 47,500 acres more to the Persons whom his Father had deluded from Scotland into this Province and to their children: and I never granted any land with more pleasure than this: for the Grant to these People when they arrived was obstructed by the fraudulent views and practices of the Father in respect to these People.[84]

Nonetheless, Campbell still wanted more—the whole 100,000 acres that his father had sought years before. London never gave in on that, so Campbell had to be satisfied with what he received. However, most of the land obtained was rather "rugged" which made road building difficult, lessening the land's value. Most of the grantees sold their shares quickly, suggesting that this whole affair had been a large speculative gambit from the start.[85]

In 1764 Colden received another surprise when a new immigrant couple met with him. William O'Brien, an actor described in Britain as both handsome and poor, had married Lady Susan Fox Strangways, the daughter of a noble and related to a powerful politician. The incongruous match rocked the imperial capital, so the young pair journeyed to New York to dwell in the wilderness among the Indians. Mrs. O'Brien's highly placed connections secured a royal grant of 60,000 acres. Colden had to be astonished when he discovered that the actor insisted upon the land being on the Mohawk River and that the territory in question had been given to Johnson. Warning Johnson to be on his guard, Colden assured him that he would do everything he could to help him but "It will remain with you to support your own Interest without delay, because I expect some peremptory orders if you do not prevent it." Rumors surged in New York that London would overturn "one or more great patents." Who knows how many New York estates might someday have been wiped out to deal with inconvenient marriages among the high and mighty in Britain. Luckily for Johnson, the O'Briens discovered that life on the frontier was not as romantic as it had seemed across the Atlantic; Johnson's property was safe.[86]

Many others had a claim to land. On October 7, 1763 the king proclaimed that all retired officers and soldiers who had served in America were entitled to a land grant, ranging from 5,000 acres for high ranking officers to 50 acres for a common soldier. This set off a rush by all those eligible to find suitable land. According to Colden, "Almost all the reduced officers and disbanded soldiers in North America have applied to me for the Kings bounty in Lands." New York saw retired officers wander about "like Noah's Dove not able to find a Spot on which to rest." Still, a young ensign with little time in the army, James Howetson, found a place to settle on the Hudson across from the vast estates of the Livingston and Van Rensselaer families. Although some officers quickly sold the land they had received for very little, others of the "great number" of grantees stayed to live in New York.[87]

Despite all the chaos stirred up by these new grants, Colden knew that the great landlords remained as entrenched as ever and wanted still another *Partition Act* to distribute their property within their families. In 1762 Colden tried to explain why he signed the new act—not doing so "would lay me under a load too heavy for me to bear alone." As a further excuse, he explained that he rushed the law to London for the king's perusal; various delays written into it would prevent any action under the law before news of a disallowal arrived. He then argued for a royal veto of the controversial law. The Privy Council was not happy with him and the law was quickly nullified. Colden was reprimanded for signing a bill lacking a clause suspending the act until the king approved it. The lieutenant governor's behavior was "the more exceptionable as so many laws of this kind have been repealed; and some of them upon representations of your own while acting in another station." Colden had now used the same trick Burnet had employed in 1726 to avoid hostility in the province—signing a bill he knew London would reject—which had so upset the younger Colden. The breathing room Colden had gained would not last long. In 1763 the Assembly lowered his salary by £200.[88]

New York's merchants were another entrenched interest that Colden had to confront. Regarding commerce, Colden had no difficulty trying to expand it. As early as 1738, he had pushed for the production of hemp in New York, but it never took hold in the colony. Another product he recommended, potash, did better. In 1761, responding to an inquiry from a British improvement society, he suggested that expert Russian producers of potash be encouraged to emigrate to America. Domestic producers did well enough. By the 1770s potash became a significant export.[89]

Colden would also be an advocate of inter-colonial trade in the Western Hemisphere. Already, New York traders had been obtaining valuable woods from the Mosquito Coast in Spanish Central America. New York merchants saw that trade as perfectly acceptable—British goods entered a new market. Surely, Colden thought, British colonists could trade with Spanish possessions as the Britons did. He wrote directly to the Spanish viceroy in Mexico protesting the treatment of a New York trader, an unprecedented move. In fact, Colden had "outlined the first program for hemispheric trade." Parliament did not go as far as the lieutenant governor had hoped.[90]

Some merchants, though, went way too far. During the war, the British government insisted upon a crackdown on illegal trade with the French enemy in the Caribbean. Such clandestine trade had been going on for years. In 1756 Alexander Colden had ended his mercantile relations with his partner who indulged "very much into an Illicit Trade for which he will some day or other Smart." When, in 1759, an informer notified Lieutenant Governor DeLancey about illegal trade, the man's identity leaked out and it took the intervention of both DeLancey and the city magistrates to save him from a mob that seemed ready to kill him.[91]

Cadwallader Colden was specifically ordered to investigate the "dangerous and ignominious Trade" and discover what tricks the smugglers used to get around the law. That smuggling existed in New York was no surprise to him, but he had been retired in the countryside so long he had no idea about the latest scams. From what he discovered, the smugglers' chief accomplices were in New Jersey and southern New England where New York smugglers brought in a huge cargo of food and received documentation giving the cargo an air of legality; bonds given in New York to ensure obedience to the law were thus voided. Then, the goods were easily dispatched to enemy territory for valuable sugar. The best way to deal with smugglers, Colden suggested later, was for naval vessels to hover around eastern Long Island and the Jersey shore to seize the vessels engaged in such activities. On land, however, Colden warned his superiors "that it is difficult to prosecute with success against the bent of the people," who thought that the English sugar islands had twisted the trade laws to their own advantage. There was also an illegal tea trade with Holland he informed London.[92]

The enforcement suggestions put a dent in smuggling but did not destroy it. When the war ended, London had to deal with the huge debt generated by the vast military machine that had defeated Britain's enemies. And this debt was truly massive. The interest on it alone was so large that it totaled well more than half of the yearly governmental budget. Having great incentive to find more revenue, George Grenville, in charge of the British treasury, sought a new law, the *Sugar Act*, to bring in more cash and clamp down harder on smugglers.[93]

News of what was transpiring in the imperial capital reached America, causing great concern. The huge influx of British money had created prosperity in the colonies. With the war over, so was the gushing military funding. The considerable sums had created a huge economic bubble that colonial economies could not sustain by themselves. Beginning in 1763 the American colonies plummeted into a severe depression that lasted for years. The proposed *Sugar Act* would disrupt trade, only making the economy worse, which Colden realized. Backing a petition sent by New York merchants, in 1764 he suggested to his superiors that a colony such as New York that sent "no staple" like desired sugar across the Atlantic was still very useful to the mother country. New York, "consisting of great numbers of free men," consumed "a vast quantity of the manufactures of Great Britain." In contrast, the English sugar colonies produced a product "entirely raised by the Hands of Slaves who consume very little or none of the Manufactures of Great Britain." If New Yorkers were impoverished and "be reduced so low that they cannot purchase clothing, they must make them and be content with what they can make."[94]

The British government did not listen to Colden's opposition to the *Sugar Act*. New Yorkers began wishing that the French had retained Canada—at least in such circumstances New York had been treated as if it was important to the Empire. Then the New York Assembly jumped in and its heated rhetoric provoked the lieutenant governor.[95]

New York's Assembly produced an address to Colden which, despite his own opposition to the *Sugar Act*, he called "undutiful and indecent." The assemblymen, "Depressed with the prospect of inevitable Ruin by the Alarming Informations we have from Home," had learned that Parliament believed it could tax Americans. The Assembly declared: "Such must be the deplorable State of that wretched people, who, (being taxed by a Power subordinate to none, and in a great measure unacquainted with their circumstances) can call nothing their Own."[96]

Before the address was formally given, Colden learned about its "tenor" and tried to convince the assemblymen to tone down their complaints. He failed. Colden, before responding to the address, stated he needed the Council's advice. The Assembly's statement even disturbed Watts. The councilors all agreed that dissolving the Assembly would do no good because the address had already been published. A dissolution would only make matters worse, and royal officials had not yet been granted their pay. The "old Gentleman," therefore, was advised "to give as soft an Answer" as possible.[97]

Colden tried his best to do that in a short response. He told the Assembly that some of their comments should not have been addressed to him. "When We consider the Blood and Treasure our Mother Country has poured forth in our defence," which, almost certainly, preserved New York, "it should make us desirious to contribute everything in our power, for her Ease and Benefit." Dutiful subjects should give "our Sentiments in every instance with gratitude and filial Submission."[98]

The lieutenant governor meant what he said. When he learned during June 1764 that the *Sugar Act* had been approved, Colden wrote that he "gave my sentiments freely, now I am to obey." He thought of at least one positive thing the *Sugar Act* would produce. New Yorkers now had to suspend "the growing luxury of this Colony." Expenses had to be cut and British goods could not be bought, "but whether this will be for the advantage of our mother Country, I am not the proper judge."[99]

Colden made sure to alert his superiors that he had no role in the Assembly's address in which the assemblymen had declared their opposition "to their being Tax'd by a British Parliament." He blamed this "disrespectful" address on the influence of the great landlords in the Assembly in which three of the manors had their own representatives. Such "Men of the greatest Opulence" had been informed that Parliament planned to hit them with a land tax, explaining their excessive zeal. Along with the landed interest, the Assembly also consisted of "the Merchants of New York, the principal of them strongly connected with the Owners of these great Tracts, by family Interest, and of Common Farmers, which last are Men easily deluded and led away with popular Arguments of Liberty and Privilege."[100]

Now that "The old man and his Assembly [were] jarring," Colden had alienated two of the most entrenched interests in New York, the manor lords and the merchants. At least, at the end of 1764, London was pleased with his "Diligence and Exactness in obeying His Majesty's Orders." When the Privy Council saw what the assemblies of Massachusetts and New York had done, it insisted that these bodies had demonstrated "the most indecent disrespect to the Legislature of Great Britain," echoing Colden. And the lieutenant governor had made another group happy—comedians.[101]

In January 1762 Colden gave special permission for a "company of Comedians" to perform a play plus "a Pantomine Entertainment in Grotesque Characters." His intervention thwarted any attempt by the mayor of New York to repeat his effort to ban such performances within the city. Colden had interceded to help actors earlier in his administration too.[102]

So actors were in Colden's debt. Unfortunately, there were not many actors in New York and no one cared what they thought anyway. More important was an on-going battle Colden had with a powerful entrenched interest—New York's lawyers. The lawyers seemed on the verge of retiring Colden—this time permanently.

NOTES

1. CC to AC, June 15, 1759, CC, "The Colden Letters on Smith's History," New York Historical Society, *Collections* 1 (1868): 181.

2. DeLancey to GC, August 30, 1746, George Clinton Papers, vol. 4, CL; JA to CC, May 7, 1751, *CP*, vol. 4, 265; circular letter to the several governors, August 4, 1760, *CLB*, vol. 1, 1–2; CC to William Pitt, August 7, 1760, *CLB*, vol. 1, 3–4; Stanley McCrory Pargellis, *Lord Loudoun in North America* (New Haven, CT: Yale University Press, 1933), 167; *DH*, vol. 4, 1054–56. I wish to thank Dr. Sunil Mehra for his information regarding asthma.

3. CC to Pitt, August 7, 1760, *CLB*, vol. 1, 3–4; Thomas M. Truxes, *Defying Empire: Trading with the Enemy in Colonial New York* (New Haven, CT: Yale University Press, 2008), 111.

4. CC to Halifax, November 11, 1760, *CLB*, vol. 1, 34–36; Andrew Burnaby, *Travels Through the Middle Settlements in North America in the Years 1759 and 1760 With Observations upon the State of the Colonies* (London: T. Payne, 1775; repr. New York: Kelley, 1970), 118–19; Klein, "Tyros," 218; Thompson, "Stamp Acts," 257.

5. CC to Halifax, November 11, 1760, *CLB*, vol. 1, 34–36; "Watchman," no. 2, February 17, 1770, *New York Journal* (Holt), April 12, 1770.

6. CC to Commissioners for Trade and Plantation, August 7, 1760, *CLB*, vol. 1, 5–6; CC to Halifax, August 11, 1760, *CLB*, vol. 1, 9–11; CC to Whytt, September 3, 1763, *CP*, vol. 6, 272–74; John Watts to James Napier, December 14, 1764, in Watts, *Letter Book of John Watts, Merchant and Councillor of New York, January 1, 1762–December 22, 1765*, New York Historical Society, *Collections* 61 (1928): 317–19; "Watchman," no. 3, March 10, 1770, *New York Journal* (Holt), April 19, 1770; New York Colony, Council, *Journal of the Legislative Council of the Colony of New York, Began the 9th day of April, 1691; and ended the [3d of April, 1775]* (Albany, NY: Weed, Parsons, 1861), vol. 2, 1426; Milton M. Klein, *The American Whig: William Livingston of New York* (New York: Garland, 1990*)*, 384–85.

7. CC to Mrs. CC, September 25, 1750, *CP*, vol. 9, 77–78; CC to Halifax, *CLB*, vol. 1, 398–99; Memorial of John Tabor Kempe to Robert Monckton, July 22, 1763, *Aspinwall Papers*, Massachusetts Historical Society, *Coll.*, 4th ser., 9–10 (1871): 480–82; William Livingston and others, *The Independent Reflector or Weekly Essays on Sundry Important Subjects More particularly adapted to the Province of New-York*, ed. Milton M. Klein (Cambridge, MA: Harvard University Press, 1963), June 14, 1753, 259–60; Catherine S. Crary, "The American Dream: John Tabor Kempe's Rise from Poverty to Riches," *William and Mary Quarterly*, 3rd ser., 14 (1957): 176–77, 179–82, 184, 186–87; Milton M. Klein, "The Rise of the New York Bar: The Legal Career of William Livingston," *William and Mary Quarterly*, 3rd ser., 15, no. 3 (1958): 355.

8. AC to Harison, March 21, August 12, 1756, Richard Harison Papers, box 2, NYHS; William Kelly to Johnson, May 2, 1756, *JP*, vol. 2, 463; CC to Johnson, January 12, 1765, *JP*, vol. 9, 528–29; AC to CC, May 8, 1756, Bancroft Coll., Colden Papers, vol. 2, 58, NYPL; AC to CC, May 8, 1756, *CP*, vol. 5, 71–74; Alexander C. Flick, *History of the State of New York* (New York: Columbia University Press, 1933–1937), vol. 2, 355.

9. Francis Bernard to AC, February 28, 1763, Francis Bernard Papers (Sparks Manuscripts), MS4, Houghton Library, Harvard University, Cambridge, MA; Henry Laurens to William Fisher, September 5, 1771, in Henry Laurens, *The Papers of Henry Laurens, August 1, 1769–October 9, 1771*, ed. George C. Rogers, Jr. and David R. Chesnutt (Columbia, SC: University of South Carolina Press, 1979), vol. 7, 561; BF to Deborah Franklin, May 27, 1757,

FP, vol. 7, 217–18; Montagu Wilmot to AC, November 10, 1764, *CP*, vol. 6, 377–78; Edward Sedgwick to CC, July 14, 1764, *CP*, vol. 6, 332–33; Esther Singleton, *Social New York under the Georges, 1714–1776* (New York: D. Appleton, 1902), 38; Thomas C. Barrow, *Trade and Empire: The British Customs Service in Colonial America, 1660–1775* (Cambridge, MA: Harvard University Press, 1967), 264.

10. BF to William Franklin, October 14, 1754, *FP*, vol. 5, 438; BF to John Foxcroft, December 2, 1772, *FP*, vol. 19, 414–15.

11. AC to Harison, March 19, August 13, 1765, Richard Harison Papers, box 2, NYHS; Harison to AC, March 9, July 7, 1767, Richard Harison Papers, box 2, NYHS; Elizabeth DeLancey to Oliver DeLancey, November 6, 1773, DeLancey Papers, Museum of the City of New York; CC to Collinson, [October 1755?], *CP*, vol. 5, 38–39; "To be Let, or Leased," *New York Gazetteer* (Rivington), February 23, 1775; "Will of Lieutenant Governor Colden," in Edwin R. Purple, "Notes, Biographical and Genealogical, of the Colden Family, and of Some of Its Collateral Branches in America," *New York Genealogical and Biographical Record* 4 (1873): 169; Singleton, *Social New York*, 55.

12. CC to Collinson, October 27, 1760, *CLB*, vol. 1, 28–30; CC to Halifax, August 11, 1760, *CLB*, vol. 1, 9–11; Council to Monckton, June 26, 1763, *Aspinwall Papers*, vol. 9, 476–77.

13. CC to Pitt, November 23, 1761, *CLB*, vol. 1, 133–35; CC to Board of Trade, May 11, 1762, *CLB*, vol. 1, 203–4; CC to Jeffrey Amherst, April 13, 1764, *CLB*, vol. 1, 320.

14. Beverly McAnear, *The Income of the Colonial Governors of British North America* (New York: Pageant Press, 1967), 19; Irving Mark, *Agrarian Conflicts in Colonial New York, 1711–1775* (New York: Columbia University Press, 1940), 43; *DH*, vol. 4, 1059.

15. "An Account of Money laid out by me," CPU, reel 2; Peter Wilson Coldham, *American Loyalist Claims Abstracted from the Public Record Office*, ed. Sally Lou Mick Haight *(Washington, DC: National Genealogical Society, 1980)*, vol. 1, 95; Saul Jarcho, "Biographical and Bibliographical Notes on Cadwallader Colden," *Bulletin of the History of Medicine* 32, no. 4 (1958): 329; James A. Wall, "Cadwallader Colden and His Homestead at Spring Hill, Flushing, Long Island," *New York Historical Society Quarterly* 8, no. 1 (1924): 11–12, 17; Eugene R. Fingerhut, *Survivor: Cadwallader Colden II in Revolutionary America* (Washington, DC: University Press of America, 1983), 23.

16. CC to Amherst, August 11, 1760, *CLB*, vol. 1, 7; CC to Henry Moore, June 23, 1761, *CLB*, vol. 1, 93; CC to John Pownall, August 12, 14, 1761, *CLB*, vol. 1, 107–8, 111; David Colden to CC, March 2, 1758, *CP*, vol. 5, 220; Amherst to CC, September 9, 1760, *CP*, vol. 5, 338–39; Amherst to Monckton, April 9, 1761, *The Northcliffe Collection: Presented to the Government of Canada by Sir Leicester Harmsworth, Bt.* (Ottawa: F. A. Acland, 1926), 118.

17. *New York Mercury* (Gaine), January 18, 1762; C. Colden to _____, April 27, 1796, Samuel W. Eager, *An Outline History of Orange County* (Newburgh, NY: S. T. Callahan, 1846–1847*)*, 246; CC to Johnson, May 3, 1762, *CLB*, vol. 1, 198; Johnson to CC, January 30, 1762, *JP*, vol. 10, 371–72. All of David Colden's daughters died of consumption, suggesting that the Colden women had a genetic weakness to tuberculosis. Wadsworth, "A Sketch," 7–8, Gordon Ford Coll., NYPL; Timothy Alden, *A Collection of American Epitaphs and Inscriptions with Occasional Notes* (New York: [S. Marks, Printer], 1814), vol. 5, 268–75; *Oxford English Dictionary*, s.v. "hectic."

18. CC to Johnson, May 3, 1762, *JP*, vol. 10, 441–42; *New York Mercury* (Gaine), May 24, 1762; *American Chronicle* (Farley), May 24, 1762.

19. Samuel Bard to CC, July 8, 1764, *CP*, vol. 6, 322–23; CC to W. Popple, September 2, 1762, *CP*, vol. 6, 193–97; CC to Johnson, June 6, 1762, *JP*, vol. 10, 467–68; BF to CC, February 26, 1763, *FP*, vol. 10, 202.

20. James Hamilton to CC, August 10, 1760, *CP*, vol. 5, 328; Fauquier to CC, August 31, 1760, *CP*, vol. 5, 333; William Bull to CC, June 6, 1761, *CP*, vol. 6, 36–37; CC to Bull, November 29, 1760, *CLB*, vol. 1, 42.

21. CC to Mrs. CC, August 17, 1760, *CP*, vol. 9, 180–81; CC to Johnson, November 3, 1760, *JP*, vol. 10, 192–93; CC to Shirley, January 20, 1761, *CLB*, vol. 1, 59; CC to Board of Trade, November 11, 1760, *CLB*, vol. 1, 33–34.

22. CC to Board of Trade, November 11, 1760, *CLB*, vol. 1, 33–34; CC to Collinson, January 10, 1761, *CLB*, vol. 1, 56; Halifax to Collinson, October 12, 1760, *CP*, vol. 5, 346–47,

New York Colony, *Calendar of New York Colonial Commissions, 1680–1770*, comp. E. B. O'Callaghan (New York: New York Historical Society, 1929), 58.

23. BF to CC, December 5, 1760, *FP*, vol. 9, 252–53; John Pownall to CC, January 10, [1761], *CP*, vol. 5, 307–8; CC to J. Pownall, August 22, 1760, *CLB*, vol. 1, 13–14; Fintan O'Toole, *White Savage: William Johnson and the Invention of America* (New York: Farrar, Straus, and Giroux, 2005), 220; Oliver Morton Dickerson, *American Colonial Government, 1696–1765: A Study of the British Board of Trade in Its Relation to the American Colonies, Political, Industrial, Administrative* (Cleveland, OH: A. H. Clark, 1912), 77–78; John A. Schutz, *Thomas Pownall, British Defender of American Liberty: A Study of Anglo-American Relations in the Eighteenth Century* (Glendale, CA: Arthur H. Clark, 1951), 20.

24. CC to J. Pownall, November 11, 1760, April 5, August 12, 1761, *CLB*, vol. 1, 38, 80–82, 107–8; Richard M. Ketchum, *Divided Loyalties: How the American Revolution Came to New York* (New York: Henry Holt, 2002), 102; Nicholas Varga, "Robert Charles: New York Agent, 1748–1770," *William and Mary Quarterly*, 3rd ser., 18 (1961): 230–31; Franklin B. Wickwire, "John Pownall and British Colonial Policy," *William and Mary Quarterly*, 3rd ser., 20 (1963): 545.

25. J. Pownall to CC, January 10, [1761], October 9, 1761, *CP*, vol. 5, 307–8, vol. 6, 83; CC to J. Pownall, April 5, August 12, 1761, *CLB*, vol. 1, 80–82, 107–8; Committee of Assembly to Charles, 1761, W. Smith, Jr., *History*, vol. 2, 268–269n.

26. J. Pownall to CC, January 10, [1761], *CP*, vol. 5, 307–8.

27. CC to Collinson, October 27, 1760, *CLB*, vol. 1, 28–30; Halifax to Collinson, October 12, 1760, *CP*, vol. 5, 346–47; CC to Halifax, March 27, 1763, Bancroft Coll., Colden Papers, vol. 2, 192, NYPL.

28. CC to Pitt, August 11, 1761, *CLB*, vol. 1, 103–5; New York Colony, *Calendar of New York Colonial Commissions, 1680–1770*, 34; CC's commission, April 14, 1761, *CP*, vol. 6, 26–27; Leonard Woods Labaree, "The Early Careers of the Royal Governors," in *Essays in Colonial History Presented to Charles McLean Andrews by his Students*, ed. Labaree (New Haven, CT: Yale University Press, 1931), 150.

29. CC to J. Pownall, May 16, 1761, *CLB*, vol. 1, 85; Collinson to CC, June 12, 1761, *CP*, vol. 6, 40; J. Pownall to CC, July 22, 1761, *CP*, vol. 6, 57–58; T. Pownall to CC, November 1, 1760, *CP*, vol. 5, 370–71; Richard Shuckburgh to Johnson, January 21, 1762, *JP*, vol. 3, 611; O'Toole, *White Savage*, 220.

30. James Murray to Monckton, January 28, 1761, Monckton Papers, University of Nottingham, UK; *Gentleman's Magazine* 52 (July 1782), 357; John Knox, *An Historical Journal of the Campaigns in North America, For the Years 1757, 1758, 1759, and 1760*, ed. Arthur G. Doughty (Toronto: Champlain Society, 1914–1916), vol. 1, 163–64; vol. 2, 243, 597; vol. 3, 78; *Oxford DNB*, s.v. Monckton, Robert.

31. Knox, *Historical Journal of the Campaigns*, vol. 1, 163–64.

32. CC to Pitt, November 22, 1761, *CLB*, vol. 1, 132–33; W. Smith, Jr., *History*, vol. 2, 258–59; Amherst to Monckton, January 26, 1762, *Monckton Papers*, University of Nottingham Department of Manuscripts, [Nottingham, UK, 1986], 18.

33. Thomas Jones, *History of New York during the Revolutionary War*, ed. Edward Floyd De Lancey (New York: New York Historical Society, 1879; repr. Cranbury, NJ: Scholar's Bookshelf, 2006), vol. 1, 225.

34. CC to J. Pownall, November 26, 1761, *CLB*, vol. 1, 137–41; CC to Board of Trade, April 7, 1762, *CLB*, vol. 1, 186–91.

35. CC to J. Pownall, November 26, 1761, *CLB*, vol. 1, 137–41; CC to Monckton, November 11, 12, 1761, *CLB*, vol. 1, 128–30; Monckton to CC, November 11, 1761, *CP*, vol. 6, 88–89.

36. CC to J. Pownall, November 26, 1761, *CLB*, vol. 1, 137–41; Monckton to Smith, c. November 15, [1761], W. Smith, Jr., *History*, vol. 2, 261; L. F. S. Upton, *The Loyal Whig: William Smith of New York and Quebec* (Toronto: University of Toronto Press, 1969), 46. On Watts see *Appletons' Cyclopaedia of American Biography*, ed. James Grant Wilson and John Fiske (New York: D. Appleton, 1894–1900), s.v. Watts, John.

37. *SM*, vol. 2, 32.

38. W. Smith, Jr., *History*, vol. 2, 259–60; CC to J. Pownall, November 26, 1761, *CLB*, vol. 1, 137–41.

39. CC to Pitt, November 22, 1761, *CLB*, vol. 1, 132–33; James Douglas to Monckton, September 20, 1761, *Monckton Papers*, University of Nottingham, Manuscript Department, 15; Amherst to Rollo, October 8, 1761, *Northcliffe Collection* (1926), 311; W. Smith, Jr., *History*, vol. 2, 258–59.

40. Jeffrey Amherst, *The Journal of Jeffrey Amherst Recording the Military Career of General Amherst in America from 1758 to 1763*, ed. J. Clarence Webster (Toronto: Ryerson Press, 1931), 280; CC to Pitt, November 22, 1761, *CLB*, vol. 1, 132–33; CC to Monckton, January 1, 1762, *CLB*, vol. 1, 144–45; James Hamilton to Monckton, July 1, 1762, *Monckton Papers*, University of Nottingham, Manuscript Department, 21; Horatio Gates to Monckton, April 3, 1762, Monckton Papers, University of Nottingham.

41. CC to Monckton, September 20, 1762, New York Colony, Miscellany Coll. Governor, box 1 A-C, NYPL; Amherst, *Journal*, 284; CC to Whytt, September 3, 1763, *CP*, vol. 6, 272–74.

42. CC to Monckton, November 12, 1761, *CLB*, vol. 1, 129–30; Jones, *History*, vol. 1, 225.

43. Sir Henry Moore to Earl of Shelburne, April 25, 1767, *NYCD*, vol. 7, 922; Monckton to Jack Monckton, November 29, 1762, Robert Monckton Papers (Northcliffe Coll.), reel C-368, Library and Archives Canada, Ottawa, Ontario.

44. Monckton to Jack Monckton, November 29, 1762, Monckton Papers (Northcliffe Coll.), reel C-368, Library and Archives Canada; Monckton to Gates, April 7, 1765, Gates Papers, reel 1, NYHS; Knox, *Historical Journal of the Campaigns*, vol. 2, 107–8; CC to Halifax, March 27, 1763, *CLB*, vol. 1, 216.

45. Monckton to Jack Monckton, April 11, 1763, Monckton Papers (Northcliffe Coll.), reel C-368, Library and Archives Canada; Watts to Gedney Clarke, May 20, 1763, Watts, *Letter Book*, 143–44; *SM*, vol. 1, 22.

46. Smith Jr. to Gates, November 22, 1763, March 9, 1764, Gates Papers, reel 1, NYHS; Watts to Sir William Baker, June 26, 1763, Watts, *Letter Book*, 149; Watts to Monckton, March 11, 1764, Watts, *Letter Book*, 234; *SM*, vol. 1, 30; Watts to Monckton, July 23, 1763, *Aspinwall Papers*, vol. 9, 483; CC to Board of Trade, July 8, 1763, *CLB*, vol. 1, 217–18.

47. Watts to Hardy, June 11, 1763, Watts, *Letter Book*, 146–47; Watts to Baker, August 11, 1764, Watts, *Letter Book*, 282–83; CC to Whytt, September 3, 1763, *CP*, vol. 6, 272–74; Johnson to CC, July 13, 1763, *JP*, vol. 4, 171.

48. Monckton to Lords of Trade, November 10, 1761, *NYCD*, vol. 7, 471; CC to Board of Trade, July 8, 1763, *CLB*, vol. 1, 217–18; Smith Jr. to Monckton, July 20, 1763, *Aspinwall Papers*, vol. 9, 479; *SM*, vol. 1, 22–23; Upton, *Loyal Whig*, 57; Martha J. Lamb, *History of the City of New York: Its Origin, Rise, and Progress* (New York: A. S. Barnes, 1877–1896); repr. New York: Valentine's Manual, 1921), vol. 2, 712.

49. Watts to Monckton, January 23, 1768, *Aspinwall Papers*, vol. 10, 599–600; CC to Halifax, November 5, 1764, *CLB*, vol. 1, 390–91; Watts to Monckton, December 10, 1763, Watts, *Letter Book*, 207; Great Britain, *Acts of Privy Council, Colonial Series*, ed. William L. Grant and James Munroe (London: H. M. S. O., 1908–1912), vol. 5, 570.

50. CC to Monckton, April 14, 1764, *CLB*, vol. 1, 321; CC to Board of Trade, April 14, 1764, *CLB*, vol. 1, 321–22; CC to Halifax, November 5, 1764, *CLB*, vol. 1, 390–91.

51. CC to Charles Ward Apthorpe, May 4, 1764, *CLB*, vol. 1, 326; CC to Halifax, May 8, 1764, *CLB*, vol. 1, 326–27; CC to Board of Trade, May 14, 1764, *CLB*, vol. 1, 328–29; CC to Sedgwick, September 21, 1764, *CLB*, vol. 1, 364–65; Apthorpe to CC, May 1, 1764, *CP*, vol. 6, 305–6; Sedgwick to CC, July 14, 1764, *CLB*, vol. 6, 332–33; Watts to Monckton, January 21, April 20, 1764, Watts, *Letter Book*, 219–20, 248–49.

52. CC to Halifax, March 27, 1763, Bancroft Coll., Colden Papers, vol. 2, 192, NYPL.

53. CC to Council, March 24, 1761, New York Colony, Council, *Journal of the Legislative Council of the Colony of New York*, vol. 2, 1429; Garden to CC, October 26, 1760, *CP*, vol. 5, 361.

54. CC, "Publick Notice is hereby Given," September 20, 1760, in *All Canada in the Hands of the English: Or, An Authentick Journal Of the Proceedings of the Army, Under General Amherst* (Boston: B. Mecom, 1760), n.p.; CC to Board of Trade, August 30, 1760, *CLB*, vol. 1,

17; CC to Amherst, November 8, 1760, *CLB*, vol. 1, 32; Klein, *American Whig*, 401; Virginia D. Harrington, *The New York Merchant on the Eve of the Revolution* (New York: Columbia University Press, 1935; repr. Gloucester, MA: Peter Smith, 1964), 308.

55. CC to Council and Assembly, October 22, 1760, New York Colony, Council, *Journal of the Legislative Council of the Colony of New York*, vol. 2, 1409–10.

56. CC to William Nicholls, March 30, 1761, *CLB*, vol. 1, 75; CC to Pitt, April 5, August 11, September 24, 1761, *CLB*, vol. 1, 75–77, 103–5, 116–17; CC to Col. Thodey, September 6, 1761, *CLB*, vol. 1, 112–13; CC to Amherst, September 3, 12, 1761, *CLB*, vol. 1, 111–12, 114–15.

57. CC to Board of Trade, April 7, 1762, *CLB*, vol. 1, 186–91; CC to Egremont, April 7, 1762, *CLB*, vol. 1, 192–93; David Syrett, "American Provincials and the Havanna Campaign of 1762," *New York History* 49, no. 4 (1968): 381.

58. Robert Livingston to Yates, July 21, 1761, Abraham Yates Jr. Papers, no. 76, NYPL; CC to Amherst, August 11, December 31, 1760, *CLB*, vol. 1, 6, 47; petition of Albany magistrates to CC, December 22, 1760, *CP*, vol. 5, 385–86; [Ralph Izard], *An Account of a Journey to Niagara, Montreal and Quebec, in 1765; or; "'Tis Eighty Years Since"* (New York: [W. Osborn], 1846), 5–6.

59. Amherst to CC, June 7, 21, 1761, *CP*, vol. 6, 38, 46–47; CC to Amherst, June 29, 1761, *CLB*, vol. 1, 94–95; CC to Johnson, June 2, July 2, 1761, *JP*, vol. 10, 276, 310–11; Flick, *History*, vol. 3, 152; William G. Godfrey, *Pursuit of Profit and Preferment in Colonial North America: John Bradstreet's Quest* (Waterloo, Canada: Wilfrid Laurier University Press, 1982), 166.

60. Amherst to CC, May 9, 1762, *Aspinwall Papers*, vol. 9, 452–53; Anthony Quackenboss to Col. Bradstreet, May 9, 1762, *Aspinwall Papers*, vol. 9, 453; Godfrey, *Pursuit*, 165.

61. CC to Amherst, May 9, 1762, *Aspinwall Papers*, vol. 9, 454; Amherst to CC, May 10, 1762, *Aspinwall Papers*, vol. 9, 454–55.

62. Col. John Bradstreet to mayor, May 31, June 1, 1762, *Aspinwall Papers*, vol. 9, 455–56; extract of letter from Capt. Winepress to Amherst, May 31, 1762, *Aspinwall Papers*, vol. 9, 457; mayor to Bradstreet, June 1, 1762, *Aspinwall Papers*, vol. 9, 457–58; Godfrey, *Pursuit*, 166.

63. CC to Lords of Trade, March 1, 1762, *NYCD*, vol. 7, 493; CC to Egremont, July 19, 1763, *CLB*, vol. 1, 220; CC to Thomas Gage, August 23, 1764, *CLB*, vol. 1, 356.

64. CC to Johnson, July 2, 1763, *JP*, vol. 10, 726–27; Johnson to CC, July 13, 1763, *CP*, vol. 6, 226; Watts to Monckton, July 23, 1763, Watts, *Letter Book*, 159; Watts to Robert Porter, August 13, 1763, Watts, *Letter Book*, 168.

65. CC to Col. Hardenbergh, July 28, 1763, *CLB*, vol. 1, 222; CC to C. Colden, Jr., August 3, 1763, *CLB*, vol. 1, 223; CC to James Clinton, December 12, 1763, HM22371, Misc. Mss., Huntington; CC to Col. Ellison, October 17, 1763, Colden Family Papers, LC.

66. CC to Johnson, January 23, 1764, *CLB*, vol. 1, 283; CC to Gov. Penn, January 10, 1764, *CLB*, vol. 1, 279–80; CC to Halifax, July 9, 1764, *CLB*, vol. 1, 335–37; CC to Johnson, December 12, 1763, Misc., box 6, CL; CC to Johnson, December 28, 1763, Misc. Personal Name Files, box 24, NYPL; CC to Johnson, December 28, 1763, *JP*, vol. 10, 988–89.

67. CC to Halifax, July 9, 1764, Bancroft Coll., Colden Papers, vol. 3, 59, NYPL; CC to Amherst, August 28, 1763, *CLB*, vol. 1, 226. For the Fort Pitt incident of June 1763, see Philip Ranlet, "The British, the Indians, and Smallpox: What Actually Happened at Fort Pitt in 1763?," *Pennsylvania History* 67, no. 3 (2000): 427–41. Elizabeth A. Fenn is as wrong about smallpox as anyone could be.

68. Halifax to CC, May 12, 1764, *CP*, vol. 6, 309–10; Johnson to CC, January 12, 1764, *CP*, vol. 6, 277; CC to Halifax, December 22, 1763, *NYCD*, vol. 7, 594; CC to Halifax, December 8, 1763, *CLB*, vol. 1, 260–61; CC to Board of Trade, December 19, 1763, *CLB*, vol. 1, 270.

69. CC to Board of Trade, October 12, 1764, *CLB*, vol. 1, 380–86; CC to Halifax, February 13, 1764, *CLB*, vol. 1, 308; "Plan for the future Management of Indian affairs," CPU, reel 2, NYHS.

70. Penn to CC, January 5, 1764, in Pennsylvania Colony, *Colonial Records of Pennsylvania, Minutes of the Provincial Council of Pennsylvania, October 15, 1762–October 17, 1771*

(Harrisburg: T. Fenn, 1852; repr. 16 vols. New York: AMS Press, 1968), vol. 9, 112; CC to Johnson, January 9, 1764, Emmet Coll., no. 1804, NYPL.

71. Penn to assembly, January 16, 1764, Pennsylvania Colony, *Colonial Records*, vol. 9, 122; CC to Johnson, January 9, 1764, Emmet Coll., no. 1804, NYPL.

72. Council minutes, January 9, 1764, Emmet Coll., no. 86, NYPL; CC to Gage, January 9, 1764, *CLB*, vol. 1, 277.

73. CC to Penn, January 10, 1764, Pennsylvania Colony, *Colonial Records*, vol. 9, 120; Johnson to Penn, January 20, 1764, *JP*, vol. 11, 18; Johnson to CC, January 27, 1764, *JP*, vol. 4, 306–7.

74. Johnson to Penn, February 27, 1764, *JP*, vol. 4, 343; Johnson to CC, February 28, 1764, *JP*, vol. 4, 345–46; CC to Penn, c. March 1764, *CLB*, vol. 1, 310–11; CC to Johnson, March 9, 1764, *CLB*, vol. 1, 311–12; John W. Jordan, "Biographical Sketch of Rev. Bernhard Adam Grube," *Pennsylvania Magazine of History and Biography* 25, no. 1 (1901), 17–18.

75. CC to Johnson, March 7, 1761, *JP*, vol. 10, 233; additional instruction to Monckton, December 9, 1761, *JP*, vol. 10, 340–42; Johnson to J. Pownall, April 18, 1763, *JP*, vol. 4, 90; CC to Lords of Trade, March 1, 1762, *NYCD*, vol. 7, 492.

76. CC to Board of Trade, March 1, 1762, November 10, 1764, *CLB*, vol. 1, 176–82, 401.

77. CC to Board of Trade, March 1, 1762, *CLB*, vol. 1, 176–82.

78. CC to Board of Trade, March 1, 1762, *CLB*, vol. 1, 176–82; Goldsbrow Banyar to Johnson, April 6, May 28, 1761, *JP*, vol. 3, 373–74, 397; "By the Honble Cadwallader Colden Esqr.," June 1, 1761, Ulster County Coll., 1666–1893, series vol. 2, box 1, folder 7, no. 56, NYHS.

79. CC to Monckton, August 8, 1762, New York Colony, Miscellany Coll., Governor, box 1, A–C, NYPL; Jones, *Vermont*, 90–91. See also *Aspinwall Papers*, vol. 9, 467–68.

80. Watts to Napier, December 14, 1764, Watts, *Letter Book*, 317–19.

81. CC to Board of Trade, August 30, 1760, December 9, 1763, *CLB*, vol. 1, 14–17, 262–65; Philip Skene to CC, August 17, 1763, *CP*, vol. 9, 187–88.

82. CC to Board of Trade, August 30, 1760, December 9, 1763, *CLB*, vol. 1, 14–17, 262–65; CC to Skene, August 18, 1763, *CLB*, vol. 1, 225–26; CC to Earl of Hillsborough, August 10, 1764, *CLB*, vol. 1, 345–47; Hillsborough to CC, June 8, 1764, *CP*, vol. 6, 313–14; minutes of Council relative to Skene's grant, August 7, 1764, *CP*, vol. 6, 335–37; Sara Stidstone Gronim, "Geography and Persuasion: Maps in British Colonial New York," *William and Mary Quarterly*, 3rd ser., 58 (2001):393.

83. CC to Hillsborough, August 10, 1764, *CLB*, vol. 1, 345–47.

84. CC to Hillsborough, August 10, 1764, *CLB*, vol. 1, 345–47.

85. Frederick B. Richards, "The Black Watch at Ticonderoga," New York State Historical Association, *Proceedings* 10 (1911): 420, 453; Robert A. A. McGeachy, "Captain Lauchlin Campbell and Argyllshire Emigration to New York," *Northern Scotland* 19, no. 1 (1999): 31, 34–35.

86. CC to Johnson, May 31, [1765], *JP*, vol. 11, 758–59; CC to Hillsborough, November 5, 1764, *CLB*, vol. 1, 399–400; Watts to Adam Drummond, November 5, 1764, Watts, *Letter Book*, 304; Charlotte Wilcoxen, "A Highborn Lady in Colonial New York," *New York Historical Society Quarterly* 63, no. 4 (1979):315, 328–30.

87. "The Proclamation of 1763," October 7, 1763, in *English Historical Documents: American Colonial Documents To 1776*, ed. Merrill Jensen (New York, 1955), vol. 9, 641; CC to Board of Trade, November 10, 1764, *CLB*, vol. 1, 401; CC to Charles, June 8, 1764, *CLB*, vol. 1, 330–31; Watts to Drummond, November 5, 1764, Watts, *Letter Book*, 304; Watts to Lasselles Clark and Daling, April 1, 1765, Watts, *Letter Book*, 343; Worthington Chauncey Ford, ed., *British Officers Serving in America, 1754–1774, Compiled from the "Army Lists"* (Boston: D. Clapp, 1894), 56. For Howetson's role in the Revolution, see *ANB*, s.v. Howetson, James. For the role of retired British officers in the Revolution, see Philip Ranlet, *The New York Loyalists*, 2nd ed. (Lanham, MD: University Press of America, 2002), passim.

88. CC to Board of Trade, January 25, 1762, *CLB*, vol. 1, 155–58; Privy Council to CC, June 11, 1762, *Aspinwall Papers*, vol. 9, 459–60; Watts to Monckton, December 10, 1763, Watts, *Letter Book*, 206; Alan Tully, *Forming American Politics: Ideals, Interests, and Institu-*

tions in Colonial New York and Pennsylvania (Baltimore: Johns Hopkins University Press, 1994), 168–69.

89. CC, "Observations on Situation," 174; CC to Templeman, February 6, 1761, Guard Books, Royal Society of Arts, London; Harrington, *New York Merchant*, 288; Samuel K. Anderson, "Public Lotteries in Colonial New York," *New York Historical Society Quarterly* 56, no. 2 (1972): 143. For the Royal Society of Arts, see "The Plan of the Society For the Encouragement of Arts, Manufactures, and Commerce," February 19, 1755, Broadside Coll., NYHS.

90. James Birket, *Some Cursory Remarks Made by James Birket in his Voyage to North America, 1750–1751* (New Haven, CT: Yale University Press, 1916; repr. Freeport, NY: Books for Libraries Press, 1971), 45–46; H. Bernstein, *Origins of Inter-American Interest, 1700–1812* (Philadelphia: University of Pennsylvania Press, 1945), 23–24, 31, 76.

91. Pitt to governor of New York, August 23, 1760, *CP*, vol. 5, 330–31; petition of George Spencer, November 26, 1761, *CP*, vol. 6, 93–95; AC to Harison, May 10, 1756, Richard Harison Papers, box 2, NYHS.

92. Pitt to New York governor, August 23, 1760, *CP*, vol. 5, 330–31; CC to Pitt, October 27, December 27, 1760, *CLB*, vol. 1, 26–28, 53; CC to Egremont, September 14, 1763, *CLB*, vol. 1, 230–31; CC to Board of Trade, December 7, 1763, *CLB*, vol. 1, 258–59; CC to Halifax, October 9, 1764, *CLB*, vol. 1, 375–76; Harrington, *New York Merchant*, 271; Barrow, *Trade and Empire*, 163.

93. Harrington, *New York Merchant*, 267–68; Allen S. Johnson, "The Passage of the Sugar Act," *William and Mary Quarterly*, 3rd ser., 16 (1959): 507–12.

94. CC to Board of Trade, March 9, 1764, *CLB*, vol. 1, 312–13; Watts to Col. Barré, January 21, 1763, Watts, *Letter Book*, 218; Harrington, *New York Merchant*, 254, 316.

95. Watts to Monckton, May 16, 1764, Watts, *Letter Book*, 254–55.

96. CC to Board of Trade, September 20, 1764, *CLB*, vol. 1, 361–64; Assembly to CC, September 11, 1764, House of Lords Papers, reel 16, Columbia University, New York City; *SM*, vol. 1, 23.

97. CC to Board of Trade, September 20, 1764, *CLB*, vol. 1, 361–64; Watts to Monckton, September 22, 1764, Watts, *Letter Book*, 291.

98. CC's answer to Assembly, September 17, 1764, House of Lords Papers, reel 16, Columbia University.

99. CC to Charles, June 8, 1764, *CLB*, vol. 1, 330–31.

100. CC to Sedgwick, September 21, 1764, *CLB*, vol. 1, 364–65; CC to Board of Trade, September 20, 1764, *CLB*, vol. 1, 361–64.

101. Watts to Napier, September 22, 1764, Watts, *Letter Book*, 293; Halifax to CC, December 8, 1764, *CP*, vol. 6, 395; "At the Court at St. James's," December 12, 1764, House of Lords Papers, reel 16, Columbia University.

102. *New York Mercury* (Gaine), January 18, 1762; Mary L. Booth, *History of the City of New York* (New York: W. R. C. Clark, 1867), vol. 1, 395.

Chapter Thirteen

Lawyers

Cadwallader Colden's battle with the New York legal profession in the 1760s has attracted much attention, mostly hostile to Colden, over the years. Though depicted as a struggle between upholders of freedom—the lawyers—and a tyrant, were the lawyers truly on the side of liberty?

Colden thought otherwise. In 1759, when criticizing William Smith Jr.'s *History*, the philosopher noted that the lawyer praised certain governors "who ruled only by the dictates of their own discretion" suggesting to Colden that the author "seems to grant that justice may be done under a despotic government." In contrast, Colden mused, "I doubt whether it be possible that justice can be done where the administration of it is in the hands of Lawyers for, tho' the Judgement given may be just, it is always attended with injustice in the expense and delay which attends it."[1]

With no illusion about the profession, Colden observed that "The lawyer, under the mask of a gown," along with supposed "wisdom as the guardian of the liberty . . . of the people, will for a fee disguise truth" whether or not this would "oppress the poor, the widow, and the orphan." Colden did not have the slightest doubt that a wealthy client, no matter how vilely he had obtained his money, would inevitably "have the ablest lawyer on his side" to attack a poor, defrauded man who would have a hard time finding "one of these guardians of . . . liberty" to protect him.[2]

A lawyer's job, Colden asserted, was "knowingly to pervert . . . Justice, in favour of the rogue, and to the prejudice of the innocent." That made the lawyer into "a good lawyer, tho' in all cases, even in defense of right, he be a sort of licensed pickpocket." (Knowing how lawyers profited from probate proceedings, Colden conveyed many of his assets—such as Coldengham—to his heirs long before his death.) Not surprisingly, lawyers were unlikely to support reform of the system. Profiting too much from the system to want to change it, they were "too powerful in the state to be easily reduced to order."[3]

Colden, however, did not oppose the study of law. As early as 1718 he ordered a prominent legal text. Two of his sons became members of the bar: John, who must have assumed that becoming a lawyer would help him perform his official duties; and Cad, who did legal work in Ulster.[4]

Nor should it be forgotten that Colden's best friend happened to be James Alexander, one of the greatest lawyers of the period. They did have a minor clash regarding law. During the George Clinton administration, the lawyer tried to explain to his friend that James DeLancey could not be suspended as lieutenant governor because he had not received his commission for that office. Colden could not accept that legal reasoning. "Men of common sense (who are not lawyers) will think it very odd" he insisted. Such "scruples" were "artificially raised in weak minds in order to defeat everything." Their friendship remained too strong to end over differences about legal mumbo-jumbo.[5]

By 1763, long after Alexander's death, Colden's opinion about lawyers had not changed and he felt a deep hostility to New York lawyers. "We have a Set of Lawyers in this Province as Insolent, Petulant and at the same time as well skilled in all the chicanerie of the Law as perhaps is to be found anywhere." Learning "the Secrets of the most considerable Families" by marrying into these "distinguished families," the lawyers gained "a general Influence." Therefore, when a suit entered a court, the involved lawyers were probably related by marriage to the presiding judge, making impartiality practically impossible especially if the royal prerogative was at issue.[6]

Colden made no secret of his feelings about New York's justice system. On November 25, 1761 Colden gave a speech before the legislature that William Smith Jr. declared was "dictated by passion" leading "to an excess of indiscriminate rage at the whole profession, Bench and Bar."[7]

In truth, Colden was not raging; he was expressing reality that the lawyers did not want to hear. After explaining that Monckton had been ordered away from New York, the lieutenant governor told the legislators:

> Complaints of the dilatory Proceedings in the Courts of Law and of the heavy Expense in obtaining Justice, are so general and frequent, that they well deserve your Attention. . . . The Delay of Justice is a Denial of it for a Time, and is often, when attended with great Expense of worse Consequence to Individuals than the absolute Refusal of Justice. The Security of Government and the well-being of Society are founded on the equal Distribution of Justice, which cannot prevail in its proper Extent, while the Expense in obtaining it, is insupportable to many.[8]

Responding to Colden, the Council indicated it would do nothing. The councilors promised to act if the "Complaints appear well grounded." Knowing their real intention, Colden replied: "It is not easy to conceive that complaints so general and frequent . . . can be without some foundation, especially when they have gone so far as to reach the Royal Ear."[9]

When Colden attempted to reform New York's legal system, lawyers sought to block him. Colden fingered some of them in particular—"Three popular Lawyers, educated in Connecticut, who have strongly imbibed the Independent principles of that Country." Although he then identified only one of them, William Smith, Jr., in 1774 John Adams named the others, John Morin Scott and William Livingston, all of whom were "children of Yale College" and were called "the Triumvirate," a name that captured the historical imagination. This trio wrote many of the pamphlets and newspaper essays that tried to stir New York against the lieutenant governor. Scott, Adams thought, was an eloquent speaker but both he and Livingston were lazy—unlike Smith.[10]

The Triumvirate smeared Colden with harsh names and ridicule in a newspaper, the *American Chronicle*, which Colden complained about to London. Being lawyers, Smith and his friends "couched the meaning" of their written remarks "in such words as they may think secures them from a criminal prosecution." Still, the Triumvirate tossed a host of insults in Colden's direction: "proud, self-conceited and all sufficient." But he was also "full of himself, imperious, ungracious, and forbiding—incapable of Friendship or Sincerity—crafty and rapacious—without Honour—void of Faith—of insatiable Avarice, and abandoned to his Passions." For good measure, they tried humor, inserting a fake ad for a law volume which explained law "in a Geometrical Manner." In case no one got the joke, they referred to a "Theodolite," a surveying tool, to link the insults to Colden more closely. The rhetoric was so over-blown that the essays had no impact and provoked no response from Colden, who let the Triumvirate ramble on.[11]

Two deaths—of George II and DeLancey—set off this legal war in New York. During the Clinton administration, DeLancey tricked the governor into presenting all the judges with commissions that they would hold as long as they practiced good behavior, thus giving them almost complete independence from the royal governor. DeLancey's death paved the way for a new chief justice with a new commission. The king's death invalidated all the other judicial commissions.[12]

In London, the imperial government had long before expressly forbidden the granting of any more good behavior judicial commissions. Instead, the bureaucrats demanded the commissions grant tenure only at the king's "pleasure," which allowed a governor to fire a judge, giving royal officials a check upon judges who ignored some aspect of the king's prerogative. Knowing what the British government wanted, Colden refused to give good behavior commissions. Robert Monckton talked about granting such commissions, but this turned out to be just talk, lucky for him. The governor of

New Jersey ignored his instructions, appointed judges under good behavior, and was fired "as a necessary example to deter others in the same situation from like Acts of Disobedience" to the king's will.[13]

Colden's political instincts had served him well again, but the New York judges had no intention of surrendering. They demanded good behavior commissions and vowed not to act until they got them. The Assembly backed the judges and, by all appearances, so did the Council. The Assembly then tried to pass a bill requiring good behavior commissions by placing the colonial courts under its control. "The Lawyers are endeavoring to raise a distinction between the authority of Commissions when they are continued by Act of Parliament and where it is done by the King's Proclamation," Colden explained, and added his opposition to a further increase in the Assembly's powers.[14]

Lieutenant Governor Colden did suggest a compromise with the Assembly. He would accept good behavior commissions—which lessened the power of the executive—if the Assembly agreed to a permanent salary for each judge. By agreeing not to change judicial salaries, the Assembly would give up any control over judges. Colden had made a radical suggestion for America—that New York create the first truly independent judiciary. (The king had supported such a system for judges in Britain.) But London rejected Colden's idea, which puzzled imperial bureaucrats. Nor, of course, would the Assembly agree to stop trying to impose its "Factious Will and Caprice."[15] The Assembly was as determined as any over-bearing monarch to keep its power.

DeLancey's death meant that the colony now needed a new chief justice. Or did it? DeLancey had not served as chief justice of New York's supreme court of judicature when he acted as governor. Colden saw no need to rush to appoint someone. DeLancey himself had told him "that a Chief Justice has more Power than a Governor." As president of the Council, Colden was merely a caretaker and the position of chief justice was "of such consequence" that he should not make the choice. Reluctant to make an appointment that would undercut the next governor—despite all the advice that he do so—Colden declined from the very beginning, leaving the opening for the imperial government to fill.[16]

Plenty of lawyers wanted the post and they all hoped for a recommendation from Colden. Two of the judges on the court sought a promotion but, as Colden wrote, he "did not know one Man of Distinction in the Place, who thought either of them qualified for the Office."[17]

The first of these judges, Daniel Horsmanden, had a long, unpleasant history with Colden or, as John Watts commented, they had "a Cordial Antipathy." No chance existed that Colden would support his candidacy. Colden did, sort of, suggest that Horsmanden's colleague, John Chambers, become chief justice. A loyal Clinton ally, he seemed the best candidate to Colden, who wrote a devastating recommendation for him: "Tho' some think that he is not of bright parts, yet from what I can learn he will be the most acceptable to the people in general."[18]

Quickly, Colden had rejected two other possible chief justices. Robert Hunter Morris no longer resided in New York. And there was another candidate—William Smith, Sr. Another loyal Clintonite, Smith had been the only lawyer willing to prosecute the thuggish Oliver DeLancey. Yet Colden refused to suggest the senior Smith's appointment, supposedly because raising a lawyer who had appeared before the other judges would be insulting to them. At least that is what Colden claimed.[19]

However, Smith had been accused of altering an official document—not something helping the prospective chief justice's cause. Perhaps the factor that most influenced Colden was that, despite thirty years of practicing law, the elder Smith was not a good lawyer. Thomas Jones observed that Smith's legal "reputation and character . . . were but slight, indifferent, and very freely spoken of." Colden's explanation thus seems like a polite excuse to turn an ally down (though it infuriated the younger Smith and his comrades). Monckton did make the senior Smith a judge, but his lack of ability appeared obvious as Watts noted: "Old S. makes no figure upon the Bench, he wants his Sons able Talents." Already by 1764 William Smith, Sr.'s health was visibly worsening; he died in 1769.[20]

London settled the issue by picking a total stranger to both New York and Colden. Upon the recommendation of Thomas Pownall, Benjamin Pratt, a Bostonian, was named New York's chief justice. Pratt had a considerable legal reputation in New England, but his "method of speaking," though it had been popular in Boston, was "by no means" what New Yorkers were used to.[21]

Although Colden had not heard of Pratt, Pratt had heard of him. "My Knowledge of your Character, has no Small Effect upon my Mind" and had encouraged the new chief justice to abandon his home and take up the office. Pratt did have some concern, like the New York judges, about serving with a commission under the king's pleasure. He did vow to accept the chief justiceship whatever his commission specified, which would be the king's pleasure.[22]

Happy that Pratt would serve on the court, Colden suspected that the New York bar would not like the presence of an outsider. "Now when these Lawyers see a chief Justice on the Bench capable to restrain them, their resentments are greatly provoked." He warned Pratt that the Assembly might play games with his salary. Urging the new chief justice to start working soon, Pratt could see if he would be paid. If not, an early arrival would allow him to complain to London very quickly.[23]

Colden's foreboding proved accurate. Determined to force the granting of good behavior commissions, the Assembly gave Pratt "not one Farthing" as he complained to Thomas Pownall. It did offer a "Pittance" of £300 in New

York money, roughly equivalent to £160 British sterling, but only if he had a good behavior commission. That would not happen. As an added complication, the other judges still refused to act under pleasure commissions, so Pratt presided over all the trials that came to the supreme court. At least Pratt saw to it that there would not be "a failure of justice" in New York.[24]

The New York assemblymen and lawyers, Colden observed, "want a Chief Justice with whom they have strong connections, and in order to obtain their end find pretences to refuse a salary to Mr. Pratt." But Colden himself came under criticism from London. He had signed an Assembly bill funding the salaries of all New York officials, including himself, that excluded Chief Justice Pratt.[25]

Both Colden and Pratt pushed the logical solution—compensate the chief justice from the quitrents paid in New York. London approved that option. Meanwhile, Pratt asked for a leave of absence to take care of personal matters in Massachusetts, which was granted. He died there in 1762. The New York Assembly and the lawyers gave up their campaign for good behavior commissions when formal instructions came from London promising the dismissal of a governor who gave such a commission. Finally, Monckton made new appointments to the supreme court, which would be headed by Horsmanden as Pratt's successor.[26]

New York's lawyers, of course, busied themselves with more than driving out interlopers from New England and, in Colden's colorful imagery, picking the pockets of their clients. The New York bar sought wealth by taking advantage of the colony's often confused land grants. As Colden wrote, "The Lawyers (some of them) purchase in every disputed Title, by this and the expence of Lawsuits they will worm People out of all their Property." Old, fraudulent purchases of Indian land constituted significant investments for the bar. The land grant dispute that most exasperated the Mohawks, the Kayaderosseras patent, had begun in 1704, well before Colden came to America. A supposed deed for the 800,000 acres of Kayaderosseras, signed by Indians, was dated in 1704; the grant was made in 1708. Whether the Indians even received the £60 for the huge land purchase is not certain. The whole process was so fake that even the perpetrators seemed embarrassed by it.[27]

After many decades, the Mohawks continued to deny the validity of the Kayaderosseras patent. By the 1760s the ownership of the disputed territory had changed greatly. Watts stated that the owners included "some of our best Lawyers" who had no intention of giving any of it back to the Indians. In 1761 William Smith, Jr. joined the Kayaderosseras proprietors. The Mohawk dilemma is obvious. They, somehow, had to triumph over a host of New York lawyers in New York courts that were friendly to the proprietors. And no court in the colony admitted into evidence the testimony of any Indian.[28]

Both Lieutenant Governor Colden and Sir William Johnson did everything they could to invalidate the Kayaderosseras patent. The Mohawks' long-simmering disgust about it increased incredibly when, in 1764, they discovered that the proprietors had placed settlers in the disputed territory. Colden tried addressing the Assembly about Kayaderosseras. The assemblymen suggested that many of the problems relating to such grants came about because many of the Dutch inhabitants did not know English very well. Finally, the assemblymen declared, they "conceive it extremely dangerous, at this late day, to enter into an Enquiry, in which Sufficient light probably Cannot be obtained to direct a just and Accurate determination, and that the Precedent . . . will render all property insecure."[29]

The Assembly's response did not surprise Colden or, for that matter, anybody else in the province. General Thomas Gage, worried about the military consequences of alienating the Mohawks, explained the state of affairs in New York well. The assemblymen "were too much concerned in Patents" for land "And I find no Person who will pretend to advise, where to prosecute" Kayaderosseras "in this Province, with the hopes of a fair and impartial Judgement; or where to find Judges and Jurors who are not interested."[30]

Given the legal hopelessness in New York, Colden thought the best way to proceed was to beseech Parliament to nullify Kayaderosseras, especially as the British government had been demanding the voiding of the grant. First writing a detailed account of all the fraud involved and dispatching it to London, Colden then recommended to Johnson that he explain to the Iroquois that "you and I have done everything in our power to do them Justice." Inevitably, justice would result "tho' it cannot be done so speedily as they expect, and we wish it may be done."[31]

Colden went on:

> If I were one of themselves, and indeed I was adopted by the Canajoharies many years since, I cannot do more for their obtaining of Justice, than I have for many years past done, but never had so much in my power to do as now, and you may assure them I will omit nothing in their favour which is in my power, and I am confident that my endeavors will in the end prove effectual. On these assurances they may rest easy.[32]

Meaning every word, Colden gave Johnson advice on what would work best as evidence. But he asked Johnson "not to mention me as any way informing you." The Iroquois had long before made sure that Johnson would be determined to act in their interests. They had given him, as a gift, a chunk of what the Kayaderosseras proprietors considered their land. Colden supported Johnson in that matter too although it, technically, seemed to violate rules about grants.[33]

However, by the middle of 1765 the Kayaderosseras proprietors appeared to be looking for a way out of their legal problems. A few years more passed before a deal could be arranged—the proprietors dropped their claim for much of the land and paid the Indians a large sum for the rest.[34]

Although the Kayaderosseras embarrassment finally ended, another fraudulent land deal, the Canajoharie patent, continued to show how New York's courts were stacked against Indians. This fraud started in 1731 when the grantees surveyed the land during the night. The Indians refused to accept this patent. In 1761 the perpetrators of the Canajoharie grant sold the "confounded patent" to George Klock and his partners. Then Klock tried to legally force off the land tenant farmers whom the Indians had placed in the area. These tenants resisted Klock's maneuver.[35]

The dispute entered the Albany courts. William Livingston, part of the anti-Colden Triumvirate, served as Klock's lawyer. A historian has succinctly summed up the legal proceedings: "no jury found enough unequivocal and overwhelming evidence to convict him of defrauding the Iroquois." Watts was blunter: "These vile Dutch will Swear any thing for one another." Johnson warned Colden that the Mohawks were "so exasperated" that he found it difficult "to restrain them from committing acts of Violence."[36]

Eager to please the Mohawks, Colden received the support of the Council against Klock. By July 1763 the lieutenant governor decided to dispose of Klock by seeking "an order from the King, and by the Kings bearing the necessary Expense of it, otherwise it cannot be carried effectually on." Financially, Klock was in better shape than the government of New York.[37]

Almost as if Klock wished to flaunt his success, in 1763 he made arrangements to travel to Great Britain with three Mohawks who would be displayed and gawked at by paying spectators. The British government, out of fear of alienating the Iroquois, wanted to stamp out this long-standing practice. When Johnson learned of Klock's plans, he warned Colden but Klock managed to leave New York with one of his exhibits. Colden was convinced that Klock had been tipped off and escaped before any inquiry could begin. The lieutenant governor also suspected that Klock must have support in Britain—otherwise his trip made no sense.[38]

Colden guessed wrong about Klock having allies across the Atlantic yet, given Klock's success in stymieing him in New York, that assumption is understandable. When Klock returned, the battle continued. By 1774 all of his partners had surrendered though he stubbornly held out. The slow legal process had not finished in 1775 when war broke out. After the American Revolution concluded, long after Colden's demise, George Klock finally won legal control of the land he had lusted after for so long.[39]

Of course, Colden could not have known that and in 1764 he had other problems to deal with. Philip Skene had complained to London officials about the substantial fees he had to pay to secure his land grant—over £700, of which some £300 went to Colden. An order came to Colden demanding to know the fees New York officials charged.[40]

Colden, who did not know the identity of the complainer, simply explained that the rates of various fees had not been changed since 1710 with the exception of chancery fees. No law had been passed on the subject since 1720. (Skene paid a huge amount in fees because he had a huge land grant.) The lieutenant governor then switched the discussion to the fees New York lawyers charged. "I believe that the Expence of Law suits in this Province yearly amounts to more than four times the support of Government."[41]

Lieutenant Governor Colden had learned that the lawyers—supported by the judges—claimed that the old fee list of 1710 no longer had legal force; they could charge any amount they thought appropriate. Surely, imperial officials could not have a full picture of the fee structure in New York without knowing about the costs of the legal system, Colden thought, and he requested information on the fees charged by both lawyers and judges. They refused to provide the details. Probably not surprised, Colden sent specifics about all fees in New York "except those taken by the attornies at Law who think themselves too high for me to reach them." The lawyers' "unreasonable Expense" led "to the oppression of the Poor, and often with the suppression of Justice as to them" Colden added.[42]

While all these affairs stirred the New York bar against Colden, no issue had the influence or fame to match Colden's opinion about one legal case, *Forsey v. Cunningham*. In this cause Colden asserted the right of the Crown to re-examine factual evidence—not just judicial errors—and to permit appeals to the king from the New York supreme court. Years later, American revolutionaries looked back at "the noble stand" of New York lawyers and judges for opposing the usurpation of "a designing Governor."[43]

Certainly, William Smith, Jr. blasted "Mr. Colden's pernicious Scheme of introducing Appeals from Verdicts." To Monckton, Smith thundered: "It falls in with the Ministerial Principle that the King's Will is Law in the Provinces."[44]

So Colden invented this doctrine. Or did he? Captain John Montresor, an able military engineer, was both Colden's friend and politically savvy. In December 1765 Montresor complained about the proceedings in the Assembly when it "indecently debated" the issue of appeals that had been stirred up by *Forsey v. Cunningham*. The soldier had to laugh after learning that the younger Smith had admitted that the whole idea had come about "through his advice, tho a person apparently on the opposite side of the question." Before the Assembly Smith would insist that no such right of appeal existed in New York.[45]

Although Smith vilified Colden for his stand in *Forsey v. Cunningham*, Smith had pushed the principle of a wide-ranging right of appeal years before. The subject of appeals had been mentioned in the New York governor's commission from the time it became a royal colony. In 1708 appeals were shifted to the governor's instructions. These early incarnations referred to appealing legal errors only. But in 1753 the instructions issued to Sir Danvers Osborn had a significant change in wording. The reference to errors disappeared, to be replaced by seemingly clear wording: appeals could be launched "in all civil causes."[46]

The new language continued into Monckton's instructions. The 33rd instruction specified that an appeal could be brought to the king in his Privy Council for a misdemeanor that incurred a fine at least £200. However, the thirty-second instruction became the pivot upon which the controversy over *Forsey v. Cunningham* will revolve and, again, it seems clear:

> Our Will and Pleasure is, that you, or the Commander in Chief of our said Province for the Time being, do in all civil Causes, on Application being made to you, or the Commander in chief . . ., for that Purpose, permit and allow Appeals from any of the Courts of common Law in our said Province.[47]

In 1755, just two years after the wording changed, William Smith, Jr. used the right of appeal in Bryant v. O'Bryan, a trespass proceeding. Smith did not base his logic on the instructions as such. He asserted that New York's Council, while sitting as a court, had the same power as the British House of Lords when it acted as a court. This would be "the initial appearance of the Coldenite interpretation" on appeals which, obviously, Colden did not invent.[48]

That appeals became a great issue in New York seems puzzling. The right to appeal for justice to the king had been avidly pursued by opponents of Puritan governments in New England. Such appeals were still occurring in New York's neighbors. Appeals in New York, Colden recalled, had been rare. In the past forty years, up to six appeals had been made to the governor in Council—all had involved alleged legal errors. One of these appeals, when Lieutenant Governor George Clarke was in command, went to the king in his Privy Council. There the suggestion of error was not considered. Instead, "a new Judgment on the Merits of the Cause was given, different from that of the Supreme Court."[49]

Forsey v. Cunningham, though, was the first appeal that was not based on legal error. Colden believed he knew why there was so intense opposition to it. Behind the protest were the great manor lords, with their vast landholdings with vague boundaries. They were "terribly afraid" about the results if lawsuits regarding their estates reached London via an appeal. So they stirred up "unreasonable apprehensions." Small landholders were very reluctant to live anywhere near one of the great manors, fearing that a rich manor lord would try to seize their property by means of a lawsuit in the biased New York courts, which Colden compared to the biased English county courts in the Middle Ages. No one could deny, Colden insisted, that New York's courts had reached "many iniquitous Verdicts." Furthermore, in 1764 independent farmers in the Evans Patent had been sued by the holders of the Minisink Patent. Not surprisingly, Judge Robert Livingston, one of the manor lords, had delivered a great "Harangue" against appeals. Colden revealed that the judge was "involved in Disputes with the poor industrious Farmers who had settled and improved the adjoining Lands." But, with an appeal to the king and Privy Council, a small farmer would have access "to a Crown where" the rich landlords "can have no undue influence."[50]

The actual facts behind *Forsey v. Cunningham* appear simple, at least the way historians have explained them. Waddell Cunningham attacked Thomas Forsey, then severely wounded him with a sword that had been concealed. The problem is that Lord Halifax, acting at the personal behest of the king, wrote Colden stating that Forsey had attacked Cunningham, explaining why swordplay took place. Presumably that was Cunningham's version of events. Judge Livingston insisted to Monckton that because of an argument between the two traders, Cunningham suddenly produced his hidden sword so Forsey "ran from him as fast as he could." Cunningham caught up "and beat him with his sword." The "provoked" Forsey suddenly had a whip which he used on his attacker who then stabbed him, causing a serious wound.[51]

If anything, the facts behind *Forsey v. Cunningham* seem very jumbled. Who struck first? What did Cunningham wear that could conceal a sword? Given that the incident happened in July 1763, it appears peculiar that he had on such a garment. And where did Forsey's whip come from? These questions explain why Colden assured Cunningham that he had presented his memorials to the councilors and, "though they as well as myself looked on your case in a Light which would have entitled you to a favourable Opinion, they thought it improper for them to intermeddle." Politics got in the way.[52]

Little is known about either combatant or the trial itself because historians have concentrated on Colden's role afterward. It is documented that Forsey was from another province. Cunningham was one of the city's "Leading Citizens" who signed (near the bottom) a proclamation honoring George III on his ascending the throne. No doubt exists that Cunningham had superb connections in London that included the king. Through Halifax, the king ordered Colden that, if Forsey died from his injuries, he should delay the sentence (which probably would have been death) "till His Majesty's Pleasure shall be known thereupon." The king's interest in the case explains why Cunningham wanted to appeal the case to the king and the Privy Council. Apparently, those judges were not as impartial as Colden claimed they were.[53]

As Cunningham's cause went on, Colden believed that "the Proceedings become more and more interesting, and appears . . . of the greatest consequence to his Majesty's authority in this Province," and even "to the Dependence of the Colonies on the Crown of Great Britain." Forsey recovered so Cunningham escaped a murder charge. Instead, he would be tried for both criminal and civil law matters. Assault and battery plus "wounding" constituted the criminal portion; Forsey asked for £5,000 damages from the defendant. Prominent lawyers—including the Triumvirate—appeared on both sides. John Morin Scott was the leading lawyer aiding Forsey, while William Livingston and William Smith, Jr. led the defense team.[54]

On October 26, 1764 Cunningham had his day in court—literally. The jury found him guilty on all counts and awarded Forsey damages amounting to £1,500 along with his costs. But the real fireworks started after the verdicts were reached and it was the younger Smith who turned this cause into a lightning rod.[55]

By the time of the trial Cunningham had left for England but, anticipating "unreasonable" damages, he had authorized Robert Ross Waddell, his attorney, to appeal for him—an attorney is not necessarily a lawyer (Waddell was his business partner). Cunningham's lawyers had earlier agreed to appeal the case as specified in Monckton's instructions—and not for legal error. Smith had to have suggested this move, which he would later, in his diary, term "that dangerous Measure." (Smith's whole version of the case represents a rare example of a man lying to his diary.) Smith also spoke to Waddell saying "that he had told Mr. Cunningham long before he had departed" that if he appealed Smith "would not be concerned in the Cause, as it was a measure he neither did, nor would Approve of." Having set the stage, Smith bailed out.[56]

Before fleeing Cunningham's cause, however, Smith gave Waddell nonsensical advice—have George Harison (Alexander Colden's in-law), a notary public who had assisted Waddell, make the motion in court requesting the appeal. According to Harison, Smith "did direct me the said Notary what to say." No notary public had been allowed to speak in a New York court since the English conquest of the colony, which Smith knew very well. The appeal was rejected; Chief Justice Horsmanden reprimanded the notary for speaking. Smith jumped in and made a nonsensical motion to reject the heavy assessed damages, the reason for the appeal, to shield himself from seeming to support it. The motion was rejected. James Duane, one of Cunningham's lawyers, made another ridiculous motion for a second trial—that never had a chance. All of Cunningham's lawyers now walked away from the case.[57]

Waddell's astonishment at what had happened is easy to understand. At one point he complained to Harison, who stood by him, that he had no lawyer "to Advise him what Measures to pursue in order to Obtain Relief." He had been "Left in the Dark;" the supreme court had displayed "the highest Contempt of the Royal Prerogative." He saw the court's action "to be a Violent Step towards Shuting the Door of an Appeal to our Most Gracious Sovereign and his Most Honourable Privy Council."[58] Now Waddell had no choice but to go to Lieutenant Governor Cadwallader Colden for help. In reality, that had been the purpose of Smith's orchestrated sideshow in the supreme court.

Smith had planned the charade from the beginning. He had misdirected Cunningham, Waddell and Harison to turn the case into a dispute about the royal prerogative. Smith knew Colden would be attracted to supporting the prerogative—as surely as a moth flying in the dark is attracted to light. Smith thought the situation presented an excellent way to drive Colden from office.

On October 30, 1764, a few days after the debacle, Colden willingly took the bait. Petitioning him for his help, Waddell explained that the supreme court had rejected both an appeal and Monckton's thirty-second instruction. Colden agreed and said he would confer with New York's attorney-general John Tabor Kempe "immediately."[59]

Kempe knew all about the case; he had been one of Forsey's lawyers. Colden, joined by both Waddell and Harison (who took notes), asked the attorney-general "to inform me what is proper for me to do in this Case" and requested he write a writ for an appeal on the merits of a legal case. Kempe knew a controversy when he saw one. He said there was no form for such a writ and that the thirty-second instruction really meant appeals about legal error.[60]

Colden could not be dissuaded that easily. His historical side surfaced as he found, in a work of history, that the Irish House of Lords had appealed "the case of Maurice Annesly" to its English counterpart. This action had helped to establish the supremacy of the British Parliament over that of Ireland he revealed. Recall that Smith had compared the New York Council with the British House of Lords. The lieutenant governor asked Kempe to verify the account. Quickly, the attorney-general searched law books and could find no reference to that affair. Instead, he located two references that contradicted it and sent the law books to Colden for his perusal. Kempe, seemingly relieved, insisted to Colden that the controversy was "not so much on a point of Law, as on the Intent of the King, Expressed in the Instruction." It was a political matter to be judged by Colden and the councilors who "will be much better able to collect the Royal Intention" than he could.[61]

Because Kempe had successfully dodged the issue, Waddell and Harison continued to lack legal advice. Even a lawyer who had committed a crime and suffered transportation to the colonies refused to help. So Waddell made up what writs were required; Colden admitted that "they may be liable to just exceptions." Nonetheless, they were sent to the supreme court.[62]

Colden summoned the Council to discuss the case, which dragged out the proceedings for over eight weeks solely "in order to give the Judges severally an opportunity to harangue" the people. Only one councilor supported Colden, Johnson, who did not attend any of the sessions.[63]

On November 14, 1764 Chief Justice Horsmanden told the Council what he thought was the best reason to ignore the submitted writs. He had sworn an oath "not to delay Justice by any Letter from the King, that Writs are Letters and that it is better to obey God than Man." Not much of a lawyer, Horsmanden, afterward, "was observed to be in frequent consultation with some of the principal Lawyers in this Place." As the process kept going, Colden thought about suspending Horsmanden from his offices. However, Horsmanden, president of the Council, was the next in line to command New York if Colden died. Remembering what had ensued when Cosby suspended Van Dam, the lieutenant governor decided not to rile the councilors any more than they were already. Besides, it would not have done any good. Of course, if London wished to fire Horsmanden, that would have been different.[64]

Meanwhile, Watts had been waxing eloquent to Monckton over the stance of the "very old Mischief Maker" on appeals. Now New Yorkers "would prefer Beelzebub himself" to Colden, the "evil Genius." During the proceedings, Watts would tell Colden that "a Jury was the Bulwark of English Freedom"—one of the charges against Colden was his supposed attack upon juries. According to Watts, the "old Gentleman . . . coldly answered and with seeming indifference 'that there were no Jurys in Scotland and he did not see but Justice was as well administered as in England,'" which Watts branded the "Scot's unconstitutional Doctrine."[65]

Whatever Watts may have believed, Colden's stand was not beyond the proper bounds of law. He was not "making French Men of us all." The councilor should not have been shocked that Colden had been influenced by Scottish law; he was born a Scot. His ideas had more of a foundation than just that source. A legal scholar has written that Colden's belief about appeals "revealed his grasp on the problem of legal uniformity in an expanding empire. The proposal had elements of Scottish law, civil law, the royal prerogative, and common law. It could be seen as derived from any of these sources." And Colden never suggested that Monckton's instructions ended juries—the charge was "inconsistent with truth." At most, Colden estimated there might be an appeal in one percent of the supreme court's cases.[66]

Eventually, the Council and Colden sat as a court to decide the appeal issue. The judges and lawyers not on the Council attended as did other spectators, swelling to an audience of one or two hundred people. These sessions degenerated into a free-for-all, with councilors conferring with lawyers. At times Colden found it impossible "to preserve the decorum of the court."[67]

The lieutenant governor thought that Horsmanden was most objectionable, so much so that his judicial colleagues feared to join in with him. Colden, however, had to change his mind: Judge Livingston surpassed even the chief justice. Livingston's "Harangue" was "industriously intruded . . . without being desired to speak." It was so bad that Colden recommended his dismissal. Overall, Colden declared, "The Judges under pretence of delivering the Reasons of their conduct" instead made "vile suggestions" that both

Colden and the Privy Council were "capable of overturning the Law and Constitution" and would even put New Yorkers into "a state of Slavery."[68]

On January 2, 1765 Colden addressed the Council, once again, to clarify his legal reasoning. It boiled down, ultimately, to a basic idea: "The King is the Fountain of Justice." His talk, unintended for publication, was not a finished, polished treatise; it was for the councilors' edification. They asked for a copy and Colden said no "several times" but at last relented. Though Colden had been suspicious of what his document might be used for, even he was taken aback at the session of January 11. The councilors had answered his "Memorandums" and put both their attack and Colden's "Paper" into the minutes. Then the Council rejected his argument that the king had authorized appeals upon the merits of a legal case.[69]

To say that Colden was upset is an understatement. Judge Livingston remarked that Colden "was not a little offended" at the use his paper was put to. Watts dismissed Colden's annoyance that his writing had been for their "own private thoughts" and that placing it in the minutes was a "Breach of Confidence." The paper had been read in public before an audience; the Council had been, formally, a court. As for Smith, he responded, with his usual exaggeration, that Colden's complaints were "Violence."[70]

Well before the Council vote against Colden's stand, an essay campaign in the newspapers had begun "with design to prejudice the People against me Personally" the lieutenant governor explained to London. Because this whole matter was initially planned to destroy Colden, such a tactic was logical. He again refused to respond to these printed assaults. "They refuse an appeal to the King and at the same time appeal to the People" he pointed out. However, the lawyers failed to achieve "the success that was expected." After weeks of unremitting political abuse, Colden knew that New Yorkers had been inflamed, "but clamours artfully raised soon subside." The operations of the government continued "in their usual manner."[71]

Nor was Colden concerned about the veiled threats against him and his family: "I and they must expect to feel the resentment (and perhaps the malice) of a powerful Body of Men." After many decades in public life, Colden and his children had become accustomed to such hints. He trusted in "the Kings Protection."[72]

Even the obvious signs that New York's lawyers were coordinating their campaign against him with their supporters in Parliament did not faze Colden all that much. In fact, British Quakers had become inflamed about news from New York. During a trial in the colony, a Quaker witness had refused to swear an oath in accordance with Quaker religious beliefs. The judge "threatened" him with jail or a fine; the Quaker, "being Intimidated,. . . took it contrary to his conscience." A disturbed Peter Collinson declared: "Our Friends Here are much troubled to be informed of Such Harsh proceedings in a Country where all profess Liberty of Conscience." The reputation of New York's lawyers across the Atlantic was not as glowing as they imagined.[73]

The Quakers could not have felt freer because of the New York lawyers' behavior, nor did Colden. The lawyers "bawl out for Liberty," he exclaimed, but they "will not allow the Governor the liberty to give his Opinion" on a judicial matter. For opposing them, they attacked him "in the vilest manner" and try "to expose him to the rage of a deluded multitude if they can." In March 1765 newspaper attacks upon the "odious" Colden (who still refused to respond) were ongoing. He believed that the lawyers who had written the latest installment "would cut a throat in the dark if they thought they could not be detected so as to be brought to Justice and punished."[74]

Clearly, the controversy over appeals had not changed Colden's thoughts about lawyers. He told Lord Halifax: "All associations are dangerous to good Government more so in distant Dominions and associations of Lawyers the most dangerous of any next to Military." To a Scottish friend, the lieutenant governor explained that "political fermentations" were needed to keep "the Political system in its full vigor." But when these disputes had been inspired "from vicious Principles of Avarice or Lust of Power" they create "corruption through the whole system, and at length its Death or Destruction."[75]

Finally, the Privy Council during July 1765 had been beseeched by Robert Charles, the Assembly's agent, about Colden's stand on appeals. The Board of Trade sent the Privy Council a lawyerly report stating that the thirty-second instruction had not been intended to be read as Colden had. The instructions for the next governor of New York specified that appeals could be allowed only for legal error.[76]

The problem with the Board of Trade's interpretation is that the board had no evidence, either way, as to why there had been a change in the thrity-second instruction back in 1753. In reality, the change had been in the instructions for Sir Danvers Osborn during one of the few periods when the British government actually wished to clean up the mess in New York. A historian has declared that "On the whole these were the strictest instructions ever given to a governor." By all appearances, the authors of the thirty-second instruction in 1753 meant it to be taken just as Colden—and originally Smith—understood it.[77]

Although the lawyers had won a battle, they had not won the war. Appeals upon the merits of legal cases had been rejected, but Colden remained in office despite the hostile essays written by the lawyers. Watts had been right about one thing—Colden had pushed his interpretation of the instructions very hard. He had known early on that the king had been greatly interested in Cunningham's fate, so the lieutenant governor could proceed knowing his office was secure. Indeed, during October 1765 Johnson learned about "the King's satisfaction with Lieutenant Governor Colden."[78]

Watts, however, was wrong when he wrote that Colden thought that "a few Weeks reading will make an old Man of Eighty a greater Adept in Law" than all of New York's lawyers. Watts's arithmetic was off. On February 7, 1765 Colden became a spry 77 years old.[79]

Meanwhile, Parliament, which had not rushed to the rescue of the New York bar, had been busy. During Colden's birthday in 1765, Parliament was in the process of approving a new tax on the American colonies.[80] The parliamentary stamp tax would make Colden's 77th year the most stressful—and dangerous—one of his life.

NOTES

1. CC to AC, June 15, 1759, CC, "The Colden Letters on Smith's History," New York Historical Society, *Collections* 1 (1868): 186–87.

2. CC, "The Reading of an Elaborate Treatise on the Eye, by the Learned and Ingenious Dr. Porterfield Is the Occasion of the Following Reflections," in *The Philosophical Writings of Cadwallader Colden*, ed. Scott L. Pratt and John Ryder (Amherst, NY: Humanity Books, 2002), 137–38.

3. CC, "An Introduction to the Study of Phylosophy Wrote In America for the Use of a Young Gentleman," in *American Philosophical Addresses, 1700–1900*, ed. Joseph L. Blau (New York: Columbia University Press, 1946), 293; Edwin R. Purple, "Notes, Biographical and Genealogical, of the Colden Family, and of Some of Its Collateral Branches in America," *New York Genealogical and Biographical Record* 4 (1873): 167.

4. CC to Innys, August 6, 1718, *CP*, vol. 1, 41; New York Colony, *Calendar of New York Colonial Commissions, 1680–1770*, comp. E. B. O'Callaghan (New York: New York Historical Society, 1929), 31; Eugene R. Fingerhut, *Survivor: Cadwallader Colden II in Revolutionary America* (Washington, DC: University Press of America, 1983), 17.

5. JA to CC, July 10, 1752, *CP*, vol. 4, 340–41; CC to JA, [July 1752], *CP*, vol. 7, 352–55.

6. CC to Egremont, September 14, 1763, *CLB*, vol. 1, 230–31; CC, *The Conduct of Cadwallader Colden, Esquire, Late Lieutenant Governor of New York: Relating to The Judges Commissions, Appeals to the King, and the Stamp Duty* (1767), in *CLB*, vol. 2, 440; Alan Tully, *Forming American Politics: Ideals, Interests, and Institutions in Colonial New York and Pennsylvania* (Baltimore: Johns Hopkins University Press, 1994), 168.

7. William Smith, Jr., *The History of the Province of New York*, ed. Michael Kammen (Cambridge, MA: Belknap Press of Harvard University Press, 1972), vol. 2, 262.

8. CC to Council and Assembly, November 25, 1761, New York Colony, Council, *Journal of the Legislative Council of the Colony of New York, Began the 9th day of April, 1691; and ended the [3d of April, 1775]* (Albany, NY: Weed, Parsons, 1861), vol. 2, 1447.

9. Council to CC, November 30, 1761, New York Colony, Council, *Journal of the Legislative Council of the Colony of New York*, vol. 2, 1448–49; CC to Council, November 30, 1761, New York Colony, Council, *Journal of the Legislative Council of the Colony of New York*, vol. 2, 1449.

10. CC to Board of Trade, April 7, 1762, *CLB*, vol. 1, 186–91; John Adams, *Diary and Autobiography of John Adams*, ed. L. H. Butterfield (New York: Atheneum, 1964), vol. 1, 105.

11. CC to Board of Trade, April 7, 1762, *CLB*, vol. 1, 186–91; CC to Halifax, April 27, 1763, *CLB*, vol. 1, 479–80; "XYZ," "Of Good and Bad Rulers," March 16, 1762, *American Chronicle* (Farley), March 20, 1762; "Advertisement," *American Chronicle* (Farley) March 20, 1762; Milton M. Klein, *The American Whig: William Livingston of New York* (New York: Garland, 1990), 408–11; Tully, *Forming American Politics*, 168.

12. Dorothy Rita Dillon, *The New York Triumvirate: A Study of the Legal and Political Careers of William Livingston, John Morin Scott, William Smith, Jr.* (New York: Columbia University Press, 1949), 57–58.

13. CC, *Conduct*, 437; "Copy of Representation from the Board of Trade to the King in Council," March 27, 1762, New Jersey Colony, *Documents Relating to the Colonial History of the State of New Jersey*, ed. William A. Whitehead (Newark, NJ: Daily Advertiser Printing House, 1880–1886), vol. 9, 361–62; W. Smith, Jr., *History*, vol. 2, 261–62; Dillon, *New York Triumvirate*, 57–58.

14. CC to Board of Trade, April 5, June 2, September 25, October 6, 1761, *CLB*, vol. 1, 79–80, 88–90, 118–20, 122; CC to Pitt, August 11, September 24, 1761, *CLB*, vol. 1, 103–5, 116–17; W. Smith, Jr., *History*, vol. 2, 270–71; Oliver Morton Dickerson, *American Colonial Government, 1696–1765: A Study of the British Board of Trade in Its Relation to the American Colonies, Political, Industrial, Administrative* (Cleveland, OH: A. H. Clark, 1912), 202.

15. Thomas Jones, *History of New York during the Revolutionary War, Edited by Edward Floyd De Lancey* (New York: New York Historical Society, 1879; repr. Cranbury, NJ: Scholar's Bookshelf, 2006), vol. 1, 229–30; Great Britain, *Acts of Privy Council, Colonial Series*, ed. William L. Grant and James Munroe (London: H. M. S. O., 1908–1912), vol. 4, 449–500; Benjamin Pratt to CC, August 22, 1761, *CP*, vol. 6, 68–69; Klein, *American Whig*, 408–9.

16. CC to Shirley, July 25, 1749, *CP*, vol. 4, 125; CC to Mrs. CC, August 17, 1760, *CP*, vol. 9, 180–81; CC to Commissioners for Trade and Plantation, August 7, 1760, *CLB*, vol. 1, 5–6; CC to Halifax, August 11, 1760, *CLB*, vol. 1, 9–11; W. Smith, Jr., *History*, vol. 2, 249.

17. CC, *Conduct*, 434.

18. Watts to Monckton, June 30, 1764, in Watts, *Letter Book of John Watts, Merchant and Councillor of New York, January 1, 1762–December 22, 1765*, New York Historical Society, *Collections* 61 (1928): 270–71; CC to Halifax, November 11, 1760, *CLB*, vol. 1, 34–36.

19. CC to Lords of Trade, October 24, 1752, *NYCD*, vol. 6, 766; Jones, *History*, vol. 1, 223–24.

20. Jones, *History*, vol. 1, 223–25; Watts to Monckton, November 24, 1763, June 30, 1764, Watts, *Letter Book*, 203, 270–71; L. F. S. Upton, *The Loyal Whig: William Smith of New York and Quebec* (Toronto: University of Toronto Press, 1969), 47.

21. Pratt to CC, August 22, 1761, *CP*, vol. 6, 68–69; Jones, *History*, vol. 1, 226–28.

22. Pratt to CC, August 22, September 14, October 3, 1761, *CP*, vol. 6, 68–69, 76–78, 81–82.

23. CC to Pratt, October 12, 1761, *CLB*, vol. 1, 123–24; CC to Board of Trade, April 7, 1762, *CLB*, vol. 1, 186–91.

24. Pratt to T. Pownall, January 7, 1762, *CP*, vol. 6, 113–15; CC to Egremont, January 12, 1762, *CLB*, vol. 1, 150–53; Pratt to William Nicoll, March 15, 1762, *CLB*, vol. 1, 174–75; Pratt to Monckton, June 22, 1762, *Aspinwall Papers*, Massachusetts Historical Society, *Coll.*, 4th ser., 9–10 (1871): 462–65.

25. CC to J. Pownall, January 12, 1762, *CLB*, vol. 1, 154–55; CC to Board of Trade, February 11, 1762, *Aspinwall Papers*, vol. 9, 159–60; Privy Council report, November 11, 1761, *Aspinwall Papers*, vol. 9, 441–47; Privy Council to CC, June 11, 1762, *Aspinwall Papers*, vol. 9, 459; New York Colony, Council, *Journal of the Legislative Council of the Colony of New York*, vol. 2, 1461.

26. CC to J. Pownall, January 12, 1762, *CLB*, vol. 1, 154–55; CC to Pratt, October 12, 1761, March 7, 1762, *CLB*, vol. 1, 123–24, 171; CC to Monckton, March 30, 1762, *CLB*, vol. 1, 183–84; Pratt to T. Pownall, January 7, 1762, *CP*, vol. 6, 113–15; Privy Council to CC, June 11, 1762, *Aspinwall Papers*, vol. 9, 495; Pratt to Monckton, June 22, 1762, *Aspinwall Papers*, vol. 9, 462–65; Jones, *History*, vol. 1, 225–28, 230.

27. Indian deed, October 6, 1704, *CP*, vol. 6, 359–60; Kayaderosseras grant, *CP*, vol. 6, 360–66; CC to Johnson, January 6, 1765, *JP*, vol. 11, 523–24; Johnson to CC, March 21, 1765, *JP*, vol. 4, 694; Georgiana C. Nammack, *Fraud, Politics, and the Dispossession of the Indians: The Iroquois Land Frontier in the Colonial Period* (Norman: University of Oklahoma Press, 1969), 53–54. For legal documents, see New York State, *Calendar of N.Y. Colonial Manuscripts Indorsed Land Papers in the Office of the Secretary of State of New York, 1643–1803*, comp. E. B. O'Callaghan (Albany, NY: Weed, Parsons, 1864; repr. Harrison, NY: Harbor Hill Books, 1987), 65, 76–77, 80–81, 87, 89, 206.

28. Watts to Johnson, [March 26, 1765], *JP*, vol. 11, 663; Upton, *Loyal Whig*, 42; Nammack, *Fraud*, 104; Bernhard Knollenberg, *Origin of the American Revolution: 1759–1766* (New York: Macmillan, 1960), 208.

29. Assembly Deliberations, October 5, 1764, *CP*, vol. 6, 356–57; Journal of Indian Affairs, [September 1764], *JP*, vol. 11, 360; Nammack, *Fraud*, 64.

30. CC to Johnson, October 15, 1764, *JP*, vol. 11, 381–82; Gage to Shelburne, October 10, 1767, in Thomas Gage, *The Correspondence of General Thomas Gage with the Secretaries of State, 1763–1775*, ed. Clarence E. Carter (New Haven, CT: Yale University Press, 1931), vol. 1, 152.

31. CC to Johnson, November 19, 1764, March 15, 1765, *JP*, vol. 11, 468–69, vol. 4, 681–82; CC to Board of Trade, November 6, 1764, *CLB*, vol. 1, 392–93.

32. CC to Johnson, March 15, 1765, *JP*, vol. 4, 681–82.

33. Johnson to CC, June 18, 1761, *JP*, vol. 3, 408; CC to Johnson, March 15, 1765, Theodorus Bailey Myers Coll., no. 78, NYPL; CC to Board of Trade, June 8, 1765, *CLB*, vol. 2, 17–18; Wanda Burch, "A Little World Formed by His Hand," *New York History* 89, no. 2 (2008): 105.

34. Johnson to CC, July 5, 1765, *JP*, vol. 11, 823–25; Gage to Hillsborough, August 17, 1768, Gage, *Correspondence of General Thomas Gage*, vol. 1, 185; Moore to Hillsborough, August 17, 1768, *NYCD*, vol. 8, 92.

35. Watts to Monckton, July 31, 1763, Watts, *Letter Book*, 165–66; David L. Preston, "George Klock, the Canajoharie Mohawks, and the Good Ship *Sir William Johnson*: Land, Legitimacy, and Community in the Eighteenth-Century Mohawk Valley," *New York History* 86, no. 4 (2005): 485, 488; Preston, *The Texture of Contact: European and Indian Settler Communities on the Frontiers of Iroquoia, 1667–1783* (Lincoln: University of Nebraska Press, 2009), 271.

36. Watts to Monckton, July 31, 1763, Watts, *Letter Book*, 165–66; Johnson to CC, March 20, 1762, *JP*, vol. 3, 652–53; Preston, "George Klock," 475; Mary Lou Lustig, *Privilege and Prerogative: New York's Provincial Elite, 1710–1776* (Madison, NJ: Fairleigh Dickinson University Press, 1995), 119.

37. Proceedings against George Clock, April 7, 1762, *JP*, vol. 3, 672–74; CC to Johnson, December 27, 1761, July 28, 1763, *JP*, vol. 10, 350, 759–60.

38. CC to Johnson, November 28, 1764, Rare Books, 111170, vol. 1 part 2, Huntington Library, San Marino, CA; CC to Johnson, May 27, 1765, *JP*, vol. 11, 754; Alden T. Vaughan, *Transatlantic Encounters: American Indians in Britain, 1500–1776* (New York: Cambridge University Press, 2006), 183–86, 218.

39. Guy Johnson to CC, August 2, 1774, *JP*, vol. 8, 1192–93; Preston, "George Klock," 498.

40. Watts to Monckton, March 30, 1765, Watts, *Letter Book*, 340; Armand La Potin, "The Minisink Grant: Partnerships, Patents, and Processing Fees in Eighteenth Century New York," *New York History* 56, no. 1 (1975): 36–37.

41. CC to Board of Trade, August 9, 1764, *CLB*, vol. 1, 340–42; CC to _____, August 16, 1764, Manuscript Collection, Ch.M.1.9 (132), Boston Public Library.

42. CC to _____, August 16, 1764, Manuscript Collection, Ch.M.1.9 (132), Boston Public Library; CC to Board of Trade, October 13, 1764, *CLB*, vol. 1, 386–89.

43. Gouverneur Morris to John Dunlap, [April 22?, 1779], Smith, ed., *Letters of Delegates*, vol. 12, 375.

44. *SM*, vol. 2, 40; Smith to Monckton, November 5, 1764, *SM*, vol. 1, 26.

45. John Montresor, *The Montresor Journals*, ed. G. D. Scull, New York Historical Society, *Collections* 14 (1881): 341–42; New York Colony, Assembly, *Journal of the Votes and Proceedings of the General Assembly of the Colony of New York, 1691–1765* (New York: Hugh Gaine, 1764–1766), vol. 2, 804.

46. CC to Board of Trade, February 22, 1765, *CLB*, vol. 1, 467–68; Leonard Woods Labaree, *Royal Government in America: A Study of the British Colonial System before 1783* (New Haven, CT: Yale University Press, 1930), 409.

47. CC, *Conduct*, 442–43.

48. Joseph Henry Smith, *Appeals to the Privy Council from the American Plantations* (New York: Columbia University Press, 1950), 220, 394.

49. CC to Board of Trade, November 7, 1764, February 22, 1765, *CLB*, vol. 1, 395–98, 467–68. For appeals in New England, see Philip Ranlet, *Enemies of the Bay Colony: Puritan Massachusetts and Its Foes*, 2nd ed. (Lanham, MD: University Press of America, 2006), 28, 63–64, 67–68.

50. CC to Board of Trade, November 7, 1764, January 22, April 13, 1765, *CLB*, vol. 1, 395–98, 446–55, 477–79; CC to Halifax, December 13, 1764, *CLB*, vol. 1, 427–34; CC to Johnson, November 19, 1764, *JP*, vol. 11, 469; Daniel J. Hulsebosch, *Constituting Empire: New York and the Transformation of Constitutionalism in the Atlantic World, 1664–1830* (Chapel Hill: University of North Carolina Press, 2005), 119–20.

51. Robert Livingston to Monckton, January 26, 1765, *Aspinwall Papers*, vol. 10, 554–57; Halifax to CC, September 5, 1763, *CP*, vol. 6, 236. For the traditional rendition see Dillon, *New York Triumvirate*, 68–69.

52. CC to Waddell Cunningham, [c. April–May 1764], *CLB*, vol. 1, 325; Halifax to CC, September 5, 1763, *CP*, vol. 6, 236.

53. CC, "A Narrative, Etc.," December 13, 1764, *CLB*, vol. 1, 436–39; "Proclamation of Accession of George III by New York Council and Leading Citizens," January 17, 1761, *CP*, vol. 6, 6–9; Halifax to CC, September 5, 1763, *CP*, vol. 6, 236.

54. CC to Board of Trade, December 13, 1764, *CLB*, vol. 1, 421–25; Daniel Horsmanden, "Court of Errors: Cunningham agt. Forsey," November 19, 1764, *CLB*, vol. 1, 407–15; Milton M. Klein, "The Rise of the New York Bar: The Legal Career of William Livingston," *William and Mary Quarterly*, 3rd ser., 15, no. 3 (1958): 351; Upton, *Loyal Whig*, 44.

55. Horsmanden, "Court of Errors," November 19, 1764, *CLB*, vol. 1, 407–15; petition of Robert Ross Waddell, October 30, 1764, *CLB*, vol. 1, 417–19.

56. CC, "A Narrative, Etc.," December 13, 1764, *CLB*, vol. 1, 436–39; *SM*, vol. 1, 24; George Harison, "George Harison's Protest: New Light On Forsey versus Cunningham," ed. Herbert A. Johnson, *New York History* 50, no. 1 (1969): 78, 78n32, 78n34.

57. Harison, "George Harison's Protest," 65–66, 78, 78n32, 79–82.

58. Harison, "George Harison's Protest," 79, 81–82.

59. Petition of Waddell to CC, October 30, 1764, *CLB*, vol. 1, 417–19; CC, "Narrative," December 13, 1764, *CLB*, vol. 1, 436–39.

60. Harison to CC, November 24, 1764, *CP*, vol. 6, 387–88; Kempe to CC, October 31, 1764, *CP*, vol. 6, 368–71; CC, "Narrative," *CLB*, vol. 1, 436–39; *SM*, vol. 1, 24–25.

61. Kempe to CC, October 31, November 16, 1764, *CP*, vol. 6, 368–71, 378; CC to Kempe, November 16, 1764, Misc. Personal Name Files, box 24, NYPL.

62. CC, "Narrative," *CLB*, vol. 1, 436–39; CC to Board of Trade, November 7, 1764, *CLB*, vol. 1, 395–98.

63. CC to Board of Trade, January 22, 1765, *CLB*, vol. 1, 446–55; Johnson to CC, December 11, 1764, *JP*, vol. 4, 615–16.

64. CC to Board of Trade, December 13, 1764, *CLB*, vol. 1, 421–25; CC, "Narrative," December 13, 1764, *CLB*, vol. 1, 436–39.

65. Watts to Monckton, November 10, December 10, 1764, Watts, *Letter Book*, 309–10, 313–14.

66. Watts to Napier, December 14, 1764, Watts, *Letter Book*, 317–19; CC to Board of Trade, January 22, 1765, *CLB*, vol. 1, 446–55; Hulsebosch, *Constituting Empire*, 119.

67. CC, "Narrative," December 13, 1764, *CLB*, vol. 1, 436–39; Watts to Monckton, January 10, 1765, Watts, *Letter Book*, 319–22.

68. CC to Board of Trade, January 22, 27, 1765, *CLB*, vol. 1, 446–55, 461–62; CC to Halifax, January 23, [1765], *CLB*, vol. 1, 456–59.

69. CC to Board of Trade, January 22, 1765, *CLB*, vol. 1, 446–55; CC to Council, January 3, 1765, *CLB*, vol. 1, 441–42; CC, "Opinion on Appeals," *CP*, vol. 7, 1; CC to Johnson, January 12, 1765, *JP*, vol. 11, 529.

70. Livingston to Monckton, January 26, 1765, *Aspinwall Papers*, vol. 10, 554–57; Watts to Monckton, January 10, 1765, Watts, *Letter Book*, 319–22; *SM*, vol. 1, 28.

71. CC to Halifax, January 23, [1765], *CLB*, vol. 1, 456–59; CC to Board of Trade, January 27, April 14, 1765, *CLB*, vol. 1, 461–62, 476–77; CC to Monckton, May 3, 1765, *CLB*, vol. 2, 2–3.

72. CC to Halifax, December 13, 1764, January 23, [1765], *CLB*, vol. 1, 427–34, 456–59.

73. CC to Halifax, December 13, 1764, , *CLB*, vol. 1, 427–34; Collinson to CC, October 7, 1764, *CP*, vol. 6, 393–94.

74. CC to Johnson, March 3, 1765, New Netherlands Coll., oldest New York, and the colonial government, 1655–1744 (microfilm), no. 69, NYHS; R. R. Livingston to Robert Livingston, March 4, 1765, Robert R. Livingston Papers, NYHS; CC to Monckton, May 3, 1765, Misc. Personal Name Files, box 24, NYPL.

75. CC to Halifax, February 22, 1765, *CLB*, vol. 1, 469–71; CC to Whytt, February 2, 1765, *CLB*, vol. 1, 465.

76. Great Britain, *Acts of Privy Council*, ed. Grant and Munroe, vol. 4, 740; vol. 5, 727–28; vol. 6, 419–20; Board of Trade on appeals from the New York Courts, September 24, 1765, *NYCD*, vol. 7, 762–63; Dickerson, *American Colonial Government*, 280.

77. Board of Trade on appeals, September 24, 1765, *NYCD*, vol. 7, 762–63; Dickerson, *American Colonial Government*, 192.

78. Watts to Monckton, February 23, 1765, Watts, *Letter Book*, 334; *JP*, vol. 4, 855.

79. Watts to Monckton, January 10, 1765, Watts, *Letter Book*, 319–22.

80. Monckton to CC, February 9, 1765, *CP*, vol. 7, 11–12; Smith to Monckton, May 30, 1765, *SM*, vol. 1, 29–30.

Chapter Fourteen

Civil War

Cadwallader Colden insisted that, during the *Stamp Act* troubles, he was "under greater difficulties that any Governor ever met with since I knew America." What happened was all his fault John Watts declared. "The Old Gentleman," Watts wrote in November 1765, had brought on the crisis "owing to his own impolitick Conduct, which is bred in the Bone." The royal governor of New Jersey, William Franklin, the son of Colden's friend, also chimed in, claiming that the lieutenant governor's "unnecessary Officiousness . . . made Matters much worse . . . than they otherwise would have been.[1]

Though Governor Franklin failed to mention that he had asked Colden to protect New Jersey's stamps, most historians agreed with him that Colden had botched everything relating to Parliament's *Stamp Act*. However, a Whig historian, David Ramsay, pointed out that the rioters had been so turbulent primarily because of their dislike of Colden's "political sentiments."[2]

The political atmosphere had been poisoned by New York's entrenched interests who saw Colden as a threat and wanted him removed because of his push for appeals. Then came their campaign to stir up hatred toward the *Stamp Act*. When the two targets of their hatred converged, the violent, shocking result should not have surprised anyone—but it did.

After years passed, a former member of New York's Council thought he understood how the New York mob had become empowered:

> The people of consideration feel too late their ill policy in having made [the mob] so consequential and omnipotent in the time of the disturbances occasioned by the Stamp Act and fear now to attempt . . . to resume the power with which they then conspired to arm the Multitude, that they now see a Monster of their own creation.[3]

319

In May 1765 the lawyers' agitation over *Forsey v. Cunningham* continued in New York. Colden thought nothing would come of it, aside from making him very unpopular. He predicted that "the People will quietly submit to the authority of Parliament and his Majesty's determination of the case in dispute relating to appeals." Indeed, there had been no disruption in the normal operations of government.[4]

The same month Robert Monckton had told William Smith Jr. that the new governor's instructions would be changed to eliminate appeals on the facts of a case. Every bit of news that came from Britain, carefully scrutinized, was sometimes wrongly analyzed driving Colden's foes into a panic that he might win. So the attacks on him did not diminish. By August 1765 a French traveler (who happened to be a spy), after dining with John Watts and General Thomas Gage, reported that Watts would succeed Colden as lieutenant governor. Watts even asserted that Colden's stand on appeals "is more detested than the Stamp Act."[5]

In early March 1765 New Yorkers already had a good idea of the *Stamp Act*'s details. Parliament had had no role in *Forsey v. Cunningham*; Colden's assertion that New Yorkers would accept Parliament's authority referred to the upcoming stamp duties. There seemed no reason to doubt that, nor any reason to think that Watts was wrong that the appeals issue would have more impact than the stamp taxes. That appeared likely even though, as Judge Robert Livingston believed, the new taxes "will heavily burthen us."[6]

Later, Colden realized how his confident assertion about New Yorkers accepting Parliament's taxing authority over the colonies was totally wrong. His stand on appeals had earned him the "most violent Resentment of the Faction" that controlled New York's courts:

> They, taking Advantage of the general Abhorence against the Stamp Act, and which had been raised by the inflammatory Papers daily published, turned the Edge of the popular Fury against the Person of the Lieutenant Governor, which before that Time they had not been able to do.[7]

The unrelenting media assault had made New Yorkers see themselves as "absolute Slaves" in the words of William Smith Jr. Trying again to mislead future generations, he wrote that "Mr. Colden's obnoxious Character added Fuel to the general Discontent—His Attempt to invade the Right of Trials by Jury in the late Appeal Cause falling in with it" and so on.[8]

"The Pr[inters] all mad," Watts commented, and they were. They had disliked DeLancey's stamp tax, which taxed newspapers as did the parliamentary version. John Holt, probably the maddest, published in mid-May 1765 one essay, "To the Printer," which denied that the colonies were "virtually represented in Parliament." Therefore, the colonies "have not given, nor can they possibly give their Consent to be there taxed, consequently that such a Tax must be arbitrary illegal and oppressive." Disturbed by this essay, Colden directed Attorney-General John Tabor Kempe to examine it. This time Kempe did not avoid the issue, telling the lieutenant governor that he thought "the Author and publisher punishable."[9]

Far worse was in the offing. What Colden dubbed "The most remarkable" of these publications, the *Constitutional Courant*, appeared in September 1765. Designed to look like a newspaper, it has been called both a "political manifesto" and a "political screed." "Shall we sit down quietly, while the yoke of slavery is wreathing about our necks? . . . Poor America! the bootless privilege of complaining, always allowed to the vilest criminals on the rack, is denied thee!," the tract trumpeted. The *Constitutional Courant* advocated violence, if necessary, to stop the stamp taxes and targeted "all those enemies and betrayers of their Country's most sacred rights, who officiously endeavour to enforce it." When the essays of the *Constitutional Courant* finally reached the mother country, they did not go over well. Especially infuriating across the Atlantic was the assertion that Parliament's authority had been "usurped" so the colonists owed no more respect to it "in this respect, than the Divan of Constantinople."[10]

Aside from publishing such essays, the printers had another trick up their sleeves—a popular medium of the day, almanacs. In order to beat the start of the stamp tax, they produced their new almanacs early. Enclosed within their pages, the printers included an alphabetical list of all the items subject to taxation by the *Stamp Act*—intending to inflame customers who did not pay attention to newspapers. Observing this multimedia campaign, Sir William Johnson commented to Colden that "The Liberty of the press is a darling Subject, generally insisted most upon, by those who most abuse it."[11]

At first Colden believed that the printers had failed "for a considerable Time" to infuriate the populace. Eventually, however, the attacks began to work. By October 1765, Colden sadly noted, "the People of this Town appeared as much inclined to Sedition and Violence as in any other of the Colonies." As Colden wrote later, "the people's spirits were inflamed to a degree of Madness by the Seditious papers which were published filled with every falsehood which malice could invent." He suggested that the "common people" would not have succumbed to hatred "had not some in high Trust privately promoted the most violent Proceedings" in print. To General Amherst, the lieutenant governor explained who these culprits were: "No man in this Place doubts who the Authors are. A few popular Lawyers whom you know well."[12]

When the *Constitutional Courant* suddenly appeared, Colden noticed that no printer had been listed, but he had a good idea whose press it had flowed from. James Parker, whose type was old and worn down, had to be the source. Colden could easily check one of his own publications printed by Parker to determine that the *Courant* was an obvious match. For good measure, Colden solicited Benjamin Franklin's opinion but Franklin, in England, had been in business with Parker and never responded. Actually, William Goddard, another printer, had produced the *Courant* using Parker's type. Nonetheless, Colden investigated and learned that Parker had brought the offending publication to the royal post office, which delivered the tract all the way from Boston to Charleston, South Carolina. As it turned out, Parker and the other printers escaped legal prosecution because both Colden and the councilors agreed that in the people's "present temper" it was best not to infuriate them any more than they were. Attorney-General Kempe feared for his safety if he tried "any such Prosecutions."[13]

One wonders how the common folks would have reacted if they had realized that Colden and Kempe had both been influential in the crafting of the *Stamp Act*. In August 1764, after Parliament had deemed a colonial stamp tax necessary, Colden had been ordered to immediately create "a List of all Instruments made use of in publick Transactions, Law Proceedings, Grants, Conveyances, Securities of Land or money" in New York so they could be slapped with a tax. Colden did his duty by directing Kempe to undertake the assignment. According to Colden, Kempe had been "diligent and accurate" and produced a "full" list which was sent off to London. Although all the governors had received the same order, Colden's letter, the first to arrive in the imperial capital, would be utilized in the actual drafting of the *Stamp Act*. Only later did New Yorkers discover what the "black List" included.[14]

Despite such distressing news and the continuing press assault, the colony of New York remained relatively calm as the summer months approached and the gentlemen involved in government fled to their country estates as usual. Colden believed his return to Spring Hill "was necessary for the preservation of my Health during the heats of summer." General Gage joined the exodus and stayed near Colden's abode. Their pleasant summer interlude would be shattered by "violent Riots" in Boston.[15]

The lieutenant governor, naturally, could not avoid public business at Spring Hill. James McEvers, who had been made distributor of New York's stamps, journeyed to Flushing in August, well before the *Stamp Act*'s start on November 1, to sign a bond required to execute the office. Then news reached New York of the Boston riots; "there was nothing talked of at York . . . but the spirited and patriotic behavior" there (at least according to the French spy) which caused the Massachusetts distributor to resign. Sir William Johnson saw the Boston events as "Violent and unaccountable Conduct;" Colden agreed. Quickly, McEvers, bombarded with threats, became "so frightened" he resigned. New York newspapers printed more details of hostility directed at the stamp distributors in Connecticut and Rhode Island. According to one historian, "The conflagration spread like a prairie fire" and led to one resignation after another.[16]

On August 30, 1765 Colden at Spring Hill learned there was trouble afoot when he received McEvers's resignation letter. He blamed the resignation on the Boston violence, "the Inflamatory Papers lately printed in the Colonies," and McEvers's wish to escape "the same Cruel Fate" meted out to the distributor in Boston. Colden declared: "I shall not be intimidated." The stamp taxes would be implemented as the law specified though the lieutenant governor realized "that great prudence is required in my conduct."[17]

Colden had understood as early as July that problems over the stamps might hit New York. On July 8, 1765 he had asked Gage for some soldiers to garrison the city's Fort George, then totally bereft of any military force. To the general, he explained that the fort needed to be in readiness to protect the city against a slave revolt—something that might arise in an unsettled time— "or a Mob." The commander-in-chief scrounged up a few soldiers to put into the deserted fort.[18]

The next month, before both McEvers's resignation and Gage's return to the city, Colden told the general he "might have occasion to demand . . . assistance for the Support of the Civil Power." New York's customs officers had also requested troops. Right after McEvers's letter reached Spring Hill, Colden received a missive from the general with bad news. The soldiers Colden needed were far away; given the slowness of land travel, the lieutenant governor had to make do with what he had. And Gage expressed his shock at what he was witnessing: "It must give every well-wisher to his Country the greatest Pain and Anxiety to see the Publick Papers crammed with Treason, the Minds of the People disturbed, excited and encouraged to revolt against the Government, to subvert the Constitution and trample upon the Laws."[19]

What Colden had predicted in 1727 had finally happened: an act of Parliament had to be enforced by military might. The problem was that Colden did not have enough military might to enforce the law. At least Gage vowed his support. "The Military can do nothing by themselves; but must act wholly and solely in obedience to the Civil Power." Colden was in charge—and just as well. Later on Gage admitted: "I must confess . . . that during these commotions . . . I have never been more at a loss how to act, to perform the Duty" he owed to his sovereign and nation without stirring up anti-military feelings. All he had to do was give "an opening" and everything that happened would be blamed on his soldiers.[20]

Colden knew what he had to do. He left "immediately" for the city and called a Council meeting. The lieutenant governor had not met with the councilors who had "not been in good humour for some time past." But he needed to consult them now. The first attempt brought in only three of the Council—Chief Justice Daniel Horsmanden along with William Smith Sr. and Watts—as all the others were still at their country homes. More councilors were needed. Finally on September 7 eight of them had arrived and

Colden briefed them on Gage's letter. The Council, however, believed that New Yorkers would not tolerate "any Riot or Tumult." The fort had a large enough garrison for a defensive posture. It was best, the councilors thought, "to shew a Confidence in the People" rather than suggesting "distrust of them" by bringing in more soldiers (who were weeks away anyway).[21]

When Colden first arrived in the city, he soon learned that Major Thomas James, an artillery officer, had by Gage's order—but without any directive from the lieutenant governor—moved howitzers, ammunition, and supplies into the fort. As Colden later observed, "This gave the first uneasiness to the people." Making matters worse, the major's "imprudent discourse" had "raised their resentment more against him than any other man in the province,"[22] rather remarkable given that Colden lived in New York.

Colden did not object to such precautions, believing that "acting with vigour seemed the more necessary as the eyes of all the other Colonies were on New York." Its capital had a garrisoned fort, General Gage's headquarters, and warships patrolled its harbor.[23]

Fort George, Colden knew, "was far from being in a proper State of Defence." No shock to Colden, in 1763 he had written to Monckton: "You know Sir the State of the Fort, that it is needless for me to mention any thing of it." Over the years the fort had been considered primarily as the site of the governor's house; its military trappings had been lessened "for the Pleasure and Conveniency of his Family." The astute French spy noticed that Fort George's guns were "in very bad order." Because the Council insisted "that there was no Danger of Riots or Mobs," Colden decided to leave the neglected fort as it was, but he did take a precaution. He obtained from Captain John Montresor a copy of his report to Gage giving suggestions how to bolster the fort's defenses. In early September, however, Montresor's report was still only for the lieutenant governor's "private perusal."[24]

In September, Colden continued to do his duty, which included giving a fugitive stamp distributor, Zacharias Hood of Maryland, "a Bed in his House" in the fort. But the lieutenant governor had to note: "I have received no kind of Directions in relation to the Stamped Papers." A change in the leadership of the British government must have been responsible for the lack of guidance from Britain. At least Sir William Johnson gave his old friend and ally his support: "The Steps You have taken for the Security of the Officers of the Crown, are as resolute, as they are necessary, for in Riots of a Mob, no Person can think himself safe unless he is one of them."[25]

Late in September, Colden received a letter, dated July 2, from the newly appointed governor of New York, Sir Henry Moore, Jamaica's former governor, then in London. Colden soon congratulated him and told him "Nothing could give me more pleasure than that you were in this Place at this time." His being on the spot "would contribute to bring the People to their senses, who seem now to be running Mad in opposition to the Stamp Act."

Assuring Moore that he had done everything possible "to have your authority properly supported," Colden added that "no man can more earnestly desire your speedy arrival than I do," not surprising given the circumstances.[26]

As September ebbed, New Yorkers, who expected Moore to arrive literally any day, did have some concern about him. A West Indian by birth, Moore came from a region rather unpopular in New York because of lingering anger over the *Sugar Act*. In early October Colden received another latter from Moore—this one dated August 9—which suggested that he would sail into New York in about two weeks. With a replacement on the way, Colden's authority declined while the crisis in New York did not calm. Though Colden hoped to transfer the administration "in perfect quietness," that seemed less and less likely. In October 1765 the Council strongly recommended against any legal action against those behind the *Constitutional Courant* for fear of "raising the Mob."[27]

With Moore not present, Colden had to deal with the crisis as it continued to develop. A *Stamp Act* Congress, branded "an illegal convention" by Colden, gathered in New York City. On September 23 the shocked Colden revealed that this congress had been "kept secret from me till lately." Not knowing the "plausable pretences" behind the meeting of various colonials, he explained to London that "their real intentions may be dangerous." The "very resolute" Colden kept delaying the Assembly's meeting to prevent its sending official delegates to the congress; some New York assemblymen, including Judge Livingston, attended anyway. The congress, seen in Britain as "directly treasonable," had no effect.[28]

While Colden and many others wondered what the ineffectual *Stamp Act* Congress would do, a more significant notice appeared in the mad printer John Holt's newspaper:

> A Meeting of the Friends to Liberty and the English Constitution, in this City and Parts adjacent, is earnestly desired, by great Numbers of the Inhabitants, in order to form an Association of All who are not already Slaves, in Opposition to all Attempts to make them so.[29]

By all appearances, this blurb resulted in the creation of the New York Sons of Liberty, a group that bedeviled Colden for the rest of his life.

Soon after, the *Stamp Act* crisis came to life. On October 23, a ship carrying the dreaded stamps entered the harbor. Even the passengers had been kept in the dark about the hated cargo. Colden had already, in early September, made a plan to protect the stamps. He had arranged with Captain Archibald Kennedy, the commander of the small naval force based in New York (and also the son of his deceased friend), to have naval officers check each vessel as it sailed into the harbor till they found the right ship. Then Kennedy's squadron would inform the ship's captain of the "great danger" his cargo was in. Colden specified that the stamp ship be anchored away from the wharf, close by the warships, "till such time as proper measures can be taken for securing the stamps from any violence," surprising a mob of 2,000 that expected an immediate docking of their target. That night, after they had dispersed, the stamps were brought ashore and into Fort George "without any guard." Colden had avoided a major confrontation because "The Demagogues were not apprised of this."[30]

Although no instructions had come with the stamps, Colden hoped to employ them "if possible," a difficult task without a stamp distributor. David Colden, his father's secretary, saw the potential for an office. No competition existed for the job as death threats were directed at anyone who tried to issue the stamps. David explained to his potential employers in London that, since he would be helping his father with the stamps—and so would "incur . . . danger and Odium"—he might as well "enjoy the advantages of that office when it is quietly submitted to . . . in a few months." David's confident prediction no doubt was caused by the still apparent calm in the city despite the threats.[31]

Nonetheless, the lieutenant governor probably had a good idea of what was coming. He commented that "I have had a difficult part to act at this time, but I hope soon to be relieved from it by Sir Henry Moore's Arrival, when I shall return to Spring Hill." This time, Colden really was looking forward to retirement as long as he received "the favour of the Crown in his old age." Despite such wistful thoughts of retirement, he would do his duty. Sir William Johnson echoed Colden's own beliefs when he wrote him: "Whilst an Act of Parliament remains in force, it is certainly the Duty of all Officers of the Crown to support it, and I have not the least reason to think that a popular Clamor will ever intimidate You."[32]

Pleasant daydreams of philosophical amusements at Spring Hill had to be brusquely pushed aside on October 31. With still no sign of Moore despite his being "daily expected," the news in New York appeared ominous. An individual came forward to alert Colden that there was talk of a plot to kill Major James and "that a Riot or Tumultuous Proceedings were intended this day or Tomorrow." Colden informed the city magistrates he would provide them "all the assistance in my power to maintain the Peace," which, frankly, was minimal. Having assumed that Moore would suddenly appear, Colden had not taken the oath to enforce the *Stamp Act* required of governors, but he could delay no longer. On October 31 he swore the oath, a day before the commencement of the stamp taxes, making the end of October—in the colonists' eyes—"the last day of Liberty."[33]

Meanwhile, everyone wanted to know what General Gage was going to do; his letters were being opened covertly. Colden, insisting that he had "no military skill," invited Gage "to take the command of the Fort, which he refused." Later, when violence erupted, Gage, outside the fort, asked Colden "to have 60 Men in readiness to March out for his defence in his House, being threatened by the Mob." Gage realized that if he ordered soldiers to fire on civilians, his career would be hurt. Even Gage's aides were outside the fort; in no way could the commander-in-chief of British forces in North America be blamed for what might happen. It would all be Colden's responsibility, by the general's design.[34]

Gage made his position clear in early November 1765: "I have hitherto only acted in my proper sphere of granting all aid and assistance to the Civil Power. Tho endeavours have been used to draw me in to be the acting Person, which while it is a Mob I shall avoid." Only if the disturbance "increases to Arms it's then Rebellion, and every Faithful subject must do his utmost and particularly belongs to me to be active in suppressing it."[35] Unless there was a full-scale armed rebellion, Colden, the officers, and men in Fort George were on their own.

When the disturbances began on November 1, they swirled for months with an occasional break in the turmoil.[36] One reason why the mobbing surged on for so long is the freakish weather of the winter and spring of 1765–1766. On May 6, 1766 James Parker described this meteorologic oddity: "Tho' we have had a very mild Winter, we have had the coldest and most backward Spring I think that ever I knew. There has not been but one warm Day properly speaking since the Month of February, and it is so cold now, that I am obliged to keep by the Fire." During the winter months, there were some cold days and it did snow, yet, overall, the weather was very warm for New York.[37]

Normally, drunken men, "in high spirits full of Old Madiera," confronted by cold, wintery weather, would have fallen asleep inside by a fireplace, but the freakish warmth encouraged the drunks to prowl about the city, hoping to find some enemy of the people with a renowned wine cellar. So the city witnessed, in Colden's words, "a savage Mob . . . such as has rarely happened in any civilized Country."[38]

The events of November 1, 1765 suggest that Colden's statement had little exaggeration in it. Already aware that serious problems were possible that evening, the lieutenant governor asked Captain Kennedy to dispatch his small detachment of marines to the fort; he complied despite his fear that, with the marines gone, his sailors might desert. Colden also asked that Montresor and another military engineer do what they could, hurriedly, to improve Fort George's defenses. Lieutenant Governor Colden lacked the authority to order the military men to work on the post so he asked Gage to give the order and the general complied. The engineers now scurried about, removing a wooden fence outside the fort itself that could shield rioters from gunfire. Other obstructions also were disposed of, giving the garrison a clear line of fire around the fort's walls.[39]

Literally, "a few Minutes before the mob came up," Colden received an anonymous diatribe by "New York" that had been posted at a coffeehouse earlier in the day. Attacking Colden for swearing the oath to enforce the *Stamp Act*, the author vowed that the tax would never be levied "so long as a Man has life to defend his injured Country." Comparing the lieutenant governor to "wicked Men of old" who plotted to murder the Apostle Paul, the writer seemed assured that as "God defeated their bloody purposes,. . . we trust he'll do Yours." "New York" also predicted: "You'll die a martyr to your own villainy, and be hanged, like Porteis upon a Sign Post, as a memento to all wicked Governors," an allusion to Colden being a Scot. An Edinburgh guard, a Captain Porteous, responsible for shooting at rioters almost twenty years before, had been lynched as his reward.[40]

As the evening began, the garrison of about 150 men watched a mob, perhaps of 2,000 "Rabble or rather Rebels," approach the fort. And this mob was badly informed about what the soldiers could do. General Gage explained the mob's "chief dependence was that the Fort would not fire as no Civil Magistrate was with them." This mistaken thinking is a reference to the parliamentary *Riot Act* (1714), which specified that, before soldiers could fire on civilians, a magistrate had to first announce the specifics of the *Riot Act* to rioters, ordering them to disperse. Yet soldiers could fire to protect themselves, and an acting governor could order soldiers to fire on a mob. This confused understanding of the law led directly, in 1770, to the Boston Massacre. But that was Massachusetts; this was New York in 1765 with Cadwallader Colden in charge.[41]

Given that many of the rioters were drunken, their lack of legal understanding is no surprise. Nor is their behavior. At first, the garrison feared that the mob's members had numerous guns. They did have some, but most only had "clubs and such like weapons." The rioters did toss "bricks and stones against the Fort" and smaller stones flied over the ramparts inside the fort itself.[42]

The mob had come prepared with its own props. An effigy of Colden had been prepared:

> In his Hand was a stamped Paper, which he seemed to court the People to receive;. . . at his Back hung a Drum; on his Breast a Label, supposed to allude to some former circumstances of his Life. By his Side hung, with a Boot in his Hand, the grand Deceiver of Mankind, seeming to urge him to Perseverance in the cause of Slavery.[43]

Both effigies again referred to Scotland. The drum conjured up the old, false story that Colden had been a drummer for the Jacobites. The label stated: "The Rebel Drummer in the year 1715." The devil effigy suggested more recent events. The boot held by Beelzebub was a not subtle allusion to the Scot Lord Bute, who had been the king's tutor and advisor and was blamed for the *Stamp Act*.[44]

As these props were paraded downtown to the fort, Colden's effigy "sat on an old Chair which a Seaman Carried." At one point Mayor John Cruger sent city constables, who knocked the effigy down. The mob did not tolerate this interference: "The persons attending ordered it to be taken up again in the most Magisterial manner, and told the Mayor etc., they would not hurt them, provided they stood out of their way." The law retreated. During the march, "now and then" some of the rioters amused themselves by "firing a pistol at the Effigy" of Colden, still "carried in a chair." The mob "went to the fort that the Governor might see his Effigy if he dare show his face."[45]

Upon arriving at Fort George, "the Mob gave several huzzas and threatened the Officers upon the wall Particularly Major James." Since the rioters believed that Colden had joined the Jacobites in 1715, "the Mob had Assurance Enough to break open the Governor's Coach house"—which was outside the fort—"and took his Coach" (more properly called a chariot) "from under the muzzle of the Cannon." The rioters placed the Colden effigy on top of his chariot and dragged it to Wall Street where "the Merchants were exceedingly Pleased." The mob returned to the fort via Broadway. When James spotted the mob, he exclaimed: "Here they come by God."[46]

Now the rioters built a gallows, hanged both effigies, and moved them. A sort of parade took place to the fort, led by Colden's chariot, followed by the effigies and the gallows, all of which were put by the gate of the fort. Seeing a "Soldier upon the walls," he was ordered "to tell the rebel drummer or Major James to Give orders to fire." Various projectiles were tossed at the fort as already related. According to Judge Livingston, a few of the mob actually managed to get "their hands on the top of the Ramparts" of the fort.[47]

By this time all of Fort George's garrison stood on the ramparts. Their professionalism impressed the lieutenant governor. "Notwithstanding of the grossest Ribaldry from the Mob" and the flying stones, "not a single word was returned from any Man in the Fort." Just as impressed, Livingston noted "the patience and temper of the officers and soldiers" especially given "the highest provocation" of "the most opprobrious language." No one saw fit to record what vile obscenities were spewed at the soldiers.[48]

Another distressing event for Colden would happen by the fort. The rioters now brought the effigies, the gallows, Colden's chariot, and some sledges a few feet further away to Bowling Green. Using the remains of the fort's disassembled fence as kindling, the mob started a bonfire fueled by the purloined property. As the press reported, "the Lieutenant Governor and his Friends had the Mortification of viewing the whole Proceeding from the Ramparts."[49]

It was bad enough for Colden having to watch the destruction of property—not all of which belonged to him. What made it worse was that while the mob created this bonfire, "a great number of Gentlemen of the Town, if they can be called so, stood round to observe this outrage on their King's Governor." He believed, as did others in the fort, that sending a small number of the garrison outside would have prevented the spectacle, "but perhaps with Bloodshed, as many of the Mob were drunk; and when once Blood is shed no Man can tell where it will end." Colden could have acted even more drastically by having the cannons and soldiers fire from the fort. Colden wrote: "in such Case many more innocent People must have suffered than the whole Number of the Guilty." In the end, the safety of "that most insolent Mob" depended upon Colden's "Prudence and Humanity." Once again, the lieutenant governor was enthused by the sterling conduct of the garrison. Though they watched what was happening, "not a single return was made in words or otherwise from any Man in the Fort while this egregious Insult was performing." The soldiers would not fire on the mob unless Colden gave them the order.[50]

Apparently, the mob decided it had dealt sufficiently with the lieutenant governor for the moment. The time had come to settle scores with someone it hated even more. While at the fort, members of the mob yelled to Major James that, as soon as the bonfire had burned itself out, "they would knock down his house." And they did. Marching up Broadway, they reached James's leased luxurious residence, Vauxhall, near the northern limit of the city. The sizable mob, "in less than ten Minutes," all but gutted it. Then the rioters devoted themselves to destroying the contents of James's home and drinking some "3 or 4 Pipes of wine," a significant task indeed. They may have consumed up to 368 gallons (one source, modestly, suggested some of the wine had been destroyed in some other way). Almost everything that could be burned fueled a second bonfire except "only one red Silk Curtain they kept for a Colour." The mob also busied itself by "threatening to take away his life in the most shameful manner." This sacking had been inspired by press reports of the earlier, similar destruction of Lieutenant Governor Thomas Hutchinson's Boston mansion, an act that had drawn an estimated 10,000 individuals who had gawked at the wreckage.[51] After the destruction of Vauxhall, the rioters assaulted "some bawdy houses." Only about 4:00 a.m. the following morning did the commotion end—for the moment.[52]

Judge Livingston had believed the rioting was over. He was wrong. The stamps remained in the fort and, as Colden related, on November 2 "the Mob continued to patrol the Streets;" the New Englanders had not left. In fact, the lieutenant governor thought the rioters were "encouraged by their late Success," so "they boldly threatened to put every Person in the Fort to Death, and at any Risk to destroy the Stamped Papers there." According to a message received by the Council, the mob now specified that its demands be delivered to Colden; he was not to enforce the stamp taxes but was supposed to tell Parliament to repeal the hated law and to send the stamps in the fort away on one of Kennedy's ships. If these demands were not met, Colden would be killed—"the People seemed determined, one and all, to set fire to the Fort," a tactic that the mob had not yet employed.[53]

Colden had summoned the Council to ask for its advice, mostly hoping for support for further strengthening of Fort George. The Council agreed and the military engineers, again, hurriedly improved the fort's defenses. This was a wise move for the mob, a participant declared, "was resolved to have the Governor Dead or Alive."[54]

During the evening of November 2, the mob reappeared and grew to a "very considerable body" of "thousands." Colden, once again, met with the Council, some of whose members, the lieutenant governor understood, had "called me an obstinate old man, in opposing the violent spirit of the People." That "opinion was every where propagated in Town." Meanwhile, his son Alexander and his family had fled to Kennedy's ship out of fear of the mob, which vowed "to destroy everything" the lieutenant governor "had both in Town and country."[55]

At this Council meeting, which lasted for two hours, Colden reiterated that he had no instructions about what to do with the stamps and again asked the councilors for their advice. The Council recommended that he calm the mob by declaring he would "do nothing" about the stamp tax and leave the matter for Governor Moore. The lieutenant governor did so. Immediately, councilors rushed out to "the Mob and declared to them what I had agreed to, on which a general huzza was given, and they dispersed in all appearance with satisfaction."[56]

Actually, the Council had wanted far more. The eager councilors had also been willing to give in to the mob on a vital point, transferring the stamps to the control of the navy. When Colden asked Captain Kennedy if he would take the stamps, he declined. Assuming that the stamps could be transported safely to the waterside seemed dubious at best under the current circumstances, the captain noted. Why move them from secure Fort George?[57]

Colden totally agreed with the mariner, seeing the demand as merely an attempt "to insult the Government." And Colden knew, as did the New Yorkers in the mob, that Kennedy's father had amassed a great deal of real estate in the city, all of which "Directors of the Mob" would have targeted as soon as he controlled the stamps. There was no need to subject Kennedy to such pressure when the stamps still remained safe where they were.[58]

Both Colden and the mob's director also knew that the naval ships would not be secure for much longer. Because the city's harbor froze during winter, the warships had to be protected from the ice by going to a wharf; their guns were unloaded making them defenseless. The rioters would then reach the sailors: "it is well known Sailors easily may be seduced." Even the Council seemed embarrassed by its request and asked that it not be recorded in the minutes.[59]

The mob, seemingly satisfied, broke up after Colden's declaration, but the rioters, in smaller groups, continued to roam about the city. Montresor related what happened afterward: "Money extracted from private people or die, others threatened their public chests, city treasure, Custom House, etc." That the individuals continued to act mobbish could not have surprised Colden, who had pointed out that "a great part of the Mob consists of Men who have been Privateers and disbanded Soldiers whose view is to plunder the Town."[60]

These still hostile persons were likely among the "strange set" of about 200 men Livingston discovered who had taken a barber's pole "dressed up with a parcel of Rags." The "mad project" they had planned, the surprised judge realized, was to employ the pole as a battering ram to force their way into the fort to seize the stamps. The news of Colden's declaration stopped the suicidal scheme. "The most turbulent" probably kept wandering around the streets.[61]

On November 3, "while the People were in Commotion," soldiers spiked various cannons around the city that rioters might employ against the fort. This news meant, one rioter believed, that Colden had "ordered the cannon of the Battery to be spiked up for the Mob should Come so far as Break out A Civil war and knock down the fort." Some of the least drunk rioters, "enraged at Mr. Colden for spiking up the guns on the Battery," now utilized high technology to aid their cause. "They contrived a machine"—an automatron—"on which there was a wooden cannon and his effigy drilling the touch hole, designing thereby, to represent him clearing the cannon which he had spiked up."[62]

That the military spiked cannons demonstrated that Colden's declaration could not end the turmoil. The same day as the spiking, General Gage's aides finally joined the fort's garrison, another bad sign. The mob's leader had, by that time, turned on John Holt, of all people, who seemed to be slacking in his devotion. The mad printer received a death threat and a promise to destroy his home, just as Major James's dwelling had been ransacked.[63]

And, of course, Colden did not escape threats. Early on November 3, a Sunday, a mysterious letter appeared by the fort's gate, supposedly from a friend of his. Although warning about treating "the guides of the People" with "an impolitic Contempt," this author probably did not yet know about the spikings. The postscript caught the lieutenant governor's attention: "You are not safe at Flushing." Colden would observe: "Could I be assured that no villanous assassin would come from this Town, I should think myself as secure at my country house as in the Fort."[64]

By November 4 the "Guides of the People" had regrouped and pushed, once again, their trap for Colden. The mob demanded that the stamps be moved to the naval ships. Various broadsides appeared that threatened the lives of all those who opposed them. Meanwhile, "stragglers" arrived in the city from surrounding areas—and they had guns. Various "Gentlemen of the Town" entered Fort George to talk with Colden "to propose some Method of Accomodation." What struck Colden was that "Fear was very evident in the Countenances of those, who the Day before expected to frighten the Lieutenant Governor into the most abject Compliances."[65]

November 5 saw no lessening of the fear. If anything, the fear mounted throughout the city. "It is given out that the Mob will storm the Fort this night," Colden stated. He doubted they would succeed but "it may be attended with much bloodshed." Judge Livingston railed "at the secret unknown party" that had threatened "such bold things." Colden vowed that, whatever happened, he hoped he would not "dishonour the Commission I have the honour to bear."[66]

Some of those who knew Livingston's secret party became fearful too. The details of the planned attack on the fort leaked out. First, the mob intended to approach Fort George under cover of burning effigies of "the Pope and pretender." When the rioters got close, the most devious part of their stratagem would be revealed. Suddenly, they planned to produce General Gage (who was still outside the fort) along with other "friends to the Government" and employ them as human shields as the attack began.[67]

The problems in New York had just about reached the point where Gage had said he would act decisively—"Acts of Rebellion"—assuming he was still at liberty to do so. Colden doubled the number of guards watching for trouble. Fifty artillerymen who happened to arrive in the city from Fort Detroit on their way to Great Britain were rushed into Fort George at 5:00 p.m. Colden made no secret that, as Gage recorded, if the rioters "come near the Fort, He will order the Troops to fire."[68]

Suddenly, city officials stepped into the crisis and decided to "acquaint" Colden "of the present dangerous State of things"—which the lieutenant governor knew very well. The municipal officials volunteered to take charge of the stamps themselves to diffuse the danger. Colden then asked the Council for its advice on the offer. Since the city was in a state of anarchy, the councilors, unanimously, agreed that the city's offer should be accepted. But Colden insisted "That the demands of the Populace would not end" with his surrender of the stamps.[69]

Colden wanted General Gage's opinion as well. He reminded the general that giving in because of "the threats of a Mob who may still make further demands greatly affects the dignity" of the royal government and probably would "encourage perpetual mobbish Proceedings hereafter." Gage responded that he agreed with his objections, but "tho' a fire from the Fort might disperse the Mob, it would not quell it." Added to the violent residents and sailors, the mob would swell with supporters from nearby colonies who, likely, would seize the considerable military supplies stored in the city. "It seems to me that a fire from the Fort would in this situation of things, be the Commencement of a Civil War" when nothing could oppose it. In this crisis, when the city's prominent citizens feared for their loved ones, it was best to "temporise" and accept the city government's proposal.[70]

According to the commander-in-chief, Colden "was undoubtedly glad of the Offer, and said in private he would accept of it." Despite what Colden thought, he "made difficulties" about the deal, which threw the city authorities into "the greatest confusion and terror." In order to understand why, one has to realize that Colden still believed that, eventually, the *Stamp Act* would be enforced. When that took place, somebody would have to distribute the stamps. Once the officials had panicked, "to prevent the Effusion of blood and the Calamities of a Civil Warr," Colden maneuvered the city corporation to agree "to make good all Such Sums of money as might be Raised by the distribution" of those stamps "as shall be lost destroyed or Carried out of the province." The city government now had to protect the hated items from destruction by a mob and, when New York finally accepted the stamp duties, the city would have to issue the stamps. Having "voluntarily" accepted them, Colden asserted, the municipal government had assumed the post McEvers had vacated. Colden's cleverness seems to have impressed Gage and frightened the city officials when they realized the implications of their agreement.[71]

The next day an anonymous broadside—lacking even an alias—announced that "We have entirely accomplished all we wanted" and called for peace. Major James soon left the city for the safer confines of Great Britain. Once the city government received the stamps, Colden noted, "all Threatening ceased."[72]

Colden's old antagonists did not take long to level charges at him. If only the lieutenant governor had just said at the start that he would do nothing about the stamps, Judge Livingston asserted, "all would have been quieted, and he would even have acquired some degree of popularity, instead of those gross and mortifying affronts." The judge insisted that Colden "had been so imprudently instrumental in raising" the mob.[73]

Lieutenant Governor Colden believed that "The acting with vigour seemed the more necessary" at the beginning of the crisis. If he had done nothing and refused to deal with the stamps, "I should have been thought mad." Besides, if the Council had not pressed its mistaken belief that no riots would happen, "it would have been much easier to prevent the first appearance of any Mob." More intensive work on Fort George, for example, might have presented a much more intimidating appearance. In fact, instructions ordering Colden to act might well have arrived from Britain, forcing him to repudiate an earlier stand, not something that would have won favor with drunken sailors and their compatriots.[74]

In the midst of such political sparring in which the lawyers were blamed for the mess by more people than just Colden, on November 13 Governor Moore arrived in New York after a difficult Atlantic crossing lasting ten weeks. (The lieutenant governor lamented that, if the governor had reached the colony two weeks earlier, "I had been freed from all this trouble and vexation.") Moore's arrival sparked sheer joy among Colden's political foes who could not have been happier if Monckton had miraculously materialized. "Everybody likes the change extremely" since they were "rid of the old man" Watts enthused. Also impressed by the new governor, the Sons of Liberty "erected Pyramids and Inscriptions" celebrating Moore's arrival, and built still another bonfire—this one to honor him.[75]

At Moore's first Council meeting, everyone but him (he claimed) thought enforcing the *Stamp Act* was impossible. Next on the agenda, the governor considered Fort George "too hostile . . . in a friend's Country" and recommended, not only its return to its earlier appearance, but that its gates be opened "as usual" to the public. Everyone agreed with the governor, including "the old man at his elbow."[76]

Watts somewhat misrepresented what happened at the meeting. The opening of the gates, Moore wrote, had been done "contrary to Mr. Colden's opinion, who endeavoured to dissuade me from it" and the lieutenant governor also felt uneasy at the gathering crowd. Although the people were not disruptive, Colden asked Moore if he "would excuse his attendance there" and he did. The governor believed that Colden had overreacted during the *Stamp Act* troubles. That was an easy stance for Moore to take—no one had used his effigy for target practice. Colden had to have been surprised when he vacated the governor's house and walked about the city—nothing happened.[77]

Not a babe in the woods, Colden knew very well what the governor was doing: "Sir Henry was resolved to make himself easy." He had neglected Colden by not asking his advice about reducing the fort's defenses before the Council meeting. Realizing that Moore's treatment of him "might be of Personal use to him with the Assembly," Colden "was willing he should take the benefit of it without opposing any of his measures."[78]

Colden thought it best that he leave and allow the governor to impugn him all he wanted to gain popularity at the lieutenant governor's expense. He met with the governor telling him, truthfully, about "the fatigues I had undergone both of Body and Mind" which "made it proper for me to desire some ease." If Moore "had no further Commands" for him—and Colden already understood the governor did not—"I was desirous to retire to my House in the Country." As Colden wrote, "My retiring seemed very agreeable to him and I took my leave."[79]

Just five days after the appearance of Moore in the colony, Colden departed for Spring Hill and stayed there. By the end of December, his enemies thought, it was as if Colden "had been in the other world (where they heartily wish him)."[80]

Colden, however, did not travel alone. His "good friends the Gentlemen of the Artillery and some others accompanied me as far as Jamaica" in Queens County. His companions seemed to be a combined bodyguard and honor guard. There, Colden related, "they dined with me, and have met me there every Week since." That Colden, in December, budged from Spring Hill to attend festivities at a distance from his home shows, once again, how mild the weather had been so far.[81]

Despite the company, Colden's trip to Flushing could not have been very pleasant. It had to be difficult for him to put aside what Peter Collinson called "the Late Mad and Tumultuous Scenes that Distressed your Mind, and embarrassed your Government." But there was more to worry about. As Colden put it, "Were it possible that these men could succeed in their hope of Independency on a British Parliament . . . (tho' they dare not declare what they think) we shall become a most unhappy People."[82]

And how would the British government react to what Johnson dubbed a "Hibernian Concert"? The colonial riots and violence against the *Stamp Act* constituted the most serious breach of the peace in the British Empire since the Jacobite invasion of 1745. In the House of Commons George Grenville insisted that "the Provinces were in Rebellion, and compared it to the Rebellion of 1745." New Yorkers who knew their history had to shudder when the news of the terrible riots in their colony was transported across the Atlantic by the mail packet *Duke of Cumberland*, named after the general who savagely suppressed the Jacobites in Scotland after their defeat. Not surprisingly, the Sons of Liberty made a point that they supported the Hanoverian succession thus emphasizing that they were not Jacobites.[83]

But Colden—and some of his enemies—had an even greater fear, which Livingston expressed to General Monckton. If Britain refused to repeal the *Stamp Act*, there was "the utmost danger, I speak it with the greatest concern imaginable, of a civil war." Colden had also remarked to General Amherst about what the forces behind the rioting "have in view." They aimed "to intimidate the Parliament into a repeal of the Stamp Act by having it believed that the Act cannot be put in execution without occasioning a civil war." Another witness to the New York riots plainly stated: "there has been a Civil War here about the Stamp Act."[84]

The phrase "civil war" had nothing to do with the class conflict so beloved by twentieth-century historians. Rather, it reflected Colden's and other observers' knowledge of English history. The English Civil War (1642–1646) resulted in a military dictator, Oliver Cromwell, seizing power. In the Glorious Revolution (1688) the sovereigns William and Mary, friends to liberty, ascended the throne. A civil war was associated with dictatorship;

a revolution saw an increase in liberty and the continued survival of the Constitution.

Cromwell's shade seemed alive in America. Dr. Benjamin Rush asserted: "You seem to feel good old Oliver's [i.e., Cromwell's] spirit in New York." Captain Montresor reported news from Hartford, Connecticut, where "a large body" had gathered to debate about "forming a new system of government." He continued: "Some were for choosing a Protector as in Oliver Cromwell's time"—Cromwell had used the title Lord Protector—while "some were for another form." The debaters "were very much divided and the consequences amongst themselves were dreaded."[85]

The dread over what the American turmoil would turn into continued to fester. In May 1775 a British army officer wrote Colden that "such of the Torys as pleases come in" to Boston, "but they are few. Parties run as high as ever they did in Cromwell's time and was there not a Red Coat in the Country they would cut one another's throats."[86]

For the rest of Colden's life, two vital questions remained to be answered. Would the troubles in America become a civil war or a revolution? Whatever the turmoil turned out to be, the second question stayed of great importance. Could one old man stop a crisis that was tearing the British Empire apart?

NOTES

1. CC to Conway, February 21, 1766, *CLB*, vol. 2, 97–100; Watts to Monckton, November 9, 1765, in Watts, *Letter Book of John Watts, Merchant and Councillor of New York, January 1, 1762–December 22, 1765*, New York Historical Society, *Collections* 61 (1928): 400–401; William Franklin to BF, November 13, 1765, *FP*, vol. 12, 369.

2. W. Franklin to CC, September 25, 1765, *CP*, vol. 7, 79–80; David Ramsay, *The History of the American Revolution* (Philadelphia: R. Aitken & Son, 1789; repr. ed. Lester H. Cohen, Indianapolis, IN: Liberty Classics, 1990), vol. 1, 62.

3. Josiah Martin to Dartmouth, November 4, 1774, in North Carolina Colony, *The Colonial Records of North Carolina*, ed. William L. Saunders (Raleigh, NC: P. M. Hale, State Printer, 1886–1890), vol. 9, 1083–84.

4. CC to Halifax, May 31, 1765, *CLB*, vol. 2, 4–5.

5. Smith to Monckton, May 30, 1765, *SM*, vol. 1, 29–30; "Journal of a French Traveller in the Colonies, 1765, II," *American Historical Review* 27, no. 1 (October 1921), 85; CC, *The Conduct of Cadwallader Colden, Esquire, Late Lieutenant-Governor of New York: Relating to The Judges Commissions, Appeals to the King, and the Stamp Duty*, in *The Colden Letter Books, 1760–1775*, New York Historical Society, *Collections* 2 (1767): 452–53; Watts to Baker, October 4, 12, 1765, Watts, *Letter Book*, 390–91; Watts to Monckton, October 12, 1765, *Aspinwall Papers*, Massachusetts Historical Society, *Coll.*, 4th ser. (1871): vol. 10, 578–80.

6. CC to Halifax, May 31, 1765, *CLB*, vol. 2, 4–5; Watts to Monckton, October 12, 1765, *Aspinwall Papers*, vol. 10, 578–80; R. R. Livingston to Robert Livingston, March 4, 1765, Robert R. Livingston Papers, reel 1, NYHS.

7. CC, *Conduct*, 452–53.

8. Smith to Monckton, November 8, 1765, *SM*, vol. 1, 30–31.

9. Watts to Monckton, September 24, 1765, Watts, *Letter Book*, 386–87; James Parker, "An Appeal to the Publick of New York," February 23, 1759, in Beverly McAnear, "James Parker versus William Weyman," New Jersey Historical Society, *Proceedings* 59 (1941): 7;

"To the Printer," *New York Gazette, or the Weekly Post-Boy* (Holt), May 16, 1765; Kemp to CC, May 31, 1765, *CP*, vol. 7, 38.

10. CC to Conway, October 12, 1765, *CLB*, vol. 2, 45–46; *Constitutional Courant* (Goddard), September 21, 1765, Ralph Frasca, "'At the Sign of the Bribe Refused': The *Constitutional Courant* and the Stamp Tax, 1765," *New Jersey History* 107, nos. 3–4 (1989): 21; Charles Lloyd, *[A Copy taken from a Pamphlet Intitluled] The Conduct of the Late Administration Examined, With an Appendix, containing original and authentic Documents.* (London, J. Almon, 1767; repr. Boston: Edes and Gill, 1767), 47. For the *Constitutional Courant*, see Merrill Jensen, ed., *Tracts of the American Revolution, 1763–1776* (New York: Bobbs-Merrill, 1967), 79–93.

11. CC, *Conduct*, 457–58; Johnson to CC, October 11, 1765, *JP*, vol. 4, 857.

12. CC, *Conduct*, 457–58; CC to Amherst, October 10, 1765, *CLB*, vol. 2, 44–45; CC to Collinson, December 16, 1765, New Netherlands Coll., oldest New York, and the colonial government, 1655–1744 (microfilm), no. 71, NYHS.

13. CC to Johnson, September 29, 1765, *JP*, vol. 11, 952–53; CC to Conway, September 23, 1765, *CLB*, vol. 2, 33–36; CC to BF, October 1, 1765, *FP*, vol. 12, 287–88; Parker to BF, May 6, July 15, 1766, *FP*, vol. 13, 263–64, 344; Ralph Frasca, *Benjamin Franklin's Printing Network: Disseminating Virtue in Early America* (Columbia: University of Missouri Press, 2006), 150; Franca, "At the Sign," 21, 28.

14. Halifax to CC, August 11, 1764, *CP*, vol. 6, 338–39; CC to Halifax, October 14, 1764, *CLB*, vol. 1, 405; Watts to Monckton, April 16, 1765, Watts, *Letter Book*, 346; Edward Hughes, "The English Stamp Duties, 1664–1764," *English Historical Review* 56, no. 222 (1941): 257.

15. CC to Conway, September 23, 1765, *CLB*, vol. 2, 33–36; CC, *Conduct*, 457–58; Watts to Monckton, June 1, 1765, Watts, *Letter Book*, 351.

16. CC to Conway, September 23, 1765, *CLB*, vol. 2, 33–36; CC, *Conduct*, 457–58; Johnson to Mrs. Cosby, September 30, 1765, *DH*, vol. 2, 823; "Journal of French Traveller," 85; *New York Mercury* (Gaine), July 1, August 26, September 2, 1765; *New York Gazette, or the Weekly Post-Boy* (Holt), September 5, 1765; Hughes, "English Stamp," 259.

17. James McEvers to CC, [August 1765], *CP*, vol. 7, 56–57; CC to Johnson, August 31, 1765, Emmet Coll., no. 10747, NYPL.

18. CC to Gage, July 8, 1765, *CLB*, vol. 2, 23; Gage to CC, July 8, 1765, *CP*, vol. 7, 46.

19. Gage to CC, August 31, 1765, *CP*, vol. 7, 57–58; Gage to Halifax, August 10, 1765, Thomas Gage, *The Correspondence of General Thomas Gage with the Secretaries of State, 1763–1775*, ed. Clarence E. Carter (New Haven, CT: Yale University Press, 1931–1933), vol. 1, 64.

20. Gage to CC, August 31, 1765, *CP*, vol. 7, 57–58; Gage to Conway, January 16, 1766, Gage, *Correspondence of General Thomas Gage*, 81–82.

21. CC to Johnson, August 31, 1765, *JP*, vol. 11, 920–22; CC to Conway, September 23, 1765, *CLB*, vol. 2, 33–36; Minutes of Council Relative to the Stamp Duties in New York, September 4, 7, 1765, *CP*, vol. 7, 59–69.

22. CC, "State of the Province of New York," December 6, 1765, *CLB*, vol. 2, 68–72; CC to George Grenville, October 22, 1768, *CLB*, vol. 2, 176–79.

23. CC, "State of Province," December 6, 1765, *CLB*, vol. 2, 68–72.

24. CC, *Conduct*, 460–61; CC to Monckton, October 7, 1763, New York Colony, Miscellany Collection Governor, A–C, box 1, NYPL; John Montressor's Report on Means of Strengthening Fort George, September 6, 1765, *CP*, vol. 7, 73–74; Montresor to CC, September 6, 1765, *CP*, vol. 7, 72; "Journal of French Traveller," 82. For an earlier comment on the fort, see "Mr. Armstrong's Report of the Fortifications at New York," April 7, 1748, C05/1096/153, LC transcript.

25. D. Colden to Zacharias Hood, September 16, 1765, *CLB*, vol. 2, 33; CC to W. Franklin, September 29, 1765, *CLB*, vol. 2, 38; Johnson to CC, September 13, October 11, 1765, *JP*, vol. 4, 843–44, 857.

26. CC to Moore, September 23, 1765, *CLB*, vol. 2, 37.

27. AC to _____, September 25, 1765, Colden Family Papers, LC; CC to James Murray, October 8, 1765, *CLB*, vol. 2, 43; CC to Conway, October 12, 1765, *CLB*, vol. 2, 45–46; Watts

to Napier, September 23, 1765, Watts, *Letter Book*, 385; Watts to Baker, September 24, 1765, Watts, *Letter Book*, 387–88; Watts to William Amherst, September 28, 1765, Watts, *Letter Book*, 389.

28. CC to Conway, September 23, 1765, *CLB*, vol. 2, 33–36; William Murdock and others to Garth, October 26, 1765, C.A. Weslager, *The Stamp Act Congress* (Newark: University of Delaware Press, 1976), 220; Thomas Whately to Grenville, October 17, 1765, in George Grenville, *The Grenville Papers*, ed. William James Smith (London: J. Murray, 1852–1853, repr. New York: AMS Press, 1970), vol. 3, 100; Nathaniel Rogers to Thomas Hutchinson, September 16, 1765, Thomas Hutchinson, *The Correspondence of Thomas Hutchinson*, ed. John W. Tyler (Boston: Colonial Society of Massachusetts, University of Virginia Press, 2014), vol. 1, 302.

29. *New York Gazette, or the Weekly Post-Boy* (Holt), October 17, 1765.

30. *New York Gazette, or the Weekly Post-Boy* (Holt), October 24, 1765; CC to Capt. Kennedy, September 3, 1765, *CLB*, vol. 2, 29–30; CC, "To the Master . . . of the Ship . . . on Board of which the Stamped Papers etc. and for the Province of New York," October 18, 1765, *CLB*, vol. 2, 47; CC, *Conduct*, 459; John Montresor, *The Montresor Journals*, ed. G. D. Scull, New York Historical Society, *Collections* 14 (1881): 336.

31. CC to Conway, October 26, 1765, *CLB*, vol. 2, 47–50; D. Colden to commissioners of the Stamp Office in London, October 26, 1765, *CLB*, vol. 2, 50–52; Watts to Monckton, October 26, 1765, Watts, *Letter Book*, 396–97; Montresor, *Montressor Journals*, 336.

32. CC to Amherst, October 10, 1765, *CLB*, vol. 2, 44–45; Johnson to CC, September 13, 1765, *JP*, vol. 4, 843–44.

33. CC to Cruger, October 31, 1765, *CLB*, vol. 2, 53; CC, *Conduct*, 460; Robert R. Livingston to Monckton, November 8, 1765, *Aspinwall Papers*, vol. 10, 559–63; Council meeting, October 31, 1765, *CP*, vol. 7, 59–69; *New York Gazette, or the Weekly Post-Boy* (Holt), October 24, 1765.

34. Johnson to Lords of Trade, September 28, 1765, *NYCD*, vol. 7, 766; CC to Amherst, [c. December 1766], *CLB*, vol. 2, 125–26; John Richard Alden, *General Gage in America Being Principally A History of His Role in the American Revolution* (Baton Rouge: Lousiana State University Press, 1948; repr. New York: Greenwood Press, 1969), 118, 120; David L. Preston, *The Texture of Contact: European and Indian Settler Communities on the Frontiers of Iroquoia, 1667–1783* (Lincoln: University of Nebraska Press, 2009), 255.

35. Gage to Major General Burton, November 5, 1765, Thomas Gage Papers, American Series, vol. 45, CL.

36. For a thorough account of the *Stamp Act* rioting, see Philip Ranlet, *The New York Loyalists*, 2nd ed. (Lanham, MD: University Press of America, 2002), 9–21.

37. Parker to BF, May 6, 1766, *FP*, vol. 13, 266; Montresor, *Montresor Journals*, 341, 343.

38. "Letter Describing the Stamp Act Riot in New York," November 2, 1765, Henry B. Dawson, ed., *New York City During the American Revolution* (New York: Mercantile Library, 1861), 42–45; CC to Shelburne, December 26, 1766, *CLB*, vol. 2, 122–23.

39. CC to Kennedy, November 1, 1765, *CLB*, vol. 2, 53; Kennedy to CC, November 1, 1765, *CP*, vol. 7, 85–86; Montresor, *Montresor Journals*, 336–37.

40. "New York" to CC, November 1, 1765, *CP*, vol. 7, 84–85; and *NYCD*, vol. 7, 774–75; F. L. Engelman, "Cadwallader Colden and the New York Stamp Act Riots," *William and Mary Quarterly*, 3rd ser., 10 (1953): 561n2.

41. Montresor, *Montresor Journals*, 337; Gage to Conway, November 4, 1765, Gage, *Correspondence of General Thomas Gage*, vol. 1, 70–71; Hiller B. Zobel, *The Boston Massacre* (New York: Norton, 1970), 52–53.

42. Gage to Conway, November 4, 1765, Gage, *Correspondence of General Thomas Gage*, vol. 1, 70–71; Livingston to Monckton, November 8, 1765, *Aspinwall Papers*, vol. 10, 559–67; CC to Board of Trade, December 6, 1765, *CLB*, vol. 2, 80.

43. Dawson, ed., *New York City*, 93–94.

44. Dawson, ed., *New York City*, 94n3; *New York Mercury* (Gaine), November 4, 1765.

45. "Letter Describing the Stamp Act Riot," November 2, 1765, Dawson, ed., *New York City*, 44–46; Livingston to Monckton, November 8, 1765, *Aspinwall Papers*, vol. 10, 559–67.

46. "Letter," November 2, 1765, Dawson, ed., *New York City*, 45–48; *FP*, 352n2.

47. "Letter," November 2, 1765, Dawson, ed., *New York City*, 45–48; Livingston to Monckton, November 8, 1765, *Aspinwall Papers*, vol. 10, 559–67; CC to Conway, November 5, 1765, *CLB*, vol. 2, 54–56; *New York Mercury* (Gaine), November 4, 1765.

48. CC to Board of Trade, December 6, 1765, *CLB*, vol. 2, 80; Livingston to Monckton, November 8, 1765, *Aspinwall Papers*, vol. 10, 559–67.

49. CC to Conway, November 5, 1765, *CLB*, vol. 2, 54–56; Livingston to Monckton, November 8, 1765, *Aspinwall Papers*, vol. 10, 559–67; *New York Mercury* (Gaine), November 4, 1765; *New York Gazette, or the Weekly Post-Boy* (Holt), November 7, 1765; "Letter," November 2, 1765, Dawson, ed., *New York City*, 46–48.

50. CC, *Conduct*, 460–61; CC to Conway, November 5, 1765, *CLB*, vol. 2, 54–56; Livingston to Monckton, November 8, 1765, *Aspinwall Papers*, vol. 10, 559–67.

51. "Letter," November 2, 1765, Dawson, ed., *New York City*, 46–49; CC to Conway, November 5, 1765, *CLB*, vol. 2, 54–56; Thomas James to CC, November 6, 1765, *CP*, vol. 7, 89–90; Livingston to Monckton, November 8, 1765, *Aspinwall Papers*, vol. 10, 559–67; *New York Gazette, or the Weekly Post-Boy* (Holt), November 7, 1765; *New York Mercury* (Gaine), November 4, 1765; *Remarkable Occurrences* [*Pennsylvania Gazette*], November 14, 1765; I. N. Phelps Stokes, *The Iconography of Manhattan Island, 1498–1909* (New York: R. H. Dood, 1915–1928), vol. 3, 981; Benjamin L. Carp, *Rebels Rising: Cities and the American Revolution* (Oxford: Oxford University Press, 2007), 82; Charles Hemstreet, *The Story of Manhattan* (New York: C. Scribner, 1916), 131–32; Engelman, "Cadwallader Colden," 572.

52. Montresor, *Montresor Journals*, 337; Livingston to Monckton, November 8, 1765, *Aspinwall Papers*, vol. 10, 559–67; Hutchinson to Richard Jackson, September 1765, Hutchinson, *Correspondence of Thomas Hutchinson*, vol. 1, 298; Richard R. Beeman, *The Varieties of Political Experience in Eighteenth-Century America* (Philadelphia: University of Pennsylvania Press, 2004), 266.

53. CC, *Conduct*, 461; Council minutes, November 2, 1765, *CP*, vol. 7, 65; Livingston to Monckton, November 8, 1765, *Aspinwall Papers*, vol. 10, 559–67; "Amicus Publico" to the printer, November 7, 1765, House of Lords Papers, 1.5/26b, microfilm, Columbia University, New York City.

54. CC, *Conduct*, 461; *Montresor Journals*, 337; Council minutes, November 2, 1765, *CP*, vol. 7, 65; "Letter," November 2, 1765, Dawson, ed., *New York City*, 48–49.

55. *New York Mercury* (Gaine), November 4, 1765; CC to Conway, February 21, 1766, *CLB*, vol. 2, 97–100; "Letter," November 2, 1765, Dawson, ed., *New York City*, 48–49.

56. "Letter," November 2, 1765, Dawson, ed., *New York City*, 48–49; Council minutes, November 2, 1765, *CP*, vol. 7, 66; "The Lt. Governor declares," November 2, 1765, Broadside Coll., NYHS; CC to Conway, March 28, 1766, *CLB*, vol. 2, 103–7.

57. CC to Kennedy, November 2, 1765, *CLB*, vol. 2, 102; Kennedy to CC, November 2, 1765, *CP*, vol. 7, 86; Livingston to Monckton, November 8, 1765, *Aspinwall Papers*, vol. 10, 559–67.

58. CC to Conway, March 28, 1766, *CLB*, vol. 2, 103–7.

59. CC to Conway, March 28, 1766, *CLB*, vol. 2, 103–7.

60. Montresor, *Montresor Journals*, 337; CC to Conway, November 5, 1765, *CLB*, vol. 2, 54–56.

61. Livingston to Monckton, November 8, 1765, *Aspinwall Papers*, vol. 10, 559–67.

62. "Letters," November 2, 1765, Dawson, ed., *New York City*, 42–45; "Watchman," No. 5, April 21, 1770, Microfiche, Early American Imprints, Evans no. 11921; *New York Gazette, or the Weekly Post-Boy* (Holt), November 7, 1765; Montresor, *Montresor Journals*, 337–38.

63. Montresor, *Montresor Journals*, 337–38; "John Hamden" to John Holt, November 2, 1765, *New York Gazette, or the Weekly Post-Boy* (Holt), November 7, 1765; Ranlet, *New York Loyalists*, 14.

64. "Benevolus" to CC, November 3, 1765, *CP*, vol. 7, 88; CC to Conway, November 9, 1765, *CLB*, vol. 2, 60–63. CC's mention of an assassin is not unbelievable. Later, in November, several hundred Sons of Liberty tracked down Zacharias Hood in Flushing and forced him to resign his office. Two groups of Liberty Boys did form on Long Island but not at Flushing. Montresor, *Montresor Journals*, 340; Ranlet, *New York Loyalists*, 50.

65. "Benevolus" to CC, November 3, 1765, *CP*, vol. 7, 88; CC, *Conduct*, 462–64; Montresor, *Montresor Journals*, 338.
66. CC to Marquis of Granby, November 5, 1765, *CLB*, vol. 2, 54; CC to Conway, November 5, 1765, *CLB*, vol. 2, 54–56; Livingston to Monckton, November 8, 1765, *Aspinwall Papers*, vol. 10, 559–67.
67. Montresor, *Montresor Journals*, 338–39.
68. Gage to Barrington, November 10, 1765, Gage, *Correspondence of General Thomas Gage*, vol. 2, 316–17; Montresor, *Montresor Journals*, 338–39; Gage to Burton, November 5, 1765, Thomas Gage Papers, CL.
69. Minutes, November 5, 1765, in New York City, *Minutes of The Common Council of the City of New York, 1675–1776* (New York: Dodd, Mead, 1905), vol. 6, 438–39; Council minutes, November 5, 1765, *CP*, vol. 7, 67–68; CC to James, November 6, 1765, *CLB*, vol. 2, 58–59.
70. CC to Gage, November 5, 1765, Thomas Gage Papers, CL; Gage to CC, November 5, 1765, Thomas Gage Papers, CL.
71. Gage to Conway, November 8, 1765, Gage, *Correspondence of General Thomas Gage*, vol. 1, 72–73; CC to Conway, November 9, 1765, *CLB*, vol. 2, 60–63; CC to mayor and corporation, November 5, 1765, New York City, *Minutes of The Common Council*, vol. 6, 439; mayor's receipt, November 5, 1765, New York City, *Minutes of The Common Council*, vol. 6, 439.
72. "To the Freeholders," November 6, 1765, *CP*, vol. 7, 91; CC to James, December 11, 1765, *CLB*, vol. 2, 64–65; CC, *Conduct*, 465.
73. Livingston to Monckton, November 8, 1765, *Aspinwall Papers*, vol. 10, 559–67.
74. CC to Conway, November 9, 1765, *CLB*, vol. 2, 60–63; CC, "State of Province," December 6, 1765, *CLB*, vol. 2, 68–72; CC to Board of Trade, December 6, 1765, *CLB*, vol. 2, 79; AC to ____, September 25, 1765, Colden Family Papers, LC.
75. Montresor, *Montresor Journals*, 339; CC, *Conduct*, 465; Moore to Dartmouth, November 21, 1765, *NYCD*, vol. 7, 789; Watts to Monckton, November 22, 1765, *Aspinwall Papers*, vol. 10, 585–86; CC to Collinson, December 16, 1765, New Netherlands Coll., no. 71, NYHS; *New York Gazette, or the Weekly Post-Boy* (Holt), November 21, 1765.
76. Watts to Monckton, November 22, 1765, *Aspinwall Papers*, vol. 10, 585–86; Moore to Conway, November 21, 1765, *NYCD*, vol. 7, 789–90.
77. Moore to Hillsborough, May 9, 1768, *NYCD*, vol. 8, 66–68; CC, *Conduct*, 465.
78. CC to Johnson, December 15, 1765, *JP*, vol. 4, 883–84; CC to Conway, February 22, 1766, *CLB*, vol. 2, 101–2.
79. CC to Conway, December 13, 1765, February 22, 1766, *CLB*, vol. 2, 66–68, 101–2; CC to Johnson, February 20, 1766, *JP*, vol. 5, 33–34.
80. Watts to Monckton, December 30, 1765, *Aspinwall Papers*, vol. 10, 586–87; CC, *Conduct*, 452–53, 465; CC to James, December 11, 1765, *CLB*, vol. 2, 64–65.
81. CC to James, December 11, 1765, *CLB*, vol. 2, 64–65.
82. Collinson to CC, March 20, 1766, *CP*, vol. 7, 104–5; CC, "State of Province," December 6, 1765, *CLB*, vol. 2, 68–72.
83. *JP*, vol. 4, 849–51; Conway to the king, December 17, 1765, George III, *The Correspondence of King George the Third From 1760 to December 1783, Printed from the Original Papers in the Royal Archives at Windsor Castle: 1760–1767*, ed. Sir John Fortescue (London: Macmillan, 1927), vol. 1, 201–2; Montresor, *Montresor Journals*, 348; Oyster Bay Sons of Liberty to New York Sons of Liberty, February 22, 1766, John Lamb Papers, reel 1, NYHS; Huntington Sons of Liberty to New York Sons of Liberty, February 24, 1766, John Lamb Papers, reel 1, NYHS; Geoffrey Plank, *Rebellion and Savagery: The Jacobite Rising of 1745 and the British Empire* (Philadelphia: University of Pennsylvania Press, 2006), 1, 54.
84. Livingston to Monckton, November 8, 1765, *Aspinwall Papers*, vol. 10, 559–67; CC to Amherst, January 13, 1766, *CLB*, vol. 2, 90–92; Croghan to Johnson, November 18, 1765, *JP*, vol. 11, 969–70.
85. Benjamin Rush to Ebenezer Hazard, November 8, 1765, Benjamin Rush, *Letters of Benjamin Rush*, ed. L. H. Butterfield (Princeton, NJ: Princeton University Press, 1951), vol. 1, 18–19; Montresor, *Montresor Journals*, 347.

86. Lt. Col. James Abercrombie to CC, May 2, 1775, Colden Family Papers, LC. This letter is in print. See Samuel A. Green, ed., "The Battle of Lexington," Massachusetts Historical Society, *Proceedings*, 2nd ser., 11 (1896–1897): 305–6. For another reference, see John Thurman, Jr. to John Markland, April 6, 1775, John Thurman, Jr., "Extracts from the Letter Books of John Thurman, Junior," ed. Benjamin H. Hall, *Historical Magazine*, 2nd ser., 4 (December 1868): 291.

Chapter Fifteen

Out, In, and Out Again

After Cadwallader Colden turned the government over and arrived at Spring Hill, he remarked: "I cannot live many years longer." The lieutenant governor, now 78 years old, insisted that "I am in the country in hopes of passing the little remainder of life at ease." It seemed a safe ambition; Sir Henry Moore was in his fifties and the thought that Colden might outlive him appeared to be a fantasy. To everyone's surprise, Colden outlasted still another governor, took the reins of power yet again, and undercut those disrupting the Empire.[1]

First, though, Colden had to avoid being fired from his office. Writing to a friendly army major, the Honorable Lucius Ferdinand Carey, a witness to Colden's deal with the city government about taking the stamps, the lieutenant governor observed: "No doubt I wish to retire, as most proper for me at my age, but I wish to do it with some dignity." Major Carey had made a "proposal" to Colden, which his son David knew about. All the interested parties agreed it should be "kept secret." From the lieutenant governor's letter, the plan consisted of Colden's stepping down in favor of the major, a man who apparently had enough influence in London, he thought, to achieve the transfer. Colden, not sure "how this can be done with a proper decorum at this distance," suggested delaying for several months to see the imperial government's reaction to the *Stamp Act* riots and who would be blamed or commended.[2] This delay ended any chance of him retiring.

Colden's prospects improved partly due to Moore's escalating problems with the opposition to the *Stamp Act*. Most historians missed the continuing crisis because of a curious incident of the next century. In 1859 the able local historian Henry B. Dawson presented a paper on the Sons of Liberty, tracing them all the way back to the English conquest in 1664 and gradually reached 1765. This was a talk before an audience so he had a limited time to speak.

After retelling the story of the *Stamp Act* rioting through November 26, 1765, Dawson, "for want of time," jumped ahead. For well over a hundred years, almost all historians closely followed Dawson's lead. These missing months are vital to understanding Colden's political survival.[3]

Put simply, Governor Moore was in a mess. The people whose counsel he had sought proved to be totally wrong, while Colden's warning that mobbish activity would continue if the mob was catered to came true. The governor even resorted to meeting with the man revealed as the mob's director, Isaac Sears, a former privateer crowned "king" of the mob. The Sons of Liberty kept asserting their power, at one point seizing control of the mail—postmaster Alexander Colden could not stop them. James Parker, who spread the *Constitutional Courant* throughout the colonies, admitted to Benjamin Franklin that "we are all afraid of the Populace for the Tail is where the Head should be, the Spirit of Independence is too prevalent, it does not subside much." As for the Sons of Liberty, Parker remarked: "It is surprising to see the Influence they have, and the Dread everyone is Under of Opening their Mouths against them."[4]

In early January 1766 Moore's authority fell to a new low when "divers Persons unknown" seized another batch of stamps still on the vessel that brought them and "feloniously" burned them. Moore's offer of a substantial reward for information leading to arrests—even from one of the culprits—brought no response. Moore realized he could get no cooperation because everyone was "under terrors."[5]

With Colden powerless in Flushing, only Captain Archibald Kennedy remained willing to enforce the law. Moore refused to advise the mariner about seizing ships that tried to leave the port of New York without the proper document—with a hated stamp. The captain did his best to shut the harbor without the governor's support. Although ships could enter, they could not depart, but the weather undermined Kennedy's efforts. A tourist described the usual New York weather: "about Christmas, or New-year's day . . . the snow generally falls, and a hard frost sets in, and continues . . . till March." True to form, on January 2, 1766 the icing compelled Kennedy's squadron to dock to be laid up for the winter. The cold stayed for much of January, preventing merchant ships from sailing through the frozen harbor. Then the weather warmed in February, melting enough ice for the traders to dispatch their ships, lacking stamped forms, into the ocean without any hindrance from the navy. Once the merchants started ignoring official documentation (and the accompanying fees), they kept up the habit for years.[6]

Because March 1766 was mostly freakishly warm (and early April too), the Sons of Liberty and their comrades took to the streets. Though Colden remained the most popular subject for effigy makers and death threats, he felt secure in Flushing. George Grenville and Generals Jeffrey Amherst and Thomas Gage were among the other worthies depicted as effigies. April turned chilly but May 7 brought "summer weather." In an apparent celebratory mood, a mob suggested barbecuing an army officer.[7]

At Spring Hill, meanwhile, Colden, cut off from the swirl of events in the metropolis, was reduced to reading newspapers, talking with visitors about mobbish transactions, and getting reports from his sons, Alexander and David. David and his family also lived at Spring Hill; his father hoped "to end my days in quietness" there, cheered by "the company of my children and Grand children." The lieutenant governor did make sure to correspond with Peter Collinson on a personal matter, his need to replace the burned chariot.[8]

A means of transportation was vital to Cadwallader Colden, who could no longer ride a horse but still needed "to take air." Exercise was "essential" to maintain his father's health, David explained to Collinson. To protect the elderly man from cold weather, a new vehicle had to be "a closed Carriage;" a style called a "Post Chariot" that had appeared in New York seemed suitable. Basically, the elder Colden wanted a "Chariot neat not gaudy fit for an old man" and assured his friend that "Your taste I am confident will please mine." Getting a new chariot had become a matter of pride for Colden who did not want to "give those who are unfriendly the pleasure to see me reduced to a mean method of going abroad." Despite what had happened, Colden now was in "good Spirits," David informed Collinson, "as can only attend a good Conscience."[9]

Thrilled to hear from the senior Colden, Collinson had been worried about him. The "New York" broadside had been reprinted everywhere in America, then spread to English newspapers where Collinson saw it. "I was truly concerned for you, yet I was persuaded of your unshaken Mind, in pursuing the paths of Equity and Moderation," he told his friend. Collinson purchased the chariot Colden had requested, even coming close to the specified price. The lieutenant governor, however, would need more assistance from Collinson. Cadwallader Colden, despite his own suspicion that his political career was probably over, had no intention of surrendering without a fight.[10]

Colden, with plenty of time on his hands at Spring Hill, wrote frequently defending his role during the riots in New York. He passed on additional information to imperial officials as to the motive behind the turmoil. Having talked with a number of "men of large Property" who had "excited this violent seditious Spirit in the People," he was convinced that they had not planned a "Revolt." Instead, they had hoped to push Parliament into repealing the hated stamp tax. "Some of them in conversation have mentioned this to me" and gave precedents where unpopular laws "had been Repealed to quiet the Minds of the People," once they displayed "their utmost dislike by Riots and Tumults." He did not know if these men "who excited this seditious Spirit in People, have it in their power to suppress it."[11]

Doubting that these now regretful instigators could stop what they had started, the lieutenant governor gave London harsh advice. "I write my Opinion more freely than I did while the administration was in my hands." According to Colden, two things were needed to quiet New York. First, Fort George had to be, again, strengthened to its pre-Moore configuration. Second, more soldiers had to be dispatched to the rebellious city. "I believe a Thousand Men may be sufficient." In Massachusetts, Governor Francis Bernard also noted that "New York has gone much beyond" Boston "in absurdity of politicks, declarations of intention to resist, and acts of mischief." He proposed the same solution as Colden—more soldiers—and hoped "that New York . . . will have the honor of being subdued first."[12]

While Colden freely gave his advice on how to restore New York to a proper respect for law and order, he sought to defend his reputation from any onslaught from his enemies. William Smith Sr. no doubt prodded by his namesake son, saw Colden as vulnerable. Not well known in London's official circles, the Smiths did have an acquaintance whom Lord Dartmouth, an important figure in colonial governance, would listen to. During one of the great preacher George Whitefield's campaigns in America, he had stayed with the Smiths. On December 6, 1765 the elder Smith wrote to the minister about the American disturbances, one of the causes of which, Smith exclaimed, was the stance "relating to appeals which has been taken by Lieutenant Governor Colden." In addition, Smith excoriated "the granting of lands" in New York, charging that Colden had taken excessive fees. Whitefield passed the letter along to Dartmouth, an evangelical Christian at whose home he had preached to an extensive number of listeners.[13]

Colden would have been astonished at that means of attack, but he had tried to ward off what he could. As he had done in 1748, he proved in an account sent to London that he had never been a Jacobite—a charge that had circulated again during the *Stamp Act* riots—and that Daniel Horsmanden had fabricated the falsehood. Luckily, Colden's old friend the marquess of Lothian still lived and the lieutenant governor referred any doubters to the one unimpeachable witness who could verify his loyalty.[14]

Leaving nothing untouched, Colden also penned "A State of the Province of New York," which sounded like a formal report sent by a sitting governor, across the Atlantic. This official-sounding document went over Colden's views about the power of the entrenched interests of New York, which he had already voiced many times. He knew, however, with the frequent shifts in the British government he might now be addressing a new audience unaware of the realities of New York. After the past had been repeated, he defended his actions relating to *Forsey v. Cunningham* and the recent riots.[15]

Primarily, Colden depended upon Collinson's connections in the imperial capital to spread the word of what had really happened. At Colden's advanced age, he assured Collinson, "My strongest wish is to end my days in retirement to enjoy my friends and follow such amusements as are fit for old age and my natural inclination to philosophic inquiries." Having served the cause of royal government for so many decades, Colden felt he deserved a pension that would add "more dignity" to his final years. He recommended that Collinson consult General Amherst as well as any friends he might have at the Board of Trade, perhaps Lord Dartmouth, to see if such hopes had any chance. Colden added his sincere wish of helping his old friend pursue, once again, his interest in botany.[16]

Amherst would be "very obliging," Collinson informed Colden, on both a pension and in another campaign—obtaining compensation for his destroyed property. The New York Assembly refused to pay up. Moore received orders from London to obtain Colden's compensation and unpaid salary. Though the governor did his best, the Assembly never gave in on the compensation issue, which inspired correspondence between Grenville and Colden. Along with the compensation question, they also discussed New York. The British politician, who became Colden's ally, believed "it most base that the Friends of Government should suffer for their Support of it."[17] Despite Grenville's aid, Colden struck out on both a pension and compensation.

At first, Colden appeared to be a superb target for a needed scapegoat, desperately sought by British officials for their own protection. In the House of Lords, Lord Camden "very severely" blasted Colden, one of "a Set of Creatures our Governors were." Accusing Colden of "suspending" one parliamentary act and of "straining one of the Articles of his Instructions," Camden, "After saying many severe Things said, This was Cadwallader Colden."[18]

Disappointing the lieutenant governor's enemies on both sides of the Atlantic, he had plenty of supporters in Britain. Aside from Amherst and Collinson's circle, the soldier who had been the senior officer in Fort George during the riots, Lt. Col. John Vaughan, was in the mother country. Vaughan did not shy away from "warmly" defending the lieutenant governor's "spirited conduct." Within Britain, the opinion spread that the events of November 1, 1765 had been "unprovoked" and "In this riot the lieutenant governor had been abused, insulted and plundered." Once the king saw the dispatches from both Colden and Gage, the monarch was pleased "that matters were not pushed" to the point of bloodshed. Overall, Gage was assured, "The Temper shewn . . . by Lict. Govr. Colden, as by the Officers there, is highly to be commended." He was not going to be retired against his wishes because he protected the stamps.[19]

If anyone appeared destined to be a scapegoat, it was Major Thomas James, but he quickly learned how to play the political games required in London. He testified before the House of Commons, potentially risky for him as New Yorkers had sent their London contacts "Everything that could be alleged against him." Such parliamentary investigations were theater, not an honest examination of facts. Answers to questions were written out ahead of time for cooperative witnesses. After James was given a large amount of money, supposedly to compensate him for his losses, he cooperated as much as possible. As Colden informed Grenville, who would not have been surprised, James "had a paper of directions given him how to answer on his examination." He followed the script well. When James read from his "written account drawn up by himself"—and, of course, it had not been—he gave "the first Mark of Discontent" as the regulation of colonial trade with the West Indies, that is, the *Sugar Act*. That law had been passed well before the disorders and before the current ministry had taken office, throwing the blame on the earlier Grenville administration. So James was in no trouble. [20]

James's testimony also shows what little interest the British government had in any finger-pointing at Colden. Major James mentioned that "the Mob" was "discontented with Colden before the Stamp Act," prompting a question from a foe of the ministry asking if the lieutenant governor "was not universally disliked." Quickly, a pro-government member jumped in, blasting "the Question as not fair." The committee debated the subject; James, who then left the hearing, would not be questioned there again. When James talked with even higher officials, he assured Colden, "I had an Opportunity of Introducing my Friend John Morin Scott whom I painted in lively Colours." (As a Triumvirate member, Scott was no friend to James or Colden.) [21]

Back in New York, Governor Moore did not know that Colden faced no danger within the British government. With the governor's problems with turbulent New Yorkers continuing, he needed a scapegoat too; Colden seemed a perfect target. In an odd dispute, Moore kept complaining that his lieutenant governor would not hand over his correspondence with London—just extracts. Colden did not send the letters because he knew who Moore's advisors were—William Smith Jr. for one. The lieutenant governor explained how this dispute started. Soon after the governor appeared,

> In order to enter into some discourse with him on the state of the Province, I shewed him the speech I had intended to have made at the opening of the Sessions [of the Assembly], He read it and returned it to me without speaking one Word on the Subject. Some time afterwards without any previous discourse he desired to have copies of my Letters to the Ministry. [22]

Alexander Colden wrote to his father, still at Spring Hill, what the governor was saying about him and his letters. Moore, who had known almost no one in New York, "had desired of you Copys of your letters to the Ministry for his information." As Alexander related, Moore tried "to excuse his Conduct by saying you had not informed him as was expected and throw the Blame off of his own shoulders as much as possible on yours." The younger William Smith would have eagerly searched through the correspondence looking for more ways to blame and attack the lieutenant governor. Colden's keeping his letters private became Moore's best excuse for the problems of his administration. When some old French claims in New York had been absorbed within bounty lands given by Colden to soldiers, Moore, once again, blamed his ignorance about the subject on Colden's refusal to share his letters. Though not a very good excuse, in Moore's defense, it was all he had.[23]

On February 18, 1766, Colden received a letter from London observing, logically, that it was "expected . . . from your knowledge of the Country and People" that he should brief Moore about "the State of Things, as the Characters and Disposition of Men in that Country," especially the judges. Promptly, Colden wrote Moore about Horsmanden and the senior Smith, blaming the weather for not coming to see him—an unconvincing excuse because of the still rather warm winter. Colden did not see him during the summer either. Governor Moore, who had not wanted any advice from his lieutenant governor, complained: "Had Mr. Colden thought fit to have done this on my arrival here I might have had an opportunity of serving His Majesty more effectually than I have done." Each passing month made Moore's excuse weaker and weaker.[24]

Actually, Moore did not need to bother scapegoating Colden. Imperial officials in London found one, Captain Archibald Kennedy. On November 8, 1765, General Gage, wanting to be certain that someone other than himself would be blamed, wrote that "the Officer who commands the King's Ships,. . . absolutely determined to refuse receiving the Stampt Papers on board." Gage also criticized Colden's similar refusal to store them on Kennedy's ships, but London was not interested in targeting Colden. When Major James testified, he was specifically asked about Kennedy and related what the sailor had told him: "he informed me he had a Note that if he took the Stamps he would be ruined." It appeared, in London anyway, that moving the stamps through mobs onto Kennedy's vessels made sense. Therefore, in March 1766 Kennedy, accused of "lack of zeal," was removed from his command.[25]

Captain Kennedy, in serious trouble, knew it. A British admiral had been court-martialed and executed for "lack of zeal" not many years before. Unaware that Gage had selected him for scapegoating, Kennedy asked Colden what he had written about him. The "extremely surprised" lieutenant governor told Kennedy that he had reported very little about him or even given his name and promised to aid him. As soon as Kennedy contacted him, Colden wrote to London explaining the circumstances and vindicating the mariner. Eventually, Captain Kennedy was cleared largely due to the "great trouble" Colden had taken.[26]

In fairness to the imperial government, some 400 letters came from America about events there regarding the *Stamp Act*. Sometimes bureaucrats across the Atlantic did not quite grasp all the details. When Colden finally heard from Henry Conway, then in charge of colonial affairs, Colden was astonished as he read his superior's letter. While overwhelmingly positive, Conway did criticize him. "There is one circumstance in your conduct, which neither his Majesty nor his servants can at all approve." This complaint involved, Conway wrote, "that you should upon any persuasion have been induced to a declaration and promise of taking no step till Sir Henry Moore should arrive." Because Colden had sworn to uphold the *Stamp Act*, this especially disturbing declaration nullified his oath as "a change of circumstances might make it practicable" to levy the stamp tax.[27]

Colden knew he had to defend his declaration as soon and as well as possible. In February 1766 he responded to Conway that "I was the least apprehensive of blame in that circumstance of my Conduct which has happened to be chiefly blamed." The lieutenant governor blamed himself for what he saw as the government's misapprehension of the circumstances. "It often happens that when the reasons of Conduct are the most evident and clear, we are apt to suppose them alike evident every where and therefore neglect to be sufficiently Explicit." Correcting his error, Colden explained that the new governor was expected at any time. Besides, Colden and everyone else on the scene knew he could not issue stamps anyway. "If any accident" had befallen Moore, ending any chance of a speedy appearance, that ended the validity of "the Promise" for "I believe no Man would have thought me perpetually bound by it." Nothing more was heard about Conway's complaint.[28]

Conway's letter convinced Colden that both the government and the king had every intention of enforcing the principle of parliamentary authority over the colonial empire. Imagine Colden's shock when Parliament did what those who had stirred up the riots had hoped would happen—it overturned the *Stamp Act*. Colden had never imagined that the hated law would be repealed "without enforcing a previous submission, because I believed it would give such a shock to the Authority of Parliament over the Colonies, as would certainly be avoided." This precedent only encouraged colonists to resist Parliament's authority upon its next assertion. For the moment, he observed, "I find I have mistook greatly." Still, "in this, as I have at all times, I submit to the Wisdom of my Superiors."[29]

Pledging obedience was one thing, being happy at the turn of events was another. Colden had been vilified on two different continents and lost property; the attacks had permeated both houses of Parliament. Printed attacks on him had saturated the mother country. Nor had he been compensated in either Britain or New York for his losses. In Parliament, Grenville pointedly demanded that Colden be given "reparation" and, in writing, told the lieutenant governor that "Your Behaviour during the former Disturbances appeared to me highly meritorious and I have more than once declared in the House of

Commons my Opinion concerning it." Grenville, however, had no power to do anything.[30]

Colden's children suggested a way to vindicate his ravished reputation. They urged their father to pen a written defense of his administration's most targeted events such as *Forsey v. Cunningham* and the *Stamp Act* riots. His friends seconded his family's advice. Therefore, in 1766 Colden wrote his defense, which had to have improved his spirits, and dispatched it to Britain in the secure hands of Captain John Montresor who sent them to the even safer hands of Collinson. The lieutenant governor limited his attacks to New Yorkers alone, taking "Particular care" not to upset anyone in any British "Ministry either past or present," something that would have been counterproductive. General Amherst, involved in the project, at first advised Collinson not to print Colden's pamphlet as there was talk in Parliament of compensating the maligned New Yorker which the writing might disrupt. Yet, again, nothing came out of Parliament and, in early 1767, the general thought the time was ripe for its publication. Colden's *Conduct* appeared after all.[31]

Having carefully plotted the best way to influence Britain's political elite, Colden had only a hundred copies circulated in Britain. Another twenty were sent to New York for Colden's use. He composed a list of parliamentarians Collinson should send a copy "under cover." It was essential not to bring copies to any offices but only to their private dwellings in London, before mid-day, and right after Parliament had met. This strategy intended to get the copy quickly to the recipient with little time for his servants to learn about it. Directing the copies away from government offices was also a wise move. Earlier, some "malicious" office clerks had gotten their hands on Colden's letters "of which a bad use has been made to my prejudice." Colden gave Collinson discretion to present copies to people he trusted; the lieutenant governor also wanted copies given to another old friend, Dr. John Fothergill, and the head of his old school, the historian Dr. William Robertson at the University of Edinburgh.[32]

Colden's allies on both sides of the Atlantic relished his "spirited" *Conduct*. Not meant for public perusal, Colden spoke frankly about his political enemies. In England, where it was "well received," Zacharias Hood, the refugee stamp distributor whom Colden had protected as long as he could, heard about the pamphlet and called on Collinson for some copies to help the man who had helped him. The happy Collinson complied and dispatched Hood to General Amherst "because he could Inform Him of Every Step of the Rioters and the Share you suffered in it."[33]

Back in America, Sir William Johnson enjoyed the "Judicious Pamphlet" which gave "a candid and circumstantial relation of transactions which the Public ought certainly to know in order to form a right Judgment of the Subjects treated." Especially pleasing to Johnson was Colden's "handsome manner" of dealing with William Smith Jr. Colden had demonstrated how Smith's history contradicted what he was now saying in 1767.[34]

However, a security breach occurred. Somehow or other, William Smith Jr. obtained a handwritten copy of *Conduct*. Colden remained clueless about how it happened. He had specified that the London printer sell none of the copies. In New York, the author gave copies only to trusted family and friends. Perhaps the leak happened because Grenville lost his original copy. Or a recipient in Britain or New York lent the pamphlet to someone claiming friendship for Colden who instead copied it for Smith.[35]

No matter how the lawyer obtained the text, he saw in it the potential for another controversy that might drive Colden from office. The lieutenant governor never intended starting an "appeal to the People," but "the malice of the Faction" created one. John Holt, who had no scruples about reprinting a work without the author's permission, published it.[36]

Late on October 20, 1767, Judge Robert R. Livingston asked grand jurors, expecting to be dismissed, if they would themselves charge the pamphlet to be libel. They answered no. Then Livingston bluntly "told them they would not be discharged till they had." When seated in court, the grand jurors again were asked about the pamphlet and "gave the same answer;" some of the jurors mentioned "they knew nothing about" the publication. Promptly, Livingston gave them one of the New York version. Chief Justice Horsmanden, whom Colden had skewered in *Conduct*, then "charged them in very strong Terms to present it." Wasting no time, on October 21 the grand jury, which parroted almost totally the words Horsmanden had used, "presented it as a very vile, infamous, false and libellous Reflection on his Majesty's Council, Assembly, Courts of Justice and the whole body of the Law in this Province." Colden had thus been charged with seditious libel, the same offense as John Peter Zenger during Cosby's administration. At least the grand jurors finally gained their freedom from jury duty. This incident confirmed everything Colden had claimed about the colony's legal system.[37]

But how could Colden be prosecuted? The Assembly had not yet seized the power of prosecuting an accused culprit for an alleged crime. In this bizarre scene, judges demanded an indictment, not New York's attorney-general. Watching the assemblymen's subsequent maneuverings, Governor Moore pointed out "their own inability to punish." Moore would have been deemed mad in London if he brought the lieutenant governor of the colony into a court and prosecuted him for seditious libel.[38]

Livingston, Horsmanden, Smith, and the others knew that, but they hoped to stir public opinion into a frenzy that, they imagined, would push Moore into bringing Colden to account for criticizing them. In December 1767 the Council and Assembly launched an investigation to look into *Conduct*; William Smith Jr. was named one of the investigators, a useful appointment as he had been behind the printing of the New York edition.[39]

On January 8, 1768 the Assembly called for the appearance of Thomas Smith (another son of the elder Smith) as well as the mad printer Holt and his spouse. Four days later, only Thomas Smith and Mrs. Holt showed up. Although the mad printer, claiming to be "indisposed," failed to appear, his absence did not bother the Assembly at all. The two witnesses told everything they knew about the pamphlet's authorship. Alexander Colden and a Colden in-law, also summoned, testified soon after.[40]

In February 1768 the Assembly dramatically revealed the results of its supposed investigation:

> That as the house has not been able to discover the author of the said pamphlet,. . . his Excellency the Governor be humbly requested, in case the author should hereafter be discovered, to order a prosecution to be issued against him, that such punishment may be inflicted on so great an offender, as the law directs.[41]

Astonished at this "Farce," Moore commented on the "great deal of pains seemingly taken to come at a discovery of what every body else but themselves appeared to be well acquainted with." The lieutenant governor's in-law, more frightened by the Assembly than Alexander was, had said he thought Cadwallader Colden had written the pamphlet. When assemblymen came to Moore with the Assembly resolution, he told them bluntly that "if they really wanted information" they should ask the lieutenant governor. Moore was sure that Cadwallader Colden would "declare to them who the author was, and save them the trouble of farther examinations." There is no reason to doubt Moore's statement that he would have immediately dissolved the Assembly when the charade started except that some important financial matters remained to be dealt with.[42]

Later, Moore expressed his surprise that Colden, concerned about these transactions, had not contacted him. Colden's motivation is clear—he did not trust Moore. The governor depended on William Smith Jr. for advice and thought highly of Judge Livingston. Frankly, both Alexander Colden and his father seemed somewhat paranoid about Moore's conduct, even suspecting him of concealing information about London's support for the long-delayed compensation for Colden's losses in 1765.[43]

Instead of relying on Moore's protection, the lieutenant governor dispatched a blizzard of letters to the imperial government including letters to Halifax, Lord Shelburne and to the prominent politician and jurist, Lord Mansfield. To Mansfield, Colden observed: "These pretended patriots of liberty are tyrants when in power." Impressed by Colden's letter, the judge "put the Letter in his Pocket, and said he would make the best use he could of it. And that he thought Mr. Colden's behaviour merited the attention and protection of all good men."[44]

Nor did Colden neglect the Board of Trade or Lord Hillsborough, now in charge of colonial affairs. He regaled the Board and pointed out that the instigators had "suggested measures for punishment and deterring others" to "shew the necessity I am under of writing to your Lordships in the manner I now do." To Hillsborough, Colden explained his theory that his foes wanted to "discredit" his pamphlet because they had heard rumors, in September 1767, that forces in the mother country wanted Colden in charge again. The curious prosecution had been dreamed up to convince their ally, the Duke of Grafton, that if Colden took command again "it would set the Colony in a flame and occasion the greatest disorders."[45]

Colden's letter writing campaign had a definite impact. Just in case Governor Moore needed reminding, in March 1768 Hillsborough told him that Colden had sent him still "another letter" on the subject. "If these Attacks upon and proceedings against this Gentleman are the effects of his dutifull attachment to the Crown during his Administration. . ., I make no doubt but His Majesty will think Himself called upon to extend his Royal Protection to him," his lordship informed the governor of New York.[46]

With such support of Colden, the campaign to destroy him with a charge of seditious libel went nowhere. Even before that news crossed the Atlantic, the odd stratagem had flopped in New York. The subject became hot gossip in the city and sparked a run to read the reprinted pamphlet. Copies were "eagerly bought up." The contents surprised some of its new readers. Colden's version of events had not been told because of the blatant press bias against him; the pamphlet for them was an eye-opener. According to Colden, "People . . . generally declare in its favour openly saying that they know the most part of it to be true and believe the other parts."[47]

Colden remained fully capable of defending himself despite his turning 80 in 1768. He had been attacking Governor Moore, starting soon after his arrival. Realizing that the governor preferred to deal with Smith and Livingston, Colden brought to London's attention a stunning mistake on the governor's part. Moore, trying to curry favor in early 1766, had gone about the city wearing homespun clothing. A New York newspaper had proclaimed: "It is better to Wear a Homespun Coat Than Lose our Liberty." Homespun clothes, created in America, would make the colonies less dependent on imports from Britain, not something a royal governor should support by wearing such items. Colden made sure to alert General Amherst that Moore had worn homespun—he had two American coats. An obvious problem for Moore, he felt it necessary to attack supposed "American Patriots" who only wore homespun. Its actual makers, the governor insisted, "never cloathed themselves with the work of their own hands" but, instead, wore "English cloth." Moore's concern demonstrated that Colden had not been "forgotten by the Ministry."[48]

In reality, the rumors swirling around New York during September 1767 that Moore's replacement was probable and that Colden—"Old Silverlocks"—would take over were factual. In June 1767 a draft letter recalling Moore had been written but not dispatched because of infighting in the government. Rumors continued to spread that Moore's time in New York had neared its end. In January 1768 General Robert Monckton wanted to return to the colony as Moore's replacement.[49]

Moore made another obvious mistake. Urged on by William Smith, Jr., the governor recommended that Judge Robert Livingston be appointed to the Council in both 1768 and 1769. Colden had made plenty of references to Livingston in his letters and officials in London decided to check the Assembly minutes they had on hand to find out for themselves what the judge stood for. They were not happy at what they found—he had voted for "violent resolves" against the policies of the imperial government. In July 1769 Hillsborough chided the governor about his lack of candor. "Tho' you have not thought fit to point them out in your correspondence," such hostile votes "could not escape the King's notice." Livingston stayed off the Council.[50]

Whether Moore was more popular in New York than London is open to doubt. Colden, not unbiased about the governor, thought in September 1766 that Moore "acts oddly" and had failed to win much approval. "A general diffidence is entertained of him" in the colony. On the other hand, in May 1769 William Smith, Jr., whom the governor had put on the Council replacing the senior Smith, insisted that "We never had a Governor in a safer Condition," which proved sadly ironic.[51]

In August 1769 Sir Henry Moore caught an epidemic disease rampaging through the area. Chief Justice Horsmanden fell ill with the same serious condition and hovered near death. Parker referred to the dangerous disease as "a Bloody Flux," indicating Moore had dysentery.[52] Suddenly, in September 1769 the governor strengthened, appearing to be in recovery from the contagion. Just as suddenly, he died on September 11. His death finally brought Cadwallader Colden back to the city; John Watts complained that the old man seemed indestructible. The cranky Watts, though, had not yet seen Colden.[53]

Colden's exile at Spring Hill had not been healthy, no shock for someone in his eighties. He had been "generally" in good health until about May 1768 when he started having fits which went away. Then on May 16 the old man "was much Convulsed" and stayed in that condition for two hours before there was any recovery. He stayed "unwell all the rest of the day, and lost the use of his Legs very much, which seemed to shock him more than any other circumstance of his Disorder." The next day Colden could not "walk at all without assistance." David assured his brother Cad that he would be sent for if necessary.[54]

The identity of this condition is not clear. The word fit could mean a recurring attack of some malady. It could also mean a temporary occurrence. Convulsions might suggest a serious of strokes, but in early June the Rev. Samuel Auchmuty visited Spring Hill and informed a nervous Cad that "The Old Gentleman has not had any return of his Fits, for a fortnight past; and appears to be as hearty and well as I have known him for some Years." Nothing else suggestive of a stroke is recorded to have happened for eight years.[55]

In September 1769, when Watts grumbled about Colden outliving Moore, the lieutenant governor had survived his own bout with dysentery (as did Horsmanden). Parker, who also came down with it, described the lieutenant governor as being "weakly and infirm" and that he almost died. Meanwhile, in northern New York Sir William Johnson feared for his friend: "I am in hopes that the Lt. Governor's Administration may be tranquil, otherwise it may Shorten the Old Gentleman's Days, as I hear he is now very infirm."[56]

Nonetheless, Colden journeyed to New York City the day after Moore's demise. As he had a problem getting on and off the East River ferry, a boat from a naval vessel brought him to the capital. This may have been caused by his bout with dysentery, but more likely came about because he was in his eighties. The 81-year-old Colden did not join Moore's funeral procession because, he reportedly said, he "was unable to walk to the church." On September 13 Colden took the oath and, William Smith Jr. wrote, "He was cheerful tho' his Speech was low and his Hearing thick."[57]

Colden had to be happy. His outliving Moore seemed miraculous and the acting governor had to be pleased by the political transformation that had rocked the colony in 1768 and 1769. David Colden noted the "strange changes in the politics of the different parties in New York."[58]

In the 1768 Assembly election the Livingston faction lost seats, when "The general cry of the people both in town and country was 'no Lawyer in the Assembly.'" Nothing could have enthused Colden more than that. John Morin Scott lost in the city while in Dutchess Judge Livingston found himself tossed out by the voters there. But there was bad news for the Coldens too. Cad, the only son of Colden ever to run for office, lost his race in Ulster to George Clinton, the son of Colden's old ally Charles Clinton.[59]

The 1768 contest settled little and politicking continued while both the Livingston and DeLancey factions tried to twist imperial issues to their own benefit. The Livingston forces sowed fear that their foes supported having a Church of England bishop in America. David Colden reported the failure of the Livingstons in the 1769 elections: "Scot has been again rebuffed; that party has again met with a Severe drubbing." To deepen the defeat, the new Assembly, dominated by the DeLanceys, rejected Judge Livingston as the representative from Livingston Manor because he did not live there. As the judge had "some of the sarcastic turn in him, which he indulged in the house with the ignorant members of it," they surely relished throwing him out of the Assembly.⁶⁰

For Sir William Johnson, the lieutenant governor summed up these elections. "Tho in the late spirited contest in the late Elections Patriotism, the Church, and the Dissenting Interests were made the Pretences, the true motive was whether the DeLancey or the Livingston Interest should have the Lead in the Assembly for the future." Although Moore favored the Livingstons, Colden dismissed them as motivated by "selfish" interests. In contrast, the DeLanceys had "more generous principles." Such parties were no surprise to Colden. During his long career in New York, all the parties were called after a prominent "Person or Family who have appeared at their Head."⁶¹

Yet the political strife did not end with the 1769 election. Later in the year, Samuel Seabury, an Anglican minister in Westchester, observed that "At present Politics seem to engross almost every body, and leave little or no Room for more serious and important Reflections." To ban Robert Livingston from the Assembly forever, in early 1770 both the Assembly and Council passed a bill prohibiting New York judges from being in the Assembly, which the House of Commons had previously done with judges in Great Britain. Colden signed the bill with no problem he claimed. Livingston accused Colden of standing aside and "suffered it to pass unnoticed."⁶²

However, the Privy Council nullified this "Innovation," which concerned Colden—at least that is what he told Hillsborough. In defense of the vetoed law, Colden emphasized that New York's judges had blatantly used "their influence" to interfere in elections against the prerogative and to boost the power of "a Party." The lieutenant governor knew that New York judges including Lewis Morris, James DeLancey, and Livingston had often played politics. "In my humble Opinion," the lieutenant governor advised, "the Judges can be of more real use to the Crown by being disinterested in all Party disputes." Left unstated was a basic fact—by signing the bill Colden had disposed of an enemy.⁶³

Whatever London thought—and the imperial government expressed its extreme annoyance that Colden had signed that bill—the Assembly refused to admit Livingston, who kept thinking he would win out. He was wrong and Colden lost no sleep over Livingston's fate.⁶⁴

With the political tide—for once—going in Colden's direction, he expected to remain as acting governor for an extended period although he stated that "From my Age it cannot be of long continuance." He had gained sympathy and support in Britain because of his stand during the *Stamp Act* troubles. Pushing his continuance in charge as a way to compensate him for the destruction of his property, Colden assumed he had crafted a winning argument.⁶⁵

In an apparent secure position, Colden began to remove colonial officials not to his liking. The first to go, Philip Livingston, Jr., Moore's secretary, who knew David Colden would be his father's secretary, beseeched the lieutenant governor to be kept in some lesser offices he held because he was the grandson of Colden's friend James Alexander. At first Colden agreed but very soon Goldsbrow Banyar, who had often helped him, was rewarded with the jobs. However, the resourceful young Livingston secured an office in the new British colony of West Florida. William Smith Jr. saw the purge as evidence that the DeLanceys were rising within this new Colden administration while the Livingston prospects were bleak. The DeLancey interest in the Assembly even increased Colden's salary.[66]

More heads rolled among the colony's sheriffs. Another Livingston ally, Harmanus Schuyler, Albany's sheriff, whom Amherst and Monckton had pushed on Colden back in 1761, was also dismissed. Albany's mayor, who had links to the declining Livingstons and had caused Colden grief about quartering there, was removed. He had publicly supported the continuance of non-importation, a stand not appropriate for a gubernatorial appointee.[67]

Colden also had the opportunity to make two legal appointments. Thomas Jones, a Tory in the English sense of the term, became the recorder, New York City's lawyer; he was a DeLancey in-law, demonstrating again Colden's tilt to the DeLancey faction. To replace the deceased William Smith Sr. on the bench, Colden selected George D. Ludlow, who became a close friend of David Colden and his family.[68]

Cleaning house, no matter how enjoyable it might have been for Colden, could not distract him from two vital issues: the colony needed a new issue of paper currency and the Assembly had to be convinced to provide for the substantial number of soldiers garrisoned in New York City after the *Stamp Act* disorders. The exasperated Moore had been unable to settle either one. It had been clear well before Moore's death that if Colden became governor again, he would have to sail on "a rough Sea."[69]

Unlike other colonies, New York's currency had been very stable. The money problems had been created by the parliamentary *Currency Act* (1764). Paper money in New England had been banned long before, but recent behavior by Virginia created the present crisis. British merchants had become fearful that colonists would pay off their debts in worthless colonial paper. Therefore, Parliament banned any colonial currency being made legal tender. Any colonial governor who accepted the creation of such money would suffer severe punishment.[70]

Realizing that New York's paper money would soon leave circulation causing serious problems in the colony's economy, Moore did his best to acquaint London of the problem the colony faced. The Assembly provided for a much smaller issue of money than it wanted, but Moore could not approve the bill because it did not include a provision suspending it until the imperial government had okayed the measure. The governor did send the currency bill to his superiors for their review. London, however, did not seem happy about the Assembly's handiwork and let a year go by with no verdict. Meanwhile, the Assembly stalled voting for supplies for New York's garrison.[71]

There the matter stood until Moore died and Colden returned to a position of power. The lieutenant governor then showed himself to be "the most astute politician of them all." First off, he informed Lord Hillsborough that he had been told by reliable sources that the assemblymen "have the passing the Bill for issuing a paper Currency, much at heart." Furthermore, "the passing of that Bill will put them in good humour" and that, if their favored bill did not become law, "it will be difficult to make them continue the Provision for the Soldiers quartered in this Province." After all, troublesome Massachusetts had stirred up difficulties over supplying troops and even the usually more agreeable South Carolina had followed that exasperating example.[72]

Having looked over the currency bill that had already been sent across the Atlantic, Colden assured Hillsborough there was nothing wrong with it. In fact, having more New York currency meant that New Yorkers could buy more British goods. The new Assembly, Colden explained, was much different from its predecessor. These assemblymen had to pass hostile resolutions to mollify the voters, he revealed, but most of the Assembly realized good relations with the mother country was "essential to their well being." And the merchants were leery of following the violent acts of the Bostonians anymore. Colden was trying to prepare his superiors for what he had already decided to do.[73]

Colden had made a deal with the DeLancey-dominated Assembly. In return for the lieutenant governor's signature on the currency bill, the assemblymen would supply the troops, much of the necessary funds coming from the loan office set up by the currency bill. No clause suspending the currency law for London's approval was included.[74]

One historian suggested that Colden believed he would be fired if he signed the currency bill. Yet the lieutenant governor at the moment appeared confident that would not happen. Back in October 1769, when he defended having a new issue, he suggested in the same letter keeping him in office in lieu of compensation for his *Stamp Act* losses. With all the praise he had received from prominent Britons after the stamp riots, Colden assumed he was in a strong—and safe—position.[75]

Even the Sons of Liberty realized that their influence had suddenly weakened. When the Assembly voted to supply the troops, the Sons, whom the garrison was in New York to watch, tried to foment trouble. One of King Sears's comrades, Alexander McDougall, attacked the Assembly in a pamphlet for, in effect, putting Colden "in the Speaker's chair" of the chamber where "his honour would have the pleasure to see how zealous his former enemies are in promoting his interest to serve themselves." The deal, McDougall trumpeted, was "only a snare to impose on the simple for it will not obtain the royal assent." As for the Assembly, led by James DeLancey (the son of the deceased lieutenant governor), "like true politicians, although they were to all appearance at mortal odds with Mr. Colden," they had now entered into "a coalition" with him.[76]

McDougall's attack did not intimidate the Assembly or dissuade Colden from signing the bill into law on January 5, 1770. He tried to impress on the authorities in London that this deal had something in it for both them and the New York assemblymen—supplies for the soldiers and money for the colonists. He related that he alerted the Council to his harsh instructions about paper currency and they "unanimously" advised him to approve the bill anyway as "absolutely necessary in the present circumstances of this Colony." Admitting that the new law was "in every part similar" to what Moore had transmitted, Colden explained away the lack of a "suspending clause enjoined by the Instruction." Since he was transmitting the signed bill immediately, and the paper currency would not be issued for quite some time anyway, the Privy Council could void it in plenty of time before the law became operational. So there was, sort of, an unstated suspending clause. Colden did not fail to mention that since this law extended for some fourteen years, the whole contentious dispute of supplying the garrison had been disposed of for a long time.[77]

To Hillsborough, Colden tried to soften the surprise of his signing the bill with an account of the great popularity of the compromise:

> It may not be improper to tell you that no Governor in chief has been at any Time attended by greater numbers on New Years Day than I was on the last with their Compliments of the Season. When what has appeared in this Place in past times is considered, my mentioning this will not be thought to proceed merely from vanity.[78]

Colden had often written to his superiors that he was popular, but this was the first time he had real evidence supporting his claims. Exciting him even more was that the Sons of Liberty had been outmaneuvered and marginalized. Do not believe the biased accounts of the New York newspapers Colden advised Hillsborough. Despite the distortions in the press reports, the public gatherings of the Sons and their allies were poorly attended, so much so that they had no impact in spite of the "pains . . . taken to work upon the prejudice of the people here" against the "unpopular" supplying of the soldiers.[79]

The Assembly, however, had disliked McDougall's pamphlet enough that it authorized Colden to offer a substantial reward of £100 for information about its authorship. Colden knew from the type that Parker had printed that seditious libel, and the reward resulted in the fingering of McDougall as the libeler. Typically, Smith in the Council recommended that McDougall be prosecuted, then vilified Colden in Parker's newspaper: "I rejoice at the Attack upon Capt. McDougall—Whatever was the Design of your old Lieutenant Governor and his Adherents in stirring up a Prosecution against that gallant Son of Liberty, it will advance . . . the grand Cause of America." The jailed McDougall linked himself to the similar prosecution of the English radical John Wilkes. Eventually, McDougall was released.[80]

On January 19, 1770 the soldiers' anger at the Sons of Liberty ("All the People of Sense in Town rail openly against them," one observer insisted) for all the abuse heaped on both them and their families finally erupted in violence. A riot in a New York City neighborhood, Golden Hill, at first produced a "very diverting . . . battle." "One Soldier with a dirty short cutlass" drove "hundreds of the brave Yorkers before him who were better armed than him." Quickly, the Sons of Liberty decided to target unarmed soldiers unaware of what was happening. Soldiers also attacked unarmed civilians. To Colden's relief, the city magistrates calmed the soldiers and those "of inferior rank" before any deaths occurred. A few weeks after the riot, Colden happily remarked that "notwithstanding the unremitted Endeavours of a Party in opposition to Government to embarrass every Transaction and to create Disturbances," things were going well in New York.[81]

The rhetoric of Colden's foes remained extreme, however. According to one enemy, Colden, a "despotic and satanical genius," had used his "long life and experience, like Satan,. . . to perplex, enslave and to tyrannize over the people of this colony." The lieutenant governor's evil conduct "must be attributed to a corrupt and tyrannical heart," which also had caused Satan "to seduce" Adam and Eve.[82]

Unlike earlier trashings of Colden, in 1770 he had a good number of determined defenders. "A Merchant" lambasted those trying to raise up hate against soldiers and Colden. "If we cannot render Mr. Colden's Administration odious," as "The Merchant" had these demagogues saying, "and breed Dissentions and Animosities amongst the People," then they had no chance in the next Assembly election. God forbid the soldiers and their families could have bread bought from the public purse. The money could be spent "so much better on some poor Inhabitants, too proud and lazy to work." After all, they needed "Rum for themselves" along with tea and "fat Turkeys." "The Merchant" remembered how the chants had changed. Not long before, these characters had been yelling: "Oh the Bishop, the Bishop! The Lord deliver us from a Bishop." Now the hypocrites had forgotten all about that and had moved on to what "is most in Vogue."[83]

While the immediate crisis had been settled in New York, Colden still had to deal with the reaction of the imperial government, which disliked what had been done as much as the Sons of Liberty. The displeased king, Hillsborough, and the Board of Trade were downright apoplectic over the missing suspending clause and the paper money. No one in London understood what Colden had succeeded in doing and the law signed by him was hurriedly nullified along with the earlier one sent by Moore.[84]

Eventually, the imperial government calmed down, soothed by General Gage's strong support of the compromise, which guaranteed supplies for the soldiers for many years. Hillsborough gave Colden his absolution:

> The merit, however, of your former services, and what you say in respect to the time fixed by the Act for its operation, which you state as an excuse for your conduct, prevail with His Majesty to forbear any further remarks of his displeasure, trusting that you will not for the future suffer yourself to be withdrawn from your duty by any motive whatever.[85]

In 1770 serving British kings for so long paid off for Colden. Moore could never had done what Colden did and stayed in office. Across the Atlantic the colony of New York suddenly became extremely popular and Parliament passed a bill, accepted by the government, that legalized the compromise forged by Colden and the Assembly. The lieutenant governor's "boldness" was excused, again, by Hillsborough, who had once called him "A meritorious old servant of the Crown": "I have reason to believe from what you allege that you erred from real good intention. I have not failed to represent your conduct in that light to His Majesty."[86]

As if those difficulties were not enough to keep Colden busy, he also had to deal with non-importation, the colonists' tool of economic warfare against parliamentary taxation. On October 31, 1765, non-importation first appeared as a way to oppose the *Stamp Act*. Unless Parliament revoked the stamp duties, the New York merchants vowed to place no new orders for British goods and to rescind older ones. Colden, thinking of his experience long before as a trader, had believed that the tactic was doomed to fail. "All the Wool in America is not sufficient to make stockings for the Inhabitants" he asserted, and insisted that "the severe Winters in North America render the production of Wool in any great quantities impracticable." Besides, if British products were not imported, Americans were fated to "pay an extravagant price for old moth eaten Goods, and such as the Merchants could not otherwise Sell." Perhaps, he thought, the merchants hoped that rioters would stop customs officers from preventing the import of foreign products.[87]

Although Colden correctly predicted the shortages and increased prices non-importation brought about, nothing in his mercantile experience had suggested how determined New Yorkers would be about boycotting British goods or the impact it had despite being overshadowed by the violence.

British merchants, shocked by non-importation, exerted their influence with Parliament to help repeal the *Stamp Act*.[88]

Because of non-importation's success, when Parliament again taxed the colonies, boycotting was resurrected in 1768. This time, the *Townshend Act* (1767) imposed small taxes on colonial imports from Britain such as tea. These duties were targeted for repeal. New York's merchants, who vigorously enforced non-importation, became bothered by the blatant cheating by merchants in other ports, most prominently, their supposed brethren in Boston.[89]

On November 22, 1769, in an apparent attempt to weaken the boycotters' resolve, Colden, in office again, addressed the Assembly and Council about "the greatest Probability" that all the Townshend taxes "imposed by the authority of Parliament" would be dropped soon. What Colden called "this desirable Event" gave the assemblymen "the most sincere pleasure." Hillsborough had dispatched the news of the government's "intention" to request Parliament to remove all except the tea duty to colonial governors some time before.[90]

Parliament, however, did not revoke most of the Townshend taxes until April 1770, long after Colden's speech, which caused a tempest within Parliament. Furious with Colden and Governor William Tryon of North Carolina (who had done something similar to Colden's exuberant speech), some members of Parliament saw a threat to their independence if governors promised their assemblies that the king or his government would bring Parliament to heel by "Influence." Meanwhile, an upset Hillsborough blasted Colden for saying the tea tax would be gone too. Colden's phrasing, especially his use of "imposed," suggested that he was critical of Parliament's claim of authority over the colonies. He had opposed the *Sugar Act* and, apparently, secretly disagreed with the *Townshend Act* too. It was a major blunder by Colden. He never directly responded to Hillsborough's attack on his speech, but did soon write:

> As I have had my Duty constantly before my Eyes, and have pursued it sincerely to the best of my ability, the thoughts of closing my Life under his Majesty's Displeasure give me great Pain, and that by any Error I may have forfeited your Lordship's regard, for with the greatest Truth, I am, My Lord, Your most obedient and faithful servant.[91]

Colden soon had good news to send the exasperated Hillsborough. Moderate merchants managed to defeat the Sons of Liberty for control of the committee that supervised non-importation. These merchants were determined not to allow the Sons to subject the city to serious violence as they had done before. In 1770 the traders learned that Parliament had overturned most of the Townshend taxes. Having already seen nasty riots in Golden Hill, they were deluged with news of cheaters who violated non-importation. Given these developments, in July 1770 the merchant committee dropped the economic boycott of all items except for the still taxed tea. Colden delayed a mail packet's sailing so it could carry a host of orders from New York merchants for now acceptable British goods. The lieutenant governor noted that the Sons of Liberty had tried "by every method in their power by Riots, Clamour and threats" to intimidate the moderate merchants, but they could not be dissuaded. Most of the city's population backed the merchants in their defiance of their home-grown demagogues and the cheaters in Boston and elsewhere.[92]

The moderate merchants' action had serious consequences. They and the Sons of Liberty had so badly split that Colden believed they could not "unite" against British policies again without great difficulty. New York's resuming the importation of most British products affected Parliament and was an important reason why it exempted New York from the harsh regulations of the *Currency Act* while leaving other colonies such as New Jersey in the lurch.[93]

To Colden, the breaching of non-importation was of "great importance." He expected that other colonies would do what the New Yorkers had done, a correct prediction. The whole affair had been a joyous one for Colden, who reflected upon the flow of events since the *Stamp Act* riots:

> The Disorders in North America began while the Administration of Government was in my hands. . . . I am happy that now while the administration is again in my Hands, the People of this Province set an example to the other Colonies of returning to their Duty.[94]

Colden's enthusiasm can be understood, but it was premature. The imperial crisis had not yet ended.

Colden's administrations also saw considerable action on other, more local matters. For example, he had not forgotten about the great manors and their wildly inflated borders. That did not mean he approved of violence against the landlords. In 1762 Colden ordered the arrest of individuals trying to seize part of the Livingstons' vast holding, Livingston Manor. The claimants fled. Nonetheless, Colden believed the Livingston title to much of the land was false. In 1767 Judge Livingston fumed that Colden "has furnished twelve folio papers against the Manor of Livingston" and in favor of a rival claimant.[95]

Among the great manors, Colden focused primarily on Claverack, a swollen territory held by the Van Rensselaer family. William Smith Jr. had manufactured a crisis for Colden with *Forsey v. Cunningham*. Two could play that game; Colden used the same technique on the Rensselaers. In one respect, Claverack—one of two huge properties held by that family—was a deserving target for the lieutenant governor. According to his calculations, a cautious analysis of the Claverack grant gave it but 23,800 acres. An overly-generous interpretation, however, pushed Claverack's size to 281,600 acres. All in all, Claverack symbolized everything fraudulent about New York's bizarre manors.[96]

In 1764 Colden convinced some British officers, due a considerable amount of bounty land, to petition for over 40,000 acres of Claverack and a neighboring—and equally dubious—grant, Westenhook. To no one's surprise, the Council rejected it. Following Colden's advice, the officers appealed to the king. The Board of Trade reasoned that "Mr. Rensselaer's claim does not appear reasonable" and ordered that the king's officials in New York seek a legal remedy there "at his Majesty's expense." The Board based its decision on an earlier Colden letter that explained that the Rensselaer claim rested on "two heaps of stones erected by the Indians in memory of their sachems buried there."[97]

In 1767 the trial took place before New York's Supreme Court; the Crown lost. If Rensselaer had been defeated, the manors of the other great landlords might be endangered. The colony's entrenched interests simply would not allow such a dangerous precedent. However, in 1772 the Rensselaers did agree to abandon their claim to 66,000 acres of Claverack; the rest stayed under their control. The officers' hope for land in Westenhook finally ended, unsuccessfully for them, in 1775.[98]

Indian land claims also continued to occupy Colden, who could not have forgotten the Wappingers. In 1721 they had ignored Governor William Burnet's ruling on a land claim which appeared to have been properly purchased from them, and used violence to prevent Colden from surveying it. In 1763 another old Wappinger sale near Fishkill in Dutchess County was disputed by an Indian, whom Colden had to remind about what had happened in the 1720s:

> I told him that near 40 years since the Indians of Fishkill and Wappingers were heard by Governor Burnet. . ., that then every thing was settled to the content of Nimham the Grand father of this Man and of the other Indians to which this Man had nothing to reply, but owned that he was then a boy and present at the Meeting.[99]

Another Wappinger land dispute created more controversy. In 1765 the Wappingers went after some land held by Beverly Robinson in Dutchess. At a Council hearing with Colden present, a councilor told sachem Daniel Nimham that Robinson had a deed. The sachem declared "that he chose to hear that Expression from the Lieutenant Governor's own Mouth first" so Colden asked an elderly Indian present, who was probably as old as Colden, if he remembered the Indian sellers who had signed the deed. He answered that he had known some of them but that he doubted they had actually signed the deed. Colden, obviously, knew the truth because "after a Short Pause" Colden stated "that Mr. Robinson had a Deed of the Land in Controversy" and told the Indians present to "return home and make themselves and the Rest of the Tribe Easy, and quiet, and give them . . . no further Trouble about the matter." In 1767 another hearing undertaken by Governor Moore confirmed Colden's earlier ruling.[100]

The Wappingers had a bad reputation in Colden's eyes; his memory was not impaired. Watts knew that, regarding the "Mysterious Business" of the colony's lands, Colden "as Governor, Surveyor General, etc. has all the information and power too in his own hands, and knows well how to make use of them" though he did not always succeed. Both he and the Council backed the cause of some Long Island Indians cheated of their land, but Attorney-General Kempe had no interest in enforcing the ruling.[101]

Curiously, the Indian trade demonstrated how the imperial government, by 1770, seemed frightened and paranoid about its North American colonies. Acting upon a suggestion of George III that the Indian trade be regulated, the New York legislature passed a law calling for all the colonies involved to meet to do so. Strongly in favor of this meeting, Colden encouraged the governors of Quebec, Pennsylvania, and other colonies in the trade to send delegates to New York in July 1770 for "a congress" to decide upon regulations for that oft-troubled commerce. Only Virginians arrived to join the New Yorkers. Colden, who invited the distinguished visitors from the South to visit him at Spring Hill, suggested they meet anyway and submit a plan for the other provinces' perusal. The delegates, however, decided their numbers were too small to conduct any business.[102]

Such meetings of colonies had happened before over the years, especially during wartime. But London now panicked over the news of an intercolonial congress. Hillsborough sent a letter of concern to the astonished Colden. He attempted to calm the imperial officials by assuring them that he did not have "the least suspicion of any prejudice to his Majesty's service" from this congress, which, ultimately, never formally met. Whenever London learned of Patrick Henry's presence as a Virginia delegate at the conference, the panic among the imperial bureaucrats must have increased. Eventually, Henry caused serious problems for London but not in New York during 1770.[103]

With all the excitement in New York about currency, supplies for the soldiers, and even the visit of a future revolutionary, some of Colden's other accomplishments have gained little notice. He strongly supported the incorporation of institutions "of public utility" for New York City. For example, the Marine Society, which aided the numerous "distressed seamen," considered Colden its founder. Another group he pushed provided for "the relief of widows and children of clergymen," who usually were poorly paid. He vigorously aided the incorporation of the New York Hospital, which also received the support of his old friend Dr. John Fothergill in Britain.[104]

Colden, however, made sure not to encourage organizations that, outwardly, appeared benevolent but might become a center of opposition to royal government. An example is the New York Society Library, seemingly a useful addition to the city's cultural life. Not only did Colden fail to join this association, he refused to lift a finger to help it. Among its members were William Smith Jr. and the other members of the Triumvirate. This apparent bastion of opposition forces did not receive a charter until 1772, when Colden was out of office.[105]

The lieutenant governor displayed similar caution about religious groups. The troublemakers in New York, Colden believed, "consist chiefly of Dissenters," that is, those who did not adhere to the Church of England, the established church in the city and three other New York counties. There were, by far, more dissenters in New York than Anglicans. Therefore, it was not "good policy" to charter some other church, which would, in effect, place it "upon an equality with the Established Church." So Colden refused to incorporate the Lutherans, the Dutch Church, and French Protestants.[106]

On the other hand, when Anglican King's College sought a royal charter, Colden eagerly did everything he could to help. Because the dissenters had many colleges, he believed that King's College deserved the royal favor. Giving a royal charter to the school (which it did obtain), was essential, he declared in 1774, "not only on account of religion but of good policy to prevent the further growth of republican principles," a blight he lamented was "already too much" prevalent in America.[107]

Another group that, by its actions, opposed such dangerous ideas, the New York merchants, who had fostered the continuance of order, also benefitted from Colden's patronage. The traders had formed a Chamber of Commerce in 1768 and knew that, if incorporated, the merchant members could explore new "Plans of Trade." On February 15, 1770 the Chamber petitioned Colden for a charter making it "a Body Politic."[108]

Colden reacted very positively to the Chamber's request and the merchants appreciated his support. As they mentioned to him, "The important Light in which your Honour views this Institution has been abundantly evinced by that Readiness so conspicuously manifest in every part of your conduct" from their first request for a charter. In March 1770 the merchant members declared themselves "submissive to the Laws, zealous for the Support of Government,. . . our happy Constitution," and the king. Colden acknowledged the Chamber as "a good institution" and was pleased that it was "incorporated during my administration."[109]

The Chamber of Commerce's support for order was quickly evident. On March 24, 1770, when the Sons of Liberty were throwing parties commemorating the *Stamp Act*'s repeal, a delegation from the Chamber came to thank Lieutenant Governor Colden for its charter. Responding, he praised the merchant members, "united with Principles of Loyalty." Furthermore, "your good Example will, at all times, have the most favourable Influence, by promoting that due Obedience to the Laws, which is essential to the Security of the Rights and Liberties of the Subject." Such sentiments were not evident at the parties of the Sons of Liberty.[110]

Leaving no doubt how popular Colden was with the Chamber, it paid for a portrait of him. At this period, largely because he had signed the bill for another issue of New York paper money, Colden was popular, highly unusual for him. Even a sculptor would commemorate him. A local artist, Patience Wright, convinced him to model for her. She produced, for display, a bust of Colden made out of wax, a fashionable art form in the mother country. And, despite what historians imply, Colden was popular with General Gage too.[111]

Gage had been supportive of Colden during his time in command of the province. The general also had been making contingency plans with the governor of Quebec, Guy Carleton, for what Colden and others feared lay in the future—rebellion. Together, Gage and Carleton wanted to repair forts such as Ticonderoga and build another near New York City to "secure the communication" between the colony of New York and Quebec, make troop movements safe along the Hudson, and "separate the Northern from the Southern colonies."[112]

Having an effective governor of New York was important to Gage, and Colden was the incumbent. It is true that, during 1772, Gage did comment that "the Old Gentleman . . . does not dislike a little Controversy, which he has been engaged in for the greatest part of his life." The general had been irritated by Colden's stand on an old dispute between the commander-in-chief and the governor of New York—which one took precedence at official ceremonies. Colden backed the governor's preeminence in the colony, a position taken by all New York governors.[113]

In 1770, however, rumors—fueled by correspondence from across the Atlantic—had it that Colden "will have the Management of this Province during his life"—Colden and everybody else assumed he would not live much longer—"and that his Majesty should have Said that so old and loyal a subject deserved that, if not a better reward for his good Services." Gage had also heard that "old Colden will be left in the Government for Life," which seemed to be a good idea to the general. On January 6, 1770 Gage wrote a letter that his biographer says "hinted" that Colden should be kept in office. Gage mentioned the *Stamp Act* crisis, Colden's coalition with the Assembly, and the New York merchants' realization that the cheating Bostonians had made them into "Dupes" over non-importation. John Richard Alden explained Gage's stand—he believed that "nonimportation would collapse if one single royal governor insisted on protecting merchants who chose to buy and sell British goods." To Gage, Colden was the royal servant who would crush non-importation once and for all.[114]

Colden, of course, would have been overjoyed to serve as governor while he lived. Well before the rumor about Colden staying in office reached the colony, on December 9, 1769 Lord Hillsborough wrote to the lieutenant governor notifying him of the appointment of a new governor, the Scot Lord Dunmore. Colden masked his disappointment by assuring Hillsborough: "It gives me great satisfaction that in this short administration I have had an opportunity of doing something of Importance for his Majesty's service" as "the promoters of Discord" had been "checked."[115]

Because Dunmore did not arrive in New York until October 18, 1770, Colden had the pleasure of presiding over an event that boded well for the future of the British Empire. Back in 1766, the idea had been suggested that a statue of William Pitt should be erected "on the Identical Spot" to mark the place where Colden's property had been burned. That would not happen. Instead, a gilt statue of George III on horseback, in the style of a Roman emperor, erected on an "elegant" base, would be placed in Bowling Green, the site of the burning. By all accounts, the king's statue was impressive. The American artist John Singleton Copley, on a trip to New York, observed: "I have seen the Statues of the King and Mr. Pitt, and I think them both good Statues." Even a visitor hostile to the king admitted that the statue in its setting presented a beautiful vista.[116]

Though Colden ignored the Pitt statue, in August 1770 he oversaw the official unveiling of George III's. Enthused, Colden was accompanied by the councilors, some of the assemblymen, General Gage, the army officers, the ministers of the various churches, city officials, and a "very large number of the principal inhabitants. Our loyalty and firm attachment and affection to his Majesty's person was expressed by drinking the King's health and a long continuance of his Reign." Guns were fired from Fort George while musicians played on its ramparts. Then "The whole Company walked in procession from the fort round the statue while the spectators expressed their Joy by loud acclamations the Procession having returned with me to the Fort." In a fitting end, "the Ceremony concluded with great cheerfullness and good humor." What a contrast, Colden must have thought, to what had happened in front of the fort in 1765.[117]

Dunmore's eventual arrival in October was also an important day for the colony. Aside from the brief administration of Sir Danvers Osborn—a rather low-ranking noble, a baronet—no noble appointed governor of New York had actually showed up to do the job since the first decade of the eighteenth century. Very few New Yorkers had had any contact with the nobility and just as few knew how the greatest nobles expected to be treated. Colden did and, as he wrote, "Everything in my Power was done to give him a Reception suited to his Rank." This included Colden paying for a dinner for his lordship and the Council. Dunmore noted: "I have the greatest reason to be pleased with the reception I have met with."[118]

The lieutenant governor was satisfied that he had put on a good show to make the governor "well pleased."[119] But Colden failed to realize that Dunmore was not what he seemed and that history would repeat itself.

NOTES

1. CC to Conway, January 14, 1766, *CLB*, vol. 2, 86–88; CC to Monckton, February 21, 1766, *CLB*, vol. 2, 96; CC to Johnson, December 15, 1765, *JP*, vol. 4, 883–84; *Oxford DNB*, s.v. Moore, Sir Henry.

2. CC to Lucius Ferdinand Carey, January 14, 1766, *CLB*, vol. 2, 92–93; New York City, *Minutes of The Common Council of the City of New York, 1675–1776* (New York: Dodd, Mead, 1905), vol. 6, 439; Worthington Chauncey Ford, comp., "British Officers Serving in America, 1754–1774," *New England Historical and Genealogical Register* 48 (April 1894), 163.

3. Henry B. Dawson, *The Sons of Liberty in New York: A Paper Read before the New York Historical Society, May 3, 1859* (Poughkeepsie, NY: Platt & Schram, 1859), 10, 111–12.

4. Moore to Dartmouth, January 16, 1766, *NYCD*, vol. 7, 807; John Montresor, *The Montresor Journals*, ed. G. D. Scull, New York Historical Society, *Collections* 14 (1881): 340; Parker to BF, May 6, June 11, 1766, *FP*, vol. 13, 265–66, 308–10.

5. Proclamation of Sir Henry Moore, January 10, 1766, *New York Gazette* (Weyman), January 13, 1766; Moore to Conway, January 16, 1766, *NYCD*, vol. 7, 805–6.

6. Patrick M'Robert, *A Tour Through Part of the North Provinces of America* (Edinburgh: Printed for the Author, 1776; repr., ed. Carl Bridenbaugh, New York: New York Times, 1968), 38; Montresor, *Montresor Journals*, 344; Watts to Monckton, January 20, 1766, *Aspinwall Papers*, Massachusetts Historical Society, *Collections*. 4th ser., 10 (1871): 588–89; Parker to BF, May 6, 1766, *FP*, vol. 13, 266; Moore to Lords of Trade, January 14, 1767, *NYCD*, vol. 7, 890–91; Gage to Johnson, July 9, 1770, *JP*, vol. 7, 796; Neil R. Stout, "Captain Kennedy and the Stamp Act," *New York History* 45, no. 1 (1964), 52–54.

7. Montresor, *Montresor Journals*, 342–44, 351–55, 357, 363, 365; CC to Board of Trade, *CLB*, vol. 2, 84–86; *New York Mercury* (Gaine), March 10, 1766; *New York Gazette, or the Weekly Post-Boy* (Holt), March 13, 1766; Parker to BF, May 6, 1766, *FP*, vol. 13, 266.

8. CC to Collinson, December 16, 1765, New Netherlands Coll., oldest New York, and the colonial government, 1655–1744 (microfilm), no. 71, NYHS.

9. CC to Collinson, December 16, 1765, New Netherlands Coll., NYHS; D. Colden to Collinson, December 17, 1765, New Netherlands Coll., NYHS; CC to Collinson, February 21, 1766, New Netherlands Coll., no. 75, NYHS; CC to Collinson, January 14, 1766, Miscellaneous Manuscripts, HM8256, Huntington Library, San Marino, CA.

10. CC, *The Conduct of Cadwallader Colden, Esquire, Late Lieutenant-Governor of New York: Relating to The Judges Commissions, Appeals to the King, and the Stamp Duty*, in *The Colden Letter Books, 1760–1775*, New York Historical Society, *Collections* 2 (1877): 460; Collinson to CC, March 20, 1766, *CP*, vol. 7, 104–5; Collinson to CC, May 16, 1766, *CP*, vol. 9, 206–7.

11. CC to Conway, February 21, 1766, *CLB*, vol. 2, 97–100.

12. CC to Conway, February 21, 1766, *CLB*, vol. 2, 97–100; Francis Bernard to Conway, January 23, 1766, Francis Bernard, *The Papers of Francis Bernard: Governor of Colonial Massachusetts, 1760–69*, ed. Colin Nicolson (Boston: Colonial Society of Massachusetts, 2007–), vol. 3, 73–75.

13. William Smith to George Whitefield, December 6, 1765, Historical Manuscripts Commission, in Great Britain, *The Manuscripts of the Earl of Dartmouth* (London: H. M. S. O., 1887), vol. 1, 331–32; William Smith, Jr., *The History of the Province of New York*, ed. Michael Kammen (Cambridge, MA: Belknap Press of Harvard University Press, 1972), vol. 1,

lviii; B. D. Bargar, "Lord Dartmouth's Patronage, 1772–1775," *William and Mary Quarterly*, 3rd ser., 15 (1958): 198; B. D. Bargar, *Lord Dartmouth and the American Revolution* (Columbia: University of South Carolina Press, 1965), 9.

14. CC to Newcastle, March 21, 1747/8, *CP*, vol. 4, 21–25; "A Narrative of some facts relative to Mr. Colden, occasioned by a Libell Printed in New York, November 4, 1765," n.d., *CLB*, vol. 2, 63–64.

15. CC, "State of the Province of New York," December 6, 1765, *CLB*, vol. 2, 68–78.

16. CC to Collinson, January 14, 1766, Miscellaneous Manuscripts, HM8256, Huntington Library; CC to Collinson, February 21, 1766, New Netherlands Coll., no. 75, NYHS.

17. Collinson to CC, May 16, 1766, *CP*, vol. 9, 206–7; Collinson to Amherst, May 17, 1766, Miscellaneous Manuscripts, HM8256, Huntington Library; Hillsborough to Moore, February 25, 1768, *NYCD*, vol. 8, 13; CC to Shelburne, December 26, 1766, October 20, 1767, *CLB*, vol. 2, 122–23, 129–31; CC to Moore, October 24, 1768, *CLB*, vol. 2, 179; CC to Grenville, October 22, 1768, Bancroft Coll., Colden Papers, vol. 4, 83, NYPL; CC to Grenville, January 6, 1769, *CLB*, vol. 2, 180–83; M. Collinson to CC, February 6, 1769, *CP*, vol. 7, 152–53; CC to Johnson, January 11, 1769, *JP*, vol. 12, 686–88.

18. "Extract of a letter from a Gentleman in London," March 28, 1766, *Boston Evening Post*, May 26, 1766. See Bernard, *Papers of Francis Bernard*, vol. 3, 153n3.

19. Charles Lloyd, *[A Copy taken from a Pamphlet Intitluled] The Conduct of the Late Administration Examined, With an Appendix, containing original and authentic Documents* (London: J. Almon, 1767; repr. Boston: Edes and Gill, 1767), 46; CC to Grenville, January 2, 1768, *CLB*, vol. 2, 151–54; extract of Conway to Gage, December 15, 1765, *CLB*, vol. 2, 128–29; Johnson to CC, May 9, 1766, *JP*, vol. 5, 206; Worthington Chauncey Ford, comp., "British Officers Serving in America, 1754–1774," *New England Historical and Genealogical Register* 49 (April 1895): 171.

20. "Committee on the American Papers," January 31, 1766, Newcastle Papers, British Museum Additional Manuscript 33030, f. 84, LC transcript; CC to Johnson, May 1, 1766, Autograph File, Houghton Library, Harvard University, Cambridge, MA; CC to Grenville, October 22, 1768, *CLB*, vol. 2, 176–79; Julie M. Flavell, *When London Was Capital of America* (New Haven, CT: Yale University Press, 2010), 140. James's testimony is printed in Great Britain, *Proceedings and Debates of the British Parliaments Respecting North America, 1754–1783*, ed. R. C. Simmons and P. D. G. Thomas (Millwood, NY: Kraus, 1982–1987), vol. 2, 121–22.

21. "Committee Papers," January 31, 1766, Newcastle Papers, British Museum Additional Manuscript 33030, f. 84, LC transcript; CC to Johnson, May 1, 1766, Autograph File, Houghton Library, Harvard University; James to CC, [December 1765?], *CP*, vol. 7, 98–100.

22. CC to Conway, February 22, 1766, *CLB*, vol. 2, 101–2.

23. AC to CC, [February 1766], *CP*, vol. 7, 93–95; Moore to Lords of Trade, November 7, 1766, *NYCD*, vol. 7, 874.

24. Conway to CC, December 15, 1765, *CLB*, vol. 2, 94–96; CC to Moore, February 18, 1766, *CLB*, vol. 2, 93–94; Moore to Conway, February 20, 1766, *NYCD*, vol. 7, 810–11; Montresor, *Montresor Journals*, 351, 365.

25. "Precis of the American Correspondence from the 31st August to the 9th November 1765," Newcastle Papers, British Museum Additional Manuscript 33030, LC transcript; Committee on the American Papers, January 31, 1766, f.84, Newcastle Papers, British Museum Additional Manuscript 33030, LC transcript; Gage to Conway, November 8, 1765, Thomas Gage, *The Correspondence of General Thomas Gage with the Secretaries of State, 1763–1775*, ed. Clarence E. Carter (New Haven, CT: Yale University Press, 1931–1933), vol. 1, 72–73; Conway to Gage, December 15, 1765, Gage, *Correspondence of General Thomas Gage*, vol. 2, 29–30; Stout, "Captain Kennedy," 44, 50.

26. CC to Kennedy, March 28, 1766, *CLB*, vol. 2, 102–3; CC to Conway, March 28, 1766, *CLB*, vol. 2, 103–7; Kennedy to CC, March 30, 1766, *CP*, vol. 7, 107; Stout, "Captain Kennedy," 55; Sarah Kinkel, "The King's Pirates? Naval Enforcement of Imperial Authority, 1740–76," *William and Mary Quarterly*, 3rd ser., 71 (2014): 29–30.

27. James to CC, [December 1765?], *CP*, vol. 7, 98–100; Conway to CC, December 15, 1765, *CLB*, vol. 2, 94–96; Stout, "Captain Kennedy," 50.

28. CC to Conway, February 21, 1766, *CLB*, vol. 2, 97–100.
29. CC to Johnson, February 20, 1766, *JP*, vol. 5, 33–34; CC to James, May 1, 1766, *CLB*, vol. 2, 108–9.
30. CC to Amherst, November 10, 1766, *CLB*, vol. 2, 118–19; Collinson to CC, April 2, 1769, *CP*, vol. 7, 137; Grenville to CC, July 28, 1768, *CP*, vol. 7, 145–46; Bernard to J. Pownall, May 30, 1766, Bernard, *Papers of Francis Bernard*, vol. 3, 151.
31. Collinson to CC, January 30, February 12, August 11, 1767, *CP*, vol. 7, 116–19, 126–27; CC to Amherst, November 10, 1766, *CLB*, vol. 2, 118–19.
32. CC to Collinson, November 10, 1766, *CLB*, vol. 2, 119–21; CC to Dartmouth, December 6, 1765, *CLB*, vol. 2, 83.
33. Collinson to CC, April 2, 1768, *CP*, vol. 7, 137; CC to _____, July 27, 1767, Gratz Coll., HSP: Johnson to CC, September 8, 1767, *JP*, vol. 5, 661.
34. Johnson to CC, September 8, 1767, *JP*, vol. 5, 661; CC, *Conduct*, 451.
35. CC to Shelburne, November 23, 1767, *CLB*, vol. 2, 131–37; Collinson to CC, April 2, 1768, *CP*, vol. 7, 137.
36. CC to Shelburne, November 23, 1767, *CLB*, vol. 2, 131–37.
37. CC to Shelburne, November 23, 1767, *CLB*, vol. 2, 131–37; CC, *Conduct*, 434.
38. Moore to Hillsborough, May 9, 1768, *NYCD*, vol. 8, 66–68.
39. New York Colony, Council, *Journal of the Legislative Council of the Colony of New York, Began the 9th day of April, 1691; and ended the [3d of April, 1775]* (Albany, NY: Weed, Parsons, 1861), vol. 2, 1635, 1640–41; New York Colony, Assembly, *Journal of the Votes and Proceedings of the General Assembly of the Colony of New York from 1766 to 1776, Inclusive* (Albany, NY: J. Buel, 1820), December 23–24, 30, 1767, 52–53, 55, 64; Dorothy Rita Dillon, *The New York Triumvirate: A Study of the Legal and Political Careers of William Livingston, John Morin Scott, William Smith, Jr.* (New York: Columbia University Press, 1949), 80.
40. New York Colony, Assembly, *Journal of the Votes (1766–1776)*, January 8, 12, and 14, 1768, 69–70, 73–74.
41. New York Colony, Assembly, *Journal of the Votes (1766–1776)*, February 6, 1768, 91.
42. Moore to Hillsborough, May 9, 1768, *NYCD*, vol. 8, 66–68.
43. Moore to Hillsborough, May 9, 1768, *NYCD*, vol. 8, 66–68; AC to CC, October 22, 1768, Colden Family Papers, box 11, NYHS.
44. CC to Halifax, January 29, 1768, *CLB*, vol. 2, 161; CC to Shelburne, November 23, 1767, January 21, 1768, *CLB*, vol. 2, 131–37, 143–45; CC to Lord Mansfield, January 22, 1768, *CLB*, vol. 2, 146–50; George Ross to Col. James Robertson, March 12, 1768, *CP*, vol. 7, 133–34.
45. CC to Board of Trade, November 23, 1767, *CLB*, vol. 2, 137–42; CC to Hillsborough, June 16, 1768, *CLB*, vol. 2, 174–75.
46. Hillsborough to Moore, March 12, 1768, *NYCD*, vol. 8, 35.
47. CC to Grenville, January 29, 1768, *CLB*, vol. 2, 157–60; CC to Mansfield, January 29, 1768, *CLB*, vol. 2, 154–57; CC to Shelburne, January 21, 1768, *CLB*, vol. 2, 143–45.
48. CC to Amherst, June 24, 1766, *CLB*, vol. 2, 110–13; Moore to Lords of Trade, January 12, 1767, *NYCD*, vol. 7, 888; *New York Gazette* (Weyman), January 6, 1766; Montresor, *Montresor Journals*, 351; Michael D'Innocenzo and John J. Turner, Jr., "The Role of New York Newspapers in the Stamp Act Crisis, 1764–66," *New York Historical Society Quarterly* 51, nos. 3–4 (1967): part 2, 356; *SM*, vol. 1, 94–97.
49. Hugh Wallace to Johnson, September 28, 1767, *JP*, vol. 5, 706; Watts to Monckton, January 23, 1768, *Aspinwall Papers*, vol. 10, 599–600; R. A. Humphreys, "Lord Shelburne and a Projected Recall of Colonial Governors in 1767," *American Historical Review* 37, no. 2 (1932), 271; Nicholas Varga, "The New York Restraining Act: Its Passage and Some Effects, 1766–1768," *New York History* 37, no. 3 (1956): 251.
50. *SM*, vol. 1, 43–44; Moore to Lords of Trade, April 22, 1768, *NYCD*, vol. 8, 59–60; Moore to Hillsborough, January 21, 1769, *NYCD*, vol. 8, 148–49; Hillsborough to Moore, March 24, July 15, 1769, *NYCD*, vol. 8, 155–56, 176–77.
51. CC to Collinson, September 12, 1766, *CLB*, vol. 2, 117–18; *SM*, vol. 1, 51; Watts to Monckton, January 23, 1768, *Aspinwall Papers*, vol. 10, 599–600.

52. Watts to Monckton, September 12, 1769, *Aspinwall Papers*, vol. 10, 618–19; Philip Livingston Jr. to Hillsborough, September 11, 1769, *NYCD*, vol. 8, 187–88; Parker to BF, September 12–13, 1769, *FP*, vol. 16, 202–3.

53. *New York Mercury* (Gaine), September 11, 18, 1769; Watts to Monckton, September 12, 1769, *Aspinwall Papers*, vol. 10, 618–19.

54. Garden to CC, c. June 1768, *CP*, vol. 7, 139–40; D. Colden to CC Jr., May 17, 1768, *CP*, vol. 9, 211–12.

55. Samuel Auchmuty to CC Jr., June 4, 1768, *CP*, vol. 7, 139; *Oxford English Dictionary*, s.v. "fit."

56. Parker to BF, September 12–13, 1769, *FP*, vol. 16, 202–3; Johnson to John Wetherhead, October 6, 1769, *JP*, vol. 7, 205.

57. *SM*, vol. 1, 53–54; CC to Hillsborough, September 13, 1769, *CLB*, vol. 2, 185–86.

58. D. Colden to his brother, January 31, 1769, Bancroft Coll., Colden Papers, vol. 4, 103–5, NYPL.

59. CC to [Hillsborough?], April 25, 1768, *CLB*, vol. 2, 167–70; John P. Kaminski, *George Clinton: Yeoman Politician of the New Republic* (Madison: University of Wisconsin Press, 1993), 15; E. Wilder Spaulding, *His Excellency George Clinton: Critic of the Constitution* (New York: Macmillan, 1938), 21; Patricia U. Bonomi, *A Factious People: Politics and Society in Colonial New York* (New York: Columbia University Press, 1971), 239–46.

60. D. Colden to his brother, January 31, 1769, Bancroft Coll., Colden Papers, vol. 4, 103–5, NYPL; Bonomi, *Factious People*, 246–58; "Watchman," No. 3, March 10, 1770, *New York Journal* (Holt), April 19, 1770; Roger J. Champagne, "Family Politics versus Constitutional Principles: The New York Assembly Elections of 1768 and 1769," *William and Mary Quarterly*, 3rd ser., 20 (1963): 59, 79.

61. CC to Johnson, January 11, 1769, *CLB*, vol. 2, 184–85; CC to Johnson, February 26, 1769, Gratz Coll., HSP; CC to Hillsborough, July 7, 1770, *CLB*, vol. 2, 221–24.

62. Samuel Seabury to Society for the Propagation of the Gospel, December 27, 1769, Society for the Propagation of the Gospel Papers, Series B, vol. 2, 176, Columbia University, microfilm; CC to Hillsborough, July 7, 1770, *CLB*, vol. 2, 221–24; Livingston to Hillsborough, December 4, 1769, *NYCD*, vol. 8, 192.

63. CC to Hillsborough, February 21, July 7, 1770, *CLB*, vol. 2, 207–12, 221–24; Hillsborough to CC, June 12, 1770, *NYCD*, vol. 8, 215–16; *SM*, vol. 1, 82.

64. Hillsborough to CC, April 14, 1770, *NYCD*, vol. 8, 210–11; Livingston to Margaret Livingston, January 11, 1771, Robert R. Livingston Papers, reel 1, NYHS; *SM*, vol. 1, 92–93.

65. CC to Grenville, October 5, 1769, *CLB*, vol. 2, 190.

66. *SM*, vol. 1, 52, 67; Johnson to CC, February 9, 1770, *DH*, vol. 2, 965; Robin F. A. Fabel, *The Economy of British West Florida, 1763–1783* (Tuscaloosa: University of Alabama Press, 1988), 168–69.

67. *SM*, vol. 1, 82, 88, 94–97; William G. Godfrey, *Pursuit of Profit and Preferment in Colonial North America: John Bradstreet's Quest* (Waterloo, Canada: Wilfrid Laurier University Press, 1982), 166.

68. James Rivington to Johnson, November 27, 1769, *JP*, vol. 7, 271; Bonomi, *Factious People*, 265.

69. Wallace to Johnson, September 28, 1768, *JP*, vol. 5, 706; Conway to Gage, May 20, 1766, Gage, *Correspondence of General Thomas Gage*, vol. 2, 37–38; Moore to Shelburne, August 21, 1767, *NYCD*, vol. 7, 948–49; Moore to Hillsborough, March 30, May 29, 1769, *NYCD*, vol. 8, 157, 169.

70. Moore to Lords of Trade, December 19, 1766, *NYCD*, vol. 7, 884–85; Jack P. Greene and Richard M. Jellison, "The Currency Act of 1764 in Imperial–Colonial Relations, 1764–1776," *William and Mary Quarterly*, 3rd ser., 18 (1961): 486–89.

71. Greene and Jellison, "Currency," 502, 511–12; Moore to Lords of Trade, March 28, 1766, *NYCD*, vol. 7, 820–21; Moore to Shelburne, January 3, 1768, *NYCD*, vol. 8, 1; Moore to Hillsborough, May 14, August 18, 1768, January 20, 1769, *NYCD*, vol. 8, 72, 96–97, 147; Joseph Albert Ernst, *Money and Politics in America, 1755–1775: A Study in the Currency Act of 1764 and the Political Economy of Revolution* (Chapel Hill: University of North Carolina Press, 1973), 268; Roger J. Champagne, *Alexander McDougall and the American Revolution in*

New York (Schenectady, NY: New York State American Revolution Bicentennial Commission, Union College Press, 1975), 18.

72. Champagne, *Alexander McDougall*, 54; Ernst, *Money*, 269; CC to Hillsborough, October 4, 1769, *CLB*, vol. 2, 187–89.

73. CC to Hillsborough, October 4, December 4, 1769, *CLB*, vol. 2, 187–89, 193–94; Ernst, *Money*, 269–70.

74. Ernst, *Money*, 270–71.

75. CC to Hillsborough, October 4, 1769, *CLB*, vol. 2, 187–89; Joseph S. Tiedemann, *Reluctant Revolutionaries: New York City and the Road to Independence, 1763–1776* (Ithaca, NY: Cornell University Press, 1997), 142.

76. Alexander McDougall, "To the Betrayed Inhabitants of the City and Colony of New York," December 17, 1764, *DH*, vol. 3, 530–31; Kaminski, *George Clinton*, 15.

77. CC to Board of Trade, January 6, 1770, *CLB*, vol. 2, 202–4; Ernst, *Money*, 272–73, 275.

78. CC to Hillsborough, January 6, 1770, *CLB*, vol. 2, 199–202.

79. CC to Hillsborough, January 6, 1770, *CLB*, vol. 2, 199–202.

80. "A Proclamation," December 20, 1769, *DH*, vol. 3, 532–34; *SM*, vol. 1, 72–76; Smith, "Copy of a late letter from an Eminent Counsellor, and a Friend to Liberty," *New York Gazette, or the Weekly Post-Boy* (Parker), March 19, 1770; Leonard W. Levy, "Did the Zenger Case Really Matter? Freedom of the Press in Colonial New York," *William and Mary Quarterly*, 3rd ser., 17 (1960): 45; Pauline Maier, *From Resistance to Revolution: Colonial Radicals and the Development of American Opposition to Britain, 1765–1776* (New York: Vintage Books, 1972), 192–93; I. N. Phelps Stokes, *The Iconography of Manhattan Island, 1498–1909* (New York: R. H. Dodd, 1915–1928), vol. 4, 818.

81. Norman MacLeod to Johnson, January 27, 1770, *JP*, vol. 12, 772–74; CC to Hillsborough, February 21, 1770, *CLB*, vol. 2, 207–12; CC to Board of Trade, February 21, 1770, *CLB*, vol. 2, 213; "To the Printer," *New York Gazette, or the Weekly Post-Boy* (Parker), February 5, 1770; Philip Ranlet, *The New York Loyalists*, 2nd ed. (Lanham, MD: University Press of America, 2002), 27.

82. "The Watchman," No. 4, March 29, 1770, Microfiche, Early American Imprints, 1st ser., Evans no. 11920.

83. "A Merchant," *The Times*, c. March 1770, Microfiche, Early American Imprints, 1st ser., Evans no. 11912, NYPL.

84. Hillsborough to CC, January 18, 1770, *NYCD*, vol. 8, 201; Ernst, *Money*, 273–76.

85. Hillsborough to CC, February 17, 1770, *NYCD*, vol. 8, 205–6; Gage to Hillsborough, February 21, July 7, 1770, Gage, *Correspondence of General Thomas Gage*, vol. 1, 248, 262; Ernst, *Money*, 276.

86. Hillsborough to Moore, July 9, 1768, *NYCD*, vol. 8, 81; Hillsborough to CC, February 17, June 12, 1770, *NYCD*, vol. 8, 205–6, 215–16; Ernst, *Money*, 278–79; Greene and Jellison, "Currency," 512–14; Ian R. Christie and Benjamin W. Labaree, *Empire or Independence, 1760–1776* (New York: Norton, 1976), 146.

87. *New York Gazette, or the Weekly Post-Boy* (Holt), November 7, 1765; CC, "State of Province," December 6, 1765, *CLB*, vol. 2, 77–78; Ranlet, *Loyalists*, 12–13.

88. Ranlet, *Loyalists*, 51; Edmund S. Morgan and Helen M. Morgan, *The Stamp Act Crisis: Prologue to Revolution*, 2nd ed. (New York: Collier Books, 1963), 331–33.

89. For a thorough account of non-importation against the Townshend duties, see Ranlet, *Loyalists*, 25-33.

90. CC to Council and Assembly, November 22, 1769, New York Colony, Council, *Journal of the Legislative Council of the Colony of New York*, vol. 2, 1711; Assembly to CC, November 29, 1769, New York Colony, Assembly, *Journal of the Votes (1766–1776)*, 13; Extract of Lieut. Governor Colden's Speech to the Council and General Assembly, November 22, 1769, House of Lords Papers, 9.4/4, reel 20, Columbia University, microfilm; Hillsborough to William Tryon, May 13, 1769, William Tryon, *The Correspondence of William Tryon and Other Selected Papers*, ed. William S. Powell (Raleigh, NC: Division of Archives and History, Department of Cultural Resources, 1981), vol. 2, 335; *NYCD*, vol. 8, 164–65; Moore to Hillsborough, July 19, 1769, *NYCD*, vol. 8, 177–78; Paul David Nelson, *William Tryon and the*

Course of Empire: A Life in British Imperial Service (Chapel Hill: University of North Carolina Press, 1990), 67.

91. Great Britain, *Proceedings and Debates of the British Parliaments*, vol. 3, 298, 323; Hillsborough to CC, January 18, 1770, *NYCD*, vol. 8, 201; CC to Hillsborough, April 25, 1770, *CLB*, vol. 2, 219.

92. CC to Hillsborough, July 7, 1770, *CLB*, vol. 2, 222–23; CC to AC, July 7, 1770, *NYCD*, vol. 8, 220; AC to Anthony Todd, July 11, 1770, *NYCD*, vol. 8, 221; CC to Hillsborough, July 10, 1770, *NYCD*, vol. 8, 218; Ranlet, *Loyalists*, 25–26, 28–32.

93. Peter D. G. Thomas, *The Townshend Duties Crisis: The Second Phase of the American Revolution, 1767–1773* (New York: Oxford University Press, 1987), 200–201; Milton M. Klein, "New York Lawyers and the Coming of the American Revolution," *New York History* 55, no. 4 (1974): 395; Ernst, *Money*, 277–78; CC to Hillsborough, September 8, 1770, *CLB*, vol. 2, 228.

94. CC to Hillsborough, July 10, 1770, *NYCD*, vol. 8, 218; CC to Hillsborough, July 7, August 18, October 5, 1770, *CLB*, vol. 2, 221–30.

95. Livingston to Robert Livingston, September 18, 1768, Robert R. Livingston Papers, reel 1, NYHS; Cynthia A. Kierner, *Traders and Gentlefolk: The Livingstons of New York, 1675–1790* (Ithaca, NY: Cornell University Press, 1992), 113; Sung Bok Kim, *Landlord and Tenant in Colonial New York: Manorial Society, 1664–1775* (Chapel Hill: University of North Carolina Press, 1978), 355.

96. Kim, *Landlord*, 349–50, 360–61.

97. Kim, *Landlord*, 360n43, 361n44; "Settlement of reduced officers," November 19, 1765, Great Britain, *Acts of Privy Council, Colonial Series*, ed. William L. Grant and James Munroe (London: H. M. S. O., 1908–1912), vol. 6, 421–22.

98. Bonomi, *Factious People*, 208–9; Kim, *Landlord*, 409, 412; *SM*, vol. 1, 227.

99. CC to Johnson, October 8, 1763, *JP*, vol. 10, 874.

100. Oscar Handlin and Irving Mark, eds., "Chief Daniel Nimham v. Roger Morris, Beverly Robinson, and Philip Philipse—An Indian Land Case in Colonial New York, 1765–1767," *Ethnohistory* 11, no. 3 (1964): 193, 204–5, 242; Georgiana C. Nammack, *Fraud, Politics, and the Dispossession of the Indians: The Iroquois Land Frontier in the Colonial Period* (Norman: University of Oklahoma Press, 1969), 75.

101. Watts to Monckton, March 16, 1765, in Watts, *Letter Book of John Watts, Merchant and Councillor of New York, January 1, 1762–December 22, 1765*, New York Historical Society, *Collections* 61 (1928): 338; Colin G. Calloway, *The Scratch of a Pen: 1763 and the Transformation of North America* (New York: Oxford University Press, 2006), 52.

102. Richard Bland and Patrick Henry to CC, July 11, 1770, Bancroft Coll., Colden Papers, vol. 4, 171, NYPL; Carleton to CC, May 30, 1770, William Nelson, *The Correspondence of William Nelson as Acting Governor of Virginia, 1770–1771*, ed. John C. Van Horne (Charlottesville: Virginia Historical Society, University Press of Virginia, 1975), 127; CC to Bland and Henry, July 11, 1770, Nelson, *Correspondence*, 124–25; statement of Bland and others, July 12, 1770, Nelson, *Correspondence*, 125.

103. Nelson, *Correspondence*; CC to Hillsborough, February 21, July 7, 1770, *CLB*, vol. 2, 210, 221–24; Hillsborough to CC, April 14, 1770, *NYCD*, vol. 8, 210–11; Bland and Henry to CC, July 11, 1770, Bancroft Coll., Colden Papers, vol. 4, 171, NYPL.

104. Election of CC to Honorary Membership in the Marine Society, June 18, 1772, *CP*, vol. 7, 182; William Allen, *An American Biographical and Historical Dictionary* (Cambridge, MA: William Hilliard, 1809), 200; "Cadwallader Colden," *Historical Magazine* 9 (January 1865): 10; Francis R. Packard, *History of Medicine in the United States* (New York: Hoeber, 1931), vol. 1, 233; Stokes, *Iconography*, vol. 4, 830; James B. Bell, *The Imperial Origins of the King's Church in Early America, 1607–1783* (New York: Palgrave Macmillan, 2004), 85.

105. Austin Baxter Keep, *History of the New York Society Library* (New York: De Vinne Press, 1908), 180.

106. CC to Lords of Trade, December 7, 1763, *NYCD*, vol. 7, 586; CC to Hillsborough, February 21, 1770, *NYCD*, vol. 8, 208; Carl Bridenbaugh, *Mitre and Sceptre: Transatlantic Faiths, Ideas, Personalities, and Politics, 1689–1775* (New York: Oxford University Press, 1962), 253.

107. CC to Tryon, August 22, 1774, Bancroft Coll., Colden Papers, vol. 4, 317, NYPL.

108. "To the Honourable Cadwallader Colden, Esqr.," February 15, 1770, John Austin Stevens, Jr., ed., *Colonial Records of the New York Chamber of Commerce, 1768–1784* (New York: John F. Trow, 1867), 76–77; "To the Honourable Cadwallader Colden," March 24, 1770, Stevens, ed., *Colonial Records*, 87–88; Philip L. White, *The Beekmans of New York in Politics and Commerce, 1647–1877* (New York: New York Historical Society, 1956), 432–33.

109. "To the Honorable Cadwallader Colden," March 24, 1770, Stevens, ed., *Colonial Records*, 87–88; CC, speech, March 6, 1770, Stevens, ed., *Colonial Records*, 78–79.

110. CC, speech, March 24, 1770, Stevens, ed., *Colonial Records*, 88; *New York Mercury* (Gaine), March 26, 1770.

111. Charles Coleman Sellers, *Patience Wright: American Artist and Spy in George III's London* (Middletown, CT: Wesleyan University Press, 1976), 37, 49–50, 228; William Dunlap, *History of the Rise and Progress of The Arts of Design in the United States*, ed. Alexander Wyckoff (New York: G. P. Scott, 1834; repr. new ed., ed. Alexander Wyckoff, New York: B. Blom, 1965), vol. 1, 151; Stokes, *Iconography*, vol. 4, 819–20, 822.

112. Carleton to Gage, February 15, 1767, Bancroft Coll., Colden Papers, vol. 3, 439, NYPL.

113. Gage to Barrington, February 4, July 1, 1772, Gage, *Correspondence of General Thomas Gage*, vol. 2, 598–99, 611. On this dispute see Moore to Shelburne, March 5, 1768, *NYCD*, vol. 8, 15; Hillsborough to Moore, May 14, 1768, *NYCD*, vol. 8, 73.

114. MacLeod to Johnson, January 6, 1770, *JP*, vol. 7, 333–34; Gage to Barrington, January 6, 1770, Thomas Gage Papers, CL; John R. Alden, *General Gage in America Being Principally A History of His Role in the American Revolution* (Baton Rouge: Lousiana State University Press, 1948; repr. New York: Greenwood Press, 1969), 186.

115. Hillsborough to CC, December 9, 1769, *NYCD*, vol. 8, 193; CC to Hillsborough, February 21, 1770, *CLB*, vol. 2, 207–12.

116. Montresor, *Montresor Journals*, 353; M'Robert, *Tour*, 5; John Singleton Copley to Henry Pelham, June 16, 1771, in Copley, *Letters and Papers of John Singleton Copley and Henry Pelham, 1739–1776* (Boston: Massachusetts Historical Society, 1914; repr. New York: Kennedy Graphics, 1970), 117; Edward Bangs, ed., *Journal of Lieutenant Isaac Bangs, April 1 to July 29, 1776* (Cambridge, MA: J. Wilson and Son, 1890; repr. New York: Arno Press, 1968), 25; Charles Inglis to Richard Hind, October 31, 1776, John Wolfe Lydekker, *The Life and Letters of Charles Inglis.* (London: Church Historical Society, 1936), 165; A. James Wall, "The Statues of King George III and the Honorable William Pitt Erected in New York City, 1770," *New York Historical Society Quarterly Bulletin* 4, no. 2 (1920): 49; Stokes, *Iconography*, vol. 4, 813.

117. CC to Hillsborough, August 18, 1770, *CLB*, vol. 2, 225–27; Wall, "Statues," 46.

118. CC to Hillsborough, November 10, 1770, *CLB*, vol. 2, 231–35; *SM*, vol. 1, 83; Lord Dunmore to Hillsborough, October 24, 1770, *NYCD*, vol. 8, 249; Bonomi, *Factious People*, 294.

119. CC to Hillsborough, November 10, 1770, *CLB*, vol. 2, 231–35.

Chapter Sixteen

Drunkard

In 1770, at the close of what had to be Cadwallader Colden's last time as acting governor, a substantial delegation of some fifty-six of "the Principal and most respected Merchants" in the city, having learned that he "intended to retire to the country, came in a Body and thanked me for my Administration." Their appreciation pleased Colden as he prepared for life at Spring Hill again. The merchants were soon followed by the Church of England ministers and most important New York Anglicans with the same mission. "Since I left the Town," the surprised lieutenant governor reported, "I have been informed that other distinguished Bodies designed to have made me the like compliments, had I not left the place sooner than was expected."[1]

These processions of New Yorkers had the air of a final farewell to an old royal servant who had been a mainstay of New York's government since before almost all of them had been born. They had good reasons to be thankful for what Colden had presided over in office. Another batch of needed New York paper money had been approved, the troops protecting them from the Sons of Liberty had been provided for, and, as Colden commented, "all kind of Rioting is greatly discouraged."[2]

None of the happy New Yorkers could have imagined that their new, noble governor would combat his elderly lieutenant governor in a legal dispute unseen since the days of Governor William Cosby or that Lord Dunmore would be hurriedly transferred far away from their colony. Nor could they have dreamed that their second gubernatorial arrival in the decade, a sickly soldier, would have to leave too. This improbable chain of events resulted in Colden—then 86 years old—returning still another time to govern the province of New York.

Given all the hatred directed at Colden over the years because of the outright lie that he had been a Jacobite, it will surprise most readers that Lord

Dunmore really was a Jacobite in 1745. The teenaged Dunmore, then merely John Murray, served as a page in the pretender's court; Murray's father was convicted of treason but spared execution. Despite this past, Lord Dunmore was welcomed by New Yorkers. About the same time, William Livingston, a Triumvirate member, wrote *A Soliloquy*, a pamphlet mocking Colden (which even some of his friends enjoyed) that brought up, once again, the absurd charge that Colden had joined the Jacobites in 1715.[3]

Dunmore, truly a survivor, got away with other problems or "weaknesses" as William Smith Jr. called them. Soon after Dunmore arrived he wrote a draft letter for the lawyer's perusal, which was verbose with "bad spelling." Smith confided to his diary: "I judge from this and former conversations that his Lordship's Education and Abilities are equally beneath his Birth." A scholar has dismissed Dunmore as "decidedly less-than-brilliant." Colden summed up the governor as "a capricious ignorant Lord."[4]

Stupidity, however, was not Dunmore's greatest weakness. He drank to excess all the time, so much so that he was clearly an alcoholic, and could become violent. New York had no shortage of governors who drank too much, George Clinton for example. But Clinton became drunk with the Hungarian Club or at home in private. Dunmore was not reluctant to be inebriated in polite society. In 1771 Smith, again in his diary, remarked that Dunmore "took too cheerful a Glass and forced it upon his Company . . . but the Company did not part without Blows."[5]

Early on in Dunmore's administration, Smith talked with the disgusted Colonel John Bradstreet, who had been with the governor, "a damned Fool," at a dinner given by the Sons of St. Andrew, a Scottish club. Bradstreet called Dunmore "a silly extravagant Buck," who, when making toasts "sunk himself to the vilest baudy Healths." According to Bradstreet, the entire gathering was "ashamed of him." This incident forced Smith to reconsider his relationship with Dunmore: "Henceforth I shall be more shy for Fear of involving my own with a Character that will be disreputable among all sorts of People, and perhaps expose what I gave him in Confidence." It can be assumed that New York's governor acted in the same fashion whenever he had access to liquor such as "an entertainment" in November 1770 given by King's College to honor him or at a celebration of St. George, the patron saint of England, held in a tavern during April 1771.[6]

Being a blatant drunkard did not enhance Dunmore's time as governor. He discovered that the Assembly remained totally "inflexible" about allowing Judge Robert R. Livingston to serve in the chamber, just as Colden had predicted. Livingston railed at Dunmore for his failure. Dunmore had just as little influence when the Assembly picked a new London agent, Edmund Burke, "a Mortification" to Dunmore. Burke, a prominent member of Parliament, was, Livingston observed, "the King's personal Enemy and is the most detested of any Man in the Opposition." This appointment, the governor feared, would damage him in the corridors of power across the Atlantic. Dunmore's own appointment of mob leader King Sears to a patronage job would have been almost as damaging in London, but luckily for Dunmore, Sears rejected the position.[7]

When Dunmore first arrived at New York, Colden had become reconciled to his retirement. "I thought of nothing but to retire and spend my few remaining Days with satisfaction." Philosophical amusements beckoned to him once again. He had abandoned metaphysics and had devoted himself to "a revisal of the Art of Logic," not a subject usually connected with New York's political figures.[8]

Unknown to Colden, highly unusual events had been coalescing in the imperial capital. In July 1770 the king had granted Dunmore a secure salary of £2,000 a year that came from the colonial tea tax and he could not accept any funds from the Assembly; no longer would a New York governor be at the mercy of the Assembly for his salary. Such a strengthening of colonial governors was long overdue, but more was in store. Lord Hillsborough sent along a copy of a declaration proclaimed by King William III in the 1690s that the monarch could give a new governor, from his commission's date, one-half of the total salary and fees received by an acting governor filling in for a deceased governor. George III decided that the financially-strapped Dunmore should receive that one-half of the money that would have otherwise gone to Colden. No other acting governor since Rip Van Dam, who had filled in for the dead Governor John Montgomerie in the 1730s, had been treated this way.[9]

The imperial bureaucrats seemed totally ignorant of a basic fact of law. A dead king's proclamation was as dead as he was or, as Colden put it, "The Declaration of King William died with him." Colden had also changed his mind about a story Governor William Burnet had told him decades before. Colden had recalled his mentor saying that a clerk had added an "of" to the form of the instructions of New York's governor, changing the income he would receive. A search of the records showed Colden to be mistaken about that. Yet Colden persisted in his belief that Burnet (and his own memory) had been correct except for one detail—the clerk had changed the wording of the copy of King William's declaration on file, not the draft instructions. This recollection would make Colden even more determined to resist what he saw as an injustice. Of course, Hillsborough and his superiors could simply have had the king issue his own declaration, making the policy legal and beyond dispute. That would have been logical, but logic was in as short supply among British bureaucrats as with New York politicians.[10]

Before Colden learned what was in store for him, Dunmore alerted Attorney-General John Tabor Kempe about the king's bounty, knowing that Colden would not just give away the money. Kempe annoyed his lordship by pointing out that all the precedents in New York argued against the scheme, which made the governor want to fire him. When Smith learned about the dispute, he talked Dunmore out of dismissing Kempe, assuring the governor that Kempe would do his job. Indeed, he would; Dunmore frightened him.[11]

Colden's surprise can be imagined when the governor told him what he expected. Suddenly, Dunmore had transformed into Cosby, while Colden had been cast into the role of Rip Van Dam. Experiencing "a very sensible uneasiness," Colden, who knew that Cosby had not won his case, refused to comply and claimed to deserve better treatment for his service. Then Dunmore mocked him, saying "If you think you have Merit with Administration ask them; for whatever you had you have lost lately." The lieutenant governor "hinted" he had reached an age "that the Favor of the Crown was nothing to him now." Dunmore, who was accustomed to people groveling before him, responded: "you had best give it up for the Sake of your Children."[12]

Dunmore, a bully, thought he could push an old man into bending to his will and directed the attorney-general to find a way to "force out the Money from Colden," and threatened Colden's family. Immediately, Kempe tried to divert the governor's attention away from Colden's children. Smith insisted that this threat was "a Joke." It is unlikely that Kempe thought that to be the case.[13]

Smith warned the governor "that Colden would complain to the Ministry." With extreme self-confidence, Dunmore, unconcerned, assured the man who would assist him in the upcoming trial that Colden "might try if he would, but he would be sure to be disappointed, for that all the Ministers had a bad opinion of him, and had expressed it very freely to him."[14]

Who composed this legion of government ministers? Lord Hillsborough had to be one of them. Colden's transgression of signing the New York paper money bill had been forgiven by this time, leaving only his approval of the bill banning judges from the Assembly. That action seems a rather weak reason to generate such opposition to Colden. It probably had more to do with Dunmore's status, which also explains why Dunmore became governor in the first place—he held a seat in the House of Lords; Hillsborough did not. Apparently, Hillsborough was groveling before someone with greater status. As if to emphasize the point, Dunmore authorized Hillsborough to be his proxy for his parliamentary seat while he was in America. Now Hillsborough could bask in the reflected glory of great nobles while sitting in the House of Lords.[15]

Hillsborough was not the only prop Dunmore counted on. Curiously, the reason goes back to, again, Cosby, and relates to the man who was prime minister when Dunmore was chosen to be New York's governor, the Duke of Grafton. When Cosby ran New York, a son of the then Duke of Grafton came to New York in his capacity as a naval officer. He and a daughter of the governor took a liking to each other and Mrs. Cosby saw an opportunity. She snuck a minster into Fort George who married them. According to one scholar, "the romantic wedding was the talk of the town for many a year."[16]

The marriage produced two sons, the eldest of whom, Augustus Henry Fitzroy, inherited the dukedom and became prime minister. Although his father died young, his mother, the former Elizabeth Cosby, lived to 1788. As the young boy grew up, his mother must have told him stories about the bad men who had persecuted his beloved grandfather, William Cosby. FitzRoy's papers include a copy of Henry Conway's letter of December 15, 1765 to Colden, which gives Conway's brief criticism of Colden's conduct during the *Stamp Act* riots. Grafton was interested in criticism of Colden. When the duke became prime minister, it can not surprise that he would be hostile to Colden, the last surviving foe of his grandfather, or that other ministers would parrot what the prime minister believed. Grafton, however, resigned his office well before Dunmore arrived in New York. Gradually, the truth about Colden reasserted itself among the ministers, which would not work to Dunmore's benefit.[17]

Convinced that the dispute would eventually be settled in London, where Dunmore's apparent influence at court and with the ministers would be overwhelming, Smith doubted that Colden would challenge the governor in a court of law. Financially, it might have made sense for Colden to give in—defending himself would be expensive. Such matters did not faze Colden; Dunmore had picked the wrong old man to bully. As Dunmore's biographer commented: "In Colden, Dunmore faced an adversary who was his superior in age, experience, and intellect." The King v. Cadwallader Colden would proceed.[18]

Colden needed a lawyer and he found James Duane, one of the more conservative lawyers in the province, who agreed to defend him. No supporter of mobs, Duane had opposed rioting at the time of the *Stamp Act* and had been willing to prosecute Alexander McDougall for his seditious writing. Already well known to Colden, who had appointed him to a lesser legal office, Duane, a friend of David's, had also represented Cad in a land dispute.[19]

Duane knew he was risking Dunmore's ire – the governor's vindictive personality did not stay secret for long. "It is not unusual to court the rising Sun, nor are the ties of Duty always strong enough to resist its Influence," Duane wrote to the lieutenant governor and continued: "This may in some measure apologize for the Caution of my Brethren." There had not been a rush of lawyers who wanted to take the side of the setting sun. Duane "had a good opinion" of Colden's cause. Therefore, "I shall not now sacrifice my Integrity or Independence to the Fear" of losing "the Esteem of a great Man, or even an Office of some profit."[20]

The forum where Colden and Duane had to battle Smith and Kempe was the most biased in Dunmore's favor, the chancery court, where Dunmore alone presided. Smith, who had steered the case there, "must be convinced of my Right," Colden insisted, because "Lord Dunmore could not recover in any other Court of Justice, or before a disinterested judge." Realizing the difficulty of Duane's task, Colden offered to hire any other lawyer he wanted to assist him. Duane, who knew all the precedents, declined the offer. He wanted to thrash Smith all by himself.[21]

During January and February 1771 the legal battle ensued. Colden noted Smith's attack:

> Mr. Smith has entered into the cause with all his soul—he is an able Disputant, and has an easiness of Principles that allows him to affirm deny or Pervert any thing with a confidence sufficient to deceive the unwary. Of this his argument affords ample Testimony.[22]

Both Colden and Duane knew Smith was a good lawyer, but they found Kempe of great interest too: "We think it easy to discover in the Attorney General's Argument, that it was a work of necessity not of choice—an endeavour to vindicate Measures and Principles which himself thinks unjust and unsupportable." What Kempe actually believed was obvious, not only to Colden and Duane, but to everyone watching the proceedings (except for the clueless Dunmore). At one time Colden had thought so little of Kempe that he had recommended his dismissal. Now Colden decided he was wrong about him. In 1774 Colden urged that the attorney-general be made a councilor.[23]

When Duane rose to counter Smith's presentation, he had to have been confident. According to Colden, "Mr. Duane in his closing argument has answered him fully; has refuted every Principle, every point of Law or Fact, by which he endeavours to support the Title of the Crown to the money demanded." Duane emphasized that the lieutenant governor's "just Rights" were being challenged "in an Expensive and unequal Course of Litigation." Colden's lawyer seemed especially fluent when he disposed of Kempe's argument that the lieutenant governor had hidden assets from Dunmore by giving them to the Colden family. Not "a Breach of Trust," Colden resented being depicted "as a fraudulent Bankrupt, who has artfully vested his Estate in others, to elude that Hand of Justice," an "unlooked for Misfortune which he cannot but lament." Colden had transferred assets to his family to avoid probate, not because he had ever imagined that some future governor would try to resurrect Cosby's discredited scam.[24]

Colden relished Duane's performance. Even better was the opinion of those who watched it. According to Colden, "The arguments have been attended by the most respectable Gentlemen in Town." And "his Performance is greatly applauded by the audience."[25]

Dunmore realized he could not rule in his favor after such a legal debacle, which explains why, after Colden entered his 83rd year, he remained "in his usual State of health and flow of Spirits." Meanwhile, someone—not Smith—suggested to Dunmore that he bring in the supreme court justices and ask for their opinions. The judges agreed, looked over the legal documents, and took their time. "The voice of the People is that the cause is so clear, the Judges must give their opinion in my favor," Colden predicted correctly. All four judges, Daniel Horsmanden and Robert Livingston included, backed Colden's position. Dunmore never gave a formal ruling in the case.[26]

Though the chancery proceeding flopped, that did not mean Dunmore had surrendered. He now set his sights on a victory in London, which he had "Driven . . . on with Vehemence." Colden called Dunmore's actions an appeal from the New York chancery court. To Colden's knowledge, it was unprecedented. Technically, whatever Dunmore's case was, it was not an appeal because Dunmore had not given a verdict to appeal from.[27]

Whatever precedent Dunmore was blazing, Colden needed people on the scene to supervise whatever the process was. He hired a London agent who had worked for Amherst, but Colden also needed a friend in the capital as insurance, a "joint Agent." Because Peter Collinson had died, Colden was in a quandary until he learned that William Samuel Johnson, the son of his friend the Anglican minister Samuel Johnson, was in London as Connecticut's agent. William Samuel Johnson willingly agreed to help Cadwallader Colden.[28]

Johnson's talks with Lord Hillsborough became almost comical. Writing back to Johnson, the astonished Colden remarked: "You say that Lord Hillsborough wished I had let him know that I expected to keep the whole profits of my administration. I should as soon have thought it necessary to Inform him that I expected to keep every part of my Estate." Despite Johnson's determined efforts, Hillsborough stated that something Colden had done had caused this strange treatment, but refused to say what it was. "I am condemned and punished without even knowing the fault of which I am accused," the exasperated Colden fumed. It was as if Colden's supposed transgression had become a state secret.[29]

With the Duke of Grafton long gone, Colden no longer seemed the epitome of evil. The Crown dropped its support of Dunmore's action, but he pressed on despite leaving New York. In 1773 an English lawyer hired by Dunmore examined the evidence and, as gently as possible, informed his client that he was wasting his time. By March 1774, Colden would learn, the whole matter had been dropped.[30]

In the meantime, Dunmore had been transferred to Virginia, a move he had not requested. Hillsborough presented the shift as a promotion for Dunmore when it was made after just a short time of his being governor of New

York. Yet, as time passed, Dunmore seemed more and more embarrassing. In June 1771 his successor William Tryon received an order from Hillsborough "to repair without Loss of Time to New York to take upon him the Administration of that Government." Tryon barely had time to finish defeating an insurgency in North Carolina, sheathe his sword, and start the arduous trip to New York.[31]

Dunmore, refusing to leave, deluded himself that he could stay on as governor though Tryon refused to swap governorships. Dunmore then went on a drunken rampage in the city. After a journey to the northern reaches of the province, his lordship returned to the capital and, with some fellows, engaged in another drunken rampage, this time attacking Horsmanden's coach—even cutting off his steeds' tails. The fancy vehicle had humiliated Dunmore, who could not afford a coach of such quality. Not surprisingly, a prominent Virginian confessed: "We entertain a very disadvantageous opinion of him from the accounts brought to us from New York."[32]

Something Dunmore did while he was sober had a much more significant impact than the damage done to the chief justice's coach. The governor had, soon after his arrival in the colony, complained that Fort George provided "little security." Colden knew that too, but Dunmore added to the insecurity. Thinking that the fort, as a living space, had to be improved for such an important personage as himself, he came up with a plan. Having the stable outside the fort was an inconvenience—that was how the mob could burn Colden's chariot—and Dunmore insisted that this inconvenience be removed. He convinced the Assembly to place the stable inside the fort and to make room for it by "Removing the Barracks out of the said fort and erecting" the quarters somewhere else. In 1775 Colden commented that the stable was inserted into the old area the barracks had occupied "and dismantled the Fort itself, which before that Time was a sufficient security against the attempts of a Mob." With the garrison's quarters now in an indefensible place, Dunmore had demilitarized Fort George. Sometimes the fate of a mighty empire can be determined by something that appeared trivial at the time.[33]

In 1771, however, the Colden family was interested in how they would interact with the new governor, Tryon. Alexander Colden observed that "His Amiable Disposition leaves no room to doubt we will be happy in having so worthy a Gentleman for our Governor." And he was not Dunmore, seemingly no longer a threat to the lieutenant governor (at least for the moment).[34]

Tryon and Cadwallader Colden stayed on good terms. In fact, Colden believed that Tryon "seems to be something like him" and considered him a friend. Though the governor had no formal education, he was well read and had an extensive library (calling to mind an earlier soldier/governor, John Montgomerie). Tryon visited Spring Hill often and, New Yorkers thought, saw Colden "as a Nestor," an elderly and wise Greek king mentioned by Homer.[35]

On the other hand, the two men had very different backgrounds. The Scot came from a family of ministers not flush with money. Tryon, whose family arrived in England with William the Conqueror, was a member of the gentry and accustomed to the privileged atmosphere of luxurious manor houses.[36]

The class difference between the two leading royal officials in New York became obvious in conversations William Smith had with Tryon. The lawyer asked the governor about Colden and Tryon responded: "I don't think . . . that Colden ever had much opportunity to know Mankind. He is rather the Scholar." Tryon added that "The sum of his Character is that of a shrewd old Fellow." Smith's idea of what not knowing mankind meant was Colden's going to college and living in "a rude neighbourhood in Ulster." That is, Colden enjoyed living among the poor farmers of the frontier, not the Livingstons, Van Renssalaers, and wealthy lawyers such as Smith. One knew mankind by dwelling among the wealthy, a world view Tryon shared.[37]

Tryon, however, was probably manipulating Smith and knew his antipathy to the lieutenant governor. The governor never totally trusted anyone, but was close enough to Colden to recommend that David, a gentleman of "good character," become a councilor, something his father would have appreciated. In 1772 Smith tried to tell Tryon that Colden had vowed to seek a reconciliation with the Sons of Liberty causing Tryon to laugh— at the councilors for being so gullible to think Cadwallader Colden wished to be a pal of King Sears.[38]

At first Governor Tryon had to deal with secondary issues. He discovered that Judge Livingston had no chance of being admitted to the Assembly; Colden had been proved correct again. And another, even older issue popped up—the land grants made in New York. Lord Dartmouth, at present handling the colonies, insisted that land grants be limited to only 1,000 acres and that the "collusive practice" of grants to supposed partners who transferred the land to, say, the governor be ended once and for all.[39]

Tryon knew all about the collusive practice. In 1772 he granted a huge amount, over 30,000 acres for thirty-two supposed partners, all of whom surrendered the land to Tryon for a pittance. The governor argued against the one man/one grant dictum by saying that could be just as shady. Dartmouth did not accept his reasoning.[40]

An Indian land purchase in 1772 also generated anger in London about Tryon's conduct (though nothing suggests fraud had occurred). The imperial government's concern about Indian land purchases faded in importance by April 1775 when London, urged on by Colden, suddenly became more flexible regarding "every reasonable request." The New Yorkers could keep the Indian land bought in 1772 as long as they gave "a disavowal of all association to obstruct the Importation or Exportation of goods to and from Great Britain," an act of desperation that was too late.[41]

Such a panic-stricken move suggests how increasingly serious the breach between the mother country and its colonies had become because of the *Tea Act* (1773), an attempt to bail out the politically influential British East India Company. Governor Thomas Hutchinson of Massachusetts crafted an overly clever scheme to subvert non-importation, and the "Unruly people" at Boston realized that the only way to subvert the ploy was to toss the taxed tea into the harbor on December 16, 1773, an action that became known as the Boston Tea Party.[42]

Immediately, other ports that would receive taxed East India Company tea praised the Bostonians. The Tea Party "has determined the Americans to perish" rather than accept taxed tea, declared one New York merchant who disliked the Sons of Liberty. If Parliament did not back down, he insisted, it "had Better declare war against the Colonies at once."[43]

Before the Tea Party, at a meeting the New York Sons of Liberty advised killing the governor and his councilors. None of the Sons were arrested because of the threat. Alexander McDougall revealed to the Bostonians what their New York allies feared—a surprise "Landing and Storing the Tea in the Fort." Colden had done that with the hated stamps in 1765. But Colden was not in charge, Tryon was. He refused to use the soldiers in New York to secure the tea and would resort to force only in the most dire circumstances. "I will run the risk of Brick Batts and Dirt and I trust that you and others will stand by me," he told a councilor. As it turned out, the crisis in New York stalled because terrible weather blew the tea ship meant for New York all the way to the West Indies. Tryon would not be in New York when that ship finally docked at its destination.[44]

William Tryon was ill and had been for some time. In 1770 he wanted to return to Britain but put the trip off because he had been named New York's governor. During August 1771 both he and his wife were very sick. By 1772 the climate of New York, so much milder than North Carolina's, had helped the Tryons. At least in the governor's case, the good effect of a healthy climate did not last.[45]

In 1772 Colden had tried, once again, to have a salary attached to his office. He had learned that the lieutenant governor of Massachusetts had a salary and pummeled Lord Dartmouth with arguments hoping to get his sympathy. Colden wrote him: "The period of my days cannot be distant." Still, Dartmouth turned him down and explained the case of Massachusetts away. Colden could not have been happy that Horsmanden's salary as chief justice in 1773 now came from the Crown, not the Assembly.[46]

During 1773 Tryon announced that he, at last, would voyage to the mother country to regain his health but only in the spring of 1774. What Tryon did not say publicly was that he thought Colden might not live that long because of his advanced age; "His Life is certainly tottering," the governor wrote, despite Colden's being "tolerably hearty and yet retaining his faculties."

Tryon explained to Dartmouth that Colden had attended only one Council meeting since he handed over the government. He had "given me expectation" that he would not attend unless he became acting governor. The lieutenant governor did suffer from a serious health problem, "a degree of inflammation on his Lungs which it is imagined as he becomes weaker, and not able to throw off that matter by [pectirating?] will be the cause of his Death."[47]

Was Colden near the end? If his sons can be believed, and there is no reason to doubt them, Cadwallader Colden was in good health. Late in 1772 David assured Benjamin Franklin that his long-time friend "enjoys a great share of Health and surprising Spirits for a Man" of his age. "He has much more Strength now than he had two Years ago." Early in 1773 Alexander wrote: "My Father Continues to have a Remarkable Flow of Spirits and Retention of all his faculties he Says he thinks he has got a New Lease of his Life" and that was still the case in July 1773.[48]

In October 1773 a friend of Sir William Johnson told him that Colden was "going to make his Appearance once more at the Helm." As can be seen, Johnson had his own sources of information. He congratulated Colden when he eventually took over from Tryon: "Tho' the various duties of such a Station must render it . . . burthensome to a Gentleman of an advanced Age . . ., Yet it is with . . . pleasure . . . that I view you once more able to enter upon these arduous duties with a portion of health . . . which the Gentleman you succeeded appears to stand in much need."[49] To Johnson, Colden was healthier than Tryon.

Indeed, the newspapers reported Colden's "good health." rather remarkable for the eighteenth century. Franklin emphasized this in 1773 when he wrote Alexander: "I admire your good Father's rare Felicity in retaining so long his Health, and Spirits, and particularly that Vigour of his mental Faculties which enables him still to amuse himself with abstruse philosophical Disquisitions."[50]

Colden did show his age. He suffered some hearing loss, but he was not deaf. Smith suspected that Colden was deaf when he wanted to be. In one case, Colden employed deafness as a way to avoid taking a stand on a personnel issue. He could not sign his name too often at a sitting, probably because of arthritis. And he continued to have problems with the ferry—the Council met for several months in Brooklyn so Colden could avoid it. But he does not seem to have needed a cane to walk. His Chamber of Commerce portrait shows him standing without a cane (but one hand is on a piece of furniture). Though that could have resulted from vanity or artistic license, it seems likely that Colden had no trouble walking except for longer distances. If Colden could not walk well enough to do the job, Smith would have mentioned it.[51]

In Smith's obituary of Colden, the lawyer depicts a man too old to be in command: "While he was last in the Chair, his Faculties were so impaired by

Figure 16.1. *Cadwallader Colden*, by Matthew Pratt. Colden in the 1770s. This portrait was created at the behest of the New York Chamber of Commerce. Engraved. PR 052 (Portrait File). ID85498d. *Collection of the New-York Historical Society.*

age, as to be entirely dictated to by others. He often fell asleep while the Council were in Debate." However, in 1774 Smith met with Colden to try and convince him to join with his Council faction. The lieutenant governor was wide awake. Granted, Colden was in his eighties and surely dozed off at times. Smith's tale of a sleepy Colden probably suggests that the Council debates were not as scintillating as the lawyer thought.[52]

Smith listed another of Colden's failings in the obituary. When the Council considered land disputes, Colden "used to retire, till we called him in, when he would concur in . . . any. . . . Resolution formed by the Majority, without ever desiring to be informed concerning the Merits of the Controversy." Cadwallader Colden had spent decades of his life arguing about the identity of individual trees and rocks. At his age, he no longer had the patience or the willingness to waste time over such minutiae while much more important issues had to be dealt with. Ignoring the specifics of new land controversies made sense to him and does not mean he was too old to be acting governor.[53]

Why then did Tryon think that Colden might soon die? His lieutenant governor had been mentioning his age for decades and kept mentioning that his life might soon be over. Someone who lived into his mid-eighties remained uncommon in the 1700s. Logically, Colden was being realistic about his eventual demise. Tryon, who had bad health, made an assumption about Colden's signs of age and illness and thought he was "tottering." Colden was in good health both for his age and the century.[54]

Tryon wanted Dartmouth to pick the acting governor if Colden died. The two choices Tryon suggested, Horsmanden and Sir William Johnson, were next in seniority on the Council. In 1769 Judge Livingston, who worked with Horsmanden, called him "very old and infirm." In 1771 even Colden called him "very infirm." Smith referred to "the withered Hand of Mr. Horsmanden." Tryon called him "tottering" too. The chief justice was in far worse shape than Colden.[55]

No one can doubt the abilities of Sir William Johnson. During the 1770s, however, he had become very ill, so ill he came close to death. A few months after Tryon left for England, Johnson died, much lamented. Nobody could match his influence with the Indians. Colden called the death of his ally "a very great Loss."[56]

Despite Colden's good health, his holding onto his office suddenly appeared unlikely. On May 2, 1774 Smith recorded information passed on to him by Judge Livingston. The story went that Colden had written to his superiors that he was just too old to govern the colony during the intense days after the Boston Tea Party and that he "expected to be removed soon." The time had finally come for Colden to retire, but, Livingston related, the lieutenant governor soon regretted making such a statement.[57]

This supposed letter of Colden has not been located. That does not mean it never existed, of course. It was unlikely that Colden would have told Livingston, a great enemy, that he was finished in New York politics—Livingston would have jumped for joy at the prospect—so the judge was told the story by somebody else. Given all these intermediaries, the account became jumbled. Tryon's letter of October 6, 1773 where he suggested Colden was not far from death—the tottering letter—likely caused a strong reaction by Lord Dartmouth. In April 1774 he referred to a "private letter" to Tryon in which Dartmouth "expressed a wish that you should not come away from your Government until you should be relieved by a Lieutenant Governor." That is, a new lieutenant governor would be named. Tryon, who liked Colden, had to have explained to him his concern and Colden agreed that his retirement in the current crisis made sense. Apparently, in March 1774 both Oliver DeLancey and another councilor, Roger Morris, were already campaigning for Colden's job; they likely heard what was happening from English connections.[58]

That Colden knew what was going on explains an otherwise mysterious letter from Thomas Howard, an official who worked in Whitehall, the administrative headquarters of the imperial government. Howard and Colden were probably brought together by William Samuel Johnson, who would have encountered Howard while serving as a colonial agent. On January 5, 1774, Howard, responding to a Colden letter, announced that he would be "extremely happy to have it in my power mutually to obtain for each other what we each of us are desirous of." Colden thought it best that he be in charge at New York for the plan to work, while Howard wanted first to consult Tryon when he was back in Britain. The letter conjures up what Colden and Major Carey were planning in 1766. So what was this new stratagem? In 1774 Colden would throw his support for Howard to replace him in office while Howard used all his influence to obtain a long-desired pension for Colden; a Council appointment for David could also have been part of the deal. Perhaps Howard would also be granted land in New York by Colden while he was acting governor.[59]

The shrewd old man, however, had never really wanted to retire—at least while he was still healthy and could do his job. He came up with a plan to stall his forced retirement. On April 7, 1774 Tryon left New York. On the mail packet was a letter from Colden to Dartmouth with surprising news. Lord Dunmore still had not given up getting money from Colden "to the astonishment of every One Here." For Colden, this was "Oppression." This time, Dunmore expected to win by "Favour" alone, "on an Appeal to the Privy Council." Alas, Colden pointed out, he was to be subjected to "an unavoidable Expense, Anxiety and Vexation very little suited to a Man at 87 [sic 86] years of Age." This incredible treatment was more substantial than just losing money:

It is reported Here that Ld Dunmore is making use of his Interest, at this Time, to get Me removed from being Lt. Govr. of the Province. I have too much Confidence in his Majesty's Goodness, and in your Lordship's Integrity, to imagine that . . . I shall be dismissed without sufficient Reason. I do not Think it improbable that Ld Dunmore may endeavour to get Me removed, in order to facilitate his oppressive Suit against Me; but this is Such a Reason, that I am certain the very Idea of it, will be held in Abhorence by your Lordship.[60]

Forced retirements are never easy, and Colden, thanks to Lord Dunmore, made any attempt to replace him impossible at least for the immediate future. On April 7, 1774, the day Tryon departed, the Council met at Colden's "Room" (in December 1773 the governor's house had been destroyed in a fire) and swore "in old Caddy" as acting governor for the fifth time. Governor Tryon had predicted "that Colden will do little." Tryon was wrong.[61]

As late as 1774 the crisis over parliamentary taxation of the colonies was not the only issue. Some were quite local and united those who disagreed on the great tax debate. On April 12, 1774, not long after Colden had taken over the province, the city's house carpenters created a petition complaining about a new law banning the building of wooden structures in much of the city to lessen the risk of fire. Roofs had to be constructed either of tiles or slate to make them fireproof. The city's council backed the carpenters as did many well known citizens such as Sons of Liberty Peter Curtenius and Peter Vandervoort as well as their archenemy, the printer James Rivington. On May 2 the "very sorely aggrieved" carpenters insisted that the new law "will prove greatly detrimental and injurious to the Inhabitants of this City." Lieutenant Governor Colden rejected the petition.[62]

Other pressing issues had intercolonial interest. The borders of New York and some of its neighbors had not yet been agreed to by the 1770s. Decades before, Colden had been instrumental in drawing the New York-Connecticut boundary and he wanted to deal with the rest. In August 1774 Pennsylvania's governor wrote to Colden about "running and marking the Lines" between their provinces. Colden quickly responded, agreeing to the project, even suggesting the proper latitude of the border. However, future events stopped this survey in its tracks.[63]

Earlier, Colden had turned his attention to a much more contentious dispute, the New York-Massachusetts boundary, which John Watts deemed "almost a civil Warr." Not an inch of this boundary had been agreed upon.[64]

In March 1762 Massachusetts men invaded Livingston Manor, which that family had controlled for some seventy years. Colden authorized a posse to arrest the rioters who had tried to expel Livingston's tenants "by Force and Violence." In 1764 Governor Francis Bernard of Massachusetts agreed to track down murderers who had fled to that colony's eastern areas, and the next year requested that Colden restrain the Livingstons from violence against those residing in the area claimed by Massachusetts.[65]

Colden knew that working out borders with these New Englanders would be tough, because "every free Man in the Charter Governments thinks that he has a Personal undivided interest in the Lands within the limits of their charter." Therefore, their assemblymen, being politicians, insisted upon "enlarging their boundaries." However, on October 22, 1764 he suggested to Bernard that the two colonies create a boundary commission as New York had done with New Jersey. The Massachusetts assembly took until March 1765 to say no.[66]

Moore resurrected the process and in 1768 Massachusetts, sort of, accepted that its western border should be twenty miles east of the Hudson River. Only in 1774, though, did Tryon and Governor Hutchinson of Massachusetts announce to their legislatures that the New York-Massachusetts borderline had finally become legal with the king's approval.[67]

Dealing with Massachusetts and its aggressive land claims was difficult, but it pales in comparison with the problems caused by what became known as the New Hampshire Grants—which covered the territory that became Vermont. In 1749 New Hampshire's governor, Benning Wentworth, granted land west of his colony's presumptive border, the Connecticut River. New York claimed the land west of the river because of its charter granted to the Duke of York in 1664. This controversy began during the administration of George Clinton when Colden was surveyor-general.[68]

On December 6, 1749 Colden advised Clinton about a letter Wentworth had sent him inquiring about New York's border. New York's surveyor-general, who knew the details of New Hampshire's royal charter, explained that that colony was "to extend no further westward than till it meets with some other of his Majesty's Government." Since New York extended to the Connecticut River by virtue of the duke's grant, New Hampshire had no right to the territory. Although Massachusetts and Connecticut extended beyond the river (and Colden had made a deal with Connecticut confirming that), New Hampshire's border did not. As some of those Wentworth had given grants to had already settled, Colden recommended that these individuals be allowed to stay on this New York land. Colden had advised the same thing regarding the Connecticut settlers in the Oblong, which had forged a deal with that colony.[69]

In 1751 Colden pointed out that the king could decide this border question because both of the disputants were royal colonies; that rendered charter claims moot. There were other reasons the king should favor New York Colden thought. New Hampshire could not defend this frontier area as well as New York, whose citizens had long been settled there. Secondly, Albany was far closer to the settlers than the populated parts of New Hampshire. Clearly, logic favored New York but, as one scholar observed, "With the exception of Colden, the New York officials appear to have been decidedly lackadaisical in this boundary matter." Little happened for years.[70]

By 1760 Governor Wentworth had to have assumed that his colony would win the disputed area in time simply because more New Englanders than New Yorkers wanted to move there. Despite the validity of New York's claim, the soil in what became Vermont was poor. Why should a New Yorker relocate to a contested place when his own colony had better land anyway? Wentworth, however, "had not counted on the activity" of Cadwallader Colden, who had just taken over command of New York from DeLancey.[71]

As Matt B. Jones has written, "Colden was not only persistent, but frank and truthful in his communications with all parties, and there is no reason to suppose that he had improperly secured any personal benefit from the disputed lands." Colden did not want Vermont to be retained by New York so he could reap a fortune in land grants. In 1761 Colden made one investment in a township in the territory. Years after his death, it was valued at $449.15. Though a goodly sum at that time, it is not outlandish by any means.[72]

Colden fought for the alleged New Hampshire Grants because he believed they belonged to New York, not New Hampshire. Amazed in 1761 that New Englanders even claimed the site of Crown Point, on the western shore of Lake Champlain, Colden bluntly told the Board of Trade: "I am clearly convinced that the Province of New York extends Eastwards as far as Connecticut River, that New Hampshire can have no pretence to the westward of that River." On December 28, 1763 Lieutenant Governor Colden proclaimed that the Connecticut River was the eastern border of New York. Most of those who have researched the subject have agreed with Colden's position.[73]

The Board of Trade considered the contested border and, as Philip J. Schwarz stated, "Colden was the only person in the colonies who had anything to do with the royal decision." The imperial bureaucrats depended upon Colden to the point of quoting him and adding his letters to their report of July 10, 1764 to George III. Their report reiterated Colden's arguments about the duke's charter, New York's levying of quitrents, and that the army officers granted land in the contested area wanted nothing to do with New Hampshire. Wentworth came under attack for his "very extraordinary Conduct." The king accepted the Board of Trade's conclusion favoring New York.[74]

To say the least, Colden was happy with the result. Watts penned that "the Old Gentleman plumes himself much upon this, as owing to his information and discernment" which it was. Watts suggested, however, a rather mercenary reason for the British decision. "They are granting away so lavishly at Home," that is, Great Britain, "that in order to make room N. Hampshire is to be shoved back it seems to Connecticut River."[75]

With official news arriving in April 1765 that New Hampshire had been beaten back (or so it appeared), New York's leaders decided the eastern part of New York had to be better organized. Then part of Albany County, the future Vermont would be sliced off into new counties. A Colden County (and a town of Colden) were suggested, but neither made the cut.[76]

Since this eastern territory was now, formally, part of New York, Colden could issue land grants and he did in 1765 (and later); the only restriction was that he could not grant land already given away by Wentworth. All of Colden's grants obeyed this directive except one to James Duane, Kempe and others. This huge grant happened to be in a section granted by Wentworth to the most prominent supporters of New Hampshire. Jones explained that this single Colden grant "was the real cause of the bitter attacks on Colden by the New Hampshire party." This grant also violated the restriction against the old trickery of land grantees signing the land away to the real, secret buyers. For New York, that remained standard practice in spite of London's wishes.[77]

In 1765 Colden urged that nobles who sought land in New York pick it in these territories. At the same time, he spoke up for "The poor people who have expended their all in making their settlements" in Vermont. They would not interfere with the nobles' plans—there was plenty of open space—and would be "of great use in furnishing Provisions." Therefore, these poor farmers' grants should be confirmed. And Colden continued pushing for the lowest fees possible. Governor Henry Moore, causing "great disgust," reversed this policy, but Colden restored it when he came back after the governor's death.[78]

During 1767 the British government ordered the suspension of land grants in Vermont until the confusion about landholding there was straightened out. Moore obeyed; Colden, Dunmore, and Tryon, supported by the Council, did not.[79]

Many of the New Hampshire grant holders remained hostile. In 1769 in a place covered by a New York grant from 1739, some sixty New Englanders forcibly prevented New Yorkers from surveying; this survey was needed to levy quitrents. These "Rioters," as Colden branded them, "resolved to defend the Limit they claimed under New Hampshire to the last drop of their Blood." The lieutenant governor ordered the arrest of this "Confederacy so insolent and dangerous."[80]

In 1774, with Colden back in charge, he intended to formally grant acreage that had been purchased from the Indians and also Vermont land. The substantial fees he received would provide for his family after his death; the king had had no interest in giving him a salary when not serving as governor or a pension. Nor had there been an explanation why the king wanted to give Dunmore his money. Smith, amazed at the 86-year-old Colden's willingness to violate his contrary instructions, noted "that Colden fears nothing and cares not what he does," and, perhaps even more startling to the lawyer, "Colden is perfectly indifferent to the Smiles or Frowns of the King."[81]

Colden assumed London would do nothing about the grants no matter what the instructions had insisted. More important problems had arisen. He was correct. In England, meanwhile, Tryon had argued against these instructions. Tryon even showed Lord Dartmouth a letter from Colden saying what he was going to do about land grants. A pleased Tryon related to his lieutenant governor, in a private letter, that Dartmouth "perused it but said not a word good, bad, or indifferent."[82]

Later in 1774, Colden brought in a slew of requests to the Council for land grants in Vermont which, according to Smith, "he seemed to have much at Heart." To Smith it appeared "that at the Rate we were going on, all the New Hampshire Lands would go contrary to the Instructions, for that the whole Country had been asked for by some Petitioner or other." Smith had exaggerated a bit, but the amount of land asked for was huge.[83]

By 1774 each side had abandoned any thought of compromise. "The New York grantees," Colden explained to Tryon, "think they have a complete title in law and that the others have none at all but usurpation." Vermont's New Englanders, Colden believed, had "become a numerous and dangerous Body of Banditti." They had, years before, already organized themselves. Colden, allegedly, had "threatened to drive the rebellious mob back into the Green Mountains, so the group named itself the Green Mountain Boys." When in 1774 New Yorkers in Vermont were attacked, Colden asked Thomas Gage to dispatch troops there; he refused so ending, for the moment, "the Intention of forcing Peace in that Quarter."[84]

In 1774 violence broke out elsewhere in New York. The long-delayed tea ship finally arrived after Tryon had left the colony. The involved merchants informed the captain they did not want the taxed tea. Unlike the stamps in 1765, which were Crown property, this tea was private property. If those merchants the tea was intended for rejected it, Colden had no authority to intervene and nobody asked him to. This ship left New York harbor in complete safety. Apparently, New York had become the only major port in the thirteen colonies not to have a tea party.[85]

If Colden breathed a sigh of relief that no tea party had been staged, the relief did not last long. On April 22, Captain James Chambers sailed into the harbor with a cargo of taxed tea that, he thought, nobody knew about. The Sons of Liberty had been tipped off by a contact in London. A mob of "Thousands" proceeded to have its own tea party and the taxed tea soon was ruined. For good measure, they burned the boxes the hated tea leaves came in. "The destruction of Captain Chamber's Tea was so unexpected and sudden that no measures could be previously thought of to prevent it," Colden explained to Dartmouth. The frightened Chambers did not complain to the lieutenant governor.[86]

The Sons of Liberty had reasserted their influence, briefly, with the New York Tea Party. Then the news of the infamous *Intolerable Acts* (1774) reached the colony. Great Britain had punished Massachusetts harshly by, among other things, altering its government and shutting Boston's port. Outraged New Yorkers feared that unjust Great Britain was provoking a "Civil Warr." A committeeman active in enforcing non-importation insisted that the Bostonians "deserve to be Hanged and Quartered if they submitted" to the closing of Boston harbor.[87]

Such criticism of the British found voice at even the highest levels of New York society. Oliver DeLancey reportedly said that "He would rather spend every Shilling of his Fortune than that the Boston Port Bill should be complied with." William Smith believed that the DeLanceys took "Advantage of the Weakness of Colden" and spoke "aloud against the Measures of Administration even at Dinner in his Presence."[88]

Exactly what Smith expected Colden to do went unsaid. The lieutenant governor knew that New Yorkers had "universally" rejected the idea "of being taxed at the pleasure of Parliament." Was he supposed to arrest the entire population? His knowledge about the unanimity against Parliament's stand made him "particularly anxious."[89]

Colden especially wanted to know how "the principal People" would respond to the *Intolerable Acts*. To Colden's joy, they showed up at a public meeting and took control of the committee established to deal with the new crisis, all "to preserve the Peace of the Colony." The Sons had been thwarted yet again. A happy David Colden noted that the new committee "prevent the violent inflammatory Measures, that some among us would run into." Watts rejoiced at "the interference of most people of weight."[90]

Nonetheless, Cadwallader Colden was not altogether happy with this cautious committee. As he wrote to Dartmouth, "These transactions are dangerous, my Lord, and illegal, but by what means shall Government prevent them? An attempt by the power of the Civil Magistrate would only show their weakness." Still more dangerous was the Continental Congress the New York committee insisted be called. Using military power in an attempt to silence such committees and this congress in Philadelphia could only cause "Troubles which it is thought much more prudent to avoid." The Congress could not be stopped. From a secret talk Colden had with his lawyer James Duane, a New York delegate to the Congress, Colden hoped that it would be moderate as was the New York delegation.[91]

Colden's hopes were dashed. The Continental Congress, according to him, resorted to "Wickedness, Extravagance and Absurdity." He talked personally to Duane and Joseph Galloway of Pennsylvania who had opposed what happened but could not stop the "most violent" such as the Virginians. The Congress endorsed non-importation and more methods of economic warfare against Great Britain.[92]

From what Colden could tell, New York as a whole seemed to agree with Duane "even in the City." The merchants were not happy with non-importation. Overall, New Yorkers were not eager to link themselves to "the dangerous and extravagant Measures" of New England. Clearly, Colden declared, New Yorkers "abhor the thoughts of a civil war, and desire nothing so much as to have an end put to this unhappy Dispute with the Mother Country." Why then did the merchants accept the dictates of the Congress? A puzzled Colden investigated and learned they feared that, if they backed away from the Congress, the Sons of Liberty would subject everyone to serious violence.[93]

These events distressed Colden enough, but he also was concerned about his eldest son. Alexander had a problem juggling his offices. James Parker complained that Alexander ran the post office like a gentleman. Because a ship could dock with mail aboard at any hour of the day or night, the office of postmaster was a twenty-four hour-a-day job, but Alexander often was not up and about. Instead, he had hired clerks who tended to be absent from their duties too. In 1772 Benjamin Franklin bluntly reprimanded Alexander about his sloppy financial records and was on the verge of firing him.[94]

Nor did Alexander have an easy time as surveyor-general. In 1771 one customer was not very satisfied with the maps he had received. Sending them to Sir William Johnson, councilor Hugh Wallace complained that "I hope they will be satisfactory, they are roughly done, but Mr. Colden is always so busy, there is no getting them done better," a complaint never made about his father. Then in 1772 at a conference with Governor Tryon, the Mohawks complained about "a piece of Land patented by Mr. Colden with which we were never before acquainted." After Tryon met with Johnson, this complaint disappeared.[95]

Obviously, Alexander could not handle his multiple positions. In January 1773 his father asked permission from Lord North for Alexander to step aside from his customs job in favor of his own son, Richard Nicholls Colden, who had left the army. Normally, North did not approve of such deals but this involved Cadwallader Colden. Because of "the Respect I have for your long Services"—and Tryon's recommendation—the young man got the job. The lieutenant governor made a point of praising his grandson's work performance and his incorruptibility. There seemed to be another Colden with a bright future in New York's government.[96]

The diminished workload did not stave off a great decline in Alexander's health. When Tryon left the colony, Alexander was so ill that his doctors thought he would die. Suddenly, one of his sons-in-law rushed to England to get his office as postmaster. Though the lieutenant governor had not given his approval for this unlikely candidacy, he did write a recommendation he thought would make no difference.[97]

With the news of Alexander's critical state of health, a replacement for him as postmaster was picked. Meanwhile, the lieutenant governor appointed

David to fill in as surveyor-general as his brother had been "disabled by sickness and bodily infirmity."[98]

In England, however, the news of Alexander's probable death unleashed a flock of vultures seeking to become surveyor-general of New York. Among the candidates in London was Edmund Fanning, Tryon's secretary. When a new postmaster reached New York, the shocked man discovered Alexander Colden was not only alive, but as his father noted, he had "surprisingly Recovered." David returned the other office to his brother.[99]

This recovery did not last long. On December 12, 1774 Alexander Colden, "universally beloved," died, and did not leave "a Man of more humane Temper, and more generous Disposition behind him." On December 14 he was buried, "attended by a numerous Train of Relations and Friends." Cadwallader Colden had now outlived all but three of his children.[100]

While mourning one son, Colden did everything he could to aid another. The day after the funeral, David Colden lobbied the councilors to support his appointment as surveyor-general. The lieutenant governor did not need the Council's approval to give his son the position, but he sought the Council's backing because he planned to violate his instructions again. Colden wished to give David a good behavior commission, not pleasure as the instructions specified. David reminded William Smith that the instructions had been destroyed when the governor's house had been ravaged by fire. "I was astonished at this Suggestion" the lawyer noted and rejected the weak argument.[101]

None of the councilors had any objection to David succeeding his brother. In contrast to his father, they liked David, but a good behavior commission rankled some of them. Cadwallader Colden tried to say that only judges had to have pleasure commissions and feigned surprise when Smith proved that was not the case. Oliver DeLancey stated "we have Nothing to do" with the appointment though everyone voiced their approval of David. On December 20, 1774 he received the office from his father under good behavior. Smith complained to his diary: "What a Villain is Colden who always professed a Zeal for the Prerogative and got his Living by it!"[102]

While New Yorkers fought over patronage, events in the British Empire continued to spiral out of control. On December 15, the day after Alexander's funeral, his father officially notified Andrew Elliot, the collector of the port, about the king's order to seize all guns, ammunition, and gunpowder that might be brought into New York harbor.[103]

Anyone who walked about the city knew how bad the crisis had become. Smith was amazed that New Yorkers expressed disrespect for George III, comparing him unfavorably with his predecessor. The lawyer predicted "That the first Act of Indiscretion on the Part of the Army or the People marked with Blood, would light up a Civil War." Alerting Governor Tryon in England to the climate in the province, Cadwallader Colden observed: "The times are full of the most interesting events. God knows what is to come of us."[104]

NOTES

1. CC to Hillsborough, December 6, 1770, *CLB*, vol. 2, 251–53.
2. CC to Hillsborough, October 5, 1770, *CLB*, vol. 2, 228–30.
3. M. Collinson to BF, March 9, 1771, *FP*, vol. 18, 58; James Corbett David, *Dunmore's New World* (Charlottesville: University of Virginia Press, 2013), 9, 12–14; Milton M. Klein, *The American Whig: William Livingston of New York* (New York: Garland, 1990), 533.
4. *SM*, vol. 1, 86, 180; CC to William Samuel Johnson, May 8, 1771, *CLB*, vol. 2, 322–23; Philip J. Schwarz, "'To Conciliate the Jarring Interests': William Smith, Thomas Hutchinson, and the Massachusetts–New York Boundary, 1771–1773," *New York Historical Society Quarterly* 59, no. 4 (1975): 307.
5. David, *Dunmore's New World*, 41; *SM*, vol. 1, 107.
6. *SM*, vol. 1, 91, 107; I. N. Phelps Stokes, *The Iconography of Manhattan Island, 1498–1909* (New York: R. H. Dodd, 1915–1928), vol. 4, 815, 819.
7. Dunmore to Hillsborough, March 9, 1771, *NYCD*, vol. 8, 265; Livingston to Margaret Livingston, January 11, 1771, Robert R. Livingston Papers, reel 1, NYHS; *SM*, vol. 1, 102–3.
8. CC to Hillsborough, November 10, 1770, *CLB*, vol. 2, 231–35; Garden to CC, c. June 1768, *CP*, vol. 7, 139–40.
9. Hillsborough to Dunmore, July 16, 1770, *NYCD*, vol. 8, 223; "Copy of His Majesty's Declaration at the Treasury Board in 1697," Chalmers Coll., New York, vol. 1, no. 21, NYPL.
10. CC's Observations, on the Bill Brought Against Him in Chancery, 1770, *CP*, vol. 9, 225; CC's Notes about the Lieutenant–Governor's Salary . . ., *CP*, vol. 9, 229–30.
11. *SM*, vol. 1, 83–87.
12. *SM*, vol. 1, 85–86; CC to Hillsborough, November 10, 1770, *CLB*, vol. 2, 231–35.
13. *SM*, vol. 1, 84–86.
14. *SM*, vol. 1, 86–87.
15. Dunmore to Hillsborough, December 5, 1770, *NYCD*, vol. 8, 256–57; David, *Dunmore's New World*, 16.
16. *Oxford DNB*, s.v. FitzRoy, Augustus Henry; Charles Hemstreet, "Literary Landmarks of New York," *Critic* 41 (1902): 164.
17. "To Lieut. Govr. Colden," December 15, 1765, Grafton Papers, Bury St. Edmunds Record Office, Suffolk, UK; *Oxford DNB*, s.v. Fitzroy, Augustus Henry.
18. *SM*, vol. 1, 85–86; David, *Dunmore's New World*, 32; Edward P. Alexander, *A Revolutionary Conservative: James Duane of New York* (New York: Columbia University Press, 1938), 31–33; Beverly McAnear, *The Income of the Colonial Governors of British North America* (New York: Pageant Press, 1967), 70.
19. Alexander, *Revolutionary Conservative: James Duane*, 36, 36n53, 95–96; Richard R. Beeman, *Our Lives, Our Fortunes and Our Sacred Honor: The Forging of American Independence, 1774–1776* (New York: Basic Books, 2013), 128–29; James Duane to CC, June 6, 1771, *CP*, vol. 7, 172; Duane to CC Jr., April 4, 1768, *CP*, vol. 9, 211.
20. Duane to CC, November 28, 1770, *CLB*, vol. 2, 273–74.
21. CC to Hillsborough, November 10, December 6, 1770, *CLB*, vol. 2, 231–35, 251–53; CC to Duane, November 26, 1770, *CLB*, vol. 2, 248–50; *SM*, vol. 1, 84–85.
22. CC to Arthur Mairs, March 9, 1771, *CLB*, vol. 2, 316–17.
23. CC to Arthur Mairs, March 9, 1771, *CLB*, vol. 2, 316–17; CC to Board of Trade, April 7, 1762, *CLB*, vol. 2, 186–91; CC to Tryon, August 2, 1774, *CLB*, vol. 2, 351–53.
24. CC to Mairs, March 9, 1771, *CLB*, vol. 2, 316–17; "Lt. Gov. Colden agt. Attorney General in Chancery (Duane)," William Smith Papers, lot 178, Colden, Cadwallader, item 2, NYPL.
25. CC to Mairs, January 17, March 9, 1771, *CLB*, vol. 2, 277–79, 316–17; Alexander, *Revolutionary Conservative: James Duane*, 31–33.

26. CC to W. S. Johnson, April 2, May 8, 1771, *CLB*, vol. 2, 319–23; AC to BF, July 2, 1771, *FP*, vol. 18, 158; David, *Dunmore's New World*, 35.

27. CC to Mairs, n.d., April 2, May 8, 1771, *CLB*, vol. 2, 254–55, 321–24.

28. CC to Mairs, November 12, 1770, *CLB*, vol. 2, 235–36; CC to W. S. Johnson, November 12, 1770, *CLB*, vol. 2, 237–39.

29. CC to W. S. Johnson, April 2, 1771, *CLB*, vol. 2, 319–21.

30. Dunmore to Dartmouth, May 25, 1773, Historical Manuscripts Commission, Great Britain, *The Manuscripts of the Earl of Dartmouth* (London: H. M. S. O., 1887–1896), vol. 2, 152; "Mr. Dunning's opinion," August 12, 1773, William Smith Papers, lot 178, Colden, Cadwallader, item 5, NYPL; M. Collinson to CC, March 11, 1774, *CP*, vol. 7, 217–18; David, *Dunmore's New World*, 36.

31. Hillsborough to Dunmore, December 11, 1770, *NYCD*, vol. 8, 260–61; William Tryon, "Journal of the Expedition against the Insurgents, April 20–June 21, 1771," in *The Correspondence of William Tryon and Other Selected Papers*, ed. William S. Powell (Raleigh, NC: Division of Archives and History, Department of Cultural Resources, 1981), vol. 2, 730.

32. Goldsbrow Banyar to W. Johnson, July 18, 1771, Tryon, *Correspondence of William Tryon*, vol. 2, 808–9; Dunmore to Hillsborough, July 9, 1771, *NYCD*, vol. 8, 278; *SM*, vol. 1, 107; Bland to Thomas Adams, August 1, 1771, Richard Bland, "Letters," *William and Mary Quarterly*, 1st ser., 5, no. 3 (January 1897): 156; David, *Dunmore's New World*, 41; Philip Ranlet, *The New York Loyalists*, 2nd ed. (Lanham, MD: University Press of America, 2002), 33; Stokes, *Iconography*, vol. 4, 822.

33. Dunmore to Hillsborough, December 6, 1770, *NYCD*, vol. 8, 259; CC to Dartmouth, May 3, 1775, *CLB*, vol. 2, 402–3; Stokes, *Iconography*, vol. 4, 817–18.

34. AC to BF, August 6, 1771, *FP*, vol. 18, 197.

35. *SM*, vol. 1, 146–47, 152–53; Johnson to CC, July 3, 1772, *JP*, vol. 8, 528; Paul David Nelson, *William Tryon and the Course of Empire: A Life in British Imperial Service* (Chapel Hill: University of North Carolina Press, 1990), 4–5.

36. Nelson, *Tryon*, 4.

37. *SM*, vol. 1, 146–47.

38. *SM*, vol. 1, 118, 148; Tryon to Dartmouth, October 4, 1774, Dartmouth Manuscripts, Staffordshire Record Office, Stafford, UK.

39. Tryon to Hillsborough, June 4, 1772, *NYCD*, vol. 8, 299–300; Dartmouth to Tryon, December 9, 1772, *NYCD*, vol. 8, 339.

40. Tryon to Hillsborough, April 11, 1772, *NYCD*, vol. 8, 293; Dartmouth to Tryon, March 3, 1773, *NYCD*, vol. 8, 356; Nelson, *Tryon*, 102–3.

41. Tryon to Dartmouth, January 5, 1773, *NYCD*, vol. 8, 342–43; Dartmouth to Tryon, November 4, 1772, April 21, 1775, *NYCD*, vol. 8, 317, 569–70; Bernard Mason, *The Road to Independence: The Revolutionary Movement in New York, 1773–1777* (Lexington: University Press of Kentucky, 1966), 49–50.

42. James Stevenson to Johnson, December 25–27, 1773, *JP*, vol. 8, 974–75.

43. Thurman to Amos Heyton, December 26, 1773, John Thurman, Jr., "Extracts from the Letter Books of John Thurman, Junior," ed. Benjamin H. Hall, *Historical Magazine*, 2nd ser., 4 (December 1868): 288.

44. *SM*, vol. 1, 158–59; McDougall to William Cooper, December 13, 1773, Boston Committee of Correspondence Papers, box 3, New York folder, no. 600, NYPL; Ranlet, *Loyalists*, 33–34.

45. Tryon to Hillsborough, January 8, 1770, Tryon, *Correspondence of William Tryon*, vol. 2, 425; Tryon to Council and Assembly, January 8, 1772, New York Colony, *Journal of the Legislative Council of the Colony of New York, Began the 9th day of April, 1691; and ended the [3d of April, 1775]* (Albany, NY: Weed, Parsons, 1861), vol. 2, 1800–1801; Council to Tryon, January 13, 1772, New York Colony, *Journal of the Legislative Council*, 1804; Tryon to Dartmouth, August 31, 1771, CO5/154/16, LC transcript.

46. CC to Dartmouth, December 1, 1772, *NYCD*, vol. 8, 327–30; Dartmouth to CC, February 3, 1773, *NYCD*, vol. 8, 347–48; Horsmanden to Dartmouth, July 23, 1773, *NYCD*, vol. 8, 391.

47. Tryon to Dartmouth, October 6, 1773, Dartmouth Manuscripts, Staffordshire Record Office. Tryon meant that Colden expectorated—spit—mucus out of his lungs. Given the prevalence of smoking at the time, spitting would not have attracted much notice.
48. D. Colden to BF, November 30, 1772, *FP*, vol. 19, 390–92; AC to Charles Stuart, January 15, 1773, Ms. Number 5028, f. 14, National Library of Scotland, Edinburgh; AC to BF, July 7, 1773, *FP*, vol. 20, 294.
49. Robert Adems to Johnson, October 25, 1773, *JP*, vol. 8, 910; Johnson to CC, April 17, 1774, *JP*, vol. 8, 1123.
50. BF to AC, June 2, 1773, *FP*, vol. 20, 220–21; *New York Journal* (Holt), March 24, 1774; *New York Gazetteer* (Rivington), March 24, 1774.
51. *SM*, vol. 1, 180, 217; Stokes, *Iconography*, vol. 4, 852.
52. *SM*, vol. 1, 179–80; vol. 2, 29–30.
53. *SM*, vol. 2, 29–30.
54. Tryon to Dartmouth, October 6, 1773, Dartmouth Manuscripts, Staffordshire Record Office.
55. Tryon to Dartmouth, October 6, 1773, Dartmouth Manuscripts, Staffordshire Record Office; Livingston to [Monckton], December 4, 1769, Livingston Family Papers, box 3, reel 1, NYPL; CC to Johnson, April 2, 1771, *CLB*, vol. 2, 319–21; *SM*, vol. 2, 41.
56. Johnson to Dartmouth, April 17, 1774, *NYCD*, vol. 8, 419–21; Gage to Dartmouth, July 18, 1774, Thomas Gage, *The Correspondence of General Thomas Gage with the Secretaries of State, 1763–1775*, ed. Clarence E. Carter (New Haven, CT: Yale University Press, 1931–1933), vol. 1, 360; CC to Dartmouth, August 2, 1774, *CLB*, vol. 2, 349–51.
57. *SM*, vol. 1, 185; Ranlet, *Loyalists*, 34.
58. Tryon to Dartmouth, October 6, 1773, Dartmouth Manuscripts, Staffordshire Record Office; *SM*, vol. 1, 179; Dartmouth to Tryon, April 6, 1774, *NYCD*, vol. 8, 415.
59. Thomas Howard to CC, January 5, 1774, *CP*, vol. 7, 200–1.
60. CC to Dartmouth, [April 1774?], *CP*, vol. 7, 220–22. This could be the letter Livingston mentioned to Smith that Colden sent. If so, it demonstrates that Smith's account was confused. See *SM*, vol. 1, 185.
61. *SM*, vol. 1, 180, 182; Smith to Philip Schuyler, April 7, 1774, *SM*, vol. 1, 182; D. Colden, Memorandum, April 7, 1773, *CLB*, vol. 2, 333; Stokes, *Iconography*, vol. 4, 844. The governor's house was never rebuilt.
62. "To the Honourable Cadwallader Colden, Esq.," May 2, 1774, New York City, "Names of the Principal Male Inhabitants of New York, Anno 1774," in *Manual of the Corporation of the City of New York for 1850*, ed. D. T. Valentine (New York: McSpedon & Baker, 1850), 427–42; New York City, *Minutes of The Common Council of the City of New York, 1675–1776* (New York: Dodd, Mead, 1905), vol. 8, 24; Stokes, *Iconography*, vol. 4, 852.
63. Penn to CC, August 11, 1774, Emmet Coll., no. 114, NYPL; CC to Penn, August 22, 1774, *CLB*, vol. 2, 355–56.
64. CC, "Observations on Situation," 178–79; Watts to Hardy, June 11, 1763, John Watts, *Letter Book of John Watts, Merchant and Councillor of New York, January 1, 1762–December 22, 1765*, New York Historical Society, *Collections* 61 (1928): 146–47.
65. CC, "A Proclamation," March 31, 1762, GLC03107.05300, Gilder Lehrman Coll., Gilder Lehrman Institute of American History, New York City; Bernard to CC, March 31, 1764, Francis Bernard Papers (Sparks Manuscripts), 3:35, Houghton Library, Harvard University, Cambridge, MA; Bernard to CC, July 20, 1765, Francis Bernard, *The Papers of Francis Bernard: Governor of Colonial Massachusetts, 1760–1769*, ed. Colin Nicolson (Boston: Colonial Society of Massachusetts, 2007–), vol. 2, 294.
66. CC to Board of Trade, January 21, 1764, *CLB*, vol. 1, 280–81; CC to Bernard, October 22, 1764, Massachusetts Archives Coll., Records, 1629–1799, vol. 4, 199, Massachusetts Archives at Columbia Point, MA; Massachusetts Colony, *Journals of the House of Representatives of Massachusetts* (Boston: Massachusetts Historical Society, 1971–1981), vol. 41, 124–25, 291–92; Bernard to CC, December 17, 1764, March 9, 1765, Bernard Papers (Sparks Manuscripts), Houghton Library, Harvard University, 4:26, 34; Schwarz, *The Jarring Interests: New York's Boundary Makers, 1664–1776* (Albany: State University of New York Press, 1979), 196–97.

67. Tryon to Council and Assembly, January 12, 1774, New York Colony, *Journal of the Legislative Council*, vol. 2, 1898–99; Massachusetts Colony, *Journals of the House of Representatives of Massachusetts* (Boston: Massachusetts Historical Society, 1971–1981), vol. 43, Part 2, 372; vol. 45, 17; vol. 48, 122; vol. 49, 8–9, 206; vol. 50, 102.

68. Matt Bushnell Jones, *Vermont in the Making, 1750–1777* (Cambridge, MA: Harvard University Press, 1939), 28, 35–36; E. Wilder Spaulding, *His Excellency George Clinton: Critic of the Constitution* (New York, 1938), 143; David Bennett, *A Few Lawless Vagabonds: Ethan Allen, the Republic of Vermont, and the American Revolution* (Havertown, PA : Casemate Publishers, 2014), 21.

69. CC to GC, December 6, 1749, George Clinton Papers, vol. 9, CL; Bennett, *Vagabonds*, 21.

70. "Surveyor General's Observations on Mr. Bradley's Report," October 14, 1751, *DH*, vol. 4, 546–47; Jones, *Vermont*, 28, 35–36; Allan R. Raymond, "Benning Wentworth's Claims in the New Hampshire-New York Border Controversy: A Case of Twenty-Twenty Hindsight?" *Vermont History* 43 (1975): 26, 32.

71. Raymond, "Benning," 28; Dixon Ryan Fox, *Yankees and Yorkers* (New York: New York University Press, 1940; repr. Westport, CT: Greenwood Press, 1979), 156.

72. Jones, *Vermont*, 66; Alexander C. Flick, *History of the State of New York* (New York: Columbia University Press, 1933–1937), vol. 5, 6; "Minutes of the Commrs. on Vermont Claims," New York Colony, *Lists of Inhabitants of Colonial New York Excerpted from The Documentary History of the State of New-York*, ed. Edmund B. O'Callaghan (Baltimore, MD, Genealogical Publishing, 1979), 294.

73. CC to Board of Trade, February 28, 1761, *CLB*, vol. 1, 66–68; CC, "A Proclamation," December 28, 1763, *DH*, vol. 4, 558–59; Bennett, *Vagabonds*, 46.

74. Board of Trade to king, July 10, 1764, in Jones, *Vermont*, 397–98; Schwarz, *Jarring*, 169–70; Raymond, "Benning," 30–31. See CC's letters to the Board of Trade of September 26, 1763, January 20, February 8, April 12, September 21, 1764, *CLB*, vol. 1, 232–37, 285–92, 304, 316–18, 365–66.

75. Watts to Monckton, October 11, 1764, Watts, *Letter Book*, 297–98.

76. CC to Wentworth, April 13, 1765, *CLB*, vol. 1, 475; Jones, *Vermont*, 76; Flick, *History*, vol. 5, 10–11; Thomas Chandler and others to CC, October 9, 15, 1765, *DH*, vol. 4, 578–81.

77. Jones, *Vermont*, 93, 102–3, 167; Virginia D. Harrington, *The New York Merchant on the Eve of the Revolution* (New York: Columbia University Press, 1935; repr. Gloucester, MA: Peter Smith, 1964), 140–41; Irving Mark, *Agrarian Conflicts in Colonial New York, 1711–1775* (New York: Columbia University Press, 1940), 46–47; Nelson, *Tryon*, 103.

78. CC to Hillsborough, June 7, 1765, January 4, 1770, *CLB*, vol. 2, 15, 197–99; Jones, *Vermont*, 62, 108–9, 167.

79. Jones, *Vermont*, 93, 166–67; Harrington, *New York Merchant*, 140–41.

80. CC, "A Proclamation," December 12, 1769, *DH*, vol. 4, 615–16; CC to John Wentworth, December 20, 1769, *CLB*, vol. 2, 196–97.

81. *SM*, vol. 1, 185–88; Richard M. Ketcham, *Divided Loyalties: How the American Revolution Came to New York* (New York: Henry Holt, 2002), 274.

82. CC to Tryon, September 7, 1774, *CLB*, vol. 2, 360–61; Tryon to CC, June 30, 1774, *CP*, vol. 7, 227; Tryon to CC, August 18, 1774, private, Bancroft Coll., Colden Papers, vol. 4, 319, NYPL; *SM*, vol. 1, 204.

83. *SM*, vol. 1, 197–98; Bennett, *Vagabonds*, 44.

84. *SM*, vol. 1, 192–93; CC to Tryon, May 31, 1774, Bancroft Coll., Colden Papers, vol. 4, 247, NYPL; CC to Gage, September 7, 1774, *CLB*, vol. 2, 357–59; CC to Dartmouth, October 4, 1774, *CLB*, vol. 2, 364–65; Bennett, *Vagabonds*, 32, 37–39.

85. *SM*, vol. 1, 184–85; CC to Dartmouth, May 4, 1774, *CLB*, vol. 2, 334–35; Ranlet, *Loyalists*, 34.

86. *SM*, vol. 1, 184–85; CC to Dartmouth, May 4, September 7, 1774, *CLB*, vol. 2, 334–35, 359–60; Ranlet, *Loyalists*, 34–35.

87. Thurman to Aaron Orme and Sons, June 21, 1774, Thurman, "Extracts," 288; "Political Memorandums relative to the Conduct of the Citizens on the Boston Port Bill," May 13, 1774, Alexander McDougall Papers, NYHS.

88. "Political Memorandums," May 13, 1774, Alexander McDougall Papers, NYHS; *SM*, vol. 1, 188.

89. CC to Dartmouth, June 1, 1774, *CLB*, vol. 2, 339–41.

90. CC to Tryon, May 31, 1774, *CLB*, vol. 2, 341–43; D. Colden to Tryon, June 1, 1774, *CLB*, vol. 2, 343–44; Watts to Monckton, May 30, 1774, *Aspinwall Papers, Massachusetts Historical Society. Collections* 4th ser., 9–10 (1871), vol. 10, 710–11.

91. CC to Dartmouth, July 6, August 2, October 5, 1774, *CLB*, vol. 2, 346–47, 349–51, 366–68; Alexander, *Revolutionary Conservative: James Duane*, 104; Ranlet, *Loyalists*, 36–37, 195n79.

92. CC to Dartmouth, November 2, December 7, 1774, *CLB*, vol. 2, 369–75.

93. CC to Dartmouth, November 2, December 7, 1774, *CLB*, vol. 2, 369–75; Ranlet, *Loyalists*, 41.

94. Parker to BF, June 11, July 15, 1766, *FP*, vol. 13, 308–10, 344; BF to AC, December 2, 1772, *FP*, vol. 19, 399; BF to John Foxcroft, October 7, 1772, *FP*, vol. 19, 320.

95. Hugh Wallace to Johnson, February 17, 1771, *JP*, vol. 7, 1145; Indian Congress, July 28, 1772, *NYCD*, vol. 8, 304–10; New York State, *Calendar of N.Y. Colonial Manuscripts Indorsed Land Papers in the Office of the Secretary of State of New York, 1643–1803*, comp. E. B. O'Callaghan. (Albany, NY: Weed, Parsons, 1864; repr. Harrison, NY: Harbor Hill Books, 1987), 473.

96. Lord North to CC, March 25, 1773, *CP*, vol. 7, 186–87; CC to Dartmouth, November 2, 1774, *CLB*, vol. 2, 369–71.

97. John Antill to CC, September 7, 1774, *CP*, vol. 7, 247–48; CC to Tryon, July 6, August 2, December 7, 1774, *CLB*, vol. 2, 348–49, 351–53, 375–76.

98. Antill to CC, September 7, 1774, *CP*, vol. 7, 247–48; New York Colony, *Calendar of New York Colonial Commissions, Book VI (1770–1776)*, ed. Kenneth Scott (New York: National Society of Colonial Dames, 1972), 17.

99. C. Williamos to [Dartmouth], July 12, 1774, Historical Manuscripts Commission, Great Britain, *Manuscripts of the Earl of Dartmouth*, vol. 2, 218; Edmund Fanning to Dartmouth, September 12, 1774, Great Britain, *Manuscripts of the Earl of Dartmouth*, vol. 2, 225; Antill to CC, September 7, 1774, *CP*, vol. 7, 247–48; CC to Tryon, September 7, 1774, *CLB*, vol. 2, 361; Stokes, *Iconography*, vol. 4, 867.

100. *New York Gazetteer* (Rivington), December 15, 1774; *New York Mercury* (Gaine), December 19, 1774.

101. *SM*, vol. 1, 204–6.

102. *SM*, vol. 1, 204–6; New York Colony, *Calendar of New York Colonial Commissions, Book VI (1770–1776)*, ed. Scott, 19.

103. CC to Andrew Elliot, December 15, 1774, *CLB*, vol. 2, 376.

104. *SM*, vol. 1, 192; CC to Tryon, June 2, 1774, Bancroft Coll., Colden Papers, vol. 4, 263, NYPL.

Chapter Seventeen

Finis

When the year 1775 dawned, Cadwallader Colden remained "in good health" despite the rapid approach of his 87th birthday.[1] Determined to bring about a reconciliation between the exasperated colonies and their mother country, Colden kept battling to avoid the rupture of the British Empire, by force if necessary, until at last he could battle no more.

Colden and his allies had to deal with a basic reality that changed the political and social dynamics in New York. General Thomas Gage had withdrawn almost all of the soldiers who had protected New Yorkers, for years, from the Sons of Liberty. Because New Yorkers were "in general moderate, and well affected to all Measures but Taxations," the troops, he thought, were not needed there. The general also stripped New Jersey and Pennsylvania of their soldiers and left a hundred men and their officers from the Royal Irish regiment to garrison Fort George. Gage, largely responsible for the master plan for dealing with rebellion by holding the city and the line of the Hudson, had abandoned it. Instead, he concentrated the vast bulk of his available force to defend Boston, a "little seaport" with no strategic significance.[2]

Captain John Montresor called Gage's obsessive hoarding of soldiers in Boston a "Blunder," and Henry White, a New York councilor, expressed his view that leaving New York City devoid of protection was a major mistake. An American in England, hostile to the British government, sagely observed: "It is fortunate for America that the Governing powers of this Country have had as much folly as wickedness in their conduct."[3]

While New York no longer figured in Gage's plans, his foes understood its importance. On February 25, 1775 William Lee thundered from London about the "New York Traitors." The British ministers had decided to make New York "a place of Arms, to secure that Colony with the assistance of James DeLancey, Colden, John Watts, etc.," all "to prevent any communication or assistance from Virginia, or any of the other colonies getting to New England." Seizing New York was essential Lee advised, and the next year he remained even more adamant. Nothing was more essential than "not to lose a moment in securing this important post," New York, "which in the hands of the enemy must cut the continent in twain, and render it almost impossible for the northern and southern colonies to support each other."[4] Apparently, only the commanders of the British army and navy in America thought Boston was pivotal, not New York.

In the meantime, Colden, at the helm of New York, had been expressly told by Lord Dartmouth to "not fail to embrace every opportunity that offers of writing to me" with the news "of all public Occurrences" there. Only New York had provided any encouragement to the British. Colden complied, writing often to Dartmouth and to William Tryon, who was trying to improve his health. Tryon's health remained poor despite sojourning to the therapeutic waters at Bath, and the possibility existed that he could not return to New York. In that case, rumors in London pointed to British general John Burgoyne as Tryon's replacement.[5]

Whoever finally assumed the reins of power, Colden had to face a serious problem in New York. The lieutenant governor "was afraid of a civil War" and would do everything he could to stop it from igniting. Lord Dartmouth had stated that the colonists should follow the British Constitution and petition their gracious rulers about their complaints. The way to do so was via the elected representatives of their own colony, not an extra-legal body such as the Continental Congress. Fearful that New Yorkers might create another illegal group, a "provincial Congress," Colden decided to call the New York Assembly into session. As he told Dartmouth, "the measures pursued as well by the southern as eastern Provinces puts the Moderate and peaceable Disposition which prevails among the Majority of the People of this Province daily to the trial."[6]

Nonetheless, Colden remained confident that "there is still a good Majority of the most respectable People in this Place" against violence. For evidence, he knew what had happened when Andrew Elliot had confiscated a cargo of illegally imported weapons and gunpowder. Although the Sons of Liberty raised a mob against the port's collector, the merchants, buttressed by many sailors, backed him and the contraband stayed out of the hands of the troublemakers.[7]

The councilors, however, did not share Colden's confidence about the Assembly. Some believed that it might actually endorse the Continental Congress, but Colden thought he had a good plan in case the assemblymen leaned that way and against "prudent Measures." He could always "prorogue" the Assembly, that is delay its meeting for a time in the hope that Parliament might diffuse the crisis somehow. Yet Colden did take a precaution—urging Guy Johnson, Sir William Johnson's nephew now handling Indian affairs, to come to the legislative session. An assemblyman, Johnson was a definite anti-Congress vote if he could come. He could not.[8]

Then came another question: should Colden address the Assembly? William Smith Jr. called such a speech "inexpedient" because it would immediately force the issue. Governor Thomas Hutchinson of Massachusetts had only made things worse when he gave an "Argumentative Speech" to his assembly. When the councilors told Colden their concerns about his speech draft, he was "much confounded." Over the next few meetings he presented more drafts for their consideration, and pointed out "that he thought he could not excuse himself in unnoticing the present confusions."[9]

Overall, the Council toned down Colden's drafts. He had blamed the Presbyterians for the crisis; the Presbyterian Smith mentioned that Anglicans backed the Congress too. That charge disappeared along with some others. As Colden read aloud successive drafts, Smith wrote—"the poor old Man summed up his Powers." The lawyer saw Colden as an elderly man using what remained of his strength to deal with this risky matter.[10]

The old man had more strength left than Smith imagined. After promising the councilors he would not go against their wishes, on January 11, 1775 Colden told the Council he would do just that. Although he did agree to delete some upsetting wording, the speech he delivered to the Assembly was his (if toned down somewhat).[11]

On January 13, 1775 Colden addressed a joint meeting of the Assembly and Council:

> We cannot Sufficiently lament the present disordered State of the Colonies. The Dispute between Great Britain and her American Dominions, is now brought to the most Alarming Crisis, and fills every Humane Breast with the deepest Affliction. It is to you, Gentlemen, in this anxious moment, that your Country looks up for Counsel; And on you it, in a great Measure, depends to Rescue her from Evils of the most Ruinous Tendency.[12]

The assemblymen should look at the complaints of Americans impartially, Colden advised the people's representatives. Then

> If you find them to be well grounded, pursue the Means of Redress which the Constitution has pointed out. Supplicate the Throne, and our Most Gracious Sovereign will hear and Relieve you with Paternal Tenderness. But I entreat you, as you regard the Happiness of your Country, to discountenance every measure, which may increase our Distress.[13]

It was essential, Colden proclaimed, to restore "Harmony, with that Power with which you are Connected by the Ties of Blood, Religion, Interest and Duty, prove yourselves, by your Conduct on this Occasion, earnestly sollicitous for a Cordial and permanent Reconciliation."[14]

Colden's speech went over well, although no one can tell how many New Yorkers went about singing "Loyal York," a song probably composed by James Rivington. The ditty compared Colden to Apollo, who had been "sent to reconcile" brothers. While not quite Olympian, Colden became legendary among loyalists. Some years after his death, a refugee loyalist from South Carolina referred to "the good old Cadwallader Colden."[15]

The lieutenant governor received a far greater reward than a ditty. Despite all the concern before his speech, a pro-Congress assemblyman "counted Noses so well that there was a Majority but of one against them, besides the speaker, who did not Vote." With the prospect that most of the still absent members did not back their cause, the friends of Congress decided to try their luck before they were swamped. Almost two weeks after the speech, on January 26, the New York Assembly refused to endorse the Congress by one vote. No other colony rejected it.[16]

"Worthy old Silver Locks . . . when he heard that the Assembly had acted right, cried out, 'Lord, now lettest thou thy servant depart in peace.'" The deist Colden had quoted a hymn, *Nunc dimittis*. Suddenly, "a bystander cried out 'Well done old Silver Locks.'"[17]

The enthused Colden wanted to send the good news to London immediately. Rather than wait for a mail packet to arrive, he dispatched the news, his speech, and the addresses of the Assembly and Council to him on the first trading ship headed to the imperial capital. However, the petitions to the king and Parliament would not be ready for awhile. The lieutenant governor told Dartmouth that "the loyalty and firmness of the Assembly of this Province, and of the People in general, will appear in a very striking light." Colden did caution him that "The sentiments of the new Parliament is a Matter of great importance." Clearly, Colden hoped that the members of Parliament would ameliorate the imperial dispute. To Tryon, he rejoiced: "We are at this Time entirely Quiet, while all our Neighbours appear to be in the utmost Disorder and Confusion."[18]

Soon, reaction to the proceedings in New York flowed from around America. The pro-Congress Charles Lee referred to the "eleven polluted members of the Assembly of New York." When that did not seem harsh enough, he called them "contemptible," but then settled upon the "prostitute eleven of New York."[19]

The British high command saw things differently. To Colden, Admiral Samuel Graves wished "that your Honor may experience the high satisfaction to see [the colonists] lay aside their senseless opposition to their indulgent Mother Country, and Unite in endeavouring to restore Publick Tranquility and a due subjection to the Laws among themselves."[20]

If anything, General Gage was even more enthusiastic than his naval colleague. Thrilled that New Yorkers had given the Massachusetts "Royalists" new hope and that reconciliation was still possible, he told the 87-year-old Colden: "I sincerely pray that New York may continue to pursue the road she is in, and merit the distinction of the loyal Province; and the saviour of America; and that you may live to see the completion of the good work you have so happily begun."[21]

When Colden's dispatch reached London, the news of the Assembly's rejection of Congress, his speech and the addresses "filled every heart with joy." Tryon informed Colden that his speech and the addresses "were approved by those in Power" including the king. George III was "greatly pleased, with the Loyalty and Temperate Conduct . . . of his faithful Subjects in . . . New York." On March 14, 1775 the Assembly's agent Edmund Burke revealed to James DeLancey: "I find that Ministry place their best hopes of dissolving the Union of the Colonies and breaking the present spirit of resistance, wholly in your Province."[22]

In British eyes, New York had become their most important colony. The problem with all this hope breaking out, however, is that no one in Britain had yet seen the Assembly's petitions. On March 1, 1775 Colden expressed his fear that the Assembly would include complaints about legislation such as the *Boston Port Act* and the *Quebec Act*. His concern was justified. Trying to be as positive as possible, Colden related to Dartmouth that the Assembly refused to send a delegation to the Second Continental Congress, but the petitions he sent to Britain, almost as negative as those of the Congress, rejected the primacy of the British Parliament. Despite praising the petitions, Colden had no illusion about their future rejection.[23]

Eventually, when New Yorkers learned that their Assembly's petitions had gotten nowhere in the halls of power in Britain, many decided that the mother country would never be interested in seriously considering colonial grievances. Colden was, perhaps, the most disappointed New Yorker. In August 1774 he all but begged, in very cautious language, that Parliament back away from its claim that it could tax colonials.[24] Without that concession, Colden knew that reconciliation could not happen.

Earlier, Colden discovered he could not wean New Yorkers away from congressional non-importation. In order to break this "Association" that had created an economic boycott, Colden needed some ship captain to actually ask him for help. Because the trading ships carried private property of either some merchant or the captain, the lieutenant governor had to have a request for help, which he would eagerly give to undermine "the violent party." Colden believed the colonial government was not "too weak" to do so.[25]

The day after the Association's deadline of February 1, 1775 for importing, the *James* from Glasgow, Scotland, entered the harbor with mostly coal. This ship, the first since the deadline passed, constituted an opportunity for Colden. If landed, its cargo would violate non-importation. When the ship's Captain Watson seemed unwilling to comply with the Association, a mob appeared on shore and untied the *James*' mooring. Now the captain thought "the ship to be in danger." A boat, "with armed Men," kept an eye on the *James* as well. Watson, spooked, ordered his mate to take the ship away from the wharf.[26]

Colden now had a pretext to act. Forcing the Scottish ship to leave the wharf was an "act of Outrage and Violence," and Colden did have a naval vessel he could employ, the *Kingsfisher*. A sloop with sixteen guns, the *Kingsfisher* was not a huge warship, but it would do. Because the harbor was not icy, the sloop could sail into action. The lieutenant governor consulted the Council, which though "shy," did agree that an inquiry be made to see if the *James* wanted help. Promptly, Colden ordered the *Kingsfisher*'s Captain James Montagu "to go down to the ship and to offer the Master your assistance. The sooner this is done I think the better."[27]

When sailors of the *Kingsfisher* boarded the *James*, the mate declined any assistance from the navy. But Colden must have also told Montagu to find out if the *James* had received a "clearance"—a legal authorization to leave the harbor. Because the mate had no such document, its departure was illegal and the *Kingsfisher* brought the *James* back to the wharf—as Colden had wanted.[28]

The return of the *James* made the Sons of Liberty unhappy and, with few soldiers left in the city, the Sons could act as they wished. Seizing the captain of the *James*, they paraded him about the city. Though not hurt, he was frightened to death. Colden, however, would not let the vessel slip away without the necessary clearance. Despite other merchants' advice, the owners of the cargo obtained the necessary documentation, and the *James* sped off to Jamaica to dispose of the cargo there.[29]

To say that Colden was "shagreened"—as he did—that the Scottish ship had not broken the Association is an understatement. He characterized its captain as "a stupid Body who would neither make a complaint nor ask for assistance." The cargo's owners lacked the "Resolution enough to Demand their Goods, so that it was impossible for Government to interfere to any good purpose."[30]

Briefly, the lieutenant governor's spirits soared again when an English ship approached the harbor. According to information he received, this captain was "a spirited Man, and has said he will land his Cargo," just what Colden wanted to hear. "If he makes application, we shall give him all the assistance We have." Yet Colden suffered disappointment again as this captain sailed off to Nova Scotia, without asking for assistance. These victories buoyed the Sons of Liberty, giving "them great Spirits," and were "a strong Counterpoise to the Conduct of the Assembly."[31] Colden knew of another way to forestall civil war.

While the *Kingsfisher* was useful to have about, a sloop did not project enough power to control the harbor and protect traders still willing to do business with Britain. Colden wanted much more. On February 20, 1775

Colden wrote to Admiral Graves for a much more powerful vessel. Though most New Yorkers sought reconciliation, some did not. "We have among Us a set of violent Spirits . . . who lay hold of every occasion to raise Mobs and excite sedition," Colden explained to the sailor. New York's "Friends to Government" deserved to be "Protected" and the few troops in the colony could not do so. Besides, closing the Hudson to troublemakers from more southern colonies who had vowed to help Massachusetts was essential. Sending a warship with significant firepower, aided by smaller ships such as the *Kingsfisher*, could "obstruct the Passage of the River." Colden also looked forward to having the large contingent of marines a big ship carried to supplement, if necessary, the handful of soldiers on shore.[32]

Graves agreed that a government should protect "its declared friends" especially since "the opposition" would "excite" its followers "to the most desperate Acts." The admiral had been thinking along the same lines as Colden and had resolved to send to New York a powerful ship of the line, the *Asia*, equipped with sixty-four cannons. Graves warned Colden to keep this "profound secret" to heighten its shock value. "The sudden arrival of this ship at New York may . . . have the effect to surprize and, perhaps, intimidate." Graves understood how New Yorkers would react upon seeing the weaponry of a ship of the line. According to a South Carolinian, "There are but three towns, of any consequence, that could be hurt by the English fleet:" Charleston, Boston, and New York City. New Yorkers knew that very well, but when would the *Asia* arrive? Graves was in no hurry—perhaps at the end of March, perhaps much later in the spring. It would get there—eventually.[33]

Colden's desire for a large, powerful warship in the harbor helps put in perspective his common assertions that most of New York was loyal for which he has often been criticized by historians. Colden knew very well that there was no support for recent British policies in New York. He could have had no delusions after an official ceremony at the statue of George III on March 2, 1775, when he and the other participants left "amidst the Hisses of the people."[34]

Although New Yorkers disliked British policies and backed non-importation, they also backed their Assembly's effort to forge reconciliation. Even as late as the summer of 1775, according to a British observer on Long Island, "the general voice is peace and friendship with England upon fair and equitable terms."[35]

Merchant John Thurman summed up well the attitudes of New Yorkers:

> most of the Inhabitants in this Place are averse to any Violence and wish to Support Law and order we are abused by our neighbors because we do not run into the same violent measures with them yet. I dare be bold to say this province would be as firm in any constitutional opposition to unconstitutional Impositions as any of them.[36]

Both the need for law and order and the fear of what a civil war would bring in its wake weighed heavily on New Yorkers. Everyone knew that the Sons of Liberty had a violent streak, which they had often demonstrated; the fear of civil war had become more intense among New Yorkers. Thurman declared that "nothing but ruin and distress can be got by either side by Civil War." Even the least imaginative could guess that, if war broke out, their city and province would turn into a battlefield and become "the Seat of War in America."[37] The reason Colden could call New Yorkers loyal is that they knew if the king's government fell, all the evils visited upon England because of its civil war, including despotism, would engulf them too. King Sears received his nickname for a reason.

New Yorkers, Colden understood, could not defend themselves against forces of disruption in their current, weak state. "With a proper Military Power," Colden asserted, "I think this Province would continue to set a good Example" to its erring sister colonies, "but without that protection I fear even the best Friends of Government will not care to risk their personal safety and expose their Families to continual Terrors and alarms." Just a few hundred more soldiers would "have very salutary Effects."[38]

The lieutenant governor was not alone in wanting a reversal of the foolish mistake in leaving New York undefended. Soldiers for the province had "been requested to be sent by [James] DeLancey, and his band of traitors, Cooper, White, Colden, and Watts, to aid them in securing New York for the Ministry." Seeing Colden's name is no shock. Councilors Henry White and Watts along with Myles Cooper, the president of King's College, are not all that surprising either. Yet heading the list is James DeLancey, who controlled the Assembly. The champion of the people knew what had to be done as well as Colden did. In Boston, General James Robertson, who had been stationed in New York for many years and also understood what was happening there, had been pushing, unsuccessfully, for the *Asia* to be sent quickly to New York.[39]

Colden tried to be subtle with General Gage. Rather than ask him directly for more troops, Colden asked him to peruse his letter of February 20, 1775 to Admiral Graves requesting more naval support. In this letter to Graves Colden included one sentence really intended for the commander-in-chief himself: "we have had at least one Regiment ever since the Peace till now." Gage, however, did not react to it, other than to send the letter to Graves.[40]

More direct with Lord Dartmouth, on March 1 Colden declared that "The moderate Inhabitants" of New York "have constantly expressed a Wish that We had a more formidable military Power in the Place, to awe the Licentious and encourage the Friends of Government." While the thought that the troublesome men "really fighting the King's Troops is so full of madness and folly" that it was difficult to take "seriously," it was also true that "a neglect of proper precautions may encourage the wild enthusiasts to attempt what they would not otherwise venture upon." Colden would have been pleased to know that, even as his letter was being composed, the British government was preparing a fleet bringing substantial reinforcements to not only Gage at Boston, but to Colden at New York too. For once, London was doing something both sensible and correct.[41]

Then in March 1775 Vermont exploded. In Cumberland County, created by New York, a "daring Riot" took place. This area was not in turmoil over land titles; instead, Colden believed, "It is a contagion spread from Massachusetts Bay." The New Englanders closed a court and were strengthened by arrivals from both New Hampshire and Massachusetts which "made them too powerful for the Magistrates." Some New York officials were carted off and jailed in Massachusetts. By April 1775 New Englanders were preventing New Yorkers from entering the county.[42]

Apparently, this riot was an act of desperation. As more and more of the Vermonters developed their land, they wished to enjoy the fruits of their labor in peace. The violence of the Green Mountain Boys was something these settlers could do without. The Green Mountain Boys had largely been defeated; support for New York had been growing. This latest round of violence was a last attempt to stem the tide. Colden was winning over Vermont, but his victory will soon be overshadowed by another act of violence.[43]

Colden believed that "the Bennington Mob" could be stopped only "by force" and there was a secondary effect of sending soldiers to Cumberland. Having the British military "so near the Borders of Massachusetts Bay" was "unavoidable for bringing the eastern colonies under submission to Great Britain or any legal authority."[44]

This time Gage, fearing "that anarchy may spread from" Vermont "over the whole province," ordered General Carleton to send troops to Ticonderoga and Crown Point; New York had to supply some soldiers of its own to help. This joint expedition never happened. Colden was told all this by James Robertson on April 21, 1775, because Gage had delegated him to write as the commander-in-chief was "fully employed at present." Indeed he was.[45]

Before the firestorm blazed in Massachusetts, Dartmouth had ordered colonial governors, at all costs, to stop their citizens from choosing members of the new Continental Congress, which he bluntly termed "an illegal Convention," that was planned for May 1775. When Colden informed the Council about this demand, Smith convinced them all that Colden show Dartmouth's letter to Assembly leaders and explain "that the Congress was not pleasing to the King and forbidden by the minister." Although the Assembly did not select congressional delegates, Dartmouth's letter became public knowledge almost immediately, stirred up more support for the Congress, and a New York delegation was picked in an extra-legal fashion.[46]

Colden's own faith in the British government had to be shaken by the fate of David Colden's succession to the office of surveyor-general. On January 3, 1775 the lieutenant governor informed Dartmouth about David becoming surveyor-general and explained away the good behavior commission. The lieutenant governor, emphasizing what he had done for Britain over so many years, reminded Dartmouth of "The Manner in which I have supported the Supreme authority of Parliament" and his suffering from "The odium of a popular Party." Most of all, Colden saw his son's appointment as "a lasting Instance of the Favour I received in my old Age, for the past services of my Life."[47]

Cadwallader Colden did not know that Governor Tryon had heard very quickly of Alexander Colden's death and saw it as a patronage opportunity for a close personal ally, his secretary Edmund Fanning.[48] In Tryon's defense, he knew about David's fragile health and could not have imagined him trudging about the countryside surveying. Because David could hire surveyors to do the actual work, he did not have to do any trudging himself.

When Dartmouth received Colden's letter, he checked with the British Treasury which controlled the position and discovered that Fanning had already been granted it. There was nothing that could be done. As for Tryon, he had to be surprised when letters informed him about David's appointment. Tryon gave his lieutenant governor a sharp reprimand for giving David a good behavior commission, but also remarked that David's succession as surveyor-general "was a measure very Natural and what I could not disapprove."[49]

Throughout the colonial history of New York, a royal commission had always trumped an appointment made in the colony. Colden, though, was not going to let such precedents threaten the future prospects of his crippled son. On June 20, 1775 Fanning came to Colden expecting to be sworn in as surveyor-general. To Fanning's amazement, Colden refused and told him "he should do nothing against his Son and that he thought Lord North's Hand ought to have been counter-signed to the Sign Manual." Lord North, it seemed, had not followed procedure to the letter. This had to be true. North held two of the most important offices in the British government at the same time—prime minister and head of the Treasury—and, not surprisingly, had little time to spare to do such routine work as signing commissions thus explaining the error. When Tryon came back to New York, he had to have talked with Fanning; there was no further mention of his royal commission. David Colden would be surveyor-general as long as there was a royal New York, but, already by June 1775, the once fought-for position had become almost meaningless.[50]

Back in England, by March 1775 rumors swirled about significant political changes planned for New York. Arthur Lee, a Virginian in the mother country, wrote letters, some of which purported to be meant for Cadwallader

Colden, that were really propaganda. Though they contained paranoia about a colonial bishop and that the New York Assembly had been bribed, these supposed letters did have some significant information about New York. Lee asserted:

> The DeLanceys, Watts, Coldens, and the leaders of the party are to be rewarded much higher, by places of honour, profit, and pensions, viz. Watts to be Lieutenant Governor, in the room of old Colden, who resigns on a pension, Cruger to be of the Council, also a young Colden, McEvers, and some of the Watts. Large grants of land are also to be given . . . [These scoundrels, Lee asserted,] are most assuredly assisting the ministers in devising plans for disuniting America, which are communicated by Colden officially. . . . [51]

In 1774 Cadwallader Colden had commented on what he knew was coming sooner or later, his retirement. He had managed to stall retirement for some time but the subject was in the air. Writing to Dartmouth, Colden observed:

> I have reason from your Lordship's Letter to suppose there is a Design to appoint another Lieut. Governor of this Province. I trust in his Majesty's Justice that when he is pleased to dismiss an old Servant, he will bestow such gracious Testimonies as will evince that tho' he may think me too old to serve him at a Time when the task is become uncommonly arduous, I have not forfeited his royal Protection and Favour.[52]

The testimonies Colden wished as an acknowledgment of his service are clear. First, he wanted a pension, which was being discussed in London. In fact, during 1775 the imperial government had suddenly gotten generous—two Anglican ministers had received pensions of £200 a year for writing some pro-British pamphlets. Finally, Colden appeared to be in line for one too. Second, the lieutenant governor desired that David, who had already been nominated by Tryon, be named to the Council as Lee suggested would happen. These two testimonies would have made the old man happy to retire, permanently, to Spring Hill.[53]

Lee had good insight into New York affairs because he had a member of Colden's extended family as a source. Young Aly DeLancey had grown up and had married Ralph Izard, a South Carolina planter. Her grandfather liked the young man and had trusted him to help with his defense against Dunmore when the couple travelled to London.[54]

In Britain, Izard developed important connections with Lord North and the political opposition. Among Americans, he had ties to members of the Continental Congress and associated with Arthur Lee. Izard had spent enough time in New York to be familiar with its major figures and made only one mistake in what he told Lee—the New York Council already had a Cruger.[55]

These well-laid plans fell apart very suddenly. In 1775 Dartmouth passed along new orders for Gage. He was supposed to deal with the nascent rebellion in Massachusetts and seize two of the leaders, John Hancock and Samuel Adams, who were in the town of Lexington, well away from Boston. The general decided on a preemptive strike; a force would be sent first to Lexington to nab the two outlaws and then to Concord, where weapons and other war materials had been stashed. On April 19, 1775 American blood was spilt in both communities, sparking open war.[56]

The firestorm ignited by Lexington and Concord spread throughout the American colonies, hitting New York on April 23. David Colden, a few years later, recalled this "event, which produced the most violent change in the temper and conduct of the people of this Province. The greatest confusion and total prostration of Government succeeded."[57]

On April 24 Lieutenant Governor Colden, asking the councilors for their advice, plainly stated what had happened:

> Last Night a Number of Persons violently Seized 530 stand of Arms which belonged to the City and were Lodged in the City Hall, that they also Seized the public powder House, and have put a Guard of fifty Men to maintain it; that they have been Parading thro the Town this Day, and have Proclaimed a meeting of the Inhabitants this Afternoon, in order as it is said to chuse Military Officers, when they declare their Intention is to oblige his Majesty's Troops, which are now in the Barracks in this City, to lay down their Arms.[58]

When Izard in London heard what had happened, he aptly declared: "The people of New York have taken the Government out of Mr. Colden's hands." Nor did the chaos soon end. Months later, a female member of the Livingston clan lamented: "Times are very distressing here that we know not where to flee." A New England diarist reported the latest news: "Gov. Colden of N. York, it is said, has said that if there had been a few ships, they would have supported the Friends of Government but now all was irretrievably lost!" Colden did complain to Dartmouth about the *Asia*'s late arrival: "I really think the Countenance of that Ship would have" succeeded in "encouraging some and discouraging others." The lieutenant governor also knew "that if the same Number of Regular Troops had been here" as in the past, "this change of Measures and Prostration of legal authority had not happened."[59]

This collapse of royal authority in New York would not have lasted as long as it did, even without large numbers of soldiers, if one circumstance had been different. When the *Stamp Act* riots loomed in 1765, Cadwallader Colden entered Fort George with the small handful of soldiers in the city. Knowing Colden, he would have done the same thing in 1775, this time with the soldiers of the Royal Irish who had been left to garrison the fort, creating an eighteenth century Alamo. He knew that Fort George "was a sufficient security against the attempts of a Mob," which he again faced in 1775. The lieutenant governor would have been joined by some volunteers, councilor John Harris Cruger for example. Cruger soon began serving with distinction as a loyalist army officer.[60]

Colden's last stand defense would have made it politically impossible for Gage to divert reinforcements headed to New York. Colden did remark, "A reinforcement of four strong Regiments may indeed make a favourable change in the Face of affairs Here." Because the rebel forces in the city were little better than an armed mob, these fresh regiments could have seized southern New York. What the British needed a huge armada and army to do in 1776 could have been accomplished, with little cost, in 1775. Therefore, the British army could have concentrated in 1776 on seizing the line of the Hudson when the rebel army was still amateurish, a year before it was tried in 1777.[61]

Colden could not stop the outbreak of war, but he might have made it short and unsuccessful because the British would have controlled New York and split New England away from the other rebellious colonies. The War of Independence would have gone down in history as just another of the unsuccessful rebellions that briefly disrupted the British Empire and would have received a different name, perhaps the great tea rebellion. The problem, of course, is that Lord Dunmore demilitarized Fort George. There could be no last stand as the detachment Colden had at his disposal was "too small to make any formidable Opposition to the violences of the People" with no secure base to protect them. Instead, Colden had to watch the humiliation of the Royal Irish.[62]

Besieged in their insecure barracks, the harassed soldiers had to keep up a constant guard. When the officers arrested a deserter, and the New Englanders in New York discovered what had happened, the Royal Irish had to release the culprit amidst a threat of their barracks being torched. After losing some of the Royal Irish themselves to desertion, it was decided that the remaining soldiers had to be evacuated to the *Asia*, which arrived in late May. Colden instructed the officers to keep their intended movement "Secret... to give the People the least Notice you possibly can of it."[63]

Despite the permission of the rebel authorities, the short march on June 6 did not go well. A few unarmed men stopped the Royal Irish in their tracks, searched their baggage carts, and removed weapons in them. Ensign John Peter DeLancey, eager to fight the "mob," had equipped his gun with a bayonet but was ordered by a senior officer to remove it. Concerned by this "high Insult and Outrage," Colden demanded that the seized weapons be returned; they were, but the damage to British prestige had already been done. "I am sorry to find these wicked Men daily get the Better of Magistrates and Congresses and Committees, and do whatever their extravagant Passions lead to," the lieutenant governor exclaimed.[64]

At least General Robertson in Boston was doing everything he could to give Colden enough military strength to influence the course of events. On May 4 the general informed David Colden: "The madness of some of the inhabitants of N. York has had a better effect than my sollicitations, and has hastened the departure of the *Asia*." (Yet the warship still did not enter New York harbor until May 26.) Robertson, full of enthusiasm at the prospect of aiding Cadwallader Colden, had wanted to be on board the *Asia* "to cooperate with the Governor in reestablishing government in the province." The means Robertson wanted to employ involved sending two regiments to assist Colden, one from Canada, one from East Florida. "I was complimented out of my request" the general complained.[65]

On the same day Gage floated an idea. He told the lieutenant governor that a regiment had been transferred from Canada to Crown Point, and tried to cheer him with the prospect of that regiment joining him in the chaotic capital of the province. More realistic, Colden had to explain that a single regiment would probably find it difficult, if not impossible, to traverse the whole expanse of New York in the current, disrupted atmosphere. The handful of troops he had earlier asked for would be useless now; a more substantial number was required.[66]

Gage voiced confidence in Colden's "prudence in this Critical juncture; Time, and circumstances must be your guide." He did what he could and consulted with the Council, which was about as defeatist as possible. On April 24, 1775 the Council met to decide "What is to be done?" Calling in the militia officers, the judges, and city officials, the Council learned that the militia would do nothing but that the colony remained quiet beyond the city's outskirts. On May 1 the councilors insisted that Colden send Gage a minute of their meeting, during which they begged the general to avoid any more bloodshed, advice that did not go over well, and Colden tried to keep away from the frightened councilors the reality that Gage would never have agreed to that. Colden made no secret of the "total prostration of government."[67]

While Colden could not do anything forceful at least until the arrival of the *Asia*, he did what he could to help the king's cause. Mail service to and from Boston had been ended; "All Intelligence to Government is intercepted;" all letters were opened. So Colden pursued imaginative ways to distribute the dispatches Gage sent him. In one case, taking advantage of Sir John Johnson (Sir William's son) being in the city, Gage's critical mail would be delivered to Canada by an Indian. And Gage wanted Colden to have the British version of Lexington and Concord published in New York. The lieutenant governor sent it off to the king's printer, Hugh Gaine, who first agreed to print it but then reneged. Only in June did the nervous printer finally put the account into his newspaper.[68]

Colden had another duty to perform—notifying his superiors in London what had happened in New York. Of all Colden's letters to London, this letter of May 3, 1775 to Dartmouth had to have been the most difficult to write. "In all my correspondence," the lieutenant governor insisted, "I have studied to give your lordship an exact idea of the real situation of the province and of the most material transactions of the people." Sadly, he continued: "The accounts which I have now to give will almost entirely destroy the expectations you have had reason to entertain of the conduct which this province would pursue." Trying his best to demonstrate that his positive reports were not just the wishful thinking of an old man, Colden pointed to the actions of the Assembly. However, the weakness of the civil magistrates and the insignificant military garrison had made "the leaders of the people insolently bold and daring." With nothing to protect "The friends of order," they had to submit to save themselves.[69]

The lieutenant governor's assertion of the danger the king's friends were in was well founded. The would be dictator King Sears had been prowling the city with an armed gang and he was only the best known. After the exposure of James DeLancey and Watts as being among those who called for more troops for New York, there was serious talk of shooting them. Both soon left for Britain. After a British newspaper printed a letter—that the mob did not like—with Oliver DeLancey's initials, he "was frequently mobbed" despite being cleared by a panel of friends of the people that included James Duane. Although the elder DeLancey stayed, many others joined Watts in fleeing to the mother country. "No one dare now print write or speak a word in favour of Government" Cad declared at Coldengham after he had been intimidated into signing the Continental Association.[70]

Cadwallader Colden had borne witness to "the Horrors and Calamities of a Civil War which has already had such terrifying Effects." Unlike so many others, though, the lieutenant governor had not been mobbed. This apparent immunity is the more marked because he was not staying in the ruined governor's house but, almost certainly, in his daughter Elizabeth's home at Whitehall near the fort. His safety was due partly to his popularity and that the city committee had ordered that he not be asked to sign their association. As the king's governor, an attack on him could be considered treason, which few of the rebellious New Yorkers at this time wanted to risk.[71]

Nonetheless, there was little Colden could do. Because "Congresses and Committees had taken the entire direction of the Government," he found it "extremely disagreeable" to be "a Spectator of the Proceedings and confusions in Town, which I had it not in my Power to prevent." On May 5, 1775 Colden announced to the Council his desire to return to Spring Hill, which he did. He met the Council again but at Brooklyn in Kings County which remained quiet as had Flushing and Queens County in general. Flushing was dominated by Quakers, who showed little interest in joining the rebellion against the mother country.[72]

Despite Colden's absence from the troubled city, he was able to make an appeal for peace. On May 13 some of the city's committeemen met Colden in Jamaica, the county seat of Queens. These leaders emphasized to Colden that they had restored order to the city but complained of "ministerial misconduct" and feared that "the streets of New York may be deluged with blood." They believed that Colden "will do everything in your power to avert" such a disaster and begged him to ask General Gage "that expected troops will not come and land in New York."[73]

An emotional Colden addressed the committeemen, assuring them that peace with Britain was still possible and that Parliament was willing to discuss "any real grievances." The lieutenant governor urged them to seek a solution with the British government. He feared for the welfare of New Yorkers

> over whom I have so long presided as the immediate representative of their august Sovereign, with whom I have lived the term of a long life, and among whom I leave all that is dear and valuable to me. I am impelled by my duty, and a most zealous attachment to the interest and safety of this people, to exhort you not to irritate the present enraged state of their minds, nor suffer them to plunge into labyrinths, from whence they can neither advance nor retreat, but through blood and desolation.[74]

The lieutenant governor stated unequivocally that he had not "the least intimation" about troops coming to New York, turning it into another Boston, and promised to write to General Gage. Colden guessed that this report had been "invented" just "to facilitate the introduction of an armed force from Connecticut, which I am told is meditated."[75]

That Colden meant what he said is obvious from the press reports of his speech. The *New York Mercury* related that "His Honor in giving his Answer was so affected that he shed many Tears." Even a critical report remarked that "His reply was unsatisfactory, though given with tears." Colden's speech worked as a Livingston commented after it: "The most turbulent Spirits amongst us do not expect the arrival of any Troops at present."[76]

This speech had such an impact that the mad printer, John Holt, felt he had to attack Colden:

> To know what confidence this colony ought to put in the assurances given to our committee, by a certain person who fills a high post in this government, it will be sufficient to read the extracts of the letters he wrote to the ministry, and which have been exhibited before the parliament.[77]

On May 18 Colden kept his promise to write Gage. Sending along to the general a copy of the addresses, the lieutenant governor thought they were self-explanatory. He invited Gage to send a response, if he wished, and it would be passed on. Colden still had no idea that soldiers were, indeed, sailing to New York, but he soon learned the truth.[78]

The long delayed *Asia* finally arrived in the harbor on May 26, 1775. A grumpy Colden complained to Dartmouth: Admiral Graves had assured him "that I might expect the *Asia* here by the 1st of April. I am heartily sorry she was not, for I really think the Countenance of the Ship would have had a good effect." To demonstrate the effect Colden was writing about, the ship of the line "moored before New York," giving troublemakers an excellent view of the guns that made every ship of the line a floating fortress. Though the *Asia*'s captain, George Vandeput, would be ordered to shell "the house of that traitor Sears," the ship only gave a demonstration of its firepower on August 24, 1775 when the rebels removed cannons from the Battery. The *Asia* fired a broadside which hit some houses near Elizabeth's Whitehall home. Izard revealed that her unmarried daughters "happened unluckily, to be in town for that night only. They were not hurt, but returned to Westchester, next morning, terribly frightened."[79]

When the *Asia* first anchored in New York, Vandeput immediately made contact with Colden, secure at his estate in Queens. The captain offered the lieutenant governor the assistance of his warship "towards supporting the legal Authority of Government" and protecting the king's friends. Captain Vandeput agreed to "consult" with him about what the *Asia* could do to fulfill those objectives. On May 27, 1775 Colden lamented to the sailor: "I only regret that the Admiral did not find it Consistent with his Majesty's Service to send Me so necessary an Aid much sooner."[80]

Vandeput told Colden about the substantial reinforcements headed to the colony. Two regiments each were slated for both New York City and Albany, which would give Colden enough firepower to restore royal rule. Oddly, the dispatches from London delivered by the *Asia* gave no hint about this important news. Supposedly, these soldiers "were not to act but to support and defend the Friends of Government." Whatever the intention, protection of these embattled men would lead, very fast, to the spilling of blood which Colden realized. But he predicted that "whenever a sufficient protection appears it will be found that His Majesty has many true and loyal subjects who are at present compelled to acquiesce in the plans of opposition."[81]

Although Colden's hopes had to be raised, they would soon be dashed. These troops had been sent to New York, not because New Yorkers had requested them, but to isolate New England from the other colonies. However, Gage had been given permission to divert the soldiers from New York to strengthen Boston still more. Because this substantial army planned for New York "could be of little use in the present Situation of that Province," Gage wanted them in Boston; Admiral Graves had a warship find this New York bound fleet and bring it to Boston.[82] With the successful diversion to Massachusetts of these four regiments, the British campaign to defeat the rebellion was already doomed.

In June 1775 direct responsibility for the province passed from Colden to William Tryon when the governor returned. On June 26 Tryon regained "the diminished authority the Lieutenant Governor had to transfer to me" the governor alerted Dartmouth. Once Tryon learned that the reinforcements were not coming, there was little he could do. To welcome Tryon back, Colden hosted a dinner after the governor's swearing in but attended no other Council meetings. On July 3, 1775 Colden concluded his official duties by writing to Lord Dartmouth with intelligence gathered before Tryon's arrival. In what would be the lieutenant governor's last letter to London, Colden also proclaimed his loyalty: "I entreat your Lordship to believe that I [have] the firmest attachment to His Majesty's Person and Government."[83]

Tryon might as well have stayed in Bath. His situation in the city deteriorated quickly, and on October 30 he hurriedly went on board a merchant ship to avoid being taken prisoner by the rebels. Colden, among those royal officials cleared to visit Tryon on board the vessel, did not do so. The lieutenant governor had left for Queens long before and never returned to the city. Climbing onto a ship away from the docks would have been nearly impossible for him anyway. By April 1776 Tryon's effigy was being burned in the city's streets. Soon his refuge, along with the *Asia* and other warships that had joined it, sailed out of the harbor. Technically, that meant that Colden was, once again, acting governor, but the royal government he had served for so long no longer existed.[84]

Meanwhile, across the Atlantic, Izard had been following events in New York. Informed by his mother-in-law that Cadwallader Colden's health remained good—amazing considering what he had just gone through—Izard, on September 10, 1775, wrote Colden an astonishing letter:

> You have had a great deal of trouble, and have conducted yourself to the satisfaction of all parties. This is a very difficult matter, and requires more than ordinary abilities to accomplish. . . . [Americans had been betrayed] by a man whose family was brought into this Kingdom, for the purpose of abolishing tyranny, and securing the liberties of the people. He has, as far as he could, defeated the intention. America has acted wisely in not trusting her cause to his justice and honor. If she had—she would have found herself in the situation of Aesop's sheep, when they committed themselves to the custody of a wolf.[85]

The South Carolinian had more to say as he stressed his belief that Americans would be "severed" from the British "forever." If he had not gone far enough with that, he declared his support for the Continental Congress while attacking the New York Assembly. Then Izard gave the old man news he thought was unknown to him:

> There has been some very unfair management at New York, and if the scheme of disuniting that Province from the rest of America had been accomplished, I can assure you, that your office of Lieutenant Governor would have been transferred to a certain gentleman, and you would have been left, after your long, troublesome, and faithful services, with another proof of the wickedness and ingratitude of the Ministry of this Country.[86]

Whatever Izard hoped his letter might achieve, Colden was not going to change the decision he had made six decades before in his father's church. Though no doubt exasperated by this report that no pension was coming his way, Colden remained a loyal subject of his king. If the lieutenant governor had needed any other demonstration of the great strength of the rebel cause, he got it with the revelation that rebel support was present even within his own family. This letter did not stop Colden from aiding his king within the county of Queens.

In September 1775 the rebels discovered they had significant resistance in Queens. They tried to collect guns from refusers of the Association in two towns, Hempstead and Jamaica, and were surprised at what happened. According to one rebel officer, William Williams:

> The people conceal all their arms that are of any value; many declare they know nothing about the Congress nor do they care anything for the orders of the Congress; and say that they would sooner lose their lives, than give up their arms, and that they would blow any man's brains out that should attempt to take them from them.[87]

Not many areas of the thirteen colonies had enough supporters of the British, who became known as loyalists, to enable them to intimidate the rebels so blatantly, but Queens County was one of them. The Church of England had been established there, and both Jamaica and Hempstead had substantial Anglican congregations complete with ministers to urge them on. The ministers served as able leaders of the loyalist cause in Queens. Deference to high-placed people remained important in the 1770s, and it should not be forgotten that the Coldens resided in Queens.[88]

Governor Tryon attributed much of the credit for the loyal conduct of Queens to his lieutenant governor and David. The opposition of the Coldens was known to the rebels. As the harassed Major Williams commented, "We also have it from good authority, that Governor Colden" on September 24, 1775 "sent his servant"—probably a slave—"round to some of the leading people" urging "them to arms." Not surprisingly, a loyal militia officer told the spooked Williams that if rebel soldiers had shown up in Hempstead, they would have regretted it. The lieutenant governor would have used his influence extensively in the county.[89]

More shock was in store for the rebels, and David Colden helped to cause it. In November 1775 a special election would be held to pick the new Queens delegation to the New York Provincial Congress. The election took place—the county rejected having any representation. According to Judge George D. Ludlow of Queens, David "Exerted all his influence in Queens County to keep the Inhabitants there true to their Allegiance [and] Contributed to prevent Delegates being sent to Congress." Apparently, there were speeches made before the actual voting. Ludlow's loyalist brother declared that David "was one of about 12 or 14 who made a Protest against a Provincial Congress." Governor Tryon summed up David's activity: "It was owing to his exertions and those of the Loyal Gentlemen of the County that the Inhabitants opposed the General Defection."[90]

A happy Cadwallader Colden informed Tryon of the "remarkable" loyalist victory at the election. At first the loyalists were "unwilling even to shew that kind of submission to the Authority of the Congress, which holding a Poll for an Election in consequence of their Order, seemed to express." Their initial plan was "only to Protest" against the election. Instead, they changed their minds "on the Day of Election." They insisted on a poll "for Deputies, or No Deputies," which resulted in a crushing landslide against deputies: 747 (77 percent of the total) against, 221 (23 percent) for. The victory margin was 526 votes, some 54 percent.[91]

If anything, the actual margin of loyalist dominance in Queens was underrepresented even by that lopsided margin, the lieutenant governor believed:

> I am assured that a much greater Number in the County, join in Sentiments with the Majority, but the Report of their running so much a Head on the Poll made many think it was unnecessary to go from Home. The Resolution to hold a Poll was taken so suddenly, and the Weather at the Time so very bad, occasioned much Difficulty in getting the proper Notice throughout the County. This Considered, with the prevailing Temper of the Times, sets the spirited Conduct of our People in a Light that does them great Honor.[92]

Cadwallader Colden's glee was short-lived. As Governor Tryon mentioned later, the people of Queens "did not submit until their Leaders were carried off Prisoners to Congress." That dragnet, in January 1776, netted most of the leaders; David Colden managed to escape from the clutches of the rebels. He hid out until the summer of 1776 when he obtained "Refuge" with British forces that had seized Staten Island.[93]

David's father had not been arrested. He had never been asked to sign the Continental Association so he was not on the rebels' list of those who refused. When Cadwallader Colden celebrated his 88th birthday on February 7,

1776, he had to have missed his youngest child, but David's wife, Ann, and their family remained at Spring Hill.[94]

The early months of 1776 did not bode well for those who remained loyal to Great Britain. Watching this deterioration, the Izards, during March, from Bath begged Elizabeth to "remove from so turbulent a scene as America presents" and stay with them for some years. Elizabeth would not desert her family or her elderly father.[95]

Other New Yorkers had to make similar decisions. Before William Smith left the city for his country estate, he urged Chief Justice Daniel Horsmanden to also "retire from the Metropolis as an obnoxious Crown Officer." Horsmanden displayed "an anxious, helpless Despondency," Smith thought. The judge's demeanor was not surprising because King Sears had threatened to hang him. In March 1776 Horsmanden, who survived until 1778, told Smith that he "wished for the arrival of General Washington, and seemed to derive some Hope from his Generosity as a Gentleman."[96]

By the end of June and early July 1776, even Cad at Coldengham saw his personal situation fall apart. A nearby rebel committee arrested "this scoundrel" because his own local committee was either under "some undue Influence, or destitute of spirit." The rebels knew very well who his father was. In August Cad was forced to beg the New York Convention for his freedom:

> One great reason that I am so solicitous to have my discharge is, that I want to be at liberty to go to see my honoured ancient father once more, who I am sure must be overwhelmed with grief and anxiety, at this critical moment, for the fate of a country in which he must soon leave all that is dear to him.[97]

The rebels, however, were not going to release a colonel of the Ulster militia. Cad remained a prisoner for years.[98]

Much had happened elsewhere. After finally abandoning Boston in March 1776, the first elements of a huge British expedition seized Staten Island on July 2. Eight days later, it was announced to the rebel army in New York City that the thirteen colonies had declared their independence by rejecting the authority of the British monarch and Parliament. The soldiers "totally demolished immediately" the statue of George III that Colden had unveiled years before. General Washington strongly disapproved of this act of violence. Even "the meanest planters," Governor Tryon complained, were "persecuted and tyrannized over."[99]

Still, women could travel around southern New York with comparative ease. About mid-August Elizabeth and her daughters came to Spring Hill to visit the family patriarch. What they found had to be distressing. Cadwallader Colden was seriously ill. Details are lacking. He could have suffered a stroke. Given his age, the chaos about him could well have brought one on. An obituary, not written by the family, published in the *New York Mercury* during October 1776 stressed that his mind was still clear enough to follow what was happening. This statement suggests that his mind surviving in his circumstances was unusual; this could hint at a stroke. Elizabeth, however, said that her father had an "illness" which appears to point to Colden's lung ailment which Tryon had described—and which Colden had to have told him about.[100]

Whatever the cause, Cadwallader Colden lingered on. Elizabeth, who was one of her father's executors, decided to take some precautions. A British attack on Long Island was a certainty and looting could be expected. She buried his cash on hand, about £1,000 New York money plus various warrants from the colonial treasury, bonds, and records of loans. (Because there were no banks, wealthy men lent their money; some seventy-three individuals had yet unpaid loans from Colden.) All told, his liquid assets came to almost £19,500. Some of the paper currency was damaged from its time underground.[101]

Due to Cadwallader Colden's condition "and the unhappy situation of affairs" Elizabeth and her daughters were "obliged ... to prolong" their stay at Spring Hill "beyond the time she intended," and then they could not leave it. The DeLancey women would not see their Westchester home for years. This long sojourn at Spring Hill saved them from the horrors that soon engulfed southern Westchester.[102]

The dreaded British invasion of Long Island finally started on August 22, 1776. Although the king's army approached the western boundary of Queens, they moved through the Jamaica Pass, then swept back to the westernmost part of the island, sparing Spring Hill and Flushing from the fate of a battlefield. Those areas the army entered suffered at the hands of Britain's German mercenaries, the Hessians. According to one British observer, "It is impossible to express the Devastations which the Hessians have made upon the Houses and Country Seats of some of the Rebels," but the Hessians also inflicted "several Depredations ... upon the Friends of Government."[103]

Nonetheless, the Battle of Brooklyn was a tremendous victory for British arms. The rebel soldiers fled Long Island at the end of August. Surveying the result, a British general predicted: "if a good Bleeding can bring those Bible-faced Yankees to their Senses, the Fever of Independence should soon abate."[104]

Another victory was in store for the British, who landed on September 15 upon the island of Manhattan as the remnants of the rebel army ran. New York City was entirely empty except for a handful of Anglicans. According to the obituary in the *Mercury*, Colden "had the Satisfaction, before his Departure, to know, that the Arms of his Prince had prevailed, in a signal instance over the Forces of the Rebels."[105]

Perhaps of more importance to the old man, who was slowly slipping away, was that the British victory on Long Island enabled his son David to return to his side. That meant that David and his family (including Cadwallader D. Colden, then a young boy) and Elizabeth and her unmarried daughters were with him when he died. As an account probably from Colden family tradition had it, on September 20, 1776—sometime before midnight—Cadwallader Colden "complained neither of pain of body, nor anguish of mind, except on account of the political troubles . . . which he then saw overwhelming the country. He retained his senses till the last moment, and expired without a groan" at the age of 88 years. Ultimately, Colden died of old age or, as the *Mercury* obituary had it, "He died full of Days."[106]

Colden had specified in his will "that my Body be interred in a private manner, with as little expense as with Common Decency may be." He was buried at Spring Hill.[107]

Barely a few hours after Colden's death, a terrible fire—suspected to be arson perpetrated by New Englanders—ravaged much of New York City. This added destruction delayed Governor Tryon from writing to London about Cadwallader Colden's fate. On September 24 the governor passed on the news: "Lieut. Governor Colden departed this life at Flushing. This makes a Vacancy in the Council." This terse announcement seems inadequate as a final mention of an individual of whom it was said, he "probably contributed more than any other single man to the development of early New York."[108]

NOTES

1. Abercrombie to CC, May 2, 1775, Samuel A. Green, ed., "The Battle of Lexington," Massachusetts Historical Society, *Proceedings*, 2nd ser., 11 (1896–1897): 306.

2. Gage to Dartmouth, August 27, September 2, October 30, 1774, Thomas Gage, *The Correspondence of General Thomas Gage with the Secretaries of State, 1763–1775*, ed. Clarence E. Carter (New Haven, CT: Yale University Press, 1931–1933), vol. 1, 368, 370–71, 382; CC to Dartmouth, November 2, 1774, *CLB*, vol. 2, 369–71; Julie M. Flavell, *When London Was Capital of America* (New Haven, CT: Yale University Press, 2010), 235; I. N. Phelps Stokes, *The Iconography of Manhattan Island, 1498–1909* (New York: R. H. Dodd, 1915–1928), vol. 4, 868.

3. John Montresor, *The Montresor Journals*, ed. G. D. Scull, New York Historical Society, *Collections* 14 (1881): 136; Henry White to Tryon, December 7, 1774, Historical Manuscripts Commission, Great Britain, *The Manuscripts of the Earl of Dartmouth* (London: H. M. S. O., 1887–1896), vol. 2, 237; Ralph Izard to Watts, December 12, 1775, Ralph Izard, *Correspondence of Mr. Ralph Izard, of South Carolina, From the year 1774 to 1804; with a Short Memoir*, ed. Anne Izard Deas (New York: C. S. Francis, 1844), vol. 1, 170–71.

4. William Lee to Richard Henry Lee, February 25, 1775, in Lee, *Letters of William Lee, 1766–1783*, ed. Worthington Chauncey Ford (Brooklyn, NY: Historical Printing Club, 1891; repr. 3 vols. in 1, New York: Burt Franklin Research, 1968), vol. 1, 128; W. Lee to John Hancock, January 22, 1779 [*sic* 1776], John Hancock and Torry Hancock Papers, William R. Perkins Library, Manuscript Dept., Duke University, Durham, NC.

5. Dartmouth to CC, September 7, 1774, *NYCD*, vol. 8, 487; Tryon to CC, March 2, 3, April 15, 1775, *CP*, vol. 7, 267–68, 272, 283; Arthur Lee to Izard, February 19, 1775, Izard, *Correspondence of Mr. Ralph Izard*, vol. 1, 49; Tryon to Dartmouth, January 19, 1775, Historical Manuscripts Commission, Great Britain, *Manuscripts of the Earl of Dartmouth*, vol. 2, 261.

6. Dartmouth to CC, September 7, 1774, *NYCD*, vol. 8, 487; CC to Dartmouth, January 4, 1775, *CLB*, vol. 2, 377–79; *SM*, vol. 1, 206–7; B. D. Bargar, *Lord Dartmouth and the American*

Revolution (Columbia: University of South Carolina Press, 1965), 149–52; Philip Ranlet, *The New York Loyalists*, 2nd ed. (Lanham, MD: University Press of America, 2002), 48; Bruce E. Steiner, *Samuel Seabury, 1729–1796: A Study in the High Church Tradition* (Oberlin; [Athens]: Ohio University Press, 1971), 151–52.

7. CC to Dartmouth, January 4, 1775, *CLB*, vol. 2, 377–79; Ranlet, *Loyalists*, 77.

8. CC to Dartmouth, January 4, 1775, *CLB*, vol. 2, 377–79; CC to Guy Johnson, January 13, 1775, *CLB*, vol. 2, 379–80; CC to Tryon, February 1, 1775, *CLB*, vol. 2, 391; *SM*, vol. 1, 206–8; Steiner, *Samuel Seabury*, 151–52.

9. *SM*, vol. 1, 206–8.

10. *SM*, vol. 1, 206–8, 207–9; Leopold Launitz-Schürer, Jr., *Loyal Whigs and Revolutionaries: The Making of a Revolution in New York, 1765–1776* (New York: New York University Press, 1980), 131–32.

11. *SM*, vol. 1, 207–9.

12. New York Colony, *Journal of the Legislative Council of the Colony of New York, Began the 9th day of April, 1691; and ended the [3d of April, 1775]* (Albany, NY: Weed, Parsons, 1861), vol. 2, 1942–43.

13. New York Colony, *Journal of the Legislative Council*, vol. 2, 1942–43.

14. New York Colony, *Journal of the Legislative Council*, vol. 2, 1942–43.

15. Frank Moore, *Songs and Ballads of the American Revolution* (New York: D. Appleton, 1856; repr. New York: New York Times, 1969), 74–76; Louisa Susannah Wells, *The Journal of a Voyage from Charlestown, S.C., to London During the American Revolution* (New York: New York Historical Society, 1906; repr. New York: Arno Press, 1968), 41.

16. CC to Gage, January 29, 1775, *CLB*, vol. 2, 381–82; CC to Dartmouth, February 1, 1775, *CLB*, vol. 2, 382–84; Ranlet, *Loyalists*, 49.

17. "Extract of a letter from New York, to a Gentleman in Boston," January 30, 1775, Peter Force, *American Archives* (Washington, DC: M. St. Clair Clarke and Peter Force, under the authority of Acts of Congress, 1837–1853), 4th ser., vol. 1, 1203; Wells, *Journal*, 41.

18. CC to Dartmouth, January 21, February 1, 1775, *CLB*, vol. 2, 380–81, 383–84; CC to Tryon, February 1, 1775, *CLB*, vol. 2, 391–92. This Assembly also granted CC a salary which contravened imperial policy, but the happy British government allowed him and Tryon to keep it. *SM*, vol. 1, 211; Beverly McAnear, *The Income of the Colonial Governors of British North America* (New York: Pageant Press, 1967), 13–14.

19. Charles Lee to Va. Provincial Congress, n.d., Charles Lee, *The Lee Papers*, New York Historical Society, *Collections* 4 (1871): vol. 1, 172–78.

20. Samuel Graves to CC, February 25, 1775, *CP*, vol. 7, 266.

21. Gage to CC, February 26, 1775, Bancroft Coll., Colden Papers, 1722–1775, vol. 5, 133–35, NYPL.

22. "Extract of a letter from London, to a Gentleman in New York," March 4, 1775, Force, *American Archives*, 4th ser., vol. 2, 29; *New York Mercury* (Gaine), February 6, 1775; Tryon to CC, March 2, 1775, *CP*, vol. 7, 267–68; Edmund Burke to James DeLancey, March 14, 1775, in Burke, *Edmund Burke, New York Agent with his letters to the New York Assembly and intimate correspondence with Charles O'Hara, 1761–1776*, ed. Ross J. S. Hoffman (Philadelphia: American Philosophical Society, 1956), 262–63.

23. CC to Gage, February 20, April 2, 1775, *CLB*, vol. 2, 385–87, 407–9; CC to Dartmouth, March 1, April 5, 1775, *CLB*, vol. 2, 388–90, 395–98; CC to Tryon, April 5, 1775, *CLB*, vol. 2, 398–400; Bargar, *Lord Dartmouth*, 149–52; Ranlet, *Loyalists*, 49.

24. James Murray to Rockinghan, July 18, 1775, John E. Tyler, ed., "A British Whig's Report from New York on the American Situation, 1775," in *Narratives of the Revolution in New York: A Collection of Articles from the New-York Historical Society Quarterly*, New York Historical Society, *Collections* 85 (1975): 21; John Harris Cruger to Henry Cruger, Jr., July 5, 1775, Historical Manuscripts Commission, Great Britain, *Manuscripts of the Earl of Dartmouth*, vol. 2, 326–27; Ranlet, *Loyalists*, 44.

25. CC to Dartmouth, March 1, 1775, *CLB*, vol. 2, 388–90; *SM*, vol. 1, 209–10.

26. *New York Journal* (Holt), February 9, 1775, William Bell Clark and others, eds., *Naval Documents of the American Revolution* (Washington, DC: GPO, 1964–), vol. 1, 85–86, 86nl; Clark and others, *Naval Documents*, 88; James Montagu, log for *Kingsfisher*, February 8, 1775,

Clark and others, *Naval Documents*, 83; A. B., "To the Printer," *New York Journal* (Holt), February 16, 1775.

27. CC to Montagu, February 8, 1775, *CLB*, vol. 2, 384–85; *SM*, vol. 1, 209–10; Graves to Philip Stephens, March 4, 1775, Clark and others, *Naval Documents*, vol. 1, 123–24.

28. A. B., "To the Printer," *New York Journal* (Holt), February 16, 1775; *SM*, vol. 1, 210; CC to Montagu, February 9, 1775, *CLB*, vol. 2, 385. Nothing in writing states that CC told Montagu to demand a clearance; Montagu's log entries regarding the incident are very brief and silent on the matter. There was no other legal way that the *James* could be brought back. The order, given verbally, probably was conveyed by the person who brought CC's letters to Montagu, probably David, CC's secretary. Perhaps CC suspected he might be stretching his authority by targeting one ship in particular. This would explain both CC's silence and Montagu's. See Montagu's log for February 8–9, 1775, Clark and others, *Naval Documents*, vol. 1, 83, 85. In addition, this silence may have been intended to avoid serious rioting. In 1768 Boston officials seized a ship owned by John Hancock for a minor violation, causing violence. Ian R. Christie and Benjamin W. Labaree, *Empire or Independence, 1760–1776: A British-American Dialogue on the Coming of the American Revolution* (New York: Norton, 1976), 109–11.

29. *SM*, vol. 1, 210; A. B., "To the Printer," *New York Journal* (Holt), February 16, 1775; *Kemble's Journals, 1733–1789*, New York Historical Society, *Collections* 16 (1883): 41–42; CC to Dartmouth, March 1, 1775, *CLB*, vol. 2, 388–90.

30. CC to Gage, February 20, 1775, *CLB*, vol. 2, 386–87.

31. CC to Gage, February 20, 1775, *CLB*, vol. 2, 386–87; CC to Dartmouth, March 1, 1775, *CLB*, vol. 2, 388–90.

32. CC to Graves, February 20, 1775, *CLB*, vol. 2, 387–88.

33. Graves to CC, February 26, 1775, Bancroft Coll., Colden Papers, vol. 5, 139–41, NYPL; Izard to George Dempster, August 1, 1775, Izard, *Correspondence of Mr. Ralph Izard*, vol. 1, 114.

34. Stokes, *Iconography*, vol. 4, 876. For an example of such criticism of CC, see Joseph S. Tiedemann, *Reluctant Revolutionaries: New York City and the Road to Independence, 1763–1776* (Ithaca, NY: Cornell University Press, 1997), 210.

35. Murray to Rockingham, June–July 1775, Tyler, ed., "British Whig's Report," 18; Ranlet, *Loyalists*, 50.

36. Thurman to Remington and Briggs, February 18, 1775, John Thurman, Jr., "Extracts from the Letter Books of John Thurman, Junior," ed. Benjamin H. Hall, *Historical Magazine*, 2nd ser., 4 (December 1868): 291.

37. Thurman to Markland, April 6, 1776, Thurman, "Extracts," 291; Peter Vandevoort to Nathaniel Shaw, Jr., Clark and others, *Naval Documents*, vol. 1, 240; CC to Dartmouth, November 2, 1774, *CLB*, vol. 2, 369–71.

38. CC to Gage, April 13, 1775, *CLB*, vol. 2, 411–12.

39. "Extracts from Bradford's Pennsylvania Journal of April 26, 1775," New York, 1775, Microfiche, Early American Imprints, 1st ser., Evans no. 14028; James Robertson to D. Colden, May 4, 1775, Bancroft Coll., Colden Papers, vol. 5, 255–57, NYPL; Tiedemann, *Reluctant*, 224.

40. CC to Gage, February 20, 1775, *CLB*, vol. 2, 386–87; CC to Graves, February 20, 1775, *CLB*, vol. 2, 387–88; Gage to CC, February 26, 1775, Bancroft Coll., Colden Papers, vol. 5, 133–35, NYPL, and *CP*, vol. 7, 266–67.

41. CC to Dartmouth, March 1, 1775, *CLB*, vol. 2, 388–90; W. Lee to Izard, March 4, 1775, Izard, *Correspondence of Mr. Ralph Izard*, vol. 1, 54.

42. CC to Dartmouth, April 5, 1775, *CLB*, vol. 2, 396–98; CC to Tryon, April 5, 1775, *CLB*, vol. 2, 398–400; CC to Gage, April 2, 13, 1775, *CLB*, vol. 2, 407–12; *SM*, vol. 1, 215.

43. David Bennett, *A Few Lawless Vagabonds: Ethan Allen, the Republic of Vermont, and the American Revolution* (Havertown, PA: Casemate Publishers, 2014), 65–67.

44. CC to Dartmouth, April 5, 1775, *CLB*, vol. 2, 396; CC to Gage, April 13, 1775, *CLB*, vol. 2, 410–12.

45. Robertson to CC, April 21, 1775, Bancroft Coll., Colden Papers, vol. 5, 219–21, NYPL.

46. *SM*, vol. 1, 212–13; Roger J. Champagne, *Alexander McDougall and the American Revolution in New York* (Schenectady, NY: New York State American Revolution Bicentennial Commission, Union College Press, 1975), 80–81.

47. CC to Dartmouth, January 3, 1775, *CLB*, vol. 2, 376–77.

48. Tryon to Dartmouth, January 19, 1775, Historical Manuscripts Commission, Great Britain, *Manuscripts of the Earl of Dartmouth*, vol. 2, 261.

49. Dartmouth to CC, February 1, 1775, *NYCD*, vol. 8, 530–31 and *CP*, vol. 7, 261–62; Tryon to CC, [February 1775?], *CP*, vol. 7, 262–63.

50. *SM*, vol. 1, 228c; Memorial of David Colden, [1784], Colden Family Papers, box 12, no. 2, NYHS; Andrew Jackson O'Shaughnessy, *The Men Who Lost America: British Leadership, the American Revolution, and the Fate of the Empire* (New Haven, CT: Yale University Press, 2013), 68–69.

51. "Communicated by a Letter from a Worthy American Patriot in London to his Friends in this Country," March 15, 1775, New York State, *Calendar of Historical Manuscripts relating to the War of the Revolution in the Office of the Secretary of State* (Albany, NY: Weed, Parson, 1868), vol. 1, 1; Paul H. Smith and others, eds., *Letters of Delegates to Congress, 1774–1789* (Washington, DC: GPO, 1976–2000), vol. 4, 55n2.

52. CC to Dartmouth, June 1, 1774, *CLB*, vol. 2, 341.

53. Secretary Pownall to Reverend Drs. Cooper and Chandler, April 5, 1775, *NYCD*, vol. 8, 569.

54. D. Colden to Mairs, June 18, [1771], *CLB*, vol. 2, 328; Flavell, *When London Was Capital of America*, 18–19; Julie M. Flavell, "American Patriots in London and the Quest for Talks, 1774–1775," *Journal of Imperial and Commonwealth History* 20, no. 3 (1992): 351, 354.

55. Julie M. Flavell, "Lord North's Conciliatory Proposal and the Patriots in London," *English Historical Review* 107, no. 423 (1992): 309, 313–16, 320; Flavell, "American Patriots in London," 351; O'Shaughnessy, *Men Who Lost*, 58.

56. There are many accounts of the fighting that started the War of Independence. See, for example, Christie and Labaree, *Empire*, 242–46.

57. D. Colden to William Eden, October 23, 1778, Bancroft Coll., Colden Papers, vol. 5, 223, NYPL; Ranlet, *Loyalists*, 52.

58. Stokes, *Iconography*, vol. 4, 882.

59. Izard to Dempster, June 25, 1775, Izard, *Correspondence of Mr. Ralph Izard*, vol. 1, 93–94; C. Lawrence to Robert Livingston, Jr., August 31, 1775, Livingston-Redmond Papers, reel 6, microfilm, Columbia University, New York City; Ezra Stiles, *The Literary Diary of Ezra Stiles, D.D., LL.D., President of Yale College*, ed. Franklin Bowditch Dexter (New York: C. Scribner, 1901), vol. 1, 555; CC to Dartmouth, June 7, 1775, *CLB*, vol. 2, 419–26.

60. CC to Dartmouth, May 3, 1775, *CLB*, vol. 2, 402–3; Daniel Parker Coke, *The Royal Commission on the Losses and Services of American Loyalists, 1783–1785*, ed. Hugh Edward Egerton (Oxford: Printed for presentation to the members of the Roxburghe Club, [by H. Hart at the University Press], 1915), 376.

61. CC to George Vandeput, June 1, 1775, *CLB*, vol. 2, 417.

62. CC to Dartmouth, May 3, 1775, *CLB*, vol. 2, 402–3.

63. CC to Major Isaac Hamilton, May 27, 1775, *CLB*, vol. 2, 413–14; *SM*, vol. 1, 221–22; Gage to Major Isaac Hamilton, May 7, 1775, *CP*, vol. 7, 293; Hamilton to CC, May 26, 1775, *CP*, vol. 7, 297–98; "Extract of a letter to a gentleman in Philadelphia," May 10, 1775, Force, *American Archives*, 4th ser., vol. 2, 547–48.

64. CC to Hamilton, June 9, 1775, *CLB*, vol. 2, 426–27; CC to Whitehead Hicks, June 9, 1775, *CLB*, vol. 2, 427–28; Hamilton to CC, June 8, 1775, *CP*, vol. 7, 300–301; Stokes, *Iconography*, vol. 4, 892; John McKesson to George Clinton, June 7, 1775, Clark and others, *Naval Documents*, vol. 1, 628; Steven M. Baule, *Protecting the Empire's Frontier: Officers of the 18th (Royal Irish) Regiment of Foot During Its North American Service, 1767–1776* (Athens: Ohio University Press, 2014), 130–31, 156.

65. Robertson to D. Colden, May 4, 1775, *CP*, vol. 7, 290; Ranlet, *Loyalists*, 54.

66. Gage to CC, May 4, 1775, *CP*, vol. 7, 291; CC to Gage, May 31, 1775, *CLB*, vol. 2, 415–16; Ranlet, *Loyalists*, 54.

67. *SM*, vol. 1, 221–23, 227–28, 238; Gage to CC, May 16, 1775, Colden Family Papers, LC; CC to Dartmouth, May 4, 1775, *CLB*, vol. 2, 404–5; CC to Gage, May 4, 1775, *CLB*, vol. 2, 406–7; Council minute, May 1, 1775, *CP*, vol. 7, 287–89.

68. CC to Dartmouth, May 3, 1775, *CLB*, vol. 2, 402–3; CC to Carleton, May 3, 1775, *CLB*, vol. 2, 403–4; CC to Gage, May 31, 1775, *CLB*, vol. 2, 414–16; Gage to CC, April 29, 1775, *CP*, vol. 7, 287; Gage to CC, May 16, 1775, Colden Family Papers, LC; Alfred Lawrence Lorenz, *Hugh Gaine: A Colonial Printer-Editor's Odyssey to Loyalism* (Carbondale: Southern Illinois University Press, 1972), 94.

69. CC to Dartmouth, May 3, 1775, *CLB*, vol. 2, 401–3.

70. R. R. Livingston to Margaret Livingston, May 3, 1775, Livingston Family Papers, box 3, reel 1, NYPL; CC Jr. to Myles Cooper, July 15, 1775, Historical Manuscripts Commission, Great Britain, *Manuscripts of the Earl of Dartmouth*, vol. 2, 330; *SM*, vol. 1, 222–23; statement of Duane and John Jay, April 29, 1775, Force, *American Archives*, 4th ser., vol. 2, 445–46; Coke, *Royal Commission*, 116; CC to North, May 4, 1775, *CLB*, vol. 2, 405; Ranlet, *Loyalists*, 53–54, 105.

71. CC to Dartmouth, May 4, 1775, *CLB*, vol. 2, 404–5; Stokes, *Iconography*, vol. 4, 865; Carl Becker, *The History of Political Parties in the Province of New York* (Madison : University of Wisconsin Press, 1909; repr. 1960), 200.

72. CC to Vandeput, May 27, 1775, *CLB*, vol. 2, 413; *SM*, vol. 1, 223; G. Taylor, *A Voyage to North America Perform'd by G. Taylor of Sheffield in the Years 1768, and 1769* (Nottingham, UK: S. Creswell for the Author, 1771), 71; Stokes, *Iconography*, vol. 4, 885.

73. "To the Honourable Cadwallader Colden, Esq.," May 11, 1775, *New York Journal* (Holt), May 18, 1775.

74. "His Honour's answer," May 13, 1775, *New York Journal* (Holt).

75. "His Honour's answer," May 13, 1775, *New York Journal* (Holt).

76. *New York Mercury* (Gaine), May 15, 1775; Henry Onderdonk, Jr., *Documents and Letters Intended to Illustrate the Revolutionary Incidents of Queens County* (New York: Leavitt, Trow, 1846; repr. Port Washington, NY: I. J. Friedman Division, Kennikat Press, 1970), 28; Robert C. Livingston to Robert Livingston, Jr., May 31, 1775, Livingston-Redmond Papers, reel 6, microfilm, Columbia University.

77. *New York Journal* (Holt), May 18, 1775.

78. CC to Gage, May 18, 1775, *CLB*, vol. 2, 412.

79. CC to Dartmouth, June 7, 1775, *CLB*, vol. 2, 419–26; Graves to Stephens, June 16, 1775, Clark and others, *Naval Documents*, vol. 1, 691; Graves to Vandeput, September 10, 1775, Great Britain, *Documents of the American Revolution, Colonial Office Series, 1770–1783*, ed. K. G. Davies (Shannon, Ireland: Irish University Press, 1972–1981), vol. 11, 104; Izard to William O'Brien, October 16, 1775, Izard, *Correspondence of Mr. Ralph Izard*, vol. 1, 132; Ranlet, *Loyalists*, 54–55.

80. Vandeput to CC, May 26, 1775, *CP*, vol. 7, 298; CC to Vandeput, May 27, 1775, *CLB*, vol. 2, 413.

81. CC to Vandeput, June 1, 1775, *CLB*, vol. 2, 417; CC to Dartmouth, June 7, 1775, *CLB*, vol. 2, 419–26; *SM*, vol. 1, 228d–230.

82. Dartmouth to Gage, April 15, 1775, Gage, *Correspondence of General Thomas Gage*, vol. 2, 194; Gage to Dartmouth, June 12, 1775, Gage, *Correspondence of General Thomas Gage*, vol. 1, 402; Tiedemann, *Reluctant*, 216.

83. CC to Dartmouth, July 3, 1775, *NYCD*, vol. 8, 588–89; Tryon to Dartmouth, July 4, 1775, *NYCD*, vol. 8, 589–90; *SM*, vol. 1, 228d–231, 233.

84. Tryon to Dartmouth, November 11, 1775, *NYCD*, vol. 8, 643; Richard Henry Lee to Charles Lee, April 1, 1776, in Lee, *Lee Papers*, vol. 1, 367–68; Washington to Hancock, April 15, 1776, Clark and others, *Naval Documents*, vol. 4, 836; Stokes, *Iconography*, vol. 4, 915; Ranlet, *Loyalists*, 55.

85. Izard to CC, September 10, 1775, Izard, *Correspondence of Mr. Ralph Izard*, vol. 1, 125–28.

86. Izard, *Correspondence of Mr. Ralph Izard*, vol. 1, 126–28.

87. Major William Williams to Committee of Safety, September 25, 1775, Force, *American Archives*, ser. 4, vol. 3, 912; Joseph S. Tiedemann, "Communities in the Midst of the American

Revolution: Queens County, New York, 1774–1775," *Journal of Social History* 18, no. 1 (1984): 58; Ranlet, *Loyalists*, 63.

88. Ranlet, *Loyalists*, 61–62.

89. Tryon to Dartmouth, December 6, 1775, *NYCD*, vol. 8, 645–46; Williams to Committee of Safety, September 25, 1775, Force, *American Archives*, 4th ser., vol. 3, 912; Ranlet, *Loyalists*, 63.

90. Alexander Fraser, ed., *United Empire Loyalists: Enquiry Into the Losses and Services in Consequence of their Loyalty, Evidence in the Canadian Claims* (Toronto: Legislative Assembly of Ontario, L. K. Camero, 1905), vol. 2, 855, 860; Tryon for David Colden, June 29, 1784, AO13/64/p. 70, reel 72, NYPL; CC to Tryon, November 12, 1775, CO5/1107/61–62, LC transcript; Ranlet, *Loyalists*, 62.

91. CC to Tryon, November 12, 1775, CO5/1107/61–62, LC transcript.

92. Joseph Tiedemann has suggested that Queens County was actually neutral. CC, however, gave persuasive reasons why the loyalist turnout was not even higher. Modern day turnouts are also lowered by bad weather and confidence that a question in dispute is going to be settled by a huge majority. Given the long distance men had to travel to vote at the time, such reasons had even more relevance, as did the sudden change in plan. Tiedemann's use of an address of October 21, 1776 from Queens to suggest that loyalists were overwhelmed by neutral nonsigners is misguided. Every man had to swear an oath of allegiance to stay; signing an address was not part of the process. Nonetheless, the number of signers is impressive anyway. If Queens' voting against the New York Congress does not make it a loyal county, then there were no loyalists in America. William Howe to George Germain, September 3, 1776, Great Britain, *Documents of the American Revolution*, ed. Davies, vol. 12, 217–18; Tiedemann, "Communities," 58, 60–61.

93. Tryon to D. Colden, June 29, 1784, AO13/64/70, reel 72, NYPL; Fraser, ed., *United Empire Loyalists*, vol. 2, 855; Edwin G. Burrows and Mike Wallace, *Gotham: A History of New York City to 1898* (Oxford: Oxford University Press, 1999), 227.

94. Edwin R. Purple, "Notes, Biographical and Genealogical, of the Colden Family, and of Some of Its Collateral Branches in America," *New York Genealogical and Biographical Record* 4 (1873): 178.

95. Alice Izard to E. DeLancey, March 23, 1776, DeLancey Papers, 49.48.69, Museum of the City of New York.

96. *SM*, vol. 2, 41; *New York Mercury* (Gaine), September 28, 1778.

97. Robert Boyd, Jr. to General George Clinton, July 3, 1776, George Clinton, *Public Papers of George Clinton*, ed. Hugh Hastings (New York and Albany: State of New York, 1899–1914), vol. 1, 246; CC Jr. to Nathaniel Woodhull, August 22, 1776, New York State, *Journals of the Provincial Congress, . . . Committee of Safety, and Council of Safety of the State of New York* (Albany, NY: Weed, Parsons, 1842), vol. 2, 279–80; Michael Diaz, "'Can you on such principles think of quitting a Country?': Family, Faith, Law, Property, and the Loyalists of the Hudson Valley During the American Revolution," *Hudson River Valley Review* 28, no. 1 (Autumn 2011): 7.

98. Tryon's commission to CC Jr., March 18, 1774, Colden Family Papers, LC; Joseph Bragdon, "Cadwallader Colden, Second: An Ulster County Tory," *New York History* 14, no. 4 (1933): 417.

99. Inglis to Hind, October 31, 1776, John Wolfe Lydekker, *The Life and Letters of Charles Inglis* (London: Church Historical Society, 1936), 165; Tryon to Germain, August 14, 1776, *NYCD*, vol. 8, 684; A. James Wall, "The Statues of King George III and the Honorable William Pitt Erected in New York City, 1770," *New York Historical Society Quarterly Bulletin* 4, no. 2 (1920): 50; Thomas J. Fleming, *1776: Year of Illusions* (New York: Norton, 1975), 344–45; Ranlet, *Loyalists*, 64–65.

100. Mrs. E. DeLancey to Washington, October 1, 1776, Force, *American Archives*, 5th ser., vol. 2, 894; *New York Mercury* (Gaine), October 14, 1776. Gaine was not then printing his paper which was a propaganda sheet put out by Ambrose Serle, secretary to Admiral Richard Howe, the British naval commander. Serle guessed wrongly that CC was in his 90s, and other newspapers reprinted the false information. See *Connecticut Journal*, November 13, 1776. If the family had written the piece, CC's age would have been given as 89; CC gave his age based

on the Julian year 1687. That is what William Allen, *An American Biographical and Historical Dictionary* (Cambridge, MA: William Hilliard, 1809), 200, does. Lorenz, *Hugh Gaine*, 108.

101. Fraser, ed., *United Empire Loyalists*, vol. 2, 858; Gordon S. Wood, *The Radicalism of the American Revolution* (New York: A. A. Knopf, 1992), 69. The accounts of bonds, notes, and cash are in CPU, reel 2, NYHS.

102. E. DeLancey to Washington, October 1, 1776, Force, *American Archives*, 5th ser., vol. 2, 894; Howe to Washington, October 4, 1776, George Washington, *The Papers of George Washington, Revolutionary War Series, August–October 1776*, ed. Philander D. Chase (Charlottesville: University Press of Virginia, 1994), vol. 6, 468, 469n1; Washington to Howe, October 6, 1776, Washington, *Papers, Revolutionary War Series*, vol. 6, 489; Ranlet, *Loyalists*, 134–35.

103. Edward H. Tatum, Jr., ed., *The American Journal of Ambrose Serle, Secretary to Lord Howe, 1776–1778* (San Marino, CA: Huntington Library, 1940; repr. New York: New York Times, Arno Press, 1969), 77, 86–87.

104. James Grant to Richard Rigby, September 2, 1776, in Alastair Macpherson Grant, *General James Grant of Ballindalloch, 1720–1806* (London: A. M. Grant, 1930), 85–86.

105. Inglis to Hind, October 31, 1776, Lydekker, *Life and Letters of Charles Inglis*, 167; *New York Mercury* (Gaine), October 14, 1776.

106. "Copy of an Account of Cash," September 23, 1776, CPU, reel 2, NYHS; [D. Colden to New York legislators], January 15, 1784, Colden Family Papers, box 11, NYHS; Allen, *American Biographical and Historical Dictionary*, 200; *New York Mercury* (Gaine), October 14, 1776; Timothy Alden, *A Collection of American Epitaphs and Inscriptions with Occasional Notes* (New York: [S. Marks, Printer], 1814), vol. 5, 268–75; Purple, "Notes," 167; A. James Wall, "Cadwallader Colden and His Homestead at Spring Hill, Flushing, Long Island," *New York Historical Society Quarterly* 8, no. 1 (1924): 16. See also the list of dates in Colden Family Papers, box 11, NYHS. Allen's stated death date for CC, September 28, is a typographical error.

107. New York City, *Abstracts of Wills on File in the Surrogate's Office, City of New York*, New York Historical Society, *Collections* 33 (1900): 56–57. In 1780 a young woman related to the marquess of Lothian was buried at Spring Hill, a continuation of the links between the two families. The account is confused as the Coldens did not have a burial vault there and the mansion's name is incorrect. *Royal Gazette* (Rivington), January 15, 1780; Wall, "Cadwallader Colden and His Homestead at Spring Hill," 14.

108. Tryon to Germain, September 24, 1776, *NYCD*, vol. 8, 685; Ranlet, *Loyalists*, 68; Arthur E. Sutherland, review of *John Millar of Glasgow*, by William C. Lehmann, *Harvard Law Review* 74, no. 7 (May 1961): 1482.

Afterword

Cadwallader Colden had survived only long enough to see the beginning salvos of a long war. By the time the conflict ended, New York had changed greatly in some ways that he would have approved. Although New York remained infested with lawyers, the time of the great manor lords had ended. Most of their great holdings would, eventually, come into the hands of smaller farmers as Colden had wanted. Regarding the Iroquois, however, the independent state of New York took a path much contrary to his hopes. In 1765 Colden, concerned that the Iroquois had gained too much power over other tribes, sought "some method . . . to check their ambition." Years after Colden's demise, the state's new rulers forced the Iroquois off much of their land—not a method Colden would have approved of. The land grab even affected the Iroquois who had backed the rebel cause.[1]

Nor did the change of government in New York win the approval of some of Colden's acquaintances. John Watts stayed in England and never returned to New York. William Smith Jr. departed his birthplace, finally settling in Canada. In 1785 a mutual friend brought up Smith with his old Triumvirate partner William Livingston, the governor of New Jersey. "I spent some time Lately with your Old friend Governor L[ivingston]," Smith was told. "He never mentioned your name tho I gave many openings." In contrast to Watts and Smith, Colden's surviving children wanted to try to stay in republican New York.[2]

Elizabeth and her daughters had been marooned at Spring Hill, unable to retrieve anything from Westchester, and suffered heavy losses in the fire of 1776. Anarchy soon descended upon Westchester, dominated by "lawless Banditti." By 1778 Elizabeth had been able to move her furniture to British-occupied territory. Only her loyalist sons in the British military used her estate during the war.[3]

In 1783, after a peace treaty had been signed, Elizabeth and a daughter returned to her Westchester home despite its being "a most horrid place to be in at present." They were protected by "some of the American Army." It helped, of course, that when her son-in-law Ralph Izard had come back from Europe, he had become a congressman. The presence of the Izards had been "a most fortunate Circumstance on more accounts than one."[4]

Izard could do nothing to help Elizabeth's loyalist sons. When one of them had been reluctant to leave Westchester, he received "a severe whipping." Her most infamous son, James DeLancey, the colonel of a notorious loyalist unit, "DeLancey's Cowboys," had been attainted by the rebels. With no hope of salvaging his property, James sailed away to Britain. His mother "parted with him, never expecting to see him again." She was right.[5]

In the midst of such dislocation, Elizabeth became ill. David Colden wrote to her: "It is not surprising my dear Sister that the Trials you have encountered in some months past, should have had a bad Effect on your Health." When her youngest brother left for England, Elizabeth felt "a painfull sensation" because of his need to go to the mother country. Apparently, Elizabeth died in 1784.[6]

Due to the British defeat, David Colden faced an even more perilous fate than his sister. In 1776, after Queens had been regained from the rebels, David Colden took a prominent step demonstrating his loyalty. He presented an address to William Tryon, signed by 1,293 Queens residents, looking "forward to the time, when the disobedient shall return to their duty." The loyalists sought "the King's most gracious protection, torn from us by the hand of violence" and that their loyal "county may be declared at the King's peace."[7]

Soon, David began working with Judge George D. Ludlow in the "Police on the Long Island." The judge later wrote that David's service in the police gave "general satisfaction in consequence of his upright and steady conduct" and had not "left an enemy there." Overall, Ludlow summed up, "his exertions through the war have been of great service . . . in bringing forward the resources of the Island as in preserving the Peace and determining controversies."[8]

Valuable though his police work may have been, it did not pay very well. His office of surveyor-general brought in even less. He redeemed some of his father's pay warrants, but was still not doing well financially. In 1780 David offered two adult slaves for sale, a wise investment for any prospective buyer, he insisted, as "neither [is] in the least infatuated with a desire of obtaining freedom by flight, which so unhappily reigns throughout the generality of slaves at present."[9]

The rebel government of New York, seeking revenue, in 1779 confiscated the property of prominent loyalists. As Cad Colden reminisced later, "My father's dying before the confiscation law took place was rather fortunate for his family, otherwise all would have gone." But David Colden had been "intimately . . . connected with him, and shared in his public character." Unable to seek vengeance upon the dead lieutenant governor of New York, Cad remarked, "our rulers fell upon poor David, and banished him from the country." While wealthy merchants might have held cash, movable goods, or ships—easily removed from rebel territory—David noted in 1783 "that it has not been in my power to secure any Part of my Estate." He had invested heavily in land and had received Spring Hill from his father in 1770. Practically everything David possessed was vulnerable to seizure: "My Loss in this public Cause is great; it is my All."[10]

David had hoped to stay in New York at Spring Hill. If the rebels wanted to execute him, then so be it. The peace treaty between Great Britain and the United States had specified that loyalists such as David Colden could stay and keep their property. The state of New York ignored the treaty.[11]

Colden scraped everything of value from his property that he could, but he had to borrow heavily "for the Support of a large Family." By October 1783 he wrote: "I have not now any Thing in Store to make Provisions for them or myself." If he could not get the attainder revoked, he had no choice but to seek compensation for his confiscated property.[12]

For awhile, David's friends had convinced him that staying in New York, risking "Death as a Felon," was not wise. Then he resolved, once again, to stay. On November 19, 1783 he appealed to New York's governor George Clinton to defend his conduct and asked for his "Protection." It was not forthcoming. Nor was there ever an answer to that letter and a second one. In late November 1783 David, deciding not to risk his safety, left for New Jersey before the new rulers of southern New York arrived.[13]

Within the safe confines of New Jersey, a state that did not list David Colden among its enemies, he learned that James Duane had returned to New York. Seeing an opportunity, David wrote a "friendly" and "civil Letter" to Duane delivered by David's son, who "was promised an Answer" which never came. Soon, David learned that his old friend "thought I had acted the Part of a Man drunk with Zeal." Duane refused to put anything in writing complimentary to the attainted loyalist. An appeal to the New York legislature, claiming the protection of the peace treaty, had no impact either. It was small comfort that David's new neighbors in New Jersey did not hate him. "We meet with civility from every Body and attention from some."[14]

Finally, David realized the time had come to seek help across the Atlantic. Taking young Cadwallader D. Colden with him, David had "a favourable passage of 21 Days." On June 28, 1784 he alerted his sister to his having borne "the Sea Life remarkably well (better than Cad)." Arriving at Falmouth, they journeyed east through Cornwall and Devonshire and were shocked at the poverty they saw about them—even in communities represented in Parliament. At an impressive castle in Exeter, the two Americans ran into other New Yorkers, Roger Morris and members of the Bayard family. "Its pleasant to meet any Body one knows in a strange Land," David noted.[15]

After about four days the Coldens reached London. Word spread quickly about their arrival among the loyalist refugees and, David remarked, "in less than two Hours I had a Company of my American Friends around me." Elizabeth's son, James DeLancey, John Watts, and Captain Archibald Kennedy showed up, while Judge Ludlow lived just down the street. The next day, Cadwallader Colden's old enemy, Oliver DeLancey, visited and, David informed Elizabeth, "I assure you no one has expressed a more warm concern for me, and immediately carried me in his Coach to visit Govr. Tryon and Sir Henry Clinton." DeLancey knew about David's infirmities and that renting a coach strained his reduced finances.[16]

And so did General James Robertson who visited David on June 28 and that very day "carried me [in his coach] to visit on Lord Amherst." An old friend of the family, Amherst was away but, in a letter, assured Colden that he would "do all he can to promote his wishes" regarding compensation. These days in London were happy ones for David. As he observed to Elizabeth on June 28, he "had a run of many more of my old Friends and Acquaintances, than I could now have in New York." Of course, no one knew that David Colden would be dead in twelve days.[17]

Ignorant of the future, David's son did some sightseeing with Judge Ludlow and others, but David could not join them as he had "to go about in a Coach (both because I have not . . . breath to walk, and if I had, would never find my Way)" in the strange city. He reminded his wife to sell "old Iron" at Spring Hill to pay debts, but not the furniture as such high quality items were unavailable in Nova Scotia where he expected his family to find refuge.[18]

Seeing the great buildings of the imperial capital was not the reason the Coldens had traveled so far. Compensation for Colden property had to be obtained. David submitted a memorial to start the process and solicited testimonials from friends in Britain. Both General Guy Carleton and Andrew Elliot, who had been New York's lieutenant governor, willingly backed David. William Tryon testified to his loyalty and "his deplorable Situation." Oliver DeLancey said of David: "No Man deserves a higher testimonial for his probity and there is no one whose fate is more generally lamented." James Robertson, a former governor of New York, noted: "His Merit and distresses lead me to Judge him an object worthy of the Attention and bounty of Government."[19]

David Colden did not live to see the fate of his application. Despite his apparent good health on his Atlantic voyage, the trip, he revealed to his sister, "laid the foundation of a Cold that is still very troublesome to me, having much increased my asthmatic Complaints." To his wife, David explained that he was troubled with a "load of Phlegm" that "oppressed" him, but believed the phlegm "will now soon be brought up, and then I shall be quite well." Not realizing the seriousness of the problem, he died on July 10, 1784. Judge Ludlow remarked: "I little expected when Mr. Colden joined us ... a few weeks since ... that the thread of his life as well as misfortunes would be so suddenly and fatally cut." Ludlow, who became New Brunswick's chief justice, thought that David's "Misfortunes hastened his Death." At the funeral, aside from young Cadwallader David, David Colden's nephew James DeLancey was the only relative present.[20]

On July 7, 1784 David's brother Cad wrote him a letter that he never saw. Having just visited David's family at Spring Hill, he reported that everyone was healthy and in better "Spirits than I had reason to expect." Even "the Neighbors about them are very kind." Everything was so quiet at Spring Hill that the "Second family in the house"—the slaves—could not be detected. However, the scene there changed quickly. The disastrous news of David's death and the seizure and sale of Spring Hill were hard for Ann Colden, overwhelmed by the difficulties of her time, to take. "What is to become of this poor Man's Family," a friend of David's wrote, "whose all was Sacrificed for his Attachment to the British Government?" He added, "It is as Helpless a Family as You can conceive." In New Brunswick, Chief Justice Ludlow declared: "The situation of that unfortunate family is a heavy weight on my mind."[21]

Ann Colden had seen Cadwallader Colden's confiscated mansion "as her own ... where She Once thought to find a Refuge in any misfortune." Now homeless, Ann and her daughters journeyed to Coldengham where Cad took them in. Spring Hill became the property of William Cornwell, a "yeoman," for £1,800. (The Cornwells had other property in Flushing at that time but sold that and Spring Hill within a few years.)[22]

The distraught Mrs. Colden sought mercy from the New York legislature, a daunting task, by writing "a very pathetic Petition" to the legislators. She regretted that her husband "should have incurred the displeasure of his country" and had "the Pleasing hope that the Virtues of the Man will plead in every human Breast for Errors not of the Heart but of Opinion only." She wanted "Dower," payment for a widow's financial interest in her husband's estate. She, after all, had not been attainted. The petition was not only signed by Coldens but also "by all the Most Respectable Inhabitants" of Flushing, "Particularly the Noted Whigs." That fact did not matter—the legislators rejected the petition at once.[23]

Meanwhile, Cadwallader David, a young teenager, had been stranded in England bereft of his father. Alice Christy Colden, the boy's sister, feared for him: "My brother ... will call for my tenderest concern. Dear Unfortunate Boy, what must be his situation. Alone in a strange Country without a Relation and (had not the good Judge Ludlow taken him) without a Friend."[24]

Luckily, Chief Justice Ludlow had not yet departed London to assume his duties in New Brunswick. Young Cadwallader D. Colden's prospects were so poor, Ludlow thought, that the only alternative for him was joining the British army. Before leaving England, the judge arranged for the boy to stay with a Colonel Farrington, a poor choice for a guardian. Ludlow had not been able to leave much cash for Cad's upkeep and the chief justice learned later that "Col. Farrington was rather tired of keeping him, or of contributing to his support and gave him leave or rather wished [Cad] to go."[25]

To Ludlow's surprise, Cadwallader David Colden departed for New York where he planned to study law. The justice learned, as he wrote to a returned loyalist, Peter Van Schaack, that "Caddy's return . . . was by your, and all his friends' advice." By going back to the United States, Ludlow feared that the boy had endangered any chance for compensation for his father's losses. A claimant had to live in British territory. At least the chief justice found some good news in another tragedy for the Colden family. The boy's mother, Ann Colden, had died. Her "obstinate adherence" to personal "independence" and her rejection of charity would "have ruined them all." "Now their friends can step in for their benefit."[26]

Because of the urgent need for Cadwallader David to reside in British territory for compensation, Ludlow "sent for young Colden to be brought up in the Law under my Eye." Legally "binding him a Clerk to a Lawyer" in a British colony convinced those responsible for compensation funds that Ludlow was right about the Colden family wishing to remain British. Cad and his sisters, following Ludlow's advice, came to New Brunswick and he became their guardian. Ludlow assured the compensation officials "that the young man himself has no thoughts of returning."[27]

In 1787 compensation, finally, was granted to the young Coldens. Their father had estimated his loss to be £10,282. His claim was reduced to £2,720, of which £2,100 was for Spring Hill and its associated land. With all of David's children minors, the money went to Ludlow. When the young people received the money, Cadwallader David and, apparently, all of his sisters returned home—to New York.[28]

Cadwallader D. Colden prospered in New York as the first full-time lawyer in the history of the Colden family. When hatred of loyalists began to subside, the heirs of David Colden began to triumph in New York. By April 1787 all of their father's unsold property was returned to them. Although the Coldens in 1796 sued in an attempt to regain Spring Hill, they were unsuccessful. In addition, Cadwallader David did not forget the plight of his loyalist DeLancey relatives. In 1803 he served as one DeLancey widow's lawyer in her legal struggle to secure her dower rights.[29]

David's son would rack up more firsts in the family's history. Cadwallader David was named a district attorney twice and was the first Colden elected to a state assembly and the New York state senate. He entered the halls of the

American Congress. In 1818 this son of an attainted loyalist became New York City's mayor and pushed for the Erie Canal. Much of its eventual pathway had been publicized by his grandfather so many years before. Cadwallader D. Colden became a writer, producing a biography of Robert Fulton, the inventor of the steamboat, an invention which would have fascinated his grandfather.[30]

Mayor Colden also engaged in speculation as his grandfather had but not in land. Cadwallader David succumbed to two types of speculation that boomed in the nineteenth century: stock in steamboat and canal companies. He was not as cautious a speculator as his grandfather had been. After the mayor's death in 1834, an eminent New York jurist wrote of his fate: "He was a man of Genius and Vivacity and of ardent and generous feelings, and amiable disposition, but he checked and eventually destroyed his Progress to Prosperity and Fortune, by a restless love of political office and a sanguine Zeal for Stock Speculations."[31]

Cadwallader Colden Jr. became the last survivor of Lieutenant Governor Colden's children. Although Cad had, eventually, been forced to enter British-occupied New York City, his namesake son, who had married the daughter of a prominent rebel, took care of Coldengham after Cad's departure, which probably saved it from confiscation. His son's fortuitous marriage helped lessen the hatred toward Cad when the war finally ended.[32]

On July 26, 1783 Cad wrote to Governor George Clinton, reminding him of "Our long and intimate acquaintance (even from your childhood)," and announced his pleasure that "many Gentlemen who come to this City" had informed him "that upon all Occasions you make honourable mention of me." Cad delayed returning to Coldengham, but he discovered that what he had surmised about Clinton was true. The governor had concluded, during 1777, that only "hearsay" evidence existed against Cad. Though David received no mercy from the rebels, Cad did. He returned, in peace, to Coldengham, "the safest place from Madness of all kinds."[33]

There, at Coldengham, Cad watched the young republic stumble along under the Articles of Confederation. In 1783 General George Washington returned his military commission to the Congress, an act that would have astonished Cad's father, who had written in 1749 that "There is no instance that men willingly part with power."[34] Washington did just that.

In 1787 a new Constitution was drafted that created a balance among its branches. The legislative branch could not overwhelm the executive, a problem that Lieutenant Governor Colden had identified in the government of a royal colony such as New York. Washington, a man who had walked away from power, became the republic's first president.

By 1790 Cad was still not certain whether the War of Independence had been a civil war or a revolution. He hoped that it had been a revolution, but it was still too soon to know.[35]

In 1795 Cad had become convinced that he had not lived through a civil war. Clearly, George Washington was a friend of liberty. With the aid of Alexander Hamilton, Cad was able to meet President Washington. Cad, who was suffering from heart palpitations (he died in 1797), could not express everything he wanted to say to Washington in person. So on February 10, 1795 Cad wrote to him, thanking the president "for indulging me in paying my Respects at an Unusual Hour."[36]

Cad continued:

> I could not think of leaving the City Without Seeing the Man of Whom all the World Said So Much, and whose Character (even in the Worst of times) I ever held in high Veneration. This Veneration increases with the Daily Occasions given for Every True honest Hearted American to Love and Adore you. Your Love for your Country. . . . Were not More Conspicuous in Defending your Country in Time of War Then Since in Saving it from the Calamitys of War.[37]

Yet Cad had not finished:

> Pray Accept this Faint tribute of Praise from an Old Individual Who Expects Soon to leave a Numerous Offspring of Sons and Daughters, their Children and Grand Children with this Pleasing Idea, that they With grateful hearts may long Enjoy the Blessings that you have Prepared for, and are endeavouring to Secure to the Citizens of America, for which God Reward You Amen.[38]

To Cad, the war was a revolution after all. Perhaps even the shade of his father, wherever it was, came to agree.

NOTES

1. CC to Johnson, June 13, 1765, *JP*, vol. 11, 786–88; Louise B. Dunbar, "The Royal Governors in the Middle and Southern Colonies on the Eve of the Revolution: A Study in Imperial Personnel," in *The Era of the American Revolution*, ed. Richard B. Morris (New York: Columbia University Press, 1939; repr. New York: Harper & Row, 1965), 221; Philip Ranlet, "New York, Indian Policy of," in *Encyclopedia of United States Indian Policy and Law*, ed. Paul Finkelman and Tim Alan Garrison (Washington, DC: CQ Press, 2009), vol. 2, 595–98.

2. William Smith, Jr., *The Diary and Selected Papers of Chief Justice William Smith, 1784–1793*, ed. L. F. S. Upton (Toronto: Champlain Society, 1963), vol. 1, 15; Thurman to Smith, September 8, 1785, John Thurman, Jr., "Extracts from the Letter Books of John Thurman, Junior," ed. Benjamin H. Hall, *Historical Magazine*, 2nd ser., 4 (December 1868): 294. On loyalist emigration, see Philip Ranlet, "How Many American Loyalists Left the United States?" *Historian* 76, no. 2 (2014): 278–307.

3. D. Colden to Henriette Colden, September 15, 1783, David Colden, "Letter of David Colden, Loyalist, 1783," ed. E. Alfred Jones, *American Historical Review* 25, no. 1 (October 1919): 85; E. DeLancey to Washington, October 1, 1776, Peter Force, *American Archives*, 5th ser. (Washington, DC: M. St. Clair Clarke and Peter Force, under authority of Acts of Congress, 1837–1853), vol. 2, 894; Howe to Washington, October 4, 1776, George Washington, *The Papers of George Washington, Revolutionary War Series, August–October 1776*, ed. Philander D. Chase (Charlottesville: University Press of Virginia, 1994), vol. 6, 468; Washington to Howe, October 6, 1776, Washington, *Papers, Revolutionary War Series*, vol. 6, 489; Ondine

E. LeBlanc, ed., "The Journal of the 'Rebel Lady': Katharine Farnham Hay's Account of Her Trip to New York City, 1778," Massachusetts Historical Society, *Proceedings*, 3rd ser., 109 (1997): 113–14; Thomas Fleming, *1776: Year of Illusions* (New York: Norton, 1975), 308.

4. D. Colden to H. Colden, September 15, 1783, D. Colden, "Letter," ed. Jones, 85; D. Colden to E. DeLancey, September 13, 1783, Colden Family Papers, box 11, NYHS.

5. D. Colden to H. Colden, September 15, 1783, D. Colden, "Letter," ed. Jones, 84–85.

6. D. Colden to E. DeLancey, September 13, 1783, Colden Family Papers, box 11, NYHS; E. Colden to D. Colden, May 19, 1784, Colden Family Papers, box 11, NYHS.

7. D. Colden to Tryon, October 21, 1776, Henry Onderdonk, Jr., *Documents and Letters Intended to Illustrate the Revolutionary Incidents of Queens County* (New York: Leavitt, Trow, 1846; repr. Port Washington, NY: I. J. Friedman Division, Kennikat Press, 1970), 129.

8. George D. Ludlow, statement on David Colden, AO13/64/ 74, reel 72, NYPL.

9. "Account of Bonds and Notes," October 1, 1776, Colden Papers, reel 2, NYHS; Onderdonk, *Documents and Letters*, 146.

10. C. Colden to _____, April 27, 1796, Samuel W. Eager, *An Outline History of Orange County* (Newburgh, NY: S. T. Callahan, 1846–1847), 246; D. Colden to Tryon, November 18, 1783, AO13/97/337, reel 105, NYPL; D. Colden to H. Colden, September 15, 1783, D. Colden, "Letter," ed. Jones, 81–82; G. D. Ludlow statement, June 25, 1784, AO13/64/74, reel 72, NYPL; AO12/25/296–97, reel 7, NYHS.

11. D. Colden to Carleton, October 24, 1783, British Headquarters Papers, no. 9430, box 37, NYPL; D. Colden to H. Colden, September 15, 1783, D. Colden, "Letter," ed. Jones, 81–82, 86.

12. D. Colden to Carleton, October 24, 1783, British Headquarters Papers, no. 9430, box 37, NYPL.

13. D. Colden to E. DeLancey, October 13, December 28, 1783, Colden Family Papers, box 11, NYHS; [D. Colden to Clinton], November 19, 1783, Colden Family Papers, box 11, NYHS; D. Colden to _____, January 15, 1784, Colden Family Papers, box 11, NYHS.

14. D. Colden to E. DeLancey, December 28, 1783, Colden Family Papers, box 11, NYHS; [D. Colden to New York legislature], January 15, 1784, Colden Family Papers, box 11, NYHS; D. Colden to Anne DeLancey, January 20, 1784, Colden Family Papers, box 11, NYHS.

15. D. Colden to E. DeLancey, June 28, 1784, Colden Family Papers, box 11, NYHS.

16. D. Colden to E. DeLancey, June 28, 1784, Colden Family Papers, box 11, NYHS.

17. D. Colden to E. DeLancey, June 28, 1784, Colden Family Papers, box 11, NYHS; Amherst to D. Colden, July 8, 1784, Colden Family Papers, box 11, NYHS.

18. D. Colden to Nancy [Ann Colden], June 27, 1784, Misc. Personal Name Files, box 24, NYPL.

19. Tryon, statement, March 22, 1784, AO13/97/337, reel 105, NYPL; Memorial of David Colden, [1784], Colden Family Papers, box 12, NYHS; Tryon, statement, June 29, 1784, AO13/64/70, reel 72, NYPL; Oliver DeLancey, statement, June 25, 1784, AO13/64/73, NYPL; Robertson, statement, June 28, 1784, AO13/64/75A, reel 72, NYPL.

20. D. Colden to E. DeLancey, June 28, 1784, Colden Family Papers, box 11, NYHS; G. D. Ludlow to E. DeLancey, July 15, 1784, Colden Family Papers, box 11, NYHS; Cadwallader D. Colden, "My Father's Burial," Colden Family Papers, box 11, NYHS; D. Colden to Nancy [Ann Colden], June 27, 1784, Misc. Personal Name Files, NYPL; Schedule of the Landed Property of the late David Colden, Esq., AO12/25/296, reel 7, NYHS; Lorenzo Sabine, *Biographical Sketches of Loyalists of the American Revolution with an Historical Essay*, 2nd ed. (Boston: Little, Brown, 1864; repr. 2 vols., 2nd ed., Baltimore: Genealogical Publishing, 1979), vol. 1, 329; Peter Wilson Coldham, *American Loyalist Claims Abstracted from the Public Record Office*, ed. Sally Lou Mick Haight (Washington, DC: National Genealogical Society, 1980), vol. 1, 95–97.

21. CC Jr. to D. Colden, July 7, 1784, Colden Family Papers, box 11, NYHS; John Watts, Jr. to Peter Van Schaack, December 8, 1784, Peter Van Schaack Papers, LC; G. D. Ludlow to Van Schaack, January 10, 1785, Peter Van Schaack Papers, LC. The slaves' fate is not clear. Presumably, they were soon sold by their now poverty-stricken mistress.

22. Ann Colden to New York legislature, November 9, 1784, Peter Van Schaack Papers, LC; Henry Onderdonk, Jr., comp., "Flushing-Tax List 1784," *Long Island Historical Society*

Quarterly 2, no. 3 (July 1940): 81, 85; C. Colden to _____, April 27, 1796, Eager, *Outline History of Orange County*, 246; Harry B. Yoshpe, *The Disposition of Loyalist Estates in the Southern District of the State of New York* (New York: Columbia University Press, 1939), 45–46, 121, 137; Alfred R. Hoermann, *Cadwallader Colden: A Figure of the American Enlightenment* (Westport, CT: Greenwood Press, 2002), 188.

23. J. Watts, Jr. to Van Schaack, December 8, 1784, Peter Van Schaack Papers, LC; Ann Colden to New York legislature, November 9, 1784, Peter Van Schaack Papers, LC; Henry Onderdonk, Jr., *Queens County in Olden Times* (Jamaica, NY: C. Welling, 1865), 67.

24. Alice Christy Colden to Anne Delancey, [1784], Colden Family Papers, box 11, NYHS.

25. Alice Christy Colden to Anne Delancey, [1784], Colden Family Papers, box 11, NYHS; AO12/101/17, p. 203, reel 25, NYHS; Alexander Fraser, ed., *United Empire Loyalists: Enquiry Into the Losses and Services in Consequence of their Loyalty, Evidence in the Canadian Claims* (Toronto: Legislative Assembly of Ontario, L. K. Camero, 1905), vol. 2, 859.

26. G. D. Ludlow to Van Schaack, October 16, 1785, Peter Van Schaack Papers, LC.

27. G. D. Ludlow to Van Schaack, April 2, 1786, Peter Van Schaack Papers, LC; Schedule of the Landed Property of the late D. Colden, AO12/25/295, reel 7, NYHS; American Loyalists Collection, microfilm, vol. 29, 453, reel 9, NYPL; Fraser, ed., *United Empire Loyalists*, vol. 2, 859.

28. American Loyalists Coll., vol. 29, 451–52, reel 9, NYPL; American Loyalists Coll., vol. 11, 204–5, reel 3, NYPL; Edwin R. Purple, "Notes, Biographical and Genealogical, of the Colden Family, and of Some of Its Collateral Branches in America," *New York Genealogical and Biographical Record* 4 (1873): 178–79.

29. John Jay to Alexander Hamilton, March 4, 1796, Alexander Hamilton, *The Papers of Alexander Hamilton, January 1796–March 1797*, ed. Harold C. Syrett (New York: Columbia University Press, 1974), vol. 20, 58; Yoshpe, *Disposition*, 110; Catherine Snell Crary, "Forfeited Loyalist Lands in the Western District of New York—Albany and Tryon Counties," *New York History* 35, no. 3 (1954): 253; Edward P. Alexander, *A Revolutionary Conservative: James Duane of New York* (New York: Columbia University Press, 1938), 220n35.

30. Purple, "Notes," 179–80; William Dunlap, *Diary of William Dunlap (1766–1839): The Memoirs of a Dramatist, Theatrical Manager, Painter, Critic, Novelist, and Historian*, New York Historical Society, *Collections* 64 (1931): 687–88.

31. James Kent, "The Elite of the New York Bar as Seen from the Bench: James Kent's Necrologies," ed. Donald M. Roger, *New York Historical Society Quarterly* 56, no. 2 (1972): 218.

32. Michael Diaz, "'Can you on such principles think of quitting a Country?': Family, Faith, Law, Property, and the Loyalists of the Hudson Valley During the American Revolution," *Hudson River Valley Review* 28, no. 1 (Autumn 2011): 8.

33. Clinton to president of New York Convention, May 4, 1777, George Clinton, *Public Papers of George Clinton*, ed. Hugh Hastings (New York and Albany: State of New York, 1899–1914), vol. 1, 797; CC Jr. to Clinton, July 26, 1783, Clinton, *Public Papers*, vol. 8, 221–22; D. Colden to H. Colden, September 15, 1783, D. Colden, "Letter," ed. Jones, 85; CC Jr. to D. Colden, July 7, 1784, Colden Family Papers, box 11, NYHS.

34. CC to Catherwood, November 21, 1749, *CP*, vol. 4, 162.

35. Ranlet, *Loyalists*, 160.

36. CC Jr. to Washington, February 10, 1795, George Washington, *The Papers of George Washington, Presidential Series, October 1, 1794–March 31 1795*, ed. Edward G. Lengel (Charlottesville: University Press of Virginia, 2013), vol. 17, 513–14, 514n; Joseph Bragdon, "Cadwallader Colden, Second: An Ulster County Tory," *New York History* 14, no. 4 (1933): 421.

37. CC Jr. to Washington, February 10, 1795, Washington, *Papers, Presidential Series*, vol. 17, 513–14.

38. CC Jr. to Washington, February 10, 1795, Washington, *Papers, Presidential Series*, vol. 17, 513–14.

Bibliography

ARCHIVES AND MANUSCRIPTS

Canada

Library and Archives Canada, Ottawa, Ontario
    Robert Monckton Papers (Northcliffe Collection)

United Kingdom–England

Bury St. Edmunds Record Office, Suffolk
    Grafton Papers
Lincolnshire Archives, Lincoln
    Letters of James DeLancey to the Heathcotes
Royal Society of the Arts, London
    Guard Books
Staffordshire Record Office, Stafford
    Dartmouth Manuscripts
University of Nottingham, Nottingham
    Monckton Papers

United Kingdom–Scotland

National Library of Scotland, Edinburgh
    Ms. Number 5028 f. 14

United States

Adriance Memorial Library, Poughkeepsie, NY

Livingston Family Correspondence Collection
Boston Public Library, Boston, MA
   Manuscript Collection
William L. Clements Library, Ann Arbor, MI
   American Science and Medicine, Box 1
   George Clinton Papers
   Sir Henry Clinton Papers
   Thomas Gage Papers
   Miscellaneous
   Quaker Collection
Columbia University, New York City
   House of Lords Papers (microfilm)
   Samuel Johnson Papers
   William Samuel Johnson Papers
   Livingston-Redmond Papers (microfilm)
   Spec. Mss. Coll., Typographic Library
Cornell University, Ithaca, NY
   George Hyde Clarke Papers, Box 30, folders 2–3
Gilder Lehrman Institute of American History, New York City
   Gilder Lehrman Collection
Historical Society of Pennsylvania, Philadelphia
   Benjamin S. Barton Papers
   Etting Collection
   Gratz Collection
   James Logan Papers
Houghton Library, Harvard University, Cambridge, MA
   Autograph File
   Francis Bernard Papers (Sparks Manuscripts)
   Hyde Collection
Huntington Library, San Marino, CA
   Benedict Collection
   Loudoun Papers
   Miscellaneous Letters and Manuscripts
   Rare Books
Library of Congress, Washington, DC
   Colden Family Papers
   Peter Van Schaack Papers
Library of Congress Foreign Reproductions, Washington, DC
   Bodlein Library
   Champante Papers
   British Museum
   Journal of J. L. of Quebec Merchant, 28605
   Letters to Peter Collinson, 28727

Newcastle Papers
Colonial Office (transcripts)
Society for the Propagation of the Gospel, Letter Series B

Massachusetts Archives at Columbia Point, Boston, MA
Massachusetts Archives Collection, Records 1629–1799

Museum of the City of New York
DeLancey Papers
Livingston Papers
Real Estate Collection

Newberry Library, Chicago
Ayer Manuscripts

New Jersey Historical Society, Newark
Robert Hunter Morris Papers

New York Historical Society, New York City

James Alexander Papers
Beekman Family Papers
Broadside Collection
BV Oblong Tract
George Clinton Papers
Cadwallader Colden Papers (unpublished), 2 reels
Colden Family Papers, Boxes 11–12
Connecticut and New York Boundary Papers relating to the Oblong, 1733, Boxes 1–2
Horatio Gates Papers
Richard Harison Papers, Box 2
Robert Hunter Papers
John Lamb Papers
Robert R. Livingston Papers
Alexander McDougall Papers
New Netherlands Collection, oldest New York, and the colonial government, 1655–1744 (microfilm)
Orange Country, NY
Orange County, NY—Minisink
Public Record Office, Audit Office 12/25, 101, reels 7, 25
Rutherfurd Family Collection, Box 8, folder 1
Rutherfurd Papers (microfilm)
Ulster County Collection, Series 2, Box 1, folder 7

New York Public Library, New York City
James Alexander Papers, John Peter Zenger Trial Collection
American Loyalists Collection (microfilm)
Bancroft Collection, Colden Papers, 1722–1775, Vols. 169–173
Boston Committee of Correspondence Papers, Box 3, no. 600

British Headquarters Papers, Box 37
Chalmers Collection–New York
Emmet Collection
Gordon Lester Ford Collection
Livingston Family Papers
Misc. Personal Name Files, Box 24
Theodorus Bailey Myers Collection
New York Colony Miscellany Collection Governor, Box 1
Public Record Office, Audit Office 13/64, 97, reels 72, 105
William Smith Papers, Lot 178
Abraham Yates Jr. Papers
William R. Perkins Library, Duke University, Durham, NC
John Hancock and Torry Hancock Papers
Princeton University Libraries, Princeton, NJ
Alexander Papers, Box 10, folder 32

NEWSPAPERS AND MAGAZINES

American Chronicle (Farley)
Boston Evening Post
Connecticut Journal, November 13, 1776
Constitutional Courant (Goddard)
The General Magazine and Historical Chronicle (Franklin)
Gentleman's Magazine
London Magazine
The Monthly Review
New England Weekly Journal
New York Evening Post (DeForeest)
New York Gazette (Bradford)
New York Gazette (Weyman)
New York Gazette, or the Weekly Post-Boy (Holt)
New York Gazette, or the Weekly Post-Boy (Parker)
New York Gazetteer (Rivington)
New York Journal (Holt)
New York Mercury (Gaine)
New York Weekly Journal (Zenger)
Pennsylvania Gazette
Royal Gazette (Rivington)

PRIMARY SOURCES

Adams, John. *Diary and Autobiography of John Adams*. Edited by L. H. Butterfield. 4 vols. New York: Atheneum, 1964.
Addison, Joseph. *The Letters of Joseph Addison*. Edited by Walter Graham. Oxford: Oxford University Press, 1941.
Alexander, James. *A Brief Narrative of the Case and Trial of John Peter Zenger* (1736). Edited by Stanley Nider Katz. 1736. Reprint. Cambridge, MA: Belknap Press, 1963.
———. *Wheras on the 13th day of this Instant March.* March 24, 1735/6. [New York]: [John Peter Zenger], 1736. Microfiche. Early American Imprints. 1st ser. Evans no. 3980.
Alexander, James, and William Smith Sr. *The Complaint of James Alexander and William Smith to the Committee of the General Assembly of the Colony of New York*. [New York: John Peter Zenger, 1735?].
———. *The Vindication of James Alexander . . . and of William Smith.* New York: John Peter Zenger, 1734.
Amherst, Jeffrey. *The Journal of Jeffrey Amherst Recording the Military Career of General Amherst in America from 1758 to 1763*. Edited by J. Clarence Webster. Toronto: Ryerson Press, 1931.
Andrews, Wayne, ed. "In Flocks, Like Ill-Boding Ravens: Being an Account of the Tragic End of Sir Danvers Osborne, Bart." *New York Historical Society Quarterly* 35, no. 4 (1951): 405–7.
The Argyle Papers. [Edited by J. Maidment.] Edinburgh: T. G. Stevenson, 1834.
Armstrong, Alan W., ed. *"Forget not Mee and My Garden...": Selected Letters, 1725–1768 of Peter Collinson, F.R.S.* Philadelphia: American Philosophical Society, 2002.
Aspinwall Papers. Massachusetts Historical Society. *Collections*. 4th ser., 9–10 (1871): 480–92; 588–89.
Bangs, Edward, ed. *Journal of Lieutenant Isaac Bangs, April 1 to July 29, 1776*. Cambridge, MA: J. Wilson and Son, 1890. Reprint. New York: Arno Press, 1968.
Bartram, John. *The Correspondence of John Bartram, 1734–1777*. Edited by Edmund Berkeley and Dorothy Smith Berkeley. Gainesville: University Press of Florida, 1992.
———. *Memorials of John Bartram and Humphry Marshall, with Notices of Their Botanical Contemporaries*. Edited by William Darlington. Philadelphia: Lindsay & Blakiston, 1849.
Bartram, William. "Travels in George and Florida, 1773–74, A Report to Dr. John Fothergill." Edited by Francis Harper. American Philosophical Society. *Transactions*, n.s., 33, no. 2 (November 1943): 121–242.
Berkeley, George. *The Works of George Berkeley, Bishop of Cloyne*. Edited by A. A. Luce and T. E. Jessop. Vol. 5. London: Nelson, 1953.
Bernard, Francis. *The Papers of Francis Bernard: Governor of Colonial Massachusetts, 1760–1769*. Edited by Colin Nicolson. 5 vols. to date. Boston: Colonial Society of Massachusetts, 2007–.
Betts, Joseph. "A Letter from the Rev. Mr. Joseph Betts, M.A. and Fellow of University College, Oxon to Martin Folkes, Esq." Royal Society. *Philosophical Transactions* 43 (1744–1745): 91–100.
Birket, James. *Some Cursory Remarks Made by James Birket in his Voyage to North America, 1750–1751*. New Haven, CT: Yale University Press, 1916. Reprint. Freeport, NY: Books for Libraries Press, 1971.
Bland, Richard. "Letters." *William and Mary Quarterly*, 1st ser., 5, no. 3 (January 1897): 149–56.
Bobin, Isaac. *Letters of Isaac Bobin, Esq., Private Secretary of Hon. George Clarke, Secretary of the Province of New York, 1718–1730*. Albany, NY: J. Munsell, 1872.
Botein, Stephen, ed. *"Mr. Zenger's Malice and Falshood": Six Issues of the New-York Weekly Journal, 1733–34*. Worcester, MA: American Antiquarian Society, 1985.
Brodhead, John Romeyn. *Documents Relative to the Colonial History of the State of New-York*. Edited by Edmund B. O'Callaghan and Berthold Fernow. 15 vols. Albany, NY: Weed, Parsons, 1853–1887.

Buranelli, Vincent, ed. *The Trial of Peter Zenger*. New York: New York University Press, 1957.

Burke, Edmund. *Edmund Burke, New York Agent with his letters to the New York Assembly and intimate correspondence with Charles O'Hara, 1761–1776*. Edited by Ross J. S. Hoffman. Philadelphia: American Philosophical Society, 1956.

Burnaby, Andrew. *Travels Through the Middle Settlements in North America in the Years 1759 and 1760 With Observations upon the State of the Colonies*. London: T. Payne, 1775. Reprint. New York: Kelley, 1970.

Burnet, Gilbert. *Bishop Burnet's History of His Own Time*. 6 vols. 2nd ed. Oxford: Oxford University Press, 1833.

Burnet, William. "Observations of the Eclipses of the First Satellite of Jupiter, Communicated by His Excellency William Burnet, Esq.; Governor of New York, F.R.S." Royal Society. *Philosophical Transactions* 33 (1724–1725):162–65.

Byrd, William. *The London Diary (1717–1721) and Other Writings*. Edited by Louis B. Wright and Marion Tinling. New York: Oxford University Press, 1958.

Carlyle, Alexander. *Anecdotes and Characters of the Times*. Edited by James Kinsley. London: Oxford University Press, 1973.

———. *The Autobiography of Dr. Alexander Carlyle of Inveresk, 1722–1805*. Edited by John Hill Burton. London: T. N. Foulis, 1910. Reprint. Bristol, UK: Thoemmes, 1990.

Clark, William Bell, and others, eds. *Naval Documents of the American Revolution*. 11 vols. to date. Washington, DC: GPO, 1964–.

Clinton, George. *Public Papers of George Clinton*. Edited by Hugh Hastings. 10 vols. New York and Albany: State of New York, 1899–1914.

Coke, Daniel Parker. *The Royal Commission on the Losses and Services of American Loyalists, 1783–1785*. Edited by Hugh Edward Egerton. Oxford: Printed for presentation to the members of the Roxburghe Club, [by H. Hart at the University Press], 1915.

Colden, Cadwallader. *An Abstract from Dr. Berkley's Treatise on Tar-Water with some Reflections Thereon, Adapted to Diseases Frequent in America*. New York: J. Parker, 1745.

———. "An Account of the Climate of New York." In *Documents Relative to the Colonial History of the State of New-York*, edited by Edmund B. O'Callaghan and Berthold Fernow, vol. 5, 690–92. Albany, NY: Weed, Parsons, 1853–1857.

———. "An Account of the Earthquake felt in New York, Novem. 18, 1755, in a Letter from Cadwallader Colden, Esq.; to Mr. Peter Collinson, F.R.S." Royal Society. *Philosophical Transactions* 49, part 1 (1755): 443.

———. "Account of the Government of the New England Colonies." In *The Letters and Papers of Cadwallader Colden*, vol. 9, 245–51. New York: New York Historical Society, 1937.

———. "Address to the Freeholders and Freemen of the Cities and Counties of the Province of New York On Occasion of the ensueing Elections for Representations in General Assembly." In *The Letters and Papers of Cadwallader Colden*, vol. 3, 312–28. New York: New York Historical Society, 1919.

———. "Affairs of New York and New Jersey, Under the Joint Governors." New Jersey Historical Society. *Proceedings* 9 (1860–1864): 92–94.

———. "Cadwallader Colden on the Trade of New York; 1723." In *The Documentary History of the State of New-York; Arranged Under Direction of the Hon. Christopher Morgan, Secretary of State*, edited by Edmund B. O'Callaghan, vol. 1, 714–21. Albany, NY: Weed, Parsons, 1849.

———. "Cadwallader Colden's History of William Cosby's Administration as Governor of the Province of New York and of Lieutenant-Governor George Clarke's Administration Through 1737." In *The Letters and Papers of Cadwallader Colden*, vol. 9, 281–355. New York: New York Historical Society, 1937.

———. *The Colden Letter Books, 1760–1775*. New York Historical Society. *Collections* 9–10 (1876–1877).

———. "The Colden Letters on Smith's History." New York Historical Society. *Collections* 1 (1868): 181–235.

———. "Colden's Letter on the Principles, etc." *Monthly Review* 21 (November 1759): 397–403.

———. "Colden's Observations on the Balance of Power in Government." In *The Letters and Papers of Cadwallader Colden*, vol. 9, 251–57. New York: New York Historical Society, 1937.

———. *The Conduct of Cadwallader Colden, Esquire, Late Lieutenant-Governor of New York: Relating to The Judges Commissions, Appeals to the King, and the Stamp Duty*. In *The Colden Letter Books, 1760–1775*. New York Historical Society. *Collections* 10, (1877): 431–67.

———. "Continuation of Colden's History of the Five Indian Nations, for the years 1707 through 1720." In *The Letters and Papers of Cadwallader Colden*, vol. 9, 359–434. New York: New York Historical Society, 1937.

———. "The Cure of Cancers, From an eminent physician at New-York." *Gentleman's Magazine* 21 (July 1751): 305–8.

———. "Dr. Colden's Cure." Edited by Jacob Judd. *New York Historical Society Quarterly* 45, no. 3 (1961): 251–53.

———. *An Explication of the First Causes of Action in Matter, and, of the Cause of Gravitation*. New York: James Parker, 1745 [sic 1746].

———. "Extract of a Letter from an eminent Physician of the Province of New York, concerning an Indian Remedy for the Venereal Disease." *Gentleman's Magazine* 27 (September 1757): 405–6.

———. "Extract of a Letter from Cadwallader Colden, esq. to Dr. Fothergill, concerning the throat distemper." *American Museum* 3 (January 1788): 53–59.

———. "Farming on the Hudson Valley Frontier: Cadwallader Colden's Farm Journal, 1727–1736." Edited by Jaquetta M. Haley. *Hudson Valley Regional Review* 6, no. 1 (March 1989): 1–34.

———. "Farther Account of the Phytolacca." *Gentleman's Magazine* 22 (July 1752): 302.

———. *The History of the Five Indian Nations Depending on the Province of New-York in America* (1727, Part 1; 1747, Part 2) New York: T. H. Morrell, 1866. Reprint. Ithaca, NY: Great Seal Books, 1958.

———. *The History of the Five Indian Nations of Canada*. . . . 2nd ed. London: John Whiston, 1747.

———. *The History of the Five Indian Nations of Canada*. . . . 3rd ed. 2 vols. London: Lockyer Davis, 1755.

———. *The Interest of the Country in Laying Duties: Or A Discourse, showing how Duties on some Sorts of Merchandize may make the Province of New-York richer than it would be without them*. New York: J. Peter Zenger, 1726.

———. "An Introduction to the Study of Phylosophy Wrote In America for the Use of a Young Gentleman." In *American Philosophical Addresses, 1700–1900*, edited by Joseph L. Blau, 287–310. New York: Columbia University Press, 1946.

———. "A Letter about Governors." In *The Letters and Papers of Cadwallader Colden*, vol. 9, 241–44. New York: New York Historical Society, 1937.

———. "Letter on Smith's History." New York Historical Society, *Collections* 2 (1869): 203–12.

———. *The Letters and Papers of Cadwallader Colden*. New York Historical Society. *Collections* 50–56, 67–68 (1917–1923, 1934–1935).

———. *A Memorial concerning the Furr-Trade of the Province of New York. Presented to his Excellency William Burnet, Esq.; . . . by Cadwallader Colden, Surveyor General of the said Province, the 10th of November, 1724.* In Papers relating to an act of the Assembly of the Province of New York. New York: William Bradford, 1724.

———. "Money Circulating in New York Prior to 1704." Edited by Paul M. Hamlin. *New York Historical Society Quarterly* 40, no. 4 (1956): 361–67.

———. "New Method of Printing." *American Medical and Philosophical Register* 1 (April 1811): 439–50.

———. "Observations on the Situation, Soil, Climate, Water Communications, Boundaries etc. of the Province of New York . . . 1738." In *The Documentary History of the State of*

New-York; Arranged Under Direction of the Hon. Christopher Morgan, Secretary of State, edited by Edmund B. O'Callaghan, vol. 4, 169–81. Albany, NY: Weed, Parsons, 1851.

———. "Observations on the Yellow Fever of Virginia, with some Remarks on Dr. John Mitchell's Account of the Disease." *American Medical and Philosophical Register* 4 (1814): 378–83.

———. "Of the First Principles of Morality, or of the Actions of Intelligent Beings." In *The Philosophical Writings of Cadwallader Colden,* edited by Scott L. Pratt and John Ryder, 99–120. Amherst, NY: Humanity Books, 2002.

———. *The Philosophical Writings of Cadwallader Colden.* Edited by Scott L. Pratt and John Ryder. Amherst, NY: Humanity Books, 2002.

———. "Plantae Coldenghamiae in Provincia Noveboracensi Americes sponte crescentes, quas ad methodum Cl. Linnaei Seruralem, anno 1742. etc. Observavit and descripfit." *Acta Societatis Regiae Scientiarum Upsaliensis* 4 (1743/1749): 81–136.

———. "Plantae Coldenghamiae In Provincia Noveboracensi Americes sponte crescentes Pars Secunda." *Acta Societatis Regiae Scientiarum Upsaliensis* 5 (1744/1751): 47–82.

———. *The Principles of Action in Matter, the Gravitation of Bodies, and the Motion of the Planets, explained from those Principles.* London: R. Dodsley, 1751.

———. "Publick affairs, 1744–45." In *The Letters and Papers of Cadwallader Colden,* vol. 9, 251–57. New York: New York Historical Society, 1937.

———. "Publick Notice is hereby Given." In *All Canada in the Hands of the English: Or, An Authentick Journal Of the Proceedings of the Army, Under General Amherst.* 19–20. Boston: B. Mecom, [1760].

———. "The Reading of an Elaborate Treatise on the Eye, by the Learned and Ingenious Dr. Porterfield Is the Occasion of the Following Reflections." In *The Philosophical Writings of Cadwallader Colden,* edited by Scott L. Pratt and John Ryder, 121–50. Amherst, NY: Humanity Books, 2002.

———. "The Second Part of The Interest of the Country in Laying Duties Addressed more particularly to the City." In *The Letters and Papers of Cadwallader Colden,* vol. 9, 267–79. New York: New York Historical Society, 1937.

———. *Selections from the Scientific Correspondence of Cadwallader Colden with Gronovius, Linnaeus, Collinson, and Other Naturalists.* Edited by Asa Gray. New Haven, [CT]; B. L. Hamlen, 1843.

———. "Sir, According to my Promise. . . ." *Pennsylvania Gazette,* January 11, 1743/4, Part 1; January 26, 1743/4, Part 2; February 2, 1743/4, Part 3.

———. *Sir, In my Former I frankly informed you. . . .* [New York, John Peter Zenger], 1728.

———. "The State of the Lands in the Province of New York, In 1732." In *The Documentary History of the State of New-York; Arranged Under Direction of the Hon. Christopher Morgan, Secretary of State,* edited by Edmund B. O'Callaghan, vol. 1, 377–89. Albany, NY: Weed, Parsons, 1849.

———. "To the Authors of the *Monthly Review,*" July 7, 1760, *Monthly Review* 23 (November 1760): 380–87.

———. *To The Honourable Adolph Philipse, Esq.* [New York, John Peter Zenger], 1728.

———. *A Treaty between His Excellency The Honourable George Clinton, . . . And The Six United Indian Nations, and other Indian Nations depending on the Province of New-York.* New York: James Parker, 1746.

Colden, Cadwallader, and Hugh Graham. "The Correspondence of Cadwallader Colden and Hugh Graham on Infectious Fevers (1716–1719)," edited by Saul Jarcho. *Bulletin of the History of Medicine* 30, no. 3 (May–June 1956): 195–212.

Colden, Cadwallader, and others. *Governor and Company of Connecticut, and Moheagan Indians, By Their Guardians. Certified Copy of Book of Proceedings Before Commissioners of Review, MDCCXLIII.* London: W. and J. Richardson, 1769.

Colden, Cadwallader D. "For the Port Folio." *Port Folio,* n.s., 3rd ser., 3 (January 1810): 33–34.

Colden, David. "Letter of David Colden, Loyalist, 1783." Edited by E. Alfred Jones. *American Historical Review* 25, no. 1 (October 1919): 79–86.

Colden, Jane. *Botanic Manuscript of Jane Colden, 1724–1766*. Edited by Harold W. Rickett and Elizabeth C. Hall. New York: Garden Club of Orange and Dutchess Counties, 1963.
Coldham, Peter Wilson. *American Loyalist Claims Abstracted from the Public Record Office*. Vol. 1. Edited by Sally Lou Mick Haight. Washington, DC: National Genealogical Society, 1980.
Connecticut Colony. *The Public Records of the Colony of Connecticut*. 15 vols. Edited by J. Hammond Trumbull. Hartford: University of Connecticut, 1850–1890.
Copley, John Singleton. *Letters and Papers of John Singleton Copley and Henry Pelham, 1739–1776*. Boston: Massachusetts Historical Society, 1914. Reprint. New York: Kennedy Graphics, 1970.
"Copy of a Letter from D.B. to C.C." *General Magazine and Historical Chronicle* 1, no. 3 (March 1741): 200.
Croghan, George. "The Opinions of George Croghan on the American Indian." Edited by Nicholas B. Wainwright. *Pennsylvania Magazine of History and Biography* 71, no. 2 (1947): 152–59.
Dann, John C., ed. *One Hundred and One Treasures From the Collections of The William L. Clements Library: A Celebration of Seventy-five Years, 1923–1998*. Ann Arbor: Clements Library, University of Michigan, 1998.
Dawson, Henry B., ed. *New York City during the American Revolution*. New York: Mercantile Library, 1861.
Defoe, Daniel. *A Brief History of the Poor Palatine Refugees*. London: J. Baker, 1709. Reprint. Los Angeles: William Andrews Clark Memorial Library, University of California, 1964.
Dunlap, William. *Diary of William Dunlap (1766–1839): The Memoirs of a Dramatist, Theatrical Manager, Painter, Critic, Novelist, and Historian*. New York Historical Society, *Collections* 64 (1931): 687–88.
Einstein, Albert. "Ether and the Theory of Relativity." In *The Collected Papers of Albert Einstein*. Vol. 7. *The Berlin Years, 1918–1921*, translated by Alfred Engel, 74–75, 113–118, 130, 149, 160–81. Princeton, NJ: Princeton University Press, 2002.
Extracts from Bradford's Pennsylvania Journal of April 26, 1775. New York, 1775. Microfiche. Early American Imprints. 1st ser. Evans no. 14028.
Fontaine, John. *The Journal of John Fontaine: An Irish Huguenot Son in Spain and Virginia, 1710–1719*. Edited by Edward Porter Alexander. Williamsburg: Colonial Williamsburg Foundation, University Press of Virginia, 1972.
Force, Peter. *American Archives*. 4th and 5th ser. 9 vols. Washington, DC: M. St. Clair Clarke and Peter Force, under authority of Acts of Congress, 1837–1853.
Fothergill, John. *Chain of Friendship: Selected Letters of Dr. John Fothergill of London, 1735–1780*. Edited by Betty C. Corner and Christopher C. Booth. Cambridge, MA: Harvard University Press, 1971.
Franklin, Benjamin. *The Papers of Benjamin Franklin*. Edited by Leonard W. Labaree, William B. Wilcox, Ellen R. Cohen, and others. 43 vols. to date. New Haven, CT: Yale University Press, 1959–2019.
Fraser, Alexander, ed. *United Empire Loyalists: Enquiry Into the Losses and Services in Consequence of their Loyalty, Evidence in the Canadian Claims*. 2 vols. Toronto: Legislative Assembly of Ontario, L. K. Camero, 1905.
Fyfe, J. G., ed. *Scottish Diaries and Memoirs, 1550–1746*. Stirling, Scotland: E. Mackay, 1928.
Gage, Thomas. *The Correspondence of General Thomas Gage with the Secretaries of State, 1763–1775*. Edited by Clarence E. Carter. 2 vols. New Haven, CT: Yale University Press, 1931–1933.
Galen. *Galen on the Therapeutic Method, Books I and II*. Translated by R. J. Hankinson. Oxford: Clarendon Press, 1991.
George III. *The Correspondence of King George the Third From 1760 to December 1783*. Vol. 1. *Printed from the Original Papers in the Royal Archives at Windsor Castle: 1760–1767*. Edited by Sir John Fortescue. London: Macmillan, 1927.
Goodfriend, Joyce D., ed. "New York City in 1772: The Journal of Solomon Drowne, Junior." *New York History* 82, no. 1 (2001): 25–52.

Grant, Anne. *Memoirs of an American Lady with Sketches of Manners and Scenery in America as They Existed Previous to the Revolution*. 2 vols. London: Longman, Hurst, Rees, and Orme, 1808. Reprint. New York: Research Reprints, 1970.

Great Britain. *Acts of the Privy Council, Colonial Series*. Edited by William L. Grant and James Munroe. 6 vols. London: H. M. S. O., 1908–1912.

———. *Calendar of State Papers, Colonial Series, America and West Indies*. Edited by W. Noel Sainsbury and others. 45 vols. to date. London: H. M. S. O., 1860–1994.

———. *Calendar of Treasury Books and Papers, 1731–1734*. Vol. 2. Edited by William A. Shaw. London: H. M. S. O., 1898.

———. *Documents of the American Revolution, Colonial Office Series, 1770–1783*. Edited by K. G. Davies. 21 vols. Shannon, Ireland: Irish University Press, 1972–1981.

———. *The Manuscripts of the Earl of Dartmouth*. 3 vols. London: H. M. S. O., 1887–1896.

———. *Proceedings and Debates of the British Parliaments Respecting North America, 1754–1783*. Edited by R. C. Simmons and P. D. G. Thomas. 6 vols. Millwood, NY: Kraus, 1982–1987.

Green, Samuel A., ed. "The Battle of Lexington." Massachusetts Historical Society. *Proceedings*, 2nd ser., 11 (1896–1897): 305–6.

Grenville, George. *The Grenville Papers*. Edited by William James Smith. 4 vols. London: J. Murray, 1852–1853. Reprint. New York: AMS Press, 1970.

Halsey, Francis W., ed. *A Tour of Four Great Rivers: The Hudson, Mohawk, Susquehanna and Delaware in 1769, Being the Journal of Richard Smith*. Port Washington, NY: I. J. Friedman, 1964.

Hamilton, Alexander. *Gentleman's Progress: The Itinerarium of Dr. Alexander Hamilton, 1744*. Edited by Carl Bridenbaugh. Chapel Hill: University of North Carolina Press, 1948.

Hamilton, Alexander. *The Papers of Alexander Hamilton*. Vol. 20. *January 1796–March 1797*. Edited by Harold C. Syrett. New York: Columbia University Press, 1974.

Hamlin, Paul M., ed. "'He Is Gone and Peace to His Shade': William Smith, Historian, Posthumously Boils Lieutenant Governor Cadwallader Colden In Oil." *New York Historical Society Quarterly* 36, no. 2 (1952): 161–74.

Handlin, Oscar, and Irving Mark, eds. "Chief Daniel Nimham v. Roger Morris, Beverly Robinson, and Philip Philipse—An Indian Land Case in Colonial New York, 1765–1767." *Ethnohistory* 11, no. 3 (1964): 193–246.

Harison, Francis. *To the Right Worshipful, the Mayor, Aldermen and Commonalty of the City of New York*. New York: William Bradford, 1734.

Harison, George. "George Harison's Protest: New Light on Forsey versus Cunningham." Edited by Herbert A. Johnson. *New York History* 50, no. 1 (1969): 61–82.

Hesselius, Gustavus. "'With God's Blessings on Both Land and Sea': Gustavus Hesselius Describes the New World to the Old in a Letter from Philadelphia in 1714." Translated by Carin K. Arnborg. *American Art Journal* 21, no. 3 (1989): 5–11.

Horsmanden, Daniel. *A Letter from Some of the Representatives in the Late General Assembly of the Colony of New-York to His Excellency Governor C———n*. New York: James Parker, 1747.

———. *The New York Conspiracy*. New York: James Parker, 1744. Reprint. Edited by Thomas J. Davis. Boston: Beacon Press, 1971.

———. *The New York Conspiracy Trials of 1741: Daniel Horsmanden's Journal of the Proceedings with Related Documents*. Edited by Serena R. Zabin. Boston: Bedford/St. Martin's, 2004.

Hutchinson, Thomas. *The Correspondence of Thomas Hutchinson*. Vol. 1. *1740–1766*. Edited by John W. Tyler. Boston: Colonial Society of Massachusetts, University of Virginia Press, 2014.

———. *The History of the Colony and Province of Massachusetts-Bay*. Edited by Lawrence Shaw Mayo. 3 vols. London, 1768. Reprint. Cambridge, MA: Harvard University Press, 1936.

Inglis, Charles. *The Life and Letters of Charles Inglis*. Edited by John Wolfe Lydekker. London: Church Historical Society, 1936.

The Interest of City and Country To Lay No Duties. New York: John Peter Zenger, 1726.

Bibliography

[Izard, Ralph]. *An Account of a Journey to Niagara, Montreal and Quebec, in 1765, or; "'Tis Eighty Years Since."* New York: [W. Osborn], 1846.

Izard, Ralph. *Correspondence of Mr. Ralph Izard, of South Carolina, From the Year 1774 to 1804; with a short Memoir.* Vol. 1. Edited by Anne Izard Deas. New York: C. S. Francis, 1844.

Jefferson, Thomas. *Notes on the State of Virginia.* [Paris], 1785. Reprint. Edited by William Peden. Chapel Hill: University of North Carolina Press, 1954.

———. *The Papers of Thomas Jefferson.* Vol. 9. *November 1785–June 1786*; Vol. 10. *June 1786–December 1786.* Edited by Julian P. Boyd. 39 vols. Princeton, NJ: Princeton University Press, 1954.

Jensen, Merrill, ed. *English Historical Documents.* Vol. 9. *American Colonial Documents to 1776.* New York: Eyre & Spottiswoode, 1955.

———, ed. *Tracts of the American Revolution, 1763–1776.* New York: Bobbs-Merrill, 1967.

Johnson, Samuel. *Samuel Johnson, President of King's College: His Career and Writings.* Edited by Herbert Schneider and Carol Schneider. 4 vols. New York: Columbia University Press, 1929.

Johnson, Sir William. *The Papers of Sir William Johnson.* Edited by James Sullivan and others. 14 vols. Albany: University of the State of New York, 1921–1965.

Jones, Thomas. *History of New York during the Revolutionary War.* Edited by Edward Floyd De Lancey. 2 vols. New York: New York Historical Society, 1879. Reprint. Cranbury, NJ: Scholar's Bookshelf, 2006.

"Journal of a French Traveller in the Colonies, 1765, II." *American Historical Review* 27, no. 1 (October 1921): 70–89.

Kalm, Peter. *The America of 1750: Peter Kalm's Travels In North America, The English Version of 1770.* Edited by Adolph B. Benson. 2 vols. New York: Wilson-Erickson, 1937.

Kemble's Journals, 1773–1789. New York Historical Society, *Collections* 16 (1883).

Kent, James. "The Elite of the New York Bar as Seen from the Bench: James Kent's Necrologies." Edited by Donald M. Roger. *New York Historical Society Quarterly* 56, no. 2 (1972): 199–237.

Knox, John. *An Historical Journal of the Campaigns in North America, For the Years 1757, 1758, 1759, and 1760.* Edited by Arthur G. Doughty. 3 vols. Toronto: Champlain Society, 1914–1916.

Laurens, Henry. *The Papers of Henry Laurens.* Vol. 7. *August 1, 1769–October 9, 1771.* Edited by George C. Rogers Jr. and David R. Chesnutt. Columbia: South Carolina Historical Society, University of South Carolina Press, 1979.

Law, Robert. *Memorialls; Or, The Memorable Things that Fell Out Within This Island of Brittain from 1638 to 1684.* Edited by Charles Kirkpatrick Sharpe. Edinburgh: Archibald Constable, 1818.

LeBlanc, Ondine E., ed. "The Journal of the 'Rebel Lady': Katherine Farnham Hay's Account of Her Trip to New York City, 1778." Massachusetts Historical Society. *Proceedings*, 3rd ser., 109 (1997): 102–22.

Leder, Lawrence H., ed. "Robert Hunter's Androboros." *Bulletin of the New York Public Library* 68 (1964): 153–90.

Lee, Charles. *The Lee Papers.* New York Historical Society, *Collections* 4 (1871): vol. 1, 172–78.

Lee, William. *Letters of William Lee, 1766–1783.* Edited by Worthington Chauncey Ford. 3 vols. Brooklyn, NY: Historical Printing Club, 1891. Reprint. 3 vols. in 1. New York: Burt Franklin Research, 1968.

Linnaeus. *A Selection of the Correspondence of Linnaeus and Other Naturalists, from the Original Manuscripts.* Edited by Sir James Edward Smith. 2 vols. London: Longman, Hurst, Rees, Orme, and Brown, 1821.

Livingston, Robert R. "Mr. Robert R. Livingston's Reasons against a Land Tax." Edited by Beverly McAnear. *Journal of Political Economy* 48, no. 1 (1940): 63–90.

Livingston, William. *A Review of the Military Operations in North America.* London: R. and J. Dodsley, 1757.

———. *A Soliloquy.* New York: [Samuel Inslee and Anthony Car], 1770.

Livingston, William, and others. *The Independent Reflector or Weekly Essays on Sundry Important Subjects More particularly adapted to the Province of New-York*. Edited by Milton M. Klein. Cambridge, MA: Harvard University Press, 1963.

Lloyd, Charles. [*A Copy taken from a Pamphlet Intitluled] The Conduct of the Late Administration Examined, With an Appendix, containing original and authentic Documents*. London: J. Almon, 1767. Reprint. Boston: Edes and Gill, 1767.

Logan, James. "A Quaker Imperialist's View of the British Colonies in America: 1732." Edited by Joseph E. Johnson. *Pennsylvania Magazine of History and Biography* 60, no. 2 (1936): 97–130.

M'Crie, Thomas, ed. *Memoirs of Mr. William Veitch and George Brysson. Written by Themselves*. Edinburgh: W. Blackwood, 1825.

M'Robert, Patrick. *A Tour Through Part of the North Provinces of America*. Edinburgh: Printed for the Author, 1776. Reprint. Edited by Carl Bridenbaugh. New York: New York Times, 1968.

Massachusetts Colony. *Journals of the House of Representatives of Massachusetts*. Vols. 41–50. Boston: Massachusetts Historical Society, 1971–1981.

Mather, Cotton. *The Angel of Bethesda*. Edited by Gordon W. Jones. Barre, MA: American Antiquarian Society, 1972.

McAnear, Beverly. "James Parker versus William Weyman." New Jersey Historical Society. *Proceedings* 59 (1941): 1–23.

———, ed. "Personal Accounts of the Albany Congress of 1754." *Mississippi Valley Historical Review* 39, no. 4 (1953): 727–46.

"A Merchant." *The Times*. c. March 1770. Microfiche. Early American Imprints. 1st ser. Evans no. 11912.

Mitchell, John. *The Contest in America between Great Britain and France with Its Consequences and Importance*. London: A. Millar, 1757. Reprint. New York: Johnson, 1965.

———. "A Letter from John Mitchell to Cadwallader Colden." Edited by Theodore Hornberger. *Huntington Library Quarterly* 10, no. 4 (1947): 411–17.

Monckton, Robert. University of Nottingham Department of Manuscripts. *Monckton Papers*. [Nottingham, UK]: University of Nottingham, [1986].

Montresor, John. *The Montresor Journals*. Edited by G. D. Scull. New York Historical Society. *Collections* 14 (1881).

Moore, Frank. *Songs and Ballads of the American Revolution*. New York: D. Appleton, 1856. Reprint. New York: New York Times, 1969.

Morris, Lewis. *The Papers of Lewis Morris*. Edited by Eugene R. Sheridan. 3 vols. Newark, NJ: New Jersey Historical Society, 1991–1993.

Morris, Robert Hunter. "An American in London, 1735–1736." Edited by Beverly McAnear. *Pennsylvania Magazine of History and Biography* 64, nos. 2–3 (1940): 164–217, 356–406.

Munk, William, ed. *The Roll of the Royal College of Physicians of London. Comprising Biographical Sketches of All the Eminent Physicians, Whose Names Are Recorded in the Annals from the Foundation of the College in 1518 to Its Removal in 1825, from Warwick Lane to Pall Mall East*. Vol. 2. *1701 to 1800*. London: Royal College, 1878.

Nelson, William. *The Correspondence of William Nelson as Acting Governor of Virginia, 1770–1771*. Edited John C. Van Horne. Charlottesville: Virginia Historical Society, University Press of Virginia, 1975.

New Jersey Colony. *Documents Relating to the Colonial History of the State of New Jersey*. Vols. 1–8. Edited by William A. Whitehead; Vols. 9–10. Edited by F. W. Ricord and W. Nelson. Newark, NJ: Daily Advertiser Printing House, 1880–1886.

New York City. *Abstracts of Wills on File in the Surrogate's Office, City of New York*. New York Historical Society, *Collections* 33 (1900): 56–57.

———. *Manual of the Corporation of the City of New York*. New York: New York Common Council, 1870; 1871.

———. *Minutes of The Common Council of the City of New York, 1675–1776*. 8 vols. New York: Dodd, Mead, 1905.

———. "Names of the Principal Male Inhabitants of New-York. Anno 1774." In *Manual of the Corporation of the City of New York for 1850*, by D. T. Valentine, 427–42. New York: McSpedon & Baker, 1850.

New York Colony. *An Act for the Easier Partition of Lands held in Common.* New York: William Bradford, 1726. Microfiche. Early American Imprints. 1st ser. Evans no. 2787.

———. *Calendar of New York Colonial Commissions, 1680–1770.* Compiled by E. B. O'Callaghan. New York: New York Historical Society, 1929.

———. *Calendar of New York Colonial Commissions, Book VI (1770–1776).* Edited by Kenneth Scott. New York: National Society of Colonial Dames, 1972.

———. *The Documentary History of the State of New-York; Arranged Under Direction of the Hon. Christopher Morgan, Secretary of State.* Edited by Edmund B. O'Callaghan. 4 vols. Albany, NY: Weed, Parsons, 1849–1851.

———. *Documents Relative to the Colonial History of the State of New-York.* Edited by Edmund B. O'Callaghan and Berthold Fernow. 15 vols. Albany, NY: Weed, Parsons, 1853–1887.

———. *Ecclesiastical Records State of New York.* Edited by Hugh Hastings. 7 vols. Albany, NY: J. B. Lyon, State Printer, 1901–1916.

———. *Lists of Inhabitants of Colonial New York Excerpted from The Documentary History of the State of New York.* Edited by Edmund B. O'Callaghan. Baltimore, MD: Genealogical Publishing, 1979.

———. *State of New York: Messages from the Governors, Vol. 1, 1683–1776 Colonial Period.* Edited by Charles Z. Lincoln. Albany, NY: J. B. Lyon, 1909.

New York Colony. Assembly. *Journal of the Votes and Proceedings of the General Assembly of the Colony of New York, 1691–1765.* 2 vols. New York: Hugh Gaine, 1764–1766.

———. *Journal of the Votes and Proceedings of the General Assembly of the Colony of New York from 1766 to 1776, Inclusive.* Albany, NY: J. Buel, 1820.

New York Colony. Council. *Calendar of Council Minutes, 1668–1783.* Compiled by Berthold Fernow. Albany: University of the State of New York, 1902. Reprint. Harrison, NY: Harbor Hill Books, 1987.

———. *Journal of the Legislative Council of the Colony of New York, Began the 9th day of April, 1691; and ended the [3d of April, 1775].* 2 vols. Albany, NY: Weed, Parsons, 1861.

New York State. *Calendar of Historical Manuscripts relating to the War of the Revolution in the Office of the Secretary of State.* 2 vols. Albany, NY: Weed, Parsons, 1868.

———. *Calendar of N.Y. Colonial Manuscripts Indorsed Land Papers in the Office of the Secretary of State of New York, 1643–1803.* Compiled by E. B. O'Callaghan. Albany, NY: Weed, Parsons, 1864. Reprint. Harrison, NY: Harbor Hill Books, 1987.

———. *Journals of the Provincial Congress, . . . Committee of Safety, and Council of Safety of the State of New York.* 2 vols. Albany, NY: Weed, Parsons, 1842.

———. *Report of the Regents of the University on the Boundaries of the State of New York.* Edited by Daniel J. Pratt. 2 vols. Albany, NY: Argus, 1874–1884.

Norris, Isaac. "The Journal of Isaac Norris, During a Trip to Albany in 1745, and an Account of a Treaty Held There in October of That Year." *Pennsylvania Magazine of History and Biography* 27, no. 1 (1903): 20–28.

North Carolina Colony. *The Colonial Records of North Carolina.* Edited by William L. Saunders. 10 vols. Raleigh, NC: P. M. Hale, State Printer, 1886–1890.

The Northcliffe Collection: Presented to the Government of Canada by Sir Leicester Harmsworth, Bt. Ottawa: F. A. Acland, 1926.

Ogilvie, John. "The Diary of the Reverend John Ogilvie, 1750–1759." Edited by Milton W. Hamilton. *Bulletin of the Fort Ticonderoga Museum* 10, no. 5 (1961): 331–85.

Onderdonk, Henry, Jr. *Documents and Letters Intended to Illustrate the Revolutionary Incidents of Queens County.* New York: Leavitt, Trow, 1846. Reprint. Port Washington, NY: I. J. Friedman Division, Kennikat Press, 1970.

———, comp. "Flushing-Tax List 1784." *Long Island Historical Society Quarterly* 2, no. 3 (July 1940): 81–87.

———. *Queens County in Olden Times.* Jamaica, NY: C. Welling, 1865.

"A Packet of Old Letters (found in old Poughkeepsie Court House; Livingston, Beekman families; 1732–1755)." Dutchess County Historical Society. *Year Book* 6 (1921): 26–61.

Palmer, Obadiah, and others. *Obadiah Palmer, Nehemiah Palmer, Sylvanus Palmer . . . and Henry Cock, Complainants Against Jacobus van Cortland and Adolph Philipse, Defendants, In Cancellarie Novae Eborac.* New York: William Bradford, 1727.

Patten, Robert. *The History of the Rebellion in the Year 1715.* 4th ed. London: James Roberts, 1745.

Pennsylvania Colony. *Colonial Records of Pennsylvania, Minutes of the Provincial Council of Pennsylvania.* Vol. 9. *October 15, 1762–October 17, 1771.* Harrisburg: T. Fenn, 1852. Reprint. 16 vols. New York: AMS Press, 1968.

Pike, Samuel. *Philosophia Sacra: Or, the Principles of Natural Philosophy. Extracted from Divine Revelation.* London: Printed for the Author, 1753.

Pownall, Thomas. *A Topographical Description of the Dominions of the United States of America.* Rev. ed. of London: J. Almon, 1776. Pittsburgh: University of Pittsburgh Press, 1949.

Ramsay, David. *The History of the American Revolution.* 2 vols. Philadelphia: R. Aitken & Son, 1789. Reprint. Edited by Lester H. Cohen. 2 vols. Indianapolis, IN: Liberty Classics, 1990.

The Report of the Committee of His Majesty's council, to whom it was Referred, to examine and make enquiry, touching a letter found and in the house of Mr. Alexander in New-York, on Friday the first day of February, 1733/4. New York: William Bradford, 1734.

Robson, George. *An Elegy Upon The Death of that Godly, Pious and Painful Minister, Mr. Alexander Colden Late Minister of the Gospel at Oxname.* Edinburgh: Thomas Lumisden and John Robertson for the Author, 1739.

Rush, Benjamin. *Letters of Benjamin Rush.* Edited by L. H. Butterfield. 2 vols. Princeton, NJ: Princeton University Press, 1951.

Rutherfurd, Livingston. *Family Records and Events: Compiled Principally from the Original Manuscripts in the Rutherfurd Collection.* New York: De Vinne Press, 1894.

Smith, Paul H., and others, eds. *Letters of Delegates to Congress, 1774–1789.* 26 vols. Washington, DC: GPO, 1976–2000.

Smith, William, Jr. *The Diary and Selected Papers of Chief Justice William Smith, 1784–1793.* Edited by L. F. S. Upton. 2 vols. Toronto: Champlain Society, 1963.

———. *Historical Memoirs . . . of William Smith.* Edited by William H. W. Sabine. 3 vols. New York: New York Times, Arno Press, 1956–1971.

———. *The History of the Province of New York.* Edited by Michael Kammen. 2 vols. Cambridge, MA: Belknap Press of Harvard University Press, 1972.

Smith, William, Sr. *Some Observations on the Charge given by the Honourable James DeLancey, Esq.; Chief Justice of the Province of New-York, to the Grand Jury.* New York: J. Peter Zenger, 1733/4.

Stevens, John Austin, Jr., ed. *Colonial Records of the New York Chamber of Commerce, 1768–1784.* New York: John F. Trow, 1867.

Stevenson, Joseph, ed. *Documents Illustrative of the History of Scotland: From the Death of King Alexander the Third to the Accession of Robert Bruce (1286–1306).* 2 vols. Edinburgh: H. M. General Register House, 1870.

Stiles, Ezra. *The Literary Diary of Ezra Stiles, D.D., LL.D., President of Yale College.* Edited by Franklin Bowditch Dexter. 3 vols. New York: C. Scribner, 1901.

Swift, Jonathan. *The Correspondence of Jonathan Swift, D.D.* Edited by Francis Elrington Ball. 6 vols. London: G. Bell and Sons, 1910–1914.

Talcott, Joseph. *The Talcott Papers.* Edited by Mary Kingbury Talcott. Connecticut Historical Society, *Collections* 4–5 (1892–1896).

Tatum, Edward H., Jr., ed. *The American Journal of Ambrose Serle, Secretary to Lord Howe, 1776–1778.* San Marino, CA: Huntington Library, 1940. Reprint. New York: New York Times, Arno Press, 1969.

Taylor, G. *A Voyage to North America Perform'd by G. Taylor of Sheffield in the Years 1768, and 1769.* Nottingham, UK: S. Creswell for the Author, 1771.

Thurman, John, Jr. "Extracts from the Letter Books of John Thurman, Junior." Edited by Benjamin H. Hall. *Historical Magazine*, 2nd ser., 4 (December 1868): 283–97.
Tryon, William. *The Correspondence of William Tryon and Other Selected Papers*. Edited by William S. Powell. 2 vols. Raleigh, NC: Division of Archives and History, Department of Cultural Resources, 1981.
Tyler, John E., ed. "A British Whig's Report from New York on the American Situation, 1775." In *Narratives of the Revolution in New York: A Collection of Articles from the New-York Historical Society Quarterly*. New York Historical Society. *Collections* 85 (1975): 12–24.
Van Dam, Rip. *The Arguments of the Council for the Defendant, In Support of a Plea to the Jurisdiction*. New York: John Peter Zenger, 1733.
Van Dam, Rip, and others. *Heads of Articles of Complaint by Rip Van Dam Esq; Against His Excellency William Cosby, Esq*. Boston: John Peter Zenger, 1734.
———. Heads of Articles of Complaint made . . . on Thursday, the 30th of May, 1734 to the Committee of Grievances, New York?, 1734.
Veitch, Mrs. William. *Memoirs of Mrs. William Veitch, Mr. Thomas Hog of Kiltearn, Mr. Henry Erskine and Mr. John Carstairs*. Edinburgh: [Free Church of Scotland], 1846.
Warren, Peter. *The Royal Navy and North America: The Warren Papers, 1736–1752*. Edited by Julian Gwyn. London: Navy Records Society, 1975.
Washington, George. *The Papers of George Washington, Colonial Series*. Edited by W. W. Abbot. 10 vols. Charlottesville: University Press of Virginia, 1983–1995.
———. *The Papers of George Washington, Presidential Series*. Vol. 17. *October 1, 1794–March 31, 1795*. Edited by Edward G. Lengel. Charlottesville: University Press of Virginia, 2013.
———. *The Papers of George Washington, Revolutionary War Series*. Vol. 6. *August–October 1776*. Edited by Philander D. Chase. Charlottesville: University Press of Virginia, 1994.
"Watchman." No. 4, March 29, 1770. Microfiche. Early American Imprints. 1st ser. Evans no. 11912.
"Watchman." No. 5, April 21, 1770. Microfiche. Early American Imprints. 1st ser. Evans no. 11921.
Watts, John. *Letter Book of John Watts, Merchant and Councillor of New York, January 1, 1762–December 22, 1765*. New York Historical Society, *Collections* 61 (1928).
Wells, Louisa Susannah. *The Journal of a Voyage from Charlestown, S.C., to London During the American Revolution*. New York: New York Historical Society, 1906. Reprint. New York: Arno Press, 1968.
Whytt, Robert. *Physiological Essays*. Edinburgh: Hamilton, Balfour and Neill, 1761.
W. K. "A Letter to the Authors of the *Monthly Review*." *Monthly Review* 21 (December 1759): 500–512.
———. "To the Authors of the *Monthly Review*." *Monthly Review* 23 (November 1760): 387–89.
Wodrow, Robert. *The History of the Sufferings of the Church of Scotland from the Restoration to the Revolution*. Edited by Rev. Robert Burns. 4 vols. Glasgow: Blackie, Fullarton, 1828–1830.
Wraxall, Peter. *An Abridgment of the Indian Affairs Contained In Four Folio Volumes, Transacted in the Colony of New York, From the Year 1678 to the Year 1751*. Edited by Charles Howard McIlwain. Cambridge, MA: Harvard University Press, 1915. Reprint. New York: Benjamin Blom, 1968.

SECONDARY SOURCES

Afinogenov, Gregory. "Lawyers and Politics in Eighteenth-Century New York." *New York History* 89, no. 2 (2008): 143–62.
Akers, Charles W. Review of *The Reinterpretation of Early American History: Essays in Honor of John Edwin Pomfret*, by Ray Allen Billington. *Journal of American History* 54, no. 1 (1967): 88–89.

Alden, John R. "The Albany Congress and the Creation of the Indian Superintendencies." *Mississippi Valley Historical Review* 27, no. 2 (1940): 193–210.

———. *General Gage in America Being Principally A History of His Role in the American Revolution*. Baton Rouge: Lousiana State University Press, 1948. Reprint. New York: Greenwood Press, 1969.

Alden, Timothy. *A Collection of American Epitaphs and Inscriptions with Occasional Notes*. 5 vols. New York: [S. Marks, Printer], 1814.

Alexander, Edward P. *A Revolutionary Conservative: James Duane of New York*. New York: Columbia University Press, 1938.

Allen, William. *An American Biographical and Historical Dictionary*. Cambridge, MA: William Hilliard, 1809.

American National Biography. 24 vols. New York: Oxford University Press, 1999.

Anderson, Samuel K. "Public Lotteries in Colonial New York." *New York Historical Society Quarterly* 56, no. 2 (1972): 133–46.

Appletons' Cyclopaedia of American Biography. Edited by James Grant Wilson and John Fiske. 7 vols. New York : D. Appleton, 1894–1900.

Baker, C. H. Collins, and Muriel I. Baker. *The Life and Circumstances of James Brydges, First Duke of Chandos, Patron of the Liberal Arts*. Oxford: Clarendon Press, 1949.

Bardi, Jason Socrates. *The Calculus Wars: Newton, Leibniz, and the Greatest Mathematical Clash of All Time*. New York: Thunder's Mouth Press, 2006.

Bargar, B. D. *Lord Dartmouth and the American Revolution*. Columbia: University of South Carolina Press, 1965.

———. "Lord Dartmouth's Patronage, 1772–1775." *William and Mary Quarterly*, 3rd ser., 15 (1958): 191–200.

Barrow, Thomas C. *Trade and Empire: The British Customs Service in Colonial America, 1660–1775*. Cambridge, MA: Harvard University Press, 1967.

Baule, Steven M. *Protecting the Empire's Frontier: Officers of the 18th (Royal Irish) Regiment of Foot During Its North American Service, 1767–1776*. Athens: Ohio University Press, 2014.

Beattie, John M. *The English Court in the Reign of George I*. Cambridge: Cambridge University Press, 1967.

Beauchamp, William M. *The Life of Conrad Weiser*. Syracuse, NY: Onondaga Historical Association, 1925.

Becker, Carl Lotus. *The History of Political Parties in the Province of New York*. Madison : University of Wisconsin Press, 1909. Reprint. 1960.

Beeman, Richard R. *Our Lives, Our Fortunes and Our Sacred Honor: The Forging of American Independence, 1774–1776*. New York: Basic Books, 2013.

———. *The Varieties of Political Experience in Eighteenth-Century America*. Philadelphia: University of Pennsylvania Press, 2004.

Bell, James B. *The Imperial Origins of the King's Church in Early America, 1607–1783*. New York: Palgrave Macmillan, 2004.

Benjamin, Marina. "Medicine, Morality and the Politics of Berkeley's Tar-water." In *The Medical Enlightenment of the Eighteenth Century*, edited by Andrew Cunningham and Roger French, 165–92. Cambridge and New York: Cambridge University Press, 1990.

Bennett, David. *A Few Lawless Vagabonds: Ethan Allen, the Republic of Vermont, and the American Revolution*. Havertown, PA : Casemate Publishers, 2014.

Berkeley, Edmund, and Dorothy Smith Berkeley. *Dr. Alexander Garden of Charles Town*. Chapel Hill: University of North Carolina Press, 1969.

———. *Dr. John Mitchell: The Man Who Made the Map of North America*. Chapel Hill: University of North Carolina Press, 1974.

Bernstein, Harry. *Origins of Inter-American Interest, 1700–1812*. Philadelphia: University of Pennsylvania Press, 1945.

Bernstein, Peter L. *Wedding of the Waters: The Erie Canal and the Making of a Great Nation*. New York: W. W. Norton, 2005.

"Biographical Sketch of the late Honourable Cadwallader Colden, formerly Lieutenant-Governor of New-York with an Account of His Writings." *American Medical and Philosophical Register* 1 (January 1811): 297–303.
Black, George F. *The Surnames of Scotland: Their Origin, Meaning, and History*. New York: New York Public Library, 1946.
Black's Law Dictionary With Pronunciations. 5th ed. Edited by Henry Campbell Black. St. Paul, MN: West Publishing, 1979.
Blake, John B. "Yellow Fever in Eighteenth Century America." *Bulletin of the New York Academy of Medicine*, 44, no. 6 (1968): 673–86.
Blau, Joseph L. *Men and Movements in American Philosophy*. New York: Prentice-Hall, 1952.
Bodle, Wayne. Review of *Cadwallader Colden: A Figure of the American Enlightenment*, by Alfred R. Hoermann. *William and Mary Quarterly*, 3rd ser., 60, no. 2 (2003): 446–48.
Bonomi, Patricia U. *A Factious People: Politics and Society in Colonial New York*. New York: Columbia University Press, 1971.
———. "New York: The Royal Colony." *New York History* 82, no. 1 (2001): 5–14.
Booth, Mary L. *History of the City of New York*. 2 vols. New York: W. R. C. Clark, 1867.
Botein, Stephen. "Cicero as Role Model for Early American Lawyers: A Case Study in Classical 'Influence.'" *Classical Journal* 73, no. 4 (1978): 313–21.
Bown, Stephen R. *Scurvy: How a Surgeon, a Mariner, and a Gentleman Solved the Greatest Medical Mystery of the Age of Sail*. Chichester, UK: Summersdale, 2003.
Bragdon, Joseph. "Cadwallader Colden, Second: An Ulster County Tory." *New York History* 14, no. 4 (1933): 411–21.
Brasch, Frederick E. "The Newtonian Epoch in the American Colonies (1680–1783)." American Antiquarian Society, *Proceedings* 49 (1939): 314–32.
Breslaw, Elaine G. *Dr. Alexander Hamilton and Provincial America: Expanding the Orbit of Scottish Culture*. Baton Rouge: Louisiana State University Press, 2008.
Brett-James, Norman G. *The Life of Peter Collinson, F.R.S., F.S.A.* London: E. G. Dunstan, 1925.
Bridenbaugh, Carl. *Mitre and Sceptre: Transatlantic Faiths, Ideas, Personalities, and Politics, 1689–1775*. New York: Oxford University Press, 1962.
Brock, Helen. "North America, a Western Outpost of European Medicine." In *The Medical Enlightenment of the Eighteenth Century*, edited by Andrew Cunningham and Roger French, 194–216. Cambridge and New York: Cambridge University Press, 1990.
Brock, William R., and C. Helen Brock. *Scotus Americanus: A Survey of the Sources for Links between Scotland and America in the Eighteenth Century*. Edinburgh: Edinburgh University Press, 1982.
Brown, Michael. *The Wars of Scotland, 1214–1371*. Edinburgh: Edinburgh University Press, 2004.
Bryant, G. J. "Scots in India in the Eighteenth Century." *Scottish Historical Review* 64, no. 177 (April 1985): 22–41.
Bryce, Peter H. "Sir William Johnson, Bart., The Great Diplomat of the British-French Frontier." *Quarterly Journal of the New York State Historical Association* 8, no. 4 (1926): 352–73.
Buffington, Arthur H. "The Canada Expedition of 1746: Its Relation to British Politics." *American Historical Review* 45, no. 3 (April 1940): 552–80.
———. "The Policy of Albany and English Westward Expansion." *Mississippi Valley Historical Review* 8, no. 4 (1922): 327–66.
Buranelli, Vincent. "Governor Cosby and His Enemies (1732–36)." *New York History* 37, no. 4 (1956): 365–87.
———. "Governor Cosby's Hatchet–Man." *New York History* 37, no. 1 (1956): 26–39.
Burch, Druin. "Death Beds." *Natural History* 117, no. 10 (November 2008): 16–18.
Burch, Wanda. "A Little World Formed by His Hand." *New York History* 89, no. 2 (2008): 103–10.
Burrows, Edwin G., and Mike Wallace. *Gotham: A History of New York City to 1898*. Oxford: Oxford University Press, 1999.
"Cadwallader Colden." *Historical Magazine* 9 (January 1865): 9–13.

Cajori, Florian. *A History of the Conceptions of Limits and Fluxions in Great Britain from Newton to Woodhouse.* Chicago: Open Court, 1919.
Calloway, Colin G. *The Scratch of a Pen: 1763 and the Transformation of North America.* New York: Oxford University Press, 2006.
———. *White People, Indians, and Highlanders: Tribal Peoples and Colonial Encounters in Scotland and America.* New York: Oxford University Press, 2008.
Carp, Benjamin L. *Rebels Rising: Cities and the American Revolution.* Oxford: Oxford University Press, 2007.
Caulfield, Ernest. *A True History of the Terrible Epidemic Vulgarly Called The Throat Distemper Which Occurred in His Majesty's New England Colonies Between the Years 1735 and 1740.* In *Disease and Society In Provincial Massachusetts: Collected Accounts, 1736–1939*, 1–113. New York: Arno Press, 1972.
Champagne, Roger J. *Alexander McDougall and the American Revolution in New York.* Schenectady, NY: New York State American Revolution Bicentennial Commission, Union College Press, 1975.
———. "Family Politics versus Constitutional Principles: The New York Assembly Elections of 1768 and 1769." *William and Mary Quarterly*, 3rd ser., 20 (1963): 57–79.
Chaplin, Joyce E. *The First Scientific American: Benjamin Franklin and the Pursuit of Genius.* New York: Basic Books, 2006.
Christie, Ian R., and Benjamin W. Labaree. *Empire or Independence, 1760–1776: A British-American Dialogue on the Coming of the American Revolution.* New York: Norton, 1976.
Clark, Sir George. *A History of the Royal College of Physicians of London.* 3 vols. Oxford: Clarendon Press for the Royal College of Physicians, 1964–1972.
Clarke, T. Wood. "The Negro Plot of 1741." *New York History* 25, no. 2 (1944): 167–81.
Clive, John, and Bernard Bailyn. "England's Cultural Provinces: Scotland and America." *William and Mary Quarterly*, 3rd ser., 11 (1954): 200–213.
Cokayne, George E. *The Complete Peerage Or a History of the House of Lords and All Its Members from the Earliest Times.* Vol. 8. *Lindley to Moate.* Edited by Vicary Gibbs and others. Rev. ed. London: St. Catherine Press, 1932.
Comrie, John D. *History of Scottish Medicine.* 2nd ed. 2 vols. London: Baillière, Tindall & Cox, Wellcome Historical Medical Museum, 1932.
Cowan, Ian B. *The Scottish Covenanters, 1660–1688.* London: V. Gollancz, 1976.
Crary, Catherine Snell. "The American Dream: John Tabor Kempe's Rise from Poverty to Riches." *William and Mary Quarterly*, 3rd ser., 14 (1957): 176–95.
———. "Forfeited Loyalist Lands in the Western District of New York—Albany and Tryon Counties." *New York History* 35, no. 3 (1954): 239–58.
Craven, Wesley Frank. *The Colonies in Transition, 1660–1713.* New York: Harper & Row, 1968.
Crick, B. R., and Miriam Alman, eds. *A Guide to Manuscripts Relating to America in Great Britain and Ireland.* London: British Association for American Studies, Oxford University Press, 1961.
Crosby, Alfred W. Jr. *The Columbian Exchange: Biological and Cultural Consequences of 1492.* Westport, CT: Greenwood Press, 1972.
Cunningham, Andrew, and Roger French, eds. *The Medical Enlightenment of the Eighteenth Century.* Cambridge and New York: Cambridge University Press, 1990.
David, James Corbett. *Dunmore's New World.* Charlottesville: University of Virginia Press, 2013.
Davies, Norman. *The Isles: A History.* New York: Oxford University Press, 1999.
Davis, Thomas J. *A Rumor of Revolt: The "Great Negro Plot" in Colonial New York.* New York: Free Press, 1985.
Dawson, Henry B. *The Sons of Liberty in New York: A Paper Read before the New York Historical Society, May 3, 1859.* Poughkeepsie, NY: Platt & Schram, 1859.
Delbourgo, James. *A Most Amazing Scene of Wonders: Electricity and Enlightenment in Early America.* Cambridge, MA: Harvard University Press, 2006.
Denny, Margaret. "Naming the Gardenia." *Scientific Monthly* 67, no. 1 (1948): 17–22.
Devine, T. M. *The Scottish Nation, 1700–2000.* New York: Penguin Books, 1999.

Diaz, Michael. "'Can you on such principles think of quitting a Country?': Family, Faith, Law, Property, and the Loyalists of the Hudson Valley During the American Revolution." *Hudson River Valley Review* 28, no. 1 (Autumn 2011): 3–29.
Dickerson, Oliver Morton. *American Colonial Government, 1696–1765: A Study of the British Board of Trade in Its Relation to the American Colonies, Political, Industrial, Administrative*. Cleveland, OH: A. H. Clark, 1912.
Dickinson, H. T. "The Poor Palatines and the Parties." *English Historical Review* 82, no. 324 (1967): 464–85.
Dickinson, William Croft. *Scotland from the Earliest Times to 1603*. New York: Th. Nelson, 1961.
Dictionary of American Biography. 22 vols. New York: Charles Schribner, 1928–1958.
Dillon, Dorothy Rita. *The New York Triumvirate: A Study of the Legal and Political Careers of William Livingston, John Morin Scott, William Smith, Jr.* New York: Columbia University Press, 1949.
D'Innocenzo, Michael, and John J. Turner Jr. "The Role of New York Newspapers in the Stamp Act Crisis, 1764–66." *New York Historical Society Quarterly* 51, nos. 3–4 (1967): Part 1, 215–31; Part 2, 345–65.
DiVirgilio, Justin. "Rum Punch and Cultural Revolution: The Impact of the Seven Years' War in Albany." *New York History* 86, no. 4 (2005): 435–49.
Dix, Morgan. *A History of the Parish of Trinity Church in the City of New York*. Vol. 1. *To the Close of the Rectorship of Dr. Inglis, A.D. 1783*. New York: G. P. Putnam, 1898.
Dixon, John. "Cadwallader Colden and the Scottish Enlightenment in Transatlantic Context." *Eighteenth-Century Scotland: The Newsletter of the Eighteenth-Century Scottish Studies Society* 23 (Spring 2009): 7–10.
Donnan, Elizabeth. "Eighteenth-Century English Merchants: Micajah Perry." *Journal of Economic and Business History* 4, no. 1 (November 1931): 70–98.
Draper, Theodore. *A Struggle for Power: The American Revolution*. New York: Times Books, 1996.
Duffy, John. *Epidemics in Colonial America*. Baton Rouge: Louisiana State University Press, 1953.
Dunbar, Louise B. "The Royal Governors in the Middle and Southern Colonies on the Eve of the Revolution: A Study in Imperial Personnel." In *The Era of the American Revolution*, edited by Richard B. Morris, 214–68. New York: Columbia University Press, 1939. Reprint. New York: Harper & Row, 1965.
Dunlap, William. *History of the Rise of Progress of The Arts of Design in the United States*. 2 vols. New York: G. P. Scott, 1834. Reprint. New ed. Edited by Alexander Wyckoff. 3 vols. New York: B. Blom, 1965.
Eager, John M. "An Early Canal." *Historical Magazine* 8, no. 3 (March 1864): 114–15.
Eager, Samuel W. *An Outline History of Orange County*. Newburgh, NY: S. T. Callahan, 1846–1847.
Edwards, George William. *New York as an Eighteenth Century Municipality, 1731–1776*. New York: Columbia University Press, 1917. Reprint. New York: AMS Press, 1968.
The Encyclopedia Britannica: A Dictionary of Arts, Sciences, and General Literature. 9th ed. 25 vols. Edinburgh: Adam and Charles Black, 1875–1889.
Engelman, F. L. "Cadwallader Colden and the New York Stamp Act Riots." *William and Mary Quarterly*, 3rd ser., 10 (1953): 560–578.
Ernst, Joseph Albert. *Money and Politics in America, 1755–1775: A Study in the Currency Act of 1764 and the Political Economy of Revolution*. Chapel Hill: University of North Carolina Press, 1973.
Estes, J. Worth. "Therapeutic Practice in Colonial New England." In *Medicine in Colonial Massachusetts, 1620–1820*, Colonial Society of Massachusetts. *Publications* 57 (1980): 289–383.
Fabel, Robin F. A. *The Economy of British West Florida, 1763–1783*. Tuscaloosa: University of Alabama Press, 1988.
Fara, Patricia. "'A Treasure of Hidden Vertues': The Attraction of Magnetic Marketing." *British Journal for the History of Science* 28, no. 1 (1995): 5–35.

Fiering, Norman S. "Early American Philosophy vs. Philosophy in Early America." Charles S. Peirce Society. *Transactions* 13, no. 3 (Summer 1977): 216–37.
Fingerhut, Eugene R. *Survivor: Cadwallader Colden II in Revolutionary America*. Washington, DC: University Press of America, 1983.
Finnegan, David. "What Do the Depositions Say About the Outbreak of the 1641 Rising?" In *The 1641 Depositions and the Irish Rebellion*, edited by Eamon Darcy, Annaleigh Margey, and Elaine Murphy, 21–34. London: Brookfield, 2012.
Fiore, Jordan D. "Jonathan Swift and the American Episcopate." *William and Mary Quarterly*, 3rd ser., 11 (1954): 425–33.
Flavell, Julie M. "American Patriots in London and the Quest for Talks, 1774–1775." *Journal of Imperial and Commonwealth History* 20, no. 3 (1992): 335–69.
———. "Lord North's Conciliatory Proposal and the Patriots in London." *English Historical Review* 107, no. 423 (1992): 302–22.
———. *When London Was Capital of America*. New Haven, CT: Yale University Press, 2010.
Fleming, Thomas J. *1776: Year of Illusions*. New York: Norton, 1975.
Flexner, James Thomas. *Lord of the Mohawks: A Biography of Sir William Johnson*. 2nd ed. Boston: Little, Brown, 1979.
Flick, Alexander C. *History of the State of New York*. 10 vols. New York: Columbia University Press, 1933–1937.
Ford, Worthington Chauncey, comp. "British Officers Serving in America, 1754–1774." *New England Historical and Genealogical Register* 48–49 (1894–1895): 163, 171.
———, ed. *British Officers Serving in America, 1754–1774, Compiled from the "Army Lists."* Boston: D. Clapp, 1894.
Fox, Dixon Ryan. *Yankees and Yorkers*. New York: New York University Press, 1940. Reprint. Westport, CT: Greenwood Press, 1979.
Fox, Edith M. *Land Speculation in the Mohawk Country*. Ithaca, NY: Cornell University Press, 1949.
Fox, R. Hingston. *Dr. John Fothergill and His Friends: Chapters in Eighteenth Century Life*. London: Macmillan, 1919.
Frasca, Ralph. "'At the Sign of the Bribe Refused': The *Constitutional Courant* and the Stamp Tax, 1765." *New Jersey History* 107, nos. 3–4 (1989): 21–39.
———. *Benjamin Franklin's Printing Network: Disseminating Virtue in Early America*. Columbia: University of Missouri Press, 2006.
French, Roger K. "Ether and Physiology." In *Conceptions of Ether: Studies in the History of Ether Theories, 1740–1900*, edited by G. N. Cantor and M. J. S. Hodge, 111–34. Cambridge: Cambridge University Press, 1981.
———. *Robert Whytt, the Soul, and Medicine*. London: Wellcome Institute, 1969.
Fry, Peter, and Fiona Somerset. *The History of Scotland*. London: Routledge, 1982. Reprint. New York: Routledge, 1995.
Gerlach, Don R. *Philip Schuyler and the American Revolution in New York, 1733–1777*. Lincoln: University of Nebraska, 1964.
Gibney, John. *The Shadow of a Year: The 1641 Rebellion in Irish History and Memory*. Madison: University of Wisconsin Press, 2013.
Gifford, George E., Jr. "Botanic Remedies in Colonial Massachusetts, 1620–1820." In *Medicine in Colonial Massachusetts, 1620–1820*, Colonial Society of Massachusetts. *Publications* 57 (1980): 263–88.
Gipson, Lawrence Henry. *The British Empire Before the American Revolution*. 15 vols. Caldwell, ID: Caxton Printers; New York: A. A. Knopf, 1936–1970.
———. *Lewis Evans*. Philadelphia: Historical Society of Pennsylvania, 1939.
Gitin, Louis Leonard. "Cadwallader Colden as Scientist and Philosopher." *New York History* 16, no. 2 (1935): 169–77.
Godfrey, William G. *Pursuit of Profit and Preferment in Colonial North America: John Bradstreet's Quest*. Waterloo, Canada: Wilfrid Laurier University Press, 1982.
Goldsmith, Donald. "Dark Energy Crisis." *Natural History* 117, no. 10 (December 2008–January 2009): 30–34.

———. "Turn, Turn, Turn." *Natural History* 115, no. 10 (December 2006–January 2007): 20, 22, 24–26, 60.
Golinski, Jan. *British Weather and the Climate of Enlightenment*. Chicago: University of Chicago Press, 2007.
Goodfriend, Joyce D. *Before the Melting Pot: Society and Culture in Colonial New York City, 1664–1730*. Princeton, NJ: Princeton University Press, 1992.
Graham, Ian Charles Cargill. *Colonists from Scotland: Emigration to North America, 1707–1783*. Ithaca, NY: Cornell University Press, 1956.
Grant, Alastair Macpherson. *General James Grant of Ballindalloch, 1720–1806*. London: A. M. Grant, 1930.
Grant, Alexander. *The Story of the University of Edinburgh During Its First Three Hundred Years*. 2 vols. London: Longmans, Green, 1884.
Gray, Alexander. "The Old Schools and Universities in Scotland." *Scottish Historical Review* 9, no. 34 (1912): 113–38.
Greene, Evarts B. "New York and the Old Empire." *Quarterly Journal of the New York State Historical Association* 8, no. 2 (1927): 121–32.
Greene, Jack P., and Richard M. Jellison. "The Currency Act of 1764 in Imperial-Colonial Relations, 1764–1776." *William and Mary Quarterly*, 3rd ser., 18 (1961): 485–518.
Greene, John C. "Some Aspects of American Astronomy, 1750–1815." *Isis* 45, no. 4 (1954): 339–58.
Gronim, Sara S. "At the Sign of Newton's Head: Astronomy and Cosmology in British Colonial New York." *Pennsylvania History* 66, supp. (1999): 55–85.
———. "Geography and Persuasion: Maps in British Colonial New York." *William and Mary Quarterly*, 3rd ser., 58 (2001): 373–402.
Gwyn, Julian. *An Admiral for America: Sir Peter Warren, Vice Admiral of the Red, 1703–1752*. Gainesville: University Press of Florida, 2004.
Haan, Richard. "The Problem of Iroquois Neutrality: Suggestions for Revision." *Ethnohistory* 27, no. 4 (1980): 317–30.
Haig, James. *Topographical and Historical Account of the Town of Kelso, and of the Town and Castle of Roxburgh*. Edinburgh: Fairbairn, 1825.
Hall, Elizabeth C. "The Gentlewoman, Jane Colden, and Her Manuscript on New York Native Plants." In *Botanic Manuscript of Jane Colden, 1724–1766*. Edited by Harold W. Rickett and Elizabeth C. Hall, 17–21. New York: Garden Club of Orange and Dutchess Counties, 1963.
Hallock, Thomas. "Male Pleasure and the Genders of Eighteenth–Century Botanic Exchange: A Garden Tour." *William and Mary Quarterly*, 3rd ser., 62 (2005): 697–718.
Hardy, Anne. "Scarlet Fever." In *The Cambridge World History of Human Disease*, edited by Kenneth F. Kiple, 990–92. Cambridge: Cambridge University Press, 1993.
Harlow, Alvin F. *Old Towpaths: The Story of the American Canal Era*. New York: D. Appleton, 1926. Reprint. New ed. Port Washington, NY: Kennikat Press, 1964.
Harrington, Virginia D. *The New York Merchant on the Eve of the Revolution*. New York: Columbia University Press, 1935. Reprint. Gloucester, MA: Peter Smith, 1964.
Hay, D. "England, Scotland and Europe: The Problem of the Frontier." *Royal Historical Society, Transactions*, 5th ser., 25 (1975): 77–91.
Heaton, Claude E. "Medicine in New York during the English Colonial Period." *Bulletin of the History of Medicine* 17, no. 1 (1945): 9–37.
Hedrick, Ulysses Prentiss. *A History of Agriculture in the State of New York*. Albany, NY: New York State Agricultural Society, 1933. Reprint. New York: Hill and Wang, 1966.
———. *A History of Horticulture in America To 1860*. New York: Oxford University Press, 1950.
Heimann, P. M. "Ether and Imponderables." In *Conceptions of Ether: Studies in the History of Ether Theories, 1740–1900*, edited by G. N. Cantor and M. J. S. Hodge, 61–83. Cambridge: Cambridge University Press, 1981.
Hemstreet, Charles. "Literary Landmarks of New York." *Critic* 41 (1902): 158–65.
———. *The Story of Manhattan*. New York: C. Scribner, 1916.

Henretta, James A. *"Salutary Neglect": Colonial Administration Under the Duke of Newcastle.* Princeton, NJ: Princeton University Press, 1972.

Hepburn, A. Barton. *Artificial Waterways of the World.* New York: Macmillan, 1914.

Herbert, Eugenia W. "Smallpox Inoculation in Africa." *Journal of African History* 16, no. 4 (1975): 539–59.

Hinderaker, Eric. *The Two Hendricks: Unraveling a Mohawk Mystery.* Cambridge, MA: Harvard University Press, 2010.

Hindle, Brooke. "Cadwallader Colden's Extension of the Newtonian Principles." *William and Mary Quarterly*, 3rd ser., 13 (1956): 459–75.

———. "A Colonial Governor's Family: The Coldens of Coldengham." *New York Historical Society Quarterly* 45, no. 3 (1961): 223–50.

———. *The Pursuit of Science in Revolutionary America, 1735–1789.* Chapel Hill: University of North Carolina Press, 1956.

———. "The Quaker Background and Science in Colonial Philadelphia." *Isis* 46, no. 3 (1955): 243–50.

Hoermann, Alfred R. *Cadwallader Colden: A Figure of the American Enlightenment.* Westport, CT: Greenwood Press, 2002.

———. "Cadwallader Colden and the Mind-Body Problem." *Bulletin of the History of Medicine* 50, no. 3 (1976): 392–404.

———. "A Savant in the Wilderness: Cadwallader Colden of New York." *New York Historical Society Quarterly* 62, no. 4 (1978): 271–88.

Hoffer, Peter Charles. *The Great New York Conspiracy of 1741: Slavery, Crime, and Colonial Law.* Lawrence: University Press of Kansas, 2003.

Hollingsworth, Buckner. *Her Garden Was Her Delight.* New York: Macmillan, 1962.

Hornberger, Theodore. "Samuel Johnson of Yale and King's College: A Note on the Relation of Science and Religion in Provincial America." *New England Quarterly* 8, no. 3 (1935): 378–97.

Hughes, Edward. "The English Stamp Duties, 1664–1764." *English Historical Review* 56, no. 222 (1941): 234–64.

Hulsebosch, Daniel J. *Constituting Empire: New York and the Transformation of Constitutionalism in the Atlantic World, 1664–1830.* Chapel Hill: University of North Carolina Press, 2005.

Humphrey, David C. "Urban Manners and Rural Morals: The Controversy Over the Location of King's College." *New York History* 54, no. 1 (1973): 4–23.

Humphreys, R. A. "Lord Shelburne and a Projected Recall of Colonial Governors in 1767." *American Historical Review* 37, no. 2 (1932): 269–72.

Hünemörder, Markus. *The Society of the Cincinnati: Conspiracy and Distrust in Early America.* New York: Berghahn Books, 2006.

Hunter, Michael. *Boyle: Between God and Science.* New Haven, CT: Yale University Press, 2009.

Hurlbutt, Robert H. III. *Hume, Newton, and The Design Argument.* Rev. ed., 2nd Landmark ed. Lincoln: University of Nebraska Press, 1965.

Hutton, Ronald. *Charles the Second: King of England, Scotland, and Ireland.* New York: Clarendon Press, 1989.

Isaacson, Walter. *Benjamin Franklin: An American Life.* New York: Simon & Schuster, 2003.

———. *Einstein: His Life and Universe.* New York: Simon & Schuster, 2007.

Jackson, Clare. *Restoration Scotland, 1660–1690: Royalist Politics, Religion and Ideas.* Rochester, NY: Boydell Press, 2003.

Jacobs, Wilbur R. "Cadwallader Colden's Noble Iroquois Savages." In *Colonial Legacy*, edited by Lawrence H. Leder, vol. 3, 34–58. New York: Harper & Row, 1973.

Jarcho, Saul, "Biographical and Bibliographical Notes on Cadwallader Colden." *Bulletin of the History of Medicine* 32, no. 4 (1958): 322–34.

———. "Cadwallader Colden as a Student of Infectious Diseases." *Bulletin of the History of Medicine* 29, no. 2 (1955): 99–115.

———. "The Therapeutic Use of Resin and of Tar Water by Bishop George Berkeley and Cadwallader Colden." *New York State Journal of Medicine* 55, no. 6 (1955): 834–40.

Johnson, Allen S. "The Passage of the Sugar Act." *William and Mary Quarterly*, 3rd ser., 16 (1959): 507–14.

Johnson, Herbert A. "The Rule of Law in the Realm and the Province of New York: Prelude to the American Revolution." *History* 91, no. 1(301) (2006): 3–23.

Johnson, Joan. *Princely Chandos: James Brydges, 1674–1744*. Gloucester: Sutton, 1984.

Jones, Adam Leroy. *Early American Philosophers*. New York: Macmillan, 1898. Reprint. New York: F. Ungar, 1958.

Jones, Inga. "'Holy War'? Religion, Ethnicity and Massacre During the Irish Rebellion, 1641-2," In *The 1641 Depositions and the Irish Rebellion*, edited by Eamon Darcy, Annaleigh Margey and Elaine Murphy, 21–34. London; Brookfield, 2012.

Jones, Matt Bushnell. *Vermont in the Making, 1750–1777*. Cambridge, MA: Harvard University Press, 1939.

Jordan, John W. "Biographical Sketch of Rev. Bernhard Adam Grube." *Pennsylvania Magazine of History and Biography* 25, no. 1 (1901): 14–19.

Judd, Gerrit P. *Members of Parliament, 1734–1832*. New Haven: CT: Yale University Press, 1955.

July, Robert W. *The Essential New Yorker: Gulian Crommelin Verplanck*. Durham, NC: Duke University Press, 1951.

Kaminski, John P. *George Clinton: Yeoman Politician of the New Republic*. Madison: University of Wisconsin Press, 1993.

Kastner, Joseph. *A Species of Eternity*. New York: Knopf, 1977.

Katz, Stanley Nider. "Between Scylla and Charybdis: James DeLancey and Anglo-American Politics in Early Eighteenth-Century New York." In *Anglo-American Political Relations, 1675–1775*, edited by Alison Gilbert Olson and Richard Maxwell Brown, 92–108. New Brunswick, NJ: Rutgers University Press, 1970.

———. *Newcastle's New York: Anglo-American Politics, 1732–1753*. Cambridge, MA: Harvard University Press, 1968.

———. "Newcastle's New York Governors: Imperial Patronage during the Era of 'Salutary Neglect.'" *New York Historical Society Quarterly* 51, no. 1 (1967): 7–23.

———. "The Politics of Law in Colonial America: Controversies over Chancery Courts and Equity Law in the Eighteenth Century." *Perspectives in American History* 5 (1971): 255–84.

Keep, Austin Baxter. *History of the New York Society Library*. New York: De Vinne Press, 1908.

Ketchum, Richard M. *Divided Loyalties: How the American Revolution Came to New York*. New York: Henry Holt, 2002.

Keys, Alice Mapelsden. *Cadwallader Colden: A Representative Eighteenth-Century Official*. New York: Columbia University Press, 1906. Reprint. New York: AMS Press, 1967.

Kidd, Charles, and David Williamson, eds. *Debrett's Peerage and Baronetage*. London: MacMillan, 2003.

Kierner, Cynthia A. *Traders and Gentlefolk: The Livingstons of New York, 1675–1790*. Ithaca, NY: Cornell University Press, 1992.

Kim, Sung Bok. *Landlord and Tenant in Colonial New York: Manorial Society, 1664–1775*. Chapel Hill: University of North Carolina Press, 1978.

Kimball, Everett. *The Public Life of Joseph Dudley: A Study of the Colonial Policy of the Stuarts in New England, 1660–1715*. New York: Longmans, Green, 1911.

Kinkel, Sarah. "The King's Pirates? Naval Enforcement of Imperial Authority, 1740–76." *William and Mary Quarterly*, 3rd ser., 71 (2014): 3–34.

Klein, Milton M. *The American Whig: William Livingston of New York*. New York: Garland, 1990.

———. "Archibald Kennedy: Imperial Pamphleteer." In *The Colonial Legacy*, edited by Lawrence H. Leder, vol. 2, 75–105. New York: Harper & Row, 1971.

———. "The Cultural Tyros of Colonial New York." *South Atlantic Quarterly* 66, no. 2 (1967): 218–32.

———. "Democracy and Politics in Colonial New York." *New York History* 40, no. 3 (1959): 221–46.

———, ed. *The Empire State: A History of New York*. Ithaca, NY: Cornell University Press, 2001.

———. "New York Lawyers and the Coming of the American Revolution." *New York History* 55, no. 4 (1974): 383–407.

———. "Politics and Personalities in Colonial New York." *New York History* 47, no. 1 (1966): 3–16.

———. "Prelude to Revolution in New York: Jury Trials and Judicial Tenure." *William and Mary Quarterly* 3rd ser., 17, no. 4 (1960): 439–62.

———. "The Rise of the New York Bar: The Legal Career of William Livingston." *William and Mary Quarterly*, 3rd ser., 15, no. 3 (1958): 334–58.

Klepp, Susan E., ed. *"The Swift Progress of Population": A Documentary and Bibliographical Study of Philadelphia's Growth, 1642–1859*. Philadelphia: American Philosophical Society, 1991.

Klinefelter, Walter. "Lewis Evans and His Maps." American Philosophical Society. *Transactions*, n.s., 61, no. 7 (1971): 3–65.

Knittle, Walter Allen. *Early Eighteenth Century Palatine Emigration: A British Government Redemptioner Project to Manufacture Naval Stores*. Philadelphia: Dorrance, 1937.

Knollenberg, Bernhard. *Origin of the American Revolution: 1759–1766*. New York: Macmillan 1960.

Koeppel, Gerard. *Bond of Union: Building the Erie Canal and the American Empire*. Cambridge, MA: Da Capo Press, 2009.

Korty, Margaret Barton. "Benjamin Franklin and Eighteenth-Century Libraries." American Philosophical Society. *Transactions*, n.s., 55, part 9 (1965): 1–83.

Kraus, Michael. "Scientific Relations between Europe and America in the Eighteenth Century." *Scientific Monthly* 55, no. 3 (1942): 259–72.

Kraus, Michael, and Davis D. Joyce. *The Writing of American History*. 2nd ed. Norman: University of Oklahoma Press, 1985.

Labaree, Leonard Woods. "The Early Careers of the Royal Governors." In *Essays in Colonial History Presented to Charles McLean Andrews by his Students*, edited by Labaree, 145–68. New Haven, CT: Yale University Press, 1931.

———. *Royal Government in America: A Study of the British Colonial System before 1783*. New Haven, CT: Yale University Press, 1930.

Lamb, H. H. *Climate History and the Modern World*. New York: Methuen, 1982.

Lamb, Martha J. *History of the City of New York: Its Origin, Rise, and Progress*. 3 vols. New York: A. S. Barnes, 1877–1896. Reprint. 3 vols. New York: Valentine's Manual, 1921.

Landsman, Ned C. *Scotland and Its First American Colony, 1683–1765*. Princeton, NJ: Princeton University Press, 1985.

La Potin, Armand. "The Minisink Grant: Partnerships, Patents, and Processing Fees in Eighteenth Century New York." *New York History* 56, no. 1 (1975): 29–50.

Launitz-Schürer, Leopold, Jr. *Loyal Whigs and Revolutionaries: The Making of a Revolution in New York, 1765–1776*. New York: New York University Press, 1980.

———. "Slave Resistance in Colonial New York: An Interpretation of Daniel Horsmanden's New York Conspiracy." *Phylon* 41, no. 2 (1980): 137–52.

Leach, Douglas Edward. *Roots of Conflict: British Armed Forces and Colonial Americans, 1677–1763*. Chapel Hill: University of North Carolina Press, 1986.

Leder, Lawrence H., ed. *The Colonial Legacy*. Vol. 2. *Some Eighteenth-Century Commentators*. New York: Harper & Row, 1971; Vol. 3. *Historians of Nature and Man's Nature*; Vol. 4. *Early Nationalist Historians*. New York: Harper & Row, 1973.

———. "A Neglected Aspect of New York's Forgotten Century." *New York History* 37, no. 3 (1956): 259–65.

———. *Robert Livingston, 1654–1728, and the Politics of Colonial New York*. Chapel Hill: University of North Carolina Press, 1961.

Lehmann, William C. *John Millar of Glasgow, 1735–1801: His Life and Thought and His Contributions of Sociological Analysis*. Cambridge: Cambridge University Press, 1960.

Lemay, J. A. Leo. *The Life of Benjamin Franklin*. Vol. 2. *Printer and Publisher, 1730–1747*. Philadelphia: University of Pennsylvania Press, 2006.

Lepore, Jill. "How Longfellow Woke the Dead." *American Scholar* 80, no. 2 (2011): 33–46.
———. *New York Burning: Liberty, Slavery, and Conspiracy in Eighteenth-Century Manhattan*. New York: Knopf, 2005.
Levy, Leonard W. "Did the Zenger Case Really Matter? Freedom of the Press in Colonial New York." *William and Mary Quarterly*, 3rd ser., 17 (1960): 35–50.
———. *Emergence of a Free Press*. New York: Oxford University Press, 1985.
Lipscomb, Diana. "Women in Systematics." *Annual Review of Ecology and Systematics* 26 (1995): 323–41.
Lokken, Roy N. "Cadwallader Colden's Attempt to Advance Natural Philosophy Beyond the Eighteenth-Century Mechanistic Paradigm." American Philosophical Society. *Proceedings* 122, no. 6 (December 1978): 365–76.
Lokken, Roy N., and James Logan. "The Scientific Papers of James Logan." American Philosophical Society. *Transactions*. n.s., 62, no. 6 (1972): 1–94.
Lorenz, Alfred Lawrence. *Hugh Gaine: A Colonial Printer-Editor's Odyssey to Loyalism*. Carbondale: Southern Illinois University Press, 1972.
Lustig, Mary Lou. *Privilege and Prerogative: New York's Provincial Elite, 1710–1776*. Madison, NJ: Fairleigh Dickinson University Press, 1995.
———. *Robert Hunter, 1666–1734: New York's Augustan Statesman*. Syracuse, NY: Syracuse University Press, 1983.
Lyndon, James G. "The Great Capture of 1744." *New York Historical Society Quarterly* 52, no. 3 (1968): 255–69.
MacDonald, Alan R. *The Jacobean Kirk, 1567–1625: Sovereignty, Polity, and Liturgy*. Brookfield, VT: Ashgate, 1998.
Macdougall, Norman. *James III: A Political Study*. Edinburgh: John Donald, Humanities, Press, 1982.
MacKenzie, John M. "Empire and National Identities: The Case of Scotland." Royal Historical Society. *Transactions*. 6th ser., 8 (1998): 215–31.
Mackie, R. L. *King James IV of Scotland: A Brief Survey of His Life and Times*. Edinburgh: Oliver and Boyd, 1958.
Maier, Pauline. *From Resistance to Revolution: Colonial Radicals and the Development of American Opposition to Britain, 1765–1776*. New York: Vintage Books, 1972.
Marambaud, Pierre. *William Byrd of Westover, 1674–1744*. Charlottesville: University Press of Virginia, 1971.
Mark, Irving. *Agrarian Conflicts in Colonial New York, 1711–1775*. New York: Columbia University Press, 1940.
Mason, Bernard. *The Road to Independence: The Revolutionary Movement in New York, 1773–1777*. Lexington: University Press of Kentucky, 1966.
Matthews, John A., and Keith R. Briffa. "The 'Little Ice Age': Re-Evaluation of an Evolving Concept." *Geografiska Annaler Series A: Physical Geography* 87, no. 1 (March 2005): 17–36.
Mayor, Adrienne. *Greek Fire, Poison Arrows and Scorpion Bombs: Biological and Chemical Warfare in the Ancient World*. Woodstock, NY: Overlook Duckworth, 2003.
McAnear, Beverly. *The Income of the Colonial Governors of British North America*. New York: Pageant Press, 1967.
McGeachy, Robert A. A. "Captain Lauchlin Campbell and Argyllshire Emigration to New York." *Northern Scotland* 19, no. 1 (1999): 21–46.
McManus, Edgar J. *Black Bondage in the North*. Syracuse, NY: Syracuse University Press, 1973.
Messenger, Charles. *History of the British Army*. Greenwich, CT: Brompton Books, 1986.
Middleton, W. E. Knowles. *A History of the Thermometer and Its Use in Meteorology*. Baltimore: Johns Hopkins University Press, 1966.
Moglen, Eben. "Considering *Zenger*: Partisan Politics and the Legal Profession in Provincial New York." *Columbia Law Review* 94, no. 5 (1994): 1495–524.
Moody, T. W., F. X. Martin, and F. J. Byrne, eds. *A New History of Ireland*. Vol. 3. *Early Modern Ireland, 1534–1691*. Reprint with corrections. Oxford: Clarendon Press, 1978.

Moore, George H. *Collegium Regale Novi Eboraci: The Origin and Early History of Columbia College.* New York: G. H. Moore, 1890.
Morgan, Edmund S., and Helen M. Morgan. *The Stamp Act Crisis: Prologue to Revolution.* 2nd ed. New York: Collier Books, 1963.
Morgan, William Thomas. "An Eighteenth-Century Election in England." *Political Science Quarterly* 37, no. 4 (1922): 585–604.
Morse, James M. "Colonial Historians of New York." *New York History* 23, no. 4 (1942): 395–409.
Murray, Archibald K. *History of the Scottish Regiments in the British Army.* Glasgow: Thomas Murray, 1862.
Nammack, Georgiana C. *Fraud, Politics, and the Dispossession of the Indians: The Iroquois Land Frontier in the Colonial Period.* Norman: University of Oklahoma Press, 1969.
Nash, Gary B. *The Urban Crucible: Social Change, Political Consciousness, and the Origins of the American Revolution.* Cambridge, MA: Harvard University Press, 1979.
Naylor, Rex Maurice. "The Royal Prerogative in New York, 1691–1775. *Quarterly Journal of the New York State Historical Association* 5, no. 3 (1924): 221–55.
Neffe, Jürgen. *Einstein: A Biography.* Translated by Shelly Frisch. New York: Farrar, Straus and Giroux, 2007.
Nelson, Paul David. *William Tryon and the Course of Empire: A Life in British Imperial Service.* Chapel Hill: University of North Carolina Press, 1990.
Nelson, William. *William Burnet, Governor of New York and New Jersey, 1720–1728: A Sketch of his Administration in New York.* New York: N.p., 1892.
New Catholic Encyclopedia. 2nd ed. 15 vols. Detroit: Thomson/Gale, 2003.
Nobles, Gregory H. "Straight Lines and Stability: Mapping the Political Order of the Anglo-American Frontier." *Journal of American History* 80, no. 1 (1993): 9–35.
Norton, Marcy. *Sacred Gifts, Profane Pleasures: A History of Tobacco and Chocolate in the Atlantic World.* Ithaca, NY: Cornell University Press, 2008.
Norton, Thomas Elliott. *The Fur Trade in Colonial New York, 1686–1776.* Madison: University of Wisconsin Press, 1974.
"Notes on the Erie Canal." *Bulletin of the Business Historical Society* 6, no. 5 (1932): 6–13.
Olson, Alison Gilbert. "Governor Robert Hunter and the Anglican Church in New York." In *Statesmen, Scholars and Merchants: Essays in Eighteenth-Century History presented to Dame Lucy Sutherland,* edited by Anne Whiteman, John S. Bromley, and Peter G. M. Dickson, 44–64. Oxford: Clarendon Press, 1973.
O'Shaughnessy, Andrew Jackson. *The Men Who Lost America: British Leadership, the American Revolution, and the Fate of the Empire.* New Haven, CT: Yale University Press, 2013.
O'Toole, Fintan. *White Savage: William Johnson and the Invention of America.* New York: Farrar, Straus, and Giroux, 2005.
Otterness, Philip. *Becoming German: The 1709 Palatine Migration to New York.* Ithaca, NY: Cornell University Press, 2004.
Oxford Dictionary of National Biography. 61 vols. New York: Oxford University Press, 2004.
Oxford English Dictionary. 12 vols. Oxford: Clarendon Press, 1961.
Packard, Francis R. *History of Medicine in the United States.* 2 vols. New York: Hoeber, 1931.
Paltsits, Victor Hugo. "A Scheme for the Conquest of Canada in 1746." American Antiquarian Society. *Proceedings,* n.s., 17 (1905–1906): 69–92.
Panek, Richard. "Probing the Biggest Mystery in the Universe." *Smithsonian* 41 (April 2010): 30–37.
Pargellis, Stanley McCrory. *Lord Loudoun in North America.* New Haven, CT: Yale University Press, 1933.
Parrish, Susan Scott. *American Curiosity: Cultures of Natural History in the Colonial British Atlantic World.* Chapel Hill: University of North Carolina Press, 2006.
Peck, Amelia, ed. *Interwoven Globe: The Worldwide Textile Trade, 1500–1800.* Exhibition catalogue. Metropolitan Museum of Art, New York, September 16, 2013–January 5, 2014. New Haven, CT: Yale University Press, 2013.

———. "The Verplanck Room: Coldenham, New York, 1767." In *Period Rooms in The Metropolitan Museum of Art*, edited by Amelia Peck and others, 205–11. New York: Metropolitan Museum of Art, 1996.
Peterson, Arthur Everett. *New York As An Eighteenth Century Municipality Prior to 1731*. New York: Longmans, Green, 1917. Reprint. 2 vols. New York: AMS Press, 1968.
Plaag, Eric W. "New York's 1741 Slave Conspiracy in a Climate of Fear and Anxiety." *New York History* 84, no. 3 (2003): 275–99.
Plank, Geoffrey. *Rebellion and Savagery: The Jacobite Rising of 1745 and the British Empire*. Philadelphia: University of Pennsylvania Press, 2006.
Plumb, J. H., and others. *The English Heritage*. St. Louis, MO: Forum Press, 1978.
Popper, Deborah Epstein. "Poor Christopher Colles: An Innovator's Obstacles in Early America." *Journal of American Culture* 28, no. 2 (2005): 178–90.
Porter, Roy. *Disease, Medicine and Society in England, 1550–1860*. 2nd ed. Cambridge: Cambridge University Press, 1993.
———. *Health for Sale: Quackery in England, 1660–1850*. Manchester, UK: Manchester University Press, 1989.
Pound, Arthur. "Charles Clinton: The First of the American Clintons." *Quarterly Journal of the New York State Historical Association* 12, no. 4 (1931): 375–89.
Preston, David L. "George Klock, the Canajoharie Mohawks, and the Good Ship *Sir William Johnson*: Land, Legitimacy, and Community in the Eighteenth-Century Mohawk Valley." *New York History* 86, no. 4 (2005): 473–99.
———. *The Texture of Contact: European and Indian Settler Communities on the Frontiers of Iroquoia, 1667–1783*. Lincoln: University of Nebraska Press, 2009.
Pryde, George S. "Scottish Colonization in the Province of New York." *New York History* 16, no. 2 (1935): 138–57.
Purple, Edwin R. "Notes, Biographical and Genealogical, of the Colden Family, and of Some of Its Collateral Branches in America." *New York Genealogical and Biographical Record* 4 (1873): 161–83.
Ranlet, Philip. "The British, the Indians, and Smallpox: What Actually Happened at Fort Pitt in 1763?" *Pennsylvania History* 67, no. 3 (2000): 427–41.
———. *Enemies of the Bay Colony: Puritan Massachusetts and Its Foes*. 2nd ed. Lanham, MD: University Press of America, 2006.
———. "How Many American Loyalists Left the United States?" *Historian* 76, no. 2 (2014): 278–307.
———. "New York, Indian Policy of." In *Encyclopedia of United States Indian Policy and Law*, edited by Paul Finkelman and Tim Alan Garrison, vol. 2. Washington, DC: CQ Press, 2009.
———. *The New York Loyalists*. 2nd ed. Lanham, MD: University Press of America, 2002.
———, ed. "Richard B. Morris's James DeLancey: Portrait in Loyalism." *New York History* 80, no. 2 (1999): 185–210.
———. "A Safe Haven for Witches? Colonial New York's Politics and Relations with New England in the 1690s." *New York History* 90, no. 1 (2009): 37–57.
———. "Typhus and American Prisoners in the War of Independence." *Mariner's Mirror* 96, no. 4 (2010): 443–54.
Rao, Joe. "The Southern Cross." *Natural History* 105 (May 1996): 67.
Raymond, Allan R. "Benning Wentworth's Claims in the New Hampshire-New York Border Controversy: A Case of Twenty-Twenty Hindsight?" *Vermont History* 43 (1975): 20–32.
Reinhold, Meyer. "Opponents of Classical Learning in America during the Revolutionary Period." American Philosophical Society. *Proceedings* 112, no. 4 (August 15, 1968): 221–34.
Richards, Frederick B. "The Black Watch at Ticonderoga." New York State Historical Association. *Proceedings* 10 (1911): 367–464.
Riley, I. Woodbridge. *American Philosophy: The Early Schools*. New York: Russell & Russell, 1958.

Robinson, Andrew. *The Last Man Who Knew Everything: Thomas Young, the Anonymous Genius Who Proved Newton Wrong and Deciphered the Rosetta Stone, Among Other Surprising Feats*. New York: Plume, 2006.
Rogers, Alan. *Empire and Liberty: American Resistance to British Authority, 1755–1763*. Berkeley: University of California Press, 1974.
Ruttenber, E. M. *History of the Town of Newburgh*. Newburgh, NY: E. M. Ruttenber, 1859.
Ruttenber, M., and L. H. Clark. *History of Orange County, New York*. Philadelphia: Everts & Peck, 1881.
Sabine, Lorenzo. *Biographical Sketches of Loyalists of the American Revolution with an Historical Essay*. 2nd ed. Boston: Little, Brown, 1864. Reprint. 2 vols. 2nd ed. Baltimore: Genealogical Publishing, 1979.
Savelle, Max. *Seeds of Liberty: The Genesis of the American Mind*. New York: Knopf, 1948.
Scanlon, James Edward. "British Intrigue and the Governorship of Robert Hunter." *New York Historical Society Quarterly* 57, no. 3 (1973): 199–211.
Schneider, Herbert W. *A History of American Philosophy*. New York: Forum Books, 1946.
Schutz, John A. *Thomas Pownall, British Defender of American Liberty: A Study of Anglo-American Relations in the Eighteenth Century*. Glendale, CA: Arthur H. Clark, 1951.
———. *William Shirley, King's Governor of Massachusetts*. Chapel Hill: University of North Carolina Press, 1961.
Schwarz, Philip J. *The Jarring Interests: New York's Boundary Makers, 1664–1776*. Albany: State University of New York Press, 1979.
———. "'To Conciliate the Jarring Interests': William Smith, Thomas Hutchinson, and the Massachusetts-New York Boundary, 1771–1773." *New York Historical Society Quarterly* 59, no. 4 (1975): 299–319.
Scott, Hew, ed. *Fasti Ecclesiae Scoticanae: New edition*. 8 vols. Edinburgh: Oliver & Boyd, 1915–1950.
Sellers, Charles Coleman. *Patience Wright: American Artist and Spy in George III's London*. Middletown, CT: Wesleyan University Press, 1976.
Shammas, Carole. "Cadwallader Colden and the Role of the King's Prerogative." *New York Historical Society Quarterly* 53, no. 2 (1969): 103–26.
Shank, J. B. *The Newton Wars and the Beginning of the French Enlightenment*. Chicago: University of Chicago Press, 2008.
Shea, John Gilmary. Introduction to *Cadwallader Colden: The History of the Five Indian Nations Depending on the Province of New-York*. New York: Bradford, 1727. Reprint. New York: T. H. Morrell, 1866.
Sher, Richard B. "Scotland Transformed: The Eighteenth Century." In *Scotland: A History*, edited by Jenny Wormald, 177–208. New York: Oxford University Press, 2005.
Sheridan, Eugene R. *Lewis Morris, 1671–1746: A Study in Early American Politics*. Syracuse, NY: Syracuse University Press, 1981.
Shipton, Clifford K. *Biographical Sketches of Those Who Attended Harvard College in the Classes 1722–1725*. Boston: Massachusetts Historical Society, 1945.
Singleton, Esther. *Social New York under the Georges, 1714–1776*. New York: D. Appleton, 1902.
Skeat, Walter W., and A. L. Mayhew, eds. *A Glossary of Tudor and Stuart Words Especially from the Dramatists*. Oxford: Clarendon Press, 1914. Reprint. New York: Burt Franklin, 1968.
Smallwood, William Martin. *Natural History and the American Mind*. New York: Columbia University Press, 1941. Reprint. New York: AMS Press, 1967.
Smith, Goldwin. *England: A Short History*. New York: Scribner, 1971.
Smith, Joseph Henry. *Appeals to the Privy Council from the American Plantations*. New York: Columbia University Press, 1950.
Smith, Joseph Henry, and Leo Hershkowitz. "Courts of Equity in the Province of New York: The Cosby Controversy, 1732–1736." *American Journal of Legal History* 16, no. 1 (1972): 1–50.
Spaulding, E. Wilder. *His Excellency George Clinton: Critic of the Constitution*. New York: Macmillan, 1938.

Stearns, Raymond Phineas. *Science in the British Colonies of America*. Urbana: University of Illinois Press, 1970.
Steiner, Bruce E. *Samuel Seabury, 1729–1796: A Study in the High Church Tradition*. Oberlin; [Athens]: Ohio University Press, 1971.
Stokes, I. N. Phelps. *The Iconography of Manhattan Island, 1498–1909*. 6 vols in 12. New York: R. H. Dodd, 1915–1928.
Stout, Neil R. "Captain Kennedy and the Stamp Act." *New York History* 45, no. 1 (1964): 44–58.
Sutherland, Arthur E. Review of *John Millar of Glasgow*, by William C. Lehmann. *Harvard Law Review* 74, no. 7 (May 1961): 1482–87.
Sweet, S. H. *Documentary Sketch of the New York State Canals*. Albany, NY: Van Benthuysen, 1863.
Syrett, David. "American Provincials and the Havanna Campaign of 1762." *New York History* 49, no. 4 (1968): 375–90.
Szasz, Ferenc M. "The New York Slave Revolt of 1741: A Re-Examination." *New York History* 48, no. 3 (1967): 215–30.
Szechi, Daniel. *1715: The Great Jacobite Rebellion*. New Haven, CT: Yale University Press, 2006.
Thomas, Peter P. G. *The Townshend Duties Crisis: The Second Phase of the American Revolution, 1767–1773*. New York: Oxford University Press, 1987.
Thompson, Mack. "Massachusetts and New York Stamp Acts." *William and Mary Quarterly*, 3rd ser., 26 (1969): 253–58.
Tiedemann, Joseph S. "Communities in the Midst of the American Revolution: Queens County, New York, 1774–1775." *Journal of Social History* 18, no. 1 (1984): 57–78.
———. *Reluctant Revolutionaries: New York City and the Road to Independence, 1763–1776*. Ithaca, NY: Cornell University Press, 1997.
Tolles, Frederick B. *James Logan and the Culture of Provincial America*. Boston: Little, Brown, 1957.
———. *Meeting House and Counting House: The Quaker Merchants of Colonial Philadelphia, 1682–1763*. Chapel Hill: University of North Carolina Press, 1948.
———. "Philadelphia's First Scientist: James Logan." *Isis* 47, no. 1 (1956): 20–30.
Tonks, Paul. "Empire and Authority in Colonial New York: The Political Thought of Archibald Kennedy and Cadwallader Colden." *New York History* 91, no. 1 (2010): 25–44.
Truxes, Thomas M. *Defying Empire: Trading with the Enemy in Colonial New York*. New Haven, CT: Yale University Press, 2008.
Tucker, Louis Leonard. "President Thomas Clap of Yale College: Another Founding Father of American Science." *Isis* 52, no. 1 (1961): 55–77.
———. *Puritan Protagonist: President Thomas Clap of Yale College*. Chapel Hill: University of North Carolina Press, 1962.
Tully, Alan. *Forming American Politics: Ideals, Interests, and Institutions in Colonial New York and Pennsylvania*. Baltimore: Johns Hopkins University Press, 1994.
Tyler, Moses Coit. *A History of American Literature*. Vol. 2. *1676–1765*. New York: G. P. Putnam, 1879.
Tyson, Neil de Grasse. "Galactic Engines." *Natural History* 106 (May 1997): 66–71.
Upton, L. F. S. *The Loyal Whig: William Smith of New York and Quebec*. Toronto: University of Toronto Press, 1969.
Vail, Anna Murray. "Jane Colden, An Early New York Botanist." *Torreya: A Monthly Journal of Botanical Notes and News* 7, no. 2 (1907): 21–34.
Valentine, Alan. *Lord Stirling*. New York: Oxford University Press, 1969.
Van De Wetering, Maxine. "A Reconsideration of the Inoculation Controversy." *New England Quarterly* 58, no. 1 (1985): 46–67.
Van Doren, Carl. "The Beginnings of the American Philosophical Society." *American Philosophical Society, Proceedings* 87, no. 3 (1943): 277–89.
Varga, Nicholas. "The New York Restraining Act: Its Passage and Some Effects, 1766–1768." *New York History* 37, no. 3 (1956): 233–58.

———. "Robert Charles: New York Agent, 1748–1770." *William and Mary Quarterly*, 3rd ser., 18 (1961): 211–35.

Vaughan, Alden T. *Transatlantic Encounters: American Indians in Britain, 1500–1776*. New York: Cambridge University Press, 2006.

V [Verplank, Gulian C.]. "Biographical Memoir of Cadwallader Colden, M.D. F.R.S. Lieutenant-Governor of the Colony of New York." *Monthly Recorder* (June 1813): 149–53.

Wall, A. James. "Cadwallader Colden and His Homestead at Spring Hill, Flushing, Long Island." *New York Historical Society Quarterly* 8, no. 1 (1924): 11–20.

———. "The Statues of King George III and the Honorable William Pitt Erected in New York City, 1770." *New York Historical Society Quarterly Bulletin* 4, no. 2 (1920): 36–57.

Wallace, Margaret V. S. "'Big' Little Britain: Cadwallader Colden and His Canal." *Orange County Post*, February 20, 1967.

Waller, G. M. *Samuel Vetch, Colonial Enterpriser*. Chapel Hill: University of North Carolina Press, 1960.

Waller, Henry D. *History of the Town of Flushing, Long Island, New York*. Flushing, NY: J. H. Ridenour, 1899.

Weaver, George H. "Life and Writings of William Douglass, M.D. (1691–1752)." *Bulletin of the Society of Medical History of Chicago* 2, no. 4 (1921): 229–59.

Welch, William H. "The Interdependence of Medicine and Other Sciences of Nature." *Science*, n.s., 27, no. 680 (January 10, 1908): 49–64.

Weslager, C. A. *The Stamp Act Congress*. Newark: University of Delaware Press, 1976.

White, Philip L. *The Beekmans of New York in Politics and Commerce, 1647–1877*. New York: New York Historical Society, 1956.

Whitehead, William A. *Contributions to the Early History of Perth Amboy and Adjoining Country with Sketches of Men and Events in New Jersey During the Provincial Era*. New York: D. Appleton, 1856.

Whitford, Noble E. *History of the Canal System of the State of New York, together with Brief Histories of the Canals of the United States and Canada*. 2 vols. Albany, NY: State Engineer and Surveyor, 1906.

Wickwire, Franklin B. "John Pownall and British Canal Policy." *William and Mary Quarterly*, 3rd ser., 20 (1963): 543–54.

Wilcoxen, Charlotte. "A Highborn Lady in Colonial New York." *New York Historical Society Quarterly* 63, no. 4 (1979): 315–47.

Wilczek, Frank. *The Lightness of Being: Mass, Ether, and the Unification of Forces*. New York: Basic Books, 2008.

Willcock, John. *A Scots Earl in Covenanting Times: Being Life and Times of Archibald 9th Earl of Argyll (1629–1685)*. Edinburgh: A. Elliot, 1907.

Williams, Basil. *Stanhope: A Study in Eighteenth Century War and Diplomacy*. Oxford: Clarendon Press, 1932. Reprint. Oxford: Oxford University Press, 1968.

Wilson, James Grant, ed. *The Memorial History of the City of New-York From Its First Settlement to the Year 1892*. 5 vols. New York: New York History, 1892–1896.

Wines, Roger Andrew. "William Smith, the Historian of New York." *New York History* 40, no. 1 (1959): 3–17.

Wood, George Arthur. *William Shirley, Governor of Massachusetts, 1741–1756: A History*. New York: Columbia University Press, 1920.

Wood, Gordon S. *The Radicalism of the American Revolution*. New York: A. A. Knopf, 1992.

Wormald, Jenny. "Confidence and Perplexity: The Seventeenth Century." In *Scotland: A History*, edited by Jenny Wormald, 143–76. New York: Oxford University Press, 2005.

———, ed. *Scotland: A History*. New York: Oxford University Press, 2005.

Wright, Louis B. *The Cultural Life of the American Colonies, 1607–1763*. New York: Harper & Row, 1962.

Wroth, Lawrence C. *An American Bookshelf, 1755*. London: Oxford University Press, 1934. Reprint. New York: Arno Press, New York Times, 1969.

Wulf, Andrea. *The Brother Gardeners: Botany, Empire and the Birth of an Obsession*. London: W. Heinemann, 2008.

Yoshpe, Harry B. *The Disposition of Loyalist Estates in the Southern District of the State of New York.* New York: Columbia University Press, 1939.

Zabin, Serena R. *Dangerous Economies: Status and Commerce in Imperial New York.* Philadelphia: University of Pennsylvania Press, 2009.

Zelner, Kyle F. *A Rabble in Arms: Massachusetts Towns and Militiamen during King Philip's War.* New York: New York University Press, 2009.

Zobel, Hiller B. *The Boston Massacre.* New York: Norton, 1970.

Index

Act of Union, 12
actors, 284, 288–289
Adams, John, 299
Addison, Joseph, 25, 29
Alaska, 161
Albany, 56, 76, 77, 102, 147, 163, 164, 167, 169, 170, 171, 172, 173, 174, 175; fur smuggling of, 32–33, 33, 34, 34–35, 134, 172; Indians dislike, 32, 215; quartering crisis in, 278–280
Alexander, James, 49, 73, 79, 84, 85, 86, 88, 104, 107–108, 113, 122, 127, 143, 145, 152, 187, 203, 205, 216, 222, 224, 225, 233, 243, 245, 246, 247, 248, 250, 251, 253, 277; Assembly member, 126; Clarke opposed by, 122, 124; Clinton backed by, 195, 197, 206; Colden friend, 27, 31, 39, 53, 57, 59, 60, 72, 85, 88, 121, 123, 162, 181; Cosby foe, 28, 75, 81, 82, 83, 84, 85, 86, 190; councilor, 36, 60, 75, 89, 124, 175, 196; lawyer, 27, 28, 77, 78–79, 85, 97, 197–198, 230, 298; learning and, 97; tar water advocate, 111
Alsop, John, 57, 82, 82–83, 83, 85, 124
American Revolution. *See* War of Independence
Amherst, Jeffrey, 268, 275, 278–279, 279, 281, 283–284, 321, 336, 344, 347, 351, 354, 358, 383, 438
Anglican Church. *See* Church of England
Appalachians. *See* Highlands
Apthorpe, Charles Ward, 277
Argyle, earl and dukes of [Campbells], 8–10, 10, 36, 74, 88, 98, 203
Asia, HMS, 411, 416, 417, 418, 421, 422
Assembly of New York, 2–3, 27, 29, 29–30, 36, 38, 39, 82, 85, 123, 126, 127, 135, 154, 163, 164, 166, 172, 173–174, 176–177, 177–178, 178, 178–181, 187, 195, 195–196, 201, 202, 205, 207, 215, 216, 220–221, 221–222, 224, 229, 277–278, 300, 379, 386; Congress opposed by, 406–409, 411; currency and quartering disputes in, 358–359, 360; elections of 1768-1769 for, 356–357
Ayscough, John, 202, 203

Bacon's Rebellion, 2
Banyar, Goldsbrow, 283, 358
Barbados, 18, 87–88
Barton, Benjamin S., 3
Bartram, John, 100–101, 111, 113, 129, 149, 170, 217
Berkeley, George, 109–110, 111, 245, 248, 252
Bernard, Francis, 267, 346, 391, 392
Betts, Joseph, 251
Bevis, John, 254–255, 256
Blackbeard, 25

Board of Trade, 34–35, 49, 50, 60, 71, 80, 87, 88, 101, 124, 125, 193, 200, 201, 204, 270–271, 281, 282, 283, 312, 354, 362, 365, 393
Boston, Mass., 79, 80, 97, 113, 152, 267, 322–323, 328, 330, 337, 346, 359, 368, 386, 395–396, 405, 406, 411, 412, 418, 421–422, 425
botany, 98–100, 148–149, 151
Braddock, Sir Edward, 216, 217
Bradford, William, 79, 90
Bradley, James, 254, 255
Bradley, Richard, 2, 3, 82
Bradstreet, John, 279, 279–280, 378
Buffon, Count de, 258
Bull, William, 270
Burgoyne, John, 406
Burke, Edmund, 378, 409
Burnet, Bishop Gilbert, 8, 31
Burnet, Gov. William, 30, 31–32, 32–33, 33–34, 34–35, 35–37, 38, 39, 48, 49, 50, 54, 58, 72, 97, 101, 225, 243, 250, 268, 286, 365, 379

Canajohare Patent, 304
cancer, 109
Carleton, Guy, 346, 413, 438
Catherwood, John, 199, 201
Chambers, John, 193, 300
chancery court, 27, 37–39, 59, 78, 83, 84, 85, 85–88, 89, 381, 383
Chandos, Duke of, 72, 73, 83, 84, 87
Charles, Robert, 188, 271, 312
Chrystie, Andrew, 130
Chrystie, David (father-in-law), 14–15, 17, 137, 144; wife of, 17, 136
Chrystie, James, 11, 17, 137
Church of England, 8, 15, 109, 144, 145, 147, 154, 155, 156, 221, 241, 242–243, 356, 361, 367, 377, 383, 407, 423, 426
Clap, Thomas, 253
Clarke, George, 36, 46, 48–49, 50, 51, 52, 58, 59, 61, 63, 73, 77, 83, 85, 89, 122, 123, 124, 125, 126–127, 129, 130, 132, 133, 161, 162, 202, 232, 277, 306
Clinton, Charles, 47–48, 219, 356
Clinton, Capt. [Admiral] George, 87, 133–134, 147, 161–162, 162; children of, 180, 181, 196, 197, 204; governor of New York, 162, 163, 163–164, 165, 166, 167–169, 170, 170–171, 172, 173, 173–178, 179, 180, 181, 187–188, 189–191, 191, 192–193, 193, 194, 194–195, 196–198, 199–200, 201, 202–204, 204, 205, 206, 229, 230, 272, 273, 298, 378; paranoia of, 202–204, 204, 224; shot at, 179–180, 188; wife of, 181, 193, 199, 202, 206
Clinton, Gov. George (of Ulster), 48, 356, 437, 441
Colden, Rev. Alexander (father), 8, 9, 9–10, 10, 11, 12, 13–14, 15, 18, 74, 137, 242
Colden, Alexander [Sandie] (son), 18, 137, 144, 144–145, 146–147, 152, 153, 177, 197, 204, 206, 213–214, 216–217, 219, 222–223, 225, 226, 227, 229, 233, 243, 265, 266–267, 268, 270, 277, 283, 286, 308, 331, 344, 345, 353, 381, 384, 387, 397–398, 414
Colden, Alice (daughter), 111, 148, 150, 177, 269
Colden Mrs. Alice Chrystie (wife), 11–12, 14–15, 15, 17, 19, 30, 48, 55, 74, 104, 128, 145, 147, 147–148, 152, 177, 178, 207, 222, 224–225, 226, 227, 242, 266, 268–269
Colden, Cadwallader, 1–5; Albany conference, 170–171, 173–174; Assembly and, 2–3, 39, 220, 221; Assembly spoken to by, in 1775, 407–408; astronomy and, 19, 30–31, 250–251, 254–255; beats the drum, 13–14; Beelzebub preferred to, 310; biochemistry and, 255; birth of, 10, 21n16, 21n17, 119n78; blockhouses and, 219, 220, 224, 228–229; Burnet and, 31–32, 32–33, 33–34, 34–35; business career of, 12, 13, 17–18, 19, 30; chariot of, 276, 329, 345, 384; civil war feared by, 336–337, 406, 410, 419; Clarke supported by, 123, 124; Clinton picks as advisor, 166–169; cold, thoughts about, 112, 145, 147, 203, 219, 336, 345; colleges, thoughts about, 154–156; committeemen addressed by, 420–421; Cosby, opposed to, 71, 78, 79–89, 90; Council and, 59; death of,

425–426, 426–427; deist beliefs of, 11, 241, 242; Dunmore, dispute with, 379–383, 390–391; education of children by, 143–144, 144–145; electricity and, 112–113; enemies wish him dead, 335–336; Enlightenment and, 97, 98–111; and ether, 244, 252, 259; family origins, 7–10; farming by, 54–56; *Forsey v. Cunningham* and, 305, 305–306; French, his feelings about, 32, 33, 277; French and Indian War dealt with by, 277–278, 278–280; Gage respects him, 368–369; and God, 249–250, 252; governmental theories of, 2–3, 50, 441; health of, 104–105, 268–269, 345, 355–356, 357, 386–389, 389–390, 405, 422, 425–426; Hunter and, 19, 25–27, 29–30; immigration of, 12; impeachment of, threatened, 59, 60; independent judiciary suggested by, 300; Indian land deals reformed by, 125–126; Indians and, 32; Indian trade, report on, 33–34; Iroquois, his histories of, 34, 134–136; Jacobite, accused of being, 179, 179–180, 232, 328, 329; land reform and, 36; land speculation of, 52–53, 76–77; on lawyers, 297–299, 312; leak to media, 79–81; lieutenant governor, became, 272; lieutenant governorship sought by, 175, 188, 189, 195, 197, 199, 271; and light, 242, 258; loyalty proclaimed by, 422, 423; manor lords, critic of, 46–47, 51, 285–286; map of New York, 33, 225, 284; marries, 14; medical education and practice of, 11, 15, 17, 30; mutinous army feared by, 176–178; Newton, opposed on inertia by, 166, 253; Parliament's taxes opposed by New York, 363, 396, 408–409; Philipse attacked by, 39; Queens loyalism encouraged by, 423–424; Satan, compared to, 361; Scotland revisited by, 13–14, 17; seditious libel, accused of, 351–354; slavery and, 18, 22n28, 128–129, 152–153, 217, 222, 423; Smith's history attacked by, 231–233, 234; Smith Jr.'s antagonism to, 231; soldiers, wants more, 405, 412–413, 417, 418; Stamp Act rioting and, 326, 327, 328, 329, 330, 333; surveyor-general, 47–51, 61–63, 126, 197–198, 200, 201; trade policy and taxes debated by, 35, 37; Tryon characterizes him, 385; Ulster frontier warfare and, 217–219, 220, 223, 223–224; Vermont and, 393, 393–394, 394–395, 413

Colden, Cadwallader D. (grandson), 3, 4, 427, 437–438, 438–439, 439, 441

Colden, Cadwallader Jr. [Cad] (son), 11, 137, 144, 146, 146–147, 150, 164, 190, 243, 265, 280, 298, 348, 355–356, 356, 419, 425, 436–437, 439, 441–442

Colden, Catherine (daughter), 148, 222, 269

Colden, David [Davie] (son), 113, 143, 144, 151, 153–154, 213, 222, 229, 255, 283, 326, 343, 345, 355, 356, 358, 381, 385, 387, 390, 396, 397, 398, 414, 415, 416, 418, 423–424, 424–425, 426–427, 436–439, 440, 441; electricity and, 153, 255; health of, 151, 153; slaves of, 436, 439, 443n22; wife of, 425, 439, 440

Colden, Elizabeth [Bettie]. *See* DeLancey, Elizabeth [Bettie]

Colden, James (brother), 10, 18, 130, 136, 137, 152

Colden, Jane [Jennie] (daughter), 101, 143, 148–151, 153, 154, 177, 222

Colden, Jane Hughes (mother), 10, 11, 18, 137, 242

Colden, John (son), 104, 147–148, 157n26, 190, 201, 268, 298

Colden, Richard Nicholls (grandson), 397

Colden, Rev. Robert (grandfather), 8, 10

Colden, Sarah (daughter), 104

Coldengham [Coldingham], 7, 53–56, 100, 101, 104, 105, 123, 128, 148, 151, 207, 215, 217, 218, 222, 223, 226, 227, 228, 230, 268, 297, 419, 425, 441

Colhoun, Alexander, 164, 170–171, 194, 203

Collinson, Peter, 97–98, 99, 100, 101, 105, 109, 112, 113, 134, 135, 149, 198, 200, 203, 213, 245, 247, 251, 254, 255, 271, 272, 311, 336, 345, 346–347, 347, 351, 383

Connecticut, 61–63, 135, 241, 249, 299, 322, 383, 391, 392, 420; Hartford, 335; Ridgefield, 62, 63, 72–73, 84
Continental Congress, 396, 397, 406, 407, 409, 413, 422
Conway, Henry, 350, 381
Cornbury, Lord, 46; alleged transvestism of, 87, 95n70
Cosby, William, 10, 28, 46, 63, 71, 73–77, 77–80, 80, 82–83, 83, 84–85, 86, 86–87, 87–90, 90, 121, 122, 124–125, 133, 161, 162, 163, 310, 352, 377, 380–381, 382; daughter of, 380–381; sexual charges against, 86–87; son of, 127; wife of, 73, 74, 84–85, 87, 89, 122, 380
Council of New York, 2, 3, 77, 78, 79–80, 80, 84, 88, 89, 90, 122, 128, 163, 164, 166, 167, 174–175, 176, 178, 191–192, 193, 205, 224, 229, 273, 276–277, 277, 298, 334, 387–389, 390, 391, 407
Cromwell, Oliver, 336–337
Crown Point, 90, 163–164, 171–172, 172, 173, 176, 193, 215, 220, 225, 229, 283, 393, 413, 418
Cruger, John Harris, 416, 417
Cunningham, Waddell, 307–308, 309, 312
Currency Act, problems caused by, 358–360, 362, 364, 368

Dartmouth, Lord, 346, 347, 385, 386, 387, 389, 390, 395, 396, 406, 408, 409, 412, 413–414, 414, 415, 416
Davis, Thomas J., 129
Dawson, Henry B., 343–344
DeLancey, Alice [Aly] (granddaughter), 146, 148, 225, 415
DeLancey, Elizabeth [Bettie] (daughter), 27, 74, 130, 131, 132, 133, 144, 145–146, 147, 147–148, 152, 167, 203, 224, 419, 421, 425, 425–426, 427, 436, 438
DeLancey, Chief Justice James, 52, 61, 77, 78–79, 80, 81, 113, 123, 132, 146, 162, 163, 165, 178, 187, 221, 230, 231, 270, 273, 299, 300, 357; acting governor, 206, 207, 214, 214–216, 216, 217, 222, 226–227, 227, 228, 228–229; asthma of, 172, 265; censorship of press by, 216; death of, 265, 266, 267, 268, 270; lieutenant governor, 188, 189, 190, 200, 204, 205, 219, 298; opposes Clinton, 165, 166, 167, 172, 173, 174–175, 180–181, 181, 196, 197, 199; temper of, 146, 191–193
DeLancey, James (son of chief justice), 266, 360, 405, 409, 412, 419
DeLancey, John Peter, 416
DeLancey, Oliver, 187, 193, 195, 196, 227, 265, 301, 390, 396, 398, 419, 438
DeLancey, Peter, 145–146, 146, 196, 203, 224
DeLancey, Stephen, 33, 35, 36–37, 61
Delaware River, 218
Descartes, Rene, 243, 244, 247, 249, 252
Douglass, William, 97, 104–105, 113, 152
drafts, 177, 278
Duane, James, 308, 381, 381–382, 382, 394, 396, 419, 437
Dunmore, Lord, 123–381, 369, 369–370, 377–378, 379, 381–382, 382, 383, 383–384, 390–391, 394, 417; drinking of, 378
Dutchess Co., 220, 355, 365
Dutch in New York, 30, 42n21, 60, 102, 103, 131, 134–135, 144, 152, 164, 174, 278, 304
dysentery, 355, 356

Earth, 100, 116n29, 250; wobble of, 254
Einstein, Albert, 243, 258
Elliot, Andrew, 277, 398, 406, 438
Erie Canal, 57, 441
Euler, Leonhard, 247, 254
Evans Patent, 230, 230–231, 274, 283, 307

Fanning, Edmund, 398, 414
Ferguson, Adam, 257
Flushing, 45, 229, 235, 268, 275, 322, 332, 336, 340n64, 344, 419, 426, 427
Fontaine, John, 25, 56
Forsey, Thomas, 307–308
Fort George, 25, 122, 130, 268, 324, 326, 326–327, 327, 328, 329–331, 331, 332, 333, 333–334, 334, 335, 346, 347, 369, 381, 384, 386, 405, 416–417
Fothergill, Dr. John, 105, 135, 149, 152, 351, 367

Fox, Dixon Ryan, 97
Franklin, Benjamin, 97, 101, 112–113, 113, 129, 147, 153, 154, 155, 178, 200, 214, 216, 241, 245, 246, 248–249, 254, 255, 270, 322, 344, 387, 397
French and Indian War, 216–230, 265, 280
French in Canada, 33–34, 35, 90, 101, 109, 129, 135, 163–164, 167, 169, 171, 171–172, 172, 176, 178, 200–201, 214, 215, 216, 217, 217–218, 225, 229, 250, 268, 277–278, 287
fur trade, 32–35, 163

Gage, Thomas, 280–281, 282, 303, 320, 322, 323, 324, 326–327, 327, 328, 332, 333–334, 344, 345, 349, 362, 368–369, 369, 395, 405, 408, 412, 413, 416, 418, 421; as human shield, 333
Galen, 31
Galloway, Joseph, 396
Garden, Alexander, 101, 149, 150, 253, 256, 277
Gates, Horatio, 273, 276
George I, 57
George II, 57, 129, 266, 278, 299, 398
George III, 3, 14, 266, 307, 312, 329, 347, 354, 362, 366, 379, 393, 398, 409, 411; statue of, 369, 425
Glorious Revolution, 3, 10, 336
Grafton, Duke of, 354, 380–381, 383
Graves, Samuel, 408, 411, 412, 421, 422
Grenville, George, 287, 336, 344, 347, 350–351, 352
Greyhound, HMS, 196–197
Gronovius, Johann Friedrich, 98, 99, 113, 148, 149, 169, 245

Halifax, Lord, 73, 195, 198, 200, 204–205, 206, 213, 225, 265, 267, 270, 271–272, 280–281, 307, 312, 353
Halley, Dr. Edmund, 15
Hamilton, Alexander, 442
Hardy, Sir Charles, 214, 217, 219–221, 222, 223, 224, 226, 273–274
Harison, Francis, 71–73, 76–77, 79, 80, 81–82, 83, 84–85, 125
Harison, George, 267, 308–309, 309
hemp, 35, 72, 286
Hendrick, 214, 215, 217

Henry, Patrick, 100, 366
Highlands, 56–57, 216, 217, 223
Hill, Elizabeth (aunt), 12, 17, 18, 26–27, 63, 79, 136, 137, 144, 145
Hillsborough, Lord, 354, 357, 359, 360, 362, 363, 366, 369, 379, 380, 383, 383–384
Hindle, Brooke, 26, 143, 243
Hoermann, Alfred R., 4, 11
Holland, 9, 99, 131, 169, 287
Holland, Edward, 193–194
Holt, John, 320, 325, 332, 352, 353, 420
Hood, Zacharias, 324, 340n64, 351
Horsmanden, Daniel, 73, 80, 83, 84, 89, 113, 130, 133, 162, 164, 174–175, 175, 178, 179, 181, 189, 190, 192, 214, 221, 232, 276, 281, 300, 302, 309–310, 310, 323, 346, 349, 352, 355, 356, 383, 384, 386, 387, 425; smears Colden, 179, 180
Hudson River, 45, 53, 56, 57, 102, 127, 169, 215, 220, 223, 368, 392, 405, 417
Hungarian Club, 162, 166, 181, 196, 265, 378
Hunter, Robert, 19, 25–26, 26–27, 29–30, 30–31, 31–32, 32, 34, 35, 38, 45, 47, 48, 71, 97, 101, 243
Hutchinson, Thomas, 128, 330, 386, 392, 407

immigrants, 12, 30, 36, 45, 98
impressment, 174, 278, 279
Indians, 32, 33, 34, 109, 110, 125–126, 134–135, 164, 169, 170–171, 191, 201–202, 213, 216, 217, 218, 221, 222–223, 223–224, 226, 227, 228, 229–230, 231, 280, 280–281, 302, 304, 366, 389, 418. *See also* Iroquois; River Indians; Wappinger Indians
Intolerable Acts, 395, 396
Ireland, 8, 9, 45
Iroquois, 34, 77, 100, 109, 125–126, 135, 147, 163, 164, 166, 169, 170, 171, 173, 200–201, 214, 214–215, 215, 217–218, 223, 280, 302, 304, 397, 435
Izard, Ralph, 415, 416, 421, 422–423, 425, 436

Jacobites, 13–14, 14, 17, 28–29, 75, 88, 130, 132, 132–133, 179, 189, 336, 346, 377–378
James, Major Thomas, 324, 326, 329, 330, 334, 347–348, 349
James II, 3, 8, 10, 13
Jedburgh, Lord [William Kerr], 10, 13–14, 36, 74, 88, 189, 346
Jefferson, Thomas, 258
Jews, 39, 193
Johnson, Guy, 406–407
Johnson, Sir John, 418
Johnson, Rev. Samuel, 111, 241, 242, 245, 246, 249, 250, 253, 383
Johnson, Sir William, 170, 173, 179, 201, 201–202, 215, 216, 219, 226, 269, 270, 272, 277, 279, 280, 281, 282, 284, 303, 304, 309, 312, 322, 324, 326, 336, 351, 356, 357, 387, 389, 397; on liberty of the press, 321
Johnson, William Samuel, 383, 390
Jones, Matt B., 393, 394
Jones, Thomas, 48, 243, 273, 275, 301, 358
Julian calendar, 21n16, 119n78

Kalm, Peter, 99, 101, 109
Kastner, Abraham, 247
Kayaderosseras Patent, 302–304
Keith, Sir William, 30, 31
Kelso, Scotland, 10, 11, 13, 14, 14–15
Kempe, John Tabor, 231, 266, 277, 309, 319, 322, 366, 379–380, 381, 382, 394
Kennedy, Archibald, 27, 30, 31, 33, 63, 74, 77, 78, 89, 90, 127, 202, 276, 277, 283, 325
Kennedy, Capt. Archibald, 325, 327, 331, 344, 349, 438
Keys, Alice M., 4, 34
King George's War, 162, 169, 191
King's College, 156, 367, 378, 412
Kingston, Ulster Co., 76, 226
Klein, Milton M., 1, 4, 231, 234
Klock, George, 304

Laurens, Henry, 267
lawyers, 1, 297, 300, 301, 302, 303, 305, 308, 309, 310, 311, 311–312, 312–313, 320, 335, 356, 435; drawn to fraudulent land patents, 302; fees of, 297, 305

Leder, Lawrence H., 4
Lee, Arthur, 414–415, 415–416
Lee, Charles, 408
Lee, William, 405–406
Lepore, Jill, 132, 133
Liebnitz, Gottfried, 248, 249
Linnaeus, Carolus, 98, 98–99, 101, 149
Livingston, Philip, 83, 86, 167, 171, 172–173, 174, 175, 176, 190, 201
Livingston, Robert, 51, 190
Livingston, Judge Robert R., 51, 190–191, 276, 305, 310, 311, 320, 325, 329, 330, 332, 333, 334, 336, 352, 353, 354, 355, 356, 357, 364, 378, 383, 385, 389, 389–390
Livingston, William, 51, 230, 231, 299, 304, 308, 378, 435
Livingston Manor, 51, 356, 364, 391
Logan, James, 19, 25, 26, 30, 31, 45, 71, 97, 121, 245, 246, 248–249
Lokken, Roy, 250, 252, 255
London, 9, 11, 12, 13, 15, 17, 30, 86, 87, 88, 135, 144, 156, 197, 198, 199, 251, 268, 351, 383, 395, 407, 438, 440
Long Island, 45, 151, 152, 267, 286, 340n64, 366, 411, 426
longitude, 250
Lords of Trade. *See* Board of Trade
Lothian, Marquess of. *See* Jedburgh, Lord
Loudoun, Lord, 225, 225–226, 227, 228, 229, 235
loyalism, 423, 436, 436–437, 437, 438, 439; compensation for loyalists, 438, 440
Ludlow, George D., 358, 424, 436, 438, 439, 439–440

Macclesfield, Earl of, 251, 252, 253, 254–255
manor lords, 45, 46–47, 49, 50, 51, 60, 75, 173, 225, 234–235, 285–286, 288, 391, 435
Mansfield, Lord, 353
Maryland, 17, 216, 324
Massachusetts, 58, 128, 132, 169, 171, 176, 191, 302, 322, 327, 346, 359, 386, 395, 408, 413, 422; boundary with New York, 391–392

Matthews, Vincent, 81, 82, 82–83, 127, 133
McDougall, Alexander, 359–360, 360–361, 381, 386
McEvers, James, 322–323, 323
Minisink, 222–223, 229, 230
Minorca, 73, 86
Mitchell, Dr. John, 9, 101, 106, 109, 113, 135, 203
mobs, 3, 145, 205, 319, 323, 324, 325, 326, 327–334, 334, 344, 345, 348, 351, 361, 363, 381, 384, 395, 406, 417
Mohawk River, 56–57, 89, 125
Monckton, Gov. Robert, 272–276, 277, 279, 282, 283, 298, 299, 302, 305, 306, 308, 309, 320, 324, 335, 336, 355, 358; wound of, 272, 276
Montagu, Capt. James, 410, 429n28
Montgomerie, Gov. John, 46, 50, 57, 58–59, 60–61, 63, 71, 72, 74, 77, 79, 85, 97, 232, 274, 379, 384
Monthly Review, 252, 256
Montresor, Capt. John, 305, 324, 327, 332, 337, 351, 405
Moore, Sir Henry, 57, 324–325, 326, 335, 343, 343–344, 346, 347, 348–349, 350, 352, 353, 354, 354–355, 356, 358, 358–359, 362, 366, 392, 394
Morris, Chief Justice Lewis, 27, 31, 60, 61, 73, 77, 78, 79–80, 85, 86, 87, 88, 126–127, 133
Morris, Lewis Jr., 36, 59, 60–61, 85, 104, 124, 126–127, 133, 196, 199, 274, 357
Morris, Robert Hunter, 87, 199–200, 204, 216, 217, 301
Morris, Roger, 390, 438
Murray, Joseph, 127, 165, 174, 193

Nash, Gary, 231
Newburgh, 57, 103, 146, 147, 154, 155, 156, 177, 221, 243
Newcastle, Duke of, 38, 73, 79–80, 80, 87, 88, 128, 133, 161, 188, 188–189, 189, 198, 204
New Hampshire, 128, 392–394, 413
New Hampshire Grants. *See* Vermont
New Jersey, 130, 152, 165, 199, 215, 216, 217, 220, 222, 229, 281, 286, 300, 319, 405, 435, 437

Newton, Sir Isaac, 11, 18, 31, 166, 243–244, 244–245, 245, 246, 248, 252, 256, 257, 258, 259
New York, colony of, 1, 19, 26, 32, 57, 97, 99, 100, 101, 102, 123, 128, 129, 143, 215, 217, 362; appeals to the king, 305–306, 312, 320; climate of, 101–103, 116n29, 165, 327, 344, 386; independence of, feared, 60, 127, 166–167, 176, 336, 426; reform of, 75–76; salary of governor of, 27, 50, 127, 205, 379; Stamp Act rioting in, 328–334, 343–344, 344
New York Chamber of Commerce, 367–368, 387
New York City, 19, 25, 33, 47, 56, 76, 85, 103, 108, 127, 129, 130, 144–145, 145, 149, 151, 152, 177, 180, 206, 215, 222, 325, 405, 421
New York State, 435, 436–437, 437
non-importation, 358, 362–363, 363–364, 368–369, 385–386, 396, 409–410, 411
North, Lord, 397, 414, 415
North Carolina, 363, 384, 386

Oblong, 61, 62–63, 72, 72–73, 82, 83, 84, 84–85, 85–86, 89, 125, 127, 392
O'Callaghan, Edmund B., 4, 272
Oglethorpe, James, 129, 135
Ohio River, 214, 215–216, 217
Orange Co., 48, 213, 215, 216, 216–217, 218, 220, 223, 224, 225, 228, 229
Osborn, Sir Danvers, 205–206, 217, 306, 312, 369
Oswego, 33–34, 163, 202, 280
Oxnam, Scotland, 10, 13, 18

Palatines, 29
Parker, James, 179, 221, 245–246, 321–322, 327, 344, 355, 356, 361, 397
Parliament, 10, 40, 87, 163, 205, 286, 288, 309, 311, 313, 320–321, 323, 326, 328, 336, 345, 350–351, 358, 362, 363, 378, 396, 406, 408, 409, 414, 420, 437
Pelham, Henry, 189
Pennsylvania, 12, 19, 26, 30, 57, 81, 98, 100, 215, 216, 221, 225, 247, 248, 270, 280, 366, 391, 396, 405; moves Indians into New York, 281–282

Perry, Micajah, 72, 86, 127
Philadelphia, 12–13, 18, 19, 25, 26, 30, 31, 79, 86, 97, 112, 113, 128, 152, 215, 396
Philipse, Adolph Esq. [Ape], 35–36, 36, 38–39, 58–60, 61, 62, 72, 82, 83, 84–85, 85, 127, 162, 164
Pike, Samuel, 253
Pitt, William, 272, 369
Pontiac's Rebellion, 280–281
Popple, Alured, 74, 86, 88
Pownall, John, 270–271, 271
Pownall, Thomas, 103, 206, 217, 271, 272, 301
Pratt, Benjamin, 301–302
Presbyterian Church, 7–8, 8, 11, 14, 156, 242, 407
Purple, Edwin R., 1

Quakers, 12, 19, 25, 97, 100, 137, 145, 216, 221, 311–312, 420
quartering, 278–279, 358, 359, 360, 361, 362
Quebec, 366, 368
Queens Co., 124, 229, 336, 419, 421, 422, 423, 426; loyalism in, 423, 424, 436
quitrents, 46, 49, 51, 75–76, 82, 204–205, 235, 393

Rhode Island, 128, 132, 146, 322
rhubarb, 18, 30, 98, 153
River Indians, 171, 219, 220, 222, 223
Rivington, James, 391, 408
Robertson, Gen. James, 412, 413, 418, 438
Robertson, William, 257, 351
Robinson, Beverly, 365–366
Roddam, Robert, 196
Royal Irish, 405, 416, 417
Royal Navy, 30, 161, 222
royal prerogative, 1, 4, 36, 37, 39, 58, 79, 86, 163, 196, 204, 270, 308–309, 398
Royal Society, 15, 17, 19, 98, 152, 245, 254
rum, 32, 162, 361
Rush, Benjamin, 337
Rutherfurd, John, 163–164, 167, 171, 172, 173, 174, 176, 181, 199, 245, 248, 251

Schuyler, Harmanus, 279, 358
Schuyler, Peter, 35–36, 47
Schwarz, Philip J., 393
Scotland, 2, 7–11, 12, 13–14, 18, 23n44, 136–137, 137, 152, 163, 242, 257, 328, 336, 409
Scott, John Morin, 299, 308, 348, 356
scurvy, 99, 110
Sears, Isaac [King], 344, 359, 379, 385, 412, 419, 425
Seabury, Samuel, 357
Shea, John Gilmary, 1
Shirley, William, 171–172, 191, 198–199, 201, 270
Shuckburgh, Richard, 194, 203
Skene, Philip, 284, 304
Slaughter Massacre, 223, 224
slave revolt (1741), 128–133, 140n57; compared to Salem witchcraft, 131–132, 133
smallpox, 111, 151–153, 169, 281, 293n67
Smith, William Jr., 35, 45, 53, 130, 166, 195, 230, 242, 273–275, 276, 284, 299, 302, 308, 320, 346, 348, 348–352, 352, 353, 354, 355, 356, 358, 361, 364–367, 378, 385, 387, 389, 389–390, 394, 395, 396, 398, 407, 425, 435; appeals and, 305–306, 308, 309, 312; Colden rejects his version of history, 231–234, 297, 352; Dunmore's court case and, 381, 381–382, 383; endangers Coldengham, 230–231; resents Colden's lack of wealth, 231
Smith, William Sr., 81, 83, 84, 121, 124, 127, 195, 199, 223, 226, 232, 281, 301, 323, 346, 349, 355, 358
Sons of Liberty, 325, 336, 340n64, 344, 359, 360, 361, 362, 363–364, 367–368, 377, 385, 395, 396, 397, 405, 406, 410, 412
South Carolina, 101, 149, 253, 267, 270, 359, 408, 411, 415; Charleston, 12, 322, 411
Spanish Empire, 129, 131, 217, 286
Stirling, Lord [William Alexander], 277, 281
Spring Hill, 268, 275, 322–323, 326, 335–336, 345, 355–356, 366, 377, 384, 415, 419, 426, 427, 437, 439, 440
stamp tax, 319; of New York, 215, 234, 265, 320; of Parliament, 313, 319, 320,

321, 322, 325, 326, 328, 329, 331, 334, 335, 336, 344, 363, 367, 386
Staten Island, 47, 281, 282, 424
St. Lawrence River, 33
Sugar Act, 287–288, 325, 348, 363
Swift, Jonathan, 25, 26, 29, 248
syphilis, 109, 117n55

tar water, 109–110, 110–112, 118n58, 245
Tea Act, 386
tea parties, 386, 395; in Boston, 386, 395; in New York, 395
throat distemper, 104–105, 105
Thurman, John, 411, 412
Tiedemann, Joseph, 432n92
Townshend Acts, 363
Trinity Church, 155, 156, 243
Triumvirate, 299, 304, 308, 367, 378, 435
Tryon, Gov. William, 363, 377, 384, 384–385, 386, 386–387, 389, 390, 391, 392, 394, 395, 397, 398, 406, 409, 414, 415, 422, 423–424, 424, 425, 426, 427, 436, 438; land grants and, 385
tuberculosis, 89, 269, 290n17
Tyler, Moses Coit, 1, 3, 5, 34
typhoid, 170
typhus, 117n53

Ulster Co., 48, 53, 54, 71, 76, 81, 86, 100, 101, 128, 131, 147, 177, 181, 190, 196, 205, 213, 215, 216, 217, 218, 219, 220, 221, 222, 223–224, 225, 226, 228, 229, 243, 280, 298, 356, 385, 425
University of Edinburgh, 8, 11, 18, 98, 104, 155, 242, 243, 256, 257, 258, 259, 351

Van Dam, Rip, 63, 77–78, 79, 80, 89, 90, 122, 123, 124, 310, 379, 380
Vandeput, Capt. George, 421
Van Rensselaer family, 285, 364–365

Vaughan, Lt. Col. John, 347
Veitch, William, 9, 10
Vermont, 392, 393, 394–395, 413
Verplanck, Gulian C., 3
Virginia, 2, 161, 170, 214, 216, 270, 358, 366, 383–384, 396, 406, 414

Waddell, Robert Ross, 308, 309
Wallace, Hugh, 397
Wappinger Indians, 48, 65n13, 365
War of Independence, 1–2, 34, 57, 103, 304
Warren, Peter, 89, 162, 165–166, 171–172, 188, 194, 195, 201, 204
Washington, George, 216, 425, 441, 442
waterspouts, 13, 101
Watkins, Hezekiah, 221
Watts, John, 274, 276, 280, 281, 283, 300, 301, 310, 311, 313, 319, 320, 323, 335, 355, 356, 366, 391, 393, 405, 412, 419, 435, 438
Wentworth, Benning, 392, 393, 394
Westchester Co., 131, 152, 167, 180, 196, 224, 421, 426, 435–436
West Florida, 358
White, Henry, 405, 412
Whitefield, George, 343
Whytt, Robert, 256–257
William III and Mary, 10, 77, 87, 336; proclamation of William III, 77, 379
Wines, Roger, 231–232
Wraxall, Peter, 189, 203

yellow fever, 105–109, 113, 117n53, 169
Young, Dr. Thomas, 5, 12, 258

Zenger, John Peter, 79, 80–81, 87, 90, 104, 124, 352

About the Author

Philip Ranlet received his PhD in history from Columbia University and is Adjunct Associate Professor of History at Hunter College, where he has been teaching since 1982. An authority on early New York, he has previously written *The New York Loyalists*, 2nd ed. (Lanham, MD: University Press of America, 2002), as well as a biography of a native New Yorker who became a great historian, *Richard B. Morris and American History in the Twentieth Century* (Lanham, MD: University Press of America, 2003). He has also written extensively on colonial New England, American Indians, the prison ships of the American Revolution, and diseases such as smallpox and typhus.

www.ingramcontent.com/pod-product-compliance
Lightning Source LLC
Chambersburg PA
CBHW070005010526
44117CB00011B/1436